The Great War in Post-Memory Literature and Film

Media and Cultural Memory/ Medien und kulturelle Erinnerung

Edited by
Astrid Erll · Ansgar Nünning

Editorial Board
Aleida Assmann · Mieke Bal · Vita Fortunati · Richard Grusin · Udo Hebel
Andrew Hoskins · Wulf Kansteiner · Alison Landsberg · Claus Leggewie
Jeffrey Olick · Susannah Radstone · Ann Rigney · Michael Rothberg
Werner Sollors · Frederik Tygstrup · Harald Welzer

Volume 18

The Great War
in Post-Memory
Literature and Film

Edited by
Martin Löschnigg and Marzena Sokołowska-Paryż

DE GRUYTER

ISBN 978-3-11-048600-1
e-ISBN (PDF) 978-3-11-036302-9
e-ISBN (EPUB) 978-3-11-039152-7
ISSN 1613-8961

Library of Congress Cataloging-in-Publication Data
A CIP catalog record for this book has been applied for at the Library of Congress.

Bibliographic information published by the Deutsche Nationalbibliothek
The Deutsche Nationalbibliothek lists this publication in the Deutsche Nationalbibliografie;
detailed bibliographic data are available on the internet at http://dnb.dnb.de.

© 2014 Walter de Gruyter GmbH, Berlin/Boston
Cover illustration: Photo of the camera projector: Bartosz Mierzyński; "A British heavy gun in action", Courtesy of the Library of Congress, LC-USZ62-136097.
Typesetting: PTP-Berlin Protago-T$_E$X-Production GmbH, Berlin
Printing and binding: CPI books GmbH, Leck
♾ Printed on acid-free paper
Printed in Germany

www.degruyter.com

Table of Contents

Marzena Sokołowska-Paryż and Martin Löschnigg
Introduction: "Have you forgotten yet? ..." —— 1

Part 1: 'Entrenched'(?) Perspectives: The Legacy of the Great War

Margot Norris
Revisiting *All Quiet on the Western Front* —— 17

Caroline Perret
Wilfred Owen and His War Poetry in *Wilfred Owen: A Remembrance Tale* and *Regeneration/Behind the Lines* —— 29

Ross J. Wilson
It Still Goes On: Trauma and the Memory of the First World War —— 43

Marlene A. Briggs
Working Through the Working-Class War: The Battle of the Somme in Contemporary British Literature by Alan Sillitoe and Ted Hughes —— 59

Paul Skrebels
A Poisonous Paradox: Representations of Gas Warfare in Post-Memory Films of the Great War —— 81

Ty Hawkins
The Great War, the Iraq War, and Postmodern America: Kevin Powers' *The Yellow Birds* and the Radical Isolation of Today's U.S. Veterans —— 95

Part 2: The Challenge of Form: How to 'Remember' the Great War?

Thomas F. Schneider
The Two "All Quiets": Representations of Modern Warfare in the Film Adaptations of Erich Maria Remarque's *Im Westen nichts Neues* —— 109

Marek Paryż
"I shall lie broken against this broken earth": William March's *Company K* on the Screen —— 121

Michael Paris
The Great War and British Docudrama: *The Somme*, *My Boy Jack* and *Walter's War* —— 135

Martin Löschnigg
"Like dying on a stage": Theatricality and Remembrance in Anglo-Canadian Drama on the First World War —— 153

David Malcolm
The Great War Re-Remembered: Allohistory and Allohistorical Fiction —— 171

Phil Fitzsimmons and Daniel Reynaud
Comics/Graphic Novels/Bandes Dessinées and the Representation of the Great War —— 187

Jean Anderson
What Price Justice? French Crime Fiction and the Great War —— 201

Part 3: Identities: The Great War and National Post-Memories

Sherrill Grace
Remembering *The Wars* —— 219

Hanna Teichler
Joseph Boyden's *Three Day Road*: Transcultural (Post-)Memory and Identity in Canadian World War I Fiction —— 239

Christina Spittel
Nostalgia for the Nation? The First World War in Australian Novels of the 1970s and 1980s —— 255

Clare Rhoden
Even More Australian: Australian Great War Novels in the Twenty-First Century —— 273

Daniel Reynaud
National Versions of the Great War: Modern Australian Anzac Cinema —— 289

Richard Slotkin
The "Lost Battalion" of the Argonne and the Origin of the Platoon Movie: Race, Ethnicity, and the Transformation of American Nationality —— 305

Maurizio Cinquegrani
Place, Time and Memory in Italian Cinema of the Great War —— 321

Marzena Sokołowska-Paryż
The Great War and the Easter Rising in Tom Phelan's *The Canal Bridge*: A Literary Response to the Politics of Commemoration in Ireland —— 335

Angela Brintlinger
The Great War through 'Great October': 1914/1917 in Russian Memory —— 349

Part 4: Interrogations: Cross-Cultural and Trans-Historical (Re)Interpretations of the Great War

Geert Buelens
"They wouldn't end it with any of us alive, now would they?": The First World War in Cold War Era Films —— 365

Richard Smith
Post-Colonial Melancholia and the Representation of West Indian Volunteers in the British Great War Televisual Memory —— 385

Anne Samson
Fictional Accounts of the East Africa Campaign —— 397

Alicia Fahey
Voices From the Edge: De-Centering Master Narratives in Jane Urquhart's *The Stone Carvers* —— 411

Brigitte Johanna Glaser
Women and World War I: 'Postcolonial' Imaginative Rewritings of the Great War —— 427

Contributors —— 443
Index of Names —— 451
Index of Titles —— 455

Marzena Sokołowska-Paryż and Martin Löschnigg
Introduction: "Have you forgotten yet? ..."

Military historian Richard Holmes once complained that the Great War was "far too literary" a conflict (xvii), meaning not just the enduring popularity of wartime and interwar literature, but also "another burst of writing" after the Second World War (12), which gained momentum throughout the subsequent decades, producing works of fiction which by now have become canonical in Great War studies, such as Timothy Findley's *The Wars* or Pat Barker's *Regeneration*. However, the First World War has become as much a 'cinematic,' 'televised' and 'theatrical' conflict as it remains a 'literary' war, and one can hardly imagine studying the subject today without having seen *Gallipoli*, *La vie et rien d'autre*, *Blackadder Goes Forth* or *Oh! What a Lovely War*. Notwithstanding the many other social, political and military conflicts which have torn the twentieth and twenty-first centuries, the sheer number of books, plays and films which are continuously being produced on the Great War is the most manifest "evidence that this huge and terrible war still casts its chilly shadow over our own times," as even Holmes admitted, despite all his reservations regarding the "inaccuracies [...] and stereotypes" inevitable in fiction (12–13).

Though pinpointing the exact beginning of the post-memory phase must inevitably be arbitrary, it can be tentatively assumed that since the late 1950s/early 1960s the subject matter of the Great War was gradually taken over by authors, playwrights and filmmakers for whom this conflict was a historical event located in a distant past and not a part of their own experience, though a connection was strongly felt through family (hi)stories and/or strong national identification. The term 'post-memory' refers, first and foremost, to the time span we are interested in, but it serves also to differentiate between the cultural representations of the Great War based on memory (Great War veterans continued to write memoirs and/or fiction after the Second World War, they appeared in documentaries, and their testimonies became a staple part of historical accounts) and those literary and film representations that are imaginative (re)constructions of the war, necessarily based on historical research. In other words, by 'post-memory' we mean literally 'after memory,' indicating the absence of a first-hand empirical connection to the war depicted in literature, on the screen, or on the stage.

The title of our volume must, of course, evoke immediate associations with Marianne Hirsch and her definition of "postmemory," yet this is positioned very firmly within "the personal, collective and cultural trauma [of the Holocaust]" (5), and tied to Eva Hoffman's idea of "the second generation [as] the hinge generation" (1). It is therefore far too restricted to be applied to the phenomenon we wish to explore in this volume. The seemingly unimportant insertion of a hyphen thus serves to express that 'post-memory' is an expansion – rather than a simple borrowing – of Hirsch's concept. The volume brings together chapters on writers and filmmakers representing successive post-memory generations (with an emphasis on the plural), and the importance of time and place for understanding why and how they chose to 'return' to this distant conflict. The Great War has haunted artistic imaginations with its traumatic implications primarily in Western Europe and, to a certain extent in the U.S. However, it has also inspired authors and filmmakers to promote a strong and proud sense of national identity, predominantly in Canada and Australia. The Great War remains a relatively side-tracked conflict in the literature and film of the nations of Eastern and Central Europe, as well as Russia. One can detect in post-memory literature and film a discernible need to include hitherto marginalized perspectives for reasons of race or gender, and restore the necessary prominence to unduly 'forgotten' Great War battlefields. What is more, though it is undoubtedly true that every single novel, play, feature film or docudrama can be said to perform a commemorative function, inducing us to 'remember,' it is equally true that these imaginative 'returns' to the Great War are strongly influenced by the current socio-political circumstances and contemporary versions of national history, telling and showing us as much about the period in which they were produced as about the reality and significance of the past military conflict. In other words, the present volume intends to show the Great War in post-memory literature and film as "[a] multiplicity of social experiences and representations, in part contradictory and ambiguous, in terms of which people construct the world and their actions" (Confino 1399).

One may refer at this point to Australian novelist David Malouf's definition of "fictive histories," which aptly identifies the issue of the inevitable contemporizing of the past: "our only way of grasping our history – and by history I really mean what has happened to us, and what determines what we are now and where we are now – the only way of really coming to terms with that is by people's entering into it in their imagination, not by the world of facts, but by being there." Adapting Malouf's definition for the purposes of this volume, the following can be said about post-memory literature and film about the Great War:

> [...] of course it's not the real world, it's not the way it was in [1914–1918], it's a way that [1914–1918] appears in the significance it has [in the time of the author, dramatist or filmmaker]. The readers are then able to take all of that into their consciousness and their imaginations so that it's moved out of the world of fact into something like the world of experience – but more like dream experience than real experience. [...] That's the extent to which it's a different history: it's a dream history, a myth history, a history of experience in the imagination. And I keep wanting to say societies can only become whole, can only know fully what they are when they have relived history in that kind of way. (Interview)

There are reasons, however, for which we prefer to refer to post-*memory* and not fictive *history*. Though we fully embrace Malouf's definition, it was formulated to identify a trend in prose fiction, whereas this volume also includes chapters that put the imaginative (re)constructions of the Great War in literature and film under close historical scrutiny. We have also decided to include discussions on the Great War in docudrama and documentary, in full agreement with Wulf Kansteiner that "memory's relation to history remains one of the interesting challenges in the field" (184).

Our understanding of "post-ness" derives from Hans-Georg Gadamer's concept of "historical consciousness" which "no longer listens sanctimoniously to the voice that reaches out from the past, but, in reflection on it, replaces it within the context where it took root in order to see the significance and relative value proper to it. This reflexive posture towards tradition is called interpretation" (111). It is, however, post-*memory* that we feel indicates more powerfully the need to create what Eva Hoffman has called "a sense of living connection" with the past (qtd. in Hirsch 1). The issue at stake here is what Mark Salber Phillips calls "historical distance," a concept equally valid for literary and film studies as it is for academic and popular histories: "every form of [...] representation must position its audience to some relationship of closeness to or distance from the events and experiences it describes" (95). Post-memory literature and film reinterpret and redefine the Great War but – at the same time – they create and perpetuate an empathic connection with this past, and endow it with a significance for the present. Re-working Hirsch's definition, one can see the following purpose of post-memory literature and film:

> [to establish] [a] relationship that the generation[s] after those who witnessed [the Great War] bear [...] to those came before, experiences they 'remember' only by means of the [novels, plays, films, TV series] among which they grew up. [And] these experiences [are intended to be] transmitted to them so deeply and affectively as to *seem* to constitute memor[y] in [its] own right. [Post-memory's] connection to the past is thus not actually mediated by recall but by imaginative [constructions]. (5)

The question at the heart of this volume is to what extent literature and film about the Great War created so many decades after the conflict, and reflecting the vantage points of different nations, effectively establish new "dimension[s] of our relationship with the past" (Phillips 96), and what strategies are employed to diminish the "ideological" and "affective" modes of historical distance, allowing "the past [to be] presented as a place of emotional and ideological engagement?" (Phillips 92). And we use the term post-*memory* because, as Kerwin Lee Klein has so rightly noted, "memory appeals to us [...] it projects an immediacy we feel has been lost by history" (129), remembering nonetheless that "[collective memory] is as much a result of conscious manipulation as unconscious absorption and it is always mediated" (Kansteiner 180).

The volume is divided into four sections, reflecting what we consider to be the most important preoccupations within the vast field of post-memory literature and film about the Great War. Section one ("'Entrenched'(?) Perspectives: The Cultural Legacy of the Great War") brings together chapters which examine the complex workings of trans-historical cultural interdependence. It is indisputable that there can be no in-depth understanding of the Great War without recourse to its wartime and inter-war cultural representations. From the point of view of present-day readers and viewers, however, the Great War literary and filmic canon is inevitably filtered through post-memory literature and film. As T. S. Eliot wrote, "no poet, no artist of any art, has his complete meaning alone. His significance, his appreciation is the appreciation of his relation to the dead poets and artists. You cannot value him alone; you must set him, for contrast and comparison, among the dead," but, as the poet emphasizes, it is also the case that with every new work of art, "the ideal order" of the previous "existing monuments" is altered: "The existing order is complete before the new work arrives; for order to persist after the supervention of novelty, the whole existing order must be, if ever so slightly, altered; and so the relations, proportions, values of each work of art toward the whole are readjusted; and this is conformity between the old and the new" (44–45). Margot Norris's discussion of Delbert Mann's *All Quiet on the Western Front* and Caroline Perret's analysis of Gillies MacKinnon's *Regeneration/Behind The Lines* and Louise Hooper's documentary about Great Britain's most renowned soldier poet demonstrate how such productions deliberately and effectively convince us of the timelessness and universality of Great War literature in its most canonical anti-war version, as represented, most poignantly, by Erich Maria Remarque and Wilfred Owen. Concomitantly, these chapters foreground the degree to which post-memory productions function as the inseparable cultural supplement to the Great War's literary and cinematic legacy, perpetuating this legacy, but also adding new interpretative contexts. The subsequent chapters by Ross J. Wilson on "cultural trauma" in British, Canadian, and Australian prose fiction, film and documentary, and Marlene A. Briggs on "regional trauma" in the writings of Alan Sillitoe and Ted Hughes, authors defined by their mutual industrial Northern-English working-class background, investigate the extent to which post-memory literature and film remain 'entrenched' in the epistemological paradigms created by wartime and inter-war cultural representations, as well as the motivations behind this seemingly continuous need to validate the futility-oriented version of the Great War. The section concludes with chapters questioning the trans-historical adaptability of the established cultural images of the Great War. Paul Skrebels takes under scrutiny the representations of gas warfare in post-memory film, highlighting the fact that the use of poison gas, as a uniquely Great War battlefield weapon, rendered it a problematic subject for film-makers, aiming for a more universally-applicable message about the threat of weapons of mass destruction and the inhumanity and impersonality of industrialized warfare. Ty Hawkins's analysis of Kevin Powers's *The Yellow Birds* proves that the literature generated by military conflicts subsequent to the Great War, though always looking back to the cultural legacy of this paradigmatic war, necessitates the construction of its own representational models in order to capture the distinctiveness of the socio-political and military circumstances of the contemporary conflict as well as the psychological costs of fighting a different war.

Section two ("The Challenge of Form: How to 'Remember' the Great War?") brings to the foreground the issue of "formal distance" defined as "the wide variety of textual or other representational devices that shape the reader's experience of the text or [film]" (Phillips 97). The chapters collected in this section are united by their interest in the modes of post-memory cultural representations of the Great War and the ways in which these various modes allow for an empathic immersion into the past and/or a contemporary encoding of this – by now very distant – military conflict. The opening chapter by Thomas Schneider offers an in-depth comparative analysis of the technical, structural and iconographic aspects of the two adaptations (so far) of *All Quiet on the Western Front* as war films in their own rights, shaped less by their founding text as by their directors' politically-determined visions of how modern warfare should be shown on the screen. Marek Paryż's chapter follows the same line of argumentation, showing the degree to which Robert Clem's adaptation of William March's *Company K* creates its own autonomous aesthetics and ideology, answering the demands of its own time rather than adhering to the historical context of the original text. Most importantly, however, these two chapters show the supremacy of the generic prerequisites of the war film to the criterion of fidelity in the case of these particular film adaptations, and they both raise the important question about the capacity of the visual medium to engage the viewer more powerfully than the written word. In turn, Michael Paris looks at the rise of the convention of the docudrama and its increasing importance in shaping popular perceptions of the Great War by combining purported historical veracity with fictive dramatizations. Performativity as a means of both constructing a sense of national identity as well as revising national history is an issue at the heart of Martin Löschnigg's discussion of Anglo-Canadian drama. The stage cannot be ignored as one of the more important venues for perpetuating post-memories of the Great War, with contemporary dramatists employing a variety of strategies intended either to diminish or to enhance the alienation effect endemic to contemporary theatre, constructing divergent theatrical models of representing history in order to create a post-memory understanding of the past. The intricate relationship between history and post-memory is foregrounded in David Malcolm's chapter devoted to the hitherto sidelined academic and popular modes of 're-imagining' the events of 1914–1918. While the Great War features prominently in allohistories as one of the most important turning points of the twentieth century, it rarely appears in allohistorical fiction, and the reason appears to reside in the impossibility of imagining a future-present that does not involve the slaughter on the Western Front. If re-writing the history of the Second World War (the victory of the Third Reich) does not obliterate the Holocaust, the re-writing of the First World War carries the danger of 'un-writing' the 'truth' of the conflict located in the realities of trench warfare in Flanders and France. The concluding chapters investigate the ways in which the Great War is re-remembered in representational modes which are all too often relegated to the status of entertainment-oriented literature. Phil Fitzsimmons and Daniel Reynaud invite us to the world of comics/graphic novels/*bandes dessinées* (the proliferation of terms indicating the problematic status of the genre) in order to show the importance of popular culture in shaping/reshaping contemporary understandings of the Great War. Using the example of French literature, Jean Anderson convincingly argues that the comfort of reading crime fiction relating to the Great War resides in its ability to promote an ideal of justice, though this ideal will inevitably vary, depending on the period in which the texts were written. Concomitantly, the chapter focuses on the impact of the conventions of detective fiction on the wartime and post-memory representations of the Great War.

The term 'post-memory' as used in this volume bears considerable overlap with that of 'cultural memory.' Well before the centenary, the First World War finally and completely passed from what Jan Assmann (48–66) has called "communicative memory," an inter-generational memory conveyed mainly through oral tradition (and thus commensurate, to some extent, with Marianne Hirsch's concept of – unhyphenated – 'postmemory'), into "cultural memory," a form of collective memory which is based on symbolic objectivation. The cultural memory of the war is expressed and perpetuated by literature and film, the visual arts, memorials and the rituals of commemoration. However, the relation between the cultural memory of the war and its media is reciprocal, as media (in the widest sense) have not only represented but also decisively shaped the war's remembrance. In this respect, there has also been a great deal of mutual influence between cultural history and the arts. If cultural historians have drawn on the literature and art of the First World War, contemporary writers, artists and filmmakers have necessarily acknowledged their indebtedness not only to their wartime forebears, but also to works of cultural history. Thus, for instance, Paul Fussell's classic, if also much criticized, *The Great War and Modern Memory* of

1975 stands in the background of a number of recent novels on the Great War, as do the accounts by Erich Maria Remarque, Robert Graves, Siegfried Sassoon and others. This complex relationship between earlier and later sources, and the reciprocity which characterizes the cultural memory of the war and its mediation, are the reason why many of the essays in the present volume also engage with sources from the time of the Great War or shortly after, addressing the question of how these sources have contributed to shaping the post-memory image of the war.

Since Jan and Aleida Assmann proposed the concept of cultural memory, their categories have been modified and refined by a number of scholars (see for instance Manier and Hirst), not least because media such as film and television complicate the binary division into communicative and cultural memory. What is more important for an understanding of post-memory conceptions of the Great War than a rarefied catalogue of different 'memories,' however, is an awareness of the intricate connection between cultural memory and history. "History," as Henry James reminds one, "is never, in any rich sense, the immediate crudity of what 'happens,' but the much finer complexity of what we read into it and think of in connection with it" (182). James's statement is impressively borne out by representations of the First World War in both cultural history and the arts, as these representations transcend the historical to include myth. Indeed, as Jan Assmann has emphasized, cultural memory is "mythical history" transmitted through "ceremonial communication, mediated texts, icons, dances, rituals, formalized language(s)" ("Communicative and Cultural Memory" 117), and recent examples of literature and film on the First World War clearly illustrate the interaction of the historical and the mythical in its cultural memory. 'Myth' is a notoriously vague term which has been used to include a wide range of cultural and sociological meanings. Roland Barthes and Claude Lévi-Strauss emphasize its explanatory function, regarding myths as culturally engendered imaginaries which, according to Lévi-Strauss, "appear to attenuate [the] crying illogicality of reality" (3). Evidently, this is of major relevance for representations of the experience of the front-line in World War I, an experience which has in many ways become synonymous with the illogical and absurd. Accordingly, Fussell shows that the war engendered a turning "towards myth, towards a revival of the cultic, the sacrificial, the prophetic, the sacramental and the universally significant" (121). In the context of the cultural memory of the war, Bernard Bergonzi refers to myth as "actions, persons, events, stories which escape from their historical background and have the continuing power to haunt our imagination" (8). In this sense, the front-line in the Great War has brought forth a distinct mythology of its own, which is manifested in the images which have become firmly 'entrenched,' as it were, in the public imagination, images of mud-swamped trenches, of the shell-cratered no man's land between the lines, and of soldiers clambering 'over the top' to be mowed down by machine guns. This iconography has underlined the liminality of the war experience, as symbolized most potently by no man's land, an absolute borderline whose transgression meant the sacrifice of a whole generation of young men, sent to perish in the mud. Indeed, as Francis Spufford has pointedly put it, "[w]e assign to [...] [World War I] the meaning of murderous absurdity; it has the permanent function in the culture of reducing military glory to the equivalent of an invitation to walk into the blades of a combine harvester" (12).

Images of World War I as an epitome of "murderous absurdity" have been at odds with those interpretations which have conceived of the war as a national foundation myth or a national 'master narrative.' As "[n]ation-states produce narrative versions of their past which are taught, embraced, and referred to as their collective autobiography" (Aleida Assmann 101), the Great War of 1914–1918 has figured as a milestone on the road to nationhood especially in Canada and Australia. The papers in section three of the present volume ("Identities: The Great War and National Post-Memories") investigate how post-memory literature and film represent the role of the war in the transformation of early twentieth-century (colonial) societies into (multi-ethnic and multi-cultural) modern nations. They analyse the renderings (and questionings) of national mythologies about the war, concentrating, for obvious reasons, on Canada and Australia, but also dealing with post-memories in the U.S., Ireland, Italy, and Russia. In the case of the latter, as in that of other major belligerents (France, Germany, Austria-Hungary and its successor states), national memories of the war were partially eclipsed by the events that followed, which may account for the relative scarcity of post-memory literature and film on World War I in those countries, as compared to Britain, Canada and Australia. In any case, it accounts for a complexity of historical and cultural remembrance which deserves extensive study by cultural historians.

In the cultural memory of Britain, the Great War has come to signify the end of the old Edwardian world, which thus came, *pace* T. S. Eliot, not with a whimper, but with the bang of 1914. In spite of World War II, whose toll on the population exceeded that of its predecessor, the First World War has thus remained Britain's traumatic war, as the Vietnam War has proved for the U.S. In the same way, recent representations of the Great War in the countries of the former British Empire, especially in Canada and Australia, have tended to engage with the significance of the war as the death-knell of the old imperial world and the birth of modern nations. Although, figuratively speaking, the war had imprinted the Old World anew on the maps of countries which had already entered the road to decolonization, their military support of the mother country undoubtedly accelerated developments towards national sovereignty. First and foremost, however, the foundational mythology of the war which emerged in these countries proved functional with regard to post-war concerns, fulfilling the emotional needs of societies which had suffered loss and bereavement on an unprecedented scale.

The role of the Great War in the cultural memory of Canada is dealt with, in this section, by Sherrill Grace and Hanna Teichler. Grace analyses Timothy Findley's seminal novel *The Wars* (1977), which initiated further literary investigations of the significance of World War I (and of war in general) as a Canadian national narrative. Published in the late 1970s, *The Wars* stands before the backdrop of an emphasis on 'Canadianness' in the country's literature and arts during that decade, and of the war fought by Canada's neighbour in Vietnam. This seems to have engendered a need (as expressed in Findley's novel) to question public attitudes towards war, including the validity of a national foundation myth based on World War I. Most importantly, however, *The Wars*, as Grace argues, carries with it a "narrative imperative to bear witness" to the detrimental effects of war on humanity. The fact that the Canadian 'master narrative' of the Great War has tended to exclude marginalized groups such as for instance the country's First Nations people, is discussed by Teichler, whose chapter focuses on a novel which has brought the participation of Native Canadians in the war to the attention of a wide readership, Joseph Boyden's *Three Day Road* (2005).

Like the major writers of the Great War themselves, post-memory literature and film have either searched for a 'true' anti-mythical and anti-heroic (post-)memory of World War I, or have thematized the contested nature of the memory as such. In this respect, too, there are many similarities between representations of the war in recent Australian and Canadian fiction and film. The chapters by Christina Spittel, Clare Rhoden and Daniel Reynaud in this section analyse how Australian novels and films especially since the 1980s have rendered Gallipoli and the Anzac myth, and their function as a national narrative conveying images of 'Australianness.' As they show in their discussions, the myth has been questioned, while at the same time the need for national narratives seems to have remained unbroken. As a result, it seems that 'Anzac' has now become inclusive with regard to Australia's multicultural society, and even reconciled with the demands of a social consensus which condemns war.

The heterogeneity of U.S.-American society is reflected in the personnel of Platoon Movies, a type of war film which developed during World War II. Richard Slotkin shows how the multi-ethnic make-up of these movies is anticipated by the 'Lost Battalion,' composed mainly of recent immigrants, and the Harlem Hellfighters, an African American unit, in the First World War. In retrospect, the military exploits of these units appear of symbolic significance, pointing to the mythologizing of multi-ethnicity on the one hand, and the actual status of racial and ethnic minorities (black Americans and new immigrants) on the other, whose expectations of civil equality for their loyalty to the nation were disappointed after the war. Among the European belligerents, Italy was one of the youngest nations, formed in the second half of the nineteenth century through the unification of very diverse regional traditions. Maurizio Cinquegrani compares earlier Italian war films and memoirs with Great War films of the 1970s to show how the 'memories' created and shaped by film reconstruct the past with regard to a present determined by national needs. The same applies to the Irish situation, as Marzena Sokołowska-Paryż shows in her discussion of Tom Phelan's novel *The Canal Bridge* (2005). Phelan emphasizes the Great War context of the 1916 Easter Rising, and portrays the ambivalence of Ireland's remembrance of both events – mythologizing the Dublin victims while repressing the memory of the Irish dead in the 'British' war in France and Flanders. Concluding this section, Angela Brintlinger deals with Russia's 'forgotten war' on the examples of Alexander Solzhenitsyn's *August 1914* (1971) and the novel *Moonzund* (2008) by Valentin Pikul.' What emerges from these texts is that the subordinate position of World War I in the Russian cultural memory can only partially be explained by the fact that this was an 'imperialist' war ignored by Soviet Russia, tied up with Revolution and Civil War.

Section four ("Interrogations: Cross-Cultural and Trans-Historical (Re)Interpretations of the Great War") is concerned with post-memory literature and films which render the Great War within larger temporal or spatial frameworks, investigating the ideological dimensions of its remembrance especially in Cold War and post-colonial contexts, and emphasizing perspectives which historical accounts have tended to neglect or have only recently begun to consider more extensively. Geert Buelens shows how the latent threat of a truly global conflagration during the Cold War era fostered anti-heroic images of the Great War, including the rendering of desertion and the portrayal of front-line soldiers as victims of a 'war machine' or of their own general staff as important themes, in post-1945 films on World War I. In this chapter, Buelens also discusses films from the former Eastern bloc countries to point to the tension between ethnic nationalism and Communist internationalism, whose difference to the 'internationalism' of the Habsburg Empire is emphasized in his examples. With regard to Western Europe, he shows how the needs for Franco-German reconciliation as a prerequisite for European integration have shaped the depiction of the 'other' in Great War films, and how British productions have explored the class-based and imperialist associations of the war, including Britain's role *vis a vis* the Irish. The imperialist dimension of the war also stands in the centre of Richard Smith's chapter, which deals with the little-known contribution of Caribbean soldiers to Britain's war effort on the example of three (very) recent British television documentaries and docudramas. What emerges from these sources is a conflict between empire loyalty among West

Indians (in spite of the often depressing social conditions at home), and British reluctance to acknowledge to the full the valour of imperial troops because of a fear of pressure for self-determination in reward for their services, not to speak of institutionalized racism in the British Army. As Smith shows, these aspects of the West Indian war experience are important for understanding the positioning of Caribbeans in the course of the twentieth century as colonial subjects, independent citizens, and, in the case of the many post-World War II immigrants, British nationals. In the chapter by Anne Samson, the (post-)colonial dimension of the war is further explored through a discussion of literary and filmic representations of the war in East Africa. The novels from different sides and time periods as surveyed by Samson demonstrate how this colonial 'sideshow' to the war in Europe developed its own dynamics and memory, freighted with issues of national identity and (post-)colonial ideologies.

In the case of Canada, the country's war effort did not only give rise to a narrative of national emancipation, but was also to channel divisions of class, region, ethnicity and race into a national Anglo-Canadian culture. In a political sense, the memory of the war functioned to create a nation which was to be homogeneous in character. On the example of Jane Urquhart's *The Stone Carvers* (2001), by now one of the best-known Canadian novels on World War I, Alicia Fahey shows how post-memory fiction has undermined this 'unifying myth' of the war by rendering marginalized perspectives on the war, icluding those of women, of French Canadians, of the First Nations people and of 'ethnic' immigrant communities, like the descendants of German immigrants in Urquhart's novel. In particular, Fahey concentrates on the way Urquhart renders the memory of Vimy Ridge, a part of the Battle of Arras in spring 1917 in which an 'all Canadian' contingent gained an important victory, and a focal point in Canada's collective memory of the war. *The Stone Carvers* is also one of the novels discussed by Brigitte Glaser, who shows how in World War I fiction from countries of the former British Empire post-colonial issues are often closely aligned with those of gender. Drawing on a selection of novels mainly from Canada and Australia, but also including Doris Lessing's fictionalized family memoir *Alfred and Emily* (2008), Glaser discusses literary representations of the war experience of nurses and of women on the home front, together with portrayals of the impact of the war on the (female) artistic imagination, as in C. K. Stead's 'biofiction' on New Zealand-born Katherine Mansfield (*Mansfield: A Novel*, 2004). As Glaser argues, her selected texts display an intricate connection between the limited agency of their female protagonists in wartime and the relational nature of their experience with their positioning on the margins of the empire.

The scope of the chapters in the present volume testifies to the on-going interest of writers and filmmakers in what historians have come to regard as the Ur-catastrophe of the twentieth century – a catastrophe, however, whose political, social and cultural implications escape unequivocal description:

> And yet, one might argue that, in its implosive and disintegrative power, the Great War [...] did have a positive side. By subverting context it liberated text. By undermining old authority, it released creativity. It threw us all back upon ourselves. In that sense it was and remains the great emancipatory adventure-experience of the modern age, open to all, invoking all, involving all, democratic, symbolic, and inescapable. It is the representative event of [the twentieth] century. (Eksteins 317)

It is this profound ambivalence of the war and its role as a catalyst in the development of modernity that – one may safely say – will continue to exert a challenge for literature and film well beyond the centenary.

References

Assmann, Aleida. "Canon and Archive." *A Companion to Cultural Memory Studies*. Eds. Astrid Erll and Ansgar Nünning, 2010. 98–107.
Assmann, Jan. *Das kulturelle Gedächtnis. Schrift, Erinnerung und politische Identität in frühen Hochkulturen*. Munich: Beck, 1999 [1992].
Assmann, Jan. "Communicative and Cultural Memory." *A Companion to Cultural Memory Studies*. Eds. Astrid Erll and Ansgar Nünning. 109–118.
Bergonzi, Bernard. "The First World War: Poetry, Scholarship, Myth." *English Literature of the Great War Revisited: Proceedings of the Symposium on the British Literature of the First World War*. Ed. Michel Roucoux. University of Picardy Press, 1986. 7–18.
Confino, Alon. "Collective Memory and Cultural History: Problems of Method." *The American Historical Review* 102. 5 (1997): 1386–1403.
Eksteins, Modris. "Memory and the Great War." *The Oxford Illustrated History of the First World War*. Ed. Hew Strachan. Oxford: Oxford University Press, 1998. 305–317.
Eliot, T. S. "Tradition and the Individual Talent." *The Sacred Wood: Essays on Poetry and Criticism*. London: Methuen, 1920. 42–53.
Erll, Astrid, and Ansgar Nünning, eds. *A Companion to Cultural Memory Studies*. Berlin and New York: De Gruyter, 2010.
Gadamer, Hans-Georg. "The Problem of Historical Consciousness." *Interpretative Social Science: A Reader*. Eds. Paul Rabinow and William M. Sullivan. Berkeley: University of California Press, 1979. 103–160.
Hirsch, Marianne. *The Generation of Postmemory: Writing and Visual Culture After the Holocaust*. New York: Columbia University Press, 2012.
Holmes, Richard. *Tommy: The British Soldier on the Western Front 1914–1918*. London: Harper Perennial, 2005.
Holmes, Richard. Interview by Patrick Bishop. *Tommy: The British Soldier on the Western Front 1914–1918*. 2–15.
James, Henry. *The American Scene*. Ed. Leon Edel. Bloomington: Indiana University Press, 1969.
Kansteiner, Wulf. "Finding Meaning in Memory: A Methodological Critique of Collective Memory Studies." *History and Theory* 41. 2 (2002): 179–197.
Klein, Kerwin Lee. "On the Emergence of *Memory* in Historical Discourse." *Representations* 69: Special Issue: Grounds for Remembering (2000): 127–150.
Lévi-Strauss, Claude. *The Raw and the Cooked. Introduction to a Science of Mythology*. Trans. John and Doreen Weightman. Vol. 1. New York: Harper and Row, 1969 [1964].
Malouf, David. Interview by Helen Daniel. *Australian Humanities Review* (edited transcript). http://www.australianhumanitiesreview.org/archive/Issue-Sept-1996/intermal.html (15 June 2013).
Manier, David, and William Hirst. "A Cognitive Taxonomy of Collective Memories." *A Companion to Cultural Memory Studies*. Eds. Astrid Erll and Ansgar Nünning. 253–262.
Phillips, Mark Salber. "History, Memory, and Historical Distance." *Theorizing Historical Consciousness*. Ed. Peter Seixas. Toronto: University of Toronto Press, 2006. 86–102.
Spufford, Francis. "The War that Never Stopped." *Times Literary Supplement* 22 (1996): 12.

Part 1: **'Entrenched'(?) Perspectives: The Legacy of the Great War**

Margot Norris
Revisiting *All Quiet on the Western Front*

The epigram to Erich Maria Remarque's 1929 novel *All Quiet on the Western Front* states bluntly that "This book is to be neither an accusation nor a confession, and least of all an adventure, for death is not an adventure to those who stand face to face with it" (n.p.). In a sense, this statement serves as a warning to filmmakers, particularly filmmakers of war movies that inevitably end up functioning as adventure stories, intentionally or not. The novel was published in Germany eight years after the ending of World War I under the title *Im Westen nichts Neues*, followed by an English translation published by Little, Brown, and Company in 1929. Within a year, Lewis Milestone directed a film bearing the same title as the novel, which went on to win Academy Awards for best film and best director, as well as nominations for screenwriting and cinematography. Almost forty years later, Delbert Mann directed a remake of *All Quiet on the Western Front* for television. This 1979 film earned a Golden Globe Award for best motion picture made for television, as well as an Emmy Award for outstanding film editing for a limited series or special. A third remake of *All Quiet on the Western Front*, starring Daniel Radcliffe and directed by Mimi Leder, was to have begun in 2012.[1] Given that both Milestone and Mann retained Remarque's exact title for their films, it is fair to evaluate their adaptations with respect to their fidelity to the clearly stated intention and message of the 1929 novel. And yet, given this obligation to avoid adventure in the interest of promoting a strong anti-war and pacifist agenda, how can the medium of film, with its inherent requirement to transform words and images into spectacle, possibly comply? We are effectively obliged to examine, evaluate, and critique adaptations from the political perspective of their polemical agenda, methodology, and success, and a systematic comparison with the narrative and poetic strategies of the original is required for such a critique. At the same time, such a strategy of comparison also benefits from setting the films into the larger contexts of their historical moments and those of their directors.

Charles Silver, the curator of the New York Museum of Modern Art's film department, posted a review on the occasion of the July 2010 screenings of the Milestone film at the museum. In it he reminds us that "Hollywood could hardly have been more jingoistic in the period surrounding the First World War." It may have required a decade for enthusiasm about the war to cool sufficiently to publish a critical novel like Remarque's in English, and to make a film like Mile-

---

[1] Andrew Kelly discusses various projects to re-release the Milestone film in 1939, 1950, and 1984 in Germany, and in the 1990s in Holland (cf. 150–155).

stone's not only acceptable but also highly popular. Lewis Milestone's complex background may well have contributed to his sympathy for Remarque's response to the war. Born Lev Milstein in Russia and raised in Odessa, Milestone was educated in Belgium and Berlin, and was fluent in German and Russian. After emigrating to the U.S. before this country's entry into the war he volunteered for the Army Signal Corps and worked as a maker of short educational films for soldiers in the service.[2] Delbert Mann too served in the U.S. military, although his war experience belonged to a different era. Mann was born in Lawrence, Kansas in 1920, that is, after the end of World War I. After graduating from Vanderbilt University in 1941 he enlisted and became a bomber pilot in the U.S. Air Force, for which he flew numerous missions in the European Theater of Operations. Neither filmmaker appears to have experienced hand-to-hand combat of the kind that Paul Bäumer endures in the novel. However, their war experiences may nonetheless have given them sufficient insight into the salient message of Remarque's novel to have compelled their quite faithful translations of its themes, narrative strategies, emotional temper, and war scenes into their films.

In order to offer a systematic analysis of how the films adapt the Remarque novel, it may be helpful to divide the discussion into a series of related topics and specific techniques and scenes that present them. In contrast to Remarque's deliberately disjointed narration, Milestone unfolds the story of Paul Bäumer in a linear fashion, while the Mann film stays with the sequence of the original. I will therefore first contrast the openings of the three works and their effects on the reader and viewer. The Milestone film's changed opening calls attention to the abuse of authority at home and in the military in relation to the soldier, making the point that the psychological violence endured by soldiers comes not only from the danger of guns and bombs but also from the hierarchical nature of the service itself. The contrast between such figures as the teacher Kantorek and the postman Himmelstoß with the kindly Katczinsky illuminates how conflicts about power, intrinsic to the causes of war, are already operative on the social level of both the home front and the military. We will then shift to the vulnerability of soldiers by looking at the figure of the wounded young Kemmerich, whose death and its aftermath are simultaneously treated with a significant combination of poignancy and dismissiveness. The wounding and death of Kemmerich has its counterpart in the wounding and death of Gerard Duval, the French soldier Paul stabs in a shell hole, a moment that transforms the killing of the enemy from an act of heroism into an experience of traumatizing guilt. A contrast between the scene of

---

[2] George Mitchell writes that Milestone "was first assigned to the Army's training film unit at Columbia University. After a time there he was transferred to Washington where he worked in the laboratory and learned to cut film" (43).

war and the scene of civilian civic and domestic life readdresses the intractable divide between the two that in itself transforms the soldier's state of being into a psychological no man's land. Finally, the hopelessness of camaraderie, of soldiers attempting to care for each other and support each other as they are relentlessly killed and lost ends in all three versions of *All Quiet on the Western Front* in the solitary death of Paul Bäumer.

Much of the power of the Milestone film comes from the highly ironic contrast between its opening celebration of soldiers amid excitement about war and the shock of seeing these sentiments defiled by the gruesome reality that ensues. Following an enigmatic conversation about casualties, the film opens with soldiers marching to the sound of band music, while women jubilantly throw flowers at them and people cheer them as they go off to fight. We generally associate such scenes with the celebratory welcome of returning soldiers who are being thanked for their service and sacrifice. By preempting this order, the film turns the cheering and celebration into an example of credulous naiveté and innocence, of failing to grasp that war is not a symbolic or cultural exercise but a deliberate production of bodily and material injury and death. This early innocence will intensify both the irony of the later misery in the trenches, and lay the ground for the alienation Paul will feel when he returns home on leave after a time at the front. This introduces the pacifist political argument that war is produced by an inherent discrepancy between its idealistic promotion and its actual cruel activity. As the scene shifts to a classroom, this promotion is intensified by the exhortation of a schoolteacher telling young boys that "The Fatherland needs leaders" and that enlistment will be "the glorious beginning to your life." The boys can hardly contain their rabid enthusiasm to enlist after this exhortation. This opening fails to emphasize the crucial element of impending death in the famous Latin line, *Dulce et decorum est pro patria mori*, "It is sweet and right to die for your country."

Remarque opens his novel very differently, with a strange moment of contentment spoken by a soldier "five miles behind the front." The voice, which will be revealed to belong to Paul Bäumer, goes on to say that "Yesterday we were relieved, and now our bellies are full of beef and haricot beans" (1). Being at the front does not look so bad, judging from the double portions of sausage and bread, until we learn that the double rations are the product of the loss of half the company of young men. They went out as a group of a hundred and fifty and came back as eighty – hence the surplus of provisions. We can see here that Milestone preserves Remarque's strategy of opening with a moment of acute irony, although he chooses a different set-up for delaying and then producing it. Interestingly, Mann uses both techniques. He has the narrative voice introduce Katczinsky at the outset – "He is known as Kat" – and himself, "My name is Paul Bäumer. I am eighteen years old." Paul then introduces his friends, one by one and by name, so that we become familiar with their faces and their plans for the future, to study theology, become a forester, return to wife and farm. This opening is followed by scenes of the frightening life in the trenches, the whistles that announce attacks, the soldiers charging, the retreat, and dragging a soldier with a wounded leg back into a trench. Mann then echoes Milestone by having a flashback to a peaceful classroom before the war, where a distracted Paul begins drawing a little bird that has come to the window, while a teacher exhorts support for Germany, the land of Beethoven, Schiller, and Goethe. This teacher is far less rabid than Milestone's, and he even offers Paul a friendly cigarette when he keeps him after class. "You are a dreamer," he tells Paul, but now "you have duties as a man." "Of course you'll enlist," he exhorts and predicts, and of course Paul does. The Mann film, like Remarque's opening, produces an earlier interior view of the protagonist's delicate but grounded sensibility. In spite of the battle scenes, this opening is more realistic than the polemical beginning of the Milestone film, a difference that also owes something to the disparate technical features of the two films.

These technical differences reflect the different film-making eras in which the two movies were produced. George J. Mitchell begins his discussion of the making of the Milestone film by stating "*All Quiet on the Western Front*, produced by Universal Pictures in 1930, is considered today to be a landmark motion picture" (41). This is because it was one of the earliest Hollywood films to include the new medium of sound, which was introduced only in 1927. Given its recent departure from silent films, the Milestone production still relies on the over-dramatization and visual exaggeration that had come to characterize silent film. Its depictions of modern warfare are therefore unusually vivid and powerful – at moments verging on the histrionic – a characterization not inappropriate for the disturbing nature of the material.[3] The battle scenes were filmed in the hills north of Laguna Beach, California, an area now known as a tourist resort but at that time the undeveloped land of the Irvine Ranch – a setting that in black and white works surprisingly well to convey the spiritual wilderness of the trenches. Delbert Mann filmed the television movie in Czechoslovakia, making it one of the first American films set in the then Communist bloc. This gives the village scenes particularly a quite authentic simulation. Mann's 1979 film is in color, a feature that may strike us as almost unnatural for a World War I representation, since our general visual images of that period are based on black and white photographs and therefore tend to take black and white form in our imagination. Andrew Kelly's dismissive report on the Mann version argues that World War I films should inherently be made in black and white: "Trench combat has always been best seen in black and

---

[3] Mitchell gives a great deal of credit for the film's art to the cinematographer Arthur Edeson, who had invented a quieter camera that could be mobilized to film scenes (cf. 46–47).

white: monochrome conveys the brutality and the starkness, the sheer awfulness, of the trenches and of No Man's Land; colour seems to give it glamour" (156). Although he makes no reference to color, Scott Frisina strongly disagrees in his IMDb review. He argues that the Mann film "brilliantly captured the horror of World War I," and that "This is a dirty film. Bäumer, Kat and the others almost always have mud and dirt caked on their hands and uniforms." Indeed, there is no "glamour" to the color of the Mann film, which ensures that the soldiers' drab uniforms blend into the equally bland brown and black and grey surrounding of the trenches. In spite of being a "color" film, the Mann film's hues are virtually monochromatic with the exception of the blue of the French uniforms, which helpfully differentiates the combatants.

One might argue that both Milestone and Mann compensate for the specificities of their media in opposing ways that nonetheless serve to maintain fidelity to the Remarque novel. While the visual exaggerations of the black and white film compensate for the lack of realism that color might impart to make both war's violence and celebration highly dramatic, the Mann film seems to work hard to tone down overly dramatic actions in the interest of preserving the strange quietude of the Remarque novel, its inevitably noisy and chaotic battlefield scenes notwithstanding. This may partly result from the more faithful narrative sequencing of the action, and partly from its focus on the psychological effects of life on the brutal front in the sensitive Paul Bäumer portrayal by Richard Thomas. Mann had after all directed the 1955 film *Marty*, based on the novel by Paddy Chayefsky, that won both an Academy Award for Best Picture and a Palme d'Or at the Cannes Film Festival.[4] Ernest Borgnine, who won a surprising Oscar for the lead in that film, was chosen by Mann to play the important part of the sympathetic Stanislaus Katczinsky in the Remarque film. Although Richard Thomas is known chiefly for his role as John Boy Walton in the television series *The Waltons*, he had earlier played Fleming in a 1951 television adaptation of Stephen Crane's *The Red Badge of Courage*. Like Remarque, Mann follows the opening scene and the flashback to the schoolroom with the soldiers' visit to the hospital to see their friend Kemmerich. However, he adds an effective link between the opening rescue of a soldier with a wounded leg, and the depressing discovery that Kemmerich's leg

---

4 Kelly's brutal review of the Mann film, which he calls "a generally pointless production," argues that "[i]t was poorly reviewed and sank quickly." He cites two negative reviews, but pointedly fails to mention either the Golden Globe award or Emmy award the film received. Margalit Fox's *New York Times* obituary for Delbert Mann also neglects to mention the Golden Globe and Emmy awards his *All Quiet on the Western Front* received, instead giving a lengthy discussion of a 1968 incident when football fans were furious that a Raiders and Jets game was interrupted to show Mann's film *Heidi* on schedule.

has been amputated. Mann also adds an ironic detail to the setting that may be more familiar as an image of the American Civil War than World War I – namely a church used as a field hospital.[5]

Both films preserve Remarque's use of ironic contrast between the seemingly idyllic moments of soldiers enjoying blessed moments of quiet camaraderie in a field, smoking or playing cards, and the sadness they will encounter in the hospital setting. Mann gives this scene a rare infusion of bright color, as he dots the grass with red poppies and blue flowers, and lets Paul close his eyes and remember school day picnics on the grass with pretty girls and accordion music. This daydream is brutally interrupted by a comrade telling him that they are going to see Kemmerich – the soldier whose leg was wounded in the earlier attack. Remarque's hospital scene derives much of its power from the discrepancy between the role that material possessions, Kemmerich's stolen watch and highly desirable boots, play in the exchanges and concerns of the soldiers, and the mortality and physical pain that dominate as the larger reality of the scene. "[A]nybody can see that Kemmerich will never come out of this place again," Paul thinks to himself in the novel (14). In the Mann film, the soldiers' first visit to Kemmerich remains hopeful in spite of his pain. "Pain is your ticket home," one of the fellows tells him. Paul even makes drawings of the church hospital and Kemmerich after the visit. But his friend Müller reminds him that their friend will not need his boots again: "Why should an orderly get them, and not one of his friends." Paul has a flashback to a talented Kemmerich performing brilliant gymnastics, followed by the boy telling him that "They've amputated my leg" on his return visit to the hospital. Kemmerich now clearly knows he's going to die and disposes of his possessions. "If you find my watch, send it home," he tells Paul, breathing heavily, and "Give Müller my boots." Richard Thomas's painfully subdued demeanor expresses the trauma of recognizing that his friend is dying, and that he can do nothing more than offer platitudes until it is over and orderlies hurry to remove him to clear the bed for another patient. That moment of strained speech to his dying friend produces a powerful and effective sense of helpless grief, making it one of the most brilliant moments of Richard Thomas's acting in the film. Mann now inserts a flashback to the scene where amid joyful music the boys in their Sunday best, with bouquets of flowers in their lapels, are seen off on the train by a tearful Frau Kemmerich, begging Paul to take good care of her son. This intensifies the dreadful irony of the boy's unceremonious end in the presence of his impotent friend, who can do nothing to save him or spare him.

---

[5] For a photograph of an American Army field hospital inside the ruins of a church in France, see http://en.wikipedia.org/wiki/File:Field_hospital_WWI.jpg.

Because it progresses in chronological order, the Milestone film moves from the soldiers' jubilant enlistment, to scenes of their brutal discipline in a recruit camp before taking them to the front, their first skirmishes, and the wounding and death of Kemmerich. This re-arrangement of the sequence of the action has the powerful effect of having the viewer share the soldiers' loss of innocence as they go from patriotic joy to the grim reality of military discipline, and to the horrifying damage inflicted on the body by armed conflict. Remarque's sequence in the novel actually puts the bullying and tormenting by the recruit trainer Himmelstoß as a bracket around the boys' hospital visits to the wounded Kemmerich. The effect of ordering events this way is to stress the illogicality of military training, which brutalizes the boys while doing nothing to enhance their survival skills in the field. The miseries of warfare are shown to be doubled forms of cruelty: the abuse by authority and the pain and death inflicted by enemy arms. Remarque further contrasts Himmelstoß's futile and sadistic training with Kat's resourcefulness in scavenging and finding food for his men, further intensifying the disparity between military authority and hierarchy and its practical operation on the ground if it is to be effective in promoting survival at the front. Mann's sequencing is closer to Remarque's than to Milestone's. After the death of Kemmerich and Paul's flashback to the boys' departure from home by train, the flashback continues with the scenes of Himmelstoß making the soldiers throw themselves in the mud over and over again, hitting their hands with his pole as they present arms, and waking Paul in the middle of the night to run up and down stairs in his underwear in punishment for a moment of resistance. This hews quite closely to Paul's account in the novel. In all three productions, Remarque's, Milestone's, and Mann's, the soldiers' ambush and beating of Himmelstoß as he leaves a pub at night, gives both the men and the reader a rare moment of satisfaction that justice has been done. This in turn contrasts with the overwhelming sense of all three productions, that war itself offers no such satisfaction, and produces no justice whatsoever.

The irony of Himmelstoß's brutality is that his training is perfectly useless to the soldiers heading for the front. When they meet Kat in the Mann film, he first tells them that they'll need to work hard to forget everything they've learned in their basic training. He urges them to get some sleep before taking them out on their first patrol, where they will be traumatized by a horrific scene of wounded horses. The scene is as horrible in the film as it is in the novel, where the "screaming of the beasts" goes on and on until the men hold their ears in agony. Remarque writes, "It's unendurable. It is the moaning of the world, it is the martyred creation, wild with anguish, filled with terror, groaning" (62). The horses are finally shot, and Detering, the farmer, curses at the sight. "Like to know what harm they've done," he says in the novel (64) – a statement made ironic by the fact that the same thing can be said of the recruits who will later be killed by shelling and in a gas attack. The mercy killing of the wounded horses sets up another even more traumatic moment when a very young and very scared recruit is badly wounded during a gas attack. Kat knows he will not survive, and he and Paul think it best to euthanize the boy when medics arrive to take him away. The novel makes it clear that the boy will face the same fate as the screaming horses: "In an hour he will become a bundle of intolerable pain. Every day that he can live will be a howling torture" (72). The mercy killing of the horses magnifies the agony of dying soldiers who are refused a similar kindness. "Such a kid," Kat says of the young boy in the book. "Just a baby," he says in the film. However, the theme of euthanasia also sets up the larger grim truth which Paul voices in the Mann film, that soldiers are not only victims but also killers: "We can destroy and kill," "We turn into thugs and murderers." And it is here that *All Quiet on the Western Front* produces one of its most unique and valuable insights, which differentiates it from more conventional war novels and films in which the enemy is either reprehensible or abstract and in a sense invisible, while the soldiers they attack and fight against are represented as innocent victims whose own violence is defensive and justified. In the famous scene depicting Paul's killing of a French soldier with the intimacy of a close-up, the moral binary of wartime enemies is thoroughly confounded.

Remarque's novel sets the death of Kemmerich and Paul Bäumer's killing of the French soldier so far apart that the two deaths function almost like bookends – a structure preserved by both the Milestone and the Mann films. The point, of course, is to transfer the poignancy of Kemmerich's death to the other side, to emphasize that the deaths of enemy soldiers are just as dreadful and bitterly sad as the deaths of comrades. In the Mann film, Paul hides in a ditch because there are soldiers in blue, signifying they are French by their uniforms, moving above him. Suddenly a blue clad soldier jumps into Paul's ditch, and Paul instinctively stabs him. The man is not dead, but he is incapacitated and Paul literally has blood on his hands. He wants to leave but cannot because the shooting continues, and as a result he will be trapped with the dying French soldier for hours. The soldier cannot speak but he looks at Paul, he moves his head, he moans. Paul holds his hands over his ears. He clearly finds it painful to listen to the moaning of the dying soldier, as he and his comrades earlier found it intolerable to listen to the screaming of the wounded horses. Finally, he moves toward the man to comfort him and try to help, removing his helmet, unbuckling his belt, opening his jacket and shirt, of course soaked in blood. Mercifully, the French soldier finally dies, but this in no way defuses Paul's anguish. "I didn't want to kill you," he tells the man. "I will write to your family," he tells him in a desperately sad bid to offer some reparation. But as he searches the man's paper his anguish becomes only more intense. There is a photo that makes it clear that the man has a wife and a little girl. And his papers give his name and his profession. "I have killed Gerard Duval, a printer," Paul says. By having Duval never speak, Remarque avoids any sentimentality and offers instead a sentiment which is appropriate, which a reader can understand and with which he or she can empathize. The enemy is just another version of the self, a virtually identical version of the self, with a name, a profession, a family. The inanity of war, in which human beings are obliged to kill other human beings like themselves is poignantly dramatized in this scene.

Before the fighting that leads to Paul's killing of Gerard Duval, we see Paul in a ditch during a shelling, spotting a completely terrified Himmelstoß cowering helplessly, unable to move even though the men must get out of there. Paul is obliged to slap him to get him moving, an ironic reversal of roles, in a sense, with the further irony that Paul strikes only to save his former tormentor, not to discipline him. After this terrible battle sequence is over, it is the cowardly Himmelstoß who is unaccountably awarded a medal – intensifying the irony even more. The grim fighting is followed by a break during which the soldiers swim in a stream when they are distracted by female laughter and a friendly "*Bonjour*" from a group of passing French women. What ensues is a curious reprise of the picnic fantasy Paul was seen to enjoy earlier in the day, but with an odd twist. The soldiers bring the women some bread and sausage, and the famished women fall on the food, devouring it gratefully in large chunks. This draws our attention to the theme of hunger throughout Remarque's novel and its film versions. One of Kat's notable accomplishments is the scavenging of food for his men, which is ever in short supply.[6] In turn, the women's hunger is a reminder that war also causes tremendous hardships to the civilian populations on both sides. When Paul returns home after recovering from his injury in the hospital, he ironically brings bread, cheese, and butter to his own family, who are clearly struggling. The scene with the French women ought to be erotic, with the nearly naked men and the ensuing hand-holding and embracing between the soldiers and the girls. However, the emphasis is on compassion, on the humane encounter their meeting offers both sides, instead of what ought to be an enemy collision. Discussing this scene in the Milestone film, Andrew Kelly writes: "The scene with the French women is particularly important in stressing the point about the futility of international differences" (162).

---

[6] A decade after the publication of *All Quiet on the Western Front*, the dramatist Bertolt Brecht produced the play *Mother Courage and her Children* about a woman who travels the battlefronts of the Thirty Years' War with a canteen wagon allowing her to profit from the soldiers' need for food and supplies.

Both the Milestone and Mann films also preserve the desolate nature of the interval of Paul's visit to his home town and his family. The Mann film shows damaged buildings, looking very authentic, thanks to the Czechoslovakian setting. As in the book, the visit curiously presents Paul with a strange gender divide. Remarque has Paul note that "My mother is the only one who asks questions. Not so my father. He wants me to tell him about the front; he is curious in a way I find stupid and distressing" (165). His mother is ill, perhaps dying, and his sister struggles with her care and the insufficient provisions. His father, on the other hand, wants to show off Paul's uniform and take pride in his son while the mother is literally worried sick about him. The village men continue with their totally unrealistic and untenable patriotic cant without bothering to ask Paul to infuse their fatuity with his experience. The men think they know best and resist becoming enlightened. The women sense the truth of the violence and the cruelty of war, but must be spared confirmation of their terrified intuitions, obliging Paul to lie to them, to make it sound as though things are not too bad, and will not be worse in future. Mann also preserves Paul's painful lie to Kemmerich's mother that her son died instantly and never suffered. Even when she insists and demands "I want the truth," he takes the oath that will in a sense seal his own doom: "May I never come back if he wasn't killed instantly." This lie ends up haunting not only Paul but all three productions of *All Quiet on the Western Front*: the novel, the Milestone film and the Mann film. Remarque ends Paul's first person narration with the titular army report, "All quiet on the Western Front," on the day of Paul's death. As long as Paul narrates his story, we are reassured that he is alive. Once we are given the sentence "He fell in October 1918", however, we know that he is gone. Still, the third person voice comforts us just as Paul comforted Kemmerich's mother, telling us that he fell forward and looked as if he were sleeping, and that turning him over, "one saw that he could not have suffered long." We are as fatuous if we believe this as Kemmerich's mother if she believes Paul. No one dies quietly at the front, and in the end the novel and the movies lie to us just as Paul was obliged to lie, to keep grief at his inevitably cruel death from imploding us emotionally.

There is one more devastating casualty to deal with before we come to the death of Paul and to the end of the story, and that is the death of Kat. In the novel Paul suffers the same delusion that he tried to foster in Kemmerich, that Kat will be all right, that he has only an injured leg, that he has only fainted rather than being "stone dead," as the medics tell him. In the Mann film, the experience is just as difficult for Paul to negotiate. He first reassures Kat that he'll soon be in a comfortable bed in the hospital, although he knows from having been in hospitals that no wounded soldier is ever comfortable. He is so desperate to get Kat to the medics that he somehow manages to carry the much larger, bulkier man to the bombed out church that is full of corpses. There he is told "You could have spared yourself that. He's stone dead." Paul, incredulous, tries to give Kat water to drink, and when he realizes that his friend is actually gone, he keeps saying "He was talking. Twenty minutes ago. He was talking." The novel renders this experience of Paul's as the most poignant in his life. He cannot bear to be separated from the only person in his life who understands what he has gone through, who inspired him and comforted him and gave him hope. He gets Kat's address so that they can stay in touch and visit after the war, and even thinks of shooting himself in the foot so that he can accompany Kat to the hospital. He is so shaken when Kat is dead that the orderly asks with bafflement, "You are not related, are you?" "No, we are not related," Paul thinks, although the reader, who has accompanied the men on their terrible journey, and who is also now intimately connected to them, understands perfectly that Paul and Kat were more intimately related by their common experience than any blood relatives or family members could ever be. The film extends a similar intimacy to the viewer.

After the death of Kat, Paul himself is in effect emotionally dead. His classmates are all gone. Kat is gone. It is autumn and there is talk of an armistice. The reader, aware of the history of World War I, knows that the war did indeed end on 11 November 1918. Paul dies on 11 October, we are told in the Mann film – exactly a month earlier. Before his end Paul tells us in the novel, "Let the months and years come, they can take nothing from me, they can take nothing more" (295). He has lost everyone and everything: "I am so alone, and so without hope that I can confront them without fear." Both the Milestone and the Mann film faced a great challenge in deciding how to represent the death of Paul on the screen, since it is not pictured but only offered with a speculative comment in the novel. Milestone's decision was brilliant: to have a butterfly descend on the lid of a can, and have Paul shot by a sniper at the moment he reaches to touch the butterfly, "a timeless symbol of beauty and innocence" as Richard Firda calls it (103). The butterfly harks back to a collection of mounted butterflies seen on Paul's earlier visit home. Mann clearly cannot appropriate Milestone's butterfly, so he substitutes an effective variant. We first encountered Paul in a classroom drawing a bird outside the schoolroom window while his teacher vigorously promoted the war to his students. Paul, the dreamer, was distracted by the bird. And so, the Mann film ends with Paul once more writing or drawing in a notebook while the war surrounds him, distracted by the sight and sound of a bird when he is shot. It is a tribute to both the director Delbert Mann and to the actor Richard Thomas that the Paul Bäumer of the American television film preserves the sensitivity, the emotional delicacy and empathy, of Erich Maria Remarque's memorable protagonist in *All Quiet on the Western Front*.

References

Firda, Richard Arthur. *All Quiet on the Western Front: Literary Analysis and Cultural Context*. New York: Twayne Publishers, 1993.

Frisina, Scott A. "Simply War." Reviews and Ratings for *All Quiet on the Western Front* (TV). http://www.imbd.com/title/tt0078753/reviews (6 June 2013).

Fox, Margalit. "Delbert Mann, Director, Is Dead at 87." *New York Times* (13 November 2007). http://www.nytimes.com/2007/11/13/art/13 mann.html (6 June 2013).

Kelly, Andrew. *Filming 'All Quiet on the Western Front'*. London: I. B. Tauris Publishers, 1998.

Mitchell, George J. "Making *All Quiet on the Western Front*." *Bloom's Critical Interpretations: Erich Maria Remarque's 'All Quiet on the Western Front.'* Ed. Harold Bloom. New York: Infobase Publishing, 2009. 41–55.

Remarque, Erich Maria. *All Quiet on the Western Front*. Trans. A. W. Wheen. New York: Ballantine Books, 1996.

Silver, Charles. "Lewis Milestone's *All Quiet on the Western Front*." *Inside Out:* A MoMA/MoMaPS1 Blog. http://www.moma.org/explore/inside_out/2010/07/27/lewis-milestones-all-quiet-on-the-western-front (6 June 2013).

Filmography

All Quiet on the Western Front. Dir. Delbert Mann. Marble Arch Productions, 1979.
All Quiet on the Western Front. Dir. Lewis Milestone. Universal Pictures, 1930.

Caroline Perret
Wilfred Owen and His War Poetry in *Wilfred Owen: A Remembrance Tale* and *Regeneration/Behind the Lines*

This chapter deals with the representations of British poet Wilfred Owen and the uses of his most celebrated war poems in two very different types of British films. Gillies MacKinnon's feature film *Regeneration*/U.S.: *Behind the Lines* (1997), based on British author Pat Barker's novel of the same title, tells the story of WWI officers sent from the trenches to Craiglockhart Military Hospital for the treatment of war-related neurotic disorders, devoting considerable attention to the famous meeting of Wilfred Owen (Stuart Bunce) and Siegfried Sassoon (James Wilby).[1] The film deals with a wide range of issues, including the development of military psychiatry, the conflict between generations, class distinctions between officers and soldiers, duty and courage as opposed to the horror of war, and, last but not least, war poetry in its functions of telling the 'truth' of the soldiers' experience and of being a form of protest against the mass slaughter on the Great War battlefields. In the BBC documentary entitled *Wilfred Owen: A Remembrance Tale* (dir. Louise Hooper, 2007), presenter Jeremy Paxman travels to the former battlefields of France in order to elucidate how the most horrendous conditions of trench warfare generated some of the most compelling poetry in English. The journalist juxtaposes the language of poetry with the language of jingoism and wartime propaganda. The documentary includes actual WWI images and footage as well as dramatic re-enactments of the poet's life, with Samuel Barnett performing the role of Wilfred Owen. Though the films' aesthetic approaches and narrative strategies obviously differ, they share a similar concern with the question of expressing the hell of war truthfully, as well as a comparable tendency towards the blurring of boundaries between historical facts and poetry, and the use of biographical details to give an aura of authenticity to the story.

First aired by BBC One in November 2007, and later shown on BBC Four in November 2008 and 2010, the documentary is a tribute to the author of "some of the greatest war poetry ever written," and "the second most studied poet in Britain [after Shakespeare]." It is ironical, Paxman states, that though Owen

---

[1] *Regeneration* is the original British title, while *Behind the Lines* is the American title. It would also be interesting to note that Stuart Bunce played 2nd Lieutenant Frederick Radley of the 1/5th (Territorial) Battalion of the Norfolk Regiment in *All the King's Men* (dir. Julian Jarrold, 1999), where his character recited Rupert Brooke's "If I should die" at the grave of a killed British soldier at Gallipoli.

"reinvented war poetry," there was not one collection of his works published prior to his death at the age of twenty-five. Some of his poems would be included posthumously in the anthology *Wheels* of 1919, edited by poet Edith Sitwell, who also published a small selection of his poems in 1920, with an introduction written by Siegfried Sassoon. It would take a few decades, however, until Owen's reputation as "the greatest poet of the First World War" was to become firmly established. The poems included in the documentary, "Dulce Et Decorum Est," "The Last Laugh," "The Show," "The Sentry," "Strange Meeting," "Anthem for Doomed Youth," and "Insensibility" were chosen for being most representative of the realities of trench warfare, in particular its deafening sounds and violence, the gas attacks, the No Man's Land and mutilated landscape, and the weapons of the war. In addition, the chosen poems tell us about Owen's personal combat experiences, his fear of death, and his coping mechanisms. The film *Regeneration* likewise makes use of Owen's poetry: "Anthem for Doomed Youth," "Greater Love," "Dulce Et Decorum Est," "The Calls," and "The Parable of the Old Man and the Young." This choice of poems underscores the anti-war message of the film in opposition to State propaganda, and more subtly, the ambiguity of feelings on the part of Owen – and Sassoon. While underlying the worse horrors of war, resulting in the unnecessary loss of young lives as well as the physical and psychological traumas of the surviving soldiers, the film deals with the pride in sacrifice and the sense of duty on the part of the officers and soldiers.[2]

The commemorative documentary is introduced by the preface Owen wrote for his intended collection of fifty war poems: "This book is not about heroes. English poetry is not yet fit to speak of them. Nor is it about deeds, or lands, nor anything about glory, honour, might, majesty, dominion, or power, except War. Above all I am not concerned with Poetry. My subject is War, and the pity of War. The Poetry is in the pity." Owen rejects the political and military rhetoric which justifies and glamorizes war and argues for a warning and humanising role that poetry should play amidst its horrors, not just those of WWI, but those of any military conflict. Paxman voices over the footage of unprecedented carnage: "WWI brought the fruits of the industrial age to killing, massed it, mechanised it, and turned it into wholesale slaughter. Between 1914 and 1918, nine million men were to die." The fact that "Owen gave a voice to these men" is acknowledged by the complementary images of soldiers going 'over the top.' Generally, the documentary shows Owen transforming from a sensitive young man troubled

---

[2] In contrast to Barker's novel, MacKinnon's adaptation begins and ends with Owen, who is moreover given a greater role than Sassoon. For a detailed comparison of the novel and the film adaptation see Westman.

by the "rough" men he had to command into a perfect soldier and efficient officer respectful of his fighting men and defender of their cause.

The first poem to appear in the documentary is "Dulce et Decorum Est" (October 1917 – March 1918). It is read with passion, first by Paxman, with accompanying archival footage of soldiers in the trenches, and then by Samuel Barnett, in the role of Owen, looking straight at the camera, as if the poet himself were talking – across time – directly to us, the contemporary viewer, in order to establish a physical and emotional proximity between the viewer and his message. The images of soldiers in the trenches fade into a dramatic re-enactment of a gas attack. The title is taken from a well-known quotation from one of the ancient Roman poet Horace's "Odes," *dulce et decorum est pro patria mori*, that translates into "it is sweet and fitting to die for one's country." In opposition to this rallying call to war, often used at the start of WWI, Owen focuses on one of the worst horrors of the Great War: a gas attack. As such, "Dulce et Decorum Est" has become one of the most iconic pleas of the anti-war cause, and its choice as the first poem to appear in the documentary indicates the sharing of such a stance by Paxman. The lines "But someone still was yelling out and stumbling / And floundering like a man in fire or lime [...] / Dim, through the misty panes and thick green light / As under a green sea, I saw him drowning" is a poetic, and yet precise rendering of the effects of being gassed by chlorine, described in the documentary as "drowning in one's phlegm" by military historian Taff Gillingham. Owen's language is direct and realistic, aiming for the shock effect, and leaving the reader with disturbing images, such as "froth-corrupted lungs," the "sores on innocent tongues," i.e. the regurgitated substances in the soldier's mouth, the dying man's face being "like a devil's sick of sin," the burning of live tissue with "lime," as well as the "hoots" of the "five-nine" explosive shells, the guttering sounds made by the dying man. The poem uses the pattern and rhyming of a French sonnet, but then breaks its conventions down to accentuate the profoundly chaotic nature of the event as well as despair at the collapsing moral order. While the first part of the poem is written in the present as the action unfolds and the soldiers are trying to come to terms with the assault, the second part is written as though Owen were distancing himself from the horror, as if in a "dream," but one from which the reader can experience a powerful sense of compassion, but also a feeling of revolt. Indeed, Owen concludes with an ironical use of the Roman motto, calling it "the old lie" being told "To children ardent for some desperate glory" (*The Poems* 117).

On arrival in France in 1917, Owen wrote about his initial reaction to his mother: "there is a fine heroic feeling about being in France." He was as yet unaware, Paxman states, that the "life expectancy of an officer on the front line was [then] measured in days." Owen was soon to face the realities of trench warfare. A year earlier, the infamous Somme offensive had been launched. As Paxman emphasizes, propaganda played its part: "films of the greatest historical event that has ever yet been pictorized were watched by awe-struck citizens," but "the worst horrors were never shown," such as the "60,000 casualties" on the very first day of the battle. Owen was "appalled by the shattered landscape," a shock that gave rise to the poem "The Show," the title referring to the army slang for battle. As in "Dulce et Decorum Est," the idea of war reporting is again present, with a personal involvement particularly noticeable through the use of the pronouns "I" and "my." Owen is very specific and concrete about what the combat involves: once the men come out of the relative safety of the trenches, they are confronted by a ground "cratered like the moon with hollow woe," "the horror of harsh wire," "hidden holes" – the remnants of exploded landmines, and "foul openings" – the corpses which lay in no-man's land. The "slimy paths" also tell the reader that WWI soldiers lived and died in mud, heads to the ground ("intent on mire"). Adding to these descriptions, a similarity is made between the battered landscape and the mutilated bodies and minds of the men by means of half-rhymes and the breaking up of some of the stanzas (for instance, lines 10–13), as well as specific phrases personifying the landscape, such as "myriad warts," "sweats of dearth," and "fitted with great pocks and scabs of plagues." This resemblance between the shattered battleground and the bodies and souls of the men is evoked in the documentary footage accompanying the reading of "The Show," as well as in the introductory scene of *Regeneration*.

Moreover, throughout the poem, 'Death' is the soldiers' companion, with a particularly brilliant half-rhyme depicting the landscape as "a sad land, weak with sweats of dearth." Such is the chaos that the men are no longer identifiable as human beings and seem to be in a transmuted state, they are "long-strung creatures" and "[b]rown strings [...] with bristling spines." Words related to movement and action also seem animalistic or sub-human, such as "migrants," "slowly uncoiled," and "writhed and shrivelled." Generally, the image of a terrifying living hell is evoked by an ambiguous sensation of distance and reality, typical of nightmares: the vision is one from "a vague height," the experience "[a]s unremembering how I rose or why," and the description uncertain with "It seemed" (*The Poems* 132). At the centre of "The Show," there is the notion of a loss of identity, the soldier being insignificant in the face of historical events. His life itself is worthless, not in his eyes, nor the public's, but in the eyes of the politicians who have made the decision for the nation to go to war and for the massacre to continue. The latter is the result of a choice "of whose life *is* a life, and whose life is effectively transformed into an instrument, a target, or a number, and is effaced with only a trace remaining or none at all" (Butler ix–x).

According to Paxman, Owen's poetry developed as a reaction against the legitimation of WWI by the nation state and military power, supported by some intellectuals such as Rudyard Kipling and Rupert Brooke, as well as against the "romantization" (Paxman's own words) of warfare at the time, evident in such pervasive hymns as "Jerusalem." After his one-year stay at Craiglockhart, Owen considered the function of poetry as testimony more important than ever before, as pointed out by the journalist: "Owen was determined to go back to the front, as it would give him the authority to speak. As an officer, he felt a responsibility to lead his men; as a poet, he felt it his role to bear witness to their suffering and courage." The sonnet "Anthem for Doomed Youth," written between September and October 1917, is a mournful elegy to young soldiers whose lives were unnecessarily lost in WWI and thus a plain anti-war statement. The octet consists of a list of the deafening sounds of trench warfare – "monstrous anger of the guns," "stuttering rifles' rapid rattle," whose alliteration echoes the sound itself, "wailing shells"– set against the restrained atmosphere of the church. Symbolic of the sanctity of life and death, religious imagery abounds: the "passing-bells" tolled to announce someone's death, the "orisons" or funeral prayers, "voice of mourning," "choirs," "candles" – lit in the room where a body lies in a coffin, "holy glimmers of goodbyes," "pall" – a coffin cloth. This juxtaposition suggests the inadequacy and pointlessness of organized religion when confronted with such butchery. Indeed, the expression "die as cattle" conjures up the image of a slaughterhouse. In particular, the word "mockeries" seems to articulate such a tension, and the "choirs of wailing shells" is an astonishing metaphor uniting both God's and the Devil's world, while "patter out their hasty orisons" denotes disrespect. As such, the poem is a clear rejection of the religion with which Owen was brought up. Progressively, the poem moves away from the fighting front to funeral rituals conducted by the families of the dead "from sad shires," the English counties and countryside from which a large proportion of the soldiers came, and with "bugles," commonly played at military funerals. The tone and the pace quieten from harsh fervour to regretful and solemn reflection, until the poem quietly closes with the "drawing down of blinds," whose corresponding dimming of the light is echoed in the dusk descending onto earth in a finite and slow gesture, as though to let the dead person lie in peace (*The Poems* 76).

Paxman's opening comment on Owen's verse being "far, far more vivid than any war reporting can ever be" posits Owen's poetry, and the documentary itself, within the "question of the epistemological position to which we are recruited when we watch or listen to war reports" (Butler xii). Incidentally, this question seems also to be suggested by the poignant footage of a soldier carrying a man (or is it a body?) on his back and looking at the camera, his eyes void of understanding. Butler contends that the state regulates the understanding which the public has and receives of violence by framing a certain version of reality. In this perspective, she suspects that the framing act becomes a part of "the materiality of war and the efficacy of its violence" (Butler xii–xiii). It is common knowledge that WWI marks the beginning of what will become "image propaganda" ("Le vrai contre le faux," Gervereau 91). Thus it is potent that Owen's poetry is very descriptive of the specificity of war, its weapons, both mechanical and chemical, their effects on the human body and psychology. Those were, of course, absent from state propaganda, and I would agree with Butler that with regard to the normative images chosen by the State, these censored images form "a rubbish heap whose animated debris provides the potential resources for resistance" (xiii). They do so even more convincingly, I would think, as they are seen through the 'eyes' of the reader's imagination, thus avoiding the pitfalls that "graphic depictions can sometimes do no more than [lead to] sensationalism and episodic outrage" (Butler xiv).[3] Moreover, the reader is given the space to own these images mentally – almost physically – by means of a profound appeal to his/her senses. This is, I believe, the strength of poetry as opposed to photography and film, as it enables "a normative evaluation of a war" in Butler's terminology, so that the public can indeed question the validity of such an enterprise (xv). It therefore seems redundant, to come back to our discussion of Paxman's documentary, that the image of gassed soldiers is shown as the poem is read out, as it cancels its suggestively poignant effect and reduces it to "graphic depiction." In this sense, this documentary perfectly exemplifies contemporary image-oriented and performance-oriented culture, as the reading of poems is always accompanied by photographic images, documentary footage, or re-enactment, as if poetry – on its own – were no longer sufficient to convey the message.

Moreover, Butler believes, as I do, that "[t]here is no thinking and judgement without the senses, and there is no thinking and judgement about war without the senses assuming a social form [...]. Waging war in some ways begins with the assault on the senses; the senses are the first target of war" (xvi). Paxman's comment that Owen embodied the opposition between war and poetry, a core idea of his argument, reflects the belief that poetry becomes a part of the framing – or rather the re-framing of war. The tension between war and poetry is 'embodied' in Owen's tribute to the men who fought and his anger against "the armchair generals and war-mongers who sent young men off to die," his dignifying and celebrating of "those who had to do the fighting."

---

[3] I am talking here about the difference between the passive 'seeing' of photographic or film images and an 'imagining' of the scene described in the case of poetry, which forces the reader to become emotionally and ethically involved.

The appreciation and resonance of Owen's poetry with contemporary soldiers is illustrated in the documentary with an interview with Major Justin Featherstone, an Iraq war veteran and recipient of the Military Cross, who remarks: "[H]e speaks with an honest, almost blunt vision of what being a soldier is about." This is also eloquently articulated in Paxman's conclusion:

> It was not until the 1960s that Owen's poetry really gained popularity. His unflinching depiction of war spoke powerfully to the protest generation. But these poems speak to every generation which chooses to listen. [...] What Owen does is to enable us to understand that war is about more than the strategies of generals or the manufactured animosity of politicians. His lasting memorial is to enable us to understand the human experience of war, in short, the pity of war.

To illustrate this point, a photograph of the soldiers in Owen's battalion, the 2nd Manchesters, is shown in the documentary. In this group portrait, while the feeling of camaraderie between the men is palpable, the soldiers look exhausted and ragged.[4]

This type of war photograph, the one which avoids the graphic depiction of war itself, is particularly poignant. According to Roland Barthes in *Camera Lucida*, the photographic image is already beyond the present moment to convey the pathos of past times. It "does not necessarily say *what is no longer*, but only and for certain *what has been*" (85). It is, by its very nature, located in history, but in this very specific instance it is also looking implicitly at the perspective of death, it almost acts as one entry in the visual diary of the narrative of death, something the documentary does not fail to exploit. This point is also made by Susan Sontag in *On Photography*: "Photographs state the innocence, the vulnerability of lives heading towards their own destruction, and this link between photography and death haunts all photographs of people" (70). This haunting resonance, it would seem, would produce in the viewer an understanding of the vulnerability and finite nature of human life. Then this characteristic of Jacques Derrida's concept of "absolute pastness," to be applied here to the photograph, would be the condition for the grievability of its subjects, whose lives are in the process of non-being, and therefore for the compassion of the viewer towards the afore-mentioned subjects. This in itself could be quite a political outcome for the photograph. Indeed, the photograph can be an "invitation [...] to pay attention, reflect [...] examine the rationalizations for mass suffering offered by established powers" (Sontag 117). However, like Laurent Gervereau in *Les Images qui mentent*,

---

4 Later in the documentary, Paxman would explain Owen's emphatic description of his friendship and respect in his last letter to his mother a few days before his death when sheltering in a forester's house in Ors.

I believe that there is a remedial dialogue between image and text, an exclusive efficiency of the pair of image and text, whether the latter is written or spoken (cf. 312–313). True understanding can only come from narrative, explanation and information, and this is beautifully demonstrated by both Hooper's documentary and MacKinnon's film.

The effectiveness of both films derives from their structure, following what André Bazin has termed the "ideological documentary of montage," whose "aim is less to present than to demonstrate," since "[it has] the flexibility and precision of language." In this method, images and text are treated as raw materials that are re-arranged so as to demonstrate the desired argument (Bazin 34). Of course, in the case of propaganda, this is a 'dangerous' technique, as it "lends the logical structure of discourse to the images and the credibility and evidence of the photographic image to the discourse. The viewer has the illusion of being present at a visual demonstration, when it is in fact only a sequence of [fragmentary views] which are held together only by the cement of the accompanying words" (Bazin 35). In the documentary, however, this method leads to a convincingly humanist message, whose foundation of evidently well-researched information lends an aura of objectivity to what is shown. The use of photographs, footage, and re-enactment as well as poetry enables the viewer to share the journalist's anti-war views.

In both *Remembrance Tale* and *Regeneration*, the year Owen spent at Craiglockhart is foregrounded as the most formative period of his life. In April 1917, Paxman explains, Owen was on the front line to hold a railway line as a German shell struck the embankment and projected him into the air only to land him amidst the scattered remains of a close friend. Following the incident, Owen suffered from shell-shock. The documentary shows images of suffering patients, demonstrating how the "body simply could not take the stress of intense modern warfare any longer." According to Professor Edgar Jones from the Maudsley Hospital in London, which was set up in January 1916 for the purpose of treating shell-shocked cases, neurasthenia involves a range of very extreme symptoms: "tremor, shakiness, loss of sensations, headaches, general loss of nerves," which, as the documentary images demonstrate, affects body functions so severely that it is a struggle to walk or even stand. We also learn from *Regeneration* that mutism was another symptom, and as it was considered to be a sign of blocked memory, hypnosis was used following Freud's lead. Professor Edgar Jones explained that it originated from the constant thought of losing one's life as well as tension between performing one's duty and saving one's life. The soldier, therefore, unconsciously created symptoms in order to leave the front line. Some early treatments were monstrous, pitiless and inhuman, including the application of electric shock. Dr Yealland in London, for instance, terrified the soldiers to restore their function, as the pain of the jolt was hoped to be worse than the fear of going back to the front. Owen was luckier as he was treated in the progressive Craiglockhart Hospital for officers near Edinburgh. While innovative Dr H. J. Brock used occupational therapy to reconnect the soldiers with their natural environment and the idea of friendship, he encouraged Owen to edit the hospital magazine *Hydra* and write again. With this method, he rightly hoped, Owen would confront the horrors of war and re-live his nightmares in poetry as part of his recovery process. According to Paxman, "the saving of Owen's sanity was really the making of him as a poet." This period of intense creativity was also enhanced by his meeting with Siegfried Sassoon, who assisted him redrafting the poem, substituted "doomed" for "dead," and found the well-known by-name of "patient minds." (The amended manuscript copy, in both men's handwriting, may be found at the British Library, as indicated in Paxman's visit there.)

In *Regeneration*, the focus is on the despair and anguish of the patients suffering from shell-shock. The preferred method of William H. Rivers is to encourage the officers to speak about their nightmares and hallucinations. The viewer of the film is thus confronted with horrors of war through his/her own imagined images, which I believe puts into practice again the internalisation of our senses discussed earlier. In one sequence, for instance, we learn of Burns, who cannot eat because of his memory of rotten flesh, or of the experience of having to live with the skulls of dead soldiers embedded in a trench. In this manner, the viewer is completely immersed with the sensual engagement necessary for a more profound understanding of the war.[5] Throughout the films, there are short sequences which deal with the issues raised earlier, such as the opposition between war and poetry; the "terrifying, noisy, suicidal" military strategy [sic] which would let soldiers walk in broad daylight while being shot at and which would eventually sacrifice, according to Prior, "15,000 lives" – some as young as 17, with asthma or even tuberculosis – "for an advance of 500 yards of mud"; the social-class hierarchy of the army – which would even be reflected in the psychological symptoms of suffering patients; the compassionate portrayal of neurasthenia as a mental wound, as opposed to the military presentation of it as a weakness; the issue of the lack of recognition of the soldier's individuality. In the film, the latter point is carefully being re-addressed by Sassoon and Prior, who both make sure that they name and identify their victim friend, whose dying circumstances have triggered hallucinations and mutism. The film, however, pushes these ideas even further with the character of Prior, who, formerly mute, becomes the most virulently outspoken of all the patients. In an argument reminiscent of Antonin Artaud's "Van

---

5 Except in the case of Prior's trauma, whose cause is shown to the viewer in very graphic details.

Gogh: the Man Suicided by Society," he reverses the general consensus, arguing for the madness of the war decision-makers.

Paxman explains how Owen decided to join up and train as both a soldier and an officer following the "frantic recruitment campaign" initiated by British War Minister Lord Kitchener to attract volunteers, and the propaganda onslaught, with the popular press filled with patriotic slogans and "jingoist tosh" about a war that would end by Christmas. Paxman adds that Owen was concerned that a German victory would threaten English culture, and he wanted to save the language of Keats and Shakespeare. This is the most important piece of information given by Paxman about Owen's motivations for enlisting, as the war was indeed propagated as a "liberation war." Butler's statement about the necessity to define the criteria used for the validity and justifiability of current conflicts waged in the Middle-East in order to develop an efficient opposition applies here: WWI was thought to be "an inevitability," "or even a source of moral satisfaction," and it is in this sense that popular support was then being "cultivated and maintained" (ix). It was also the reason why it was such a difficult war to oppose. Siegfried Sassoon's example is telling: as a recognised poet and officer decorated with the Military Cross, he publicly condemned the on-going conflict as a "war of aggression and conquest" in his "Public Statement of Defiance" in July 1917. In order to avoid court-martial, he was transferred to Craiglockhart. Sassoon was thus effectively silenced, his case clearly showing the power of the State to 'neutralize' anti-war sentiment. In fact, Sassoon was rebelling against the artifice of what Butler defines as "victimisation":

> If a particular subject considers her- or himself to be by definition injured or indeed persecuted, then whatever acts of violence such a subject commits cannot register as 'doing injury,' since the subject who does them is, by definition, precluded from doing anything but suffering injury. As a result, the production of the subject on the basis of its injured status then produces a permanent ground for legitimating (and disavowing) its own violent actions. (179)

Moreover, both Owen and Sassoon were aware of the ambivalence of their moral position when, while strongly against the war, they decided, after their stay at Craiglockhart, to go back to the front to fulfil their duty to protect the soldiers under their command – a decision which is made very explicit in both the documentary and film. Such an act demonstrates that they understood the clear distinction "between (a) that injured and rageful subject who gives moral legitimacy to rageful and injurious conduct, thus transmuting aggression into virtue, and (b) that injured and rageful subject who nevertheless seeks to limit the injury that she or he causes, and can do so only through an active struggle with and against aggression" (Butler 172).

However, I would further emphasize a point which is not made in the documentary, and only alluded to in the film, namely that both Owen and Sassoon also had some unconscious reasons to go back to the front, which can only be explained by survivor's guilt. In *Mourning and Melancholia*, Sigmund Freud allocates the role of the super-ego to the process of internalising and transforming the lost other as a recriminating voice. This voice then speaks exactly what the ego would have said to the other if the latter had stayed alive (cf. 243–258). This dialogue is precisely what is at play in "Strange Meeting," whose following lines best exemplify this point:

> "Strange friend," I said, "Here is no cause to mourn."
> "None," said the other, "Save the undone years,
> The hopelessness. Whatever hope is yours,
> Was my life also; I went hunting wild
> After the wildest beauty in the world,
> Which lies not calm in eyes, or braided hair,
> But mocks the steady running of the hour,
> And if it grieves, grieves richlier than here" (*The Poems* 125).

For Emmanuel Levinas, ethical responsibility originates from an anxiety, itself due to an ambivalent choice which continues to be unresolved. This ambiguity could have been settled through the acceptance of the predominant choice – in this case, the one of killing, but instead, it gives rise to an ethical choice that seeks to preserve life rather than destroy it:

> There is an anxiety of responsibility that is incumbent on everyone in the death or suffering of the other (*autrui*). The fear of everyone for themselves in the mortality of everyone does not succeed in *absorbing* the gravity of murder committed and the scandal of indifference to the suffering of the other (*autrui*). Behind the danger that everyone runs for themselves in an insecure world, there dawns the consciousness of the immediate immorality of a culture and a history. (164)

Moreover, following Theodor Adorno one has to be aware that war and violence waged in the name of peace and civilisation may reveal their own barbarism, even when they are rationalised by assuming and sometimes constructing the savage impulses and human inferiority of the "enemy":

> The affront against taste and consideration, from which no good act is exempt, completes the leveling, which the powerless utopia of the beautiful opposes. From the beginnings of mature industrial society, the allegiance to evil was not only the precursor of barbarism, but also a mask of the good. Its dignity passed over to evil, by drawing all hatred and all resentment of the social order to itself, an order which drilled the good into its members, so that it could be evil without punishment. (88)

This was precisely Sassoon's point when faced with the argument of German militarism. In *Regeneration*, his character comments: "In the name of civilisation, men are being sent to [...] slaughter. [...] Martyrdom is a dirty swindle," because war is managed by businessmen who are only concerned with their own interests.

On the one hand, the argument about the treatment of soldiers as mere fighting machines is made quite forcibly in one of the scenes in *Regeneration*. Soldiers were cured of neurasthenia through electric shock in order to be 'repaired' as quickly as possible and go back to the front. On the other hand, the point of view which sees the soldiers as anonymous is reinforced by Paxman's visit to one of the 200 cemeteries in the Somme – with 7,000 graves each – and his comment on the fact that two-thirds of the graves are occupied by unknown soldiers, nameless and unidentified. In the conclusion of his documentary, he even states:

> It seems to me that these beautifully-tended war cemeteries tell something of a lie. With their immaculately straight ranks and their uniformed head-stones, they seem to suggest that all soldiers are the same, and they are not. Some of them were tall, some were short, some were fat, some were thin, some were sporty, some were bookish, some probably were fearless, and many were utterly terrified.

In this sense therefore, following on Butler's argument about "livable and grievable lives," the cemeteries do not seem to be so much of an homage to the suffering and death of the victims, but tend to show that these lives were never considered lives in the first place, have never been really lost, and can never be truly and sincerely grieved (1).[6] According to Butler, "[t]he 'being' of life is itself constituted through selective means; as a result, we cannot refer to this 'being' outside of the operations of power, and we must make more precise the specific mechanisms of power through which life is produced" (1). In addition to exploiting the tension between the Allies and Germany, WWI revealed and reinforced the class segregation and social norms so predominant in British society, as the army hierarchy followed the standard pyramidal structure of social classes in Britain: the soldiers were working-class and/or from the colonies, the officers middle-class, and the higher-grades from the upper-class, thus following a decreasing degree of risks – and value – to their lives.

I have shown through the study of two very different types of British films that Wilfred Owen's poetry is to be located, not so much within a claim for non-violence, but as the revelation of the tension between the overpowering of the sovereignty of the British state and its upper-class on the one hand and the horrific realities of war which were escaping an ill-informed and largely complacent

---

[6] There is a case to be argued for the renaming of all the tombs from the long lists of the deceased owned by the state.

audience in England on the other. Thus, beyond the horrors of the huge number of the dead and wounded of WWI, legitimized by the nation-state and military principle, Owen's poems demand a moral response. As they formulate and occupy different forms of affects, from intense passion and anger to deeply-felt pity, they touch our senses. Owen's poetry is not only an appeal and a form of 'war reporting,' but also a means for the poet to survive psychologically. More importantly, Owen's poetry stands as a memorial to the human power of interpretation, deconstruction, and expression, which, in the face of an oppressing dominant ideology, one that justifies warfare with the prospect of peace, found a very unique voice, but one that would speak to millions then and now. However, Owen does not just oppose the dominant ideology; his poetry exposes its mechanisms and discursive dimension. Butler's conclusion for her analysis of poems written by prisoners in Guantánamo applies here: "[...] the poems resist that sovereignty [...] [and] clearly have political consequences [...], they remain proof of stubborn life, vulnerable, overwhelmed, their own and not their own, disposed, enraged, [...]. [They are] critical acts of resistance, insurgent interpretations, incendiary acts that somehow, incredibly, live through the violence they oppose" (62).

Acknowledgments

With all my most sincere thanks to Helena Scott for her constant help and support, and to Nadège Clark for her friendship.

References

Adorno, Theodor. *Minima Moralia: Reflections from Damaged Life.* Trans. E. F. N. Jephcott. London: Verso, 2005.
Barthes, Roland. *Camera Lucida: Reflections on Photography.* Trans. Richard Howard. New York: Hill and Wang, 1982.
Bazin, André. *Qu'est que le cinéma?* Paris: Les Éditions du CERF, 2003.
Butler, Judith. *Frames of War – When is Life Grievable?* London and New York: Verso, 2009.
Freud, Sigmund. *Mourning and Melancholia.* Trans. James Strachey. London: The Hogarth Press, 1957 [1917].
Gervereau, Laurent. *Les Images qui mentent.* Paris: Seuil, 2011.
Levinas, Emmanuel. "Peace and Proximity." *Emmanuel Levinas: Basic Philosophical Writings.* Eds. Adriaan T. Peperzak, Simon Critchley, and Robert Bernasconi. Bloomington: Indiana University Press, 1966. 161–170.
Owen, Wilfred. *The Poems.* Ed. Jon Stallworthy. New York and London: Norton, 1985.
Sontag, Susan. *Regarding the Pain of Others.* New York: Farrar, Strauss and Giroux, 2003.
Westman, Karen W. "Generation, Not Regeneration: Screening Out Class, Gender, and Cultural Change in the Film of *Regeneration.*" *Critical Perspectives on Pat Barker.* Eds. Margaretta Jolly, Sharon Monteith, Ronald Paul and Nahem Yousaf. Columbia: University of South Carolina Press, 2005. 162–174.

Filmography

Regeneration. Dir. Gillies MacKinnon. Norstar Entertainment, 1997.
Wilfred Owen: A Remembrance Tale. Dir. Louise Hooper. British Broadcasting Corporation, 2007.

Ross J. Wilson
It Still Goes On: Trauma and the Memory of the First World War

1 Popular Memory of the First World War: Australia, Britain and Canada

The First World War casts a long shadow from its outbreak to the present day. Within former combatant nations, such as Australia, Britain and Canada, the conflict of 1914–1918 possesses an almost mythical status (cf. Fussell 5; Vance 7; Winter 6). To even mention the battles of the war, such as the Somme, Vimy or Gallipoli, within these states is to seemingly conjure, almost automatically, visions of devastated, debris-strewn landscapes, suffering soldiers enduring the torrent of industrialised warfare and strong emotions of pity, sadness, anger and national pride (cf. Todman; Thomson). This is the 'popular memory' of the conflict; defined as the wider perceptions of the populace, emerging from tradition and culture, which are placed in contrast to the practices of the professional or academically rigorous pursuit of 'history' (Popular Memory Group et al. 205). This contrast between history and memory with regard to the First World War is especially acute amongst the Anglophone nations that contributed to the British Army. Indeed, the very remembrance of the war of 1914–1918 within these societies is accompanied by a veil of sorrow and sentimentality that scholars have found almost impenetrable (cf. Bond). This common remembrance of the conflict has been harshly critiqued, albeit perhaps accurately, as the 'rats, gas, mud and blood' image of the war, as this perception reinforces the apparently widely-held belief of a fiery, bloody conflict that caused the deaths of hundreds and thousands of men with a corresponding impact upon bereaved families at home (cf. Corrigan). However, this popular memory of the First World War, considered to be held by individuals, groups and communities in these nations has been the subject of a sustained assessment from historians over the past three decades.

Within Australia, Britain and Canada, a number of studies have sought to demonstrate the ways in which the popular memory of the conflict can be contested (cf. Sheffield, Corrigan, Todman). Revisionist historians have sought to provide a reassessment of the First World War beyond the established tropes of disillusionment and despair. Rather than the images of troops experiencing the horror and brutality in the maelstrom of war, studies have focused on the camaraderie, loyalty and determination present within the ranks. Some historians have even demonstrated the opportunities for enjoyment in wartime and the willing participation of soldiers in all aspects of military service, including the killing of enemy combatants (cf. Bourke). Whilst the popular memory focuses upon the waste of life, with the military and political elite considered to favour ill-considered tactics to break through the opposing lines of trenches, military historians have examined the conflict as an operational success. These studies have demonstrated that new technologies were incorporated successfully into troop manoeuvres, which not only revealed the awareness of conditions in the field, but also ensured the eventual triumph of the British Imperial Army and its allies in 1918. This success of the military operations is a fundamental point made by revisionist historians to counter the notions of futility that have seemingly rendered the cessation of hostilities in November 1918 as a "forgotten victory" (cf. Sheffield).

These studies have also examined the fabricated nature of the popular memory of the conflict within former combatant societies. These analyses have argued that the conceptions held regarding the First World War are the product not of history but of an acceptance of cultural forms. Post-war memoirs, novels, film and television programmes which represent the war, whether through scenes of the battlefields with stoic, suffering soldiers, or behind the lines with shell-shocked victims of the conflict are regarded as the source of the popular 'misconceptions' of the conflict. These media are considered to promote limited views of the war, focusing on shock and emotion as cynical ploys to garner the attention of their audiences (cf. Badsey). Whether it is Paul Gross's film *Passchendaele* in Canada, the classic television comedy *Blackadder Goes Forth* in Britain or Peter Weir's iconic film *Gallipoli* in Australia, the depictions of the war are critiqued by historians who regard the limited and clichéd expressions as fuelling a public misunderstanding. In short, the popular perception of the conflict is a 'media-ted memory.' This popular memory is also a distinct post-war creation, emerging not from the battlefields themselves but through the representations of the conflict after 1918. For example, in Britain the memoirs of Siegfried Sassoon, Edmund Blunden and Robert Graves are regarded as setting the scene for the portrait of the war as an exercise in futility and disillusion resulting in the tragic deaths of hundreds and thousands of young men (cf. Bond 5–7). This creation of memory has been judged by revisionist historians who have demonstrated that the popular remembrance of the conflict in this period, and indeed up to the present day, has reflected more about those engaged in the process of remembering than it does about the events of 1914 to 1918.

However, in the desire to stress the nature of the 'invented tradition' of this popular memory, scholars have frequently disregarded or derided the significance that this memory holds within the societies which honour it. Despite the similarities in form that the popular memory holds across the three nations, focusing on the brutality, horror and trauma of war, the manners in which it is employed are quite different. In Australia, the popular memory of the war is ingrained within notions of national identity. The remembrance of the sacrifice made by the Australian and New Zealand Army Corps (ANZACs) is regarded as the foundation myth for the nation, to mark it as separate and distinctive from Britain as its colonial ruler (cf. Thomson 9). From this body of men are considered to emerge the defining aspects of the national character; of strength, perseverance, anti-authoritarianism, 'mateship' and humour. In Britain, the popular memory serves as an equally important part in the formation of identity. The image of the suffering soldier in the trenches has been used to mobilise political identities, as left-wing elements have drawn upon the notion of incompetent upper-class officers sending wave after wave of working-class men to their deaths in a pointless attack to highlight abuses of power and the neglect of society by authorities (cf. Wilson). In Canada, the conflict also serves as a means of portraying a national character. The service and dedication of Canadian troops, particularly on the battlefields of Beaumont Hamel and Vimy Ridge, have been seared into the popular consciousness as examples *par excellence* of national heroism, victory and romantic individualism (Vance 5–6). Therefore, whilst the popular memory has been the object of debate and a target for revision, commentators have overlooked the function and utility of this remembrance.

This purpose is especially significant in the consideration of the persistence of this popular memory. Despite the attempts of scholars to challenge the widely held perceptions of the war in Australia, Britain and Canada, it is the image of 'mud, blood, rats and gas' that still holds sway. Remembering the battlefields of the First World War as a devastated arena of industrialised conflict where individuals suffered horrendous torments in the tumult of artillery and machine guns, whilst serving varying purposes across these societies, has proven to be quite intractable. Therefore, rather than seeking to unsettle public perceptions, the issue for consideration should be why the popular memory focuses on the trauma of the war. In this regard the cultural representations are paramount. Whilst novels, film and television have been analysed as the source of memory, they perhaps more accurately reflect widely held beliefs regarding the war (Wertsch 17). Certain representations of the conflict find favour over others because they are perceived as representing the 'truth' of the war. This truth is the horror of the war; this is the trauma that is communicated and valued by the consumers of these cultural forms. Indeed, whilst the purposes of cultural representations in Australia, Britain and Canada are drawn upon for differing agendas, it is the depiction of the horror and brutality of the war that forms a consistent thread.

To assess this commonality, the theories associated with cultural trauma can be used to investigate not how the representations of the war have shaped popular memory, but how novels, film and television have enabled the communication of trauma which is expressed within the popular memory (cf. Eyerman 5). Such an approach rejects the notion that individuals and communities are passive consumers of media, but that these representations are frames through which active agents assert particular visions of the past (cf. Wertsch 8). Notions of cultural trauma are particularly useful in this respect, as they enable an alternative perspective on popular memory, not as a misunderstanding of the past, but as a vital component of identity: "Cultural trauma occurs when members of a collectivity feel they have been subjected to a horrendous event that leaves indelible marks upon their group consciousness, marking their memories forever and changing their future identity in fundamental ways" (Alexander 1). Following Breuer and Freud's diagnosis of the ability of trauma to form the individual (6), scholars have harnessed this approach to demonstrate the utility of "trauma" as a mode of analysis (Caruth 17). In this fashion, trauma forms a means of communicating communal concepts of both an individual and a collective sense of self. This holds true to the work of Novick, who assessed the contemporary focus towards "victimhood" and trauma as a means of defining identity as opposed to a classical concern for the brave and victorious (214).

Cultural trauma defines itself through a variety of media; from novels and films to monuments and commemorative practices. The significance of these representations or actions is their capacity to sustain a sense of shock, bereavement and suffering (cf. Smelser 31–32). The similarity within these depictions and the repeated motifs they contain demonstrates the existence of common perceptions about a historical event and the desire to maintain and perpetuate these values. In effect, it reasserts what is already held to be self-evident by contemporary audiences and then requires that audience to serve as witnesses to this trauma; to bear the truth of the past into the present by testifying to its significance. Cultural forms act as a means to focus attention on this historic pain and distress. Indeed, forms of media that enable the communication of this trauma are valued above others and are, therefore, brought within a wider symbolic network with associated meanings attached to them. Following this agenda, the popular memory of the First World War in Australia, Britain and Canada can be regarded within this framework of cultural trauma. This popular memory is not derived from media representations, rather those representations reflect the trauma that is communicated within that popular memory.

Through an assessment of recent novels, film and television productions, this study will highlight how trauma serves as a fundamental aspect of these media because of the uses of a traumatic past to mobilise issues of identity in the present. Evidence for this assessment will be taken from after 1998, when the marking of the eightieth anniversary of the Armistice was perceived to encourage a public engagement with the trauma of war with an explicit effect on notions of

national, regional and political identification (cf. Audoin-Rouzeau and Becker 5). These notions of identity are forged through particular elements provided within cultural representations of the war. For the purpose of this study, these elements can be classed as:
- Suffering of soldiers – the depiction of troops enduring the anguish, alienation and disillusion of the war.
- Desolated battlefields – the imagining of a hellish, war-torn landscape where the maelstrom of conflict is inflicted upon its inhabitants.
- Witness perspective – the provision of a vantage point from which the audience is required to carry the burden of memory.

Within a variety of media, these features form the basic characteristic of the representations of the First World War. Whilst scholars have highlighted how such familiar scenes demonstrate the clichéd nature of the popular memory of the war of 1914–1918, this overlooks how these repetitive elements enable the communication and maintenance of a sense of trauma (cf. Hanna). Through an assessment of these key features, the ability of representations to perpetuate trauma within Australia, Britain and Canada will not be considered as the cynical product of a capitalist entertainment industry, but as the result of a desire within wider society to preserve this particular means of engaging with the past.

2 The Suffering of Soldiers

The communication of suffering within representations of the First World War constitutes the most prominent aspect of film, television and novels regarding the conflict. The sculptural, textual or visual depiction of soldiers' bodies tormented by war is a noticeable aspect of the contemporary depictions of the First World War. However, from 1998 onwards, there has emerged a distinctive focus on the pain of the individual and their status as the 'victim' of the war. This tendency has been expressed through a variety of media within Australia, Britain and Canada. For example, the British film *The Trench* (dir. William Boyd, 1999) focused on the experience of a detachment of soldiers stationed in the front lines just before the advance made on the catastrophic first day of the Battle of the Somme, 1 July 1916. The film's characters, with the protagonist only sixteen years of age, are shown living in the squalor of a trench with the ever-present fear of death. The indifference of the military and social elite within the film is palpable as is the viciousness of the war upon the soldiers as life and limb are lost to the shells and bullets of the enemy. The entirety of the film is played out in the tragic circumstance of the impending fate of the soldiers, as the order to 'go over the top' during the climactic scenes of the motion picture brings death to the remaining members of the section. The suffering of the characters, both physical and psychological, is the focus of the film, with the protagonist's status as a minor emphasising the sense of pity and sorrow which is evoked in his death at the conclusion of the film.

A similar theme of suffering can be observed in the British horror film *Deathwatch* (dir. Michael Bassett, 2002) and the television films *All the King's Men* (dir. Julian Jarrold, 1999) and *My Boy Jack* (dir. Brian Kirk, 2007). In each of these cases, the British soldiers are victimised; abandoned to die at the hands of some malevolent supernatural force in the case of the former or the 'old lie' of patriotism and sacrifice in the case of the latter two. The suffering of soldiers also forms the central aspect of the Australian film *Broken Sun* (dir. Brad Haynes, 2008), where a traumatised former soldier of the ANZACs meets an escaped Japanese prisoner of war in the outback during the Second World War. The experiences of the Australian soldier are shown in flashback sequence as the brutality of the battlefields of the First World War cast the individual within a 'victim' status which is compared to the internment of the Japanese soldier. The character, however, exhibits the strength, fortitude and endurance which are assumed to typify the Australian soldier, despite the trauma which they have endured. The same sense of victimhood pervades the Canadian film *Passchendaele* (dir. Paul Gross, 2008). Within this motion picture, the protagonist is shown to suffer the horrors of war in France only to be returned home to be used to spur the enlistment campaign in Canada. After rejoining the army, the hero whilst mortally wounded retrieves a comrade from the battlefield upon his back, who by the perversity of a shell explosion, appears to have been crucified. The Christian imagery of the scene emphasises the nature of suffering in the war as a higher level of sacrifice. In effect, the trauma of the war is portrayed within a moment of national tragedy.

Appropriately, the notion of suffering and victimhood was used to critique the British Broadcasting Corporation's (BBC) reality television programme *The Trench* (dir. Dominic Ozanne, 2002). In this series, a group of young men were recruited, trained and then stationed in a recreated trench system to 'relive' the experiences of their ancestors. Questions of taste and decency were directed at the programme as the inability of replicating the unique suffering of soldiers in the war of 1914–1918 was considered beyond the ken of modern society. In contrast, the Canadian Broadcasting Corporation's (CBC) television programme *The Great War* (dir. Brian McKenna, 2007) received a far warmer reception for its use of modern-day descendants of First World War servicemen to recreate battle scenes, to undertake a pilgrimage to the cemeteries and memorials and to dramatise the events from wartime letters and diaries. In this manner, the trauma of the conflict was relived in the present; it was evoked and experienced for a contemporary Canadian audience to maintain a sense of shock and bereavement. Similarly, the Australian Broadcasting Corporation's (ABC) *Australians at War* (dir. Geoff Burton, 2001), a series examining the effect of warfare on the nation, focused on the uses of a current generation of Australians to narrate the letters and diaries of 'Diggers' stationed at Gallipoli. These accounts emphasised the "despair, endurance and horror" of the Dardanelles Campaign, which were revealed to the audience as a means of extolling the significance of this anguish for the nation: "'Who'll come a-fighting the Kaiser with me' brings to the screen an Australia we have forgotten or simply did not know existed, and by its end, we are brought to a belief that it was an Australia we should continue to cherish" ("Australians at War").

This emphasis on the tragic suffering of soldiers is especially present within the programming associated with the ninetieth anniversary of the cessation of hostilities. For example, the BBC documentary *The Last Day of World War One* (dir. John Hayes Fisher, 2008) revealed the personal stories of soldiers who were killed in battle after the signing of the Armistice on 11 November 1918. The presenter of the programme, Michael Palin, who shared his own family history of loss during the conflict, detailed the lives and deaths of those killed on the last day of the war whilst interviewing surviving family members. The trauma of the war was thereby detailed as a contemporary phenomenon, lived and felt in the present. Similarly, in Australia, the Special Broadcasting Service (SBS) aired the documentary *Not Forgotten* (dir. Jane Jeffes, 2008). Narrated by Mark Lee, the lead of the iconic 1981 ANZAC film *Gallipoli*, the programme featured accounts from soldiers and their families as the experience of joining up, service and bereavement were explored. In this manner, the sense of suffering and victimhood were paramount. Nevertheless, the premise of the programme was to reiterate the place of this trauma within the national consciousness, to examine "the legacy of grief, loss and remembrance, to make sure these men are Not Forgotten."

The perpetuation of the sense of shock at the scale of loss and distress wrought during the war is evident. Through the image of the suffering soldier this historical trauma is evoked. However, the function of this trauma within each of these societies is considerably different. Within Britain, the pain and anguish of the soldier in the trenches is sacrosanct; however, its place as the exemplum of suffering enables its mobilisation for a variety of causes. Demonstrating an association with this trauma promotes a range of regional, national and political identities (cf. Wilson). To be connected to this historic trauma is seen to legitimise a sense of self, whether individual or collective. Indeed, Scottish and Welsh troops are remembered for their suffering, left-leaning politicians commemorate the sacrifices of the working-classes and conservative elements praise the national fortitude and service demonstrated on the battlefields (cf. Bond). Within Canada and Australia, this sense of victimhood with regard to the Great War provides a formative event through which a national character is defined. Whilst this trauma can serve an exclusionary agenda, disbarring others from a national narrative by proclaiming it the decisive point for the state, it also constitutes a means of organising identities in opposition towards authority (cf. Thomson; Seal). Media representations of the battlefields do not create or manipulate these perceptions of suffering; they reflect the trauma that is already present within society which is used by contemporary populations to legitimise a sense of place and identity.

3 Desolated Battlefields

Across a variety of recent media, the constant aspect of the Great War which is reiterated is the devastated landscapes of the battlefields. Soldiers are victims in the theatres of war, subject to the horrendous processes of industrialised combat. The imagery of the war-torn, debris-strewn battlefields containing an otherworldly combination of the living and the dead emphasises the sense of suffering for those who served within these arenas. For example, the Canadian novel *Three Day Road* (2005) by Joseph Boyden is replete with scenes of horror and trauma from the conflict as it features a Cree Indian veteran attempting to come to terms with his war experiences. Within the novel, the death, destruction and brutality of the war is contrasted with the indigenous practices of the Cree in harmony with the environment. The Western Front is portrayed as a dehumanising place, which transforms another Cree Indian into a murderous figure who stalks the battlefields scalping his enemies, leading his commanding officer to observe "like your heathen ancestors" (26). This corruption of the landscape through war, which leads to the corruption and victimisation of the individual, is a feature of other contemporary war fiction. In the young adult novel *Private Peaceful* (2003) by the British author Michael Morpurgo, the life of the protagonist, Thomas Peaceful, is detailed for the reader as he sits in a trench on the Western Front. The bleak, death-ridden battlefields become a place of torment for the hero and his friends as lives are cut short by both the machine guns of the enemy and the firing squad of the British Army as a comrade is executed for refusing an order during an advance. This action is played out just before the beginning of the Battle of the Somme (1916), which will inevitably bring the death of Private Peaceful himself. The portrayal of the war landscape as a broken, desolate and tragic arena where fatalities are inevitable, heightens once again the sense of victimisation and suffering associated with the conflict. It maintains the sense of trauma that pervades the First World War within Australia, Britain and Canada.

Similar uses of the battlefields as a 'hellscape,' where humanity is suppressed and soldiers forced to endure the torment of both artillery barrages, gas and rifle bullets whilst also afflicted by the incompetence or indifference of the political and military elite can be located across the former combatant societies. In the 2007 Australian novel *Barbed Wire and Roses* by Peter Yeldham, the story of a 'golden youth' being sent to fight in the bloody trenches of Gallipoli and the Somme is retold through the diaries of a veteran which are discovered by a grandchild. This familial connection demonstrates the extant trauma of the conflict, as the descendant journeys to France to uncover the mystery of his grandfather's disappearance. Within the novel, the battlefields are rendered into a perverse arena of indiscriminate killing, where horrific scenes of warfare render young men into shell-shocked victims, incapable of understanding their actions or place in this theatre of war. Such an approach reduces the moral culpability of soldiers in wartime and emphasises their innocence in the context of their military role: "It was exciting to be on our way at last [...] but we were such innocents. We had no idea of the hell that lay ahead. Even if we had known, what could we have done about it?" (1).

In the 1998 British romantic novel *Angels of Mercy* by Lyn Andrews, the lives of men and women are altered inexorably by their experiences of the front, which changes individuals through the barbarism they witness. In the same way, the British author Ben Elton's 2005 novel *The First Casualty* emphasised the transformative effect of the battlefields, where in the violent flow of artillery shells and bullets, the 'truth' of the suffering of individuals is revealed. In this book, the hero of the novel rejects the pursuit of the war on moral grounds but is forced to go to the battlefields to investigate the murder of a prominent, nationalistic poet. The protagonist discovers that this individual, formally the darling of the establishment, was poised to denounce the conflict as an absurd waste of human life. It is this theme of the 'truth' of the war, of the horrendous battlefields which dehumanise the individuals which is reiterated throughout the novel: "Look at us. We're sheep, that's what. Sheep to the bleeding slaughter. We can't win this war, not the poor bloody infantry. We just sit around hoping to cop a Blighty so's [sic] we can stagger home crippled, grateful not to be dead" (43). The presence of the battlefields, haunting the minds of the soldiers, their families and returning veterans is explored in the Canadian novel *Broken Ground* (1998) by Jack Hodgins. In this assessment, the theatre of war on the Western Front is highlighted as the formative point for the 'national character' as a group of former servicemen establish a settlement on the bleak, desolate landscape of Vancouver Island. The service, sacrifice and endeavour of the soldiers are mirrored in the creation of a community, whilst the threat of a forest fire to engulf their work evokes the nightmarish scenes of Vimy Ridge.

In further novels from Canadian authors such as Jane Urquhart's *The Stone Carvers* (2001) or Frances Itani's *Deafening* (2003), the battlefields form a landscape of suffering for soldiers, emphasising the tragedy and the trauma of the war for those who served and their families, but the devastated war landscape haunts these works rather than occupying their focus of concern. This mode of engaging with the conflict reflects the place of the war in Canadian national memory as a poignant, lingering presence that informs others of place, belonging and self (cf. Vance 8). The battlefields are an arena of martyrdom, where the endurance of the war shapes the identities of those who fought, those at home and their descendants to the present day. This is a central feature of the Australian novel *Tea Tree Passage* (2001) by Robyn Burrows, where the legacies of the Great War, represented by the looming horror of the battlefields, cast a long shadow over several generations of inhabitants in South West Australia. The presence of the war landscape, its effect on subsequent generations, and its persistence in the minds of succeeding generations is detailed in the British novelist Adam Thorpe's *Nineteen Twenty-One* (2001). However, this account engages not with the continuance and shared sense of trauma but with the impossibility of the descendants of the war generation to comprehend such an event. Within this narrative, the protagonist is an aspiring writer who misses out on the war but seeks to obtain a grasp on the truth and understanding of the conflict after the Armistice in an attempt to place himself alongside those who suffered. By interviewing traumatised soldiers and visiting the battlefield sites where the remains, both human and material, can be clearly seen, the central character realises his inability to write of the Armageddon; such is the suffering of those who inhabited the fields of conflict.

In this manner, the desolate battlefields become a cultural tool in which to stress the significance and the singularity of the trauma of the First World War. For Australian, British and Canadian novelists the war landscape is an arena of identity, formed through the suffering of soldiers; the battlefields are revisited, either in person or through some spectral presence, to justify the character and identity of individuals. The 'truth' of the war, demonstrated in the horror and brutality witnessed by its participants, casts these individuals as 'victims' of the conflict. This sense of victimhood emphasises the trauma of the war, which is demonstrated as continuing, felt and experienced by successive generations in the present. Therefore, although many of these novels engage in events after the cessation of hostilities in November 1918, through these fictional accounts the First World War is certainly not over. Indeed, the appearance of the devastated war landscape as a device which haunts society evidences a desire to demonstrate that this is a historical trauma that is lived with.

4 The Witness Perspective

The extra-media function of these novels, television programmes and films is, therefore, to maintain a sense of trauma regarding the First World War within contemporary society. This trauma is not evoked because it is somehow an 'easier' or more 'accessible' history to comprehend. Indeed, these media reflect the manner in which this past still engages with the present. This sense of trauma is maintained through these media rather than formed through them. Rather than place the assumption that media are vacuously consumed by a credulous public, it is perhaps more appropriate to consider these materials as a frame or lens through which the past can be viewed (cf. Wertsch 12). These cultural forms enable contemporary populations to serve as witnesses to this historic trauma, to carry the burden of memory into the present. The model of the witness is therefore highly appropriate to the study of the memory of the First World War. As witnesses, this memory is imparted to individuals, groups and wider society in the expectation that the testimony of this audience will maintain the 'truth' of this history. This perspective is promoted both implicitly and explicitly within the cultural representations of the First World War. For example, the British novelist Pat Barker explores this issue directly in *Another World* (1998). This fictional work describes the last few days of the life of a veteran of the conflict as he slowly descends into senility and the memory of the conflict begins to seep into the present. As the horror and trauma of the war are lived once more by the old soldier, his family, who observe the last few moments of the veteran's life, adjust to what the dying man means to those he leaves behind. In effect, the novel represents the wider memory of the conflict in former combatant countries writ small. As the last of the veterans pass away, the First World War goes beyond 'living memory,' providing a means by which contemporary society can maintain the remembrance of the war by serving as witnesses to the past.

This point of reflection is provided not just through novels but the wider array of media representations of the conflict. ABC's programming for the 2005 commemoration of the Dardanelles campaign evidences this approach. In *Revealing Gallipoli* (dir. Wain Fimeri), modern audiences were provided with a detailed assessment of perhaps Australia's most revered scene of conflict. Drawing upon detailed computer graphics alongside the accounts of servicemen, the programme assessed the 'horrors' of the war for a contemporary audience: "First-hand accounts tell viewers what Gallipoli looked, felt and smelled like, and remarkable 3D archival images bring these scenes to life. Animated maps illustrate the forbidding terrain the soldiers faced, and illuminate the strategies behind the conflict" ("Revealing Gallipoli"). This documentary enabled its viewers to become witnesses to the past, testifying to the significance of the conflict and its place within Australian society. CBC's 2000 landmark television documentary, *Canada: A People's History* also provided its audience with a means to witness the past. In this multipart programme, Canada's history was narrated with the events of the First World War occupying their own episode entitled "Ordeal by Fire." Within this account, the programme once again used contemporary letters and diaries to demonstrate the war's significance for those who fought, for those back home and for the current generation of Canadians: "The horror, bravery and sacrifice of trench warfare are evoked in Canada's great battles: Ypres, the Somme, Vimy Ridge, Courcelette and Passchendaele ("Ordeal by Fire").

The witness perspective is highly significant because it enables the continuation of the trauma of the First World War. It is this sense of trauma that holds political, social and symbolic value; it provides a means of identification and it ensures that the memory of the conflict does not lapse into history. Maintaining the traumatic memory of the conflict as current, felt and experienced is vital in asserting its emblematic value. This is a point overlooked by revisionist historians who seek to critique the popular memory of the war as historically inaccurate: "The point is not to remember the past trauma as exactly as possible: such 'documentation' is a priori false, it transforms the trauma into a neutral, objective fact, whereas the essence of the trauma is precisely that it is too horrible to be remembered, to be integrated into our symbolic universe" (Žižek 272). Nietzsche's critique of western cultural systems which rely upon a lingering sense of trauma is, therefore, quite apparent in this context; if something is to remain in the memory, it must be burnt in, it must never cease to hurt (61).

5 Conclusion

The popular memory of the First World War across Australia, Britain and Canada is often referred to in a disparaging manner, with some commentators assuming that the public perception of the 'rats, gas, mud and blood' of the battlefields is born out of a simplistic acceptance of novels, film and television programmes which depict the conflict. However, to challenge these ideas, the study of the popular memory of the 1914–1918 war can assess how the memory functions within those societies which still honour it. In this approach, the memory of the war is regarded as not a passive consumption but an active choice, made by individuals, groups and communities who desire to remember the war in this manner because it fulfils a purpose, it has utility. This popular memory is mobilised to affirm issues of identity and place within these societies. Therefore, the cultural representations of the conflict can be assessed to demonstrate how this popular memory is sustained and focused through media, not constructed by them. This effect is achieved through the portrayal and focus upon the trauma of the war. Through the images of suffering soldiers, the devastated battlefield landscapes or the enabling of a witness perspective, a sense of cultural trauma is maintained. This provides a means for contemporary populations to experience and feel the events of the First World War as a continuing disturbance. The attempts to revise the popular memory of the conflict do not consider how the trauma of the war possesses a totemic value for populations. Therefore, despite the passing of the last veterans and the ever-increasing distance of the events of 1914–1918 to the present, the war still goes on.

References

Alexander, Jeffrey. "Toward a Theory of Cultural Trauma." *Cultural Trauma and Collective Memory*. Eds. J. C. Alexander, R. Eyerman, B. Giesen, N. Smelser and P. Sztompka. Berkeley: University of California Press, 2001. 1–59.
Andrews, Lyn. *Angels of Mercy*. London: Headline, 1998.
Audoin-Rouzeau, Stéphane, and Annette Becker. *14–18, Understanding the Great War*. Trans. Catherine Temerson. New York: Hill and Wang, 2002.
"Australians at War." ABC. http://www.australiansatwar.gov.au/television/index.html. (12 January 2002).
Badsey, Stephen. "Blackadder Goes Forth and the 'Two Western Fronts' Debate." *Television and History*. Eds. G. Roberts and P. M. Taylor. Luton: University of Luton Press, 2001. 113–125.
Barker, Pat. *Another World*. London: Viking Press, 1998.
Bond, Brian. *The Unquiet Western Front*. Cambridge: Cambridge University Press, 2002.
Bourke, Joanna. *An Intimate History of Killing: Face-to-Face Killing in Twentieth-Century Warfare*. London: Granta Books, 1999.
Boyden, Joseph. *Three Day Road*. Toronto: Penguin, 2005.
Breuer, Josef, and Sigmund Freud. *Studies on Hysteria*. London: The Hogarth Press, 1895.
Burrows, Robyn. *Tea Tree Passage*. Sydney: Harper Collins, 2001.
Caruth, Cathy. *Unclaimed Experience: Trauma, Narrative, History*. Baltimore: Johns Hopkins University Press, 1996.
Corrigan, Gordon. *Mud, Blood and Poppycock: Britain and the First World War*. London: Cassell, 2003.
Elton, Ben. *The First Casualty*. London: Bantam Press, 2005.
Eyerman, Ron. *Cultural Trauma: Slavery and the Formation of African American Identity*. Cambridge: Cambridge University Press, 2001.
Fussell, Paul. *The Great War and Modern Memory*. Oxford: Oxford University Press, 1975.
"The Great War." CBC. http://www.cbc.ca/greatwar/. (21 October 2007).
Hanna, Emma. *The Great War on the Small Screen: Representing the First World War in Contemporary Britain*. Edinburgh: Edinburgh University Press, 2009.
Hodgins, Jack. *Broken Ground*. Toronto: McClelland and Stewart, 1998.
Itani, Frances. *Deafening*. Toronto: Harper Collins, 2003.

Morpurgo, Michael. *Private Peaceful*. London: Harper Collins, 2003.
Nietzsche, Friedrich. *On the Genealogy of Morals*. Trans. Walter Kaufmann and Reginald Hollingdale. New York: Random House, 1969.
Novick, Peter. *The Holocaust in American Life*. Boston: Houghton Mifflin, 2000.
"Ordeal by Fire." CBC. http://www.cbc.ca/history/EPISHOMEEP12LE.html. (19 November 2000).
Popular Memory Group, et al. "Popular Memory: Theory, Politics, Method." *Making Histories. Studies in History-Writing and Politics*. Eds. R. Johnson, G. McLennan, B. Schwartz and D. Sutton. London: Routledge, 1982. 205–252.
"Revealing Gallipoli." ABC. http://www.abc.net.au/tv/guide/netw/200504/programs/ZY7664A001D24042005T193000.html. (23 October 2005).
Reynaud, Daniel. *Celluloid Anzacs: The Great War Anzac Debate Through Australian Cinema*. Melbourne: Australian Scholarly Publishing, 2007.
Seal, Graham. *Inventing Anzac: The Digger And National Mythology*. St. Lucia: University of Queensland Press, 2004.
Sheffield, Gary. *Forgotten Victory. The First World War – Myths and Realities*. London: Headline, 2001.
Smelser, Neil. "Psychological Trauma and Cultural Trauma." *Cultural Trauma and Collective Memory*. Eds. J. C. Alexander, R. Eyerman, B. Giesen, N. Smelser and P. Sztompka. Berkeley: University of California Press, 2001. 31–59.
Thomson, Alistair. *Anzac Memories: Living with the Legend*. Oxford: Oxford University Press, 1994.
Thorpe, Adam. *Nineteen Twenty-One*. London: Vintage, 2001.
Todman, Dan. *The Great War: Myth and Memory*. Stroud: Sutton, 2005.
Urquhart, Jane. *The Stone Carvers*. Toronto: McClelland and Stewart, 2001.
Vance, Jonathan. *Death So Noble: Memory, Meaning and the First World War*. Vancouver: University of British Columbia Press, 1997.
Wilson, Ross. "The Trenches in British Popular Memory." *Interculture* 5. 2 (2008): 109–118.
Winter, Jay. *Sites of Memory, Sites of Mourning: The Great War in European Cultural History*. Cambridge: Cambridge University Press, 1992.
Yeldham, Peter. *Barbed Wire and Roses*. Sydney: Penguin, 2007.
Žižek, Slavoj. *For They Know Not What They Do: Enjoyment As a Political Factor*. London: Verso, 2002.

Filmography

All the King's Men. Dir. Julian Jarrold. British Broadcasting Corporation, 1999.
Australians at War. Dir. Geoff Burton. Australian Broadcasting Corporation, 2001.
Blackadder Goes Forth. Dir. Richard Boden. British Broadcasting Corporation, 1989.
Broken Sun. Dir. Brad Haynes. JackaFilms, 2008.
Canada: A People's History. Dir. Serges Turbide. Canadian Broadcasting Corporation, 2000.
Deathwatch. Dir. Michael Bassett. ApolloMedia, 2002.
Gallipoli. Dir. Peter Weir. Australian Film Commission, 1981.
The Great War. Dir. Brian McKenna. Canadian Broadcasting Corporation, 2007.
The Last Day of World War One. Dir. John Hayes Fisher. British Broadcasting Corporation, 2008.
My Boy Jack. Dir. Brian Kirk. Ecosse Films, 2007.

Not Forgotten. Dir. Jane Jeffes. Firefly Productions, 2008.
Passchendaele. Dir. Paul Gross. Damberger Film and Cattle, Co., 2008.
Revealing Gallipoli. Dir. Wain Fimeri. Australian Broadcasting Corporation, 2005.
The Trench. Dir. Dominic Ozanne. British Broadcasting Corporation, 2002.
The Trench. Dir. William Boyd. Arts Council of England, 1999.

Marlene A. Briggs
Working Through the Working-Class War: The Battle of the Somme in Contemporary British Literature by Alan Sillitoe and Ted Hughes

> No great voice was lifted against this internal ripping to pieces of a country.
>
> Alan Sillitoe, *Raw Material*

The battle of the Somme (1 July–19 November 1916), with its aura of hermetic and harrowing experience, both invites and repels imaginative engagement. The first day of the battle alone resulted in approximately 60,000 British casualties. Military historian John Keegan declares that the Somme is the "greatest military tragedy" in the "national military history" of Britain (299). The offensive served as the first trial for many citizen volunteers who enlisted with brothers, colleagues, or friends from the same area in 'Chums' or 'Pals' battalions, resulting in the decimation of the adult male population of towns and villages (Keegan 290). As Sharon Ouditt affirms, "The turning point in the conventional narrative of the war, and often in their reimaginings, comes with the battle of the Somme" (248). British writers Alan Sillitoe (1928–2010) and Ted Hughes (1930–1998), contemporaries, friends, and relatives of Somme veterans, share a fascination with this battle.[1] Historical trauma holds children and others in its orbit; even when an event precedes birth, its ruptures continue to impact the lives of descendants. The pathways of second-generation response to the Somme thus warrant sustained attention. Sillitoe and Hughes address the intergenerational legacies of this extreme event, particularly the staggered challenges of mourning mass death: as another descendant avows, "it is impossible not to be stricken silent or moved to the point of tears by the knowledge of what happened on the Somme" (Harris 145). By taking up this historical trauma across a generational divide, they reshape the transmission and reception of the Great War.

Although Keegan proclaims the Somme a "tragedy" for the nation, Sillitoe and Hughes deem it a regional trauma, especially for those from the North of

---

[1] On the friendship between Sillitoe and Hughes, see Sillitoe's short memoir ("Ted Hughes ..." 259–261).

England (299).² They do not conceive of the battle as a point of violent origin. Instead, they probe intersections between the traumatic histories of industrial labour and industrial warfare: the Somme, a complex site of traumatic memory, exposes the historical continuities between commodity production and cannon-fodder. In his fictional memoir *Raw Material* (1972), Sillitoe likens the Somme to a civil war in which popular outlaws such as Robin Hood, Wat Tyler, and Captain Swing go missing in action (100). And in *Elmet* (1994), an expanded version of the poetic sequence *Remains of Elmet* (1979), Hughes juxtaposes the mechanized production of nineteenth-century textile mills and the mass death of attrition battles, so that dread becomes a primal inheritance, a "mother-tongue" (116; line 13). In opposition to the forgetting that accompanied rapid social and technological changes in the birthplace of the industrial revolution, Sillitoe and Hughes insistently recall the unacknowledged and "unwritten emotional [histories]" of local communities in Nottingham and Yorkshire that overdetermine losses at Gommecourt and High Wood, respectively (Sillitoe, *Raw Material* 125). They suggest that the melancholic preoccupation with the Somme, in part, derives from the unresolved issues of industrialization and deindustrialization.

The history of the North encompasses the rise and fall of the working classes in the birthplace of the industrial revolution: hence, this population exemplifies the emergence and decline of the Western industrial social order. The shocking upheavals of interpersonal relationships, labour practices, and local spaces famously analyzed by Friedrich Engels in *The Condition of the Working Class in England in 1844* recede into a narrative of social progress in the contemporary deindustrialized world. Prior to the reorganization of capitalism in twenty-first century global markets, Geoff Eley and Kenneth Nield reckon that class politics "[achieved] its purchase from the 1880s to 1960s," validating the importance of this category to generations that preceded, coincided and followed the Great War ("Farewell..." 18).³ Obviously, the common basis of this appeal by Sillitoe and Hughes deserves critical attention although appeals to class are distinc-

---

2 Russell restricts his study of Northern England to the seven counties of Cheshire, Cumberland, Durham, Lancashire, Northumberland, Westmorland and Yorkshire, although he concedes that other counties may also be relevant, including Nottinghamshire (16). In this connection, Sillitoe clarifies, "Being neither north nor south, Nottinghamshire is defined more by history than by spectacular topography. It is the key to the country, geographically, mentally and strategically" (*Alan Sillitoe's Nottinghamshire* 104).

3 Roberts offers a capsule description of industrial working-class life that emphasizes collectivity, continuity, security, and tradition (80–82). However, recent theorists of class introduce terms to accentuate fundamental changes in the social and political conditions of post-industrial labour. In this connection, see Hardt and Negri on the "multitude" (106–107) and Standing on the "precariat" (7).

tive in each context: Sillitoe perceives the workers as dormant historical agents while Hughes emphasizes the bleak continuities of class oppression. Rather than subscribing to "the hierarchical view of society as a seamless web," or a "triadic version with upper, middle and lower collective groups," these writers often resort to a "dichotomous, adversarial picture, where society is sundered between 'us' and 'them'" (Cannadine 19–20). Both men advance claims for historical redress in the absence of the specific social formations and institutions that shaped the first half of the twentieth century. Sillitoe and Hughes delineate variable practices of working through the intergenerational legacies of loss, legacies inextricably bound to the formerly entrenched yet nearly forgotten social divisions of Western industrial modernity.

Dominick LaCapra reworks Freudian psychoanalytic vocabulary in his scholarship on extreme events: he specifies acting out and working through, processes linked to melancholia and mourning, respectively, as "interrelated modes of responding to loss or historical trauma" (*Writing History...* 65). How may relatives of veterans attempt to work through the Somme, a site associated with mass death widely perceived to be "[unjustifiable]" and, notwithstanding the proliferation of memorials, characterized by "[deficits] in the ritual process" (LaCapra, *Writing History...* 215)? In particular, how may descendants and other invested groups grapple with the regional and social divisions that exposed working-class soldiers to differential modes of death and injury? Sillitoe and Hughes debunk triumphal discourses of the Great War and the postwar rhetoric of consolation that informs public expressions of mourning. These writers foster a skeptical attitude to official memorial cultures in keeping with their critiques of social disparities: in this view, commemoration tends to serve "political elites" rather than enabling "dominated groups to contest their subordinate status" (Winter 319, 320). Remembering the working-class men killed at the Somme entails resistance to sanctioned expressions of loss. As LaCapra explicates in *History, Literature, Critical Theory*, working through may necessitate "immanent critique involving the type of transformative political action that engages and changes specific political institutions and practices" (158), including but not limited to commemorative institutions and practices.[4] In prose and poetry, Sillitoe and Hughes reconstitute

---

[4] In this connection, LaCapra mentions Adorno, who states, "The past will have been worked through only when the causes of what happened then have been eliminated. Only because the causes continue to exist does the captivating spell of the past remain to this day unbroken" (LaCapra, *History, Literature...* 158; Adorno 103). LaCapra describes "working through" as "both a narrative and other-than-narrative psychosocial and political practice of articulation. Working through should not be understood, as it often is, in stereotypical ways as purely psychological and as the simple alternative to, or binary opposite of, compulsive repetition, acting out, or even impossible mourning. Nor should it be equated with closure, therapeutic cure, healing all

class, an increasingly controversial and fragmentary category, as a fundamental problem in their efforts to work through the conjoined political and psychosocial legacies of the Somme, legacies that may be suppressed by conventional protocols of remembrance.

Progressive ideas of history associated with deindustrialization as well as unitary models of the nation linked to state commemoration disavow the conflictual legacies of class pivotal to the mobilization of total war in 1914–1918. Efforts to recover class experiences therefore play a central role in the postmemorial projects of Sillitoe and Hughes undertaken from the 1970s to the 1990s. The histories of labour reframe their stories of war: they contest hierarchies of value that denigrate the experiences of working people at the Somme through the narratives of troubled survivors, namely Edgar (Sillitoe) and Walt (Hughes). Even as they stress the impasses of collective dynamics and the oscillations of intergenerational transmission, each writer effectively works through the working-class war in so far as he remains committed to the self-reflexive exploration of affective, empirical, and ethical problems derived from the dynamic interaction of social hierarchy and industrial warfare. They hold various institutions accountable for the violence of mass death and its aftermath in vulnerable populations: Sillitoe excoriates the military while Hughes suspects the state. Taken together, these writings illuminate the legacies of the Somme with respect to particular communities, generations, and subcultures. In this manner, they identify internal conflicts and unspoken investments that perpetuate preoccupations with the Great War. By disrupting familiar stories of the battle even as they dramatize its compulsive symptoms within individuals and groups, they unsettle the past in productive ways through creative and critical modes of repetition (cf. LaCapra, *History, Literature...* 162–163). Together, Sillitoe and Hughes clarify the challenges that the Somme poses to collective mourning processes in Britain, even as their narratives and poems differentiate regional losses from national statistics, enabling distinct albeit interrelated articulations of a shattering event.

---

wounds, and dialectical transcendence of a traumatic past or problem. Rather, with crucial differences depending on subject-positions, it offers the possibility of enacting variations in repetition that may be significant (at times decisive) enough to bring about effective change, including transformations that, in context, may well be disruptive or even traumatic [...]" (*History, Literature...* 162–163).

1 Alan Sillitoe: *Raw Material*

As Sillitoe discusses, the deaths of over 11,000 men from the Sherwood Foresters permanently changed life in Nottinghamshire. His "memoir-novel" *Raw Material*, the result of over twenty years of research, chronicles "the spiritual devastation of two families by the Great War" ("Maps and the Great War" 37). More generally, he decries the rending of the nation by the battle: "No great voice was lifted against this internal ripping to pieces of a country" (*Raw Material* 102). The book has seventy-three chapters divided into three parts; Sillitoe expanded its contents three times (1974; 1978; 1979). Part Two, which consists of twenty-nine chapters, considers the history of the Sillitoe family, including the experiences of his uncle Edgar at the Somme with the Sherwood Foresters. In addition, Sillitoe familiarized himself with military records and national narratives, reading "Official Histories of the Great War, unit and regimental accounts, personal memoirs, social histories, rolls of honour and memorial books," as well as "maps, diaries, documents and training manuals" (vi–vii). His immersion in these diverse sources bolsters his trenchant critique of the battle: he maintains that class hatred determined reckless military strategy. Throughout, he advocates for ordinary people.[5] In the end, he calls *Raw Material* "a historical novel": "If I claimed to write the truth I would have told a lie. If I said I had written lies it would not have been the truth" (189). As military strategy and family memoir dovetail, Sillitoe accepts "the dilemma of uncertainty" in his quest for "truth" (32).[6] Thus, he acknowledges that his own investments and projections facilitate the partial recovery of the past. *Raw Material* constitutes an innovative effort to work through the political and psychosocial legacies of historical trauma by a second-generation descendant.[7]

Sillitoe rectifies the exclusions of official history by foregrounding the experiences of a deserter in his book. Edgar, "the darling of the family," was his mother's favourite, "a slim and handsome young man" with "wavering dark eyes" (88). He

---

[5] Sillitoe sheds light on his title: "That the raw material of the past consists of ordinary people is a truism, yet it seems a little more true of Nottingham than anywhere else. The idiosyncratic and often turbulent nature of its inhabitants produced a more vivid past than most places" ("Foreword" xvii).

[6] Sillitoe begins the book with the legless man whom he remembers from childhood: different stories explain his injury. His father alleges that the man survived an explosion at the Somme, signaling the resonance that this battle acquired for Sillitoe from an early age (*Raw Material* 8).

[7] As Tucker ventures, "At the end of the 1990s Alan Sillitoe's work had not been accorded the mainstream attention it deserved. [...] Everything he writes bears witness to the violence and suffering of our culture" (425).

enlisted in 1914 but deserted twice, seeking refuge with his family.[8] In contrast to disillusioned narratives by middle-class volunteers, desertion functions as a staple of working-class war stories. Due to his prior flights, Edgar's battalion commander threatens him with court-martial. Poised between execution and slaughter, he goes over the top at Gommecourt: "None of us knew what we were doing. Or what to expect. We were all done in" (94). Avoidance and disobedience give rise to Edgar's survival strategies on the Somme: "With a dogged sort of insanity and courage he stayed in a shell-hole between the opposing trenches, hoping to surrender to the Germans as soon as it was possible" (97). Yet, in Sillitoe's estimation, Edgar acts as a foil for the majority of English soldiers at the Somme, who emerged from trenches "in wave after wave, dogged, determined, unimaginative, with complete trust in their officers" (97). In his tribute to the desperate efforts of his uncle to stay alive, Sillitoe rejects conventional accounts of self-sacrificing heroism and military prowess. In the process, he discredits the assumption that only exceptional lives merit the interest of posterity. As he protests, "Ordinary people also deserve the benefit of history" (189). Sillitoe installs a marginal figure at the centre of his diligent reconstruction of the Somme, encouraging readers to comprehend desertion and surrender as modes of courage.

Marxist social history, popularly known as "History from Below," influences Sillitoe's reconstruction of the Somme. Its most famous practitioners, historians Christopher Hill, E. P. Thompson, and Eric Hobsbawm, three of the founders of the journal *Past & Present* (1952), provide insights into the complex history of class that preoccupies Sillitoe. Thompson published *The Making of the English Working Class* (1963), a study of the self-creation of the industrial working class (1780–1832).[9] *Raw Material* shares Thompson's ethical mission to dignify those lost to history in what might be termed "the unmaking of the English working class" (1914–1918).[10] To mark the absence of the canny instincts and values of working

---

[8] In an interview, Sillitoe explains: "Lots of my family went into the army and they were all deserters. They just didn't have anything to do with it. One or two did, however. One got killed, you know. But the majority, no. There's a working-class tradition which says that you join the army because that's the only way of getting out of your local area. Another tradition says you never join the army under any circumstances" (in Halperin 187–188).

[9] Thompson complains: "Only the successful [...] are remembered. The blind alleys, the lost causes, and the losers themselves are forgotten. I am seeking to rescue the poor stockinger, the Luddite cropper, the 'obsolete' hand-loom weaver, the 'utopian' artisan, and even the deluded follower of Joanna Southcott, from the enormous condescension of posterity" (12).

[10] As Eley and Nield outline, "during the heyday of social history those inspired by Thompson rested their case on the way working people processed their experience of exploitation over generations to produce in the end a collective consciousness of class, which then could serve as the foundation of radical or revolutionary politics" (*The Future of...* 190). Building on poststructural-

people from the battle, he compiles a list of symbolic casualties, folk heroes and popular figures of insurrection missing, dead, or injured at the Somme, and he presents them in the format of an obituary from *The Times*:

L/Cpt John Cade	7th Buffs
Pte Robert Hood	11th Sherwood Foresters
Pte Robert Kett	8th Norfolk
Pte Edward Ludd	5th Sherwood Foresters
Sgt William Posters	7th Sherwood Foresters
Pte Thomas Straw	London Rifle Brigade
Cpt George Swing	7th Royal West Kent
Pte Richard Turpin	1st Essex
Cpl Walter Tyler	2nd Essex (100)

Sillitoe invokes a long tradition of sedition ranging from the historical leader of the social uprising of 1381, Wat Tyler, to the imaginary rebel who incited labour riots in 1830, Captain Swing.[11] Hobsbawm analyzes the oppositional role of these social bandits, "men who bring justice to the people," as figures central to "remembered history" rather than "official history" (145). They signify a collective loss, an extinguished tradition of social insurgency, which, as Hill argues, was the rule rather than the exception in British history: "Popular revolt was for many centuries an essential feature of the English tradition" (11). The Somme offensive, however, disrupted a shared history founded on rebellious figures that embodied resistance to power. As such, the battle decisively impacted popular struggles: "History from Below" allows Sillitoe to grapple with the dis/continuities of class oppression.

Sillitoe situates the Somme within a narrative of internal class conflicts rather than international antagonisms: "Never before had such an assault been made of class against class" (109). He does not dispute the basis for war, but the methods by which it was fought. As Sillitoe states, "the British Army should have called on a nation of poachers instead of a nation of cricketers" (100). He lauds the poacher, the outlaw figure who defies the sanctity of inherited wealth and private property. In his view, this preindustrial social typology also encapsulates the wily

---

ist critiques of Thompson, they conceptualize class in terms of both social discourses and material determinations. Hence, Eley and Nield uphold practices of "sociocultural" history attuned to the methods of both cultural and social history (*The Future of...* 201).

11 As Griffin summarizes, "the fear generated in 1830 converted Captain Swing into a spectral presence that continued to wreak terror on the minds of farmers and the rulers of rural England. Over and above Swing's continuities and revivals, it was as a concept that Swing most meaningfully lived on" (325).

working-class subject of the industrial order. Significantly, Sillitoe judges that the French, unlike the English, "did not obey their officers so blindly"; they adopted an improvisational approach to their own survival reminiscent of the guerilla tactics of English rebels (96). The poacher, a model of stealth and self-reliance, contrasts with the public formalities of the Eton gamester. Yet, as the Somme reveals, instead of valorizing the cunning of the poacher who evaded detection as a rule, the British upper class elevated the rule-bound transparency of cricket above the lives of soldiers. In this manner, the military command deprived the people of their collective storehouse of knowledge based on a healthy instinct for self-preservation. Hence, poachers populate Sillitoe's list of bandits on the victim roll of the Somme. The stark contrast between the opposing world-views of the cricketer and the poacher organizes his scathing critique of military strategy at the Somme.

According to Sillitoe, the staff officers pursued misguided strategies at odds with the survival of the infantry in modern industrial warfare. In particular, he denounces Douglas Haig, the controversial general who planned the Somme offensive as "Britain's number one war criminal" (114). Lengthy bombardments exposed British soldiers to danger by advertising the intention to attack, permitting the enemy to make elaborate defensive preparations (102). To make matters worse, excessive reliance on massed attacks precluded other forms of tactical ingenuity. The British allocated "the best seats" to the Germans in the theatre of war, so that the infantry often occupied the low ground, making the men "clear and unmistakable targets" as they advanced in formation (111, 97). Officers coerced soldiers over the top at gunpoint, often in broad daylight on ground overlooked by the enemy, yet they neglected to train them in the "art of retreat": Sillitoe concludes that the men were not even "taught to stay alive" (114, 99). He infers that commanders valued the forms of military discipline above the realities of human life. Despite the appalling casualties on the first day of the Somme, they pronounced the offensive a success because the men "had died rather than run away": "For every officer killed or wounded on the first day of the battle of the Somme, twenty-two other ranks fell with him" (99, 107). The "suicidal maxim" that "the best defence lies in the attack" supported the belief that the "longer the casualty lists," the nearer to victory (112, 113). Sillitoe presumes that British commanders treated their own troops like enemies. Furthermore, the putative tactical supremacy of an obsolete cavalry reinforced class stratification: in contrast to the "lower-class craftsmen and clerks and slum-dwellers" of the infantry, the cavalry, "the élite of the army," embodied the glory of war (106). The New Army, squandered en masse, preserved the gentlemanly ethics of fair play and maintained social hierarchies at its own expense. Thus, Sillitoe condemns the brutal reduction of the infantry to materiel.

Yet *Raw Material* articulates an ambivalent approach to the working class that complicates classifications of commanders and soldiers as perpetrators and victims, respectively. Ironically, ordinary people enlisted to achieve social change but their deaths consolidated the unjust order that they sought to overthrow. Whereas Thompson portrays the working class as a group "present at its own making" during the early nineteenth century (9), Sillitoe envisions them as a group self-conscious of their full maturity in 1914: "They did not fight for England *as it was*. They fought to *change* England" (104). Mass enlistment potentially enabled a ritual moment of transition from aristocratic to populist rule. But massed assaults on the Western Front devastated the troops and dissolved their dreams of the commons: "Such people were thrown away with prodigal distaste because they were coming to the point of stepping into their own birthright" (108). In particular, the Somme cropped the "flower of mankind," namely "people who had been perfected by more than a century of the Industrial Revolution" (108). Sillitoe links the regimented factory hand and the passive trench soldier: "The men of 1914 were slaughtered, and indeed allowed themselves to be slaughtered – which was the fatal flaw in their perfectibility" (108). Sillitoe impugns the destruction of the New Army by military and political elites as a self-interested act of class extermination. In short, the Somme exemplifies the (self) betrayal of a class as well as a generation.

For Sillitoe, the shell hole that hides his uncle Edgar for three days represents a primal encounter with death, the definitive experience of the Somme survivor. Paying homage to this experience, he figures his postmemorial labour in the terms of trench warfare: as Sillitoe endeavors to "[dig] the ground," he also seeks to "drop into the hole" he has made (92). As he reflects on Edgar's experiences, he wonders whether or not he would have enlisted: "I too might have allowed myself to be drummed into the slaughter" (125–126). Sillitoe reconstructs Edgar's fragmentary story from brief encounters with his uncle and reported dialogues with others, shifting between collective and individual registers. Additionally, he draws on imagined conversations, the "unstated views" of people in his community, "the composite reactions to catastrophe of those whose words are not supposed to matter as far as history is concerned" (125). The trench-map of the Gommecourt salient "marked by the advancing death-lines of the Sherwood Foresters" that he displays in his study recalls his uncle's ordeal as well as the sufferings of his regiment (177).[12] Yet, when he travels to France, he refuses the prospect of psychological closure afforded by his pilgrimage. Despite his geo-

---

12 As Sillitoe discloses, the "northern part of the Gommecourt salient was of personal interest, because when two battalions of the Sherwood Foresters (the 5th and the 7th, of the 46th North Midland Division) went into the attack there on July 1st 1916, my uncle Edgar was one of the young

graphical proximity to the battle, he does not visit the field where the Germans captured Edgar: "I didn't want to disturb his shadow, which must still have been on it" (124). The contingencies that culminated in Edgar's survival inspire awe in his nephew. Instead of walking the ground, he peers at the area with binoculars, noting its natural regeneration. The cemeteries at Gommecourt, however, elicit powerful emotions of anger and sorrow: "the feeling is one of bewilderment and pity that brings tears like a wall of salt up to the eyes" (128). He contemplates the traumatic experiences of his uncle in light of the unresolved histories of the War: "We haven't finished here yet, nor in any way understood it" (126).

Accordingly, Sillitoe narrates Edgar's experience of battle on 1 July 1916 in the present tense:

> The hole is in France. It is ten feet across and five feet deep. Edgar lies in it, rotting with terror though still sound in every limb, encompassed by the squalid rammel of the battlefield. Three corpses are on the anal lip of the crater, their khaki uniforms stained red and purple. [...] Edgar has ammunition, but no rifle. The overcast sky is a vast and awful noise of bursting shells. [...] A massacre is taking place. (92)

Sillitoe locates his uncle in the midst of the clamour and squalor of mechanized killing. He comprehends Edgar's experience in no-man's-land as "a state of question without answer," and "a feat of adoration for the scarred earth" (169). His watch continues to revolve during the terrifying ordeal of combat: as he reports, "It was with me at Gommecourt, and in Germany. Went all the time I was under fire. Would you believe it? Hasn't gone for years now" (149). Edgar carries this inoperative token of social time for decades, actively resisting standard chronologies. After the Great War, shattered norms and purposive dissidence define Edgar's life. His combat experiences result in an indigent postwar existence.[13] Although he returns to work as an upholsterer, his wife deserts him after a few months and his binge drinking bankrupts the family business. Eventually, he dies alone in the hospital at the age of sixty (150). His itinerant life comprised of principled drift, drink, and poverty proves that the body of this broken social bandit, unlike his spirit, survives the Somme.

Sillitoe's last meeting with Edgar takes place on a bus in Nottingham: he shares his first book of poems, and, in exchange, his uncle gives him his pocketwatch. Sillitoe obeys his instructions to repair it: "I still wear it, and it keeps fair time" (150). H. M. Daleski treats Edgar's watch as an important symbol: Sillitoe "continuously carries with him the memory of the Great War" (142). It remains

---

soldiers, and suffered an experience which he was unable to talk about for the rest of his life" ("Maps and War..." 5).

13 See "Uncle Ernest," a short story inspired by Edgar's life (Sillitoe, *Collected Stories* 37–46).

a crucial talisman in his creative vocation. Yet the gift has a political as well as a personal significance for the author. The broken timepiece marks the lost moment of collectivity in 1914 when mass enlistment potentially heralded the end of the aristocratic order. Although Sillitoe repairs the watch, the relic of Gommecourt symbolizes interclass violence. He fashions an enduring metaphor for British society from the contrast between the brave 'lions' of the infantry and the inept 'donkeys' of the High Command: "The third and small hand on the dial of [the watch] pushes the seconds behind as it hurries on an endless donkey-like journey into the future" (175).[14] The hand that keeps the "donkey" time of the Somme foretells looming calamity: Edgar's watch represents the threat of classed extermination rather than social emancipation. Sillitoe discerns the legacies of the Somme in the lost trajectories of working-class revolt in 1970s Britain. Moreover, he deplores continuities between past and present elites: "the men who organised the Somme massacres [...] still run the country" (187). He indicts the persistence of material inequalities in an effort to reclaim an insurgent role for the working class, historical agents who may facilitate the partial working through of their losses. Thus, Sillitoe identifies political and psychosocial impasses that attest to the unresolved historical trauma of the Somme.

2 Ted Hughes: *Elmet*

In a commentary on his poem, "A Masque for Three Voices" (1990), Ted Hughes, "the son of an infantryman," highlights the effects of the Great War on "the tribal lands of the north": "the impact was naked, with no intellectual anodyne available, no social anaesthetic, certainly not for the very young" (*Collected Poems* 1219). As Tom Paulin remarks, "Hughes's continuing treatment of this subject makes him appear like a shocked survivor of that war" (254). More pointedly, Jon Stallworthy contends that Hughes inaugurated a "second phase of major literature centred on the Somme," where Walter Farrar, his maternal uncle, went over the top in July 1916 (106).[15] As Stallworthy construes, the Somme signifies a specific series of military objectives although it often stands for "modern mechanized warfare" in general: Hughes engages with both the historic and symbolic

---

[14] Sillitoe traces the origin of this famous phrase: "'Punch,' in 1855, said that the Crimean Army was an army of lions led by donkeys. The same was even more true in the Great War, and it was proved many times, one occasion surely being the attack against Gommecourt" (*Raw Material* vi; cf. 106).

[15] Hughes's correspondence with Godwin in the late 1970s indicates that his uncle Walt also inspired his work on the Calder Valley (Godwin 117).

import of this battle (108). Regional concerns motivate him to revisit the Somme and the Great War in *Elmet*, an expanded version of *Remains of Elmet*, which includes sixty black and white photographs by Fay Godwin.[16] *Elmet* adds eight poems previously collected in *Wolfwatching* (1989) as well as "Six Young Men" from his first volume, *The Hawk in the Rain* (1957). As a result, it offers a sustained consideration of the enduring impact of the conflict on his Yorkshire birthplace, the Calder Valley, especially in "Walt," "First, Mills," "The Sheep Went on Being Dead," and "Slump Sundays." Hughes's apprehension of losses preceding his birth, including the histories of industrialization prior to the Somme, played a formative role in his imagination. While the landscape bears the traces of communities formerly tied to manufacturing, the disappearance of the industrial working class obstructs processes of working through cumulative losses. In contrast to Sillitoe's vision of subversive prewar subcultures, Hughes regards the Calder Valley as a site of serial shocks engendering disordered group dynamics following recurrent victimization.

"Walt" relates the miraculous survival of Hughes's uncle at High Wood, an infamous site of bloodshed during the battle of the Somme. The veteran's testimony punctuates the lyric. When he encounters a German prisoner on his way to the front lines, Walt confesses: "I felt his eye curse me" (*Elmet* 98; line 5). The evil eye, a common superstition, imposes meaning on the random nature of mechanized warfare. In the midst of Walt's charge through No Man's Land, a bullet strikes him in the groin, forcing him to take cover in a shell-hole. Another bullet grazes his forehead and another ["clips"] him (line 12). Hughes personifies the weapons of war: "Bullet after bullet / Dug at the crater rim, searching for him" (lines 10–11). Industrial conflict conferred agency on machines rather than passive soldiers: bullets bring Walt's life to a stand still, until, inexplicably, the sniper stops shooting. Trapped within the crater until nightfall, Walt revisits the Calder Valley: "He walked about that valley, as he lay / Under High Wood in the shell-hole" (lines 24–25). His immobility under the duress of combat contrasts with his mental ramblings in his native place:

> He went walks
> Along the Heights Road, from Peckett to Midgley,
> Down to Mytholmroyd (past Ewood
> Of his ancestors, past the high-perched factory
> Of his future life.) (lines 13–17)

---

16 Notably, Armitage designates *Remains of Elmet* Hughes's "single most important publication, a kind of concordance to the whole of his work" (6).

The local topographies of Yorkshire displace the mortal danger of global strife in Picardy. Walt conjures cherished landscapes marked by genealogical continuity and childhood memory, the compass of his life. From beneath the ground in France, he passes the "high-perched factory" where he will work.[17] Hindsight thus structures this account by a second-generation descendant. Walt survives the Somme to participate in the manufacture of textiles, the declining industry pivotal to the formation of the regional working class.

Unlike Hughes, who evokes the specters of carnage in the Yorkshire moors, Walt transposes his home and the battlefields. Yet uncle and nephew travel together to French agricultural lands, the former scenes of conflict: "We stood in the young March corn / Of a perfect field" (lines 27–28).[18] The regenerated earth belies the ferocious fighting that ravaged the ground where thousands of men once ran, crawled, and dropped. Walt aims to find the spot where he nearly perished: as Edward Hadley extrapolates, "The geographical locale does not manage to connect Hughes's uncle with his pre-war self [...] the *living* veteran is trying to locate the part of him which 'died' on the battlefield" (33). Walt squints at the horizon as if through field glasses: ecological and historical changes alter his relationship to the spaces of battle: he "frowned uphill towards the skyline tree-fringe / As through binoculars / Towards all that was left" (lines 37–39). Unlike his elderly uncle, who remains uncertain of the terrain, the poet connects history and geography through the pilgrimage: "I knew the knot of scar on his temple" (line 26). The ground explains the origin of the scar but fails to register the psychosocial aftermath of combat, as evident in Walt's temporal dissociation and spatial disorientation.[19] The "misty" horizon of the resurrected field converges with the blurry vista of an unlikely old age (line 34). The poem dramatizes the challenges

---

17 According to Middlebrook, Walt ran the "family textile business": "The Farrars grew wealthy buying and selling property, and built a great house called Ewood Hall. Their fortune had diminished with the collapse of the textile industry, though when Hughes was a boy the family still owned remnants of land that had once been part of the Ewood estate" (10, 64).
18 See "My Uncle's Wound," an earlier Hughes poem based on their trip to the battlefields: "The fields, as they changed, were still finding dead men – / Richer dark patches in the pale watercolour wheat" (*Collected Poems* 100; lines 27–28). Although the ending asserts the power of memory in the second generation, Kendall interprets "My Uncle's Wound" as evidence of "the poet's ambition to appropriate the experience for himself" due to "profound jealousy that he can never achieve the authority of the combatant poet" (201).
19 Hughes includes "The Atlantic," the second part of "Walt," in *Wolfwatching* but excludes it from *Elmet*: "He seems to be touching at a wound he dare not touch" (*Collected Poems* 772; line 64). Also see his "National Ghost": "And somewhere in the nervous system of each survivor the underworld of perpetual Somme rages on unabated, ready to reabsorb the man completely at the right moment of alcohol or drug" (*Winter Pollen* 70–71).

of working through the Somme for the returning veteran unable to reconcile his experiences of home and front.

In "First, Mills," Hughes associates industrial production in Yorkshire with cenotaphs, the empty tombs of slain soldiers. He likens the railway station to a "bottomless wound" that "bled [the] valley to death" (*Elmet* 22; lines 4–5). Hughes compares the Calder Valley to a lacerated body subject to mortal throes. The railway facilitated emigration, export and the intensive exploitation of resources, enabling woolens and worsted to be shipped around the globe. But the railway also inflicted the "fatal wound," carrying men from the north to training camps in the south, where they boarded ships to France (line 6). On 1 July 1916, for instance, the 10th West Yorks suffered 710 casualties, the highest number of any single battalion on that fateful day (Reed 121). Hughes registers the emotional agonies of local households, glimpsed from outside, with "faces whitening / At the windows – even the hair whitened" (lines 6–7). The poet conveys mass bereavement on an unprecedented scale through prior images of predation and violation, namely the incursion of the Angles into the Celtic territory of Elmet in the fifth century: "The towns and the villages were sacked" (line 12). However, in this case, invading warriors do not immolate the local population and plunder the town. Instead, state authorities take sons from their mothers through conscription and propaganda: "The whole land was quietly drained" (line 8).[20] Neil Roberts grasps "the powerful interanimation of the themes of class and war" in Hughes's work," as evident in his conception of the Great War as a civil war: in this respect, "First, Mills" implies that exploitation impels national interests in the region (155, 157).[21]

In the wake of mass death, floods of tears disintegrate interior and exterior worlds alike: "Everything fell wetly to bits / In the memory / And along the sides of the streets" (lines 13–15). Physical deterioration follows psychic collapse; even memory degenerates. Collective grief erodes the valley, turning it into a channel: "Over this trench / A sky like an empty helmet / With a hole in it" (lines 16–18). Those left behind remain bound to the unseen deathscapes of the Western Front through imaginations compelled by absence. The region embodies the melancholia of its stricken populations, exposing the hollow nature of annual rites of remembrance such as the two minutes of silence on Armistice Day. Hughes

---

[20] Hughes emphasizes divisions between region and nation in this line: compare the revised version of this lyric in *Elmet* to the original poem in *Remains of Elmet* (34).
[21] In "Unfinished Business," Hughes concurs with Sillitoe: "The real enemy is the Public Monster of Warmongering Insensibility at home. For England, the Great War was, in fact, a kind of civil war (still unfinished – which helps to explain its meaning for modern England, its hold on our feelings [...])" (*Winter Pollen* 43).

juxtaposes the long history of the area, subjected to the escalating instrumentalities of industrial labour and industrial warfare, and externally-mandated displays of public mourning: "And now – two minutes' silence / In the childhood of earth" (lines 19–20). Rote gestures contradict the scale and scope of communal loss that extends to ecologies and networks: while the dead soldiers from West Yorkshire lie buried elsewhere, the "childhood of earth" serves as the empty tomb for the Calder Valley, the terminus of natural and social renewal. If rituals function to contain grief, Hughes demonstrates how grief exceeds its ceremonial expressions, suffusing the earth. And if memorials function to symbolize loss, Hughes shows how their literal proliferation and metaphoric expansion illustrate their failures as transitional objects. Cenotaphs typically occupy urban spaces or public grounds; here, their disembodied forms colonize communal lands and private bodies. Official memorials legitimate forgetting because they elide adversarial relationships between groups and regions. In this respect, commemoration, understood as a 'grammar' of national identity, relegates the ethical problems attendant upon mass death in the North to silence (Winter 319). Hughes's impassioned critique of national commemoration reveals the political and psychosocial impediments to working through the working-class war.

"The Sheep Went on Being Dead" repudiates the central image of pastoral: the shepherd peacefully tending his flock.[22] Instead, Hughes conducts a postmortem in "a fallen land" with a "broken spine" and "arthritic remains" (*Elmet* 63; lines 3, 18). Godwin's photograph of a decomposing sheep skeleton, a complex image of the community in ruins, condenses the history and (mis)fortunes of the area. Generations of labourers lived through cropping, shearing, spinning and weaving "as each stage of production was mechanised and brought within the ambit of the factory system" (Gregory 259). The North depended almost exclusively on wool, whether bred in England or imported from abroad, but the workers in industries derived from the intensive exploitation of this raw material could not anticipate impending regional crisis: they were "A people fixed / Staring at fleeces, blown like blown flames" ("Wild Rock", *Elmet* 32; lines 10–11). The poet anatomizes the solitary end of the animal:

> And how the sheep's baggage
> Flattened and tried to scatter, getting flatter
> Deepening into that power
> And indrag of wet stony death. (lines 11–14)

---

[22] Twiddy classifies poems in *Remains of Elmet* as "reverse pastoral elegies" that address "the decay of an alienated civilization" without recourse to "the consolations of nature" (55, 57).

Similarly, the local farms, once "a single strength," are now "Tumbled apart, forgetting each other – " (line 20). The disintegration of the sheep and its organs recalls the collapse of sustainable farming in the region; moreover, the disaggregation of the land anticipates the decomposition of class. The history of Yorkshire industry and the technological warfare that mobilized the district both take the sheep as a central symbol. Sacrificial overtones lend special pathos to analogies between the mass deaths of the trenches and the slaughter of helpless, huddled animals. To reinforce this melancholy connection, Hughes powerfully merges "The throb of the mills and the crying of lambs / Like shouting in Flanders" in his inextricable exploration of industrial labour and communal desolation (lines 21–22).[23] In response to the incursions of "hikers' heels," the writer crafts microhistories of place stressing the forgotten affective and somatic legacies of the working-class war (line 26).

"Slump Sundays" restages scenes from Hughes's childhood in the Calder Valley during the Great Depression of the 1930s. "Slump" refers to industrial decline and psychic depression in the Valley. The textile industry and military mobilization simultaneously bolstered and broke the region, as Hughes suggests. In the first stanza, natives consume ritual foods in silence at a funeral feast: the work of mourning extends beyond one particular loss, a singular beloved person, to encompass serial losses in the local population, including generations of textile workers, soldiers, the unemployed, and their descendants. The invisible bonds uniting the mourners seem to be incarnated at the table: "The valley god / Was pulling itself together / In the smokers' haze" (*Elmet* 116; lines 6–8). However, the spirit of place, imaged as a form in the smoke, provides no durable basis for renewal: the group can neither relinquish nor summon the "valley god." As Kai Erikson elucidates, "one can speak of traumatized communities as distinct from assemblies of traumatized persons": "traumatic experiences work their way so thoroughly into the grain of the affected community that they come to supply its prevailing mood and temper" and "dominate its imagery" (185, 190). Speculating on the successive traumas in the region, Hughes observes, "Possibly, among the survivors and the children of the survivors of the industrial horde, that sense of a paralysing defeat, the shock of massacre, was sealed by the years of the Great Depression" (*Collected Poems* 1219). Those who survived gruesome battles in Belgium and France returned to mass unemployment and the fear of another global war. Hughes fuses class and region in his catalogue of historical ruptures that demoralize successive generations.

---

23 Historically, the region of Flanders encompasses territory in both Belgium and France; French Flanders borders the Somme region.

During the "Slump," workers no longer run the mills. Instead, these derelict sites house the trapped energies of lives lost to service abroad:

> Souls were mouldering
> Inside those great barns – the seed-corn
> Lugged back from the Somme.
>
> It served for a mother-tongue. (lines 10–13)

This "mother-tongue," a wordless dread apprehended from birth, establishes nativity in this group defined by collective loss.[24] Exposure to the affects, behaviours, and sensations of cumulative grief becomes a primal inheritance, the basis of intimacy. Agricultural practices superseded by textile manufacture continue to resonate in metaphors that communicate the premature loss of a generation. Not surprisingly, smell dominates this poem: the scent of decay saturates the air. The area abounds with fungi, mildews, molds and mushrooms, saprovores without green leaves or flowers consuming dead material and multiplying through spores. Accordingly, the myriad modes of collapse in the wake of the Somme translate into an inability to preserve, protect, and regenerate. The dead burden the language of the inhabitants; rotting seed becomes "Oracular spore-breath": "The homegrown hallucinogen / Of a visionary defeat" (lines 13, 15–16). In contrast to the cyclic reproduction that takes place through sowing and reaping, Hughes conceives of cultural reproduction through the retrograde processes of degeneration. The spores perpetuate an atmospheric haze, serving as a trope for the transmission of trauma within the community. Hughes outlines a closed cycle of reproduction that forecloses the future, overtaking consciousness and annihilating hope. Lost lives and possibilities consume this group unable to work through its entangled histories of oppression. Hughes couples the sterile landscape with the dying community to embody the processes of class decomposition that exacerbate collective melancholia.

The speaker emerges in this blighted landscape, awoken by the overpowering smell of fungus, "in a goblin clump / Of agaric" (lines 18–19). The mills and the Somme possess the languishing inhabitants and shadow vanishing institutions: these intertwined objects that precede birth almost wholly subsume the child's imagination. The notes to *Elmet* list the Great War as one of many "cataclysms" for the population: "Gradually, it dawned on you that you were living among the survivors, in the remains" (11). Significantly, Hughes dates this awareness from early childhood: "When I came to consciousness there in the 1930s, the

---

24 Norfolk Cemetery, France, includes the graves of soldiers who served in Yorkshire battalions (Reed 116).

process was already far gone, though the communities seemed to be still intact, still entirely absorbed by the life of the factories – or by the slump" (11). In this manner, Hughes underscores the deferred dynamics of bearing witness to war trauma. Caught between reverie and reality, "a scraggy sheep at the moor-edge" suddenly assumes "the wild look of a hope / Returning from no man's land" (lines 21, 23–24). The young boy's dream condenses the palpable yet incomprehensible fantasies of the community. The return of the dead, an impossible longing, animates hope; the sheep, a metaphor for slaughter and a material resource in woollen production, somehow survives mass death and economic collapse. The poet simultaneously relays his temporal distance from, and his psychological proximity to, the horrors of industrial carnage, deftly divulging how the transmission of trauma takes place through cumulative affects, gestures, and sensations. Hughes's postmemorial poetics, his recursive lyrics on the numbing battles that altered his conceptions of family, region, and country, convey his profound understanding of the individual and collective consequences of the Somme. *Elmet* enacts a belated and partial process of working through historical trauma even as it resorts to biological and ecological frames of reference to signify the interdependent and intractable losses of the region.

3 Conclusion

Sillitoe and Hughes ponder the fundamental problem of class in their retrospective engagements with the Somme. Both writers situate the Great War within an extended temporal horizon in order to reassess its causes and effects in specific contexts: they investigate the political and psychosocial cleavages that contradict narratives of national unity and social progress. Sillitoe contrasts the battle of the Somme with the battle of Waterloo: "If Waterloo was won on the playing fields of Eton, the British class war was fought out on the Western Front with real shells and bullets" (*Raw Material* 107). In indignant chapters from *Raw Material*, the Nottingham writer assails the political violence that scarred his uncle, Edgar Sillitoe, and silenced other survivors. People in Yorkshire, as Hughes recounts, endured despite the invasions of the Angles and the revolutions of industry; yet following the Great War, when "a single bad ten minutes in no man's land would wipe out a street or even a village," local residents, including his uncle Walter Farrar, remained insensible to the rhetoric of Allied victory (*Elmet* 11). In his disturbing lyrics, Hughes bares the psychosocial violence that crippled communities and generations. For both men, the long-term ramifications of working-class agency and oppression bear decisively upon the mass deaths and mass bereavements of the Somme: Sillitoe and Hughes reexamine the battle in light of the catastrophic impacts of industrialization and deindustrialization.

Although we commemorate the centenary of the Great War (2014), contemporary British writers reveal that the Somme is still, at least in part, an "unwritten" history (Sillitoe, *Raw Material* 125). Silitoe and Hughes recognize the battle as a profoundly ambivalent site of mourning, one complicated by variable affiliations to class and locality. Their efforts to dignify afflicted individuals and groups regret lost opportunities for "transformative political action" in the past even as they promote the painful and problematic task of working through historical trauma in the present (LaCapra, *History, Literature...* 158). This burden falls to the disoriented denizens and dazed survivors in Sillitoe and Hughes. Varying modalities of affect – outrage and shock – galvanize their respective genealogies of the Somme. As postindustrial conflicts and new social formations supplant industrial warfare and the working class, the battle may be ostensibly forgotten even as its unconscious dynamics influence twenty-first century culture and politics. *Raw Material* laments the fact that "no great voice" denounced the destruction of British working people in the Great War: however, Sillitoe and Hughes, the descendants of veterans, compel us to acknowledge the conjoined traumatic legacies of industry and war that continue to haunt the North (Sillitoe 102).

Acknowledgments

Thanks to Jon Stallworthy and Jay Winter for thoughtful comments on an earlier version of this chapter.

References

Adorno, Theodor W. "The Meaning of Working Through the Past." *Critical Models: Interventions and Catchwords*. Trans. Henry W. Pickford. New York: Columbia University Press, 2005. 89–103.

Armitage, Simon. "The Ascent of Ted Hughes: Conquering the Calder Valley." *Ted Hughes: From Cambridge to Collected*. Eds. Mark Wormald, Neil Roberts, and Terry Gifford. Houndmills: Palgrave Macmillan, 2013. 6–16.

Cannadine, David. *Class in Britain*. New Haven: Yale University Press, 1998.

Daleski, H. M. "Alan Sillitoe: The Novelist as Map-Maker." *Essays on the Contemporary British Novel*. Eds. Hedwig Bock and Albert Wertheim. Munich: Max Hueber Verlag, 1986. 137–152.

Eley, Geoff and Keith Nield. "Farewell to the Working Class?" *International Labor and Working-Class History* 57 (2000): 1–30.

Eley, Geoff and Keith Nield. *The Future of Class in History: What's Left of the Social?* Ann Arbor: University of Michigan Press, 2007.

Erikson, Kai. "Notes on Trauma and Community." *Trauma: Explorations in Memory.* Ed. Cathy Caruth. Baltimore: Johns Hopkins University Press, 1995. 183–199.

Godwin, Fay. "Interview with Fay Godwin." By Terry Gifford. *Thumbscrew* 18 (2001): 114–117.

Gregory, Derek. *Regional Transformation and Industrial Revolution: A Geography of the Yorkshire Woollen Industry.* London: Macmillan, 1982.

Griffin, Carl J. *The Rural War: Captain Swing and the Politics of Protest.* Manchester: Manchester University Press, 2012.

Hadley, Edward. *The Elegies of Ted Hughes.* Houndmills: Palgrave Macmillan, 2010.

Hardt, Michael and Antonio Negri. *Multitude: War and Democracy in the Age of Empire.* London: Penguin, 2004.

Harris, John. *The Somme: Death of a Generation.* 1966. London: White Lion, 1975.

Hill, Christopher. *The World Turned Upside Down: Radical Ideas During the English Revolution.* London: Temple Smith, 1972.

Hobsbawm, Eric. *Bandits.* New ed. London: Weidenfeld & Nicolson, 2000 [1969].

Hughes, Ted. *Collected Poems.* Ed. Paul Keegan. London: Faber, 2003.

Hughes, Ted. *Elmet.* Photographs by Fay Godwin. London: Faber, 1994.

Hughes, Ted. *Remains of Elmet: A Pennine Sequence.* Photographs by Fay Godwin. London: Faber, 1979.

Hughes, Ted. *Winter Pollen: Occasional Prose.* Ed. William Scammell. London: Faber, 1994.

Keegan, John. *The First World War.* Toronto: Key Porter, 1998.

Kendall, Tim. *Modern English War Poetry.* Oxford: Oxford University Press, 2006.

LaCapra, Dominick. *History, Literature, Critical Theory.* Ithaca, NY: Cornell University Press, 2013.

LaCapra, Dominick. *Writing History, Writing Trauma.* Baltimore: Johns Hopkins University Press, 2001.

Middlebrook, Diane. *Her Husband: Hughes and Plath – A Marriage.* New York: Viking, 2003.

Ouditt, Sharon. "Myths, Memories, and Monuments: Reimagining the Great War." *The Cambridge Companion to the Literature of the First World War.* Ed. Vincent Sherry. Cambridge: Cambridge University Press, 2005. 245–260.

Paulin, Tom. *Minotaur: Poetry and the Nation State.* Cambridge, MA: Harvard University Press, 1992.

Reed, Paul. *Walking the Somme.* London: Leo Cooper, 1997.

Roberts, Ken. *Class in Contemporary Britain.* 2nd ed. Houndmills: Palgrave Macmillan, 2011.

Roberts, Neil. "Class, War and the Laureateship." *The Cambridge Companion to Ted Hughes.* Ed. Terry Gifford. Cambridge: Cambridge University Press, 2011. 150–161.

Russell, Dave. *Looking North: Northern England and the National Imagination.* Manchester: Manchester University Press, 2004.

Sillitoe, Alan. *Alan Sillitoe's Nottinghamshire.* Photographs by David Sillitoe. London: Grafton, 1987.

Sillitoe, Alan. *Collected Stories.* London: Flamingo, 1995.

Sillitoe, Alan. Foreword. *A Centenary History of Nottingham.* Ed. John Beckett. Manchester: Manchester University Press, 1997. xvii–xviii.

Sillitoe, Alan. "Interview with Alan Sillitoe." By John Halperin. *Modern Fiction Studies* 25. 2 (1979): 175–189.

Sillitoe, Alan. "Maps and the Great War." *A Flight of Arrows: Opinions, People, Places*. London: Robson, 2003. 32–38.
Sillitoe, Alan. "Maps and War – A Preface." *Topography of Armageddon: A British Trench Map Atlas of the Western Front 1914–1918*. Peter Chasseaud. Lewes, East Sussex: Mapbooks, 1991. 4–5.
Sillitoe, Alan. *Raw Material*. 4th ed. London: W. H. Allen, 1979 [1972].
Sillitoe, Alan. "Ted Hughes: A Short Memoir." *The Epic Poise: A Celebration of Ted Hughes*. Ed. Nick Gammage. London: Faber, 1999. 259–261.
Stallworthy, Jon. *Survivors' Songs: From Maldon to the Somme*. Cambridge: Cambridge University Press, 2008.
Standing, Guy. *The Precariat: The New Dangerous Class*. London: Bloomsbury, 2011.
Thompson, E. P. *The Making of the English Working Class*. New York: Vintage, 1966 [1963].
Tucker, John L. "Alan Sillitoe." *British Writers: Supplement V*. Eds. George Stade and Sarah Hannah Goldstein. New York: Scribner's, 1999. 409–425.
Twiddy, Iain. *Pastoral Elegy in Contemporary British and Irish Poetry*. London: Continuum, 2012.
Winter, Jay. "Commemorating War, 1914–1945." *The Cambridge History of War: Volume 4, War and the Modern World*. Eds. Roger Chickering, Dennis Showalter, and Hans Van de Ven. Cambridge: Cambridge University Press, 2012. 310–326.

Paul Skrebels
A Poisonous Paradox: Representations of Gas Warfare in Post-Memory Films of the Great War

The First World War has left us with two dominant and lasting impressions regarding its special place in the history of warfare. One involves the seemingly endless lines of trenches in which the opposing forces faced off against each other, stretching not only from the English Channel coast to the Swiss border, but along other fronts as well. The other arises out of the first sustained employment of chemical weapons, principally in the form of poison gas, in an attempt to break the stalemate of trench warfare. This is not to say that trenches and gas have not featured in other wars as well; armies have habitually dug themselves in, particularly during sieges, while poisonous chemicals have made their presence felt, albeit relatively rarely, on battlefields since the Great War. Nevertheless, probably because "gas was one of the very few genuine new weapons of the First World War" (Haber 13), it is from that war that we have inherited our principal post-memorial images of chemical warfare, and those images in turn serve to inform our more general ideas about war in the modern age.[1] The figure of the soldier in helmet and gasmask, for example, still epitomises for us the technological sophistication of the weaponry and the anonymity of the mass conscript armies with which we now equate military power, and which underwent their full gestation during the period 1914–1918. From the drawings of Otto Dix depicting storm troops attacking across no man's land, to the sinister force wielded by Darth Vader in the *Star Wars* science fiction movies, the combination of helmet and respirator has remained a powerful formula for evoking fear and terror in the viewer.

The aim of this chapter, therefore, is to investigate the ways gas warfare has been represented in post-memory films about the First World War. It will interrogate the methods and authenticity of those representations, and posit some conclusions about the actuality of gas warfare as opposed to the place it has come to occupy in our cultural consciousness. To do this, the discussion is premised on two key paradoxes which became apparent during the research process: 1) That

---

[1] The quotation from I. E. Haber, son of one of the chief German engineers of chemical warfare, Fritz Haber, goes on to state that gas was "unique in that it was not used in the next war" (13). Given his father's work which eventually led to the development of Zyklon B, and the use to which that gas was put in the next world war (albeit unforeseen by Haber senior), this is a very ingenuous claim, and one which this chapter confronts at its conclusion.

despite its significance in any account of combat in the Great War, gas warfare has been largely under-represented in post-memory cinema (indeed, in cinema generally) dealing with the war; 2) That the more literally 'authentic' cinematic representations of gas warfare try to be, the less historically accurate they actually are. Furthermore, it emerges from this study that some of the more figurative or 'metaphorical' representations actually come closer to the truth of the experience of gas warfare and to its effectiveness as a weapon in the overall scheme of the Great War.

1 The First Paradox: The Under-Representation of Gas Warfare

The unexpected reticence of filmmakers to include elements of gas warfare in their works is perhaps nowhere better illustrated than in their complete absence from the otherwise very powerful original film version of Erich Maria Remarque's *All Quiet on the Western Front* (1930). This is despite the fact that Remarque's novel contains a number of episodes involving gas, some of which, as will be shown later, make their way in a bowdlerised form into the 1979 remake. Instead, director Lewis Milestone and screenwriter Maxwell Anderson chose to present a war of trenches, shell-bursts and machine-gun bullets, of which there are plenty, but without so much as a mention of gas. Over a quarter of a century later and approaching the post-memory era, an equally moving evocation of the futility of trench warfare set within the context of the callousness of military justice, Stanley Kubrick's *Paths of Glory* (1957), made its appearance. A highly acclaimed film in its own right, *Paths of Glory* takes its cue from Milestone – as well as from the Humphrey Cobb novel on which it is based – by presenting another unforgettable recreation of a war of senseless bayonet attacks through merciless artillery barrages and into the muzzles of machine guns, but without the slightest whiff of gas.

However, a decade later a Great War film of similarly epic proportions, but this time with gas warfare central to its theme, was made. Alberto Lattuada's *Fräulein Doktor* (1968) is a joint Italian-Yugoslav production with British actors – most notably Kenneth More – in the lead roles. Unfortunately, unlike some of its predecessors it was not well received, either critically or at the box office (cf. Williams), and so has rather slipped into the dustbin of history.[2] A "[s]illy espi-

---

[2] As far as I can ascertain, at the time of writing *Fräulein Doktor* has not even been released onto the market in DVD format.

onage film" according to one source (Scheuer 255), its dramatic action consists of the supposed activities of an apparently real-life but enigmatic German PhD-turned-femme fatale, variously identified as Elsbeth Schragmuller or Annemarie Lesser (cf. Williams). One of her assignments in the story is to serve her country's war effort by seducing and assassinating a female French scientist in order to steal the formula for a new and deadly gas. This she manages, the climax of the film being the employment of this weapon as the opening gambit in the German army's *Kaiserschlacht* offensive of Spring 1918 on the Western Front. Lines of gas cylinders, operated by soldiers in rubberised protective suits and the obligatory helmets and gasmasks, release filthy-coloured clouds of poisonous matter onto the Allied lines. Within minutes the mainly Belgian soldiers occupying the opposing trenches are covered in suppurating blisters or gagging for air. Panic spreads and they abandon their positions after token resistance, allowing the triumphant German stormtroops to stride across no man's land, fully masked and protected against the vile stuff, all to an eerie music score by Ennio Morricone. The episode looks very realistic and convincing, apparently in keeping with the "fine period reconstruction" which is the film's one "saving grace" (Scheuer 255).

At about the same time, Joan Littlewood's agit-prop theatrical production, *Oh! What a Lovely War*, was being turned into a film. In keeping with the original play's staging in the style of Brecht and Piscator, Richard Attenborough's *Oh! What a Lovely War* (1969) consists of a series of set pieces alternating between naturalistic scenes and song and dance numbers designed to highlight the folly and ultimate tragedy of the First World War. The use of gas gets a brief reference in a song sung by British troops in the earlier phases of trench warfare: no steel helmets are on issue but they are wearing the clumsy 'hypo' or 'PH' helmets – early forms of gas protection consisting of chemical-impregnated cloth hoods with glass eyepieces. When these are removed on the 'all-clear' from the sergeant, the men break into "Bombed last night," a song containing a verse about gas with the line, "Cause phosgene and mustard gas is much too much for me," and ending with:

> They're warning us, they're warning us,
> One respirator for the four of us.
> Thank your lucky stars, three of us can run,
> So one of us can use it all alone.

The scene concludes with a pep-talk by a staff officer who attempts to excuse the casualties suffered by the unit through their own gas: "rather nasty – damned wind changing. But these mishaps do happen in war, and gas can be a war-winning weapon."

The film's surreal ending has one of the central characters donning the so-called Small Box Respirator (SBR), the British gasmask issued from late 1916 onwards, which in various improved forms remained in use into the Second World War and beyond. In helmet, mask and full equipment he wanders out into no man's land, "between the tapes marking the decontaminated path through the mustard gas field" (Haber 232). In a scene which bridges life and death, reality and fantasy, the soldier passes through the gas and smoke to a field of poppies which dissolves into a vast military cemetery of white crosses, and so presumably into the cultural memory.

Jack Gold's *Aces High* (1976) is, as the name suggests, a film dealing with the air war above the trenches. Nevertheless, it gestures towards the sufferings of the 'poor bloody infantry' in a scene in which some airmen are travelling to their base in a French officer's staff car. The car has to give way to a column of French infantrymen; one group is wounded: their eyes are bandaged and they make their way along in a grotesque conga-line, each with a hand on the shoulder of the man in front for guidance. This type of image has long been something of a WWI commonplace, chiefly through the impact of the 'super-picture' *Gassed* (1919), painted by American artist John Singer Sargent as a commission for a proposed Hall of Remembrance (it now hangs in the Imperial War Museum, London). It shows British soldiers whom Sargent himself had witnessed after a mustard gas attack, "shuffling" along in a line into a dressing station. Destined to become "one of the most famous of all First World War pictures," *Gassed* was "for the next twenty years [...] to be widely reproduced, both as a tribute to the endurance of the fighting man and as anti-war propaganda" (Harries 99). However, in *Aces High* no information is provided about how the *poilus* received their wounds. They pass quickly by the halted car and are seen no more, and any allusion to *Gassed* or similar images from the war is left for the viewer to determine.

Delbert Mann's remake of *All Quiet on the Western Front* (1979) offers a heavy-handed, almost naïve attempt to emphasise the horrors of war by outdoing Remarque at his own project. Thus in addition to working through a checklist of stereotypical incidents involving artillery, machine guns and rats – including a ludicrous flame-throwing sequence in which a French crew strolls around no man's land, casually spraying Germans with fire without any hint or fear that they themselves might be shot at – the fears inherent in chemical warfare are fully exploited. As if the standard bogeyman in helmet and respirator warning of the gas attack were not enough, there is also a voice-over narration by Remarque's protagonist Paul Bäumer, announcing "Gas – the most feared, the most obscene weapon of all!" – words nowhere to be found in Remarque's text. Masks are fumbled for and put on with the help of one's comrades, more shells explode, presumably bringing the gas, the yellow cloud passes over, and masks are removed. The voice-over continues in words more or less Remarque's, albeit gathered from elsewhere in the book: "The new recruits give us more trouble than they are worth. Between five and ten of them get killed to every old hand, and they get killed simply because they are so inexperienced. They know nothing, so they die like flies." One of these recruits duly knocks his helmet into a shell-hole and dives after it, the voice-over already having informed us that it is "Better to take your chances in the open rather than stay in the hollows and low places where the vapours settle." The veterans replace their masks and drag out the recruit, choking and gasping as though instantaneously and very seriously gassed. The old soldier Katczinsky ("Kat") reaches for a rifle in a bid to put the recruit out of his misery, but he's too late; a highly observant and very speedy stretcher team arrives and takes the agonised victim off to a casualty clearing station. Kat murmurs in anguish, "That baby! Just a baby!", while the others ponder the youth's fate. There immediately follows a sequence where a corpse in a handcart is dumped unceremoniously into a shell-hole with other bodies as the rain turns everything to mud and slime, and which seems to derive as much of its effect from a similar subject in "a work of Otto Dix" (Haber 232) as from Remarque. There are no other instances of gas attacks for the remainder of the film, although Remarque includes several more occasions in the book.

In 1997 the first novel in Pat Barker's much-lauded *Regeneration* trilogy was turned into a film, directed by Gillies MacKinnon. In a story where poets Siegfried Sassoon and Wilfred Owen are thrown together amid the confines of Craiglockhart psychiatric hospital, expectations might run high regarding the inclusion of something about the effects of gas on the bodies and minds of its victims. And indeed there is a scene tailor-made for just such an exploration. Owen is working on a draft of his poem "Dulce et Decorum Est," and we both see and hear the lines commencing, "Gas! Gas! Quick, boys! – an ecstasy of fumbling / Fitting the clumsy helmets just in time." However, instead of evoking the kind of graphic scene in which the remake of *All Quiet on the Western Front* revels, *Regeneration* holds back, choosing instead generalised images of the patients with no obvious signs of gassing. Furthermore, when Barker's fictional protagonist, Lieutenant Prior, undergoes hypnosis therapy, the trauma that is released proves not to have been caused by gas at all, but involves a soldier being blown to smithereens by a direct hit from a high explosive shell, with Prior and his men left literally to shovel up the remains. Gas is not foregrounded as a special problem at any stage in this film, despite its potential for dramatic or sensationalist exploitation.

This brief survey demonstrates two key aspects about representations of gas warfare in post-memory cinema – in fact, in the cinema of any period. The first is that they are far less common than might be expected, given the importance of chemical weapons for the military conduct of the Great War.³ The second is that even the small sample available for analysis reveals a considerable diversity of representation, some of it within a realistic *mise en scène*, some of it more stylised or figurative. But conventional cinematic realism is not a measure of the actuality of the experience being reproduced on the screen, and this in turn gives rise to the remaining paradox, by means of which the examples summarised above are analysed in closer detail.

2 The Second Paradox: Authenticity Does Not Equal Accuracy

The spectacular gas attack with which the Germans launch their offensive at the climax of *Fräulein Doktor*, as realistic as it is made to appear, consists of elements of both fantasy and actuality which result in a representation that operates at the level of myth rather than history. Myth, according to Roland Barthes's formulation, "is constituted by the loss of the historical quality of things: in it, things lose the memory that they once were made" (142). The constituent elements of myth – which Lévi-Strauss terms "mythemes" (104) – consist of "empty language":

> [myth] removes signs from their context, hiding the process of attaching signifier to signified. It thus strips signs of their richness and specificity. The function of myth is to empty reality of the appearance of history and of social construction. The initial sign is 'rich' in history. Myth functions by depriving it of history and turning it into an empty form to carry a different meaning. (Robinson)

The mythemes that constitute the gas attack in *Fräulein Doktor* are a series of signifiers drained of their original significance and assembled for a particular dramatic purpose. Identifying these mythemes and restoring their historical specificity – thereby "unmasking" the myth (Barthes 127) – reveals a surprisingly high degree of inaccuracy in the ways gas warfare has been represented.

First, the cylinders used to release gas in *Fräulein Doktor* were certainly used by both sides from the outset to launch so-called "cloud gas" (Haber 12), but the

---

3 In 2008 the film *Haber* was released, covering Fritz Haber's transition from "the father of modern agriculture" to "the father of chemical warfare" (*Haber*, DVD cover blurb). Although evocative and very well made, at only some 30 minutes long it doesn't qualify as a feature film. Its story ends with the first release of chlorine gas from the German trenches at Ypres in April 1915, without following up the effects of the attack.

logistics involved in such attacks made it a far from ideal method, nor a particularly secretive one:

> The German cloud-gas attacks always took place in quiet sectors. Their new [in 1915] tactics called for immense preparation and the procedure never varied. The Gaspioniere and their bulky equipment were ordered to proceed to a particular area where they dug in the cylinders and waited for suitable weather. Their activities attracted attention and what the Allies did not observe themselves they got from prisoners and deserters. Thus they were always forewarned and on the alert when the Germans released gas. (Haber 88)

This situation applied even to the very first use by the Germans of cloud gas. As all the major sources point out, the Allied high command had plenty of warning about, and opportunity to pre-empt, a forthcoming German gas attack on the Ypres front on 15 April 1915.[4] Such inherent disadvantages soon led to the development of other modes of delivery. Chief among these was the firing of shells filled with liquefied chemicals by standard artillery field guns into the enemy lines. The chemicals escaped from the ruptured projectile casings and vaporised in the open air, obviating the problem of blow-back onto one's own trenches by adverse winds – the situation alluded to in *Oh! What a Lovely War* – and guaranteeing accurate targeting and thus more efficient use of the weapon. So convinced did the Germans become of the advantages of gas shells that they gave up employing cylinders altogether; their last major cloud gas discharge on the Western Front occurred in August 1916 (Haber 177), a full eighteen months before the events portrayed in *Fräulein Doktor*.

Next, the depiction of troops wearing specialised protective clothing in action (aside from gasmasks, of course) is inaccurate. When they were developing gas weapons for the first time in early 1915, the Germans considered using "Draeger's oxygen breathing sets [...] of the standard mine rescue type," but because of their bulk did not even end up issuing them to the specialist gas pioneer units, let alone to the infantry (Haber 32).[5] When they followed up those first gas offensives in April 1915, German troops had to make do with simple padded cloth facemasks only,[6] and by 1918 were still relying on the regulation-issue respirator and nothing else. Oddly enough, this question of protective clothing and masks points us towards the crucial ideological dimension of myth-making. Although emptied

---

4 According to Butler, no action was taken by the Allies because they doubted that the Germans would "flout international law" (5 n. 3), and because they had little idea as to how advanced science was in providing chemical weapons on such a scale.
5 Draeger apparatus was issued to some specialist units as early as 1914, but mostly for tunnel digging activities (cf. Mouchet 15–17).
6 This is a feature accurately depicted in the short film, *Haber*.

of its specific historical significance, the mythical signifier is "full" when it provides the form for what Barthes calls the "concept" (127), that is, the "ideological meaning," because, says Geraghty, "myths are created to represent nations and peoples who themselves have their own political and social agendas" (192). In costuming the attacking forces in rubberised capes, hoods and masks, the producers of *Fräulein Doktor* overlook the fact that Germany under the blockade of the Royal Navy was undergoing all manner of shortages regarding food and other commodities, and that by 1917 it had no rubber to spare even for gasmasks, let alone fancy protective gear. So it was that the very satisfactory M15 and M16 *Gummischutzmasken* models of respirator, so-named for being made of rubberised cloth, were replaced from June 1917 onwards by the inferior M17 and M18 *Lederschutzmasken*, which substituted face masks of chemically-treated sheepskin (cf. Mouchet 15–16; Haber 196), a commodity available in quantity through Germany's more agrarian ally, Bulgaria (cf. Haber 195).

In reality, it was the British who had the resources to issue "various kinds of capes, overalls, and gloves" to their "decontamination squads," while the Germans had to make do with "paper fabrics and impregnated leather gloves, both useless, but they had nothing else" (Haber 202).[7] In its equipping the Germans with elaborate anti-gas accoutrements, on the other hand, *Fräulein Doktor* deflects the issue of the morality of gas warfare away from the Allies and squarely into the German camp. It promotes a concept of the 'evil Hun' who will stop at nothing to win the war, despite the fact that during WWI the Entente nations went head-to-head with the Central Powers in developing chemical weapons of equal and arguably greater lethality and effectiveness. Nevertheless, a German general in the film spurs on his soldiers by declaring, "The French did not dare to use this gas, but we dare! It will clear them like rats! Attack!" (*Fräulein Doktor*). His forces advance through the clouds of deadly gas clad in helmets, masks and protective clothing in an eerie melange of a Dix etching and a premonition of the imperial storm troopers from George Lucas's *Star Wars* (1977). And as if that image were not powerful enough, the attackers include *Uhlans* – cavalry-

---

7 Haber makes the additional point – which by implication further discredits the depiction of attacking German soldiers in *Fräulein Doktor* – that experiments by Hitler's forces before WWII showed that "rubber fabric was too hot, oiled cloth too heavy" (202). He says that it was only around 1940 that suitable clothing of this kind was developed by the British for their Air Raid Protection gas team personnel. A lightweight "gas cape" was also issued at that time to the British military, but it found use only as a substitute waterproof garment (cf. Davis 242–245). This is in direct contrast to the rubberised groundsheets and "ponchos" issued as waterproofs by the British army during both world wars, which were often used as a form of gas protection in WWI in the manner portrayed in *Fräulein Doktor*. Consequently, these ponchos are often (incorrectly) referred to as "gas capes" in both contemporary and current literature.

men armed with lances – riding horses fully caparisoned in their own specially-designed protective gear. Their appearance evokes the sinister Teutonic knights in Sergei Eisenstein's *Alexander Nevsky* (1938), and even further back in cinematic history, those self-styled "knights of the burning cross," the Ku Klux Klansmen in David W. Griffith's *Birth of a Nation* (1915).[8] The concept being subscribed to in *Fräulein Doktor*, therefore, is of the Germans as ruthless 'techno-warriors,' or in today's terms, as unscrupulous terrorists capable of deploying weapons of mass destruction in the service of their own ideological purposes.

The other important mytheme involves the use of mustard gas itself. Despite the film's main premise, no 'secrets' of mustard gas were stolen from anyone – French lesbian scientist or otherwise – by the Germans, who arrived at the formula through the efforts of Fritz Haber and his associates. While this nonsense might be excused on the grounds of creating a more interesting and titillating drama, it also arises out of, and in turn contributes to, the popular attitude expressed in the 1979 *All Quiet on the Western Front* version's description of gas as "the most obscene weapon of all." Positioning its development within a context of espionage and deception helps underline the perceived moral turpitude of the German general staff, which has no qualms about inflicting this "cruel and unlawful weapon" (Butler 7) on unsuspecting Allied troops.

Mustard gas, of course, was only one of "over thirty chemical substances, gases, liquids and solids" (Butler 9) developed as weapons during the course of the war, and employed with equal enthusiasm by both sides. Mustard gas (chemical name dichlorodiethyl sulphide) was actually first used by the Germans in July 1917 – seven months before the *Kaiserschlacht* – along the Ypres sector, in artillery shells marked with the yellow cross that would give the gas its nickname (Haber 111).[9] It is evident, then, that in terms of its origin, timing and delivery, mustard gas is completely misrepresented in *Fräulein Doktor*; but so too is its operational deployment. In some quite spectacular aerial shots, the film shows a section of the Allied trenches being isolated along the flanks by high explosive shell-bursts, while the main frontal attack consists of a cylinder-launched mustard gas cloud immediately followed up by the infantry and cavalry. This is almost the diametrical opposite of the tactics actually employed. The British official history of the March 1918 offensive makes it clear that mustard gas "was not employed in the bombardment" that opened the infantry attack, but was instead "used earlier

---

8 To the objection that the Klansmen are the "good guys" in his film, we need only note that Griffith himself pulls no punches about the organisation's tactics. The title card that follows the very first shot of some KKK types in their hooded robes and on caparisoned horses reminds us: "Their first visit to terrorize a negro disturber and barn burner" (*Birth of a Nation*).
9 The French call it 'yperite,' a term also used in some Anglophone sources, such as Butler.

for shelling areas to prevent use being made of them or defences constructed in them" (Edmonds 158 n. 2). In other words, yellow cross gas was used to isolate sections of the front or areas behind the lines while, depending on the kind of operation, high explosive shells or a 1:1 mix of high explosive with other gases – "part being lethal [usually phosgene] and part being lachrymatory" (158 n. 2) – were used in the main attack. Not only that, but saturation with mustard gas automatically rendered any sector a "no-go" area: "if the German infantry would have to cross these areas, the gas shelling was discontinued at least three days before the attack" (158 n. 2). Preparatory to the actual Operation Michael, the Germans used mass mustard gas shelling to "'box in' the British guns [...] silencing them, and preventing relief from getting through to the crews" (Haber 215). The depiction in *Fräulein Doktor* of German troops advancing into freshly mustard-gassed enemy positions, in protective clothing they never actually possessed, is thus a complete figment of the filmmaker's imagination.

Tactics, however, are certainly to be of less interest to audiences than the physical effects of chemical weapons, and three of the films under discussion present these in graphic fashion. In *Fräulein Doktor*, only minutes after contact with the gas cloud, the Allied soldiers' exposed areas of skin begin to blister and peel, and they writhe in pain as though chemically burnt. The result is mass panic and flight, allowing the Germans to advance into the opposing trenches with only moderate opposition. A comparison with the findings in a report by a British medical officer following the first use of mustard gas by the Germans on the night of 12–13 July 1917,[10] reveals just how much the film sensationalises the effects of the gas, both physically and psychologically. According to the report, apart from a few who "experienced nausea and vomited" during the actual bombardment, "the immediate effects produced by the gas were quite trifling," and "so slight as to be practically unnoticed by many men," most of whom actually managed "to have gone to sleep after the gas bombardment was over" (Butler 39). It was only "two to five hours later" that "they were awakened with pain in the eyes which rapidly became intolerable" (39). This was accompanied by running noses and eyes, along with frequent sneezing, "as if they had a violent cold in the head," often with severe irritation or burning of the throat followed by nausea and persistent vomiting (39). Some hours after this, the vesicant effect kicked in and characteristic skin blisters began to appear "on the lower part of the face," "on the backs of the thighs and buttocks and even on the scrotum" (40). The cause of all of this was identified as "some substance allied to mustard oil" (39), which "was given off from the shells in the form of a mist [...] and so

---

[10] Report dated 17 July 1917 by Major C. G. Douglas RAMC, of the British Gas Directorate, quoted at length in Butler (39–41).

did not penetrate into the lungs as does a gas" (40). Nevertheless, around half of the cases "gradually developed severe pulmonary symptoms" (40–41), which although "very different to those of acute pulmonary oedema" produced by other toxic gases such as phosgene, caused a number of deaths and made mustard gas "a far more serious poison" than the symptoms presented "in the earlier stages would lead one to expect" (41).

Serious, without a doubt, but given the timeframe involved for the symptoms fully to develop, probably not good cinema, at least from the point of view of creating effective battle scenes. Where a filmmaker is able to exploit a suitably cinematic image, as in the evocation of Sargent's *Gassed* painting in *Aces High*, the emphasis shifts away from the specifics of a mustard gas attack towards a more generalised effect. According to Haber, "It does not matter that the blindness disappeared and the blisters only lasted ten days," the fact is that the painting "struck a chord" in the viewer (230); gas has been transformed into a metonym for the horrors of modern warfare rather than a specific weapon in its own right. In this respect, the line of wounded *poilus* in *Aces High* can be regarded as a surreal image rather than a recreation of the actual circumstances of gassing. The line of soldiers has as much kinship to the Dance of Death that concludes Bergman's *The Seventh Seal* (1957) as it has to Sargent's gassed soldiers.

This sacrifice of historical accuracy and specificity in the interests of 'good' cinema is particularly evident in the remake of *All Quiet on the Western Front*, although the film draws to a certain degree on the novel's own tendency to generalise about gas warfare. The various chemical weapons employed during the war had differing characteristics and effects, but can be broadly categorised as either "persistent" substances such as mustard and lachrymatory gases – "usually liquids which evaporated slowly" – and "non-persistent" substances such as chlorine and phosgene in the form of "clouds which drifted along with the wind" (Davis 238). The non-persistent chemicals, some of them compounds of arsenic and cyanide, are particularly deadly when ingested in concentrated amounts, but of course dissipate and become less harmful in "mixing with larger quantities of air" (238). Haber maintains that "Remarque was obsessed by the symptoms of cyanosis – his injured always have blue faces – and by the mental shock of gas injury" (232). This approach certainly seems to inform the gassing scene in the 1979 *All Quiet on the Western Front*, which has considerable shock value but does not contribute much to a historical understanding of chemical warfare. The combination of the German soldiers' wearing the pre-war spiked *Pickelhaube* helmets with full-face gasmasks would suggest the period that Butler classifies as "The cloud gas and tear gas shell period," lasting from the outbreak of chemical warfare in April 1915 to August 1916 (14). In particular, the film sequence coincides with "the great clouds of chlorine plus phosgene" launched from "December 1915 to August 1916" (14), by which time the Germans had introduced the full facemask M15 and M16 respirators. And while the film's juxtaposition of the gassed recruit being carried off by a stretcher team followed by the dumping of corpses would seem to rule out any hope of recovery, the combination of intensive gas drill and protection in the form of improved respirators which both sides were very quick to implement as a reaction to chemical warfare, was making the cloud-gas phase increasingly redundant by late 1916 (Haber 177).

Thus, another aspect of the paradox in the representations of gas warfare is that the supposedly realistic 1979 version of *All Quiet on the Western Front* equips its German soldiers anachronistically with the later and less efficient *Lederschutzmaske*, and in the fate of the recruit implies that safety during gas attacks hinged more on individual experience and common sense than anything else. On the other hand, the anti-realistic musical *Oh! What a Lovely War* not only accurately charts the progression from PH helmet to Small Box Respirator (SBR) in the British forces, but depicts the attention to rigidly enforced anti-gas drills and procedures which relegated chemical warfare to "no different from the other aspects of the local and wasteful character of trench warfare" (Haber 227). That the SBR was "a complex piece of equipment" and "the best respirator then available" (99) was no doubt because the British "overrated toxicity, and adapted masks which over-protected" (45). But they also were attuned to the psychological dimensions of this "novel danger" (45): "The troops' confidence must not be undermined by gas. If the men thought they were defenceless they might panic and retreat" (41) – exactly as they do in *Fräulein Doktor*. A measure of the priorities operating on both sides is evident in the production and issue of respirators even before that of steel helmets; the troops would have to make do with their *Pickelhauben*, kepis and 'gor-blimey' hats for a little longer into the conflict, because unlike gas, head wounds from artillery were "considered among the occupational risks of soldiering" (41).[11]

For this reason, in none of the films under consideration are the relative proportions of gas warfare versus more conventional forms better restored than in *Regeneration*. As already noted, its storyline seems perfectly set up to make gas the source of Lieutenant Prior's trauma; that it refuses to do so and instead locates the origins of his condition in the effects of high explosive artillery is a far more accurate representation of the conditions of modern war, whatever our pre-

---

11 The French Army was a little exceptional in being quick to introduce a steel helmet, the famous "Adrian," in September 1915 (*World War Helmets*), but slow to issue a modern, one-piece respirator, the M2, in March 1916; however, it did develop crude two-piece face pad-plus-goggle gasmask sets from the earliest days of cloud gas attacks (Lejaille).

dispositions might be towards so-called "'*armes déloyales*' – 'unfair weapons'" (Haber 231). For "gas was no wonder weapon":

> Moreover, as the war progressed it was proved to be surprisingly non-lethal: while more than a third of men hit by shell splinters and bullets were killed, fewer than one in 20 of gas casualties died. [...] [T]hough there were those who were permanently disabled, 93 per cent of all gas casualties returned to duty, most of them within a few weeks. (Sheffield 209–210)

For the ordinary soldier, then, gas in the context of the Great War became just another in the considerable arsenal of weapons arrayed against him, to be dealt with – as clearly demonstrated in *Oh! What a Lovely War* – using the appropriate training and equipment.

There is one final aspect of the paradox, however, which rescues the so-far much maligned *Fräulein Doktor* from complete dismissal, while at the same time exposing the mythemes that inform our own twenty-first century position in relation to chemical warfare. If you take away those iconic symbols of modern techno-war, the gasmasks and helmets and other protective gear, the climactic scene in *Fräulein Doktor* is quite an acceptable representation of that very first chlorine gas attack in April 1915, which caused so much injury and panic among the troops who were its victims. Indeed, gas has emerged primarily as a weapon for use on the unprotected and unsuspecting. So it is that our attitudes to chemical weapons have been shaped since the Great War: by its use on civilians in Iraq and elsewhere by their own governments; by its employment in random terrorist attacks such as the release of Sarin gas in the Tokyo subway; and more tellingly, by its contribution to the Holocaust of WWII in the form of poisoning by chemicals such as Zyklon B, developed as an agricultural pesticide out of the work of Fritz Haber himself. For us, gas warfare has become something inflicted on the defenceless by those with the technology to do so, all in the name of a particular ideology. Consequently, in our twenty-first century nightmares, the anonymous and terrifying figure in the helmet and mask is more appropriately employed in films such as *The Boy in the Striped Pyjamas* (2008), dropping poison gas pellets into an extermination block full of naked, innocent civilians.

References

Barthes, Roland. *Mythologies*. Trans. Annette Lavers. New York: Noonday Press, 1972.
Butler, A. G. *The Australian Army Medical Services in the War of 1914–1918*. Volume 3: *Problems and Services*. Canberra: Australian War Memorial, 1943.

Davis, Brian L. *British Army Uniforms and Insignia of World War Two*. London: Arms and Armour Press, 1983.
Edmonds, J. E. *Military Operations, France and Belgium 1918: The German March Offensive and its Preliminaries*. London: Macmillan, 1935.
Geraghty, L. "Creating and Comparing Myth in Twentieth-Century Science Fiction: *Star Trek* and *Star Wars*." *Literature Film Quarterly* 33. 3 (2005): 191–200.
Haber, I. E. *The Poisonous Cloud: Chemical Warfare in the First World War*. Oxford: Clarendon Press, 1986.
Harries, Meirion and Susie. *The War Artists: British Official War Art of the Twentieth Century*. London: Michael Joseph, 1983.
Lejaille, Arnaud. "La protection française polyvalente contre les gaz de combat." 1re partie *Militaria* 226 (2004): 24–31; 2e partie *Militaria* 237 (2005): 25–31; 3e partie *Militaria* 241 (2005): 51–55.
Lévi-Strauss, Claude. "The Structural Study of Myth." *Literary Theory: An Anthology*. Eds. Julie Rivkin and Michael Ryan. Oxford: Blackwell, 1998. 101–115.
Mouchet, Yves. "Les masques à gaz allemands de la Grande Guerre." *Militaria* 220 (2003): 15–19.
Remarque, Erich Maria. *All Quiet on the Western Front*. Trans. A. W. Wheen. London: Mayflower-Dell, 1963 [1929].
Robinson, Andrew. "Roland Barthes's *Mythologies*: A Critical Theory of Myths." http://ceasefiremagazine.co.uk/in-theory-barthes-2/. (30 September 2011).
Scheuer, Steven H., ed. *Movies on TV: 1978–79 Edition*. New York: Bantam, 1977.
Sheffield, Gary, ed. *War on the Western Front in the Trenches of World War 1*. Botley: Osprey, 2007.
Williams, John W. "The Films of 'Fräulein Doktor.'" http://www.principia.edu/users/els/departments/poli_sci/film_politics/fraudoc.htm. (16 November 2012).
World War Helmets: Référence de casques de 1915 à nos jours. http://world-war-helmets.com/home.php. (16 November 2012).

Filmography

Aces High. Dir. Jack Gold. EMI Film Distributors, 1976.
Alexander Nevsky. Dir. Sergei Eisenstein and D. I. Vassiliev. Mosfilm, 1938.
All Quiet on the Western Front. Dir. Delbert Mann. Marble Arch Productions, 1979.
All Quiet on the Western Front. Dir. Lewis Milestone. Universal Pictures, 1930.
The Birth of a Nation. Dir. D. W. Griffith. David W. Griffith Corporation, 1915.
Fräulein Doktor. Dir. Alberto Lattuada. Paramount, 1968.
Haber. Dir. Daniel Ragussis. Cinespire Entertainment, 2008.
Oh! What a Lovely War. Dir. Richard Attenborough. Paramount, 1969.
Paths of Glory. Dir. Stanley Kubrick. United Artists, 1957.
Regeneration. Dir. Gillies MacKinnon. Norstar Entertainment, 1997.
The Seventh Seal. Dir. Ingmar Bergman. AB Svensk Filmindustri, 1957.
Star Wars. Dir. George Lucas. Twentieth Century Fox, 1977.

Ty Hawkins
The Great War, the Iraq War, and Postmodern America: Kevin Powers' *The Yellow Birds* and the Radical Isolation of Today's U.S. Veterans

In his seminal study, *The Great War and Modern Memory* (1975), Paul Fussell locates a ubiquitous structural paradigm for narratives of industrialized mass conflict that first arises en masse with the literature of World War I.[1] This structure opens with an innocent headed off to war – typically, an embarrassingly young man who sees in combat the prospect of a glorious entrée into manhood. In ironic fashion, this structure will force its protagonist to confront a liminal period wherein he discovers war to be wholly subversive of his expectations. This confrontation, then, precipitates a final period of consideration, wherein combat narratives' protagonists descend, rather than ascend, into adulthood – their coming-of-age journeys rooted in loss, rather than gain. It is precisely this innocence-experience-consideration structure that U.S. Army veteran Kevin Powers' autobiographical Iraq War novel, *The Yellow Birds* (2012), sets in motion. Powers turns to representational strategies that depend heavily on those Great War writers use. In fact, Tom Wolfe blurbs that Powers has written, "The *All Quiet on the Western Front* of America's Arab wars," although the particular Great War writer who exerts the most influence over *The Yellow Birds*, in terms of stylistics as well as thematics, is Ernest Hemingway, not Erich Maria Remarque. In Powers, as with many works emerging out of the war on terror, we can trace key commonalities that link contemporary American warfare and its literature to the Great War.

At the same time, Fussell and many other critics find the ironic experiences related in World War I narratives to be representative of the experience of modernity widely conceived – hence the birth of concepts such as a "lost generation." It is here that Powers' narrative, and the Iraq War itself, mark a radical departure from earlier literatures and conflicts. Given the presence of an all-volunteer military in America, as well as several other factors this essay traces, Powers and his novel are not members of a "lost generation," so much as they are cut off from their generation. For this reason, the innocence-experience-consideration paradigm is both representative *and* atypical of Americans' experiences of the Iraq

---

[1] In this configuration, Stephen Crane's *The Red Badge of Courage* (1895), and the U.S. Civil War itself, function as precursors. I am not sure whether that renders Crane an author of historical fiction, a futurist, or something of both.

War. In short, modern combat severs today's American veterans from a postmodern culture of distraction, fragmentation, and simulation.[2]

Powers' protagonist in this first-person narrative, John Bartle, internalizes the terrible truths of modern war, just as twentieth-century soldiers did before him. However, Bartle is cut off from his culture – not a representative everyman, but rather a forgotten stand-in. In conveying Bartle's alienation, Powers communicates what even Tim O'Brien seems not to understand about America's new wars. As O'Brien recently told Andrew Slater in an interview:

> In my era, soldiers would have been pissed if we had been lied to about WMDs to start a war. I had a chance to go to visit some wounded soldiers and I asked them if they weren't pissed about the lack of WMDs in the end. A lot of them said they didn't really think about it when they were over there, some of them guys with terrible wounds.

It is not that Bartle would not like to be "pissed," *The Yellow Birds* suggests, affixing itself so tightly to its protagonist's mind and actions that the novel borders on claustrophobia. No, the problem is that many veterans such as Bartle recognize that few civilians in America's a-historical culture wish to share any responsibility for today's wars. For this reason, *The Yellow Birds* goes about getting the modern-war experience right – borrowing at every turn from its literary inheritance – while offering little suggestion that the novel's project has implications beyond that.

The borrowing that occurs in *The Yellow Birds* begins with the first epigraph, wherein Powers offers two verses from a well-known and frequently bowdlerized U.S. Army marching cadence. This cadence's opening verse reads as follows: "A yellow bird / With a yellow bill / Was perched upon / My windowsill [...]." Having created a scene of pastoral repose, the cadence will in its next verse take a dramatic turn so as to create maximum ironic effect: "I lured him in / With a piece of bread / And then I smashed / His fucking head" (n.p.). With this first epigraph, Powers foreshadows the centrality of the pastoral to *The Yellow Birds*, a novel no less reliant on organic/machine dichotomies – with all their attendant binaries,

---

[2] Throughout this essay, my work proceeds from a rejection of the fashionable idea that Americans today live in an era of 'postmodern war.' To my mind, nothing of America's post-World War II wars suggests a fundamental deviation from aims of modern war – that is, to extend the modern project throughout the world, rationalizing and categorizing and, when necessary, subordinating, all in the name of progress. Americans do live in an age of 'limited war,' but I believe the retreat from total war is best understood as but one of modern war's many permutations, rather than as a break of some fundamental kind. I treat this issue at greater length in "Vietnam and Verisimilitude: Rethinking the Relationship between 'Postmodern War' and Naturalism," *War, Literature & the Arts* 24 (2012).

such as youth/old age and life/death – than the Great War poetry we now consider canonical. As Fussell writes of British World War I literature, "Recourse to the pastoral is an English mode of both fully gauging the calamities of the Great War and imaginatively protecting oneself against them. [...] The ironist thus has it both ways: he marks the distance between the desirable and the actual and at the same time provides an oasis for his brief occupancy [...]" (235, 239). In his treatment of Edmund Blunden, Fussell extends this idea, writing that Blunden's insistence on rendering "pre-industrial England [...] the only repository of criteria for measuring fully the otherwise unspeakable grossness of the war" functions as an act of subversion. For Fussell, Blunden's retreat to the pre-industrial past is a strategy designed to suggest "what the modern world would look like to a sensibility that was genuinely civilized" (268). Throughout *The Yellow Birds*, Powers makes a similar retreat; standing alongside, but also transcending, a host of organic/machine binaries is the text's fundamental one: innocence, which the novel conflates with Bartle's youth in the outskirts of Richmond, Virginia, versus the experience that comes from living and participating in the Iraq War's horrors. Moreover, by locating its protagonist's hometown in Virginia, *The Yellow Birds* conjoins Bartle's loss of innocence to that of America itself; both now are divorced from the legacy of Jefferson, the Declaration, and what Leo Marx identifies as the dream of a "middle landscape" (139) – only the war forces Bartle to recognize as much, while the civilians around him ignore this.[3] By constantly returning to its Virginia/Iraq dichotomy, Powers' novel places itself wildly out of step with the dominant culture of twenty-first-century America, wherein we find a breathless embrace of digital technologies, near-total separation from the natural world, and a more general complicity in begetting and maintaining the ever-present now of consumer capitalism. Powers' pastoral, with its fundamental Virginia/Iraq opposition, is no less stubbornly conservative than that which Fussell unpacks in Blunden.

The most significant effect of the pastoral in Powers is that it allows him to capture Bartle's alienation from a culture he has pledged to protect and defend unto death. Bartle is not a "representative American," as the twentieth-century

---

[3] In his landmark study, *The Machine in the Garden* (1964), Marx traces the roots of American pastoral literature all the way back to classical sources, showing that the desire for a blend of art and nature has long been key to the Western imagination. In America, Marx points out, Jefferson is the chief proponent of this blend. Marx argues that Jefferson's whole career unfolded as "his recognition of a constant need to redefine the 'middle landscape' ideal, pushing it ahead [...] into an unknown future to adjust it to ever-changing circumstances" (139). In fact, America's hold on the Western imagination always has been achieved through the pastoral; America was and is to be a place to "enjoy the best of both worlds – the sophisticated order of art and the simple spontaneity of nature" (22).

citizen-soldier mythos – and to a much larger degree than is true today, the citizen-soldier reality – would have things. Nor does Bartle occupy space at the vanguard of his culture like a Frederic Henry, who wishes he could declare a separate peace, but instead finds that the Great War taints everything. As Henry tells us in *A Farewell to Arms* (1929), the world "kills the very good and the very gentle and the very brave impartially. If you are none of these you can be sure it will kill you too but there will be no special hurry" (267). Here, Henry reports a truth about modernity he has gleaned via service on its frontlines. Dark as Henry's truth may be, Hemingway's Great War novel trades on the idea that Henry, through his participation in the war, has learned the lie embedded beneath modernity's rhetoric of perpetual progress. The novel functions as a reportorial document, relating Henry's findings to readers who may not yet have learned, but will soon be learning what Henry knows – unless these readers insist on remaining ignorant and thereby courting history's repetition. Nevertheless, the implicit suggestion throughout *A Farewell to Arms* is that a brave reader willing to be discomfited *can* and *should* learn the shortcomings of the modern project.

Powers writes in the midst of America's first attempts to fight extended modern wars in the absence of conscription. That is, Powers is writing to an America wherein "the logic of citizenship," as Beth Bailey clarifies, no longer stands alone as the dominant rhetoric to explain the rationale behind military service. Instead, four decades of the All-Volunteer Force (AVF) in America have worked to "replace" that logic with "the logic of the market" (4). Bailey continues: "The all-volunteer military [...] allows most Americans the safety of distance not only from war but from the possibility of military service, even from their fellow citizens who have volunteered to serve" (254–255). By rendering military service a 'choice,' rather than a 'duty,' American culture forces veterans themselves to bear the major responsibility for the results that derive from making this choice. Of course, this 'choice' idea figures as a facile understanding of the social and political currents that result in a young man or woman entering the military, to say nothing of the forces that result in one of these persons finding him- or herself in a combat zone. Moreover, this "logic of the market" assumes that it is acceptable – 'natural,' really – to exploit people's best intentions to serve something larger than themselves. As U.S. Army veteran Matt Gallagher writes in his memoir of service in Iraq, *Kaboom* (2010), "the same society that reared us had detached itself from us the day we signed our enlistment papers. In a volunteer military, we fought for the nation, not with it" (11).[4] It is this reality that Powers captures

---

4 In a number of texts that represent America's wars in Iraq and Afghanistan, this insight leads to a sense among military veterans that they occupy a warrior caste, at once cut off from and superior to American civilians. An example of this thinking emerges in U.S. Marine Corps veteran

by way of Bartle's isolation. At every turn, Powers connects Bartle's modern-war experience to a tradition of modern-war literature now more than a century old. At the same time, *The Yellow Birds* makes quite clear that Bartle is left alone to sort all this out. Bartle does not represent or lead his culture; he does its dirty work, before being cast aside.

When we return to Powers' epigraphs, we find that the second of two draws this from Thomas Browne: "To be ignorant of evils to come, and forgetfull of evils past, is a mercifull provision in nature, whereby we digest the mixture of our few and evil dayes, and our delivered senses not relapsing into cutting remembrances, our sorrows are not kept raw by the edge of repetitions" (n.p.). With this epigraph, Powers appears to forgive American culture for its entitlement and ignorance, rationalizing both away. Oddly, this begets a kind of liberation: eschewing any politics grander than the local, Powers creates space to experiment and the focus necessary to capture Bartle's loss. In fact, the only contemporary politics of which Powers seems truly resentful – if we even can call it a politics – appears to be the rhetoric of professionalism that pervades all things military. As he writes, we now live in an age "when even an apt resignation is readily dismissed as sentimental" (223). That said, this may be nothing more than Powers anticipating attacks on his prose, which does, in fact, stray into mawkishness. At any rate, his focus is such that he finds for the novel a central plot with a clear antagonist (war itself), protagonist (Bartle), and conflict – Bartle's struggle to retain his humanity as against war's dehumanizing pressure. In the first sentence of the novel proper, Bartle tells us, "The war tried to kill us in the spring" (3). From this line forward, the war will go on trying to kill Bartle, while he tries to resist – machine-versus-man, modern-versus-organic, and so on – just as the agent-victims of modern war before him have done.

Powers divides *The Yellow Birds* into eleven chapters that chart in an associative fashion what happens to Bartle from December 2003 to April 2009. All of these chapters take place primarily in one of five locations: Al Tafar, in Nineveh Province of Iraq; Fort Dix in New Jersey; Kaiserslautern, in Rhineland-Palatinate, Germany; Richmond, Virginia; and Fort Knox in Kentucky. Chapters rarely move between locations, creating a set-piece feel that intensifies the reader's growing awareness of Bartle's alienation. The novel begins in medias res, dropping the reader into Bartle's boots, which pace an Iraq where the war seems a permanent condition. As he states, "the war came to me in my dreams and showed

---

Nathaniel Fick's memoir, *One Bullet Away* (2005). Fick writes, "I watched my Marines talking and sleeping, and thought about their wives, children, and parents. [...] Each of those lives relied, at least a little, on my doing my job well. Our generation was often portrayed as one without consequences, without responsibility. Now, I thought, we were making up for it" (169).

me its sole purpose: to go on, only to go on. And I knew the war would have its way" (4). Here, Bartle entertains the prospect of what Fussell calls "endless war" (74), while Powers writes combat in Iraq into literary and cultural history. As Fussell contends, "The idea of endless war as an inevitable condition of modern life would seem to have become seriously available to the imagination around 1916. Events [...] obliged with the Spanish War, the Second World War, the Greek War, the Korean War, the Arab-Israeli War, and the Vietnam War" (74). And now, Powers adds, the Iraq War. From its inception, *The Yellow Birds* affirms Fussell's contention that "the drift of modern history domesticates the fantastic and normalizes the unspeakable. And the catastrophe that begins it is the Great War" (74).

The first hints that Bartle-as-narrator knows this – which in part we can attribute to the hindsight on the war experience he enjoys – arrive in the opening chapter. On the level of prose style, we find a mostly quiet indebtedness to Hemingway, which only occasionally becomes cloying, as with a sentence such as this one: "The [cigarette's] ash grew long and hung there and a very long time seemed to pass before it fell to the ground" (6). On the level of character, Powers introduces us to Private Murphy and Sergeant Sterling. These soldiers serve as foils to Bartle, who has pledged to the former's mother that he will return her son home. Murphy is a terribly young, blond-haired, country-bred innocent. For Bartle, preserving Murphy's safety comes to symbolize hope that one can escape Iraq with his or her innocence intact. Furthermore, from Bartle's perspective, the relationship with Murphy is replete with the homoeroticism Fussell identifies as part and parcel of Great War pastoral. As Fussell writes, "To the degree that frontline homoeroticism was sentimental it can be seen to constitute another element of pastoral" (276). Given as much, when Bartle pledges to Murphy's mother that he will make sure her son survives, he is also pledging to himself a post-war return to pre-lapsarian peace. This is a peace that would purify him of having been an agent-victim of a war wherein, "Nothing seemed more natural than someone getting killed" (Powers 11).

All the same, Bartle-as-narrator informs us that no such return will happen within ten pages of introducing Murphy. Therefore, by the time the novel alerts us that Sterling will embody a pole opposite Murphy, the two soldiers pulling Bartle into and out of the war, respectively, we already know tragedy is in store. That said, even had Bartle not told us, "I didn't die. Murph did" (14), we would know tragedy is coming because that is the nature of the literary inheritance *The Yellow Birds* is so eager to claim. In a way, then, the real questions of the novel – its true challenges and conflicts – are formal ones: how will Sterling come to win Bartle's heart? Also, will this movement be sufficiently dramatic to conjoin combat in Iraq with a modern-war tradition that figures even now as an attempt to wrest meaning out of the Great War's trenches? Bartle tells us that he "hated him [Sterling]. I hated the way he excelled in death and brutality and domination. But more than that, I hated the way he was necessary" (19). Sterling will win Bartle's heart because he has war on his side, and as the Great War and all modern war since testifies, industrialized mass death has a habit of overwhelming peace and love.

In fact, this is the insight Sterling pushes Bartle to accept throughout the novel. Moreover, readers see how well Bartle knows war's horrors from the novel's first page to its last. Yet knowing a supposed truth and accepting it are two different things, and Bartle cannot accept either his lost love or his lost self. He remembers first meeting Murphy as follows:

> I never intended to make the promise that I made. But something happened the day Murphy pivoted and moved through the open rank of our formation, took his place in the squad next to me and looked up. He smiled. And the sun careened off the small drifts of snow, and he closed his eyes slightly against it, and they were blue. Now, so many years distant, I picture him turning to speak, with his arms crossed behind him at parade rest, and it seems like whatever he says back there in my memory could be the most important words I'll ever hear. (32)

Bartle's love for Murphy is an idealized bond wherein all things kinetic, including sexuality, are sublimated in the service of pastoral harmony. However, we quickly learn that Bartle is also drawn to Sterling, whom he describes as kinetic to the core – a super-soldier who, like Murphy, is highly attractive, with "his cropped blond hair, his blue eyes scanning the brush at the wood line" (33). In fact, Bartle tells us that Murphy "looked a lot like Sterling in some ways [...]. But it was as if Murph was the ordinary version" (35). What Bartle knows but cannot accept is that under war's pressure, he inevitably will choose Sterling as his favorite yellow bird.

During the novel's second chapter, Bartle muses on why he joined the army in the first place. He tells us that he desired an identity but lacked the courage to define one. Instead, he adopted the identity of 'soldier,' one held in great esteem, even as it is wildly misunderstood, in the contemporary U.S. He believes he shares this reality with Murphy, given that both come from areas of Virginia well off the fast track. Bartle states:

> Being from a place where a few facts are enough to define you, where a few habits can fill a life, causes a unique kind of shame. We'd had small lives, populated by a longing for something more substantial than dirt roads and small dreams. So we'd come here, where life needed no elaboration and others would tell us who to be. (37)

Here again, Bartle faces the knowledge-versus-acceptance problem: if by his own standards he knows why he joined the army and knows this does not speak well of his character, can he accept the burden of acting on this knowledge? Should he embrace the warrior within, and like Sterling make soldiering his purpose? Should he try to preserve himself against exactly that threat by loving and caring for Murphy with ever more ardor?

Intriguingly, Murphy himself appears to accept the self-knowledge Bartle claims. When faced with the questions that plague Bartle, Murphy decides to walk Frederic Henry's route to its logical conclusion, which *A Farewell to Arms* stops short of portraying. Like Henry, Murphy declares his separate peace as a reaction against the dehumanizing pressure of war. In this, Murphy does pursue a course opposite that of Sterling, whose embrace of the war Bartle characterizes like this:

> I wasn't sure he [Sterling] wasn't crazy, but I trusted that he was brave. And now I know the extent of Sterling's bravery. It was narrowly focused, but it was pure and unadulterated. It was a kind of elemental self-sacrifice, free of ideology, free of logic. He would put himself on the gallows in another boy's place for no other reason than he thought the noose was better suited to his neck. (43)

Murphy's separate peace follows the collapse of a last-ditch effort to project his desire for pre-lapsarian stasis onto a woman he idealizes into a Madonna figure – much as Henry does with Catherine Barkley, his relationship with whom involves an aggressive attempt to create domestic stasis even as the Great War metastasizes all around him. Interestingly, Bartle also creates a Madonna, only with a key difference: Bartle falls for a German woman he meets while temporarily absent without leave (AWOL) in 2005. Therefore, Bartle's attempt at a separate peace comes after the fact. Conversely, Murphy's separate peace arrives in 2004, while he is in-country.

Bartle's pseudo-escape takes place when, "The mere thought of him [Sterling] made bile well up in a kind of raw, acidic burn at the back of my throat" (55). Moreover, Bartle's escape even involves a scene during which he enters a church, a priest offers him counsel, and Bartle determines his experiences to be beyond the man's powers of understanding. This is an old-orders-collapsing moment taken right out of Great War literature, with its obsessive emphasis on the falsity modern war has exposed in the West's grand narratives. Bartle states, "I realized, as I stood there in the church, that there was a sharp distinction between what was remembered, what was told, and what was true. And I didn't think I'd ever figure out which was which" (60). He declines even the priest's offer to pray for him before stopping into a brothel, believing, "My separation was complete" (61). In fact, Bartle's faith in grand narratives is so shaken at this point that he flirts with something like nihilism. Hoping to find respite at the bar, he immediately runs into Sterling, who is on a drunken rampage that features an assault on a female bartender. Predictably, Bartle steals a few moments of non-sexual communion with this woman, as if only to reassure himself that there must be some distinction between him and Sterling – some refutation possible to Sterling's assertion that, "'I've fucking got you, Private Bartle'" (68).

By contrast, Murphy makes the only real escape available, at least by the terms not only *The Yellow Birds* sets, but also the entire tradition of modern-war literature. Even before we learn of his death's full horror, we see Murphy anticipating his demise and trying to soften its impact on those he loves. At the same time, Bartle recounts Murphy's awareness of his own lack of control, quoting Murphy's response to a reporter who has asked for a description of one's feelings during combat:

> "It's like a car accident. You know? That instant between knowing that it's gonna happen and actually slamming into the other car. Feels pretty helpless actually, like you've been riding along same as always, then it's there staring you in the face and you don't have the power to do shit about it. And know it. Death, or whatever, it's either coming or it's not." (93)

Murphy will confront fully the fundamental truth of an infantryman's existence in modern war, which James Jones, in *World War II* (1975), describes as a "final full acceptance of the fact that [one's] name is already written down in the rolls of the already dead" (54). However, Bartle cannot let go of "the old life disappearing into the dust" (Powers 99). And like so many of the modernists, he at last will grope for art as a means of re-appropriating and renewing meaning, insisting, "It's imagination or it's nothing" (100). This is Bartle's last hope, and he clings to it even after returning to a U.S. that has become a circus show of "reality television, outlet malls and deep vein thrombosis" (101) – a nation so entrenched in artifice that it would appear inimical to Art, although *The Yellow Birds* itself testifies that perhaps Bartle is on to something here.

By turn, Murphy's acceptance of his fate functions as both a metaphorical and literal suicide. Over the course of the novel's final chapters, he confronts survivor's guilt, the finality of death, and his personal diminution as an agent-victim of the Iraq War's culture of death. To his credit, Sterling recognizes exactly what is happening, telling Bartle, "'You'd better get used to the fact that Murph's a dead man'" (155). He continues: "If you get back to the States in your head before your ass is there too, then you are a fucking dead man. I'm telling you. You don't know where Murph keeps going, but I do. [...] There's only one way home for real, Private. You've got to stay deviant in this motherfucker" (156).[5] Murphy does not "stay deviant," but instead comes "to embody an opacity I couldn't penetrate further," Bartle says (156). Bartle flirts with the idea of trading places with Murphy as a response to the survivor's guilt he knows will accompany Murphy's death. He follows Murphy around when their platoon is off-duty, too, and finds that Murphy has been leaving cartoons all over the base that attest to his presence at war, while linking this presence to earlier generations of American soldiers who did much the same with their "Kilroy was here" doodles.[6] Bartle locates the place to which Murphy has been disappearing while on base and discovers that he has been watching a beautiful female medic attempt to save wounded soldiers. Onto her, Murphy projects his last wish, telling Bartle, "'I want to go home, Bart'" (164). Bartle states, "the small area where she was; it might have been the last habitat for gentleness and kindness that we'd ever know" (164–165). He concludes that in watching this woman, Murphy expressed his most basic desire for agency: "He wanted to want" (165).

When insurgents shell the medic to death immediately after this passage of pastoral angst – an event that takes place around a chapel, just in case the reader missed Powers' earlier examination of grand narratives – Murphy gives up. He goes AWOL, naked, and wanders the streets of Al Tafar, where he is captured, tortured, killed, and mutilated. On what appears to be a company-sized search, Bartle and Sterling find Murphy's corpse and decide to carry out a plan to conceal Murphy's end that includes the murder of an Iraqi civilian witness who watches as the soldiers dump the body into the Tigris River. Not surprisingly, when he returns home, Bartle struggles mightily to adjust to civilian life, like generations of veterans before him. Yet it is here that Powers' novel differentiates itself from the tradition it has joined. Bartle will be imprisoned for his role in the cover up, but as many critics will recognize, his lot is not so different than that of, say, Philip Caputo at the end of *A Rumor of War* (1977). What distinguishes Bartle's homecoming – and what distinguishes the Iraq War from modern wars before it – is that Powers undermines any sense that Bartle's fate has larger cultural implications.

Nowhere in this entire novel does a single American civilian who is not directly affected by the war make any real effort to understand it. Outside of

---

[5] This passage may allude to Cormac McCarthy's *The Road* (2006), in which the father character admonishes himself to remember that "the right dreams for a man in peril were dreams of peril and all else was the call of languor and of death" (18).
[6] In addition to its many Great War and Vietnam War allusions, *The Yellow Birds* also converses with World War II, as we see here. At one point, Powers even includes the famous refrain of Kurt Vonnegut's *Slaughterhouse-Five* (1969), writing, "So it goes" (135).

service members and their families, no American has any stake in the fighting or even seriously considers that such a reality might be problematic. In distinction to a character such as Frederic Henry, whose war trauma stands as a vanguard position culturally, Bartle is not a member of a lost generation; rather, Bartle is lost to his generation. As he states near *The Yellow Birds*' conclusion, staring out of his jail cell's window while perched atop a stack of books, "Beyond the tree line the dull world that ignored our little pest of a war rolled on" (216). By capturing the effects upon U.S. veterans of contemporary America's uneasy marriage of modern war and postmodern culture, then, *The Yellow Birds* extends a legacy of modern-war literature rooted in the horrors of World War I, even as the novel marks a disjunction from that legacy.

References

Bailey, Beth. *America's Army: Making the All-Volunteer Force*. Cambridge, MA: Belknap Press of Harvard University Press, 2009.

Fick, Nathaniel. *One Bullet Away: The Making of a Marine Officer*. Boston: Houghton Mifflin, 2005.

Fussell, Paul. *The Great War and Modern Memory*. Oxford and New York: Oxford University Press, 1977 [1975].

Gallagher, Matt. *Kaboom: Embracing the Suck in a Savage Little War*. Cambridge, MA: Da Capo Press, 2010.

Hemingway, Ernest. *A Farewell to Arms*. Shelton, CT: The First Edition Library, n.d [1929].

Jones, James. *World War II: A Chronicle of Soldiering*. New York: Grossett & Dunlap, 1975.

Marx, Leo. *The Machine in the Garden: Technology and the Pastoral Idea in America*. London: Oxford University Press, 1971 [1964].

McCarthy, Cormac. *The Road*. New York: Vintage, 2007 [2006].

O'Brien, Tim. Interview by Andrew Slater. *Beached Miami*. Beached Miami, 28 March 2013. http://www.beachedmiami.com/2013/03/28/war-literature-author-tim-obrien/. (31 July 2013).

Powers, Kevin. *The Yellow Birds*. New York: Little, Brown, 2012.

Part 2: **The Challenge of Form: How to 'Remember' the Great War?**

Thomas F. Schneider
The Two "All Quiets": Representations of Modern Warfare in the Film Adaptations of Erich Maria Remarque's *Im Westen nichts Neues*

"At last motion picture audiences are to be handed a true version of the World War – a human narrative of the man in the trench." This is how as early as in August 1929, Universal Pictures informed the public about plans for filming Erich Maria Remarque's *Im Westen nichts Neues*, including the hint that "35,000,000 people will read this story" (Thomas 11). Parallel to the serialization of the English translation of the novel in more than 64 periodicals of the Hearst trust, the marketing of Universal set the guidelines of the intention connected to the movie: authenticity of war representation ("a true version") with an emphasis on the assertion that such an 'authentic' representation of trench warfare did not yet exist, although long awaited ("at last"). Moreover, Universal addressed a broad public, for the news was spread through NEA services in more than 700 daily newspapers in the U.S. (cf. Thomas). Throughout the complete production process of the movie *All Quiet on the Western Front*, Universal closely connected this claim for authenticity with a claim for universality, which aimed at the sovereignty of interpreting the Great War and providing a correct and leading representation of that event: "*All Quiet on the Western Front*, if made right, will stand for years as the greatest of war films. If it isn't, it will be just another picture" (Thomas 11).

Carl Laemmle, who emigrated from Swabian Laupheim to the U.S. in 1884, and Boss of Universal Pictures, acquired the film rights to *Im Westen nichts Neues* in early August 1929 from Erich Maria Remarque (cf. Kelly, *Filming All Quiet*). Consequently, within the marketing's intention and frame, the filming of the novel began on 11 November 1929 – exactly one year after the start of the serialization of the novel in the Berlin *Vossische Zeitung* and on the eleventh anniversary of the Armistice. Under the title of Arthur W. Wheen's English translation, *All Quiet on the Western Front*, the filming took place at Universal studios in 'Universal City,' Los Angeles, with Carl Laemmle Jr. put in charge as the producer by his father. After firing the directors Herbert Brenon and Paul Frejos, either for exaggerated salary demands or insufficient filming results, the Laemmles engaged the Russian born director Lewis Milestone. Milestone was eager to stay as close as possible to the novel and reworked Maxwell Anderson's first screenplay with George Abbott and Del Andrews.[1]

The authors rewrote Remarque's episodic structure (interspersed by flashbacks) (cf. Schneider, "The Greatest of War Films") into a chronological story of a group of young students, thus giving the audience the opportunity to identify with the protagonists and relive their way into the war: the ideological manipulation by their teacher at the beginning of the war, the first disillusionment with soldiering at the barracks, the first fighting at the front and the first losses. Paul Bäumer dominates the screen as much as he does the novel; and even though he is no longer the narrator in the film adaptation, he remains the spokesman for the generation of young men thrust into the hell of trench warfare. The group centered round Paul consists of students and – as in Remarque's text – experienced working class and peasant soldiers, with Stanislaus Katczinsky as their leader. One by one, the members of this close-knit group are either killed or seriously wounded, until it is only Bäumer and Katczinsky who are still alive. Their deaths constitute the emotional and ideological climax of the film: Katczinsky is killed during an air attack, whereas Bäumer is shot by a French sniper as he reaches out for a butterfly, a symbol of his lost youth. Embedded in this plot are numerous short scenes, which provide a panorama of different aspects of the soldiers' experience at the front, in the back area, in the hospital and at home. This story of individual suffering, dehumanization, and disillusionment is concluded – as in Remarque's text – by the pretended quote from the German official communiqué spoken by a voice-over narrator, which insistently emphasizes the senselessness of Bäumer's death: "All Quiet on the Western Front."

During the seventeen weeks of shooting in the fall and winter of 1929/1930, the indoor scenes were filmed at Universal City, while the 'frontline,' including a complete trench system, was rebuilt at southern California's Irvine Ranch. Milestone shot two versions of the film, one as a silent movie and one as a talkie (cf. Kelly, *All Quiet. Silent Version*). In particular, the technical innovation of placing the camera on a high crane provided Milestone and his camera operator Arthur Edeson with the opportunity to give an illusion of a 'realistic' representation of the Great War's western front, as announced by the film's marketing in August 1929. The positioning of the camera allows the viewer to see the entire battlefield from 'above,' while close-ups are used to provide the viewer with an insight into the emotions of the protagonists.

With the first (eleven minutes long) battle sequence, later included in documentaries on World War I as 'authentic' pictorial material, Milestone and his team

---

[1] The German translation of the screenplay by Jürgen Schebera is published in Schrader (289–408).

set the standards for representing modern warfare in the movies (cf. Beller). Milestone 'structured' the chaotic battle scene by assigning distinctive movements to the fighting parties in the picture frame: the attacking French run from left to right, the defending German soldiers from right to left. The effect of machine-gun fire is also shown by means of 'national' movement: in the case of the French, the camera (and the machine gun) pans from left to right as the Germans attack their trenches, and then from the viewpoint of the machine gun, from right to left.

The audience can always clearly discern what is happening on the battlefield. The shots from the camera crane give an overview of the whole battle scene, which is not available to the protagonists; thus the audience has a head start in knowledge. The consistent use of alternating long shots and close-up views on the protagonists allows for, respectively, the viewers' emotional distance from the scenes of carnage and empathic identification with the German 'heroes.' Before the scene of the attack begins, the camera moves over the heads of actors performing the roles of the waiting German soldiers, creating a bird's-eye perspective (emotional distance), but with spread-ins of the known faces of the protagonists (empathic identification). When the French soldiers reach the German trench, the perspectives also alternate: the French jump in from the right (false direction) and the camera moves backwards, either from a bottom view, which makes the audience feel as if they were in the trench themselves, or from the bird's-eye view in a backward move which alienates the viewer from the most horrific events shown.

In addition, Milestone 'structured' the battle sequence around two motifs, which serve to foreground the tragedy and complete senselessness of mass slaughter. During the day-long barrage the soldiers hold out in a dugout, where some go mad because of the constant threat to their lives. Their conversations deal mainly with food and drink, which they lack because of the barrage. Katczinsky manages to bring in some food, which lures masses of rats, killed by the soldiers with spades. Milestone resumes this motif in the hand-to-hand combat scene in the German trench during the French attack. German and French soldiers not only try to kill each other with bayonets and knives but also use spades – in modern warfare man is reduced to a rat, deprived of his humanity. The sequence closes with a panning shot on the group of the exhausted protagonists, who have returned to the position where they started their attack. The camera shows them gorging baguettes and drinking cognac which they looted in the French trench. For the individual soldier, the sense of modern warfare lies in securing his own survival and looting food. One could hardly imagine a clearer statement against any ideologically grounded support for war, achieved by means of the most innovative filmic modes.

Milestone's movie is extremely complex. On the surface, he pretends to provide a 'realistic' representation of the First World War. At the same time, however, he conveys numerous symbolic meanings, cross-references and quotes on the filmic level, which altogether express a clear, critical opinion on the events represented. The second main crater sequence shows Bäumer and the French soldier Duval, whom Bäumer has stabbed, and which serves to 're-humanize' the 'enemy' in the text as well as in the movie. By means of framing and imaging, Milestone here (as in numerous other takes) refers to Christian iconography: the Bäumer-Duval take clearly represents a Pietà scene, with Bäumer beweeping Duval, who becomes the individual Redeemer, representative of friend and foe. In contrast to the audience, however, Bäumer does not realize this, and with "war is war finally," he tries to avoid his individual obligation. Milestone here directly appeals to the audience to draw the right pacifist conclusions.

The structure of Milestone's *All Quiet on the Western Front*, even on the level of individual sequences and takes, has had an enormous influence on the genre of war movies. In *Full Metal Jacket*, Stanley Kubrick creates the same contrast between the senseless and disenchanting training in the army barracks and the soldiers' frontline experience in the Vietnam theatre of war. In Kubrick's *Paths of Glory* (1957), Peter Weir's *Gallipoli* (1981), Steven Spielberg's *Saving Private Ryan* (1998)[2] or Terrence Malick's *The Thin Red Line* (1998) – to name just a few – the structuring of the battlefield, including the unambiguous assignment of movement to the fighting parties, becomes most characteristic of the representation of the fighting – but with differing, sometimes pro-war intentions as in Allan Dwan's *The Sands of Iwo Jima* (1949). Even movies which are not known as war movies allude to *All Quiet on the Western Front*, like Paul Verhoeven's *Star Ship Troopers* (1997) and Joe Dante's *Small Soldiers* (1998).[3]

In the end, Universal succeeded in producing "the greatest of war films," as announced by the film's marketing in August 1929. Moreover, and as well as Remarque's novel, the movie is today nothing less than an icon of a pacifist position against any war at any time, and has become firmly established in popular transnational cultural memory. However, the image of World War I as provided in *All Quiet on the Western Front* is a highly structured, artificial and fictional construction, including numerous symbolic references to Christianity or the nature-machine dichotomy. Milestone, with Remarque, shaped the image of the Great War, narrowing it to the Western Front and to trench warfare. Within the complex process of reducing World War I to the theatre in France and Belgium,[4] which

---

[2] On the Omaha Beach sequence in *Saving Private Ryan* see Schneider, "Giving a Sense of War as it Really Was."
[3] Cf. http://www.imdb.com/title/tt0020629/movieconnections. (2 July 2013).
[4] See also Schneider, "In Russland."

already started in the early 1920s and which still lasts, Milestone's movie *All Quiet on the Western Front* takes a most prominent part.

When Marble Arch Productions and director Delbert Mann decided in 1978[5] to produce another movie version of *All Quiet on the Western Front* on the occasion of the fiftieth anniversary of the publication of Remarque's novel, they must have been aware of the risk that they would be confronted with two iconic pacifist artifacts and their irrevocable standing in common cultural commemoration.[6] In order to compare the 1979 film with its 1930 predecessor, and to assess the degree of its adherence to the novel, it is necessary first to establish which version of Remarque's text and the 1930 movie Mann was dealing with. In the U.S., the text of *All Quiet on the Western Front* was only available in the censored "Kindergarten" version of 1929 until as late as 1976 (cf. Owen). This version was not faithful to the German first edition of January 1929, because the translator Arthur W. Wheen had partly referred to the serialized version of the novel in the *Vossische Zeitung*, which differs significantly from the book version (cf. Murdoch). In the case of the Milestone movie, its censorship history is common knowledge. The last Universal re-issue of the movie in the early 1950s was a pro-war version supporting the U.S. engagement in the Korean War. It was known that the original version was 155 mins., which were reduced for the preview to 149 mins. However, the version shown in U.S. and some European theaters had only 139 mins. In every country where the movie was supposed to be screened it was either censored or completely prohibited.

With a small amount of research work, Marble Arch and Delbert Mann could have referred – and obviously did so – to the complete series of 1930 stills,[7] which indicate those scenes which had been part of the original version, had been omitted and are still unknown today, namely, extended scenes of drill in the barracks, scenes of gas attacks at the front, Bäumer's visit to Kemmerich's mother as well as the scene with a Major at home. In addition, in the late 1970s, Marble Arch and Delbert Mann could not see scenes which are today included in the numerous (at least six) attempts to restore Milestone's adaptation: the recruits' revenge on Himmelstoß, parts of the Duval sequence as well as parts of the sequence with the French girls, to name just a few.

---

[5] The film was financed by Sir Lew Grade and produced by Norman Rosemont, a specialist in producing re-makes for television. See Lewin and O'Connor.

[6] There has been no research work done on the 1979 movie yet, besides a short and obviously unverified slating review in Kelly, 2002. Kelly just quotes British critiques and has not seen the original version, but only the shorter European version. Taylor just gives a summary of the filming events in Czechoslovakia (cf. 151–153).

[7] A nearly complete series of the stills was published in Schneider (ed.), *Das Auge ist ein starker Verführer*, 52–190.

Marble Arch and Delbert Mann could have known the original screen play and Milestone's ideas and intention, but they must also have been aware that their U.S. audience would only know a fragment of the 1930 movie, regardless of its international pacifist reputation. Therefore, comparing the 1979 movie with one of the still incomplete restored 135 minute versions of the 1930 film, which have been produced since 1984, would mean to compare apples and oranges.[8]

It cannot be decided whether director Delbert Mann and screenplay author Paul Monash supposed the scene with Kemmerich's mother or the Major in the hometown were included in Milestone's original version or not, as well as the other lost scenes and sequences from the 1930 screen play and the stills. It is therefore impossible to establish with any certainty the extent of Mann's and Monash's intended re-making of Milestone's adaptation, and it is therefore inappropriate to talk about the 1979 movie as a 're-make.' Mann's *All Quiet on the Western Front* stands as a movie of its own, but with a clear and complex reference to Remarque's novel as well as Milestone's movie (or what parts and images of it had survived by 1979). Within the first ten minutes of the movie,[9] Mann and Monash make clear how they will deal with Wheen's English translation of Remarque's novel and Milestone's adaptation. The first takes and scenes expose the degree of dependence on the book and Milestone's version, and the amount of their own and up-to-date interpretation of the 'originals.'

After the short front credits and the famous epigraph taken from the novel, the movie begins with a total shot on an already damaged church placed on a devastated plain. Suddenly, the church is completely destroyed by a shell explosion. With this scene, Mann depicts modern warfare as a threat to civilization

---

[8] These productions include: ZDF (German TV) 1984, 135 mins.; NL 1 (Dutch TV) 1993, 128 mins.; WDR (German TV) 1995, 135 mins.; Library of Congress 1998, 133 mins.; Universal Pictures (DVD) 1999, 130 mins.; Universal Pictures (DVD) 2005/2006, 128 mins.

[9] The following analysis refers to the edition *Im Westen nichts Neues* (DVD), Munich: Concorde Home Entertainment, 2005. The DVD contains two versions: The European version for screening on European, especially German TV, which runs for 122 mins.; and the version here referred to as the "director's cut" of 150 mins. length. The "director's cut" is the original 1979 CBS/Hallmark Hall of Fame TV version, while the shorter version has been screened in European cinemas and on European TV since 1983. Even the second filming of Remarque's novel is a victim of censorship and brutal cutting. This is not the place for a detailed comparison of the two versions, but the German version excludes the following scenes: soldiers at the field kitchen; Himmelstoß as a postman; the Bäumer family dinner and prayer; the extended version of drill at the barracks; Katczinsky's front line instructions, the flame thrower in the sequence "The Front is a Cage"; the extended version of the dug-out sequence; the extended version of the discussion after the Kaiser's visit; Bäumer and Kropp at the theatre poster; Bäumer's walk through the hospital; the return of Peter Wächter from the death chamber; Bäumer takes his mother to bed; the extended version of Katczinsky's death; plus numerous shortages.

and its (Christian) values. Throughout the movie, Mann resumes this motif several times: all hospital scenes either invoke Catholic venues or are located in churches, including the last scene with Bäumer carrying the wounded Katczinsky to a hospital, where he realizes that Kat is already dead. This scene ends with a view from below, combining the portrait of a disillusioned Bäumer with the words written on the church's ceiling: "Gloria in excelsis deo." Milestone's and Mann's references to Christianity have no background in Remarque's text, but are a means by which they establish their pacifist positions, though with a significant difference. Milestone's use of Christian iconography serves to augment the anti-war message of the movie, but there is no doubt that God is still present and the Christian faith is a source of strength for the soldiers stuck in the trenches. In contrast, the pacifist tenor of Mann's movie derives from the depiction of the First World War and modern warfare in general as essentially anti-Christian; and there is no God where the soldiers are.

After the scene showing the destruction of the church, Mann's focus switches to a trench, presenting soldiers waiting for an attack. Mann takes the war for granted: there will be no introduction, no slow approach to the military or to the front line; instead the audience is to be immediately confronted with combat. It is at this moment that the voice-over narrator starts to speak, introducing Kat, Kropp, himself as Paul Bäumer, and then the remaining members of the group. This is a major point of departure from Milestone's movie, which adopts the omniscient camera-as-narrator technique as a means of presenting the actions and thoughts of other characters when Bäumer is not around. Mann's technique of voice-over is an obvious adaptation of the first person narrator in Remarque's novel, and this decision means that Bäumer is present in every scene of the movie, and it is his story and his view of the war that are rendered to the audience. It is as if he were speaking directly to us. However, this decision also creates a double perspective. The story is presented from the perspective of Bäumer, who is also present as a figure within the scenes, including the fighting. Thus rendering concrete the experiencing and narrating selves of Remarque's text, Mann is able to provide two points of view simultaneously, as it were: He places the figure of Bäumer within a scene as the experiencer and has him tell his thoughts about it as the narrator – all at the same time. This complex construction often creates conflicting meanings, which in general complicates the audience's ability to identify with the main character. The audience is challenged to monitor Bäumer's behavior, to reveal other motivations and intentions than those provided either by Bäumer or by the filmic narration. While Milestone's movie was in many respects an appeal to the audience's emotions, Mann's movie, in turn, demands of the audience intellectual engagement, a willingness to interpret Paul's war story.

The opening tracking shot showing the characters in the trench is a clear reference to Kirk Douglas's (in the role of Colonel Dax) reviewing his soldiers before the attack begins in Kubrick's *Paths of Glory*. Then Mann immediately refers to the famous battle sequence of Milestone's *All Quiet on the Western Front* (as described above) with several identical shots, an identical assignation of movement to the fighting parties (French: left to right, German: *vice versa*). In many respects, Mann's opening battle sequence (of identical length) does homage to the Milestone movie, but with some alterations: while in Milestone the French attack is stopped by machinery (a series of shell explosions approaching the camera), in Mann the attack is stopped because of French losses. And while in Milestone the German attack is motivated by the need to acquire food, Mann omitted this motif completely from his battle sequence. By referring to Milestone and Kubrick, Mann obviously identifies the battle as senseless (as in Milestone) and callously ordered by the General Staff (as in Kubrick). Mann did not need to explore and develop the scenes from Milestone and Kubrick, which were by then already an integral part of cultural memory, and thus he brings their pacifist intentions into his movie by replicating them.

As in Kubrick, the corresponding opening and closing scenes of Mann's movie create a frame for the entire war story. *Paths of Glory* concludes with Kirk Douglas shown in a tracking shot walking again through the trench, inspecting his soldiers before a new attack. Mann finishes the film with Paul Bäumer (performed by Richard Thomas) taking the part of Katczinsky and becoming now the inspector of 'his' soldiers. In both movies the circle is unbroken, war rages on endlessly. The killing of Bäumer then again closely refers to Milestone by indicating Bäumer's death with a close shot on his relaxing hand. Whether Bäumer is killed because of longing for a butterfly (in Milestone) or because of drawing a bird (in Mann) is extraneous (because of the iconic standing of Milestone's closing scene, Mann by no means could directly copy Bäumer's killing), the message of both versions is identical. By directly referring to two iconic movies on World War I as a frame Mann honors these movies, attaches his movie to their pacifist intention, and is now free to introduce new, diverse aspects of modern warfare.

In these first ten minutes of his movie, Mann sets the guidelines of how his movie is to be interpreted, but also introduces his own perspective. By referring to two iconic films about the First World War, Mann makes it obvious that he does not intend to invent a new cinematic representation of that conflict. Wherever possible, Mann directly refers to shots of the Milestone movie or even literally quotes dialogues (i.e. the dialogues between Bäumer and his mother, the French women, the regular's table at home, the closing dialogue between Katczinsky and Bäumer, Katczinsky's instructions to the recruits, and so on). However, whenever this is necessary, Mann introduces new aspects and thus re-reads Remarque's text as well as Milestone's movie.

In Mann's version, the drill at the barracks is based on revenge and counter-revenge. Himmelstoß remembers how the students annoyed him when he had worked as a postman, and the students – now recruits – pay back for the hardships of the training. Mann presents Himmelstoß as a victim of the military system himself, honored by the Kaiser with an Iron Cross, and then invited by the soldiers to take part in the discussion on war following the Kaiser's visit. In Mann, there is no distinction between the ordinary soldiers and noncommissioned officers, in the end all of them are victims of the military system and modern trench warfare.

In Mann, the Bäumer family is presented as part of pre-war military ideology when he creates a family dinner scene in which Paul's father prays for victory in this war. Kantorek, the teacher, is not a fanatical supporter of the war, but rather a discontented citizen, even if well situated in Prussian militaristic society. He does not have to manipulate his students in order to convince them to go to war, for when the students finish school, they immediately enlist. In general, Mann focuses more on civilians: in several scenes, French and German civilians can be seen, all victims of the war, either starving at home or evicted by their own armies, indicating that modern war is not confined to the front line but affects all parts of society, a total war indeed.

Remarque's novel is perfectly structured, consisting of emotionally appealing scenes alternating with gruesome depictions of the front line and of disillusioning experiences. Milestone adhered to this structure, but also introduced scenes of comic relief (and comic characters like Tjaden and partly Katczinsky), interspersed within the front line sequences. In contrast, Mann banned all comic relief from his version. Without doubt in Mann modern war is a serious experience with no possibility of respite. And if there was any hope for heroism in war, Mann destroys this illusion with a scene in which the young soldiers arrive at the front and are immediately confronted with a hospital train full of more or less severely wounded soldiers which is unloaded right in front of them. This corresponds to a scene in which Bäumer takes a walk through the hospital where he is recovering from his wounds, echoing an identical passage in Remarque's novel ending with the statement that: "A hospital alone shows what war is."

Most importantly, however, Mann extends his portrayal of modern warfare with two scenes taken from Remarque's novel. First, there is an essay-like sequence dealing with the character of industrialized warfare. The voice-over by Bäumer quotes verbatim from the second part of the novel's chapter VI: "The front is a cage." However, the camera shows more, with a deliberate focus on a flame thrower unit depicted as the symbol of industrialized warfare and the 'machine.' While Bäumer argues about chance, which "hovers over us," the flame thrower destroys everything in its way. The second scene pictures the death of Lt. Bertinck and of Leer during the fight against a flame thrower unit, which endangers the whole Bäumer unit (chapter X in the novel). Bertinck manages to destroy the flame thrower unit, but is killed by machine gun fire in the same way as Leer, who tries to save the wounded Bertinck. Finally, Bäumer destroys the machine gun. This is the one and only scene in Mann's movie when direct combat with a 'successful' but emotionally disturbing outcome is pictured. And here death comes from the 'machine', and not in hand-to-hand combat as in Milestone's battle scene. Mann's soldiers are attacked by modern weapons and they defend themselves with the same technological tools of mass destruction; and if these are not available the soldiers are trapped in a situation of complete helplessness.

In Mann's *All Quiet on the Western Front* modern warfare evolved into industrialized slaughter, depersonalizing, senseless, and seemingly endless, threatening the basic values at the heart of Western civilization. The scale of loss and the disenchantment of the survivors affects social relations, family bonds are broken, and communities are destroyed. All in all, Delbert Mann's 1979 *All Quiet on the Western Front* is much more radical in depicting the consequences of modern warfare. With slight changes and additions to Remarque's text and Milestone's 1930 movie it widens the perspective to include the technological nature of total war, as well as its social consequences. This is further enhanced by the fact that Richard Thomas, the actor who plays the leading character Paul Bäumer in this movie, also impersonated the exemplary Mid-Western likeable white youngster, John Boy Walton, in the TV series *The Waltons* (1971–1981).

Although Mann's movie deals with the First World War, it is firmly grounded in the late 1970s discussion on the Vietnam War, prompted by a series of prominent cinematic representations of the conflict, most notably Michael Cimino's *The Deer Hunter* (1978), Hal Ashby's *Coming Home* (1978) and, last but not least, Francis Ford Coppola's *Apocalypse Now* (1979), all of them providing a disenchanted and strongly pacifist portrayal of the Vietnam war in particular, and of modern warfare in general. Therefore, Mann's *All Quiet on the Western Front* is more than just a remake of Milestone's iconic 1930 movie or another adaptation of Remarque's text – the movie is obviously a commentary on the catastrophic U.S. involvement in the Vietnam War, and on the senselessness of modern warfare. It appeals to the audience's knowledge of cinematic representations of war, previous and contemporary, and respects our expectations of a 'true' depiction of warfare derived from these iconic representations. However, it also refreshes and varies these well-known images and connects them to a current historical situation. Without doubt, Mann's movie had and has a pacifist message, and it is a subtle irony that – as the credits indicate in the end – this complex and subversive movie is "Recommended by the National Education Association."

References

Beller, Hans. "Gegen den Krieg: *Im Westen nichts Neues* (All Quiet on the Western Front, 1929)." *Fischer Filmgeschichte. 2: Der Film als gesellschaftliche Kraft 1925–1944*. Eds. Werner Faulstich and Helmut Korte. Frankfurt/Main: Fischer, 1991. 110–129.

Kelly, Andrew. *All Quiet on the Western Front. Silent Version. Viewed Library of Congress, 25th–29th March, 1991*. Typescript, 4 April 1991 [unpublished], Erich Maria Remarque-Friedenszentrum Osnabrück.

Kelly, Andrew. *Filming All Quiet on the Western Front. "Brutal Cutting, Stupid Censors, Bigoted Politicos."* London, New York: I. B. Tauris, 1998; reprinted and enlarged as Andrew Kelly. *All Quiet on the Western Front. The Story of a Film*. London, New York: I. B. Tauris, 2002.

Lewin, David. "Remaking 'All Quiet on the Western Front' for TV." *New York Times* (11 November 1979): II, 31.

Murdoch, Brian. "Translating the Western Front." *ABM* (1991): 452–460.

O'Connor, John J. "TV: 'All Quiet on the Western Front.'" *New York Times* (14 November 1979): 33.

Owen, Claude R. "'All Quiet on the Western Front' – Sixty Years Later." *Krieg und Literatur/War and Literature* 1. 1 (1989): 41–48.

Schneider, Thomas F., ed. *Das Auge ist ein starker Verführer. Erich Maria Remarque und der Film*. Bramsche: Rasch, 1998 (Schriften des Erich Maria Remarque-Archivs 13).

Schneider, Thomas F. "'Giving a Sense of War as It Really Was.' Präformationen, Marketing und Rezeption von Steven Spielbergs Saving Private Ryan/Der Soldat James Ryan." *Krieg in den Medien*. Ed. Heinz-Peter Preußer. Amsterdam: Rodopi, 2005. 351–390.

Schneider, Thomas F. "'The Greatest of War Films.' *All Quiet on the Western Front* (USA 1930)." *Der Erste Weltkrieg im Film*. Eds. Rainer Rother and Karin Herbst-Meßlinger. Munich: Edition Text + Kritik, 2009. 68–89.

Schneider, Thomas F. "'In Russland. Da ist ja kein Krieg mehr.' Vom Verschwinden der Ostfront aus dem deutschen kulturellen Gedächtnis." *Jenseits des Schützengrabens. Der Erste Weltkrieg im Osten: Erfahrung – Wahrnehmung – Kontext*. Eds. Bernhard Bachinger and Wolfram Dornik. Innsbruck, Wien, Bozen: StudienVerlag, 2013. 437–450.

Schrader, Bärbel. *Der Fall Remarque. Im Westen nichts Neues – Eine Dokumentation*. Leipzig: Reclam, 1992.

Taylor, Harley U. *Erich Maria Remarque. A Literary and Film Biography*. New York: Peter Lang, 1989.

Thomas, Dan. "'All Quiet On Western Front' Goes to Flickers Without Knife." *Universal Weekly* 30 (1929): 11. http://www.imdb.com/title/tt0020629/movieconnections. (2 July 2013).

Filmography

All Quiet on the Western Front. Dir. Delbert Mann. Marble Arch Productions, 1979.
All Quiet on the Western Front. Dir. Lewis Milestone. Universal Pictures, 1930.

Marek Paryż
"I shall lie broken against this broken earth": William March's *Company K* on the Screen

This chapter explores the strategies of adapting a literary work for the screen employed in the film version of William March's novel *Company K* (1933). The film was written and directed by Robert Clem and released by Waterfront Pictures in 2004. In the context of canonical American novels about the Great War, *Company K* is an outstanding achievement, and yet it has remained relatively forgotten. What makes this book so unique is the directness in the presentation of combat experience, accomplished through a highly innovative form which draws from a variety of modernist techniques. However, some critics have completely overlooked the modernist aspects of March's novel, including it among less important, albeit "still readable," books that share "the dated quality of regimental reunion" (Aichinger 15). The recent adaptation of *Company K* provides a very good occasion for a reappraisal of the literary work and its author. Unlike Ernest Hemingway, John Dos Passos and E. E. Cummings, who enrolled in medical units, or William Faulkner and Francis Scott Fitzgerald, who went through military training but did not make it to Europe during World War I, William March was a regular Marine soldier, awarded for his acts of bravery with three medals: the French Croix de Guerre, the Navy Cross, and the Distinguished Service Cross. Philip D. Beidler thus summarizes March's war itinerary: "[He] saw his first action on the old Verdun battlefield near Les Eparges and shortly afterward at Belleau Wood, where he was wounded in the head and shoulder. He returned in time for Saint-Mihiel and for the attack on Blanc Mont, where he performed so extraordinarily as to receive the three major decorations for valor"; the end of the war was announced soon after his participation in the Meuse-Argonne (xi). It is not surprising that the adaptation puts a lot of emphasis on the autobiographical dimension of *Company K*.

Admittedly, *Company K* seems to be an unfilmable literary text for several reasons. First and foremost, as a narrative, it is radically fragmented and consists of 113 short monologues, each delivered by a different character, a soldier in the eponymous unit of the American army. On the whole, the succession of events is linear, but this does not really redeem the ultimate effect of discontinuity. The monologues share a kind of immediacy: most of them have dramatic, often drastic, overtones and abrupt endings. It is next to impossible to reconstruct the life stories of most of the soldiers-narrators; their plight is determined by the circumstances of combat, by their exposure to and participation in a continuing, unimaginable violence. If we learn some facts from one or another character's past, it is usually in order to see how brutally the war had verified his self-imaginings from the time of peace. A number of monologues display impressionistic features as they register the shocks, horrors and other disturbances experienced by the soldiers directly before they begin to narrate their stories. According to Roy S. Simmonds, "March's concept had been to write a book in which the background of the war, so vividly described in the narratives of previous writers, could be simply taken for granted, allowing him to concentrate almost exclusively on the *reactions* of men to war" (62, original italics). There are a few events recounted by several narrators, but the mutually resonating monologues do not form logically developed sequences. Rather, in a recognizably modernist fashion, March highlights the different ways of perceiving and interpreting selected episodes. It would be difficult to find for *Company K* literary analogues from around the time the book was written, though William Faulkner's *As I Lay Dying* (1930) comes to mind as a possible reference. A crucial dissimilarity between the two novels is that *Company K* does not have a narrative core of the sort we find in *As I Lay Dying*, in which most of the monologues have been ascribed to the members of the Bundren family. In fact, the major literary work whose tone and composition best correspond with March's novel happens to be a volume of poetry – Edgar Lee Masters' *Spoon River Anthology* (1915), a series of 244 monologues narrated by the deceased inhabitants of the eponymous town. The multitude of speakers, the directness and simplicity of style, the variations of tone – from the humorous, through the absurd, to the predominant tragic – are the commonalities to be found in *Spoon River Anthology* and *Company K*, which is an anthology of sorts, too, an anthology of voices that become virtually indistinguishable one from another in relating wartime cruelties. What is more, several monologues culminate in the narrator's death, and thus the reader deals with the dead who speak, just as in Masters' poetic work.

Company K's connection to modernism is not only formal, but also philosophical. In his seminal book *The Great War and the Language of Modernism*, Vincent Sherry argues that literary modernism challenged "the liberal rationalism of the previous centuries" (17). The invention of innovative literary forms expressed a heightened awareness of the phase of crisis, which the progress of history had just reached, and a deep dissatisfaction with the prevailing ways of articulating this crisis in public discourses. Needless to say, World War I was an overwhelming sign of the historical crisis. Sherry writes: "A deep mainstream of established attitudes – call it public reason, call it civic rationality – was convulsing under the effort to legitimize this war: increasingly, irresistibly, the 'reason' through which its causes were spoken ceased to mean anything" (9). The critic points to the beginning of the sixteenth century as the time when the notions of 'liberalism' and 'modernity' were combined so as to create the basis for a major – and subsequently dominant – philosophical tradition. The failure of "the political discourses of the Great War" to rationalize this conflict signified a collapse of liberal rationalism, which became a "discredited myth" (16). While highlighting the primary role of modernism in 'discrediting' the representative philosophical framework of modernity, Sherry observes that the very etymology of the word "modernism" presupposes "the consciousness of a *special* present, which is made more intense by virtue of some self-conscious *difference* from what went before" (17, original italics). Accordingly, the critic postulates "[a] historically responsible case [...] for a modernist literature [...] in a reading that identifies the timely crisis of this special event" (17). Sherry focuses his analysis on three great modernists: Ezra Pound, T. S. Eliot, and Virginia Woolf; therefore, obviously enough, his remarks do not pertain to combat narratives from that time. Nevertheless, he appears to have identified a critical consciousness that informs the prominent works of twentieth-century and contemporary American war literature and manifests itself in a tendency "to address and redirect the regimes of linguistic rationality" (17), the tendency reflected in William March's impressive multi-vocal composition in *Company K*, Joseph Heller's use of the absurd in *Catch-22*, Thomas Pynchon's disintegration of the narrative in *Gravity's Rainbow*, or Tim O'Brien's pondering how to write a true war story in *The Things They Carried*.

Thus, with the passage of time and with the emergence of later skeptical modes of thought, especially postmodernism, the critique of the presumed rationality of public discourses on war became something of a staple ideology, conveyed through a great variety of aesthetic forms. In the case of a structurally complex literary work like *Company K*, it is precisely the form that presents a true challenge to the filmmaker who embarks on its adaptation rather than the philosophy or ideology behind it. The form is a factor of the utmost significance when it comes to establishing the terms of historical representation. Accordingly, this paper examines primarily the structural solutions that Robert Clem adopts in his film version of March's novel. It is evident from the film that, first and foremost, the director aims to create a more coherent narrative in comparison with the literary source. In March's novel, the convention of the combat narrative is dissipated, so to speak, as a result of its refraction through the multitude of voices. The elements of the convention can be recognized easily, but they do not constitute a logically developed formula. In Clem's film, in turn, the employment of the convention of the combat narrative is one of the principles upon which the structure depends for its coherence. Another such principle consists in highlighting the autobiographical evidence provided by the film; in this respect, the novel is more ambivalent and, in fact, it undermines the use of autobiography through fragmentation. The third principle is the insistence on the historicity of March's account, hence the incorporation of some documentary footage into the film. In the novel, Private Joseph Delaney, its presumed 'author,' thinks to himself: "This book started out to be a record of my own company, but I don't want it to be that now. I want it to be a record of every company in every army" (13). The film seems to move away from this declared universal appeal toward a greater historical veracity.

From the very beginning, the film adaptation of *Company K* emphasizes the significance of March's biography for understanding his novel about the Great War. The opening credits are shown against the background of the photographs of the author at different ages, starting with his childhood. Three photographs depict March in an army uniform. In other words, at the earliest possible moment, the film combines the iconography of biography and the iconography of war. Before the proper plot begins, we can read several captions that impose a biographical meaning upon the story about to be presented. We can learn from these captions, for example, that "[i]n 1933 Alabama author William March, decorated three times for bravery as a U.S. Marine, published a book about his experiences in World War I" and "[b]y writing about the men he had soldiered with, March hoped to rid himself forever of the terrible memories of war." Another three captions follow at the end of the film and the most intriguing one informs us that *The Bad Seed*, March's best-known novel, tells the story of a girl who cannot differentiate right from wrong, which clearly implies that the writer's moral perspective on human existence had been determined by the experience of war. This reliance on biography as an indicator of truth value is quite at variance with what we find in the novel, which – no matter how extensively it refers to the author's biography – does not offer too many hints for assessing the truthfulness of the narrative with respect to facts. March insists that such an assessment should involve emotions and intuitions, and not just a recognition of what happened or did not happen. All in all, his *Company K* is a far cry from being a war memoir.

If the film foregrounds the truth of biography, the novel revolves around the truth of experience which cannot be ascribed to a particular person and which, moreover, is not specific in terms of nationality. In the monologue opening the novel, Delaney, the mouthpiece for March, ponders the sense of his book about the war: "With different names and different settings, the men of whom I have written could, as easily, be French, German, English or Russian for that matter" (13). He then comes up with a metaphor reflecting his idea of the war novel and envisages a variety of stories pinned "to a huge wheel, each story hung on a different peg until the circle was completed"; "Then I would like to spin the wheel faster and faster, until the things of which I have written took life and were recreated, and became part of the wheel [...] blurring, and then blending together into a composite whole, an unending circle of pain" (14). Thus conceived of,

Company K is an anti-(auto)biographical novel and shows that experience overshadows the person who goes through it. Symptomatically, the names of narrators are rather insignificant; there are simply too many of them. The names play a structural role as links between monologues, and not as signifiers of individual histories. The war has deprived the soldiers of their will, no matter how desperately they try to convince themselves that they still have it. They are defined by what happens to them or by how they react to the pressure of circumstances, and not by their individuality or achievement. The ranks of the narrators matter more than their names because the rank shapes the perspective: officers and privates think in different terms and speak in different ways. In rather few cases, we do learn some facts about the soldiers' lives before the war, but such facts are not mentioned with a view to individualization, but conversely, for the sake of typification so that a given character can be immediately identified as a student, a farmer etc. In general, March's novel depersonalizes experience, which perhaps echoes the modernist concept of impersonal literary creation, although it was employed mostly in poetic writing. Modris Eksteins writes: "The horror the soldier encountered had, after a time, little interpretative potential except in very personal terms" and thus "[a]rt became the only available correlative of this war [World War I] [...] an event, an experience" (214). The film adaptation of *Company K* recovers – or rather invents – the life stories of several characters, which is a primary structural solution in the adaptation. These life stories serve as vehicles of narrative coherence and contribute to the concreteness of historical presentation. In comparison with the truth of depersonalized experience, the truth of biography is more tangible and less prone to allegorization.

The evocation of a strong biographical context at the beginning of the film facilitates the introduction of a main character-narrator, a stand-in for William March, this function having been ascribed, predictably enough, to Delaney. The connection between the writer and his alter ego in the film is established in a metafictional scene framing the film's plot; interestingly, it does not have an equivalent in the novel. The scene in question shows Delaney in a shabby New York apartment, trying to write a book about his wartime experiences; it is the year 1928. Indeed, it was a crucial year for March, who had moved from Memphis to New York to organize a Broadway office of the Waterman Steamship Corporation and, due to an illness, began to write on a more regular basis. He even attended briefly a course in creative writing (Simmonds 31). In the film, writing is presented as a psychological ordeal, but a necessary one; evidently, the protagonist is struggling with himself, his memories, as well as with the literary medium, as he stares, hopeless and anguished, at the typewriter in front of him. Writing is supposed to bring about a therapeutic effect, though it remains uncertain if it eventually does. The ending of the film repeats the New York scene and then shows the last episode from the novel, in which it is narrated by Private Sam Ziegler, whereas in the film it features Delaney. Namely, during an automobile trip quite some time after the war, Delaney visits his old training camp and meets Sergeant Michael "Pig Iron" Riggin. They begin to remember the soldiers by whose side they fought in Europe. Delaney becomes increasingly confused because most of the names mentioned by Riggin do not mean anything to him any longer. In other words, the last episode in the novel and the film is concerned with the process of forgetting: "I stood there thinking, trying to bring up the faces of the men I used to soldier with, but I couldn't do it," says Ziegler (260). However, when Delaney, who had written a book about his company, faces a similar problem in the film, the question immediately arises whether forgetting is equated here with working through trauma with the help of writing. It does not seem to be the case, but this inconsistency expresses an important idea, also suggested by the book: that the necessity to remember and the desire to forget are coexisting – not mutually exclusive – impulses defining a complicated psychological condition.

As the last scene of the film illustrates, Clem casts Delaney in a number of episodes narrated by other characters in March's novel. As a result of such a compositional solution, Delaney emerges as a central consciousness, the function emphasized by the use of voice-over, conveying his ruminations in a detached and somewhat dull tone. It would seem that the protagonist playing such a role should represent some kind of superior moral attitude by which the excesses of others could be judged, but this is not true of Delaney in the film. He does not make any statements or express any emotions proving that he has retained a good moral sense; quite on the contrary, it seems that, just as in the case of most other soldiers, his moral sense has been numbed. Indeed, Delaney's numbness signifies the absence of any absolutely positive features that would mark him out, and this is the point: he is to be like others, not different from them. He takes for granted the necessity of violence during the war. He is an average soldier, a military version of everyman. He appears to be affable for a better part of the film until a very drastic episode in which he bumps into a German soldier in the forest, runs after him and stabs him to death in his neck with a bayonet. In the novel, the corresponding event is narrated by Private Manuel Burt. Both in the novel and the film, the memory of killing the German is a source of unbearable qualms of conscience for Burt and Delaney, respectively, as they confront the ghost of the dead soldier. Burt goes mad and, at the end of his monologue, shouts out frenziedly in response to the ghost's complaints. Delaney shouts out, too, but the following episode set in the training camp suggests that he has silenced the ghost within himself, as it were, but this is the kind of silence that powerfully disturbs him instead of composing him. Ultimately, neither Burt, who is driven mad, nor Delaney, who keeps up the appearance of sanity, can hope ever to escape this memory.

Apart from Delaney, the other soldiers who come to the foreground in the film because of their recurrent presence in successive episodes are Sergeant James Dunning, Private Emil Ayres and Private Edward Carter. Similarly to Delaney's, their portraits in the adaptation have been invented anew rather than reconstructed on the basis of the novel as a result of Clem's use of these three characters as replacements for a number of narrators from the novel. The presentation of Dunning, Ayres and Carter reflects the extent of the director's reliance on typification as a generic feature. Despite his lower rank in the hierarchy, Dunning embodies a model of army professionalism, combining a good understanding of military activities with a caring attitude toward the soldiers under his command. He is tough toward them and makes them observe the relevant standards of discipline, but this is for their own good, and he never puts their lives at risk if there is no absolute necessity. Dunning is juxtaposed with the commanding officers – Captain Matlock and Lieutenant Smith – who often give orders based on a mistaken recognition of the situation or, even worse, on caprice. In the novel, Sergeant Dunning tells a story about an officer who had a preposterous idea that American soldiers should throw stones at suspicious-looking clumps of bushes where German machine-gun nests could be hidden; in the film, it is Lieutenant Smith who comes up with the same idea. Private Ayres is a sensitive, honest and intelligent young man, struggling to convince himself that there is some sense in war in spite of the atrocities he has already witnessed. The film contrasts his youthful idealism with what might be called cynical pragmatism, articulated by Corporal Clarence Foster, with whom Ayres has a conversation about the nature of war. Ayres asks questions and expects answers, he is a seeker pestered with doubts, unlike his counterpart in the novel, who refuses to listen to those who jeer at idealism and the "love of the country" (96). Private Carter is an ambivalent character, at times scary and at other times funny, as he combines a lack of scruples with a sense of humor. In the novel, Carter narrates an episode in which he kills the lieutenant who sends him on various tasks all the time and does not allow him to rest at all. This memorable incident appears in the film, too, but Carter's presence in other episodes adds a greater ambiguity to his depiction.

The characters who appear often enough in the film, albeit less often than Delaney, Dunning, Ayres and Carter, include Captain Terence L. Matlock, Lieutenant Archibald Smith and Corporal Clarence Foster. Matlock's role in the adaptation has not been altered very much in comparison with the novel. In both the book and the film, the captain is an incompetent officer who uses his position as a pretext to compensate for the dullness of his civilian life, hence his inclination to make a fuss about discipline and to ignore other soldiers' opinions only because they have lower ranks. This disregard for others manifests itself most drastically in the central episode of the novel and the film – the execution of a group of

German POWs ordered by Matlock, who simply wants to avoid the trouble of escorting them somewhere else. Lieutenant Smith appears in two episodes that further illustrate the incompetence of commanding officers: in one he sends a group of soldiers on a mission during which they are bound to be killed, and in the other he himself is killed by a soldier whom he has treated with exceptional relentlessness. In the novel, these two episodes are ascribed to Lieutenant Fairbrother and Lieutenant Smith, respectively, therefore the excesses of the latter are magnified in the film. Stanley Cooperman observes that American novels about the Great War, written in the interwar years, often portray inconsiderate amateur officers who either "retreat from responsibility altogether" or "out-military the military in rear-echelon 'rest' camps, on troop marches, and in the combat environment itself" (91); needless to say, March's officers and their counterparts in Clem's film represent the latter type. Finally, Corporal Foster helps to extend the system that bestows power on men like Matlock and Smith, as he carries out all orders without thinking about their sense or possible consequences; it is he and his subordinates who slaughter the German prisoners. In the novel, Foster says: "Soldiers ain't supposed to think [...] the theory is, if any could think, they would not be soldiers. Soldiers are supposed to do what they are told, and leave thinking to their superior officers" (125). Interestingly, in the adaptation, these words are uttered, with utmost bitterness, by Dunning, thus gaining a strong ironic overtone. The film's Foster would certainly subscribe to such a credo, but his portrait has a certain complexity thanks to the combination of cynicism with detachment and disillusionment.

The configuration of characters in the film adaptation of *Company K* brings to mind the convention of the 'platoon movie,' a subgenre of the war film depicting a relatively small unit of soldiers who embark on a dire military mission. It is represented by such famous productions as *Platoon* (1986) or *Saving Private Ryan* (1998), but its unquestionable hallmark is *Bataan* (1943), the film that "does for the history of the combat genre" "what [*Citizen*] *Kane* did for form and narrative": "[i]t puts the plot devices together, weds them to a real historical event, and makes an audience deal with them as a unified story presentation – deal with them, *and remember them*" (Basinger 39, original italics). It must be emphasized, though, that Clem's film is devoid of the multi-ethnic and multi-national overtones that account for the American specificity in the "platoon movie" convention.[1] In the case of *Company K*, the fragmentation of the source literary text precludes the imposition of a coherent generic schema on the film adaptation, therefore the suggestion of the platoon convention signifies a contrasting point of reference. In

---

1 See Richard Slotkin's chapter in the present volume.

other words, the audience of *Company K* is constantly being reminded how very much unlike a typical platoon movie this film is. It seems that William March and Robert Clem share the awareness that narrative conventions can serve as receptacles for ideological meanings and should be used, as it were, against themselves. What makes *Company K* a sort of inverted platoon movie, apart from its innovative structure, is the absence of a well-defined and well-justified objective to which the men's efforts could be geared. When issuing orders, the commanding officers seem to be making *ad hoc* decisions or even improvising instead of working out strategic movements. In the platoon convention, the dynamics of interpersonal relations is governed by the opposing feelings of friendship and animosity, and the circumstances of combat can lead to the overcoming of antagonistic behaviors for the sake of an efficient concerted action. In *Company K*, on the contrary, negative emotions persist, while positive ones have waned or been replaced by indifference. Analogically to March's novel, the relations among the soldiers in Clem's film are strictly situational and stronger bonds cannot evolve from them. The writer and the director shed light on the erratic, the irrational and the unpredictable behind the activities of military men; this cannot be the basis for developing a sense of friendship and sacrifice.

The literary and film versions of *Company K* can both be interpreted as a critique targeted at the myth of the Marine Corps as an exceptional American military formation. The film medium has played a crucial role in the creation and strengthening of this myth. Lawrence H. Suid writes that "[o]f all the armed forces, the Marine Corps has remained the one branch that over the years has best publicized its role in the nation's martial history. Recognizing the potential of the film medium from its earliest days, the Corps made appearances in motion pictures a major part of its public relations operations" (117). The first films that established this mythologized image appeared at the time of the U.S. involvement in World War I: "Beginning with *Star Spangled Banner* (1917) and *The Unbeliever* (1918) the Marines had used dramatic films to help create the image of the Corps as an elite organization, one prepared for any eventuality" (Suid 117). By the time March wrote his novel, the cinematic depictions of the Marines had become less idealized as a result of a more general change in the genre of the war film, which moved from idealism toward realism and acquired a greater ideological ambivalence (cf. Midkiff DeBauche 152–158). However, March is not just ambivalent, but essentially radical in his revision of the myth of the Marine Corps. His soldiers do not feel distinguished in any way by where they belong within the American army. They do not talk about the exceptionality of their force, as if they were oblivious of its special status in the public imagination. The novel rejects the military myth by stripping the service in the Marine Corps of all signs of valor and heroism. In general, the revisionism of *Company K* precludes the use of literary creation as a way to help rationalize military conflict. The film adaptation is detached from the contemporary wars in which the United States has been involved; it is a historical presentation, not a current commentary, but its insistence on the impossibility – or perhaps the danger – of rationalizing war pertains to the challenges of the present no less than to the dramas of the past.

March's novel not only debunks an emergent military myth, but also interrogates and undermines the categories of historical representation and the terms of memorialization. On the whole, the itinerary of Company K reflects the movement of the American troops in Europe in the latter months of World War I, but the novel provides no information whatsoever about their strategic achievements. A very concise, matter-of-fact and ultimately reductive account of the company's activities can be found in Corporal Stephen Waller's monologue: "Company K went into action at 10:15 p.m. December 12th, 1917, at Verdun, France, and ceased fighting on the morning of November 11th, 1918, near Bourmont, having crossed the Meuse River the night before under shell fire; participating, during the period set out above, in the following major operations: Aisne, Aisne-Marne, St. Mihiel and Meuse-Argonne" (184). Some of these place names feature prominently in the twentieth-century military history of Europe, but for March they are mere markers of historical accuracy. He denies their significance as indicators of what might be called, after Nietzsche, monumental history which "relies on a vision of the past during moments of crisis and heroic conflict, and [...] reveals a penchant for the actions of heroic figures" (Landy 43). The representation of history based on such terms is a retroactive invention offering a very incomplete view of past events, but such inventions are fundamental for the processes of symbolization. In turn, symbolization plays a primary role in the reinforcement of public values through discursive practices. March resents the entrenched symbolic constructions of the meanings of war and bombards the reader with the images of the unfathomable degradation of human beings in military uniforms. As Steven Trout puts it, "*Company K*, filled with killing and suffering, shows what phrases like 'went into action' and 'major operations' mean at an experiential level" (151). However, it seems that March realizes the inescapability of symbolization, therefore he creates alternative terms for it. There is an episode in the novel – and it has been retained in the film – in which a soldier has a hallucinatory vision of Christ walking toward him through the field. The soldier shouts at him angrily but hears no response. This is March's way of undoing religious concepts and symbols that are often used to justify war.

By far, the most powerful expression of March's resentment at the symbolization of war and the forms of memorialization enhanced by it is to be found in the monologue ascribed to the Unknown Soldier. In this episode, the narrator is caught in the wire and fatally wounded: "I saw my belly was ripped open and that my entrails hung down like a badly arranged bouquet of blue roses" (178). As he lies immobilized and waiting for death, he envisages a commemorative ceremony at the Soldiers' Cemetery in his home town and is suddenly overwhelmed with anger at all the lies that have been told and will be told about combatant death. He refuses to be a pretext for such ceremonies, throws away his identification tags and destroys all personal belongings that could reveal his identity. Ironically enough, as an Unknown Soldier he becomes a central figure in a highly symbolic commemorative practice. In critical readings of *Company K*, the monologue of the Unknown Soldier is one of the most frequently discussed parts of the novel as it provides the key to March's critique of the public functions of memorialization. Steven Trout writes: "[T]he memory of the Great War preserved through official acts of remembrance is nothing more than a collection of dangerous omissions and outright falsehoods. And, not surprisingly, the Unknown Soldier emerges as the biggest lie of them all" (152). In turn, Marzena Sokołowska-Paryż claims that the novel articulates a warning against "the sanitizing effect of commemoration" and undermines the idea of anonymity as the only criterion of elevating the Unknown Soldier to the status of the representative of "all the dead in war." Moreover, there is a great moral ambivalence about the anonymity of the Unknown Soldier: "What if the Unknown Soldiers across nations are soldiers who raped women, killed prisoners of war, or tried hard to evade duties and danger?" (16).

The film leaves out the episode featuring the Unknown Soldier for an obvious enough reason: it would identify him by his appearance. It is possible to imagine the story of this nameless soldier narrated in the film by a separate voice-over, but this would be much too artificial a solution. On the whole, Clem does not aspire to equal March with respect to historical revisionism. It goes without saying that the novel *Company K* and its film adaptation seventy odd years later emerge not only from different historical contexts and aesthetic orders, but also from different frames of remembrance. Many aspects of March's revisionism would not have their original appeal nowadays. Beside this, the filmmakers presumably acted on the assumption that, on the average, contemporary Americans' knowledge about the Great War is rather limited. Therefore their decision to include references evoking monumental history is justified, even if it is at variance with the spirit of the novel. The most evident example of the presence of such references is the use of documentary footage, which essentially helps establish the iconography of the Great War in the film. After each documentary sequence, the plot is resumed in a black-and-white picture which gains color; in this way, the events of the film are more firmly inscribed into the historical situation. The incorporation of shots from a documentary film into a feature production is a familiar convention, strengthening the impression of authenticity. Monumental history is also evoked through the use of captions. There are two kinds of captions in the film: those telling the names of characters about to be portrayed and those stating place names, dates and events. The former series of captions reflects, in some way, the structure of the novel, whereas the latter introduces a set of historical references with a view to a better contextualization.

Being a low-budget independent production, Robert Clem's adaptation of *Company K* has received relatively little critical attention, but it deserves acknowledgment as an attempt to translate a complex work of literature into the language of film, suiting the expectations of contemporary audiences. The authors of the adaptation have introduced a whole range of modifications to make an apparently unfilmable literary text meet the requirements of the cinematic medium, and most of these modifications are structural. All in all, Clem's film testifies to the capacity of the genre of the combat war film, because this convention proves its functional significance in a film which so evidently aims to undo it.

References

Aichinger, Peter. *The American Soldier in Fiction, 1880–1963: A History of Attitudes Toward Warfare and the Military Establishment*. Ames: Iowa State University Press, 1975.

Basinger, Jeanine. "The World War II Combat Film: Definition." *The War Film*. Ed. Robert Eberwein. New Brunswick and London: Rutgers University Press, 2006. 30–52.

Beidler, Philip D. "Introduction." William March. *Company K*. Tuscaloosa and London: The University of Alabama Press, 2006. vii–xxvi.

Cooperman, Stanley. *World War I and the American Novel*. Baltimore: The Johns Hopkins University Press, 1967.

Eksteins, Modris. *Rites of Spring: The Great War and the Birth of the Modern Age*. New York: Houghton Mifflin, 2000.

Landy, Marcia. "The Historical Film: History and Memory in Media." *The History on Film Reader*. Ed. Marnie Hughes-Warrington. London and New York: Routledge, 2009. 42–52.

March, William. *Company K*. Intro. by Philip D. Beidler. Tuscaloosa and London: The University of Alabama Press, 2006.

Midkiff DeBauche, Leslie. "The United States' Film Industry and World War One." *The First World War and Popular Cinema, 1914 to the Present*. Ed. Michael Paris. Edinburgh: Edinburgh University Press, 1999. 138–161.

Sherry, Vincent. *The Great War and the Language of Modernism*. Oxford and New York: Oxford University Press, 2003.

Simmonds, Roy S. *The Two Worlds of William March*. Tuscaloosa: The University of Alabama Press, 1984.

Sokołowska-Paryż, Marzena. *Reimagining the War Memorial, Reinterpreting the Great War: The Formats of British Commemorative Fiction*. Newcastle upon Tyne: Cambridge Scholars Publishing, 2012.

Suid, Lawrence H. *Guts and Glory: The Making of the American Military Image in Film*. Lexington: The University Press of Kentucky, 2002.

Trout, Steven. *On the Battlefields of Memory: The First World War and American Remembrance, 1919–1941*. Tuscaloosa: The University of Alabama Press, 2010.

Filmography

Company K. Dir. Robert Clem. Indican Pictures, 2008.

Michael Paris
The Great War and British Docudrama: *The Somme*, *My Boy Jack* and *Walter's War*

At least from the mid-1920s, the pre-dominant public image of the Great War was shaped, not by literature, but by the moving image, simply because of the ability of film to reach a far greater public than the printed word, and because of the filmmakers' skill in restaging the past in a manner which completely engaged an audience and deeply involved them in the story on screen. For those too young to be involved in the war the cinema screen provided their dominant memory of what the war was like (Paris 2). Today, given the soaring production costs and shrinking audiences for cinema, the memory of the Great War is primarily disseminated by television. This chapter, then, is concerned with how some aspects of the War have been dealt with in post-memory British television docudrama.

The British television service began regular transmissions in November 1936. The British Broadcasting Company established studios at Alexandra Palace in north London, and from this location the service began broadcasting for an average of four hours daily to a remarkably small audience in the London area. However, television's involvement with the Great War began just months later when, in November 1937, a BBC outside broadcast unit covered the Armistice Ceremony at the Cenotaph in central London. On 11 November, the whole evening schedule was given over to an abridged version of R. C. Sherriff's well-known play *Journey's End*, set on the Western Front in 1918.[1] Directed by Michael Barry and starring Reginald Tate as Dennis Stanhope, the play was performed live in the studio but included filmed inserts of battle, allegedly taken from the German feature film *Westfront 1918* (dir. G. W. Pabst, 1930; cf. Jacobs). In September 1939 the Television Service was suspended for the duration of the Second World War and did not resume until 1946. But in that same year, the BBC again covered the Armistice Ceremony and has done so every year since. Understandably, in the aftermath of World War Two, producers were more interested in recent events than the Great War, consequently the first post-war production about 1914–1918 was not until 1960 – another version of Sherriff's play.

Thereafter, the approaching fiftieth anniversaries of the War beginning in 1964 saw an increasing public interest in the conflict and, as Brian Bond has noted, a "realization that the generation of First World War veterans was rapidly

---

[1] With its claustrophobic setting and small cast, *Journey's End* was an ideal play for television in the days before video and CGI. After the 1937 production, the BBC broadcast further versions in 1960 and 1980.

'fading away' and that their story had remained largely untold" (55). This resulted in a wave of new historical writing, mostly highly critical of the generals and the politicians, but largely built around the words of the veterans, and particularly in the monumental twenty-six-part television history *The Great War,* first transmitted in 1964 and attracting an average eight million viewers for each episode. Using archive footage, interviews with participants and even extracts from feature films, the series was written mainly by the conservative military historians Corelli Barnett and John Terraine, who intended to present a more positive interpretation of the war less critical of the military leaders. Alas, for their intentions, the power of those visual images of shattered landscapes and shattered men completely undermined their message and left only an overriding impression of the horror and pity of the war. As Peter Parker has noted, "the overwhelming impression left by the series with viewers was one of waste and futility" (190; cf. also Bond 68–70) – clearly, an interesting example of the power of the visual image to subvert the authors' intention. A new departure in *The Great War,* however, and in many of the newly written histories at that time was the reliance on the oral testimony of veterans – a technique which has since become a standard feature in television histories.

While the anniversaries resulted in an outpouring of new historiography of the war, and even a number of novels, it did not inspire many films, and even television seems to have been reluctant to follow up the success of *The Great War,* partly due, perhaps, to the high cost of such productions, and, partly to the public antipathy to war stories at the time because of the peace movement and the unpopularity of America's on-going involvement in the Vietnam War. Not until 1970 did a television play take up the Great War theme. This was Jack Gold's *Mad Jack,* based on the early experiences of Siegfried Sassoon, in the 'Play for Today' slot. Several drama series followed, among them *Wings,* about the Royal Flying Corps, in 1977, with a second series the following year. However, only at the end of that decade was another major drama series about the war made, the critically-acclaimed *Testament of Youth* (1979) – an adaptation of the war memoirs of Vera Brittain. This was followed by just a handful of popular dramas over the next twenty years, like the controversial series about the mutineer Percy Toplis, *The Monocled Mutineer* (1986), or the production *All the King's Men* (1999), which sought to explain the disappearance of the Sandringham Company of the Territorial Army at Gallipoli in 1915. These productions, even the largely fictional *Wings* and the rather more dubious *Monocled Mutineer,* can be termed docudramas, and it is this particular format which has become the preferred style for television productions dealing with the Great War.

'Docudrama' or 'story-documentary' – the narrative reconstruction of past events on film – is, as Alan Rosenthal has noted, almost as old as cinema. Early filmmakers often restaged historical episodes or great events using trick photography and scripted re-enactments – the charge of Teddy Roosevelt's Rough Riders at San Juan Hill in the Spanish-American War of 1898, or episodes from the Boer War (cf. Rosenthal 1–2). However, while many producers used a form of docudrama, there was little consensus about the style it should follow. In Britain docudrama was first used to explore the realities of the Great War in the 1920s by the filmmaker and ardent imperialist Harry Bruce Woolfe of British Instructional Films, when he wanted to produce a film celebrating the Royal Navy at the Battle at Jutland. Woolfe used actuality footage, models, animation and re-enacted scenes to tell the story of the engagement, and in the process created one of the most common styles of docudrama, one which now provides the basis for many history docudramas on modern television. Surprisingly popular with audiences, *The Battle of Jutland* inspired Woolfe to make five further docudramas about the war.[2] French filmmaker Léon Poirier later used a similar technique of combining actuality film and enacted reconstructions for his *Verdun, visions d'histoire* [*Verdun: Visions of History*] in 1928, and interestingly employed both French and German veterans of the battle as actors in a spirit of reconciliation. Two further films, similar in style, were made shortly afterwards in Germany by Heinz Paul: *Douaumont* (1931), which examined the fighting at Verdun from the German perspective; and *Tannenberg* (1932), which focused on the victory over the Russians. Paul varied the mix slightly – while both films used documentary footage to establish authenticity, *Tannenberg* has far more fictional episodes, but like Poirier's film *Douaumont*, employed both German and French veterans of the battle. Docudrama, then, was becoming quite widely used, but there were considerable variations of style.

As critic Michael Arlen has explained, "docudrama is a hybrid form [...] too various to be described by exact definition [...] but a story whose energy and focus have shifted from fiction to what is supposed to have actually happened" (277). No exact definition, then, but we can identify several styles of docudrama. The style used by Woolfe, Poirier and Paul might best be described as dramatized documentary – the use of both actuality footage and re-enacted scenes combined into a coherent narrative. But this was only one of several styles. Docudrama was often used by the British Documentary Movement in the 1930s. The younger, more ambitious filmmakers realised that straight documentary film had only limited appeal for audiences and that by re-engaging with the story form and taking on some elements of commercial narrative cinema, their work might find larger audiences. Their answer was to create the documentary around a traditional narrative

---

[2] The films were *Armageddon* (1923), *Zeebrugge* (1924), *Ypres* (1925), *Mons* (1926), and the *Battles of Coronel and Falkland Islands* (1927).

story line, scripted but using real people re-enacting their real life experiences: in other words, a reconstruction of their everyday experiences. Thus the authoritative 'Voice of God' commentary, which most audiences disliked, would no longer be necessary and they would be able to engage with the characters on screen in exactly the same way as they would in a popular feature film; as John Corner explained, "the result mixed informational throughput with narrative satisfactions, allowing for empathy with the main figures of portrayal" (36). After 1939 and with the government funding production they produced several critically-acclaimed, popular feature-length films like *Target for Tonight* (dir. Harry Watt, 1941) and *Western Approaches* (dir. Pat Jackson, 1944). These were among the purest form of docudrama – even going to the length of using service personnel to re-enact their real-life experiences in the film when possible.

The Documentary Movement, then, added new stylistic approaches to docudrama, particularly the fluidity of the narrative film, and some of the techniques of docudrama also found their way into mainstream cinema. After 1945, now labelled 'Social Realism,' Anglo-American narrative films frequently made use of location shooting, the use of members of the public acting in scripted stories based on everyday experience, or specific events. With the development of television after the Second World War, docudrama became a perfect style for the small screen; as a result, as Alan Rosenthal has noted, "reality-based stories, taken from topical journalism, are the most popular drama genre on U.S. and British television today" (xiii), and this is equally true for television history. While the television networks continue to produce many traditional style documentaries, the most popular television histories are usually some form of docudrama – dramatized documentaries or narrative dramas based on historical fact.[3] The purpose of this chapter, then, is to examine three recent television docudramas which have adopted different techniques to explore, respectively, a well-known battle in the Great War and two individual combatants, and to consider how far docudrama has moved on since its early days as a historical source. The produc-

---

[3] Given the varying forms docudrama has taken, definitions are difficult. There is, however, an insightful and interesting historiography on docudrama. An excellent starting point is Alan Rosenthal's edited collection *Why Docudrama: Fact-Fiction on Film and Television*, Carbondale: Southern Illinois University Press, 1999; John E. O'Connor (ed.), *Image as Artifact: The Historical Analysis of Film and Television*, Malabar: Krieger, 1990; and Pierre Sorlin, *Restaging the Past*, Oxford: Blackwell, 1980. Also useful are Paul Smith (ed.), *The Historian and Film*, Cambridge: Cambridge University Press, 1976; Robert A. Rosenstone, *Visions of the Past: The Challenge of Film to Our Idea of History*, Cambridge, MA: Harvard University Press, 1995; Colin McArthur, *Television and History*, London: British Film Institute, 1980; Harry Watt, *Don't Look at the Camera*, London: Elek Books, 1974.

tions chosen for analysis here are *The Somme* (2005), *My Boy Jack* (2007), and *Walter's War* (2008).

The Somme (dir. Carl Hindmarch) is the most complex of the three examples; it is a re-examination of 1 July 1916 – the opening day of the Battle of the Somme – from the perspective of a group of individuals caught up in the struggle. The Somme, regarded as one of the most terrible battles in a terrible war, has received considerable attention from historians, novelists and filmmakers,[4] but here Hindmarch attempts to introduce originality by focusing attention on a few participants: five British, two German, two French, and the American novelist Mary Borden, who by 1916 was running a nursing unit on the Western Front.[5] Hindmarch examines their part in the battle using their own words as recorded in letters and diaries at the time. As he explained, "We didn't make anything up: we used only the words from their letters and diaries" (qtd. in Hanna 176). The inclusion of Borden's testimony is particularly interesting. One of only a handful of eye-witness accounts of that battle by a woman, it challenges the old notion that war is an exclusively male preoccupation, as does Hindmarch's choice of the actress Tilda Swinton as narrator instead of the more usual authoritative male voice. Swinton, the daughter of a British major-general, had already been involved in several Great War projects, including Derek Jarman's film *War Requiem* (1988). While Hindmarch's sources are original and interesting, *The Somme* really brings nothing new to the story. Most of the many accounts of the battle, including most television histories, have used such personal testimony. Hindmarch had shown no interest in the war in his early career and was apparently only drawn to the subject because his grandfather had served throughout the war, but there is nothing of this personal dimension in the drama.

---

[4] See for example the official film *The Battle of the Somme* (War Office, 1916), and the written histories by Martin Middlebrook (*1 July 1916: The First Day on the Somme*, 1971), Lynn MacDonald (*Somme*, 1983), or Malcolm Brown (*The Imperial War Museum Book of the Somme*, 1996), all of which include first-hand accounts of the soldiers who fought in the battle. A collection of the Somme veteran testimonies was compiled by Joshua Levine (*Forgotten Voices of the Somme*, 2008). Of interest are also similar histories based on eye-witness accounts representing the German experience of the Somme by Jack Sheldon (*The Germans on the Somme 1914–1916*, 2005) and Christopher Duffy (*Through German Eyes: The British and the Somme 1916*, 2006). There have been noteworthy novels in which the Somme offensive prominently features, among them James Lansdale Hodson's *Return to the Wood* (1955), John Harris's *Covenant with Death* (1961), Stuart Cloete's *How Young They Died* (1969), Derek Robinson's *War Story* (1987), and Sebastian Faulks's *Birdsong* (1993), adapted to a TV series under the same title in 2012 (dir. Philip Martin). Perhaps the best-known film about the Somme is William Boyd's very clichéd *The Trench* (1999).

[5] The Anglophile Borden had lived in England for several years before the war and in 1914 had set up her own medical unit. She later used her wartime experiences as the basis for her novel *The Forbidden Zone* (1929).

The background is set when the narrator tells us that General Sir Henry Rawlinson, commander of the 4th Army, planned a joint Anglo-French attack on an eighteen mile front from the town of Serre southwards to the River Somme for the summer. The location was chosen because it was the point where the British and French sectors met. Knowing that his soldiers were inexperienced, Rawlinson's plan was simple, namely to drive the Germans from their trenches and liberate the territory behind. There is almost no mention of Sir Douglas Haig, Commander-in-Chief of the British Expeditionary Force, who had been planning the offensive for months and of his much more detailed and complicated strategic plan. However, this omission is typical of the serious limitations of this type of television history. It has become a common belief among writers and producers that audiences cannot deal with complicated historical explanations, but will switch channels if faced with anything too intellectually challenging. Here, then, the essential reasoning behind the offensive is drastically simplified and quickly dealt with so that the viewer can be hurried along to the next action sequence. In *The Somme* the main focus is on the specific experience of the chosen participants on the first day of battle. Nevertheless, such simplifications reduce the sense of the scale of the original plan and what it hoped to achieve. Haig, for example, really believed that the offensive could be the breakthrough that would win the war (cf. Bourne 60). To omit any mention of the greater strategic aims almost reduces the point of the battle to a personal whim of Rawlinson's to inflict casualties on the enemy. Certainly we have to accept that television history is a different proposition to the lecture hall or written monograph, yet the simplification here is really quite dramatic and does, to some extent distort the meaning of the battle.

Hindmarch rightly makes it clear that, unlike other European armies, Britain relied on a volunteer army until late in 1916, and that Rawlinson commanded one of these 'New Armies,' the volunteers who so enthusiastically enlisted for 'King and Country' in 1914. Thus the soldiers that fought on the Somme were essentially civilians in uniform; the Somme was to be their 'blooding.' Due to the essentially civilian nature of his soldiers, Rawlinson went for a simple plan: a massive artillery bombardment that would annihilate the German front line defences and enable the British Army to march across No Man's Land and occupy them. A diversionary attack towards Gommecourt by the 3rd Army to distract the Germans is not even mentioned in the programme. Rawlinson's strategy was to be that of 'bite and hold' – take their trenches and let the Germans try to take them back. According to Hindmarch, then, Rawlinson planned a simple battle of attrition, to 'kill as many Germans as possible' at the least cost. The build-up for the attack was extensive. New roads and light-gauge railways were built to take supplies up to the front and shells and guns assembled for what would be the greatest artillery barrage ever seen. To achieve authenticity, Hindmarch intercuts several sequences of actuality film from original newsreels and from the War Office film of the offensive, *The Battle of the Somme* (dir. Geoffrey Malins/J. B. McDowell). Here for example, we see contemporary footage of the preparations. While such a build-up gave the troops confidence in a victory ("they say it'll be a walk-over", says one character to his friends), such preparations could not be hidden from the enemy, who of course knew that an offensive was coming.

The Germans had been on the Somme since 1914 and had had almost two years to prepare elaborate defences, including deep bunkers and concrete gun emplacements. If the British General Staff actually appreciated this, they made no allowance in their calculations. As we see, in a very poor computer-generated sequence that looks rather like a second-rate video game, the enemy were confident in their defences and had recently completed a whole new defensive line just behind their front line. In the film, we see Rawlinson in a Royal Flying Corps machine above the front, examining these defences from the air, although he apparently did not think it worth revising his plan in the light of what he had found. Alongside the British, the French were also preparing for their part in the offensive. Already committed to a bitter struggle at the fortress of Verdun, the French could offer only five divisions and artillery to the Somme offensive. French artillery, however, was almost universally admired for its effectiveness, and it was the French who would achieve the only real success during the battle.

The bombardment of the enemy front line was intense – after four days Private Hans Eversmann in the German front line thought he would die but somehow held on, even though supplies were no longer getting through. On the eve of the battle, air reconnaissance suggested that the German defences had been eliminated. Rawlinson was only too happy to believe this, yet still ordered eighteen ambulance trains to stand by to evacuate his wounded. His men were less optimistic. Lieutenant Charlie May of the 22nd Manchester Battalion thought the signs were good, but still wrote a last note to his wife: "I don't want to die but I am ready [...]." His Sergeant, Richard H. Tawney, recorded in his diary that it was "a perfect evening when one could forget the war." But we see him quickly reminded of the grim reality when he walks past a work party making grave markers. Tawney, although badly wounded in the battle, survived and later became a distinguished academic and professor of Economic History.

In the trenches before zero hour, Charlie May tells his men, "Do not run – do not bunch." At 7.30 a.m., 60,000 British soldiers go over the top. The Manchesters initially make good progress across No Man's Land towards the enemy, but at 30 yards from the Germans the enemy guns open up, killing and maiming, and forcing the survivors to go to ground. Sergeant Tawney struggles back to find the reserves, but is hit and loses consciousness. Along the whole front it is the same story. Only in the French sector has progress been made. At Mary Borden's hospital a trickle of wounded men turns into a flood. The doctors treat only those who have a chance of recovery – a harsh but realistic decision. Here, Hindmarch again intercuts scenes from Malin's harrowing footage of the wounded being brought in from the 1916 film – scenes which still distress the viewer even after all these years. 60 minutes after zero hour, there have been 30,000 casualties, we are told, half the attacking forces are out of action. Notwithstanding the confused situation, Rawlinson sends in the second wave – another 60,000 men. They fare no better and most become casualties or are pinned down in No Man's Land by the murderous German guns.

At his Headquarters, Rawlinson receives conflicting reports. Optimistic dispatches are quickly followed by more realistic ones – there will be no exploitation of the breakthrough here. Only in the French sector, where the *poilus* have used more flexible tactics and close-support artillery, has there been some success. Charles Barberon, a French artillery officer, watches the German prisoners coming in – "They look happy," he observes. But who wouldn't be happy to know that they were finally out of that hell? However, when the Manchesters eventually break into the German line, they take no prisoners – as one veteran claimed, "We hadn't been told 'no prisoners' but we were given to understand that was what was wanted." The Manchesters had finally taken their objective, but Captain Charlie May was dead, Tawney was wounded, and 472 of their 820 men were dead or wounded. It was the same all along the line, and in some battalions even worse, the Devonshires had 27 unwounded out of a 1000 men. Yet, despite such casualties, the Allied commanders continued the offensive for another five months in the obstinate belief that one more push would bring victory. According to Hindmarch, then, there were no real gains, just appalling casualties.

According to Hanna, the historical advisor, Malcolm Brown, had taken Hindmarch through the 'more revisionist' aspects of recent historical research on the Somme, yet the latter nonetheless rendered a more traditional interpretation and was accused of adopting the "tragically futile offensive," and "one of Britain's worst military disasters" approach (135). Nevertheless, however it is explained, the first day on the Somme was one of the worst days in the history of the British Army, and the subsequent battle actually achieved very few of its objectives. Whether or not it was "tragically futile" depends on how one interprets the long-term outcomes. Revisionist historians comfort themselves by arguing that the Allied offensive was the beginning of the end for the German Army; that it never fully recovered from the heavy blows inflicted on the Somme. That interpretation depends upon particularly contentious evidence, and even if it is essentially correct, it still took another two years of extremely heavy fighting before this 'demoralised' army finally threw in the towel (cf. Strachan 189–190). The Somme

Offensive is a key event in the popular memory of the war in Britain.[6] A generation of young men, the brightest and the best, offered themselves on the altar of patriotism and were carelessly slaughtered by incompetent generals for little real purpose. Although *The Somme* only deals with the first day of battle in one particular area, it reinforces this deeply-entrenched memory – keen, articulate young men, all volunteers, and anxious to serve their country; unimaginative generals, represented here by Rawlinson, who think only in terms of a battle of attrition and who ignore information that might undermine their plan, and who refuse to call off the offensive even when the first phase is revealed to have failed. This conventional retelling of the Somme story is confirmed by the conventional style of the film. There is little difference between this and earlier docudramas – enacted sequences reinforced by archive footage and trick photography, in this case CGI (Computer-Generated Images). Interestingly, although using similar techniques, the BBC's *The Somme – From Defeat to Victory* (dir. Detlef Siebert, 2006), offered a far more balanced account of the battle. Siebert takes a wider view of the story and sees the Somme as the beginning of the British army's learning curve, which eventually results in the final offensive of 1918 and ultimate victory. It also deals with the subject matter in a more complex manner, unafraid of more complicated explanations. Hindmarch's film, however, is in places compulsive viewing – dramatic, well-made, well-acted and with a great sense of pace; good television but not good history, for it tells us nothing new and simply confirms our existing view. The story of one of the young British patriots is examined in a very different style of docudrama made two years later, *My Boy Jack* (dir. Brian Kirk, 2007).

My Boy Jack offers an interpretation of the death of John Kipling (known as 'Jack'), only son of the poet Rudyard Kipling, during the Battle of Loos in August 1915, and the effect on the Kipling family.[7] The drama is an adaptation of David Haig's 1997 stage play of the same title, in which Haig also played the older Kipling. The production uses conventional dramatic form and is largely based on historical records. The author has changed some minor incidents for greater impact, and conversations and motivations have been imagined. However, where there are gaps in the record, the author has produced a narrative that is both likely and persuasive. The film, however, omits act three of the play, which takes the story into the 1920s.

On the eve of the Great War, John Kipling is undergoing examination before a Naval Board but is rejected because of his poor vision. The younger Kipling had

---

6 See also *The Somme 1916 – Hell on Earth* (1993), *Battle of the Somme: The True Story* (2006), although these are perhaps better classified as 'documentaries.'

7 The story of John Kipling's death in the Battle of Loos is also the subject of Belgian author Geert Spillebeen's novel *Kipling's Keuze/Kipling's Choice* (2002, 2005).

always been intended for the Royal Navy, but long before 1914 it was realised that his poor eyesight, inherited from his father, would make this impossible. While John is undergoing this ordeal, his father is seen visiting King George V at Windsor. The author presumably uses these fictional episodes to establish the deep affection of both Kiplings for the Navy, John's desire to serve his country, his visual deficiency, and Rudyard's privileged position in society (cf. Carrington 485–486). By 1914, Kipling did not perhaps command the almost hysterical admiration of the earlier heydays of his career, but he was still hugely popular, mixed freely with the social and political elites, and was regarded as a spokesman for Britain, the Empire and the military.

Like many of his contemporaries, Kipling was a committed Social Darwinist, and for many years believed that war against Germany was a historical inevitability. He continually warned of Germany's territorial ambitions and argued that because of Germany's military prowess, Britain must adopt national conscription to enlarge the comparatively small British Army. He supported all the patriotic leagues, especially the Navy League and Lord Roberts' National Service League, which campaigned for universal conscription. Inevitable, then, that Kipling would want his son to serve and in the play is bitterly disappointed when John fails to secure a commission. He promises John he will do everything he can to help. It might seem to the viewer that it was almost a case of service by proxy. Kipling, who had so wanted to be a soldier himself, cannot and so sends his only son. A keen student of war, Kipling is knowingly assisting his son to enlist for a brutal war that could well result in his death. John, however, is very much his father's son, intensely patriotic and would, as Rudyard later tells his wife, go "because he wanted to." John could not have stood by and done nothing – he had already told his father that if he couldn't get a commission he would enlist in the ranks where standards were lower. In the docudrama we see Kipling addressing a patriotic meeting when an announcement tells the audience that Britain is at war. Kipling's dire warnings have come to pass.

The news intensifies John's ambition to gain a commission, and in the next scene, father and son are attending a medical board arranged through Kipling's War Office contacts – Rudyard uses all his influence but to no avail. John's vision, the Kiplings are told, could be a danger, not only to himself but to the men he is expected to command – a near-blind leader on the battlefield? Angry and disappointed they return to Bateman's, the Kipling home, where Carrie and John's sister Elsie are waiting. A few days later a desperate Rudyard asks his old friend 'Bobs,' Field-Marshal Lord Roberts, to intervene and "nominate John to his own regiment, the Irish Guards, and bypass a medical" and John is told to report for duty at Warley Barracks on 14 September' (Carrington 498). The scene in which Rudyard arranges a medical board for John never really happened, as

Kipling simply went to 'Bobs' and that was that. Presumably, however, the author includes it to show how desperate the Kiplings were to help John into the army. Equally fictitious are several scenes in which Rudyard attends a Government Propaganda Committee. In reality, Rudyard was continually approached to write official propaganda for the War Office, but always refused, preferring to work in his own way. These scenes are included, one assumes, so that the viewer can be informed just how desperate the situation was on the Western Front (and how dangerous for a visually-impaired and inexperienced eighteen-year-old). In the film, Carrie and Elsie are less than happy with John's appointment, clearly having hoped that he would be given a non-combat role. There seems to be some sense of resentment from both women that Rudyard has put undue pressure on his son to serve, which does not seem to have been the case in reality. Despite his youth and poor eyesight, however, John actually becomes a good officer, and we see something of his determination to become a good shot and to earn the affection of the tough Dubliners in his company. On his last leave at Bateman's John, still a few days short of his eighteenth birthday, has to ask his Father for formal permission to accompany his battalion to France. Rudyard, clearly proud of his son's achievements, agrees but Carrie and Elsie have doubts; the latter in particular feels John is far too young.

The battalion is sent to take part in the Loos offensive of September 1915. In the trenches around Lens we see John encouraging his men, checking their equipment before they go over the top, and leading them out into No Man's Land. Then amidst the smoke and flames we lose sight of John and his men, and the scene changes to a bright autumn day in Sussex; Rudyard is working in his study. The much feared telegram arrives, announcing John is "wounded and missing." Once Rudyard has recovered from his shock he has to tell Carrie and Elsie. All Elsie can say is "Why did you let him go?" The author uses the next Propaganda Committee meeting to inform the audience what a shambles Loos has been. The briefing explains that the bombardment was ineffective, there were not enough shells. The barbed wire remained intact and the German machine-guns were not silenced. 385 officers and 7861 men were killed or wounded in the first attack. It does not tell us, however, that the generals responsible were busy blaming each other and were desperately looking for scapegoats for their errors.

Rudyard and Carrie had seen so many friends lose their sons that doubtlessly "they regarded John's death as inevitable [...]. That they considered it their duty to make this sacrifice, as so many of their friends and fellow-countrymen were doing, is equally certain. What they had not prepared themselves for was the cruel uncertainty of whether their son was actually dead or not" (Holt & Holt 98). They spent much of their time over the next year trying to find out what happened and whether or not John was dead. Rudyard made use of all his contacts but every avenue failed. They took to interviewing Irish Guardsmen returning from the front but learned little more, although most had praise for John's commitment and bravery. Then, a Private Doyle from John's platoon tells them that John was wounded while attacking a German strongpoint and was hit again, while looking for his glasses, which had fallen into the mud. Doyle had been sure that John was dead, but he had been unable to recover the body. Later heavy shelling from both sides had probably covered the body. Rudyard's only comment is that John was privileged to have had the chance to do his duty, but Carrie snaps, "He was 18, alone and in pain – there's no glory in that!" The film ends with Rudyard's poem "My Boy Jack," written soon after:

> Have you news of my boy Jack?
> *Not this tide*
> When d'you think that he'll come back?
> *Not with this wind blowing, and this tide* (Kipling 216)

The Kiplings never recovered from John's death. In later years, perhaps as some form of atonement, Rudyard spent a great deal of time as a Commissioner with the Imperial War Graves Commission.[8]

My Boy Jack is a powerful drama based on documented fact, which tries to make sense of the *milieu* of patriotic excitement which prevailed in 1914. It encapsulates the war experience into one short life – the sense of duty, the desperation to serve, the blinding reality of war and death. It equally encapsulates another of the enshrined memories of the war, the armchair patriots, the old men, sending the young to die. *Jack* reminds us of Wilfred Owen's "The Parable of the Old Man and the Young," where Abraham, despite the angel's warning to stay his hand "Would not do so, but slew his son, / And half the seed of Europe, one by one" (Hibberd 69).

Certainly Kipling, the eternal man-boy, was desperately anxious for his son to serve, as he would have served himself had he been able to, but in reality Kipling, and his wife, were well aware of the realities and the short life expectancy of a junior officer at the front. Nevertheless, reality, perhaps, makes for less effective television, while *My Boy Jack*, a small, intimate, family-centred play, is ideal material for television. Realistically filmed at Bateman's, David Haig is very convincing as Kipling, but Daniel Radcliffe, although very good as Jack, will for most viewers

---

8 In March 1992, the War Graves Commission claimed that the body of John Kipling had finally been located in St. Mary's ADS Cemetery near Loos. However, the evidence for this has been contested and, on balance, it would seem that John Kipling's remains have yet to be found (cf. Holt & Holt 205–237).

still conjure up images of the wizard of Hogwarts, which might well undermine the credibility of the drama. Like *The Somme*, however, *Jack* essentially confirms our existing memory of the war, like our final *Walter's War* – another docudrama based on facts but which is far more speculative about the protagonist's military career.

Walter's War, written by British-playwright and actor Kwame Kwei-Armah, is a short (60 minute) docudrama that attempts to reconstruct the experiences of Walter Tull, a professional footballer and the first Black Englishman to be commissioned in the British Army. Walter's story has been documented to some extent (cf. Vasili), but *Walter's War* imaginatively fills in some of the gaps where the evidence is lacking. The docudrama opens with Walter, a lance-sergeant, leading his squad in a trench raid on the Western Front. Several men are killed and the others fall back. Later, Tull tells his young officer that such attacks are suicide. He is told never to contradict orders; and then more sympathetically, that in an "equal" world he would make an "excellent commissioned officer." Further attacks follow, and Tull barely escapes injury himself. The strain causes his complete collapse with 'trench fever.' Shipped back to a hospital in England, Tull drifts in and out of consciousness. His delirious state provides an opportunity for Kwei-Armah to fill in some of the early episodes of his life. His West Indian Father, a skilled carpenter, came to England, married a local girl and settled in Folkestone on the Kentish coast, and raised several children. Both his parents died early, and Walter and his brother Edward were sent to a London orphanage. While Edward was adopted by a successful dentist, Walter remained in the home. Although apprenticed to a printer, his talent for football took him first to Clapton FC and on to Tottenham Hotspurs as a professional player. In these dream sequences, we see Walter taunted by the boys in the home because of his colour, and later on the football field the racist taunts of the fans. From his biography, however, it would seem that he suffered remarkably little from deliberate racism (cf. Vasili). Football fans were, and still are, notorious for their taunts, so Walter would certainly have suffered abuse at games, but from photographic evidence, Walter was a handsome, light-skinned man with fine features, and this and his footballing ability probably helped him assimilate. In 1915 Walter enlisted in the 17th Service Battalion of the Middlesex Regiment – the 'Football' Battalion, formed to encourage sportsmen to sign up. The Battalion arrived in France in late 1915. In 1916 they were in trenches around Souchez, where presumably he took part in the actions which led to his collapse.

After release from hospital, Walter stays with his brother, Edward, who is delighted that he is out of the trenches. When Walter tells him he has been offered officer training, Edward is shocked that he would consider risking his life again for a nation which has treated him so badly. This is a curious conversation, for both brothers appear to have done remarkably well. Edward is a successful dentist with his own house, and Walter a respected professional footballer, and now a sergeant in the British Army. It almost seems that the playwright wants to make Walter a 'victim' – a warrior but for his race as well. If this is so, Walter's character in the drama undermines such a message. As he explains to his brother, "I feel it's my duty." In this he reveals himself as a patriotic Englishman and as committed as the next man to the national cause.

The next section of the film is set in 1917 at Gailes in Ayreshire, the base of the 10th Officer Training Battalion. The cadets are mostly ex-public schoolboys with a handful of older men who have been recommended from the ranks. Training is in the hands of a crusty Scottish sergeant who doesn't seem to like anyone. The Commandant tells Walter he doesn't like the idea of black officers – "Officers should be of pure European descent" (according to Army Regulations), "Negroes and persons of colour shall not exercise any actual command or power." Walter points out that as he was a lance-sergeant he has already commanded men in the field, but the Commandant replies he has only passed on orders from a white superior: "this is not about prejudice, Tull, it's simply logic. A Negro officer would affect the morale of the men." It's made clear to Walter that, although the Commandant cannot countermand his orders, he will get rid of Tull at the first mistake. It later emerges that he really only has the good of the service in mind and is really very fair-minded toward Tull. The confirmed racist of the story turns out to be a singularly unpleasant ex-Oxford student, Cadet Hummins, who shares Tull's dormitory. Hummins persuades the others to humiliate Walter by leaving out their shoes for him to clean. When the joke misfires, Hummins tells the Commandant he won't share the same room as a Negro. The Commandant replies that he does not have to and can go home whenever he likes. Hummins is later revealed as a bully and a coward, and leaves Gailes in disgrace.

Having already served at the front, Walter does well in training and gradually earns the respect of his contemporaries, despite the training sergeant's jibes about "monkeying about," and "show[ing] the white man how it's done, Tull." Eventually, Walter is completely accepted by his peers and several of the younger cadets want to know about conditions at the front, but Walter is reluctant to go into detail and simply tells them they'll be part of a team and that "friendship gets you through." On several occasions Walter is asked about his motives for serving. On leave, his brother, who clearly thinks Walter is still suffering from the effects of shell-shock, urges him to give up. But Walter is adamant: "I've never walked out on anything in my life", he replies, and is almost convinced that his path has been chosen for him. He is also questioned by Cadet Cooper, who asks him why a Negro, "treated as you are in this country, would want to be here in the first place?" Walter doesn't answer, for he has already made it clear he feels it his duty. In a rather far-fetched scene, Cooper is revealed as a communist who thinks that Tull could be a leader in a Soviet-style revolution. But Walter makes it clear that he wants only to serve his country. Successfully completing training, he is commissioned Second-Lieutenant. Before he leaves for France, he visits Eddie. Then, in a curious scene, he is given a photograph of their Grandfather. It shows a slave whose back has been viciously scarred by the whip. On the back is written, "Look how far we've come." It is a powerful and telling moment that encapsulates the journey from slave to British officer in three generations. But while Walter was descended from slaves this moment never happened. Indeed the photograph used here is a well-known one of a liberated American slave called 'Gordon' taken in 1862, and is presumably included to make a rather laboured point about the past treatment of Africans.

The final scene takes place during the German Spring Offensive of 1918, when Walter is killed leading his men during the British retreat. It was 25 March 1918. Later at Eddie's house a telegram announcing Walter's death is delivered and the drama ends. A note before the credits tells us that Walter was recommended for the Military Cross, which he was, however, never awarded. Although not referred to in the film, Walter also served in Italy, on the Piave, and was only then transferred back to the Western Front, where he died in the German offensive. Like so many other soldiers of the Great War, he has no known grave.[9]

Walter's War reflects that recent tendency of post-memory film and documentary to expose previously marginalised histories of the war. The contribution of black combatants was extensive, but their stories remain largely untold. Kwame Kwei-Armah, as a Briton of African descent, is understandably concerned to tell that story by focusing on the career of Walter Tull as representative for those unknown soldiers. However, Tull was not typical of the vast majority of the black soldiers who fought for Britain. He was a respected, professional sportsman who enjoyed a privileged lifestyle and who was widely admired for his prowess and treated as an equal by most of his white contemporaries, unlike the vast number of black troops who served in a menial capacity and were subject to exploitation and abuse. Apart from the racist taunts of the football supporters before the war, the only episodes of racism directed against Tull in the film are inventions, whether for dramatic effect or political purpose, there is no evidence for either episode. Both Kwei-Armah and Tull's biographer seem to want to use him as some

---

9 Tull has now become a figure of considerable interest – along with *Walter's War* and the Phil Vasili biography, there is also a television documentary, a children's book and a play: *Walter Tull: Forgotten Hero*, Nick Bailey, BBCTV 2008; Dan Lydon & Roger Wade Walker, *Walter Tull: Footballer, Soldier, Hero*, London: Collins Big Cat, 2011; Phil Vasili, *Tull*, first performed at the Octagon Theatre, Bolton in February 2013.

kind of symbol of white oppression (hence the anachronistic use of the photograph of the American slave Gordon), but the facts do not appear to support this assumption. What is perhaps of more interest is how the story of Britain's first black army officer is told in a manner which is a mirror image of the established conventions of the Great War story – patriot youth, the anxiety to serve, suffering and inevitable death. We can justifiably equally apply Pierre Sorlin's perceptive remarks about the cinema of the Great War to television docudrama: "In pictures, the War has been turned into myth. It is like a Greek tragedy: we can tell the story again and again; we can create new characters and circumstances; but we can change neither the plot nor the symbols which define the period" (22). *Walter's War*, then, like the other docudramas discussed here, follows those conventions which still seem to dictate not only what stories we tell about the war, but equally the manner of their telling.

References

Arlen, Michael. *The Camera Eye: Essays on Television*. New York: Farrar, Straus & Giroux, 1981.
Bond, Brian. *The Unquiet Western Front: Britain's Role in Literature and History*. Cambridge: Cambridge University Press, 2002.
Bourne, J. M. *Britain and the Great War, 1914–1918*. London: Edward Arnold, 1994.
Carrington, Charles. *Rudyard Kipling: His Life and Work*. London: Penguin, 1986.
Corner, John. "British TV Dramadocumentary: Origins and Development." *Why Docudrama? Fact-Fiction on Film and TV*. Ed. Alan Rosenthal. Carbondale: Southern Illinois University Press, 1999. 35–46.
Hanna, Emma. *The Great War on the Small Screen: Representing the First World War in Contemporary Britain*. Edinburgh: Edinburgh University Press, 2010.
Hibberd, Dominic, ed. *Wilfred Owen: War Poems and Others*. London: Chatto & Windus, 1975.
Holt, Tonie & Valmai. *My Boy Jack*. Barnsley: Pen and Sword, 2007.
Jacobs, Jason. *The Intimate Screen: Early British Television Drama*. Oxford: Oxford University Press, 2000.
Kipling, Rudyard. *Complete Verse. Definitive Edition*. New York et al.: Doubleday, 1940.
MacDonald, Lynn. *Somme*. London: Michael Joseph, 1983.
Middlebrook, Martin. *The First Day on the Somme*. London: Allan Lane, 1971.
Paris, Michael, ed. *The First World War and Popular Cinema: 1914 to the Present*. Edinburgh: Edinburgh University Press, 1999.
Parker, Peter. *The Last Veteran: Harry Patch and the Legacy of War*. London: Fourth Estate, 2010.
Sorlin, Pierre. "Cinema and the Memory of the Great War." *The First World War and Popular Cinema: 1914 to the Present*. Ed. Michael Paris. 5–26.
Strachan, Hew. *The First World War: A New Illustrated History*. London: Pocket Books, 2006.
Vasili, Phil. *Walter Tull, 1888–1918: Officer Footballer*. London: Raw Books, 2010.

Filmography

All the King's Men. Dir. Julian Jarrold. British Broadcasting Corporation, 1999.
The Battle of Jutland. Dir. H. Bruce Woolfe. British Instructional Films, 1921.
The Battle of the Somme. Dir. Geoffrey Malins and J. B. McDowell. British Topical Committee for War Films, 1916.
Douaumont: Die Hölle von Verdun. Dir. Heinz Paul. Karl Günther Panter Filmproduktion, 1931.
The Great War. Dir. Richard Bigham. British Broadcasting Corporation, 1964.
Mad Jack. Dir. Jack Gold. British Broadcasting Corporation, 1970.
The Monocled Mutineer. Dir. Jim O'Brien. British Broadcasting Corporation, 1986.
My Boy Jack. Dir. Brian Kirk. ITV, 2007.
The Somme. Dir. Carl Hindmarch. Darlow-Smithson Films for Channel 4, 2005.
The Somme: From Defeat to Victory. Dir. Detlef Siebert. British Broadcasting Corporation, 2006.
Tannenberg. Dir. Heinz Paul. Paul Filmproduktion, 1932.
Target for Tonight. Dir. Harry Watt. Crown Film Unit, 1941.
Testament of Youth. Dir. Moira Armstrong. British Broadcasting Corporation, 1979.
Verdun, visions d'histoire. Dir. Léon Poirier. Compagnie Universelle Cinématographique, 1928.
Walter's War. Dir. Alrick Riley. BBCTV, 2008.
War Requiem. Dir. Derek Jarman. Anglo International Films, 1989.
Western Approaches. Dir. Pat Jackson. Crown Film Unit, 1944.
Westfront 1918. Dir. G. W. Pabst. Bavaria Film, 1930.
Wings. Dir. Jim Goddard, Gareth Davies, Donald McWhinnie, and Desmond Davis. British Broadcasting Corporation, 1977–1978.

Martin Löschnigg
"Like dying on a stage": Theatricality and Remembrance in Anglo-Canadian Drama on the First World War

Since the landmark success of Timothy Findley's novel *The Wars* (1977), a substantial number of Anglo-Canadian novels and plays have dealt with the First World War and have significantly contributed to keeping that war alive in Canada's collective memory. However, while novels such as Jack Hodgins's *Broken Ground* (1998), Jane Urquhart's *The Stone Carvers* (2001), and Joseph Boyden's *Three Day Road* (2005) have meanwhile received much critical attention, there is very little work to date on modern Canadian drama about the Great War.[1] In this chapter, I want to analyze how recent Canadian plays have re-examined the significance of the First World War as a Canadian *lieu de mémoire* (Nora). In particular, I want to show how playwrights have engaged with one of their country's foundation myths,[2] according to which Canada came into her own as a nation in the trenches of Flanders and Northern France. Adapting a variety of dramatic genres, and creatively employing the theatrical medium for their purposes, their plays combine historical documentary, ideological criticism and performativity in a manner which is apt to render the 'constructedness' of collective remembrance and the significance of a cultural iconography of the war with regard to its ideological conception.

The plays I am here dealing with comprise a wide range of generic and theatrical modes, from tragedy (Kevin Major's *No Man's Land*, 2001) to tragicomedy (Vern Thiessen's *Vimy*, 2007) or even to vaudeville (*Billy Bishop Goes to War*, 1978), and from semi-documentary naturalism (Don Kerr's *The Great War*, 1985) to forms of 'epic' theatre (R. H. Thomson, *The Lost Boys*, 2002). In all these plays,

---

1 Donna Coates and Sherrill Grace have done important pioneering work by collecting Canadian plays about war in their two-volume anthology *Canada and the Theatre of War*, whose first volume is dedicated to the two World Wars and includes five of the Great War plays I am discussing here (*The Lost Boys*, *Soldier's Heart*, *Mary's Wedding*, *Dancock's Dance*, and *Vimy*). Grace also includes these plays (and others) in her survey of Canadian war art, literature and film in chapter two of *On the Art of Being Canadian* ("Theatres of War: Battle Fronts and Home Fronts," 55–105). Her most recent book on Canadian literature and art of the two world wars (*Landscapes of Memory, 1977 to 2007*, 2014) was forthcoming as the present volume was going into print.
2 I use 'myth' in the sense of Roland Barthes as a simplified projection of historical reality which appeals to the imagination. Myth, Barthes writes, "organizes a world which is without contradictions because it is without depth, a world wide open and wallowing in the evident, it establishes a blissful clarity: things appear to mean something by themselves" (143). On the political and military history of Canada in the two World Wars see Mackenzie and Granatstein/Morton.

however, the interrelation between historical documentation, commemoration and the 'staging' of their subject deserves detailed analysis. This is because, like much of the contemporary literature about the war in general, the plays here dealt with do not only contribute to preserving the memory of the war, but rather investigate the significance of the Great War within Canada's cultural memory, and forms of the remembrance of the war as such. As Sherrill Grace has pointed out, there is a "significant shift" in contemporary war writing, a shift "away from an earlier realism, satire, or battle action account to an art characterized by the stress laid on the *process* of remembering, on the attention to trauma aftershocks, on the need to expose a range of betrayals and lies that cost Canadian lives, on the healing power of commemoration through art [...] and on the profound impact war has had on the home front" (*On the Art* 96).

While all these aspects can be found in the plays here discussed, the emphasis on the "*process* of remembering" is strongest in R. H. Thomson's *The Lost Boys* (2002), a play which draws on the author's family history to reach back and establish connections between the past and present. Don Kerr's *The Great War* (1985), Vern Thiessen's *Vimy*, David French's *Soldier's Heart* (2002), and Kevin Major's *No Man's Land*[3] render revisionist histories of the war, questioning its mythology and illustrating the "betrayals" experienced by Canadians, the latter two plays dealing with the massacre of the Royal Newfoundland Regiment at Beaumont-Hamel on 1 July 1916. *Soldier's Heart*, Guy Vanderhaeghe's *Dancock's Dance* (1996) and Dennis Garnhum's dramatization of Findley's *The Wars* (2007)[4] all portray Canadians traumatized by the war, and so, in its own way, does John Gray and Eric Peterson's *Billy Bishop Goes to War*, a play about Canada's World War I flying ace, and one of the best-known Canadian plays in general. The home front stands in the centre of Anne Chislett's *Quiet in the Land* (1981), a play about religious pacifists of the Ontario Amish community, of Wendy Lill's *The Fighting Days* (1985), which is based on the life of social reformer and pacifist Francis Marion Beynon, and of Stephen Massicotte's *Mary's Wedding* (2002), a play which renders a scenario of World War I as envisaged by a young woman at home.

In Canada, the War of 1914–1918 entered national mythology as a milestone on the road to nationhood: "the First World War would be remembered as a for-

---

[3] *No Man's Land* is Major's dramatic adaptation of his own novel of that title, which was published in 1995, for Newfoundland's Rising Tide Theatre. It was first produced at Trinity, Newfoundland, on 1 July 2001.
[4] The play premiered at Theater Calgary in autumn 2007. Like Major's *No Man's Land*, Garnhum's dramatization of Findley is interesting as a play in its own right, which is why I include both pieces in my discussion. It should also be noted that well before this stage adaptation, *The Wars* had already been made into a film, scripted by Findley and directed by Robin Phillips in 1983.

mative event in Canadian history, one that had tempered the raw youth of the nation into a formidable adulthood" (Fisher 14). This is not least because the nation-building myth about the war fulfilled an important consolatory function, providing a way of making sense of loss and of grief (cf. Vance 9, 262). The war had to be given meaning – and Canada's many 'sites of memory,' in the literal and figurative sense, testify to the fact that this is an ongoing process. The plays here analyzed hold up the myths of the Great War to critical reassessment, for instance by setting the individual experience of their protagonists against those images which have tended to dominate the war's public remembrance. They thereby revise established historical perspectives, which have favoured elements conducive to myth-making to the marginalization (and sometimes the virtual exclusion) of others:

> History excludes what is extrasystemic in relation to a given system of interpretation, i.e. of values. Just as the military account of the tragedy could not but leave out much that was important, so the dominant narrative concerned with Canadians in World War I naturally tended to suppress the disturbing memory of an aberrant violence which followed neither the approved channels of patriotic murder nor the customary ways of resistance to 'the wars.' (Vauthier 15)

In particular, the narrative of national emancipation connected with the Great War, according to which the dominion's support of the mother country won it the respect that led to Canada's full sovereignty, has glossed over the fact that Canada's engagement in the conflict also reinforced Old World allegiances and Empire loyalties.[5] In some of the plays discussed here, the nascent nation's military involvement is therefore represented primarily in terms of a failed utopian vision – the vision of a pacific New World unburdened by the warlike history of the Old. Indeed, except for a few veterans of the Boer War, Canadians living in 1914 had never experienced armed conflict, and Canada's participation in the European war could thus be regarded as a loss of innocence on a national scale. This is the case for instance in the dramatization of *The Wars*, which thus adopts one of the central themes of Findley's text. The play necessarily lacks the meta-narrative level established by the archivist/biographer in the novel, yet like the original it also renders the experience of a sensitive young Canadian in the trenches in terms of an initiation into the abyss of human nature, a theme which is also played out on a collective (national) level, in the war. Also, as in the novel, innocence is symbolized by animals, and the protagonist's attempt at rescuing

---

5 As expressed for instance by the newspaper editor McNair in Wendy Lill's *The Fighting Days*: "Germany declared war on Britain. We couldn't have stayed out of it. We have a responsibility to the mother country" (74).

a drove of army horses from a bombardment represents an attempt at salvaging what has been lost.

In a more light-hearted manner, the notion of Canada as a non-militarist, peace-loving society coerced into belligerence by its imperial ties is expressed in *Billy Bishop Goes to War* (premiered at the Vancouver East Cultural Centre, 3 November 1978):

> *Nobody shoots no one in Canada,*
> *at least nobody they don't know.*
> *Nobody shoots no one in Canada,*
> *Last battle was a long long time ago.*
>
> *Nobody picks no fights in Canada,*
> *Not with nobody they ain't met.*
> *Nobody starts no wars in Canada,*
> *Folks tend to work for what they get.* (Gray and Peterson 44)

Billy Bishop traces the protagonist's development from naivety to insensibility, with the flying ace appearing as a comic innocent in Act I ("*We were off to fight the Hun / And it looked like lots of fun, / Somehow it didn't seem like war / At all, at all, at all,*" 19) and an icy professional in Act II: "I enjoy killing [the Hun] now. I go up as much as I can, even on my day off. My score is getting higher and higher because I like it" (73). The play is largely based on *Winged Warfare* (1918), Bishop's legend-creating memoir,[6] yet Peterson, after further research, "accurately portrayed a man who was egotistical, inhumanly ambitious and not really very likeable at all" (Greenhous 17). In spite of his many deficiencies, however, Bishop as portrayed in the play is not blind to the insanity of war, and his resigned statement that "*One thing's for sure, / We'll never be that young again*" (80) also expresses the notion of Canada's initiation into the realities of global armed conflict.

Billy Bishop is a musical drama in the manner and spirit of Joan Littlewood and the Theatre Workshop's *Oh! What a Lovely War* (1963). In contrast to Littlewood's larger-cast musical, however, *Billy Bishop* is "theatre pared down to its essentials" (Wasserman 48), a *tour de force* for one actor and a pianist (as originally performed by Peterson and Gray), with 'Bishop' telling his story and doing all the other characters without changes of costume or makeup, solely by means of vocal effects or, when telling about his exploits as a fighter pilot, the use of model airplanes.

Gray and Peterson's play abstains from explicit ideological commitment (as Gray emphasizes in his preface, the play "does not address itself to the issue of

---

6 A legend, however, that was thoroughly debunked in Paul Cowan's iconoclastic National Film Board documentary *The Kid Who Could Not Miss* (1982).

whether or not war is a good thing or a bad thing," 12), yet its humour undoubtedly works towards exposing war's absurdity. On another level, *Billy Bishop* makes a number of wryly ironic comments on Canadian colonial submissiveness and British imperial arrogance. Bishop, to whom flying appeals as an escape from the mud of the trenches ("the only way out is up," 33), at first sees little chance to fulfill his ambition: "How can I get into the Royal Flying Corps? I'm Canadian. I'm cannon fodder" (34). Conversely, British condescension to the 'colonials' is voiced by the character of Lady St. Helier, Bishop's patron:

> LADY ST. HELIER: You are a rude young man behaving like cannon fodder. Perfectly acceptable characteristics in a Canadian, but you are different. You are a gifted Canadian and that gift belongs to a much older and deeper tradition than Canada can ever hope to provide.
>
> [...]
> *Do you really expect Empire*
> *To settle back, retire,*
> *And say, "Colonials, go on your merry way"?*
> [...]
> *So Bishop, grow up,*
> [...]
> *You have your own naïveté to overthrow.* (47–52)

Perhaps the most intriguing aspect of this play is the way in which it combines echoes of the music hall entertainment of the Great War era itself with a timeframe that puts the war in a larger historical perspective, beyond the exigencies of Canadian nation-building. At the end, the air ace has become "a colonial figurehead" and a national hero (92), yet the *"dance in the sky"* (65) which he has learnt to perform with such deadly virtuosity has turned into a collective (and repetitive) *"dance of history"* (98), as the scene suddenly shifts to 1941, and to an equally murderous war, which saw Canada involved in the fighting again: "Makes you wonder what it was all for?" (101)[7]

The battle of Vimy Ridge (Easter Monday, 9 April, to 12 April 1917) occupies a prominent position with regard to Canada's nation-building myth about the war, since it was there that all four divisions of the Canadian Corps operated together, symbolizing provincial unity and the potential of a unified nation.[8] Vern Thiessen's play *Vimy* is set in a field hospital in the immediate aftermath of the battle.

---

[7] Along the same lines, Gray dedicated the play "To all those who didn't come back from the war, and to all those who did and wondered why" (16).

[8] For the 'classic' account of the Battle of Vimy Ridge see Berton, for a recent critical review of the place of Vimy in Canada's cultural memory, see Zacharias. On the Vimy memorial and Jane Urquhart's novel *The Stone Carvers* (2001), see Alicia Fahey's chapter in the present volume.

The play analyses the effects of traumatic experience as the characters, all shell-shocked and/or physically injured, try to cope with what they have gone through. It also probes the 'all-Canadian' myth about the battle as it assembles characters from all over Canada, including a nurse from Nova Scotia and a group of soldiers consisting of Mike, a "Blood Indian from Standoff, Alberta," Jean Paul, "a butcher from Montreal," Will, "a canoe-maker from Renfrew, Ontario," Sid, "a construction worker from Winnipeg", and Laurie, another Nova Scotian (2).[9] Undermining the 'unifying myth' of Vimy, Thiessen foregrounds ethno-cultural tensions within the Canadian Expeditionary Force, as in the following scene in which Jean Paul is told about an encounter with an arrogant sergeant by his friend Claude:

> CLAUDE: J'ai dit: "Sergeant, quand pensez-vous que nous irons au front?" [...]
>
> Il dit: "You speak to me in English, Private." Moi je réponds: "Je pensais que c'était un bataillon français." [...]
>
> J. P.: Ah no ...
>
> CLAUDE: Et lui, il dit: "This is a Canadian battalion, Private. We are fighting for the King of England, and you will speak to me in the King's English."
>
> J. P.: (*under his breath*) Trou de cul ...
>
> CLAUDE: That's exactly what I said. Asshole. (57)

At another point in the play, Jean Paul, the Quebecois infantryman with the Royal 22nd Regiment, the 'Van Doos' (anglicized from *vingt-deuxième*), claims that "This is an Anglo War. Everyone knows that" (11). French Canadian reservations about the war were hardened by the introduction of conscription in 1917 (see Granatstein and Hitsman), and would prove a bone of contention between Canada's two charter groups well into the post-war years (see Gordon). According to Thiessen, *Vimy* deals with questions such as "Why do we pass over some moments in our history and mythologize others? Why do we suppress some events while others scorch themselves into our minds?" ("Playwright's Note" v) Rather than subscribing to the pan-Canadian myth of Vimy, Thiessen's play, which premiered at Edmonton's Citadel Theatre on 25 October 2007, is concerned with how the war is remembered by individual groups within the Canadian national spectrum,

---

[9] Cf. *Mary's Wedding*, where the pan-Canadian make-up of the Expeditionary Force is also emphasized: "[Mary reading Charlie's letters:] 'There we were, more than 20,000 of us, from British Columbia to Nova Scotia – infantry, cavalry, artillery, all Canadians, all formed up and ready'" (19).

addressing the Anglo-French divide about the war, but also the contributions to the country's military efforts made by Native Canadians (cf. 34) or women serving as nurses.

Vimy combines tragedy and humour, and conventional and experimental theatrical elements to great effect. In his "Production Notes," the author states that this is "not a naturalistic play. Theatricality and non-realism in staging, sound, costume, lighting and design are encouraged. Although the play is poetic at times, it should be played without sentimentality or reverence" (x). As the play tends to undermine the all-Canadian myth of Vimy Ridge, Thiessen's technique aims towards fragmentation by creating repetitive, circular dialogues, and the play approaches the Pinteresque through its blending of the jocular and oppressive, and especially through ominous lacunae. Linear chronology is broken as flashbacks turn to the 'prehistory' of characters, showing what made the men enlist and how the trajectories of their lives converged at Vimy, and as the last part of the play renders an outlook upon their lives after the war, as they remember and try to cope with their experience.

The fact that group-specific recollections of the war may legitimize and enhance regional identities is borne out by the two plays which deal with Newfoundland, David French's *Soldier's Heart* and Kevin Major's *No Man's Land*. French's play is part of a dramatic cycle about the Mercer family, Newfoundlanders living in Toronto, which began with *Leaving Home* (1971). In *Soldier's Heart*, Jacob Mercer, the *émigré* protagonist of *Leaving Home*, is a sixteen-year-old struggling with his father Esau (the divided brothers of the Old Testament have become father and son), a traumatized war veteran. The time is "Monday, June 30, 1924," significantly the evening before 1 July, the day the Newfoundland Regiment was virtually wiped out during the opening of the Battle of the Somme in 1916. Most significantly, however, the "single greatest disaster in [Newfoundland] history" ("Introduction" 10) is rendered in Major's *No Man's Land*. The play emphasizes the contribution to Britain's war effort by a colony that would become a Canadian province only in 1949,[10] rendering the perspective of a closely-knit community. *No Man's Land* is commemorative, "without irony or self-reflexive frames of memory" (Grace, *On the Art* 95), underlining the fact that for Canada's youngest province, 1 July still bears other associations beside Canada Day. The play emphasizes authenticity, as many of the characters are based on historical persons, and the printed text is framed by photographs showing groups of Newfoundlanders

---

[10] At several points in the play (and especially against the British), characters emphasize that Newfoundlanders are not Canadians (cf. 28, 42). In the same way, one of David French's characters insists that the Newfoundlanders are not Canadians, but "one-hundred-percent British" (34).

in uniform, about to join the European war. It also extends the range of characters in the novel to include those at home, celebrating their spirit of solidarity yet also underlining the extent of the loss and the drain on the St. John's and outport communities.

No Man's Land was written, as the author claims in a preface, "[t]o honour the men of the Regiment who lost their lives that day, to remember the loved ones left to grieve, while at the same time presenting an honest and visually arresting piece of theater" ("Introduction" 16). Accordingly, the play is characterized by laconic dialogue and the use, to a certain extent, of the regional dialect and, at least in the original production, authentic uniforms and realistic scenery (including sandbags etc.). The setting switches between the Somme and home, with individual scenes emphasizing their connection by simultaneously presenting both settings. According to the introduction, the home front is given more space than it is in the original novel in order to "enlarge [the play's] theatrical possibilities" (16), not only with a view to interaction and contrast, as it seems, but also because the bereaved women end the play in the manner of a chorus in classical tragedy. As Major deals with the slaughter of the "July Drive," he clearly presents the 'colonials' as pawns in the plans of the bull-headed general staff, and their sacrifice as futile. The frontline scenes focus on the perspective of junior officers, and suspense is created as they become increasingly aware of what the impending attack may be like. In the meantime, however, songs, music, the pawky humour of privates and the character of "Madame, an estaminet owner" provide 'comic relief' reminiscent of the camp scenes in *Henry V*. As the tragedy unfolds in Act II, there is an increasing sense of the ominous. The soldiers desperately cling to the belief that preparations for the attack have been effective in breaking the German defenses, only to realize that they have been deceived. What emerges here is a drama of betrayal and sacrifice, and a sense that 'fate' has been playing against the Newfoundlanders: "CLARKE: The Great Push is in motion. There's no slowing it down [...]. What do we matter? We're one regiment. A few less of us means nothing. We're not from London. Or Poole. Or goddamn Bristol. There's plenty more to call up behind us" (110).

Canada's participation in the Great War was to channel divisions of class, region, ethnicity and race into a national Anglo-Canadian culture. However, the Conscription Crisis of 1917, in particular, which aggravated Anglo-French tensions about the 'reluctance' of Quebeckers to join the CEF, shows that the war was rather apt to deepen existing rifts in Canadian society, not to speak of the situation of German or Ukrainian (i.e. nominally Austro-Hungarian) immigrants. This is the larger context of Wendy Lill's *The Fighting Days* (1985), which deals with the war and the Women's Movement, and with Empire loyalties and questions of 'Canadianness.' The play's main character is (historical) Francis Marion

Beynon, a journalist, feminist and social reformer, and the author of *Aleta Dey* (1919), an autobiographical novel which is critical about the war. *The Fighting Days* is set in Winnipeg, where Beynon held the post of women's editor for *The Grain Growers Guide* (in the play *The Rural Review*), the largest weekly paper in western Canada, from 1912–1917, which is also roughly the time covered by the play. Lill's two-act play concentrates on Beynon's relationship to Nellie McClung, the foremost figure in the history of female suffrage in Canada. As the war brings into focus women's roles in early twentieth-century Canadian society, the play – like for instance Frances Itani's novel *Deafening* (2003), or, in British literature, Pat Barker's *Regeneration* trilogy (1991–1995) and, of course, Ford Madox Ford's *Parade's End* (1924–1928) – emphasizes the gender-divisions accentuated by the war. Beynon works together with McClung on Women's Vote, but comes to feel estrangement and disillusionment when McClung supports the war (in which her son is fighting) and wants to restrict the vote to Dominion-born women: "NELLIE: The only way to protect [...] our tradition [...] is to limit the vote to Empire women" (72). The issue behind this is to ensure conscription, which many among the "foreign community" (72) are against. In contrast, Beynon is shown as an idealist and a pacifist, speaking out against the war and the propagandist depiction of the conflict as a fight for freedom and democracy:

> FRANCIS: We thought we were sailing the vessel of freedom, but there seems to be a thousand others out there with the same claim. How can freedom take so many forms? I don't know what to think any more. [...] We've got the vote now, but we're too anxious or terrified to figure out what to do with it.
>
> [...]
>
> We, as women, in our first chance to use our franchise, are being asked to vote for war! To vote for sending more sons and husbands away to fight and be killed. (63, 87)

In the end, Beynon has to give in to public pressure (as rendered by letters which she receives in support of conscription), and leaves for New York.

The themes of 'war madness' and social conscience appear in various forms in many of the plays, for instance in Massicotte's *Mary's Wedding*, where quotes from Tennyson's "Charge of the Light Brigade" serve to introduce notions of misguided heroism and chivalric romance, as the play questions Canada's engagement in the European war, or in Vanderhaeghe's *Dancock's Dance*, where the opportunist orderly Keneally voices maudlin patriotic sentiment (87), starting to recite John McCrae's "In Flanders Fields," but failing to remember the words. In contrast to Keneally, the shell-shocked officer Dancock represents the type of the upright, committed soldier, who even shows a sense of fairness and respect for the enemy: "DANCOCK: The German soldier did his duty. I did mine. He [!] was an honest enemy. [...] I save my hatred for dishonest enemies. The ones who pretend to be your friend, then stab you in the back" (14). Ultimately disillusioned, Dancock expresses a painful awareness of how his sense of duty might have been misdirected (cf. 114–118).

The conflict between patriotism and, in this case, a religiously motivated pacifism is the subject of Anne Chislett's *Quiet in the Land*, first performed at the Blyth Summer Festival on 3 July 1981. The play is set among an Old Order Amish community in a farming area near Kitchener (before 1916, Berlin), Ontario, in 1917 (Act I) and 1918 (Act II). Beside the political implications of the community's attitudes and the way it was affected by conscription, Chislett explores the clash between 'modernity' and the Amish's traditionalist lifestyle as the war brings to focus the conflict between generations. In addition, it portrays the precarious situation of a German-speaking people among an increasingly hostile majority of Anglophones ("We are not German. We just speak it" 5).[11] In spite of farm deferment and exemption on grounds of religion, the Amish are subject to growing pressure and to much public hostility against 'shirkers' (24). Those who refuse to register under the Military Service Act are deported as 'enemy aliens.' In particular, however, the play deals with the conflict between Christy Bauman and his son Yock (Jacob), who expresses the longing of the young to be "part of the twentieth century" (53). As Christy becomes a bishop among his community, his religious principles harden to the point that he breaks with his son, who then joins up against the commands of their creed. Chislett's play thus renders its own version, under specific auspices, of the theme of the old sacrificing the young in the war. Paradoxically, it is Yock (rather than the Amish's religiosity) who 'redeems' his community in the eyes of the others in that he becomes a 'war hero,' while in fact he has been profoundly traumatized by his experience of the frontline. Thus, for instance, the Irish farmer O'Rourke, who has come to hate the 'German' Amish as his son has returned from the war an invalid, later retracts his invectives: "Guess nobody can call you people cowards now, eh? German lovers, neither" (80).

According to Sherrill Grace, plays like *Soldier's Heart*, *Dancock's Dance*, *The Lost Boys*, and *Mary's Wedding* "are works in which the First World War refuses to stay over there or release its victims but insists on permeating home ground and haunting the future" (*On the Art* 77). The persistence of memory and of trauma is rendered concrete in Thomson's *The Lost Boys*, which is based on letters to their

---

[11] The linguistic ambivalence which thus underlies the play (the characters are in fact supposed to be speaking Low German) is communicated to the audience for instance by having characters admit to difficulties spelling English. Also, the actors are to adopt a German accent when speaking English to their anglophone neighbours.

mother written by four great-uncles of the author who fought in Europe, where three of them died, and in Africa. Like *Billy Bishop*, *The Lost Boys* is a play for a single actor (in the original performance, the author himself), whose primary role is that of the grand-nephew, simply designated as "MAN." As the "MAN" delves into family history via the letters, the actor also impersonates his combatant great-uncles (and other characters) with the help of projections and sound effects. More than being just a dramatic reading of the letters, however, the play presents an imaginative re-enactment of individual experiences of the war and the front line, blurring the boundaries between the past and present.

One of the most memorable passages in Thomson's play renders memory concrete by presenting the image of the bones of the fallen soldiers which re-surface in a dance of death (a motif which also occurs in *Billy Bishop* and *Dancock's Dance*), a dance whose reverberations make themselves felt throughout time:

> The larger story is that the earth is not at peace. The earth is reworking its memory of war. [...] The larger story is also the dance of the dead soldiers. A hundred thousand skeletons lie unclaimed beneath the surface of the battlefields. They too are moving. Their bones dance ... ever so slowly in the shifting of earth and mud ... stepping with the frosts for more than eighty years. And as the dead men dance the decades away ... a few break company each spring and come to the surface ... (46–47)

Subtitled *Letters from the Sons, 1914–1923*, *The Lost Boys*, like Thiessen's *Vimy*, is mainly concerned with how the war has been remembered by individuals, families and communities. As the monologue of Thomson's "MAN" contextualizes the letters, the play investigates how this remembrance was refracted by the mythology of the war as well as how, in turn, mythical contexts were shaped by the 'text' of individual memories themselves. Thus, for instance, one of the most potent myths of the war, according to which the 'truth' about battle could not be communicated to non-combatants, and a chasm was thereby created between soldiers and civilians, is repeatedly emphasized: "MAN: There was so much they could not write about. [...] Is this all you can say George? You are fighting the battle of Passchendaele. Is that all you can say?" (44, 49).[12]

In a more specific sense, trauma as induced by 'incommunicable' experience is dealt with through the shell-shocked characters in *Vimy*, *Quiet in the Land*, where Yock is traumatized by his front-line experience especially as his religion fails him,[13] and also in *No Man's Land*: "Our Ned came back a man, but he is

---

[12] It must be noted here that the Stratford brothers all served as officers, so their letters, unlike those of privates, were not subject to being censored.

[13] As is indicated when he tells his father of a German soldier he had run through with his bayonet: "He was going to die right there in that mud and he knew it. He was afraid, Pa. He was afraid

a silent man who never talks about what he saw. He says nothing of the war, not even to his father" (116). Most prominently, however, trauma appears in two plays which deal, in the manner of analytic drama, with the reasons for their protagonist's derangement, French's *Soldier's Heart* and Vanderhaeghe's *Dancock's Dance*.

Soldier's Heart, whose title renders a historical term for 'shell shock' or post-traumatic stress disorder (PTSD), premiered at Toronto's Tarragon Theatre on 13 November 2001.[14] Like Jack Hodgins' novel *Broken Ground* (1998), which is set among a community of First World War veterans on Vancouver Island, French's play deals with the unearthing of traumatic experience, as Esau Mercer's suppressed memories of the war are brought to the surface. The play conveys the intensity of emotions which remembering the war generates in Esau and his fellow veteran Bert Taylor, and renders the gap between those who have experienced the fighting and those who have not. The scene is a Newfoundland railway station, where the young Jacob Mercer is about to leave home as conflicts with his traumatized father have escalated. Esau has never spoken about what has so profoundly shattered him (cf. 18, 27, 63), and his reticence is defended by Bert, the station-master like this: "Some things are off limits [...]"; "It's just that each man's experience was his own." (27) In a final confrontation, Jacob is determined to know, and the main part of the play consists of his urgent questions which are reluctantly answered by his father. In this connection, a reference to the well-known recruiting poster reading "Daddy, what did you do in the Great War?" creates a poignant irony. Gradually, the audience learns with Jacob that Esau's brother Will, who died and is buried in France, was killed by Esau, who tragically mistook him for a German: "He was my brother [...]. I was supposed to look after him. Instead, I – " (43).[15] French's play renders its sensational theme in a manner which is frequently melodramatic, yet it points to the importance of a *topos* that has been prominent in the literature of the war, including post-memory texts, namely the notion that the 'true' horror of the war could not be communicated to non-combatants. On another level, the play deals with 'healing' and the possibilities of overcoming the impact of traumatic memories. In contrast to Esau, who holds that "T'ings happen in war that can never be forgotten [...] never be

---

of facing God. He started screaming for a preacher. I wanted to tell him I understood, that I was Christian, that I was German, too. I wanted to say all those words I used to hear you read from the Bible, but I was ashamed" (94–95).

14 The printed text of the play (2002) bears a motto from Wilfred Owen's "Spring Offensive."
15 The theme of a surviving brother's feelings of guilt, although in this case simply for having 'failed' to protect his sibling from being killed in the trenches, is memorably rendered in a canonical Canadian short story, Margaret Laurence's "To Set Our House in Order" (*A Bird in the House*, 1970).

forgiven" (46), Bert and his wife have taken trips to the battlefield, and the 'pastoral' vision which the ending evokes of the scene there may perhaps be seen as a cautiously optimistic conclusion.

Guy Vanderhaeghe's *Dancock's Dance*, first performed at the Persephone Theatre in Saskatoon, Saskatchewan, on 1 April 1995, also concentrates on bringing to light the suppressed memories of its protagonist, and with them those 'truths' about the war that the public remembrance has tended to block out. The setting is the Saskatchewan Hospital for the Insane at North Battleford, in late autumn 1918, during the outbreak of the Spanish Influenza. Vanderhaeghe's surrealist device for rendering the protagonist's oppression by traumatic memories is the 'shadow' of an unnamed soldier hovering about him to a "popular tune from the First World War," performing a dance which is "[u]nsettling, a hint of subtle menace contained in it" (11). From Dancock's final confrontation with the spectre it emerges that – duty-bound as he was as an officer – he shot the soldier who refused to go over the top, leading the others to the point of mutiny. Before the attack, he had seen him dancing happily at a café behind the lines. Vanderhaeghe's play builds on (moral) ambiguities, as Dancock, clinging to his responsibility as an officer, may have been deceived about the loyalty of his men (cf. 118) and also about his own motives. However, like French, Vanderhaeghe, too, ends upon a subdued note of optimism as Dancock faces the past, and may be able to redeem it by showing sympathy for Braun, a patient with a German background, and by doing volunteer work as the flu causes an emergency in the hospital.

As the moment of crisis evoked in Vanderhaeghe's play (the soldier's refusal to 'go over the top') illustrates, *Dancock's Dance*, like the other plays discussed in this essay, relies on images which have become part of the iconography of the war, and which in turn, literature helps to anchor in Canada's cultural memory. Other than the historical explanations which authors either provide in a paratext (cf. *Vimy*, *The Lost Boys*) or have inserted into dialogues (Don Kerr's *The Great War*) or the monologues of narrator figures (Mary in *Mary's Wedding*, the Man in *The Lost Boys*), these emblematic images provide an effective and unobtrusive way of introducing themes like the contrast between the glorifying of war and the bleak reality. Similarly, at the beginning of *Soldier's Heart*, different perspectives on the war are evoked simply through the fact that "Keep the Home Fires Burning" is played on a gramophone, as Bert's English wife likes the dashing war songs, while Bert is telling Jacob of soldiers coming back from the line, bleating like sheep to signify 'slaughter.'[16] Initial enthusiasm for the war is summarily rendered by the confident assertion that it will be over by Christmas (cf. *Soldier's*

---

[16] An allusion to incidents reported during the disastrous Nivelle offensive on the Chemin des Dames (Verdun) in spring 1917, and the subsequent mutinies in the French Army.

Heart 24; *Timothy Findley's The Wars* 12, etc.), while the conditions along the Western Front are neatly captured for instance by references to the "water-pocked no-man's land" (*Mary's Wedding*, 25). The ultimate horror of trench warfare, however, is represented by soldiers dying slowly and painfully in no-man's land, caught on the barbed wire:

> DANCOCK: Out there, in No Man's Land, at night the wounded used to cry for us to come out and save them. We didn't dare. Flares opened in the black sky, turning everything bright as day. Like dying on a stage, I used to think, in the limelight, before an audience of thousands. (*Dancock's Dance* 109)

Analogies and associations between war and the theatre are manifold, as Sherrill Grace notes in her introduction to *Canada and the Theatre of War* (cf. iii–iv), from the well-worn military trope of the 'theatre of war' on the one hand, to a long tradition of theatrical representations of armed conflict on the other. In rendering war on stage, dramatists have usually, and for obvious reasons, needed to make a virtue out of necessity, as is best demonstrated by Shakespeare's prologue to *Henry V*. The majority of the plays discussed in this chapter are not set in the midst of battle – only Kevin Major's *No Man's Land*, Don Kerr's *The Great War* and Dennis Garnhum's dramatization of Findley contain battle-action sequences. In all the other instances, the fighting is discursivized in the sense that it is either reported orally or through letters, or remembered by survivors. Modern sound and visualizing technology as used in productions may greatly enhance the possibilities for 'realistic' or quasi-filmic representation, yet the basic limitations of theatre with regard to representing war remain. The 'theatre of war' will thus inevitably accentuate its own status as dramatic art – and this 'artificiality,' I should argue, runs counter to the mythologizing of its subject if we regard myth, with Roland Barthes, as the transformation of historical complexity into the "evident" (cf. note 2) of uncontested narratives. Looking at this from another angle, and with reference to a well-known *topos*, the theatricality of war-plays may well remind audiences that mythical 'givens' about war are 'stagings' for ideological purposes, and that soldiers killed for the 'birth of the nation' may indeed be regarded as soldiers "dying on a [national] stage."

The plays I am dicussing here emphasize theatricality, even if they largely remain within the frame of language- and character-based theatre and the well-made play. However, the dramatic illusion is invariably broken (mostly from theatrical necessity) either by dropping the fourth wall or, for example in Chislett's *Quiet in the Land*, through marking scenes as simultaneous by means of multiple interior and exterior sets. Usually – and again mostly due to practical (economic) necessities – the plays either have small casts of characters or actors taking over double or even multiple roles. Plays like Massicotte's *Mary's Wedding*, Thiessen's *Vimy* and the dramatization of Findley's *The Wars* also break with the principle of dramatic succession through flashbacks and overlapping time frames, even if in the last instance the very complex chronology of the original novel has been considerably straightened out.

If the ample use of documentary greatly contributes to the naturalistic element in the plays, some of them, especially *The Lost Boys* and *Mary's Wedding*, decisively depart from naturalistic modes to approach 'epic' drama of the Brecht and Piscator type. *Mary's Wedding* was first produced in Calgary, February 2002, at playRites '02, the annual festival of New Canadian Plays organized by Alberta Theatre Projects. The two main characters in Massicote's play are Charlie Edwards, a farmer's son, and Mary Chalmers, whose role blends with that of Sergeant (later Lieutenant) Flowers, a character based on a historical figure. Presenting a melodramatic love story in an unconventional form, the play, which is supposed to render the protagonist's dream, "begins at the end and ends at the beginning" (Prologue). In this sense, it is analytic like French's *Soldier's Heart* and Vanderhaeghe's *Dancock's Dance*. Set on the evening before Mary's wedding, in July 1920, her dream takes her back to the beginning of her romance with Charlie Edwards in 1914, and develops one possible outcome of events (as it seems, their relationship did not in fact come real, 59), in which Mary participates, as it were, in her lover's experiences at the front. Mary switches from narrator to protagonist and back, and the explanatory character of her narratives provides a panoramic perspective on the war which is set against the individual experience of Charlie as shared by Mary/Flowers in a blurring of the boundaries of 'dream' and 'reality.' To a lesser extent, the epic technique of *Mary's Wedding* can also be observed in *Dancock's Dance*, where the hospital's Superintendent addresses the audience, introducing the history of Dancock, who was decorated for bravery and later invalided out with "acute neurasthenia" (12). Breaking conventions of naturalistic drama, Dancock's communication with the 'shadow' of the unnamed Soldier remains hidden to the other characters.

Rendering different 'emplotments' of the war as farce, melodrama or tragedy, the plays here analyzed reflect but also criticize and transform ideological issues which have shaped its public remembrance in Canada. For this purpose, they recover histories that have tended to be neglected and marginalized. Addressing myths and images which have appealed to the collective imagination and have contributed to shaping later responses to the war, they reveal an awareness of the fact that what is historically significant has often been defined rather narrowly or determined ideologically. Undoubtedly, the Great War did play a formative role in Canada's process of nation-building, yet this process was shaped by a plurality of experiences rather than by that of white English-Canadian males fighting on the

Western Front alone. Emphasizing the plurality of responses to the war, modern Canadian plays about World War I reject mythologizing and totalizing accounts of Canada's history as a nation. In particular, they undermine notions of a unifying effect of the country's military engagement on Canadian society itself, by emphasizing instead the imperial associations of the war and the social divisions which it was apt to create.

References

Barthes, Roland. *Mythologies*. Trans. Annette Lavers. New York: Hill and Wang, 1972.
Berton, Pierre. *Vimy*. Toronto: McClelland & Stewart, 1986.
Chislett, Anne. *Quiet in the Land*. Toronto: Playwrights Canada Press, 1981.
Coates, Donna, and Sherrill Grace, eds. *Canada and the Theatre of War*. 2 vols. Toronto: Playwrights Canada Press, 2008, 2010.
Fisher, Susan. "The Study of War." *Literature and War: Special Issue of Canadian Literature*. Ed. Susan Fisher, 179 (2003): 10–14.
French, David. *Soldier's Heart*. Vancouver: Talonbooks, 2002.
Garnhum, Dennis. *Timothy Findley's The Wars*. Winnipeg: Shillingford, 2008.
Gordon, Alan. "Lest We Forget: Two Solitudes in War and Memory." *Canadas of the Mind: The Making and Unmaking of Canadian Nationalisms in the Twentieth Century*. Eds. Norman Hillmer and Adam Chapnick. Montreal & Kingston et al.: McGill-Queen's University Press, 2007. 159–173.
Grace, Sherrill. "Introduction: 'A Different Kind of Theatre.'" *Canada and the Theatre of War*. Eds. Donna Coates and Sherrill Grace. iii–ix.
Grace, Sherrill. *On the Art of Being Canadian*. Vancouver, Toronto: University of British Columbia Press, 2009.
Granatstein, J. L., and Desmond Morton. *Canada and the Two World Wars*. Toronto: Key Porter Books, 2003.
Granatstein, Jack Lawrence, and J. M. Hitsman. *Broken Promises: A History of Conscription in Canada*. Toronto: Oxford University Press, 1977.
Gray, John, with Eric Peterson. *Billy Bishop Goes to War*. Vancouver: Talonbooks, 1981 [1978].
Greenhous, Brereton. *The Making of Billy Bishop: The First World War Exploits of Billy Bishop, VC*. Toronto, Oxford: Dundurn, 2002.
Kerr, Don. *The Great War*. Toronto: Playwrights Canada Press, 1985.
Lill, Wendy. *The Fighting Days*. Vancouver: Talonbooks, 1985.
Mackenzie, David, ed. *Canada and the First World War. Essays in Honour of Robert Craig Brown*. Toronto, Buffalo, London: University of Toronto Press, 2005.
Major, Kevin. *No Man's Land: A Play*. St. Johns, NL: Pennywell Books, n. d.
Massicotte, Stephen. *Mary's Wedding*. Toronto: Playwrights Canada Press, 2002.
Nora, Pierre. "Between Memory and History: *Les Lieux de Mémoire*." Trans. Marc Roudebush. *Representations* 26 (1989): 7–25.
Thiessen, Vern. *Vimy*. Toronto: Playwrights Canada Press, 2007.

Thomson, R. H. *The Lost Boys. Letters from the Sons in Two Acts. 1914–1923*. Toronto: Playwrights Canada Press, 2002.

Vance, Jonathan F. *Death So Noble: Memory, Meaning, and the First World War*. Vancouver: University of British Columbia Press, 1997.

Vanderhaeghe, Guy. *Dancock's Dance*. Vancouver: Talonbooks, 2006 [Winnipeg: Blizzard Publications, 1996].

Vauthier, Simone. "The Dubious Battle of Story-Telling: Narrative Strategies in Timothy Findley's *The Wars*." *Gaining Ground: European Critics on Canadian Literature*. Eds. Robert Kroetsch and Reingard M. Nischik. Edmonton: NeWest Press, 1985. 11–39.

Wasserman, Jerry. "Introduction to *Billy Bishop Goes to War*." *Modern Canadian Plays*. Ed. Jerry Wasserman. 3rd ed., vol. 2. Vancouver: Talonbooks, 1994. 47–49.

Zacharias, Robert. "'Some Great Crisis': Vimy as Originary Violence." *Shifting the Ground of Canadian Literary Studies*. Eds. Smaro Kamboureli and R. Z. Waterloo, Ontario: Wilfrid Laurier University Press, 2012. 109–128.

David Malcolm
The Great War Re-Remembered: Allohistory and Allohistorical Fiction

As the volume in which this essay appears amply documents, the Great War of 1914–1918 is a recurrent subject in a wide variety of cultural products.[1] In the following, I consider one aspect of the War's presence in modern culture (postmemory) that, as Jörg Helbig and Christoph Rodiek note, has been little discussed (cf. Helbig 13; Rodiek 38), that is, texts that belong to the categories of allohistory and allohistorical fiction. Therefore, it seems appropriate to discuss the topic in general terms before proceeding to a consideration of allohistorical treatments of the Great War.

1 Theoretical Considerations

A variety of terms is used to denote the phenomenon that I wish to refer to as allohistory and allohistorical fiction. These include: virtual history, counter-factual history, alternative history, *Uchronie* (uchronia), *Allotopie* (allotopy), *Gegengeschichte*, *historia ficción*, and parahistory (cf. Ferguson *passim*; Helbig *passim*; Rodiek 25). Allohistory and allohistorical fiction are texts that depend on a 'what if' proposition. A key moment or conjunction of events is assumed to turn out differently from the documented record. For example, what if the Carthaginians had won the Second Punic War? What if the Spanish Armada had landed successfully in England in 1588, and the Spanish forces defeated the English? Such texts (historical or fictional) develop the implications of such a proposition.

Some issues of identification remain. One needs to distinguish between allohistory and allohistorical fiction, although this is not always done, and, indeed, the border between the two is blurred (as, for example, in Rodiek's otherwise excellent definition [cf. 26]). Allohistory is practised by historians, allohistorical fiction by fiction writers, and the texts are presented appropriately by their publishers. Above all, most allohistory is formulated in the third conditional ("if x had happened, then a, b, c. ..."), while allohistorical fiction is usually formulated in past tenses (predominantly the past simple). Not all examples of the allohistor-

---

[1] This matter has also been extensively discussed in Marzena Sokołowska-Paryż's study *Reimagining the War Memorial, Reinterpreting the Great War: The Formats of British Commemorative Fiction* (2012).

ical follow that distinction. Niall Ferguson's afterword to *Virtual History*, entitled "A Virtual History, 1646–1996," is predominantly written in past simple, although it is included in a book of speculations by historians, speculations formulated mostly in conditionals (cf. 416–440).

Identifying allohistorical fiction is further complicated because, in certain ways, all fiction is allohistorical, marked by alterity, as formulated by Manfred Pfister and Monika Lindner (34). Fiction, at some point, inevitably involves invented persons, settings, institutions, actions, or technologies. Novels may deploy historically documented personages, but not even the most severe and rigorous of historical novels employs only such. In Pfister's and Lindner's terminology (although they do not discuss it), the allohistorical would be marked by its status as *Alternative*, as opposed to *Alterität* (alterity) (cf. 32).

Allohistory is counter-factual history written by historians, largely couched in conditionals. It receives its fullest discussion and defence in the work of Alexander Demandt. His *Ungeschehene Geschichte: Ein Traktat über die Frage: Was wäre geschehen, wenn... ?* (History That Did Not Happen – A Treatise on the Question: What Would Have Happened If ...?, 2001) and *Es hätte auch anders kommen können: Wendepunkte deutscher Geschichte* (It Could Have Happened Differently: Turning Points of German History, 2010) contain useful definitions of allohistory and powerful arguments in favour of its practice. Hypotheticals, Demandt argues, are necessary to understand decisive moments in history, to weigh up causal factors, to justify judgments of value, and to calculate possibilities in the past (cf. *Ungeschehene Geschichte* 23). The methods of counter-factual history are no different from those of traditional history, Demandt insists, derived as they are from known events and considered in terms of plausibility (cf. *Ungeschehene Geschichte* 53, 144; *Es hätte auch anders kommen können* 21). A concern with the possible but *ungeschehen* (unhappened) has, he argues, considerable didactic merit. It suggests that deterministic views of history (Whig, Marxist, divine providence, and others) are faulty: the present could easily have been different (cf. *Ungeschehene Geschichte* 35). *Historia eventualis* also undermines the hubris of our thinking that the forces of history have us and our present dispensation as their goals (cf. 166–169). In a long introduction to his collection *Virtual History*, Ferguson mounts a similar defence of allohistory. It is anti-deterministic, and recognizes the stochastic nature of events (cf. 20–43, 44–52, 52–64, 79–90).

The most fruitful discussions of allohistorical fiction are by Jörg Helbig (1988), Christoph Rodiek (1997), and Helmut Ritter (1999). Of these, Rodiek's analysis is the most penetrating. One of the crucial features of his definition is the creation in allohistorical fiction of a coherent, plausible alternative model to what actually occurs (cf. 26). Thus, Rodiek points out, all contrafactual speculations are not necessarily *Uchronien* because they may weigh up a variety of possibilities in a discursive text (cf. 26). The question of the plausibility of the counter-factual is seen as key in all three discussions of allohistorical fiction (as it is in Demandt's and Ferguson's examinations of allohistory) (cf. Rodiek 25–26; Ritter 15–16; Helbig 32).

The scholarly neglect of allohistorical fiction is the more surprising because, as Rodiek demonstrates, over the past two hundred years there have been many texts, not only in English, that can legitimately be classed in the category. Isaac D'Israeli's "Of a History of Events Which Have Not Happened" (1835) and Charles Renouvier's *Uchronie. Tableau historique apocryphe* (1857) are among early examples (cf. Rodiek 9, 63–89), while, as Ritter points out, there is a plethora of allohistorical fiction relating to the Second World War (cf. 21, 23). Some of it is quite distinguished: Philip K. Dick's *The Man in the High Castle* (1962), Len Deighton's *SS-GB* (1978), and Owen Shears's *Resistance* (2007).

2 Allohistorical Fictions of the Great War

What is striking about allohistorical fictions of the Great War is their paucity.[2] Whereas the subject of the Second World War has generated a substantial quantity of allohistorical fiction, and some of it of high literary quality, the same cannot be said of the subject of the Great War of 1914–1918. Diligent enquiry will turn up few texts, and many of them are of low quality. The lack of allohistorical fiction relating to the Great War is surprising because the Great War was frequently predicted in fictions before 1914, in texts such as George Tomkyns Chesney's "The Battle of Dorking," first published in *Blackwood's Magazine* in 1871, and subsequently much reprinted, including during the years of the Great War, and H. H. Munro's ("Saki") novel *When William Came: A Story of London under the Hohenzollerns* (1913). Helbig notes Sir William Butler's *The Invasion of England Told Twenty Years After by an Old Soldier* (1882) and William le Queux's *The Invasion of 1910* (1906) (cf. Helbig 137–138; see also Moorcock 1977). Demandt discusses a German example, Ferdinand Grautoff's *1906. Der Zusammenbruch der Alten Welt* (1905) (cf. *Es hätte auch ...* 195–196). Thus, a war widely predicted in fiction is only exiguously remembered in *post factum* allohistorical narratives. However, there is a body of allohistorical fiction that touches on (remembers, re-remembers?) the Great War.

---

[2] I only discuss allohistorical fiction written originally in English. Thus, I exclude one of the most interesting allohistorical fictions of the Great War, Guido Morselli's *Contro-passato prossimo* (1975), translated by Hugh Shankland as *Past Conditional: A Retrospective Hypothesis* (1989).

Fantastic and anti-mimetic motifs are marked in American allohistorical treatments of the conflict.[3] For example, Fritz Leiber's short story "Catch That Zeppelin!" (1975) projects the narrator into an alternate 1937 in New York, in which cars are battery-driven, helium-powered Zeppelins fly safely, and Germany and Germans are highly regarded and a force for good in the world. Much of this has been occasioned by the Allies' decision in November 1918 not to conclude an armistice with the Central Powers, but to bomb Germany into submission and to march into and occupy its territories (thus producing a situation analogous to that in the documented world in 1945). The result is no *Dolchstoßlegende*, no reparations, and a strong League of Nations. The documented world is embodied in the comments made by the narrator's son in the counter-factual 1937, in which he imagines a different world (that is, in fact, the reader's). However, this counter-factual 1937 is presented as the product of a hallucination or a step into "another Time Stream" (Leiber 174), and the narrator returns to the documented world at the story's end. The story, thus, hovers between suggesting that there are other realities into which we can step, and that the reader cannot be sure whether the narrator did or did not step into another reality.[4]

The convention of time travel plays a role in several allohistorical fictions that touch on the Great War. In Ward Moore's "Bring the Jubilee" (1952), the Great War is only fleetingly alluded to as "the Emperor's war of 1914–16" (Moore 153). It is a small item in a counter-factual world in which the Confederacy wins the Battle of Gettysburg in 1863, and imposes a punitive peace on the United States, which is reduced to penury and backwardness. The indigence of the USA is contrasted with the flourishing economies and cultures of the Confederacy and "the

---

3 In the following discussion, I rely on the distinctions made by Andrzej Zgorzelski in his essay "On Differentiating Fantastic Fictions: Some Supragenological Distinctions in Literature" (Zgorzelski 299–307). The supragenological category of the fantastic, Zgorzelski proposes, can be taken to involve a "confrontation," present within a text, of the consensual model of the empirical world (which is a presupposition of the text) with a different one. This confrontation is always marked by surprise and unease on the part of characters, and all orders of the world in the text are presented as models without a hierarchy of authority. An anti-mimetic category, however, can be taken to include texts that aim to revise and correct the implied reader's faulty model of the empirical world, a faulty model that is presented in the text (cf. Zgorzelski 302). Other relevant supragenological categories proposed by Zgorzelski are that of the mimetic, which adheres strictly to the model of the world embodied in the implied reader's linguistic competence (for example, animals do not talk, humans cannot fly unaided), and that of the nonmimetic, which proposes a model of the world that is not textually confronted with that embodied in the implied reader's competence, but which is different from it (heroic fantasy or dystopia, for example) (cf. 302–304).

4 Rodiek (41) and Ritter (15–16) would disqualify this text and some of the others discussed here as allohistorical because of the presence of such fantastic and anti-mimetic motifs.

German Union" (155). The short novel involves time travel, and, thus, becomes clearly anti-mimetic. The protagonist-narrator, a historian, returns to 1863 from his 1950s, and unintentionally influences the outcome of the Battle of Gettysburg.

Time travel is a central motif and convention in David J. Kowalski's long novel *The Company of the Dead* (2012).[5] In this text, a character (called Wells) has, by a peculiar chain of circumstances, been projected back in time from the implied reader's 1999 to 1911. He decides to attempt to recast the events of the twentieth century, to avoid the Great War and its sequel ("there's an archduke in Europe who could do with living beyond 1914"; Kowalski 179). He starts by trying to save the *Titanic* in 1912, but only delays its sinking by a few hours, thus precipitating a quite different twentieth century. The sinking of the *Titanic*, and the new casualty list that results from the later sinking, poison relations between Britain and the USA, so that the USA does not intervene in the First World War. These are just a few of the consequences. Britain is a client state of a powerful Greater German Union that now possesses colonies all over the globe. The Southern States have seceded from the Union. North America is partially occupied by Japanese forces (103–106). Indeed, the world, rather than improving because of Wells's intervention, is headed for atomic destruction. In a very complex story material, an intrepid band of characters establish this and set out to right the disruption of Wells's actions in 1912, which they succeed in doing, thus restoring our documented order of things.

The Great War is one of a wide range of counter-factuals in Martin J. Gidron's *The Severed Wing* (2000). Here there is no time travel, but a magical disruption of time setting, in which divergent chronological levels interact. The allohistorical assumption in this text is that Theodore Roosevelt is elected to a third term as US president and brings the USA into the War in 1915. The War, thus, finishes earlier. Roosevelt refuses to accept a peace settlement that is punitive toward Germany. Walter Rathenau becomes Chancellor of a new Germany. A Republic of Poland has autonomy, although it is closely tied to Germany, and the Tsarist regime is maintained in Russia. There is no Bolshevik revolution (cf. 68, 139–141; 206). One of the central counterfactuals in a novel set in the late 1990s (cf. 2, 31) is the non-occurrence of the Holocaust. Anti-Semitism is rife, especially in the protagonist-narrator's native Poland (cf. 67), but Yiddish is a living language (as is Ladino in Salonika), not only in New York, and the state of Israel does not exist (Palestine is a British dominion) (cf. 9, 65, 105). However, one of the central motifs of the novel is the continual and mysterious disappearance of Jewish characters. The protagonist-narrator Janusz (a Polish Jew) constantly finds that persons whom he

---

[5] Written by an Australian author, published in the UK, but clearly oriented toward an American market.

has known suddenly, and inexplicably, vanish as if they had never been (see for instance, 44, 108, 112, and there are many other examples). At the novel's end, he realizes that he, too, will shortly be an absence. Throughout the novel, he has had dreams of the Holocaust, and in an epilogue we learn that Janusz has been killed, in the reader's reality, in a *Sonderaktion* in Poland in 1942 (cf. 199–205).

Among British allohistorical fictions of the Great War is Michael Moorcock's *A Nomad of the Streams of Time* trilogy, consisting of *A Warlord of the Air* (1971), *The Land Leviathan: A New Scientific Romance* (1974), and *The Steel Tsar* (1981). Owen Bastable, the central character, is a chrononaut, who travels into alternate times. In *A Warlord of the Air*, he falls unconscious in 1903 and wakes up in 1973. He returns to the early twentieth century, from which time he narrates his experiences. The 1973 that he experiences is untainted by the Great War, which in this reality never happened (cf. 22). The twentieth century has been one of peace and prosperity, at least by Major Powell's account. The British Empire is firmly in place. The USA has a substantial empire (cf. 24). In fact, the utopian presentation of a world without the Great War is substantially questioned in the novel, which sets up a counter utopia in the romantic socialism of a charismatic warlord (cf. 68). The novel returns to documented time and history at the end through an element of the narrational frame. The novel purports to be an account by a Michael Moorcock written in 1904 of a strange encounter with Bastable and a transcription of the story he tells him (cf. 1–6). The editor's note at the novel's end, by Moorcock's grandson, also Michael Moorcock, reveals that his grandfather died on the Somme in October 1916 (cf. 85). The author, thus, marks the importance of the Great War's absence in Bastable's account of the future.

The Great War of 1914–1918 is also markedly absent from *The Land Leviathan*, at least in terms of direct presentation in the body of the novel. However, the counter-factual hypothesis is that despite the establishment of a utopia of sorts in the early twentieth century, a destructive war breaks out in 1907 that leaves most of Europe and North America a desolate wasteland. Only in Africa (and on the Isle of Skye) has any substantial civilization survived, and the novel combines both apocalyptic and utopian motifs to suggest that things may improve through the conquests of Cicero Hood, the Black Attila. Yet, despite its absence from the central parts of the text, the Great War is a presence. The editor's grandfather's death in the War is referred to in the novel's opening sentence, as the narrational frame is established. Also, Bastable ironically wishes to return to his own time where "the threat of a major war is very remote indeed" (although, if Bastable does "turn up, then perhaps you should start worrying, for it could mean another war!") (25). *The Steel Tsar* presents yet another world. It is an account of "the Great War of 1941," a conflict largely between Britain and Japan. Our Great War is absent, although apocalypse is not. "I have passed through three alternative versions of our world," Bastable remarks, "and in each seen the most hideous destruction of civilization" (19).

All the above mentioned allofictions employ fantastic or anti-mimetic motifs and conventions. However, there is a group of allohistorical fictions relating to the Great War that works with different conventions. Although the history is counter-factual and undocumented, the texts stay within mimetic conventions. There is no time travel, no jumping to alternate universes.

The Great War is preempted in Robert Conroy's *1901* (2004). An ambitious Kaiser Wilhelm II decides to invade the USA to force the American government to relinquish some of its colonies acquired in the Spanish-American War of 1898. The Germans are simply monsters (cf. 20–22), and really might as well be predatory aliens. Overstretched and underestimating the will and resourcefulness of the Americans, ably led by Theodore Roosevelt, the Imperial German Army and Navy are defeated. Large parts of the novel are made up of descriptions of battles and military engagements of varying sizes (for example, cf. 135 following). At the novel's end a chastened but still powerful Germany decides to concentrate on Europe and preparations are underway for an ominous sounding Third Reich (cf. 398–401).

Similarly mimetic within a counter-factual assumption is Harry Turtledove's *The Great War: American Front* (1999). Once again, a Union defeat in the American Civil War is the starting point for allohistorical fiction. The novel shows the new World embroiled in the conflicts of Europe in 1914. Theodor Roosevelt is US president; Woodrow Wilson is president of the Confederate States of America. The USA is allied to Imperial Germany, the CSA to Britain, France, and the Dominion of Canada. There is much counter-historical detail as background – a Second Mexican War, manumission of slaves in the South (cf. 17–18). Custer is not killed at Little Big Horn and serves in this text as a parody of a Great War general – incompetent, drunken, self-aggrandizing (cf., for example, 49). Even more than *1901*, *The Great War: American Front* is full of battle episodes. Indeed, the narrative structure is repetitious: a single character is taken as a point of view, and an episode in the war is presented (a skirmish, an encounter with an armoured vehicle, the experience of occupation).[6]

Theodore Roosevelt recurs as a central character in Mike Resnick's counter-factual, but mimetic, short story "Over There" (1991). A heroic, now sadly out

---

[6] Despite the fact that this is by any stretch of the imagination a deeply boring novel, it is not without clever jokes, of the kind that allohistorical fiction favours. Thus the great early twentieth-century non-figurative art show, the New York Armory Show of 1913 (in the reader's world), has, in this novel, been organized in the South by a rich lady patron of the arts, for the Northern states are far too Germanic and Wagnerian to be interested in Picasso (cf. 69–74).

of date, Roosevelt raises a unit of former Rough Riders from the Spanish-American War to fight in France. They all perish in a hopeless charge against German machine guns. The story suggests that there is no place in modern war for Roosevelt's and his associates' romantic heroics.

The only British text in this category is Ian R. MacLeod's short novel *The Summer Isles* (1998). It offers a much more complex allohistorical treatment of the Great War subject matter than the three texts just considered. It is set in 1940, and the reader quickly grasps that this is a counter-factual 1940, although, as in the documented world, Disney's *Snow White* is showing in the cinema (cf. 244). Oswald Mosley is Home Secretary (cf. 236), German soldiers are serving in League of Nations forces (peacekeepers, one assumes) in Trans-Jordan (cf. 243), and the presidents of France and Germany are called De Gaulle and von Papen (cf. 286). The key event is the defeat of the Allies in the Great War in August 1918 (cf. 254). In a cleverly placed exposition, half-way through the text, the narrator, Griffin Brooke, a broken and ill man, reveals the main outline of the post-war settlement for Britain – loss of empire, expulsion from Ireland in 1923, hyper-inflation, and inept attempts by politicians called Baldwin, MacDonald, and Churchill to solve the nation's ills and malaise (cf. 263–264). This situation begets a British authoritarian movement led by one John Arthur (whom Brooke by chance and for complex reasons knows personally and well), a simple corporal (he claims) from the Great War who in a very undemagogic, but forceful manner speaks for those lost in a world of defeat and failure. His rise to power – he becomes Prime Minister in 1932 – echoes that of Hitler's in the reader's world, but is also intelligently different (cf. 269–271), except for its anti-Semitism, for the Jews in Britain are being hunted down and relocated to camps (in aim, death camps) on the bleak islands off the coast of Scotland (cf. 243, 257). Homosexuals, too, are persecuted, a policy that touches the narrator since he is a homosexual (cf. 235–237). The story material of the novel is more complex than it is necessary to outline here. Brooke resolves to assassinate Arthur, who actually turns out to be someone other than he pretends to be. Arthur is, in fact, murdered in a palace coup, and Britain is set to return to the international community at the novel's end. This text is an intelligent and moving treatment of what might have been Britain's history after the Great War, and of a much higher calibre than the other texts (by Conroy, Turtledove, and Resnick) discussed above.

The texts discussed above prompt general reflections on allohistorical fictions of the Great War:[7]

---

[7] The corpus is not complete. For example, Harry Turtledove has several other relevant pieces of allohistorical fiction.

- There is a marked presence of fantastic and anti-mimetic elements (motifs and conventions) in the texts discussed above. Time machines and the assumption of varied and alternate universes enable allohistorical fictions. Indeed, some commentators would, therefore, set these texts within a different category (cf. Rodiek 42), yet several texts operate within mimetic conventions.
- Allohistorical fictions problematize clear distinctions among supragenological categories of texts. Although this is not exclusively related to allohistorical fiction about the Great War, it is of some moment. Thus, Gidron's *The Severed Wing* proposes a counter-factual history of the twentieth century, and, to a considerable degree, adheres to mimetic conventions. These conventions are, however, disrupted by the mysterious and fantastic disappearances that bedevil the narrator's experiences. Paradoxically, however, these fantastic disruptions serve to institute the primacy of the documented world: the Holocaust took place; a great deal of the action is impossible. A return to the documented (and mimetic) *via* the fantastic is also engineered through time travel in *The Company of the Dead* and *Bring the Jubilee*. Similarly, borders between categories are blurred by texts like *The Summer Isles*. The world is non-mimetic, for it is ultimately as different from the reader's documented world as is Tolkien's Middle Earth, but that world in *The Summer Isles* adheres scrupulously to mimetic conventions.
- Although the Great War is present as a topic of some importance in the texts discussed, in many of them it is secondary – to the American Civil War, to the Holocaust, even to the sinking of the Titanic (although the two are connected in *The Company of the Dead*). In Moorcock's trilogy, the non-occurrence of the Great War is of some importance in the alternate universe of *The Warlord of the Air*, but is secondary to the novel's utopian agenda and frankly escapist adventure-story conventions. The same is even more true of the two subsequent parts of the trilogy. Only MacLeod's *The Summer Isles* takes the Great War and its counter-factual outcome as the starting point and central element in its story material.
- The question of quality is a vexed one in literary studies. However, it is hard for me not to draw attention to what appears to be the relatively low quality of much allofiction of the Great War. *The Great War: American Front* is dismally repetitive, the dullest kind of testosterone-loaded *récit de bataille*. *1901* is geopolitically idiotic (an incident in Venezuela perhaps *à la mode de* 1902–1903, but occupy Manhattan? – even the most hubristic Wilhelmine general or admiral would say no). Moorcock's texts are irresistibly entertaining inverted stories of colonial adventure, but not serious engagements with the subject of the Great War, or often anything else either. Of all the texts

discussed, only *The Summer Isles* focuses on the Great War in an intelligent fashion, and does so to produce a piece of fiction that is complexly disturbing and thought-provoking.

3 Allohistory and the Great War

Demandt argues that all historical accounts contain allohistorical elements, speculations as to what might have been if events had taken a different course (cf. *Ungeschehene Geschichte* 24). This can be readily seen in the hypotheticals in, as a relevant example, A. J. P. Taylor's *The First World War: An Illustrated History* (cf. 104, 109, 237, 280). However, brief speculation as to what might have happened, had the Gallipoli campaign been successful (indeed Taylor himself calls such imagining "futile," cf. 104), is on a quite different scale from the considerations of counter-factuals that Demandt himself puts forward in his books on allohistory. I wish to consider four such pieces of allohistory that relate to the Great War: J. C. Squire's *If It Had Happened Otherwise: Lapses into Imaginary History* (1932), Niall Ferguson's "The Kaiser's European Union: What If Britain Had 'Stood Aside' in August 1914" and "A Virtual History, 1646–1996" (both 1997), Robert Cowley's "The What Ifs of 1914" (1999), and Alexander Demandt's "Was wäre geschehen, wenn die Schüsse von Serajewo am 28. Juni unterblieben wären" ("What would have happened if the shots at Sarajevo on 28 June had not happened?") (in *Ungeschehene Geschichte*) and "Der erste Weltkrieg entfällt" ("There is no First World War") (in *Es hätte auch* …). As with the novels discussed in section 2 of this essay, the corpus of texts is not comprehensive. However, it is broad enough to permit a discussion of Great War allohistory.[8]

Squire's collection of essays, with contributions by Hilaire Belloc, G. K. Chesterton, Ronald Knox, André Maurois, H. A. L. Fisher, Harold Nicholson, and others, is described by Ritter as "der Beginn der literarischen Beschäftigung mit dem Kontrafaktischen" ("the beginning of literary concern with the counter-factual") (17). It blurs a distinction between allofiction and allohistory. The contributions are usually described as essays, several are written by historians, and the volume's evident intent is to contribute toward intelligent historical debate, as

---

[8] It could be argued that I am inconsistent here in including Demandt's hypotheses, which are in German, when I have only written of English-language allohistorical fiction. I would justify my inclusion of Demandt on three grounds. First, my essay is a preliminary discussion of an under-researched area, and as much relevant material as possible is necessary. Second, Demandt's discussion is very interesting. Third, one simply cannot write about allohistory without referring to Demandt. He is one of the outstanding authorities in the field.

much as to divert the reader (despite the self-deprecating subtitle), but several are presented in past simple narrative form, and, thus, are like allohistorical fictions. None of the essays directly addresses the Great War, although the absence of that conflict, its falling out of history, underlies two of the pieces in the volume: Emil Ludwig's "If the Emperor Frederick Had Not Had Cancer" (223–248), and Winston Churchill's "If Lee Had Not Won the Battle of Gettysburg" (175–196).

The first addresses one of the interesting 'what if's' of recent German history. Wilhelm I's son Friedrich succeeded to the Imperial throne in 1888. Already a very sick man, he died in that year, and was succeeded in his turn by his son, who became Kaiser Wilhelm II. The *Dreikaiserjahr* is frequently seen as a turning point in recent German history. If Friedrich III had survived, would the Reich have evolved into something much more like a constitutional monarchy? Would the tensions of the pre-1914 period have been avoided?[9] Ludwig assumes they would have been, and sets out how. Friedrich does not die in 1888, and in alliance with Bismarck avoids colonial adventures and fleet building. After Bismarck's death, indeed, he chooses to become a constitutional monarch like his grandmother, Queen Victoria. He dies on 1 August 1914. "The whole world," Ludwig writes, "mourned this wise prince. His successor, still in his handsome prime at fifty-five [Wilhelm II], ascended the throne with quiet dignity and was loyally welcomed by Europe" (248).

The non-occurrence of the Great War is similarly a central consequence of the 'what if' in Churchill's inventive rewriting of British, European, and North American history. If the South wins the Civil War, North and South become separate states. Gladstone becomes a Conservative, D'Israeli a Radical. A near war between the states is averted by Balfour's, Roosevelt's, and Wilson's formation of the English-speaking Association. The intervention of the Association in 1914 puts a stop to the build-up of aggression and averts that war too. In 1932 the German Emperor Wilhelm II convenes a Pan-European Conference in Berlin in order to advance a "project of European unity" (cf. 195).[10] The shadow of a Great War averted is very clear at the piece's end (cf. 195–196).

Ferguson's essay "The Kaiser's European Union: What If Britain Had 'Stood Aside' in August 1914" is a very different piece of allohistorical writing. In a sober and carefully documented manner it weighs up the inevitability of the 1914–1918

---

9 This is still a topic of some interest. See Joachim Mohr's essay in *Spiegel Geschichte* 3 (2013): 56–59.

10 It is worth remarking at this point that the reader will note in what follows, and indeed in what has gone before, in this essay that the outcome of a counter-history of 1914 is frequently a German-dominated or guided European union. This makes one wonder about those who question the predictive power of literature and history.

conflict. It considers, *inter alia*, the possibility of an Anglo-German entente in the early twentieth century, the role of Francophiles and Germanophobes in British ruling circles, and the substantial nature or otherwise of German pre-War ambitions. The counter-factual that Ferguson introduces (only at the end of the essay, it should be noted) is a delay in sending the British Expeditionary Force to France in the early days of the conflict. "If the BEF had never been sent, there is no question that the Germans would have won the war," Ferguson writes (276). Even if it had arrived only a little later, Paris would have fallen. Britain would still have pursued the war against Germany but without committing troops to a European bloodbath. Naval pressure would have brought about a compromise peace that would have left Germany dominant in Europe – "continental Europe would have been transformed into something not unlike the European Union we know today – but without the massive contraction of British overseas power entailed by the fighting of two world wars" (278).

In the Afterword to *Virtual History*, "A Virtual History, 1646–1996," Ferguson places a different course and outcome of the Great War (cf. 426–429) in an extended and highly inventive allohistory of three hundred years. The BEF is not sent to France; Germany wins and establishes a European Union (cf. 427). In one of the mischievous games that allohistorians can play, Ferguson sets up the real course of events as a counter-factual counter-factual: the British do intervene; a war of attrition ensues; everybody ends up unhappy: "Happily, the economic catastrophe of a long war did not become a reality" (429). According to Ferguson's chronicler, Anglo-German trouble lies ahead in the 1930s, but at least the insanity of our 1914–1918 was averted.

In "The What Ifs of 1914," Robert Cowley approaches the subject from a military historian's point of view. He sets up a range of counter-factuals. The BEF is not sent. The Germans win on the Marne (by actually following the Schlieffen Plan, rather than improvising). The French do not discover the revised German plans for encircling Paris. Sir John French panics and withdraws his troops from the line in September 1914. The Germans win the first Battle of Ypres. In a conclusion, Cowley imagines what the world would have been like without the actuality of 1914–1918. He has already suggested how a German victory early in the war could have benefitted Britain (the postponement of imperial decline, no indebtedness to the USA, incomparably fewer casualties) (cf. 267), and France (reparations certainly, but also not the slaughter of actual history, perhaps also a shock to reform French society and economy, no occupation in a second conflict) (cf. 277–278). He also proposes no Russian Revolution, and no sudden rise to world power of the USA (cf. 286). He suggests Alain Fournier, Wilfred Owen, and Ernest Hemingway might have gone on to write something more or other than they did (cf. 287).

In his brief essay in *Ungeschehene Geschichte*, "Was wäre geschehen, wenn die Schüsse von Serajewo am 28. Juni unterblieben wären?," Demandt suggests – oddly in a book about allohistory – that a conflict around 1914 was almost inevitable, given the tensions between the great powers and contemporary cultural assumptions about war (cf. 119–121). However, he also suggests that if reason had only prevailed in 1914 or thereabouts, then some developments like those indicated by Ferguson would have occurred, although Demandt goes beyond them. There would have been no Second World War. Colonial and post-colonial history might have been different and more benign. The Habsburg Empire might have evolved into a commonwealth. The Hohenzollerns, rendered democratically acceptable, might have stayed on the German throne (cf. 121).

Demandt returns to an allohistorical discussion of 1914–1918 in "Der erste Weltkrieg entfällt," chapter 14 of *Es hätte auch anders kommen können*. He spends the first ten pages of this seventeen-page essay showing that the outbreak of war around 1914 was almost inevitable (cf. 189–198), one-and-a-half pages to show how hard it would have been to conclude a peace in the middle of the war (cf. 200–201), and two pages to show how it is difficult to imagine the treaty of Versailles other than it was (cf. 204–205). However, he does suggest some counter-factuals: Germany's not mobilizing against Russia allows the Russians to 'liberate' some of their Pan-Slavic brethren. Tannenberg is avoided and so is the Russian Revolution (cf. 199). The USA does not intervene in the War. An *Erschöpfungsfriede* (peace of exhaustion) is concluded among the combatants circa 1916 (cf. 202–203). In fact, Demandt doubts whether even that would have averted a later conflict similar to that of 1939–1945, but he is prepared to consider such an eventuality. It takes a similar form to that proposed in *Ungeschehene Geschichte*: parliamentary control of the monarchy in Germany, the evolution of the Habsburg Empire into something like the British Commonwealth (cf. 203). However, in this essay, Demandt really suggests pious hopes more than concrete possibilities. If only people could have foreseen what was to come out of the catastrophe of 1914, they would have behaved differently (cf. 205).

The texts discussed above prompt some general reflections on allohistories of the Great War:

- From the beginning of allohistorical speculation in the twentieth century, the Great War has cast a shadow. Two of the essays in Squire's collection, in fact, seem to have been written with an imagined avoidance of that war in mind. Ferguson and Cowley find fruitful ways of imagining 1914–1918 differently. Indeed, for a military historian like Cowley, the opening months of the conflict alone provide sufficient counter-factual possibilities. As opposed to the work of many writers of allohistorical fiction, the Great War can take central importance in the work of allohistorians.

- The point that many writers about allohistory (and allohistorical fiction) make about the palimpsest-like nature of allohistorical writing (the actual always shows, and indeed, must show, through the counter-factual, cf. Rodiek 46) is well illustrated in historians' discussions of possible other outcomes and developments related to the Great War. The European Union is a favoured outcome (Ferguson, Cowley).[11] Indeed, Ferguson, Cowley, and Demandt all see some conflict around 1914 as almost unavoidable. Further, Demandt – a vigorous promoter of the virtues of allohistory – finds it difficult to see that *es hätte anders kommen können* (it could have been different) without a lot of wishful thinking. Actuality seems very stubborn with regard to 1914–1918.
- The matter of quality is worth returning to here. If many treatments of the Great War in allohistorical fiction are imaginatively impoverished, trivializing, and slight, the opposite is true of the work of historians. Ferguson's writing is provocative and stimulating; his prose is lucid and resourceful. Demandt is a major scholar whose reflections on allohistory are elegantly organized and forcefully expressed.

4 Conclusion

One of the less discussed, but interesting, ways of remembering the Great War is through allohistorical fiction and allohistory. The 1914–1918 War is a sporadic but recurrent topic in allohistorical fiction, although the Great War is often peripheral within such texts. Allohistory, however, does address the Great War as a central subject on a level with other important historical turning points. While allohistory relating to the Great War is of some substance, the same cannot be said of some Great War allohistorical fiction. It is predominantly marked by fantastic and anti-mimetic motifs (thus, trivializing the historical real, as Rodiek argues, cf. 43) or is often repetitive and uninventive. A comparison with the allohistorical fiction of the Second World War is instructive. It is of a higher quality and there is much more of it (cf. Ritter 21–22). It is striking that it appears to be difficult to imagine a different Great War. One can only speculate on the reasons for this. Is the trauma of 1914–1918 still too acute to be treated in fiction? Does the slaughter of the Western Front, for example, simply defy imaginative reworking? Is it very hard to imagine a future-present that does not involve Flanders fields (Demandt's attempts to do so suggest this)? Do we even not wish to? However it is understood, allohistorical fiction and allohistorical treatments of the Great War form an

---

[11] For Ludwig and Churchill, this would count as prediction, not adherence to the actual.

intriguing and little-known aspect of post-memory of the conflict, and one that merits further research and analysis.

References

Churchill, Winston S. "If Lee Had Not Won the Battle of Gettysburg." *If It Had Happened Otherwise*. Ed. J. C. Squire. 175–196.
Conroy, Robert. *1901*. New York: Ballantine, 1995.
Cowley, Robert. "The What Ifs of 1914: The World War That Should Never Have Been." *What If? Military Historians Imagine What Might Have Been*." Ed. Robert Cowley. London: Pan, 2001. 261–291.
Demandt, Alexander. *Ungeschehene Geschichte – Ein Traktat über die Frage: Was wäre geschehen, wenn …?* Göttingen: Vandenhoeck & Ruprecht, 2001.
Demandt, Alexander. *Es hätte auch anders kommen können: Wendepunkte deutscher Geschichte*. 4th ed. Berlin: Propyläen Verlag, 2011.
Ferguson, Niall. "The Kaiser's European Union: What If Britain Had 'Stood Aside' in August 1914?" *Virtual History: Alternatives and Counterfactuals*. Ed. Niall Ferguson. London: Penguin, 2011. 228–280.
Gidron, Martin J. *The Severed Wing*. Livingston, Alabama: Livingston Press at the University of West Alabama, 2000.
Helbig, Jörg. *Der parahistorische Roman: Ein literarhistorischer und gattungstypologischer Beitrag zur Allotopieforschung*. Frankfurt am Main et al.: Peter Lang, 1988.
Kowalski, David J. *The Company of the Dead*. London: Titan Books, 2012.
Leiber, Fritz. "Catch That Zeppelin!" *The Mammoth Book of Alternate Histories*. Eds. Ian Watson and Ian Whates. London: Constable and Robinson, 2010. 173–194.
Ludwig, Emil. "If the Emperor Frederick Had Not Had Cancer." *If It Had Happened Otherwise*. Ed. J. C. Squire. 233–248.
MacLeod, Ian R. *The Summer Isles*. *Breathmoss, and Other Exhalations*. Urbana, Illinois: Golden Gryphon Press, 2004.
Mohr, Joachim. "Das Dreikaiserjahr." *Spiegel Geschichte* 3 (2013): 56–59.
Moorcock, Michael. *The Warlord of the Air*. London: Ace Books, 1971.
Moorcock, Michael. *The Land Leviathan*. London: Quartet, 1974.
Moorcock, Michael. (ed.) *England Invaded: A Collection of Fantasy Fiction*. London: W. H. Allen, 1977.
Moorcock, Michael. *The Steel Tsar*. London: Granada, 1981.
Moore, Ward. "Bring the Jubilee." *The Best Alternate History Stories of the Twentieth Century*. Ed. Harry Turtledove and Martin H. Greenberg. New York: Ballantine, 2001. 152–249.
Pfister, Manfred, and Monika Lindner. "Alternative Welten: Ein typologischer Versuch zur englischen Literatur." *Alternative Welten*. Ed. Manfred Pfister. Münchener Universitätsschriften 12. Munich: Wilhelm Fink Verlag, 1982. 11–38.
Resnick, Mike. "Over There." *Roads Not Taken: Tales of Alternate History*. Ed. Gardner Dozois and Stanley Schmidt. New York: Ballantine, 1998. 80–111.

Ritter, Hermann. "Kontrafaktische Geschichte: Unterhaltung versus Erkenntnis." *Was wäre wenn: Alternativ- und Parallelgeschichte: Brücken zwischen Phantasie und Wirklichkeit*. Ed. Michael Salewski. Stuttgart: Franz Steiner Verlag, 1999. 13–42.

Rodiek, Christoph. *Erfundene Vergangenheit: Kontrafaktische Geschichtsdarstellung (Uchronie) in der Literatur*. Annalecta Romanica. Heft 57. Frankfurt am Main: Vittorio Klostermann, 1997.

Sokołowska-Paryż, Marzena. *Reimagining the War Memorial, Reinterpreting the Great War: The Formats of British Commemorative Fiction*. Newcastle upon Tyne: Cambridge Scholars, 2012.

Squire, J. C., ed. *If It Had Happened Otherwise*. London: Sidgwick and Jackson, 1972 [1932].

Taylor, A. J. P. *The First World War: An Illustrated History*. Harmondsworth: Penguin, 1966.

Turtledove, Harry. *The Great War: American Front*. New York: Ballantine, 1998.

Zgorzelski, Andrzej. "On Differentiating Fantastic Fiction: Some Supragenological Distinctions in Literature." *Poetics Today* 5. 2 (1984): 299–307.

Phil Fitzsimmons and Daniel Reynaud
Comics/Graphic Novels/Bandes Dessinées and the Representation of the Great War

One of the ways in which the Great War has been "textually packaged" (Budarick and King 355) as 'memory constructs' is within graphic novels, or 'comics,' as they have been popularly known in English, or 'bandes dessinées' in French. Before unpacking an understanding of how a selection of current British and French graphic novels actively portrays wartime experience, it is important to place the notion of the genre within its current academic currents. The terms 'comics,' 'graphic novels,' and 'bandes dessinées,' and what they each represent are a matter of continuing academic debate (Patrick 51), evidenced by the lack of a single comprehensive term to cover the genre or series of genres. While comics have been in the centre of the ongoing debate over the dividing line between high and low literature, there is also a secondary, overarching discussion which has spilled over into the understanding of what is a graphic novel, namely the discussion in the field of literary criticism on how a novel can actually be defined.

The French term 'bande dessinée' (hereafter referred to as BD) has been labelled, somewhat tongue-in-cheek, by leading BD artists Morris (Maurice de Bevere of *Lucky Luke* fame) and Pierre Vankeer as *'le neuvième art'* (the ninth art) (cf. Morris and Vankeer; Lacassin). While this may be seen as a continuance of the debate from an Anglophone perspective, from the French cultural context it represents the high respect which the genre has in French publishing, with albums usually issued in hard cover and full colour, and distributed by the most reputable book shops. BD is a diverse genre with many sub-genres, from popular entertainment albums like *Tintin*, *Lucky Luke* and *Asterix* to serious works of art-literature, all of which reflect French approaches to a text as requiring "overlaying, reading across, reading through" (McCarthy 33). In the French imagination, therefore, BDs can participate in the realm of high culture.

By contrast, in the English-speaking world, the name 'comics' is applied to the graphic novel genre despite the significant differences between the text types. The 'comic' genre implies childish entertainment and superficiality. By and large comics, like graphic novels, have not been held in high esteem in Anglo-American society, with the former often being attributed the derogative status of low culture art, and its target audience usually being considered as children and the marginally literate. The product is typically sold in cheap paper editions, often with no colour apart from the cover. The flimsy format is often seen to suggest an ephemeral life span suited to disposable, trashy literature. While this is not the case, "as comics were not originally intended for kids" (Daniels 225), the general public perception is that they lack any form of substance, and are related to childhood and adolescent memories in much the same way as fluffy toys and action figures. As we see it, this could not be further from actuality.

1 Theoretical Overview

While more recently comics have been recognized as a mode in which multiple levels of narration occur, more importantly they also represent a polyvalent curation of personal and social memories (Fitzsimmons and Lanphar). As we see it, graphic novels in particular represent a "natural container" of social memories (Fentress and Wickham 50) typical of what Hugo von Hofmannsthal termed the "dammed up force of our mysterious ancestors within us" (qtd. in Olick and Robbins 106). We would also contend that graphic novels also represent the rupturing of this mythic dam and the subsequent visually symbolic pooling of memory by "amplification through simplification" (McLeod 30). While exophoric in nature (cf. Whitlock; Groensteen), Nora believes that the current forms of visual facets form an extraordinary authoritative 'collective memory' presence in current cultures as they naturally resonate with our "intensely retinal and televisual memory" (17). While illusory, collective social memory exists; when it comes to analysis, the crucial set of questions are who wants what to be remembered, and why?

It is also our belief that in order to answer the previous questions, graphic novels have the reading potential to represent a much deeper symbolic presence. Not only are they representations of "alarm and emergency, an acute crisis of self-preservation" (Menninghaus 1), they are also "apophatic metaphors of socio-cultural transgression" (Fitzsimmons 100). In each frame, page and text the symbols and flow of symbols are designed to unsettle a reader-viewer as they are deeply "troubling stories, [...] ones that touch the core of what it means to be human" (Niemi and Ellis 8, 10). In other words, the visual facets and textual strata as both explicit and subtextual references resonate with what Dickstein calls "our secret fascination with deformity and the grotesque" (68). Layered on top of these elements is the notion that they are also carriers of socio-cultural memory often related to an author's and culture's deepest repressed fears.

Therefore they represent one form or space for expression regarding the "abject" (Kristeva, *Powers of Horror* 2), which in broad terms represents both the individual and cultural loathing and fascination with the 'other,' or the 'stranger.' The 'other' has a spectrum of interconnected representation ranging from anything that is expelled from the body through to the monsters and monstrous that inhabit our dreams, texts and cultural manifestations. As Menninghaus contends, these manifestations are the "unaesthetic," a direct outcome of our tacit awareness of our instability and disconnected nature of the 'self' (1). Any interaction with the abject can be realized as:

> a massive and sudden emergence of uncanniness [which] now harries me as radically separate, loathsome. Not me. Not that. But not nothing, either. A 'something' that I do not recognize as a thing. A weight of meaninglessness, about which there is nothing insignificant, and which crushes me. On the edge of non-existence and hallucination, of a reality that, if I acknowledge it, annihilates me. (Kristeva, *Powers of Horror* 2)

Before turning to another critical element of how the reading of graphic novels functions, it is important to reiterate that graphic novels both represent a clear example of the numerous 'crises of self and culture' that currently exist in the Western World, and a generational reaction related to existential angst. Through a visual-textual interplay, these texts negotiate the personal and cultural liminal, or "the difference within" (Bhabha 19) through an aestheticisation of the unaesthetic. Thus, graphic novels allow the monstrous, grotesque and abject to become 'threshold conductors between outside and inside' (Williams 17) as part of humanity's indefinable sense of identity.

While graphic novels shake, sift and separate notions of identity, and therefore break the "container of memories" (Kristeva, *Nations Without Nationalism* 187), like all narrative they also act as a synchronous mechanism of cultural and personal memory formation. While acknowledging the complexity of memory, graphic novels – as forms of biography – provide an entrée, albeit an often shattered one, not only into the lives of others, but as Goodnow suggests they also engender emotional responses which act as new boundaries of safety and reflection (cf. *Kristeva in Focus*). McAfee believes that in this process of reflection, a personal and cultural reconstruction is generated. In other words, "the politics of memory is opened, renewed and shared" (106). More importantly, the dark elements of existence are the ones "that stick, [...] and allow them to surface in memory and writing" (McAfee 106).

The graphic novel as a genre sits nicely in the space between the novel and the cinema, freely borrowing from the strengths of both as convenient to its purposes. Like the novel it can use written text, authorial comment and dialogue, and like film it uses images to communicate what words cannot say. It does not have the limitation of being ruthlessly linear like the cinema for, like a novel, it permits the reader to flip back at any point. This gives the graphic novel a unique representational capacity through a dynamic relationship between traditional text and a sequence of images. This kind of flexibility makes it a potent genre, especially in conceiving representations of the Great War.

Three representative texts have been selected for analysis. The first is *The Forgotten Five* (2004), a volume from the British 'Commando Comics' series. The anonymous author has created a story of a British officer and three of his men accidentally left behind upon the evacuation of Anzac Cove at Gallipoli on 20 December 1915, rescued by the extraordinary heroics of an Australian soldier also left behind. The second text selected for study is the French-language *L'Ambulance 13* (2010–2013) in four albums (with the last due for release in 2014), which tells the story of a young French doctor, Louis-Charles Bouteloup, from an aristocratic family who is assigned to the front in January 1916. The third text addressed is Jacques Tardi's classic *C'était la guerre des tranchées* (1993) (English edition: *It Was the War of the Trenches*, 2010). This book is a collection of slice-of-life vignettes, without an overarching narrative. It is however dominated by the story of Binet, which opens the book and forms its longest and most visually explorative section, but it also contains sections of textual exposition, where Tardi explains his purpose, methods or provides background information on the scenarios he creates.

These three texts represent a wide spectrum of remembering the Great War in the genre of the graphic novel, spanning from a simultaneous representation and rejection of the abject (*The Forgotten Five*), an acknowledgement of its presence as part of a mix of concepts and emotions (*L'Ambulance 13*), to a total commitment to representing the abject with maximum power (*C'était la guerre des tranchées*). Their range suggests the capacity of the genre of comics/BDs to create a memory of the Great War in a sophisticated variety of ways, according to the purposes of the authors, and to represent different realisations or resistances to the theoretical perspectives outlined above.

2 *The Forgotten Five*: The Great War as Superficial Glamorous Heroics

The Forgotten Five operates both in acceptance and denial of the abject. At a surface level it creates strangers who represent the abject, but at a thematic level it refuses to admit its existence, instead glorifying the characters and their actions in simplistic heroic terms, and maximizing national stereotypes, while paying lip service to modern anti-war notions or any concept of the horror of war. The text is representative of traditional popular British comics, published as part of the Commando Comics series (now officially titled Commando Action and Adventure) from D. C. Thomson publishing, which has been in continuous publication since 1961. While the focus is usually on British heroes, it has occasionally published comics with heroes from the USA, the Commonwealth, the Soviet Union and even from Britain's wartime enemies. It consciously posits itself in the 'Boys' Own' tradition of British publishing, "of thrilling tales of heroism, action, adventure, and pluck in the face of insurmountable odds," a format which dates back to the mid-nineteenth century, offering without any suggestion of irony "more edifying reading matter for younger readers than the lurid thrills to be found in the cheap, mass produced 'penny dreadful' magazines." The stories featured characters which Commando sees itself as heir to: "plucky young chaps doing their best, Western lawmen protecting law-abiding folks, square-jawed detectives solving fiendish mysteries, courageous pioneers blasting off into science fiction dramas, and jolly good sports who won through by playing fairly – in short, real ripping yarns!" (Commando Comics I). D. C. Thomson, a major publisher of this genre, had five very successful serials running between the world wars, even if changing tastes and competition from the USA and from other media cut the market. While other comics gradually faded away, however, Thomson's war comics series, Commando, found an enduring audience, remaining the only comics that D. C. Thomson continues to publish. Originally issued at two a month, this soon increased to four, and in 1971 to eight, where it remains today (Commando Comics II). It is one of the few successful mainstream comics publications out of the UK today, providing interesting representations of the Great War for popular audiences from a British perspective. In effect, the war setting is a convenient way of addressing the publisher's theme of noble men in action, rather than an attempt to address issues pertaining to the war in any serious way.

The Forgotten Five was originally published in 2004 as Commando 3729. It was republished in 2010 as an episode in *Anzacs at War*, a compilation of twelve Commando Comics of Australians and New Zealanders at war edited by George Low, with stories from the New Zealand Land Wars to Vietnam. Nine are set in World War Two, the most common conflict for Commando Comics. The text is in a typical format, with a standard 135 frames over sixty-eight 7 x 5 ½" pages published in black and white on cheap newsprint.

The characters follow a simple and predictable pattern. The harsh British Lieutenant Trevayne is a stickler for petty rules, and a treacherous coward until his dramatic change at the end of the story, which leads to his heroic and redemptive death. The three British soldiers, Norm, Alf and Frank, are decent, honourable types but lack much differentiation or initiative. They need constant rescuing and leading from the Australian, Sergeant Baker. The latter is the clichéd bushman-Anzac, constructed as an outsider to British military traditions while embodying in extreme form the virtues of the Australian soldier: tough, irreverent, practical, battle-hardened, and capable of impossible physical feats. Having spent two nights trapped in the open, exposed to the elements of a Gallipoli winter without food and water, he then leads the four other men over the course of several more days and nights, with only the rations of two Turks to share between them, leading three attacks on Turks, then swimming in freezing waters and repeatedly diving to free a lifeboat from a sunken ship for the men to escape in. His distinctive identity as an outsider is in part constructed by the use of much 'Aussie' slang ("cobbers," "flamin' idiot," "strewth," "Pommie," "crikey," "mate," "fair dinkum"), but notably lacking the profanity for which the typical Australian was famous. In a nod to modern sensibilities about war violence, Baker offers a token apology for bayoneting a Turk ("sorry mate, this is war"), which is as close as the text comes to exploring the moral issues of war. Putting the simple line in the mouth of its character offers a superficial moral defence of justifiable violence without having to explore it in any more detail. None of the British or Australian characters exhibit any complex emotions about their situation: it is either simple fear or heroic determination.

The presence of strangers in the text fits the definition of the abject, but only at a superficial level. Nothing is done to engage the reader with the Turks as strangers; they are drawn smaller with darkened faces, denying them any individuality or positive existence, as the audience is not intended to identify or sympathise with them. Baker, the other stranger, has his 'strangerliness' enhanced by the text, as it is a key theme of the story that Baker is a hero precisely because he is Australian rather than British. The artwork for him is in classic cartoon heroic terms, with the largely realistic art work mildly distorted in its proportions for the hero, portrayed in strong lines, square-jawed visage and an imposing physique, and seen frequently from a low angle for added emphasis. By naturalising the stranger as the hero, *The Forgotten Five* ironically turns the British characters into outsiders.

The plot is equally simplistic and unrealistic. In the best Anzac tradition of mythicising British incompetence, Baker's unit is ordered by senior officers into a hopeless attack on purely speculative military grounds, while Trevayne attempts to avoid being sent to a dangerous position, then runs at the slightest provocation, leading to the deaths of all but three of his men. Baker is able to resolve all problems facing him: the opposing Turks are killed to a man in each of the three battle encounters, and the end of the story neatly resolves everything by having Trevayne sacrifice his life to allow the others to escape, and having all four escapees survive the rest of the war. The vapidity of characterisation of the three British soldiers renders them close to sheep-like anonymity, while the odious Lieutenant Trevayne is alienated from reader sympathy until his final dramatic turn-around.

While superficially encompassing the notion of the 'other' or outsider, at a deeper level *The Forgotten Five* refuses or resists the theoretical aspects concerning graphic novels outlined in section one. Niemi and Ellis' belief that comics are designed to unsettle is undermined; or at least if *The Forgotten Five* is unsettling it is in the direction of denying the dominant British literary and historical tradition of representing the Great War as an unmitigated disaster and horror, instead making it conventionally heroic, populated with glamorous protagonists. It makes no attempt at 'touching the core of what it means to be human.' Rather, its failure to do so is what gives it a 'deeply troubling' dimension (Niemi and Ellis 8, 10). Similarly, Kristevan notions of the loathsomeness of the abject are ignored; instead, the fascination with the abject is constructed in purely positive terms. There is a striking absence in the text, an absence of home, of women and of any other desire, emotion or context in which the characters live. In short, the comic perfectly realises the simplistic aims of the publisher in creating a 'Boy's Own' story that would still sell in the modern era. It is strictly formulaic, which is well established by Commando Comics, and which refuses any engagement with a negative connotation of war. As a vehicle of cultural memory, *The Forgotten Five* represents an attempt to revive and preserve late nineteenth-century British values clustering on a romanticized Imperialism, constructing a memory of the Great War through a censored and sanitized portrayal in terms which represent an essentially pre-Great War version of the heroic.

3 *L'Ambulance 13*: A Complex Great War Representation

L'Ambulance 13 has been told in three volumes to date: Album 1: *Croix de Sang* (*Cross of Blood*, 2010), album 2: *Nom des Hommes* (*Name of Men*, 2012) and Album 3: *Les Braves Gens* (*The Brave Ones*, 2013). The concluding album, *Des Morts sans Nom* (*Nameless Dead*) has January 2014 as its release date. The scenario is by two writers, Patrick Cothias, one of France's most highly respected, award-winning scenarists, and Patrice Ordas, a scholar and art teacher, and a noted historical novelist. The artwork is by Alain Mounier and the colouring by Sebastien Bouet.

The story has room for considerable nuance compared to the restricted Commando format, because of the size of each album, at forty-eight pages of 170 x 190 mms (the standard French BD format), with between 7–10 frames per page. While the story acknowledges the abject, and makes it part of the theme, it also has more positive dimensions, particularly in its romantic sub-plot. The story involves a complex pattern of representing its characters as strangers as well as insiders. Bouteloup is by birth an insider, a member of France's political and social elite, but by character an outsider, as he resists the easy but false values of his father's rigid and socially orthodox world. Similarly, the aristocratic nun and nurse, Sister Isabelle de Ferlon, Baroness de Bach, is an insider by birth, but also a stranger, since she is from Alsace, the contested border provinces taken by Germany from France in 1870. Becoming a Catholic nun, she has suffered the rejection of her Protestant father and brother, who are officers in the German military. In character, she is also a stranger, insisting on adopting a non-political, non-nationalistic view in accordance with her spiritual vows, which puts her at odds with the French authorities in the polarising crucible of war. The complex situation the hero finds himself in is partly due to his self-serving politician-father, who is on the general staff of the medical corps. The son battles prejudice from his men and from superior officers, who hate his father's politics. His integrity in helping the wounded under fire wins him support from the rank and file, but gets him into trouble with his superiors, who assign him dangerous missions and accuse him of fraternising with the enemy when he negotiates a cease-fire to search for the wounded on the battlefield. Sister Isabelle saves him from the consequences of this at the front, which out-manoeuvres his enemies and has the charges quashed. This triggers her arrest on charges of espionage, because of her letters to her father and brother serving in the German army. The love between Sister Isabelle and the doctor adds tension, heightened by the pre-war attraction he had for Emilie, a lively young lady of poor origins who makes a living by sketching corpses, and whom he met in medical school. A number of flash-backs give added depth to the story, with incidences of Louis' younger brother dying of fever that could have been treated if his father had allowed it, the meeting with Emilie, the corpse sketcher, and a flashback by another character to a decadent pre-war ball at St Petersburg. At other times the story cuts from the front to other settings, particularly to the Bouteloup home where the reactions of the women are juxtaposed with those of the father, and to Emilie, who invites men to her home to draw them and offer sexual comforts.

The text draws in a number of historical personages, such as the legendary Lieutenant-Colonel Emile Driant, Marshals Joffre and Petain, and Marie Curie, and sets itself in historical events, including the opening days of the Battles of the Somme and Verdun, and Curie's mobile radiography units. The representations of soldiers encompass units of French colonials, pointing out the disjunction of Africans dying in France to uphold the power of the imperialist government which subjugated them. An American character even evokes the French assistance to George Washington during the American Revolution as a motivation for his involvement in France in 1916.

Both drawings and text indicate meticulous research. Like *The Forgotten Five*, *L'Ambulance 13* uses a great deal of slang, but to greater historical effect. Much of it is specific to the soldiers in the trenches of World War One, and is not necessarily readily comprehensible to modern French speakers. The language also includes profanity, which confronts the reader with what *The Forgotten Five* carefully avoids as it is concerned with maintaining a 'Boys' Own' reading audience. The colour palate of the albums is muted. In front-line scenes, the colours are predominantly in a sombre red-orange-black spectrum, except for the winter scenes, which are in a cold blue hue. Civilian scenes, both wartime and pre-war, are in muted pastel shades, none of which suggest a bright outlook.

The text addresses the abject, often with wit. In one early example, outside a brothel, a sergeant comments to the main character Lieutenant Bouteloup, "I smell meat." Bouteloup takes exception to the sergeant designating the whore as "meat," but the sergeant clarifies his meaning by noting that soldiers with money to spend on women, gambling and cigarettes can only mean an offensive is brewing, with high casualties expected. The representation of death is confronting, and not just on the battlefield. Bouteloup meets Emilie for the first time in a morgue, where she is practising her anatomy drawing skills. The spirited encounter between the two is all the more dramatic because it takes place around a starkly naked female corpse. In another foregrounding of the abject, Bouteloup has a clergyman attached to his unit to offer spiritual consolation, but the chaplain is so disaffected by the world and the war that his spiritual interventions are more cynical than uplifting. However, compromising its engagement with the abject is the fact that Bouteloup and a handful of other characters (especially his mother and sister, and Sister Isabelle) are presented in clear-cut moral terms. Bouteloup himself is drawn in heroic proportions, with a body too large for his head, and frequently from a low angle, which adds to the nobility which he is to represent.

As indicated previously, this text is rich in nuances in its depictions of war, and of the associated memory construction, within a 'true to actuality' visual and textual framework. At their core, these nuances convey perhaps the deepest sense of the abject, which we understand to be the concept of 'absence of the key elements or understandings of life.' Firstly, this applies to the portrayal of death and of humankind's avoidance of the one plight that all will face. All depictions of death reveal the issue of everyone wanting to die a good death, when in fact this is often not the case. These war deaths confront us with our deepest fear of our own death being a hovering in a twilight or liminal zone of loneliness, not touched in any way by intervention, or the pain brought on by an absence of care by medical staff and nakedness. *L'Ambulance 13* clearly portrays this fear of prolonged social castration within all of us, in which one is neither pronounced dead nor obviously alive. The text deals with one of the greatest points of the abject: that of being fully whole, while not fully there or acknowledged as belonging, being, or a being.

The second critical point which the abject raises in this text is the concept of the absent father. Carrying on the narrative tradition that the father represents either a physical or emotional absence, or both, and therefore perhaps represents the epitome of all evil (Fitzsimmons 101), in this text the key father figures appear as being absent in the sense of not having provided guidance regarding a sense of place or a genuine purpose in life. It is only in the darkest places of the abject that Bouteloup realizes that the nature of the truly heroic is an authentic engagement with others and a deep appreciation of self. The wasteland of war he encounters represents the social wastelands that produced the conflict in the first place. The evil other that Bouteloup is fighting is really the evil absence of love and acceptance within, or the Other Within and the ongoing socio-cultural memories which this predisposition carries and perpetuates. This evil is contrasted with the positive relationships that Bouteloup has, with the men in his unit, with Sister Isabelle and with Emily. The tension felt in the relationship with his mother and sister foregrounds the divided loyalties that the emotionally absent father evokes in the rest of the family.

4 *C'était la guerre des tranchées*/It was the War of the Trenches: The Abject, Centre Foreground

C'était la guerre des tranchées is merely one of Jacques Tardi's excursions into war literature. Such is the distinction of this highly respected and multi-award-winning artist that he has been decorated by the French State for his contribution to French culture. The thread of the album comes not from the discontinuous vignettes, but rather from the overarching theme of an anonymous, agonising death as experienced by his flawed and often unattractive protagonists, which is common to each element of the album. Unlike most other BD versions of the Great War, Tardi's lacks interest in telling a story as such; rather it is driven by a powerful anti-war ideology. Tardi creates a memory of the Great War through a number of processes. Firstly, he is motivated by stories from his grandfather. In particular, one story stands out: that of his grandfather carrying soup and bread to the trenches one night, being forced to take cover from an artillery bombardment. Burying himself in the oozing mud, he felt the hot soup soak through his uniform. On getting up, he discovered that the oozing mud was actually the intestines of a dead soldier. The horrific narrative is recounted by Tardi in words, and also occurs in three separate stories in the book. Tardi's second source is an archivist whom he consults when researching his work. The level of research is impressive, almost obsessive even, for example in checking details of how a court-martial and the ensuing execution might be conducted. The text itself mixes episodic narrative with pages of type-text expounding either the history of the war or explaining how Tardi went about his research. Finally, Tardi lists in an extensive bibliography all of the written and cinematic texts he has also consulted in the course of creating his work. This level of research is not unknown in creative representations of war; what is unusual is the scrupulous referencing at the end, and the overt lengths to which he goes throughout the album to highlight his research, which acts further to validate his representation of the war as a true and accurate record.

The abject is indeed the exclusive focus of Tardi's work. In his book, he strives to strip away any illusion of glory, redemption or value from the war, and portrays its abjectness with as much power as possible. His artwork, using heavy lines and mostly low-key tonality panels, confirms the darkness of his theme, and it is common for him to portray skeletons with eyeballs: a kind of living dead with staring eyes that accentuate the horror. While his settings are drawn for maximum realistic effect, his characters are the most cartoonish in the three texts under examination. He highlights the differences between the industrial nature of Great War warfare and the human beings sucked into it by contrasting a rigidly accurate depiction of military technology, rendered with clinically thin hard lines, with a depiction of humans which is frequently characterized by thick shapeless lines and minimal attempts at detail. Tardi tends towards caricature in his human faces, regardless of subject matter, but in his war BDs the caricature foregrounds the pathos of the abject through the dramatic contrast between the reality of the settings and the stylised, round-faced, jug-eared, button-nosed characters. Unusual for a French BD, the album is entirely in black and white, which adds to the starkness of his portrayal of the war.

The story of his grandfather's embrace of a corpse acts as a kind of parodic reversal of the sexual act, but this intimate embrace is entirely grotesque, precluding any kind of positive construct. It typifies the lack of real human emotional contact that Tardi emphasises in all the stories, not just those set at the Front but also those set in civilian life. The character of Binet in the opening story is not particularly pleasant. He does not seem to like anyone, resenting all of his co-tenants in his pre-war apartment, and appears to be alienated from everything except a desire to live and a curious attachment to discovering the fate of Faucheux, a comrade who disappeared while on a reconnaissance mission in no-man's-land. Yet despite this alienation, the reader is still able to empathise with his situation, allowing his death to have the kind of negative impact desired.

5 Conclusion

The Forgotten Five illustrates the trend of many British comics towards simplistic representations. War itself is glorified and reduced to a Manichean stereotype of heroes versus villains. However, the format suggests a lack of value in the text, being issued in an ephemeral binding that encourages disposability. There is also a seemingly outward distance with regard to signifying any profounder values than those of colonial 'rescuer' memorialization, and texts such as this appear to resist any genuine recognition of decolonisation (cf. Veracini, "Telling the End..."). On the other hand, the French texts illustrate the European tendency to use BDs as a more sophisticated literary/artistic tool, as both *L'Ambulance 13* and *C'était la guerre des tranchées* represent the war in great depth, exploring the moral dimensions of war and tying the action at the Front to social and political issues. The memories they create through their representations of the Great War are subtle, and emotionally and morally complex. As a hardcover product, they are made to endure, to be re-read, and even passed down. There is thus an issue in the nature of socio-cultural memory that each creates: one implies continued repression of our deepest fears through transient memory, the other offers a confronting visualisation of those same fears in a more permanent medium.

There are some similarities between the *The Forgotten Five* and *C'était la guerre des tranchées* in that, on a surface level, each reduces war to a single theme. *The Forgotten Five* reflects this singular motif through the 'crusader' or "crusader or rescue" (Spivak 284) trope that typifies the ongoing issue of 'empire narrative,' while the volumes of *C'était la guerre des tranchées* represent an immersion in the abject, with a constant flow among and between of "objects of disgust, loathing, and repulsion as well as envy and desire" (Grosz 81).

In all, the three texts demonstrate the various ideological uses to which comics/BDs can be used to create a memory of the Great War in modern contexts. While they also reveal the complexity of social memory creation and evolution, the spread of memory recreation embedded in each also reveals the counter discourse that is beginning to emerge regarding the echoes of a colonial past. This emergence clearly reveals that we tend to collectively forget and distance ourselves from the past, and ignore competing memories, conflicting discourses and truth factors. Texts such as these graphic novels allow us to remember the most abject aspects of humanity, and represent the shift towards authentic awareness. Thus, they enable us collectively "to remember, to mourn and to learn" (Pennycook 17).

References

Bhabha, Homi. *The Location of Culture*. New York: Routledge, 1994.
Budraick, John, and Debra Kind. "Framing Ideology in the Niche Media: The Koori Mails Construction of the Redfern Riots." *Journal of Sociology* 44. 4 (2008): 355–371.
Commando Comics War Comics I. http://www.commandocomics.com/editorial/the-memories/a-history-of-war-comics part-1. (23 April 2013).
Commando Comics War Comics II. http://www.commandocomics.com/editorial/the-memories/a-history-of-war-comics-part-2. (23 April 2013).
Daniels, Les. *Marvel: Five Fabulous Decades of the World's Greatest Comics*. New York: Henry Abrams, 1992.
Dickstein, Morris. *The Aesthetics of Fright. Planks of Reason: Essays on the Horror Film*. Metuchen, NJ: Scarecrow Press, 1984.
Fentress, James, and Chris Wickham. *Social Memory*. Oxford: Blackwell, 1992.
Fitzsimmons, Phil. "The Labyrinth, Lustrate and Liminal in *Requiem for a Beast*: The Monster Resurrected as Multi-Modality." *Monstrous Deviations in Literature and the Arts*. Eds. C. Santos and A. Spahr. Amsterdam: Rodopi Press, 2011. 95–110.
Fitzsimmons, Phil, and Edie Lanphar. "The Visual Framework of Wonder in 'Wonderstruck': Unpacking the Visual and Textual Elements in a Hybrid Graphic Novel." *7th Global Conference on Visual Literacy*. Athens, Greece, November 2013.
Groensteen, Thierry. "The Monstrator, the Recitant and the Shadow of the Narrator." Trans. Laurence Grove. *European Comic Art* 3. 1 (2010): 1–21.
Goodnow, Katherine. *Kristeva in Focus: From Theory to Film Analysis*. Oxford: Berghahn Books, 2010.
Grosz, Elizabeth. "The Body of Signification." *Abjection, Melancholia and Love: The Work of Julia Kristeva*. Eds. John Fletcher and Andrew Benjamin. London/New York: Routledge, 1990. 80–103.
Kristeva, Julia. *Powers of Horror: An Essay on Abjection*. Trans. Leon S. Roudiez. New York: Columbia University Press, 1982 [1980].
Kristeva, Julia. *Nations Without Nationalism*. New York: Columbia University Press, 1993.
Lacassin, Francis. *Pour un neuvième art, la bande dessinée*. Paris: Slatkin, 1982.
McAfee, Noelle. "Bearing Witness in the *Polis*: Kristeva, Arendt, and the Space of Appearance." *Revolt, Affect, Collectivity: The Unstable Boundaries of Kristeva's Polis*. Eds. Tina Chanter and Ewa Ziarek. Albany: University of New York Press, 2005. 96–112.
McCarthy, Tom. *Tintin and the Secret of Literature*. London: Granta, 2006.
McCloud, Scott. *Understanding Comics: The Invisible Art*. New York: Harper-Perennial, 1994.
Menninghaus, Winfried. *Disgust: Theory and History of a Strong Sensation*. Trans. Howard Eiland and Joel Golb. New York: State University of New York Press, 1999.
Morris, and Pierre Vankeer. "Neuvième Art, musée de la bande dessinée." *Spirou* 1392 (1964).
Niemi, Loren, and Elizabeth Ellis. *Inviting the Wolf In: Thinking about Difficult Stories*. Little Rock, AR: August House Publ., 2001.
Nora, Pierre. "Between Memory and History: *Les Lieux de Mémoire*." Trans. Marc Roudebush. *Representations* 26 (1989): 7–25.
Olick, Jeffery, and Joyce Robbins. "Social Memory Studies: From 'Collective Memory' to the Historical Sociology of Mnemonic Practices." *Annual Review of Sociology* 24 (1998): 105–140.

Patrick, Kevin. "In Search of the Great Australian (Graphic) Novel." *Australian Journal of Popular Culture* 1. 1 (2012): 51–66.

Pennycook, Alastaire. *English and the Discourse of Colonialism*. London: Routledge, 1998.

Spivak, Gayatri. *A Critique of Postcolonial Reason: Toward a History of the Vanishing Present*. Cambridge, MA: Harvard University Press, 1999.

Veracini, Lorenzo. "Telling the End of the Settler Colonial Story." *Studies in Settler Colonialism*. Eds. Fiona Bateman and Lionel Pilkington. London: Palgrave Macmillan, 2011. 204–218.

Whitlock, Gillian. "Autographics: The Seeing 'I' of the Comics." *Modern Fiction Studies* 52. 4 (2006): 965–979.

Williams, David. *Deformed Discourse: The Function of the Monster in Medieval Thought and Literature*. Exeter: University of Exeter Press, 2012.

Jean Anderson
What Price Justice? French Crime Fiction and the Great War

> If I am not evil, then somebody *else* must be. [...] Projecting evil onto an Other is the perfect way of exculpating ourselves from it.
>
> Damian Catani, *Evil: A History in Modern French Literature and Thought*

Some of the comfort of reading crime fiction for "escape and relaxation" (Cawelti 8) may be based on its reinforcement of the "just world" paradigm (cf. Lerner), according to which virtue is rewarded and evil punished. To varying degrees, crime writing has traditionally reinforced these beliefs: following the classic formula, readers are invited to identify with the champion of justice, the investigator, who acts as a vector for the most fundamental social values of law and order.[1] In this way, we are reassured that criminal behaviour (in others) will be detected and punished, and social order will be restored. The same principle arguably underlies declarations of war, particularly since the advent of World War I, which brought "total war": "the first of its kind, in which whole nations and not just their armed forces were locked together in struggle" (Welch 78). Each country's soldiers, but also the majority of its inhabitants, must believe in the justice of the initial declaration and ensuing acts of aggression (often qualified as essential self-defence). Additionally, as Coates comments, "When states employ force in defence of their particular interests they are justified in doing so only to the extent that, at the same time, their actions can be convincingly construed as a defence of an international order and a securing of the international common good" (127). In other words, the stakes must be seen as high, the enemy as a severely significant threat.

In the French context under discussion here, this Manichean simplification, the 'us and them' mentality, propounded in large part through the then relatively new media of newspapers and photography, was initially under rigid government control. As Villach has pointed out, newspapers published outrageous claims of French superiority in order to bolster nationalistic feeling, particularly in the

---

[1] It might be argued that the hard-boiled detective turns this model on its head, by blurring the lines between 'good' and 'evil,' standing somewhat outside the social structures he observes and at times noting the attraction of rule-breaking (via the *femme fatale*, for instance). Certainly the flawed detective is nothing new: however, these flaws generally serve to sharpen the reader's awareness of social norms, not to challenge them to the point of invalidation.

early stages of the war: German shells, bullets and gas attacks were harmless, the soldiers barbaric and cowardly, and certainly no match for the valiant, dedicated and happy *poilus*. These *bobards* [fantastic lies, tall tales], repeated in newspapers such as *Le Temps*, *Le Petit Journal*, *L'Intransigeant*, *Le Petit Parisien*, *L'Echo de Paris* and *Le Matin de Paris* resulted in what Villach calls "une hallucination collective" [a collective hallucination].[2]

Misrepresentation in the name of patriotism has been challenged by events of the later twentieth century, for the Americans, most notably, the wars in Vietnam and Iraq (cf. Fisher),[3] or for the French, Indochina and, increasingly as further details emerge since the turn of the millennium, Algeria (cf. Belhadjin). Governments lost wartime control over the media in many countries, and the resultant political cynicism has led to the same problematised idea of justice and authority that marks the French *néo-polar*, a genre which combines a crime story with social criticism (cf. Manchette); Morris suggests that the *néo-polar* is intimately connected to revisiting the dark years of retaliatory violence against French collaborators at all levels, up to and including government, following the 1939–1945 war (132).

Recent developments in Great War crime fiction series would seem to align these works with the *néo-polar* because a similar disillusionment is expressed, although specifically within the category of historical detective fiction. From a modern perspective, the literary representation of crime against the background of war becomes an arena for the exploration of complex principles of justice and retribution. As Hutton has claimed for World War II-focused crime fiction, this subgenre shares with the writing of history, among other elements, a concern with "the relationship between morality and legality; the potential difficulty in identifying clear-cut heroes and villains and the criteria by which to make such a judgment" (4).

In order to highlight the differences between what we might assume, from the examples cited by Villach, to be the ideologically naïve period of the early twentieth century and the more media-savvy new millennium, this essay will compare

---

[2] French media had been exposing political scandals since the 1880s, although not within a wartime framework (for example, the Boulanger, Panama and Dreyfus scandals): the 'just war' propaganda cited here was arguably all the more important to maintain national backing and in particular to support campaigns for the purchase of war bonds.

[3] Fisher's discussion focuses chiefly on the possibilities of waging a "just war," with an emphasis on more recent conflicts (Vietnam and after). I would argue that the well-known debate over the 'Weapons of Mass Destruction' in Iraq illustrates both the persistence of a perceived political need for this ideology of good versus evil, and the difficulty of maintaining it in the face of increased media exposure of a different reality, in particular one that draws attention to the fate of individuals (civilians, children).

French wartime and post-memory crime fiction. Beginning with a brief study of two investigator-heroes created by Gaston Leroux (Joseph Rouletabille and Carolus Herbert de Renich) I will investigate whether, in these works dating from 1917, such lead characters serve to establish a clear pattern of good and bad, hero and villain, 'us' and 'them,' arising from the wartime context.[4] Several writers of popular fiction, most notably Gustave Le Rouge,[5] contributed to Rouff's 1917–1920 "Collection Patrie," widely acknowledged as a purveyor of propagandistic patriotism, and we might reasonably expect this attitude on the part of writers to have permeated published crime fiction with a wartime setting, published during the Great War.[6] These works will be compared to historical crime fiction by contemporary authors Didier Daeninckx (*Le Der des ders*, 1984), Thierry Bourcy (*La Cote 512*, 2005), Patrick Pécherot (*Tranchecaille*, 2008) and Guillaume Prévost (*La Valse des gueules cassées*, 2010)[7] in order to explore issues of justice and criminality set against the background of moral indeterminacy experienced during trench warfare and its aftermath. How does the approach to the notion of justice of these post-memory writers and their characters compare with work published during the war years? How might comparing these recent writers with Leroux illuminate an evolution in the 'us and them' mentality, the sense of justice, and indeed the belief in a 'just world'? My analysis will focus on the following aspects: the representation of the Great War, attitudes towards the enemy, and finally the stories' *dénouements* and whether the principle of justice is (re)asserted in closing.

---

4 I would clarify here that the boundary between crime and espionage fiction is not clear-cut for this timeframe: indeed, early French crime writers often included elements we might now see as restricted to other genres (e.g. the supernatural).

5 Le Rouge's contributions are mentioned by Pécherot (see below). Although primarily known for science-fiction, Le Rouge also authored a series of crime novels featuring the millionaire American detective Todd Marvel, created in 1923. The majority of these were not published until the 1930s and since they do not feature the war period or its immediate aftermath, fall outside our period of interest. We note in passing, though, that the villains – Doctor Cornélius Klamm and Klaus Kristian – are foreigners.

6 From 1917–1920 and again from 1939–1940, in the "Collection Patrie" [Homeland Collection], publisher Frédéric Rouff put out a weekly series of short, novelised versions of real events of the war: their patriotism was extreme. Le Rouge authored three titles, including *Reims sous les obus*, 1917 [Rheims under the shells]: according to Welch, the September 1914 bombing of the cathedral in Rheims was considered "the height of German barbarism" (160).

7 Both Bourcy and Prévost have published further novels in their series; for reasons of concision this discussion will be limited to their first novels only.

1 In the Thick of It: Gaston Leroux

Although probably best-known today for his *Phantom of the Opera* (1911), Gaston Leroux (1868–1927) was also an internationally reputed crime novelist: his *Mystère de la chambre jaune* (1907) [*The Mystery of the Yellow Room* (1907)] introduced to a large readership, including one Agatha Christie, the gifted journalist-detective, Joseph Joséphin, known as Rouletabille. This young, ebullient and strongly analytical investigator featured in four volumes published between 1914 and 1918,[8] the first three of which deal principally with Russia and the Balkan War. The fourth, *Rouletabille chez Krupp* (serialized 1917–1918: *Rouletabille at Krupp's*, 2013), begins as Corporal Rouletabille, newly summoned from the trenches at Verdun, returns to save Paris from a super weapon that has fallen into the hands of the Germans. Stableford points out that the novel "warrants consideration as one of the central texts of the morale-boosting [literary] project" (7), promoted by the French government after three years of a war that had originally been predicted to be very short. The opening pages give the reader only the merest glimpse of his combat experiences: "il portait encore sur lui la boue de la tranchée" ["he still had the mud of the trenches on him"] (Leroux 319).[9] A cheerful Rouletabille quickly establishes (by the second page) the appropriate moral attitude as he arrives in the capital:

> D'autres, avant lui, étaient revenus et avaient montré une peine égoïste de revoir la ville dans sa splendeur sereine d'avant-guerre, à quelques kilomètres des tranchées. Ceux-là auraient voulu lui trouver un visage de souffrance en rapport avec leurs inquiétudes à eux, leurs angoisses, leur sacrifice. Rouletabille, lui, en concevait un singulier orgueil. [...] Et il se redressait dans sa crotte, dans ses vêtements boueux. (320)

> [Others before him had come back and shown selfish distress at seeing the city in its serene pre-war splendour, just a few kilometres from the trenches. They would have preferred to see it show a suffering face, in accord with their own concerns, their distress, their sacrifice. But Rouletabille felt strangely proud of it. [...] And he stood straighter in his filth, in his muddy clothes.]

By focalising the events in this way, Leroux ensures that a tone of patriotic heroism dominates from the beginning. There is, as a consequence, very little information supplied about the horrendous conditions in the trenches. It is not

---

[8] These are: *Rouletabille chez le Tsar*, *Le Château noir*, *Les Étranges Noces de Rouletabille* and *Rouletabille chez Krupp*.
[9] Although Brian Stableford's 2013 translation provides some interesting insights, like many English versions of popular fiction, it is an adaptation rather than a close translation. This translation, and all those following, are my own unless otherwise indicated.

the case that this brutal reality was unknown: the controversial revelations of Roland Dorgelès's *Les Croix de bois* (1915) and Henri Barbusse's *Le Feu* (1916) had already appeared in print.[10] Leroux's purpose is not to present a true picture, but rather to promote a kind of 'boys' own adventure' tale in which good triumphs over evil. The aim, in other words, is propagandistic rather than realistic.

Perhaps surprisingly, then, the mere fact of being German does not always equate automatically with evil: although other, minor focalisers in the novel reduce the enemy to "les Fritz" (354, 375), on one occasion Rouletabille sees beyond the stereotypes. His description of the officer supervising prisoners is sympathetic: "un gros bonhomme d'une quarantaine d'années, à figure de brique barrée d'une énorme moustache blanche [...] Pas méchant homme, doit être bon père de famille" ["a large chap in his forties, with a brick-like face crossed by an enormous white moustache [...] Not a bad fellow, most likely a good father"] (394). On the whole, however, the enemy is base and inhuman: Rouletabille's description of the Kaiser on a visit to the factory in Essen where the super weapon is being developed is, as Stableford points out, demonising (cf. 13). The Emperor has a "red face like Satan's" ("comme celui de Satan") and creates fear in the onlooker with "his hideous features" ("[s]es traits hideux") (454). He is "the soul of disaster and ruin" ("l'âme du désastre et de la ruine") (455).

Rouletabille is horrified by the destructive power of the weapon at the Kaiser's command, and by his depiction of the war as essential to defend his nation:

> Dans deux mois, si Paris n'a pas entendu notre voix d'*amitié et de pardon, Paris aura vécu!* Nous ne sommes pas des barbares! [...] Nous n'avons pas voulu cette guerre, mais puisqu'on nous l'a faite il est juste que nous en profitions pour exiger tout au moins la place nécessaire au développement de notre génie sur tous les continents! (471; italics in the original)

> [In two months, if Paris has not acknowledged our offer of *friendship and forgiveness, Paris will be no more!* [...] We did not want this war, but since it has been imposed upon us it is only fair that we take advantage of it to insist on having at least enough space to develop our genius on every continent!]

The threat is clear in the Kaiser's immoderate claims for territory, despite his protestations of friendship and the idea that Germany is merely seeking to defend itself. The super weapon that will be turned against Paris was originally developed in France for use against the Germans, who are now able to respond in kind: "l'œuvre qu'ils avaient imaginée contre nous et que nous retournons contre eux!" ["the machine they invented to use against us [Germans] and that we are turning against them!"] (472). The *bona fides* of a satanic figure is of course debatable, but

---

[10] See also van Montfrans for a discussion of pacifist writings of the period.

the fact that this enemy discourse of self-defence has a place here would seem to run counter to the one-sided view promoted by newspapers. The Manichean dialectic so evident there is clearly not universal, even in a text devoted to an anti-German cause.

In wartime, chivalry gives way to patriotism, and horrific crimes may be committed on this basis: Rouletabille beats a young woman to death in the closing pages of the novel, only to reveal in the final *dénouement* that she was in fact an impostor and a spy.[11] Far from breaking traditional codes of gallantry, the hero is confirmed as a patriot.

Another Leroux wartime novel raises the stakes by exploring the ethics of neutrality: the protagonist of the two volumes of the *Aventures effroyables du capitaine Hyx* [The Fearful Adventures of Captain Hyx] is Carolus Herbert de Renich from neutral Luxembourg. This choice serves only to strengthen the argument in favour of violence as a morally-justified response to a dishonorable enemy attack. In the second volume of the *Aventures, La Bataille invisible* (1917), Herbert is aboard a German submarine which fires twice on a merchant vessel carrying passengers, in a clear echo of the sinking of the Lusitania in May 1915.[12] The crew is not content with hitting the ship: "Nous tirions sur les naufragés!" ["We were firing on the survivors!"]. Women and children drown before the narrator's very eyes: German officers burst into applause, singing *Deutschland über alles* and drinking champagne in "ferocious delight" ("allégresse féroce"):

> Mais que dire maintenant de ces invectives, de cette bave carnassière et de ces rires triomphants sur le pont de notre sous-marin pendant qu'on se noyait devant nous? [...] Les officiers supérieurs donnaient le plus ignoble exemple du cynisme et du sadisme! (61)
>
> [But what can be said now about the insults, the predatory drooling and the triumphant laughter on the bridge of our submarine while people drowned in front of us? [...] The superior officers were setting the most ignoble example of cynicism and sadism!]

Provoked beyond reason, Herbert can no longer remain impartial and seeks revenge by strangling and drowning a young German ensign, whose youth and attractiveness are no guarantee of civilised behaviour: "un joli petit officier frais

---

[11] The figure of the woman spy is found elsewhere, for example in Le Rouge's reality-based *L'Espionne de la marine* [The Woman Who Spied on the Navy] (1917) in the Rouff series. The story of Mata Hari (executed in 1917) is no doubt also present in the popular imagination.

[12] This shocking attack, which resulted in the loss of nearly 1200 civilian lives, was instrumental in bringing the USA into the war. It was also the subject of a Rouff version, Georges Toudouze's *Le Crime du Lusitania* (1918). Leroux identifies the fictional event as an anti-French act, stating that the vessel, the *Lot-et-Garonne*, was one of the last to be built in the Gironde shipyards (*La Bataille invisible* [henceforth *BI*] 61).

comme une rose ou encore comme un petit cochon de lait" ["a pretty little officer as fresh as a rose or perhaps a little suckling pig"] (63). Over the following pages, Leroux elaborates on the theme of German wartime atrocities as a justification for Herbert's rejection of neutrality. In conversation with a Belgian doctor, the protagonist learns more about attacks by the "boches" (both speakers now use this derogatory term),[13] before the doctor's final comment that the real tragedy is that such massacres are of concern to the general public for only a few days before fading into indifference and disbelief.

Neither work fits neatly into the narrative framework of modern detective fiction: their origins as serials mean their plots have a multitude of picaresque twists and turns, mingling elements of adventure, science-fiction and spy novels. The ending of *Rouletabille chez Krupp* allows for an element of redress and return to the *status quo*, with family members falling into one another's arms, and concluding with a headline in the young reporter's newspaper: "*Si le miracle de la Marne a sauvé la France, Paris a été sauvé par le miracle de Rouletabille!*" (525; italics in the original). [*Where the miracle of the Marne saved France, Paris has been saved by the miracle of Rouletabille!*].[14] *La Bataille invisible* is less optimistic. Families are initially reunited, and a mysterious veiled Frenchwoman preaches a message of peace to French submariners and German prisoners together:

> pour que cette misère s'apaisât un jour, le jour qui ne serait point de la vengeance mais de la justice, le jour qui verrait peser dans la balance le bien et le mal, sans tricherie, sans colère et sans faiblesse! (*BI* 250)
>
> [so that this suffering might be eased one day, on a day that would not be the day of vengeance but the day of justice, the day when good and evil would be weighed in the balance, with no cheating, no anger and no weakness!]

The revelation that the woman's hands had been cut off by Germans, however, unleashes a bloody combat among her listeners: atrocities are not so easily forgotten. In terms of Herbert's personal *dénouement*, his newly refound love is now off-limits to him, since he has shot her German husband. If there is a final word here, it is surely more one of vengeance than justice, unless we are to understand that they are the same thing. What is clear, in any case, is that neither story ends

---

[13] Herbert later refers to them as "les Fritz" (*BI* 68), and another protagonist calls them "boches" (*BI* 76): both terms are used repeatedly by Herbert and others throughout the second half of the book.
[14] Maxime Vuillaume's Rouff title *Paris menacé, Paris sauvé* (1918) echoes this popular concept of the need to protect Paris at any cost.

with a sense of return to normality. Although the Rouletabille tale establishes some degree of accomplishment against enemy forces, it does not go so far as to proclaim total victory (arguably difficult to do in a work published in 1917), and the Herbert story ends on a note of incompletion and continued hostilities, despite personal safety.

2 'Remembering' the Great War: Didier Daeninckx, Thierry Bourcy, Guillaume Prévost, and Patrick Pécherot

A number of recent authors have followed in Dorgelès's and Barbusse's footsteps in representing the Great War in literary fiction, including Sébastien Japrisot in *Un long dimanche de fiançailles* (1991) and Philippe Claudel in *Les Âmes grises* (2005). Another contemporary development has seen criminal acts committed during wartime or shortly afterwards combined into works of detective fiction: arguably, Jean (Amila) Meckert's *Le Boucher des Hurlus* (1982) and Didier Daeninckx's *Le Der des ders* (1984)[15] opened the way to this post-memory subgenre that has continued to develop over the following two decades. Alongside Daeninckx, three writers from the new millennium will exemplify this: Thierry Bourcy has now published six novels in a series featuring detective Célestin Louise, "flic et soldat" ["cop and soldier"]. Guillaume Prévost's series of five thrillers features a young returned soldier, François-Claudius Simon; and Patrick Pécherot (in much the same sociocritical, left-wing vein as Amila and Daeninckx) has also explored this literary terrain.

Meckert's pioneering crime novel is set in a village, Les Hurlus, which was wiped from the map by the war. Four children of soldiers unjustly shot for insubordination set out to avenge their fathers by tracking down the general responsible for their execution. The wrongful death of soldiers at the hands of their own officers becomes a key element for dealing with the themes of military discipline, social hierarchy (officers are from the upper classes, soldiers are often ill-equipped, through lack of education, to defend themselves) and justice.

Some such wrongs may only be tackled after the war is over. In Daeninckx's *Le Der des ders,* the action takes place in peacetime, closing after the election of

---

[15] Daeninckx's title, based on the expression "la der des ders" [the last of the last, i.e. the war to end all wars] is impossible to translate directly. Both books, along with the work of Bourcy and Pécherot, are published in Gallimard's "folio policier" series.

President Paul Deschanel in early 1920. The investigation of a postwar crime leads back to the discovery of one committed in wartime. Under attack in the trenches, Colonel Fantin de Larsaudière[16] panics and puts his soldiers at risk. Labelled a coward by one of them, he shoots his accuser point-blank, then ensures that his death is registered as an execution for desertion in the face of the enemy. Hired after the war on a pretext by the colonel, René Griffon, a private investigator and returned soldier, the narrator for almost the entire story, discovers the truth. No admirer of military rank, nor motivated by a desire for revenge, he decides to reveal all:

> Je ne faisais pas ça pour me venger de tous ces connards de gradés qui nous envoyaient à la mort cent fois par jour, leurs culs bien au chaud dans les blockhaus de l'arrière. […] Si on commençait à s'ériger en justicier de cette boucherie, il fallait décimer tout le commandement, du sous-off au maréchal et ça faisait du monde! (245–246)

> [I wasn't doing it to avenge myself on all those bastards of officers who sent us off to our deaths a hundred times a day, while they kept their arses nice and warm in the bunkers well behind the lines. […] If you started trying to right all the wrongs from that slaughter, you'd have to wipe out most of the command, from the NCOs to the top brass, and that's quite a crowd!]

When the detective is killed by an anarchist bomb and the evidence destroyed, Fantin maintains his reputation for valour in post-war French society. There is no question, then, of righting any wartime wrongs publicly.

The interest here of Daeninckx's work is that it develops a series of *topoi* that become constitutive of a subgenre: a disillusioned soldier or former soldier turned detective who is marked by his experiences. Griffon has tried to forget the war, and rejects any sense of a future patriotic duty:

> En l'espace de deux ans j'avais tenté d'oublier le quotidien de la guerre. Je voulais croire que je m'en étais sorti indemne. J'en connaissais assez qui ne vivaient que dans le souvenir de la boucherie, partants comme en quatorze pour un nouveau round... (75)

> [Over the last two years I had tried to forget what life was like during the war. I wanted to believe I had got out of it intact. I knew plenty of others who still lived only through their memories of the slaughter, as ready as they had been in 1914 to go another round...]

---

16 As the 'de' in his surname indicates, he comes from a noble, although impoverished background.

Crimes are committed by one soldier against another, often by an officer against one of his men; a cover-up under the label of desertion or cowardice leads to execution 'pour l'exemple' [to serve as an example]. The court-martialled and executed soldier, as Smith has pointed out, came to represent the "quintessential example of wartime injustice" (159). The greater subtext that accompanies these features is an indictment of the idea of war as a righteous act protecting superior values; in other words, the invalidation of the concept of a just war. Corruption within the system fundamentally undermines any idea of being on the side of right. This is a long way from the jaunty patriotism or the justifiably broken neutrality of Leroux's heroes.

Guillaume Prévost's *La Valse des gueules cassées* [Waltz of the Broken-Faced Men] also uses a civilian setting, this time in the immediate postwar period, in a scenario not unlike that of Daeninckx's *Der des ders*. The protagonist-investigator, François-Claudius Simon, is a newly qualified police inspector in early 1919, still affected by a war wound to the head. His immediate superior, Chief Inspector Robineau, is a French Sherlock Holmes, a war hero renowned for his analytical skills and his political ambitions. Together, they investigate a series of murders in which the victims' faces have been mutilated, perhaps in imitation of the "gueules cassées," soldiers returned from the war with serious facial injuries.[17]

Despite his inexperience, Simon traces these crimes back to his superior, who has killed several men in an attempt to prevent the revelation that the 'heroic' conduct for which he was awarded a *Croix de guerre* medal was in fact a cover-up for cowardly behaviour. Robineau confesses to Simon, but attempts to justify his behaviour, both in the wartime episode and afterwards:

> Je m'étais engagé, oui, je désirais ardemment défendre mon pays! La patrie par-dessus tout! Mais ce jour-là [...] j'ai eu la trouille [...] Je ne pouvais tout de même pas me laisser salir pour avoir eu peur une fois dans ma vie, non? (273–274)

> [I had signed up, yes, because I was burning to defend my country! My homeland above everything else! But that day [...] I was scared [...] I couldn't just let my name be sullied because for once in my life I had been afraid, could I?]

Although the physical side of the war is largely reduced to a series of nightmarish memories that trouble the protagonist, there are multiple reminders of its brutality in the presence of war amputees ("mutilés de guerre"), both in daily life and as encountered on a visit to see the "gueules cassées" in hospital. More importantly,

---

[17] The "gueules cassées" are another recurring theme of representing the First World War: a number of documentary and fictional works have been produced, notably Marc Dugain's *La Chambre des officiers* (1999; film version by François Dupeyron, 2001).

Bourcy's story suggests, the war was not over by any means with the signing of the Armistice, and would continue to play itself out through multitudes of broken lives as people sought some form of justice, from widow's pensions and adequate disability payments, to the exposure of criminal behaviour.

Other novels with a wartime setting seek to tackle injustice as it occurs, on the battlefield, rather than to break through a successful cover-up. Thierry Bourcy's first novel in the Célestin Louise series provides relatively simple representations of right versus wrong. In *La Cote 512* [Spot Height 512], the young police inspector quickly joins up, out of a sense of solidarity first and foremost: "Je ne me sens pas de rester ici, quand les copains seront en première ligne" ["I can't see myself staying here, when my friends will be at the Front"] (14). Social barriers collapse, as Louise finds himself next to a patriotic pickpocket who declares: "on est tous dans la même galère au jour d'aujourd'hui" ["we're all in the same boat these days"] (15). Military discipline, Louise quickly decides, is not founded on moral principles but on an overwhelming need to preserve order. The grisly reality of mutilated bodies and suffering (cf. 56–57) is a revelation,[18] but Louise refuses to accept as just another "mort pour la France" ["death for France"] (73) the murder of his superior Paul de Mérange, shot in the back by a French bullet.

An embittered doctor who helps with Louise's unauthorised investigation into this death condemns the war in no uncertain terms: "La guerre est une manière d'assassinat, collectif et officiel" ["war is a form of collective, official assassination"] (81). This condemnatory viewpoint is not explicitly accepted by Bourcy's protagonist: although his and his fellow soldiers' attitude to the 'boches' is antagonistic, and the term is widely used by the characters, the book also features an episode of fraternisation (cf. 172–174). The reader is left with an image of the suffering inflicted on ordinary soldiers required to defend principles of rectitude in conditions where such justice rarely prevails. Although Louise finally solves the murder of Mérange (killed by a soldier-criminal so that his employer, the victim's brother, may have access to his wife and her money), he can pursue the case only by defying authority: "tout le monde s'en fout" ["nobody gives a damn"] (85).

The conflict between individual justice and collective interests here takes on a new slant: instead of focusing on an unjustly executed soldier, powerless against the hierarchical forces of an army acting in the name of patriotic values, Bourcy chooses to empower a soldier fixated on seeing justice done and

---

18 These kinds of details about the physical reality of war are more likely to figure in contemporary fiction than in crime writing produced during the war, when the traumatic after-effects were still unknown and realistic depictions were secondary to the promotion of patriotism.

an officer's murder avenged, despite the indifference of those around him.[19] In this novel, then, although unorthodox methods are imposed by combat circumstances, justice is enacted and the (relatively minor) wrong of one man's murder is righted. The origins of the crime are traced back to pre-war civilian life and to issues of class and wealth, and despite a few passages decrying the random violence of the Front and its dehumanising conditions, with their implied loss of justice, Louise succeeds in correctly identifying the wrongdoers, both of whom die shortly afterwards.

The most complex of the recent works is undoubtedly Patrick Pécherot's *Tranchecaille*, a multilayered polyphonic narrative that, in presenting multiple points of view, offers no certain solution. The murder of Lieutenant Landry, bayoneted in the back, was supposedly committed by Antoine Jonas, aka Tranchecaille. Captain Duparc, his defender and the principal investigator, is unsure whether the accused is a simple-minded victim of circumstances or a cunning murderer who may have killed previously. By allowing several narrators to present conflicting 'facts,' from the disillusioned Commandant de Guermantes through Duparc and former detective Corporal Bohman to Tranchecaille's trenchmates, Pécherot presents a complex and, in the end, unresolved network of clues and observations. While there is no single character focalising values throughout the narrative, Duparc's doubts are declared early, as the execution of the accused occurs on the first page of the novel:

> Justice a été rendue. Justice. [...] Je savais la justice faillible, elle est une action humaine. Aujourd'hui elle me semble pareille à ces lacs dont les reflets donnent aux choses l'apparence trompeuse de la vérité. (12)
>
> [Justice has been served. Justice. [...] I knew that justice was fallible, it's a human action. Today it strikes me as being like one of those lakes whose reflections give things a false appearance of reality].

Nor is this the only dubious aspect of the war. Guermantes himself voices the difficult reality of the trenches, expressing what is arguably a modern, retrospective opinion, although as Dorgelès's and Barbusse's works attest, the horror of warfare was not always completely glossed over: "Ce n'est plus une guerre où l'on mène des hommes, c'est un égorgeoir où l'on pousse des bêtes fourbues" ["This

---

19 This determination earns him some kudos: in the next book he is recalled to Paris to investigate the theft of Renault's top secret plans for a lightweight tank that will mean certain victory for France. However the majority of the five novels in the series see Louise back at the front. In *Les Traîtres* (2008) [The Traitors], he is forced to desert in order to pursue his investigation, in other words, he must do wrong in order to do right.

is no longer a war where you lead men, it's a slaughterhouse you drive exhausted animals into"] (22). Where justice is concerned, he is a cynic: "La justice? Quelle idée ..." ["Justice? What a joke ..."] (24). In the end, as Bohman points out, a culprit must be condemned, "pour l'ordre" ["for the sake of order"] (302): officially, this is all that matters.

Pécherot bookends *Tranchecaille*, with its multiple examples of suffering and injustice, with two impossibly positive quotations, from Henri Lavedan (1914) – "Le soldat français rit de partout" ["The French soldier laughs wherever he goes"] (n. p.) and Gustave Le Bon (1916) – "plus d'un regrettera peut-être les meurtrières tranchées" ["many may well think back fondly to the murderous trenches"] (n. p.). Both writers, somewhat shockingly for modern readers, highlight the 'fun' and good times soldiers experienced in the trenches: Pécherot thus places the issues of fairness, justice and patriotism within a framework of propagandistic enthusiasm. The implicit gap between this naïve patriotic discourse and now well-known historical reality underlines the double perspective already present in any modern reading of a Great War setting. Referring elsewhere in the novel to writers and events of the early 1900s and the war years,[20] Pécherot strongly evokes both the ways in which popular culture of the time represented the battle between good and evil, and the difficult application of justice in a military setting, while simultaneously reminding readers that we can no longer see war in such simplistic terms.

3 What Price Justice?

Daeninckx kills off his investigator and destroys vital evidence; in leaving the crime essentially unsolved while the accused is executed despite a lack of incontrovertible proof, Pécherot undermines any sense of justice being valued under combat conditions. Both Bourcy's and Prévost's detectives pursue their investigations to closure, thereby allowing some sense of retributive justice to prevail: to achieve this, however, both investigators must work outside the system and against a background of soldiers' suffering and the pointlessness of much of the fighting, as well as the brutal expediency with which punishments are inflicted for 'crimes' we might now read as psychological illness resulting from very high levels of stress.

---

20 For example, Leroux's and Allain and Souvestre's reporter heroes, Rouletabille and Fandor (146), Le Rouge's contributions to the Rouff series (147), Feuillade's 1915–1916 film series *Les Vampires* (148–149) and the Dreyfus affair of 1894 to 1906 (205–206).

For Leroux's Rouletabille, despite the small exceptions already noted, the lines of demarcation between 'us' and 'them,' right and wrong, were clearly drawn and for the most part unquestioned. Revisiting the Great War decades later is a different matter: in particular, many of these novels raise issues of class alongside those of military discipline, thereby puncturing the illusion of unity against the enemy. Alternatively, geographical separation is challenged, as investigators leave the field of battle to reach the scenes of the crimes that have triggered those committed inside the warzone. Another marked feature of the recent texts is the relative permeability of pre-war, wartime and post-war periods: instead of closing off the combat period from its lead-in and follow-up, crimes traverse these boundaries. Finally, as the popularity of these crime novels and their reframing of collective and individual justice suggests, the chronological separation between the Great War and our own era is open to challenge.

References

Belhadjin, Anissa. "From Politics to the Roman Noir." *South Central Review* 27. 1–2 (2010): 61–81.

Bourcy, Thierry. *La Cote 512. Les Aventures de Célestin Louise, flic et soldat*. Paris: Nouveau Monde, 2008.

Catani, Damian. *Evil: A History in Modern French Literature and Thought*. London: Bloomsbury, 2013.

Cawelti, John G. *Adventure, Mystery and Romance*. Chicago: University of Chicago Press, 1976.

Coates, Anthony J. *The Ethics of War*. Manchester and New York: Manchester University Press, 1997.

Fisher, David. *Morality and War: Can War Be Just in the Twenty-First Century?* Oxford: Oxford University Press, 2011.

Hutton, Margaret-Anne. *French Crime Fiction 1945–2005. Investigating World War II*. Farnham: Ashgate, 2013.

Lerner, Melvin. *The Belief in a Just World: A Fundamental Delusion*. Plenum: New York, 1980.

Leroux, Gaston. *La Bataille invisible. Aventures effroyables de M. Herbert de Renich, tome 2*. Paris: Pierre Lafitte, 1920 [1917].

Leroux, Gaston. *Rouletabille chez Krupp*. Paris: Robert Laffont, 1962 [1920].

Leroux, Gaston. *Rouletabille at Krupp's*. Trans. Brian Stableford. Encino, CA: Black Coat Press, 2013.

Manchette, Jean-Patrick. *Chroniques*. Paris: Rivages, 1996.

Morris, Alan. "*Roman noir, années noires:* The French *Néo-Polar* and the Occupation's Legacy of Violence." *Violent Histories: Violence, Crime and Identity in France from Surrealism to the Néo-polar*. Ed. David Gascoigne. Bern: Peter Lang, 2007. 131–154.

Pécherot, Patrick. *Tranchecaille*. Paris: Gallimard, 2008.

Prévost, Guillaume. *La Valse des gueules cassées*. Paris: Nil éditions, 2010.

Smith, Leonard V. *The Embattled Self: French Soldiers' Testimony of the Great War*. Ithaca, NY: Cornell University Press, 2007.

van Montfrans, Manet. "Pacifism and the European Idea: War and Inner Conflict in the Work of Léon Werth." *Ideas of Europe since 1914: the Legacy of the First World War*. Eds. Menno Spiering and Michael Wintle. Basingstoke: Palgrave, 2002. 160–176.

Villach, Paul. "Tous ces bobards dans les journaux, pendant la guerre de 14–18: un cas d'école." 18 novembre 2008. http://www.agoravox.fr/tribune-libre/article/tous-ces-bobards-dans-les-journaux-47397. (15 January 2012).

Welch, David. *Propaganda: Power and Persuasion*. London: The British Library, 2013.

Part 3: **Identities: The Great War and National Post-Memories**

Sherrill Grace
Remembering *The Wars*

All of this happened a long time ago. But not so long ago that everyone who played a part in it is dead. Some can still be met in dark old rooms with nurses in attendance. They look at you and rearrange their thoughts. They say: 'I don't remember.' The occupants of memory have to be protected from strangers.

Timothy Findley, *The Wars*

Where historians try to come to grips with a period which has left surviving eyewitnesses, two quite different concepts of history clash, or, in the best of cases, supplement each other: the scholarly and the existential, archive and personal memory. For everyone is a historian of his or her own consciously lived life inasmuch as he or she comes to terms with it in his mind.

Eric Hobsbawm, *The Age of Empire, 1875–1914*

Among other things, *The Wars* is about the function of memory and our persistence in time. The researcher is haunted and Robert Ross is the ghost, fixed in the mind at the moment of his fiery sacrifice and self-destruction.

Margaret Atwood, *An important book*

1 Timothy Findley and the First World War

Among war novels in English, Timothy Findley's *The Wars* (1977) is one of the finest. Complex in narrative structure, deeply moving in characterization, description, and its insistence on active reader participation in the processes of remembering, reconstructing, and witnessing the story, *The Wars* is a memory novel about war *avant la lettre*. It appeared in 1977, right at the beginning of what scholars would soon identify as an era obsessed with cultural memory, trauma and remembering, bearing witness, history and metafiction, landscapes of memory, and *lieux/milieux de mémoire*.[1] Its impact in Canada was immediate, and it has become an iconic text, an influential classic which has also been widely

---

[1] Among the most influential theorists of cultural memory, trauma, witnessing, metafiction and historiography are Assmann, Caruth, Chambers, Connerton, Felman and Laub, Hutcheon, LaCapra, Nora, Nünning et al., Oliver, and Sturken. I discuss these and other theorists in *Landscapes of Memory*.

translated.² Among Findley's many novels, stories, and plays, *The Wars* is the text most widely studied in high schools and universities. It has been extensively discussed by scholars, provoking much debate and controversy, and was once nearly banned;³ it has also been made into a stunning feature film and adapted as a stage play.⁴

As western nations enter a period of commemorating and remembering the Great War, it is important to revisit this novel. For Canadians, it is especially urgent to do so because direct public and political attention will be focused on this war as the war in which Canada came of age as a nation.⁵ The First World War will be celebrated at taxpayers' expense; places like Vimy Ridge with its extraordinary monument, Ypres, and Passchendaele will be remembered with reverence and national pride; November 11th ceremonies will be more solemn and elaborate than they have been since the immediate post-war years. All the more reason then to look again at the novel that, I argue, set the stage for contemporary Canadian remembrance of war, that influenced many later works about the war, and that still challenges readers to contemplate with close attention and care what it means to go to war, to die in war, and to remember war.

Before I turn to the text for a detailed analysis, however, let me place *The Wars* in the context of Findley's life and work and touch upon some aspects of its reception by scholars. This is his third novel, but it is by no means his only fictional treatment of either the First or the Second World War. It is safe to say that these two wars framed his formative years and made a profound and lasting impression on the rest of his life and on all his work. As he said in a 1980 interview, "I was

---

2 *The Wars* has been translated into more than a dozen languages, but its life in the first German translation by Annemarie Böll began somewhat awkwardly. The novel's title was changed to *Der Krieg und die Kröte* (*The War and the Toad*), presumably with reference to the toad rescued in the trenches by a Canadian soldier. See Naomi Buck.

3 In the 1980s, Findley faced a censorship threat when an Ontario high school tried to remove *The Wars* from its curriculum. The school did not carry through on this threat after the press picked up the story, but Findley became actively opposed to censorship as a result.

4 *The Wars* has received extensive critical analysis; I list some of these studies in the References; see also note 7. It was adapted by Findley and made into an excellent film in 1983, starring major Canadian actors such as William Hutt, Martha Henry, and Brent Carver (as Robert Ross), and directed by Robin Phillips with music arranged by Glenn Gould. It was adapted for the stage in 2007 by Dennis Garnhum.

5 Many historians have claimed that Canada was born, or came of age, as a nation during the Great War, usually at Vimy Ridge. See, for example, Pierre Berton. This idea took shape in the letters and reports sent home by soldiers, was quickly adopted by politicians anxious to mitigate the real costs of the war, and grew from there to become an accepted orginary story of the nation state. See also Alicia Fahey's, Martin Löschnigg's, Hanna Teichler's and Brigitte Glaser's chapters in the present volume.

infused with this period all through my childhood" (quoted in Aitken, 82). He returned obsessively to the subject of war in several novels: *The Butterfly Plague, Famous Last Words, The Piano Man's Daughter* (which Findley intended as the domestic and contextual counterpart to *The Wars*), and *You Went Away*. And he explored the subject in his earliest and latest short stories and in his first play, *Can You See Me, Yet?* When he was not writing directly about one or other of the wars, they surfaced in a character's memories or a narrator's references. In short, the two wars were never out of mind, never forgotten by Findley, and never seen uncritically through the dominant, political rhetoric of noble sacrifice, military machismo, and national glory.

Findley grew up in an upper middle-class Toronto family for which war was omnipresent. A favorite uncle was a First World War hero; an uncle by marriage also fought; neighbours' sons, brothers, and fathers fought (and did not return or returned badly traumatized); friends of Findley senior also fought; the private boys' school Findley attended celebrated their war heroes (as did schools across the British Empire). To drive the reality of the war home still more effectively, Findley's father, Allan Findley, always felt inferior to his heroic brother, and he brought his sense of failure home in the form of his alcoholism. Allan Findley would later leap at the chance to improve his position in the eyes of his family, and himself, by enlisting with the RCAF in the Second World War. The young Timothy Findley never forgot – perhaps never could forgive – his sense of being betrayed by his father's clearly eager departure. In later interviews and in several works of fiction, he returns, almost obsessively, to the pain this paternal abandonment caused him.[6]

The most important figure in this family tapestry of war, however, is without doubt the war hero Uncle Tif (see fig. 1). Lieutenant Thomas Irving Findley (1895–1933), after whom Findley was nicknamed Tiff (for Timothy Irving Frederick Findley), died early from the serious injuries he had sustained when his plane was shot down over No Man's Land in April 1918. He was declared "missing in action," but surfaced days later in the Hôpital Militaire in Ris-Orangis; French troops had rescued him. This was Lieutenant Findley's second war injury; his first was with the Canadian Field Artillery at the Somme in July 1916. He fought at Vimy Ridge, which he described in letters as a great high point, and in August 1917 he joined the Flying Corps as an "Observer." He was awarded a Military Cross. Years later

---

6 The key works in which Findley revisits this childhood trauma are the stories "War" and "Stones" and the novella *You Went Away*. For some of his reflections on his father's enlisting in the Second World War, see Buitenhuis and Gabriel. In the interview with Buitenhuis, Findley states: "I've never forgiven my dear father" (19); however, he would eventually reach a constructive reconciliation with his father through the story "Stones."

Findley would recall himself at three sitting beside uncle Tif's bedside, listening to stories, and being given candies. Such vivid childhood memories were reinforced when he was entrusted with a large leather-bound portfolio holding the letters – assembled chronologically like a journal or war diary – which Uncle Tif had written home during the war. "These letters got kept, ultimately, as a kind of family heirloom," Findley said, "and when I was about 10, they were presented to me as a gift, and I read them *then* [as] a great adventure story" (quoted in Aitken, 83, emphasis added).

Fig. 1: Lieutenant Thomas Irving Findley ca. 1915. This old photograph of Uncle Tif was cut from its original album and pasted into a collection kept by Timothy Findley's father, Allan. The caption below the photograph reads: "Steel True and Blade Straight."

When it came time to imagine a story about the war, Findley returned to these precious letters and to his Uncle Tif's stories not only for factual information about dates, places, and specific events, but also for the descriptive, emotional context he could elicit from the letters. It is safe to say that this recorded, yet personal, family history – what Hobsbawm (see epigraph) would call "existential [...] and personal memory" – informed *The Wars* at many levels. It is not, however, accurate to suggest (as some have; see Drolet) that Uncle Tif *is* Robert Ross or even the model for the character of Ross. No such equation can be supported. Thomas Irving Findley was proud of his fighting for king and country: judging from the letters he did not doubt his commanding officers; and he most certainly did not – never would have, in fact – do what Robert Ross does to protest the madness of war. Moreover, when a close study is made of the ways in which Findley incorporated materials from the letters into his narrative, it is obvious that the novel is a remarkable work of creative imagination – of art –, not an attempt to document one man's actual experiences.

Robert Ross is not Uncle Tif, but neither is he Timothy Findley in any simplistic sense. However, I make this latter claim with a bit more caution because Timothy Findley's life-long antipathy for war informs his portrayal of the character of Robert Ross, fuels the passion with which he recreates and imagines trench warfare, and drives the narrative search for meaning that commands a reader's attention and has intrigued so many critics since the novel's publication.[7] Without question, Findley conducted extensive research into the period. He loved history and read constantly; he also studied the facts of the Great War so as to get them right. It is what he did, creatively, with all his sources, that makes the novel the moving and ethically challenging work that it is.

On this occasion of remembering Findley's novel, it is, therefore, interesting to revisit the critical work inspired by the text. Indeed, tracing the main lines of this scholarship over almost four decades reminds me of the many critical methods and approaches the novel has inspired and of how richly it repays close analysis. In *Introducing Timothy Findley's The Wars*, Lorraine York, one of Findley's most perceptive critics, begins by stating that this text is "the sort of novel you look back on as a singularly important moment in the writing life of a nation" (14), and I agree. York's study is the place to begin any serious examination of the novel's themes and symbolism, most notably Findley's pervasive interest in the symbols of fire and animals. She also explores some of his published sources, a topic taken up in detail by Tom Hastings, Christopher Gittings, and

---

[7] I have examined aspects of Findley's response to war in "Border Crossings" and "Remembering Timothy Findley." In the effort to attempt an understanding of what life in the trenches must have been like, Findley slept in a water-filled ditch on his Ontario farm.

M. L. McKenzie.[8] Other critics have analysed the novel's structure (Simone Vauthier) or focused on his use of photography (Eva-Marie Kröller), which is a persistent and rich intertextual strategy in all his work, or debated a possible 'queer' reading of the text (Peter Dickinson and Terry Goldie). Donna Pennee sees the novel as Findley's first unequivocally metafictional text (cf. 39), whereas Anne Bailey argues that the metafictional or postmodernist leanings of the text are contradicted through its strategic "colonization" (89–91) by the language (images, rhetoric, references) of British modernists.

Although the critical debate about such issues is not my concern here, there is yet another Findley critic who warrants particular attention because, in my view, she has identified one of the most memorable and important features of *The Wars*: its narrative imperative to bear witness. In *Timothy Findley*, Diana Brydon stresses the point that in his work "the narrative stance is usually that of the witness" (9). She argues that witnessing, for Findley, is both thematic and aesthetic (part of his narrative strategy, cf. 3), and to this I would add that to bear witness is an essential ethical responsibility for both the artist and the reader (or audience), because in Findley's world we are all called upon to bear witness. In remembering *The Wars* I find it worthwhile to remember as well the connection Brydon makes between the researching narrator of the novel and the reader's constructed position as a co-investigator into the war and Robert Ross's actions. As Brydon reminds us, in *The Wars* Robert's "journey to Europe" is a journey into a heart of darkness (65) that Findley insists we (his readers) share. It is a journey Findley knew at second – and in some senses, at first – hand and that he would repeat and reverse (bringing that darkness home) in several of his novels.[9]

2 Beginning in the Archives

The Wars is a fictional biography and a biographical fiction. It is a fictional biography insofar as its biographee, Robert Ross, never existed outside the pages of the novel. His life-story is a fiction because he is. But I also consider *The Wars* to be a biographical fiction (not metafiction), because Findley has taken great pains to foreground all the hard research that a biographer must undertake, while at the same time reminding his readers – indeed, making his fictional biographer

---

8 While my list is not exhaustive, I provide a representative selection of critical analyses of *The Wars* in my References. See Bailey, Brydon, Cobley, Dickinson, Gittings, Goldie, Hastings, Hulcoop, Krause, Kröller, McKenzie, Pennee, Ricou, Vauthier, and York.

9 See, for example, *The Butterfly Plague, Famous Last Words*, and *Headhunter*.

remind himself – that biography *is a story*, a constructed narrative of a subject, the biographee, who must be imagined and created by someone else: the biographer.

At many points, Robert's biographer admits that he must rely on intuition and conjecture, that certain things simply cannot be told at all and that information about other things is confusing, incomplete, even contradictory. He is not the type of biographer who stresses a first person narrative position, but he does speak in what I can only call his own voice at times and he frequently addresses us. In other words, this biographer exists within the text, if not quite as a character, then most definitely as a voice and an active presence – a fictional, intradiegetic presence.[10] He is never named, but we learn from one of the transcribed interviews that constitute part of the narrative that he is a *he* (188), and we infer from other interview transcriptions that he is fairly young (compared with those he interviews), that he has no direct experience of the First World War, and that he is Canadian: He must work hard to recount with historical accuracy the facts of the war, and he must have certain British locutions and contexts explained to him. However, beyond these characteristics, we are told little about this man or, more importantly, his motivations. Why has he decided to write a biography in the first place instead of a history of the war or of the Somme? Why did he choose Robert Ross as his subject? How did he discover where to find Ross family documents? How did he gain permission to examine and quote from the court martial records, and how did he pin down the coordinates of key, elderly people who knew Robert and witnessed important events in his life?

We can guess at the answers to some of these questions by paying close attention to the life-story, which begins and ends "at the archives with photographs" (11).[11] It is a winter day – no year given – when we first see the narrator who, like

---

10 For his discussion of narrative levels, see Genette (228–310). While I am not conducting a narratological analysis of *The Wars* here, I will note that all three of Genette's levels operate in the novel: the text is presented by an impersonal extradiegetic narrator; the biographer is an intradiegetic narrator with an active, recognizable voice; and Nurse Turner and Lady Juliet are metadiegetic narrators.

11 Although the biographer's story begins and ends in the archive, the text does not. The opening section of the Prologue, narrated objectively – almost cinematically – presents the reader with a highly visual scene. We *see*, as it were, a horse, railway tracks, a dog, and then a man called Robert. After a panning shot, the focus tightens on the man, the horse, and the dog. The man mounts the black mare and, accompanied by the dog, they ride "down the road to Magdalene Wood" (10). However, they hear horses held in twelve rail cars and stop to release them. Then Robert, his mare, the dog, and the 130 freed horses ride along together. Cut to the archives and the biographer. We are not returned to this scene until near the end of the text, where the entire scene is repeated to remind us of what Robert did: "We shall all go together," said Robert (183). The final episodes and the Epilogue take Robert beyond the mutiny crisis to death and lift

any good biographer, is conducting exhaustive research into both the life of the biographee and the wider social, historical context for that life:

> You begin at the archives with photographs [...]. Boxes and boxes of snapshots and portraits; maps and letters; cablegrams and clippings from the papers. All you have to do is sign them out and carry them across the room. Spread over table tops, a whole age lies in fragments underneath the lamps. *The war to end all wars.* [...] The boxes smell of yellow dust. You hold your breath. As the past moves under your fingertips, part of it crumbles. Other parts, you know you'll never find. This is what you have. (11)

Two points here are essential to note. One is the simple fact of being *there* in an archive, looking down at "a whole age" lying "in fragments" on a table; the other is that seductive "You," which addresses, includes, and engages each individual reader. "You" and "I" are constructed as witnesses to this researcher's work; we also look at the evidence. We watch him looking at the documents, and we listen as he describes the images from 1915 – a year, long ago, that now appears as "sepia and soiled," but is nevertheless revealed, through the evidence we stare at, as full of people from the Edwardian and early Georgian eras. As we look and listen, we become imperceptibly involved in this search for the past, for a family, for one person among so many young soldiers who enlisted in the Canadian Expeditionary Force (CEF), who marched in General Sam Hughes's army, and who never came home. And right there, at the edge of one photograph, is Robert. We see him when the biographer does, and we too read his name written on the back "in the faintest ink in a feminine hand: 'Robert,'" (8) when our co-researcher (this biographer) turns the photograph over.

But photographs are tricky artifacts. They can lie. They can also provide crucial information for a biographer or an historian, and the narrator of *The Wars* performs both roles. The novel returns us to the archive and to a photograph at the end, when the archivist says it is time to leave and the biographer tells us: "You [...] arrange your research in bundles – letters – photos – telegrams" (191). Clearly, our work is still not done, and as attentive readers we will turn back to the opening prologue, with its description of Lieutenant Ross freeing one hundred and thirty horses from train cars on a track that is about to be bombed. Before we turn back, however, and before we *re*read this prologue more fully informed of its significance, the biographer shows us one last photograph: "This is the last thing you see before you put on your overcoat: *Robert and Rowena with Meg* [...]. On the back is written: 'Look! You can see our breath!' And you can" (191). *You* can and *I* can because the search for Robert Ross, his time and his place, and the meaning

---

the reader beyond the archive to thoughts of another war and the sounds of birds outside the building.

of his life and death, has involved us. Through the fictional biographer with *his* biographical fiction, Findley has breathed life into a past we thought was long dead, a past caught only in faded photographs and crumbling papers, a past all but forgotten or deliberately silenced and repressed. "I don't remember," those people who are "occupants of memory" (10) tell the biographer. Memory, then, and imagination are the tools that will make Hobsbawm's "scholarly" history come alive.

The Wars is a novel about remembering and unearthing the First World War. It is also the story of one young man who enlisted in Canada's citizen army at the age of nineteen, was made an officer, fought in France, was wounded in April 1915 at the Second Battle of Ypres, recuperated in England and then returned to the front at Bailleul, where he rebelled against his commanding officer. His 'mutiny' took the form of disobeying an order not to release horses stabled at a Signals Battery headquarters under bombardment by the Germans. He decided Captain Leather was insane, freed the trapped animals, and killed the captain when he tried to interfere. Although wounded, he fled on a black mare towards Magdalene Wood with the rescued horses and a dog, and they all took refuge in another barn. In the ensuing chaos back at Signals Battery, he was declared missing in action, but there were witnesses to what happened and he was tracked down by fellow soldiers and the military police. When he was surrounded but refused to come out, the barn was set on fire, and Robert Ross only broke out when the barn doors were opened from the outside. By this point, he and his horse were on fire; the other horses were trapped and dying. He collapsed, was arrested, nursed back to consciousness – not to health for his wounds are fatal – court martialled and convicted of murder and mutiny. He died before his twenty-sixth birthday.

These are the bare facts of Robert Ross's war experience, but the narrative search for his life-story takes the biographer (and us) not only to the archives and History, but also to the homes of two elderly women who knew Robert, to their personal memories of the past and their primary witness accounts of what happened. Marian Turner nursed Robert Ross after the fiery crisis in the barn on the road to Magdalene Wood. She is the first interviewee and primary witness presented to us through the transcript excerpts provided by the biographer at three points in his compilation of materials. Nurse Turner admired and greatly pitied Robert. She calls him a "hero," not a Billy Bishop style hero, but a man who "did the thing that no one else would even dare to think of doing [and] that to me's as good a definition of a 'hero' as you'll get" (16).[12] She knows full well that others, including Robert's younger brother, Stuart, see him as a traitor and

---

12 William Bishop (1894–1956) was a First World War pilot – a so-called 'ace' because of his high number of 'kills.' He has become a popular hero on the Canadian stage due to John Gray's and

a disgrace. Stuart refuses to meet with the biographer or participate in recuperating Robert's story or re-evaluating what happened in June 1916. Nurse Turner insists that Robert was "*un homme unique*" (16), and she warns the biographer "to be careful, searching his story out" (17). She draws an emphatic distinction between madness and sanity and between the ordinary and the extraordinary. In her opinion (and she reminds us that she was *there* in the war and has witnessed the monstrosity of the twentieth century), Robert was extraordinary and sane: "It was the war that was crazy," and men like Ludendorff, Kitchener, Foch, or later Churchill and Hitler were ordinary. They were "just the butcher and the grocer," who represented "the lowest common denominator" (17).

In the third and final transcript excerpt, Marian Turner provides some concrete facts: Robert was received at the field hospital on 18 June 1916, burned almost beyond recognition. Because the army had accused him of murder and insubordination, a Military Police officer guarded him at all times. In late August he was sent to England, tried *in absentia*, and kept at St. Aubyn's (an English estate used for convalescing officers) until he died. But Turner reveals much more than these cold facts; she confesses to a very personal remembered moment in her own life, and it makes a story that defines both her and Robert. "I wanted to help him die," she states, because she was "*ashamed to be alive*" and surrounded by such senseless mutilation and suffering. She offered Robert a lethal dose of morphine: "I will help you, if you want me to," she whispered, and he replied with two words: "'Not yet'" (189). Not yet became thereafter Nurse Turner's motto. Hope against despair was Timothy Findley's.

What Findley has his biographer juxtapose here encapsulates the ethical motivation and aesthetic design of the novel. The public facts of History will only provide just so much information – surface details, officially sanctioned truth claims, legally defined versions of events – and other sources for different kinds of histories are necessary if we hope to understand, even partially, the past or a life-story. Marian Turner gives us what only she can bear witness to: her ethical position under duress and Robert's courage. Not even the biographer intrudes to interpret her confession. Each reader is left to ponder her warnings, her philosophy, her offer of a merciful death, and Robert's "Not yet." My interpretation is that Findley means us to see her as both sane and compassionate, and to understand that Robert chose to remain alive, if he could, for the court martial. He would see his actions, the only correct response to violent insanity, through to their conclusion; he would not take an easy way out. This 'supplementing' of archival fact

---

Eric Peterson's classic play *Billy Bishop Goes to War*, which celebrates and satirizes myths about heroic Canadians in the war. Cf. Martin Löschnigg's chapter in the present volume.

with an eyewitness's personal memory is precisely what Hobsbawm identifies as the best practice in historiography for such a period.

The second eyewitness to be interviewed is Lady Juliet d'Orsey, the only surviving member of the aristocratic family who owned St Aubyn's and opened it to officers during the war. Where Nurse Turner survives on tea and sherry, Lady Juliet survives on gin and cigarettes. The biographer meets with her in the family apartment in London. She is now in her seventies (born in 1904, her dates suggest we are reading a narrative constructed in 1976 or 1977), but her memory and tongue are sharp. What's more, she has kept her diaries from the war years – a treasure trove for a biographer – and this makes her account of Robert "the most vivid and personal we have" (98). The wise biographer does not claim that the diaries are the most accurate account or the Truth, only that they are vivid and personal; however, most readers of autobiography tend to trust that such sources provide the *real* thing.[13] On the occasion of this first meeting, Robert's biographer describes the woman, her Knightsbridge home, and her welcome of him in detail. There is a servant who makes tea; the rooms are charmingly furnished with freesia on the mantelpiece and logs burning in a grand fireplace; but she keeps her visitor waiting while she listens to a church choir rehearsing Mass in St Paul's, Knightsbridge, beyond her balcony: "You wait with your briefcase and tape recorder in your hands in the middle of the rug" (99). Such context-establishing details are by no means superfluous. They set the tone and the stage for what will follow, and they serve to authenticate the scene and, therefore, confirm the reliability of the interviewee and her story.

It is immediately clear that Lady Juliet believes only "maniacs" could think Robert did anything wrong. It is also clear that from the age of twelve, when she first met Robert at St Aubyn's, she fell in love with him. She has never married and she still cherishes her memories of him from before the June 1916 crisis and during the years after it when he lay dying at St Aubyn's. Lady Juliet also has warnings for the biographer and a well-developed philosophy of life. She reminds us that the war was *then*; it happened, and "your friends were [...] murdered" (104). She dismisses with contempt people "who weren't there [but] look back" and criticise (104). And she pronounces what I see as the moral of *The Wars*, which is, finally, less a war story than a memory novel and a narrative about remembering, reconstructing, and reimagining a life caught up in war: "The thing is not to make excuses for the way you behaved – not to take refuge in tragedy – but to clarify

---

13 *The Wars* is an interesting study in fictional auto/biography, by which I mean a biographical text that includes and foregrounds autobiographical accounts. For discussions of truth claims, readers' responses, and the relationality of biography and autobiography, see work by Eakin, Egan, and Lejeune.

who you are through your response to when you lived" (103). Or, as Hobsbawm puts it, to "come to terms" in your mind with your own "consciously lived life" (5).

Many intimate and more public details about Robert Ross emerge from the interviews with Lady Juliet, and they crop up as facts in several fragments of the story. In her second, long excerpt (143–158), she reads from her diaries, confesses to her sins of spying on others, describes what she sees but cannot quite grasp at twelve, when she opens Robert's bedroom door to find him and her older sister, Barbara, making love, and she reports on many things Robert confided to her about his dead friends and his family. She watches him at meals and when he walks or rides outside; she recognizes his deep-seated anger and violence, as well as his sensitivity, courage, and intelligence; she hates her predatory sister for seducing him, and she sends him back to the front in 1916 with the symbolic gift of a candle. Of all the adults passing through St Aubyn's, Robert is the only one who pays her any attention, the only one who never dismisses her as just a child, and by this late stage in piecing together the fragments of his story we can understand why. Robert adored his sister Rowena, a hydrocephalic who never developed beyond the age of twelve, was confined to a wheel chair, and died from a fall. It was her death that precipitated his decision to enlist. Juliet reminds him of Rowena, and Rowena is the person beside him in the last photograph of the text: "ROBERT AND ROWENA WITH MEG [the pony]" (226).

Lady Juliet is, then, a crucial primary witness to the impact of the war on the British home front and to the life-story of Robert Ross. Her credibility as a trustworthy fictional witness is, therefore, critically important. Consequently, the biographer is scrupulously careful about setting the stage for this long excerpt from her interview. Because she reads aloud from her diaries, as well as addressing him (or musing to herself), he tells us that certain aspects of the interview do not survive "transition onto paper." Chief among these is her voice that quavers, cracks, and whispers or "sails off in what can only be described as song" (139). We are asked to listen for these modulations, to imagine the silences and gestures – the emotion of her remembering – that escape the page. "*I was a born observer*," she tells us, a "*Boswell in bows*," and "*these diaries will tell you what you want to know [...] the conclusions are for you to make*" (143). Indeed, these are always the claims of eyewitnesses: I was there. I saw this and that. I will report to you and ask only that you believe my story. And such is the claim – the direct appeal – of Findley's fictional biographer who, like Lady Juliet, leaves us to draw our own conclusions.

3 The Lessons of Remembering and why Robert Ross Matters

Robert Raymond Ross (1896–1922), a Second Lieutenant with the Canadian Field Artillery, has been called a hero, a traitor and murderer, and *"un homme unique."* Some of the novel's characters who remember him call him insane, a soldier who became crazed; others remember him as sane and brave, as one of those rare human beings who do what makes sense when all around them are unable to do so. There is no doubt about the bare (fictional) facts here: he did disobey orders and release horses trapped in a barn under bombardment; he did shoot and kill his commanding officer; he did kill one other soldier who tried to stop his escape; and he was grievously burned in a barn with the horses because he refused to come out when ordered to do so. The haunting question for the biographer, historian, and the reader is: why?

Robert is the elder son in a family of four children born and raised in the wealthy neighbourhood of Toronto called Rosedale, where Findley himself was born. His father manages a successful farm machinery business, Raymond/Ross Industries, a detail that recalls Findley's paternal grandfather's position with Massey-Harris.[14] His mother, who he resembles closely in many ways, is portrayed as highly sensitive, principled, and yet ruthlessly honest and determined when necessary. Mrs. Ross adores her son and is devastated when he enlists; over the ensuing months, she becomes an increasingly dysfunctional alcoholic. She openly condemns the war and despises the clergy and others who boast about sending their sons off to fight, but we are never told how she receives the terrible news of Robert's court martial and death. She does not go to England with Mr. Ross for her son's funeral. His beloved older sister, Rowena, was Robert's special companion; he felt responsible for her and when she died he both grieved her loss and blamed himself for failing her. His brother is a bit of a brute; although much younger than Robert, he is already a brash bully, and he will disown Robert after the events of 1916. The remaining sister, Peggy, is a minor figure more interested in flirtations and parties than the real life around her.

---

[14] Although I will not pause to identify every link between the novel and details from Findley's biography, a few do warrant mention. Massey-Harris was one of Canada's leading farm machinery manufacturers from the late nineteenth- to the mid-twentieth centuries. Thomas Findley (1870–1921), Findley's paternal grandfather, rose to become the president of the company before his untimely death from cancer. He had made a modest fortune by then and raised his family in a gracious Rosedale home. By all accounts he was a gentle, kindly man, much as Mr. Tom Ross is depicted as being in the novel.

The links between Robert and Thomas Irving Findley, Uncle Tif, are many, but as I noted earlier they do not support any form of identification of the character Robert with the actual First World War veteran. Like Uncle Tif, Robert attended the private boy's school Saint Andrews College and did cadet training while there; like Uncle Tif, Robert enlisted in 1915 and trained in Lethbridge, Alberta, before being shipped out on the *SS Massanabie*, the name Findley gives to Robert's troop ship. Robert's closest fellow soldiers have the names of Tif's colleagues in his war diaries – Harris and Purchas, for example (there is even a Captain Leather in Uncle Tif's diary, but he is well liked and respected) – and Robert is also wounded twice, as was Uncle Tif, the second time involving serious burns. Like Uncle Tif, Robert is briefly reported as missing in action, but the comparison ends there. In other words, Findley drew information, names, details, and aspects of trench experience from his uncle's diaries and letters, but Robert Ross is an entirely different kind of hero.

Findley's use of the diaries extends beyond these incidental echoes. As a close comparison of the text with passages from the diaries reveals, Findley incorporated descriptions of bombardment and mud, snatches of reported dialogue, examples of suffering, poor food, and terror from his uncle's material. It is what Findley does with this eyewitness accounting that demonstrates just how far the fiction has come from the raw material. One brief example will give some idea of the creative process at work while also, I believe, capturing a sense of the heightened realism and authenticity that carry over from bald reporting to a strategically developed fictional context. In an April 1916 letter to his mother, Lieutenant Findley briefly describes a particular sight: "I passed one German in our trenches that has lain wounded for four days, out in a crater in 'No-man's-land,' with nothing to eat. He was the most forlorn looking spectacle I have ever seen. I also saw a party of about twenty-five to thirty German prisoners, who came over and deserted this morning."[15] Findley has marked this passage to be used, but he changes it in small but interesting ways: "They also passed a German who had lain out in No Man's Land for four days without food. He was staring at the sky – lying on a stretcher. There was a party, too, of about twenty-five or thirty German prisoners who had deserted and come over that morning. The problem was that most of the dugouts in this section of the trench had been destroyed – so there was nowhere to sit or lie down except in the mud" (94).

---

[15] My quotation from this letter (contained in the assembled diary) is from the Findley/Whitehead *fonds* at the University of Guelph. My thanks to the archivists there for their help and to William Whitehead for his permission to quote and for the many family photographs he has put at my disposal. I would also like to thank the Social Sciences and Humanities Research Council of Canada for the research funds that make my visits to archives possible.

While many reasons might be given for the subtle difference between these passages – Findley is a creative writer, his uncle is not; Findley has a complex narrative and symbols to develop that Uncle Tif does not – the contrasting impact of the two passages is clear. The first is a brief, objective account, showing little human sympathy; the second attributes an element of subjectivity to the dying German and allows us to imagine the terrible conditions awaiting the Germans who have deserted and will now share these conditions with their former enemies. A shared humanity is being suggested here that is absent from the letters, and this shared suffering is critical for the meaning of Robert Ross's life. Later in the story, Robert and his men will experience the first use of chlorine gas (Canadians at Ypres were the first victims of this weapon). They will shelter in the bottom of a water-and-corpse-clogged crater holding their urine-soaked shirttails over their faces.[16] As they crawl out of this hell, they are watched by a German sniper lying at the crater's lip. But this young soldier does not shoot. He smiles to let the Canadians see that they can escape. When he makes a sudden move, however, Robert mistakes his intentions and kills him, only to realize after it is too late that the German was reaching for his binoculars, not his rifle. This scene at the crater complements – resonates with – the brief description of the dying German staring at the sky in no-man's-land, and the cumulative effect is to increase the sense of shared humanity that defies and defines the insanity of combat. Robert's tragic mistake, together with many other horrors he experiences, from the suicide of the gentle artist Rodwell, who rescues injured animals, to his violent rape by fellow soldiers shortly before the June 1916 crisis, confirm the narrative pressure towards condemning war and valorizing Robert's rebellion.

It is a big creative step from the matter-of-fact eyewitness letter that offers no value judgment or sign of empathy to the complex ethical dimension of the fictional biographer's remembering and reconstruction of events. Moreover, Uncle Tif's letters and diary sit in sharp contrast with the deeply empathetic and ethical remembering of Nurse Turner and Lady Juliet. If Robert Ross matters and if we can begin to comprehend the why of his actions – and I think he does and that we must try – then it is because Findley, through his fictive biographer, has so skillfully woven fiction out of facts and supplemented History with multiple histories, official public memory with private remembering. Findley and the biographer have taken care to be faithful to History, but they have also been faithful to the power of memory and its capacity to elicit from the reader what Dominick LaCapra calls "empathic unsettlement."[17]

---

16 The ammonia in urine provided a modest protection against the gas.
17 LaCapra describes this concept for managing trauma in *Writing History, Writing* Trauma: "Being responsive to the traumatic experience of others, notably of victims, implies not the ap-

Second Lieutenant Robert Raymond Ross may be heroic, but he is also a victim betrayed by the machine of the Great War. He is, like most of the other thousands upon thousands of casualties on both sides, a son sent off to fight the fathers' war. This is why Findley insisted that the rape scene (in which Robert is attacked in the baths at Desolé by fellow soldiers) be retained despite the qualms of friends and editors. This is why Mrs. Ross storms from the church, where the clergyman is exhorting men to fight for the glory of God and country. "Why is this happening to us," she cries. "What does it mean – *to kill your children*? Kill them and then go in there and sing about it?" (54) As a woman she is helpless to stop the war. War is a man's business. But she condemns and damns the fathers, the politicians, the generals. She provides, together with the other two female perspectives – Nurse Turner's and Lady Juliet's – the corrective lens through which we can assess what the biographer puts before us.

As I remember *The Wars* and as I observe my country – indeed the western world – remembering the 'war to end all wars,' I return to the stories of witnesses and to the importance Timothy Findley placed on memory and bearing witness. These personal stories and fictional accounts not only supplement (in Hobsbawm's sense) the official history of the war, they also challenge the dominant narrative; they undermine and contradict it. Perhaps most important, these accounts and fictions present us with multiple perspectives on the past, on the so-called facts, and on politically sanctioned Truth. Robert Ross, Nurse Turner, Lady Juliet, and Mrs. Ross insist that we heed their words and accept their actions. Pay attention, they cry out to us. Timothy Findley, working through Robert's biographer, insists that we resist the easy path of blind acceptance of myths of noble sacrifice for king and country, of mothers happily giving up their dear laddies, of evil enemy losers and righteous winners in war, of – in Canada's case – a young nation born on a battlefield. For Findley, nothing is born on a battlefield. It is what we do with the remembering of that obscene past that matters and (crucially) *how* we engage in and construct the narratives of remembering that will, just possibly, lead to the birth of a civil society and peace.

"The words 'pay attention' echoed through my life," Findley tells us, "and I must have heard it from a lot of people [because] it keeps coming out – 'Pay atten-

---

propriation of their experience but [...] empathic unsettlement" (41). By this he means a response that does not disable the witness of another's trauma (by reducing him or her to a self-indulgent suffering), but enables this witness to respond and act ethically to understand and assist the victim. The outcome, in narrative, of empathic unsettlement is a refusal of redemptive forms of closure that suggest happy resolutions or the transcending of trauma. *The Wars* blocks our attempt to find any form of redemption in Robert's story or in the story of war. At the same time, it encourages an empathic response that will leave a reader moved but critically engaged.

tion! Pay attention!'" (quoted in Aitken, 82). If *The Wars* and Robert Ross haunt us now in the twenty-first century (and, like Atwood, I believe they do), then it is because this fictional biography remembers a time when life, morality, and sanity were thrown away as cannon fodder, and the novel urges us to pay attention to our hauntedness and to use our memories now, in the present, to gain understanding and take responsibility for our collective future.

References

Aitken, Johan. "'Long Live the Dead': An Interview with Timothy Findley." *Journal of Canadian Fiction* 33 (1981–1982): 79–93.
Assmann, Jan. "Collective Memory and Cultural Identity." Trans. John Czaplicka. *New German Critique* 65 (1995): 125–133.
Atwood, Margaret. "An important book for many reasons." *The Financial Post* (12 November 1977): 290–295.
Bailey, Anne Geddes. *Timothy Findley and the Aesthetics of Fascism*. Vancouver: Talonbooks, 1998.
Berton, Pierre. *Vimy*. Toronto: McClelland and Stewart, 1986.
Brydon, Diana. *Timothy Findley*. New York and London: Twayne and Prentice Hall, 1998.
Buck, Naomi. "Pilgrim's Progress in Berlin." *The Globe and Mail* (5 June 2000): R3.
Buitenhuis, Peter. "The Return of the Crazy People." *Books in Canada* (December 1988): 17–20.
Caruth, Cathy. *Unclaimed Experience: Trauma, Narrative and History*. Baltimore: Johns Hopkins University Press, 1996.
Chambers, Ross. *Untimely Interventions: AIDS Writing, Testimonial, and the Rhetoric of Haunting*. Ann Arbor: University of Michigan Press, 2004.
Cobley, Evelyn. *Representing War: Form and Ideology in First World War Narratives*. Toronto: University of Toronto Press, 1993.
Connerton, Paul. *How Societies Remember*. Cambridge: Cambridge University Press, 1989.
Dickinson, Peter. "'Running Wilde': National Ambivalence and Sexual Dissidence in Timothy Findley's Fictions." *Here is Queer: Nationalisms, Sexualities, and the Literatures of Canada*. Toronto: University of Toronto Press, 1999. 39–68.
Drolet, Gilbert. "Prayers against Despair: A Retrospective Note on Findley's *The Wars*." *Journal of Canadian Fiction* 33 (1981–1982): 148–155.
Eakin, Paul John. *How Our Lives Become Stories: Making Selves*. Ithaca: Cornell University Press, 1999.
Egan, Susanna. *Mirror Talk: Genres of Crisis in Contemporary Autobiography*. Chapel Hill and London: University of North Carolina Press, 1999.
Felman, Shoshana, and Dori Laub. *Testimony: Crises of Witnessing in Literature, Psychoanalysis, and History*. New York: Routledge, 1992.
Findley, Timothy. *The Butterfly Plague*. Toronto: Penguin Books, 1986. Rev. edition 1996.
Findley, Timothy. *Can You See Me, Yet?* Vancouver: Talonbooks, 1977.
Findley, Timothy. *Famous Last Words*. Toronto: Clarke Irwin, 1981.
Findley, Timothy. *Headhunter*. Toronto: HarperCollins, 1993.

Findley, Timothy. *The Piano Man's Daughter*. Toronto: HarperCollins, 1995.
Findley, Timothy. *Pilgrim*. Toronto: HarperCollins, 1999.
Findley, Timothy. "Stones." *Stones*. Toronto: Viking, 1988. 193–221.
Findley, Timothy. "War." *Dinner Along the Amazon*. Toronto: Penguin Books, 1984. 65–81.
Findley, Timothy. *The Wars*. Toronto: Clarke Irwin, 1977.
Findley, Timothy. *The Wars*. Dir. Robin Phillips. Nielsen-Ferns International, Polyphon Film und Fernsehgesellschaft, 1983.
Findley, Timothy. *You Went Away*. Toronto: HarperCollins, 1996.
Gabriel, Barbara. "Masks and Icons: An Interview with Timothy Findley." *The Canadian Forum* (1986): 31–36.
Genette, Gérard. *Narrative Discourse: An Essay in Method*. Trans. Jane E. Lewin. Ithaca: Cornell University Press, 1980.
Gittings, Christopher E. "'What are soldiers for?' Re-Making Masculinities in Timothy Findley's *The Wars*." *Kunapipi* 18. 1 (1996): 184–191.
Goldie, Terry. "The Canadian Homosexual." *Journal of Canadian Studies* 33. 4 (1998–1999): 132–142.
Grace, Sherrill. "Border Crossings in Contemporary Canadian Responses to WW II: *Famous Last Words* and *Burning Vision*." *Riding/Writing across Borders in North American Travelogues and Fiction*. Ed. Waldemar Zacharasiewicz. Vienna: Verlag der Österreichischen Akademie der Wissenschaften, 2011. 369–389.
Grace, Sherrill. "Remembering Timothy Findley." Unpublished paper presented at the University of Vienna, 6 October 2013.
Grace, Sherrill. *Landscapes of Memory, 1977 to 2007: Canadian Literature, the Arts, and the Two World Wars*. Edmonton: University of Alberta Press, 2014.
Gray, John and Eric Peterson. *Billy Bishop Goes to War*. Vancouver: Talonbooks, 2000.
Hastings, Tom. "'Their fathers did it to them': Findley's Appeal to the Great War Myth of a Generational Conflict in *The Wars*." *Paying Attention: Critical Essays on Timothy Findley*. Eds. Anne Geddes Bailey and Karen Grandy. Toronto: ECW Press, 1998. 85–103.
Hobsbawm, Eric J. *The Age of Empire, 1875–1914*. New York: Random House, 1987.
Hulcoop, John. "'Look! Listen! Mark my Words!' Paying Attention to Timothy Findley's Fictions." *Canadian Literature* 91 (1981): 22–47.
Hutcheon, Linda. *The Poetics of Postmodernism: History, Theory, Fiction*. New York: Routledge, 1988.
Krause, Dagmar. *Timothy Findley's Novels: Between Ethics and Postmodernism*. Würzburg: Königshausen & Neumann, 2005.
Kröller, Eva-Marie. "The Exploding Frame: Uses of Photography in Timothy Findley's *The Wars*." *Journal of Canadian Studies* 16. 3–4 (1981): 68–74.
LaCapra, Dominick. *Writing History, Writing Trauma*. Baltimore: Johns Hopkins University Press, 2001.
Lejeune, Philippe. "The Autobiographical Pact (bis)." Trans. Katherine Leary. *On Autobiography*. Ed. Paul John Eakin. Minneapolis: University of Minnesota Press, 1989. 119–137.
McKenzie, Sister M. L. "Memories of the Great War: Graves, Sassoon, and Findley." *University of Toronto Quarterly* 55. 4 (1986): 395–411.
Nora, Pierre. "Between Memory and History: *Les Lieux de Mémoire*." Trans. Marc Roudebush. *Representations* 26 (1989): 7–25.
Nünning, Ansgar, Marion Gymnich, and Roy Sommer, eds. *Literature and Memory: Theoretical Paradigms, Genres, Functions*. Tübingen: Francke Verlag, 2006.

Oliver, Kelly. *Witnessing Beyond Recognition*. Minneapolis: University of Minnesota Press, 2001.

Pennee, Donna. *Moral Metafiction: Counterdiscourse in the Novels of Timothy Findley*. Toronto: ECW Press, 1991.

Ricou, Laurie. "Obscured by Violence: Timothy Findley's *The Wars*." *Violence in the Canadian Novel Since 1960*. Eds. Terry Goldie and Virginia Harger-Grinling. St. John's, NL: Memorial University Press, 1981. 125–137.

Sturken, Marita. *Tangled Memories: The Vietnam War, The AIDS Epidemic, and the Politics of Remembering*. Berkeley: University of California Press, 1997.

Thiessen, Vern. *Vimy*. Toronto: Playwrights Canada Press, 2007.

Vauthier, Simone. "The Dubious Battle of Story-Telling: Narrative Strategies in Timothy Findley's *The Wars*." *Gaining Ground: European Critics on Canadian Literature*. Eds. Robert Kroetsch and Reingard Nischik. Edmonton: NeWest Press, 1985. 11–39.

York, Lorraine. *Introducing Timothy Findley's* The Wars: *A Readers' Guide*. Toronto: ECW Press, 1990.

Hanna Teichler
Joseph Boyden's *Three Day Road*: Transcultural (Post-)Memory and Identity in Canadian World War I Fiction

> Elijah kneels in the tall grass, a young German pinned below him. The German is bleeding but still alive, looks up in shock and fear at Elijah. Just as I approach from behind, Elijah cuts hard into the soldier's solar plexus with a knife, muttering. I can't make out what he says. The man below him writhes and screams. I watch as Elijah plunges his knife once again into the man. I can see the horror in his eyes turn to the dullness of death as Elijah's hand moves to his own face.
>
> Joseph Boyden, Three Day Road

1 The Presence of the Absent

Paul Ricoeur has coined the term "presence of the absent" to refer to the several time levels which co-exist when we remember. Something that is remembered refers to a matter that is not anymore, yet appears to be returning. Ricoeur's study on memory and history draws on the Platonic theme of the representation of an absent thing in the present. The quotation from Joseph Boyden's novel *Three Day Road* (2005) portrays a killing scene from the battlefields of World War I. It has been identified as the moment when Cree Canadian soldier Elijah's deterioration into a "bloodthirsty warrior" has reached the point-of-no-return (Ulm 102–103). *Three Day Road* is a narrative of identity negotiation, construction and deconstruction, as Marco Ulm has convincingly argued. Contemporary Canada finds itself in a comparable quest for identity: continuing struggles for reconciliation with the First Nations are forcing Canadian society to question their national roots, while increasing globalization threatens national hegemony and cultural agency and thus further ratchets the discussion (cf. Ikas, "Formative Years" and "Global Realignments").[1] As this chapter will discuss, national identity evolves through narratives, and is constructed by them.[2] Joseph Boyden's

---

[1] The term *First Nations* subsumes indigenous peoples like the Cree, the Ojibway, and many others who are neither Métis, descendants from First Nations and English settlers, or Inuit.
[2] Identity in this context is understood as being a process of negotiation between different aspects and parts of identity rather than a fixed and stable entity. These parts are conditioned by our cultural environment, shaped by normative and creative structures that are transmitted

Three Day Road revisits World War I, and thus one of the formative narratives of Canadian national self-consciousness: participation in the conflict as the founding moment (cf. Ikas, "Formative Years") and the coming-of-age as a nation (cf. Grace and Coates; Kuester), although some scholars argue that there is no such moment to be pinpointed in history (cf. Rosenthal 306). Literary fiction is not only an "institution of transmission" of memory (Hirsch 105), but also constitutes a "social framework" to construct national identity through memory (Rigney 361). However, this chapter would like to seize the idea of identity negotiation within *Three Day Road* in order to extend its scope, outlining an extra-textual potency that is embedded in the narrative. In the following, processes of identity (de)construction will be discussed with regard to narratological strategies within the novel. In a second step, the productive force of narratives, of literary fiction, with respect to identity negotiation on a national level will be illustrated through the analysis of Boyden's text.

2 A Nation Forged in Fire – The Great War as a Founding Narrative

The involvement of the Canadian nation in the First World War is one example of the crucial impact of the British Empire on its colonies (cf. Angus). In the ongoing struggle to find an equilibrium between globalizing forces, the alleged demise of the local for the sake of the global, and maintaining a sense of nationality, Canada's self-perception as a nation is still founded on events of imperial history. These formative narratives are still equipped with enough discursive power to influence and trigger current debates about nationhood and citizenship (cf. Ikas, "Formative Years" 36).

The participation alongside Great Britain and the allies is mythologized as marking the 'birth' of the Canadian nation within the historical narrative.[3] The Canadian forces entered the war as imperial subjects in a dominion, and "arose from the battlefields" like phoenix from the ashes (Ikas, "Formative Years" 36). This idea of 'being born in the trenches of Europe' was built on the following

---

within the context of family, community, and society. Identity is constantly reshaped, questioned and negotiated through stories; and these narratives are connected with processes of memory and their relevance for the 'image of the self.' This notion of identity operates at the intersection of individual and collective, of the private and the public. For further reading, see e.g. Sen.

3 For further reading on the topic of Canadian World War I participation and its impact on Canadian self-consciousness, see e.g. Granatstein and Morton.

reading: Canada became fully independent in the aftermath of the Great War, due to its major successes on the battlefields, and entered the international stage as a 'worthy ally' and recognized nation. It was the moment when Canada could be regarded as a nation separate from Great Britain (cf. Grace 285). Fame and triumph that were gained by the Canadian forces made it difficult to further ignore the dominion's claims for independence (cf. Craig Brown).

However, the moment of 'grandeur' when Canada was supposedly born is mostly associated with the Anglo-Canadian population of that time. One fact still remains obliterated: joining the armed forces was not only an option for Canadian males of European descent, but enlisting was also – at some point – possible for the indigenous population. Although it was not expected, many First Nations men expressed a 'desire' to enlist and fight alongside the others:

> Like many young Indians, Albert [Mountain Horse, a Blood from Alberta] was torn between his traditional mores and the government's insistence on residential edification and assimilation [...] Albert proudly exclaimed that he was "going forth to fight for my King and Country." (Winegard 113)

The imperial government was not expecting any such tendencies at all, since it did not occur to them as logical that 'Indians' would fight a war for the colonizer. However, historian James Dempsey states that by the end of the war, about 35% percent of the capable male indigenous population had enlisted and joined the army. He continues: "This was at least equal to the proportion of non-Indian enlistment in Canada" (9). Many of them showed great prowess as snipers and trackers, since their cultural traditions – if their upbringing had not been grinded down by residential school education – would enable indigenous soldiers to 'excel' in certain aspects of warfare, if use of this verb is permissible in the context of killing and dying.[4] However, since military service was not mandatory for indigenous men, the question remains what made them enlist anyway. Dempsey quotes a letter from the Indian Department, which was in charge of 'aboriginal affairs' at that time, a letter which comments on the very reasons for indigenous enlistment:

> The Department receives testimonials of loyalty from Indian bands, and letters from individual Indians, which are fired with zealous and sincere patriotism and often display a highly intelligent interest in the progress of the war and a remarkably clear grasp of the principles which are at stake. (5)

---

[4] There is, for example, the quite famous story of Francis Pegahmagabow, an Ojibway, who was very successful in battle as a sniper. He joined the forces and killed more enemies than any other soldier in his battalion. He was awarded the Military Medal and two bars for that. Joseph Boyden gained inspiration for his novel from Francis Pegahmagabow's story.

After all, the indigenous population seemed either capable of displaying feelings of patriotism towards the colonizing forces and their warfare business outside the borders of Canada, or it was just the current situation of oppression, cultural re-education, poverty, and deprivation in general that made them enlist and fight for 'their' country.

At the beginning of his study on representations of World War I in English culture, Samuel Hynes proclaims: "The First World War was the greatest military and political event of its time; but it was also the great imaginative event" (xi). Canada, as has already been indicated, has imagined this war, or, more precisely, her participation in the war, as a decisive moment in the country's history. With this assessment, a Canadian master narrative has been stipulated – or not, since critics have often regarded a lack of such master narratives as characteristic of Canadian national identity: "While earlier Canadian literary theory had lamented the absence of a national master narrative (something comparable to the American Dream, for instance) this lack now undergoes a positive reassessment [...]. 'Disunity' becomes the Canadian strategy of unity" (Rosenthal 306). In any case, Canadian involvement in the First World War has become a framework through which a national self-consciousness is produced: a nation can no longer be perceived as a fixed entity, solely confined by natural or political boundaries, characterized through religious homogeneity (cf. Renan). It is rather a "spiritual principle" that is prone to construction and constant reassessment (Renan 19). This fabric is comprised of narratives of different kinds – being of a political, fictional, historical, individual or collective nature.[5] This "fragile narrative construct" is what constitutes national identity and is under constant (re)construction and negotiation (Rosenthal 302). The past and its stories are the resources that (mostly) inform these narratives and, as a consequence, become an issue of negotiation themselves. Narratives of the past are the source of individual and collective identity, for they locate us in time and space and within our specific culture, while at the same time producing notions of temporal, spatial and cultural experience in the process of narrating.[6] Hence, these texts (in a broader sense of the concept) also form mnemonic monuments which are never stable in

---

5 See the essays in Bhabha, which deal with the question of how a national structure is narrated within the collective realm, emphasizing both the constructed nature of national entity and the productive force of cultural productions addressing and employing stories of the past with regard to the narration of a nation.

6 Maurice Halbwachs and Aleida Assmann have shown that memory is a social phenomenon that operates at the intersection of the individual and collective. Memory is thus something that unfolds between people and through their interaction, while at the same time enabling group cohesion and (collective) identity. Stories of and from the past are important sources of this 'social' memory.

their meaning and always multifaceted in the response they evoke.[7] Events like the Great War become narratives that qualify as frameworks for this process of locating and construction: if a nation is imagined, then (grand) narratives are the means to assess, construct, invent and produce its unity (cf. Anderson). Imagination here is not meant to be an impeachment. On the contrary, it denotes the forceful productivity that accompanies narrating a nation. Seen in this light, it is understandable why the topic of the Great War has not lost its appeal. Being at least an important moment in Canadian history, World War I has become mythologized in the aftermath and was turned into a framework in order to draw on what the Canadian nation 'is made of' (cf. Grace). It offers a grand narrative to elicit a different assessment of the past and to enable a different reading of a nation's past in different contexts, as it will be further explained in the analysis of Boyden's novel.[8] These memory discourses have the power to overcome generational boundaries, and hence become narratives of post-memory reaching out beyond actual witnesses and testimonies (cf. Hirsch). These memories, or narratives of memory, are deeply embedded in the self-perception of a generation, and by transferring them, these narratives may become "memories in their own rights" to the next generation (Hirsch 103). This trans-generational potential of narratives about the past and the meaning ascribed to it further underlines the productive force and impact of images from the past, even if they do not directly

---

[7] The idea of the 'monument' as a mnemonic space, or rather place, has been revised within the field of memory studies. A monument is not necessarily a sculpture, building or tangible place where an event of the past is commemorated. Pierre Nora has identified various *Realms of Memory* of the French nation, broadening the concept of monuments towards e.g. literature (Proust), emphasizing that these monuments provoke and trigger processes of memory and, as a result, national consciousness. Drawing on this idea of multifaceted kinds of monuments, Indra Sengupta has shown that these monuments are never fixed in the reaction they provoke. In particular within the (post)colonial realm, memory evoked by monuments of whatever nature becomes a matter of perspective and (re)construction. Ann Rigney has contributed to this discourse by stressing the particular quality of literature as "portable monuments," operating as a framework for memory processes.

[8] Narratives of the First World War demonstrate a certain universal quality, for many countries had been involved in the war itself and struggled to come to terms with it in the aftermath. The war and its stories became part of many nations' historical and cultural inventory. In the process of (re)assessing national identity, these stories have functioned as frameworks enabling a location of Canada within this transnational realm of World-War-I-narratives by a (national) reframing of these stories (cf. Levy and Sznaider). Memories and their narrative representations become 'multidirectional' in the sense that they open up a productive space of meaning construction while at the same time contesting notions of ownership and interpretative agency regarding formative historical narratives (cf. Rothberg).

belong to the 'story of the self' of (contemporary) consumers, readers, recipients or relatives – whatever denotation for the post-generation is chosen.

The sense of forming part of a national structure is strongly informed by narratives of the past and the way they have been transmitted. A national identity is negotiated by various narratives, and they have the power to create an affectionate, ultimately imagined relation among each other and the national structure itself (cf. Anderson). These narratives are shaped and framed by prevailing narrative structures which have gained "a higher authoritative power" than other texts (Rosenthal 306). The reading and contextualization of those narrative frameworks may alter in the course of time; they are constantly undergoing processes of negotiation and construction. However, their poignancy and potential of creating affection may be transmitted to the next generation and thus enable a different contextualization.

Literary fiction is a very powerful platform for these processes of conveyance and negotiation, for it offers "an imaginary perspective on the real world" (Rosenthal 293). Furthermore, literature is capable of evoking an affective response to 'knowledge' about the past which may have become petrified, for it has seemingly lost its connection with the contemporary. Joseph Boyden's novel *Three Day Road* is an example of revisiting narratives of the Great War in order to reattach the reader with its national past, but from a different perspective (cf. Bölling).[9]

3 Negotiating Identity within the Novel and Beyond – Joseph Boyden's *Three Day Road*

Boyden's novel has already been identified as a text which challenges established notions of the national narrative, contesting the master narrative derived from Canadian participation in the Great War as being dominated by 'white' depictions and accounts (cf. Bölling, Glaser, Ulm). Seen in this light, *Three Day Road* inscribes indigenous participation in World War I into the Canadian historical consciousness. The text tells the story of two young Cree friends, Xavier Bird and Elijah Whiskeyjack, who embark for Europe to join the war for Canada. The two attended a Residential School and were educated by the colonizers in order to diminish their indigeneity. Xavier remained in close contact with his family and kin, whereas Elijah 'enjoyed' the cultural re-education practices more profoundly.

---

9 On earlier Canadian writing on World War I see Thompson and Novak. On Findley's *The Wars* see Kuester. For a concise survey of recent novels on the First World War and their themes, see Glaser.

In the course of army training and the war itself, Xavier re-educates Elijah in terms of basic skills that are framed to be typically, even stereotypically, 'Indian' (cf. Ulm): tracking, hunting, enduring. As a consequence, the two friends become renowned snipers. Elijah increasingly finds pleasure in killing and solace in morphine addiction, much to the dismay of his friend Xavier. Towards the end of the novel, Elijah turns *windigo*, hence impersonating the utmost evil in First Nations' mythology, a being which feeds on human flesh.[10] As Xavier's aunt Niska anticipates:

> We'd grown up on stories of the *windigo* that our parents fed us over the winter fires, of people who eat other people's flesh and grow into wild beasts twenty feet tall whose hunger can be satisfied only by more human flesh and then the hunger turns worse. (Boyden 49)

It is not only Elijah, however, who drifts into madness; rather, the entire war with its horrible numbers of casualties seems to be embedded in the *windigo* episode. In an act of despair, Xavier finally kills his friend Elijah.

The narrative itself is organized around two strands. One is dominated by the accounts of Niska, who is surprised to pick up Xavier, not Elijah, whom she had expected due to a confusion of identity.[11] *Three Day Road* continues the Canadian tradition of war novels, of historical novels, featuring the Great War as its framing narrative (cf. Bölling, Glaser, Ulm, Williams). It draws on well-established tropes and themes, such as the 'realistic' depiction of war experience (cf. Glaser), or the idea of a rite of passage from Canada, representing the youth and innocence of the protagonists, to the theatres of war in Europe in order to become a man, a warrior. In the case of the two Cree friends, it is not only a transition from Canada to Europe, it is also a crucible for them in terms of how they would cope with being immersed into the culture of the colonizer. Elijah has seemingly no difficulties to blend in with the other soldiers:

> Elijah can out-talk even the officers with his nun's English and his quick thinking. The others in our section are drawn to him and his endless stories. I am forced by my poor English to sit back and watch it all happen, to see how he wins them over, while I become more invisible. A brown ghost. (Boyden 73)

Boyden's narrative adds another meaning to the soldier's initiation, the coming-of-age as a warrior and as a Canadian. Whilst Elijah seemingly adjusts to lan-

---

10 For further reading on the subject of First Nations' mythological characters, see e.g. Gruber, "Aboriginal Oral Traditions."
11 Xavier had taken the identification tag off Elijah after having killed him. Having lost a leg, Xavier woke up in hospital and was identified as Elijah Whiskeyjack for that matter.

guage and customs, Xavier remains an outcast. The narrative interweaves these traditional elements of recounting World War I with features of First Nations' narrative techniques: The cyclical, associative emplotment of the narrative alludes to orality and oral history, and the use of indigenous mythological characters such as the trickster *Weesageechak* and the *Windigo* further strengthen this assessment (cf. Gruber, "Aboriginal Oral Traditions"). Elijah's last name is pronounced 'Whiskeyjack' by the Canadian soldiers, a phonetic allusion to the shape-shifting trickster figure in indigenous mythology:

> The other soldiers often ask Elijah about his name too. And he is happy to talk. His Cree name is Weesageechak. [...] Whiskeyjack is how they say his name, make it their own. He has told me that what they do to his name is what sounds to my ear like a longer word for *bastard*, making his name a name without a family. Weesageechak is the trickster, the one who takes different forms at will. (174)

This idea of the shape-shifting trickster figure is of particular importance: Elijah is the one who has command of English, even managing to acquire the fellow soldiers' accents, and who seemingly has no trouble blending in with the others. In addition, he has sufficiently maintained or regained some skills of his First Nations' cultural heritage. Elijah (together with Xavier) excels in tracking and sniping, but also manages to gain the other soldiers' sympathy and admiration. All these intertwined 'qualities' make him a hybrid figure, a person that exists at the in-between of various cultural forces. Like *Weesageechak*, he is capable of blending in wherever he wants. The war poisons this hybrid existence, and makes him deteriorate into the utmost evil. The trickster figure, which is positively connoted as being a productive force (cf. Gruber, "Aboriginal Oral Traditions"), ultimately fails. This reading poses the question whether the narrative seeks to convey that an existence at intersections is doomed to fail, hence suggests that hybridity is not viable.

Furthermore, the two narrative strands do not only open up a dichotomy between indigenous and 'white', they also refer to an antagonism that is well-known within the Canadian literary tradition (cf. Rosenthal, Kuester): the conflict of 'here' *versus* 'there.' As has already been suggested, Canadian existence, or more precisely, the image of Canadian existence, has been characterized by a status of in-between: Having gained independence from Great Britain, the newly arisen Canadian nation was trying to distance herself from the 'motherland.' The 'here,' referring to Canada, still felt inferior in comparison to England (cf. Rosenthal, drawing on the works of Northrop Frye), and a longing to be 'there,' or to be as allegedly superior as Great Britain.[12] Canadian society was driven to differentiate itself from this superpower, both in terms of economy and culture. However, this tension between the 'here' and 'there' was also strongly informed by a sense of inferiority towards other dominating nations and cultures. In Boyden's novel, the 'here' is represented by Niska and her stories, and thus alludes to Canada, home, tradition, family and kinship. This home is threatened by forced assimilation through the Residential School System and by the heinous living conditions that First Nations peoples faced at that time. Nonetheless, the 'here' within *Three Day Road* stands for the possibility of healing, of returning home through storytelling (cf. Williams, Ulm). The delineation 'there', however, stands for (Anglo-)European culture, the foreign countries, war, alienation, harm, pain, loss, death, and even muteness, and is represented by Xavier's narratives. *Three Day Road* hence draws on this tension between 'here' and 'there.' Most importantly, it opens up a different dimension of assessment of this 'ancient conflict' of identity: There is no clear-cut attribution of 'superior' and 'inferior' possible anymore. 'Here' is represented by the allegedly 'inferior' indigenous population, but also offers a possibility of healing and survival. 'There' is no longer an existence worth imitating, if it ever was, but has turned into a battleground. Again, identity negotiation is at the core of Boyden's narrative and, furthermore, is translated into a more differentiated notion of it.

Xavier, returning home from the war mutilated and intoxicated by morphine, is unable to speak about his experiences. Words, or language in general, seem inadequate to represent the horrific impressions of the war (cf. Löschnigg). Niska takes him on a three-day-journey on the river to bring him home to his family and kin, and while they travel, she recounts stories of her youth and Xavier's family, firmly believing in the healing powers of storytelling (cf. Williams, Gruber):

> I steer the canoe into the faster current and let us drift with it, using my paddle only as a rudder. The mist is disappearing now and I can see a long way down the bank, can keep an eye sharp for the movement of animals along the shore. Nephew cries out but then goes silent again. The sound of it, the animal fear at the very bottom of that cry, makes me think something I haven't thought about in a long time. It is the story of my childhood. Now I tell it to you, Xavier, to keep you alive. (39)

Her stories evoke reactions and allusions within Xavier which unfold within his mind, thus intertwining the two narrative strands. Niska's narrative draws a specific image of Canada, that of a home to wounded Xavier and a place where life can be regained, if one returns to nature and kinship. The Residential School

---

[12] In the course of time, Great Britain ceased to be the 'intimate rival' and was replaced by the USA.

System lingers in the background, reminding the reader that this Canada is still far from being an idyll for the indigenous population.

As this analysis has shown, *Three Day Road* opens various spaces of identity negotiation. On a narrative level, the reader observes the protagonists' struggles to reiterate familial and, as a consequence, cultural identity through the accounts of Aunt Niska. Her firm belief in the healing powers of storytelling provides a stage for Xavier's coming to terms with what has happened to him during the war, and what has become of him in its aftermath: returning as an amputee, Xavier recalls the topos of war being literally inscribed on a human body (cf. Winter, *Sites of Memory*). The brutal impact of war has changed him fundamentally. The Indian Residential School System, a narrative that lingers in the background, has contributed to turning Elijah into a *Weesageechak*, a hybrid figure capable of shape-shifting, but this form of identity is doomed to fail. It is an interesting aspect of *Three Day Road* that Xavier, the one of the two Crees who has tried to maintain as much of his indigenous identity as possible, ends Elijah's existence. Marco Ulm has raised the issue that the protagonists of Boyden's text are almost stereotypical representations of indigeneity, and that by constructing the characters in this particular manner, Boyden has attempted to dismantle these stereotypes in the first place, and has drawn attention to them. However, *Three Day Road* also reaches beyond this textual level: Contrasting Canada with the theatres of war in Europe evokes the country's struggle for identifying its status as a nation by seeking to distinguish itself from others, and links the Canada of the time of World War I with contemporary Canada and its struggle with her colonial heritage. Boyden's text locates itself within the realm of World War I fiction, but at the same time broadens the scope of this genre by re-narrating this formative narrative in a more inclusive manner. The structure of his narrative enables one to perceive another identity negotiation that is still ongoing. The Canadian nation is still grappling to come to terms with its imperial legacy, in this case concerning the treatment of the indigenous population under colonial reign. The text raises questions whether an existence in-between, represented by Elijah, is able to be resilient, hence connects his story with the status quo of First Nations in contemporary Canada. The current discourse of reconciliation resounds in the narrative, for *Three Day Road* on the one hand (re)claims indigenous inclusion within the overarching national narrative, while at the same time drawing attention to how the cultural re-education system has had a profoundly destructive impact on indigenous identity.

4 "A sad chapter in our history" – Reconciling Canada

Canada has recently witnessed a return to the very origins of the nation, in the shape of an attempt at reconciliation with that very indigenous population. The latter was subjected to an educational program aiming at outbreeding indigeneity – habits, customs, language, and beliefs – and at inculcating 'Europeanness.' This aim was pursued through a Residential School System, a network of boarding schools which were mostly operated by the churches. The system was in place until the mid-1990s, depriving thousands of indigenous children of their cultural roots.[13] Struggles about land claims and looming verdicts on monetary compensation for the victims of this system gave rise to a process of reconciliation with the indigenous population of Canada, as stipulated in a Settlement Agreement and in the constitution of the *Truth and Reconciliation Commission of Canada*.[14] By establishing this commission, Canadian authorities have followed international practices in transitional justice and the example of other truth commissions, such as the *Truth and Reconciliation Commission* of South Africa. The outcome of Canada's journey towards reconciliation is ambiguous, and the question of how to attain reconciliation has only been partially addressed. This process was emphasized to be of national interest by an apology that Prime Minister Stephen Harper issued on behalf of the Canadian government in 2008.[15] Canada has engaged in a controversial debate about the very origin of the nation, which perceives itself as liberal, democratic and open towards diversity. The narratives of the First Nations' fate and struggle for survival have merely been a footnote in the Canadian national narrative, but with this process unfolding, the indigenous population may eventually be viewed from a different perspective. In addition, the narratives that are evoked during this process of reconciliation may in turn spark a different assessment of the current living and educational situation of the First Nations. Hence, it is inevitable to take all different, contesting, and challenging narratives into account, for reconciliation may not be attained solely by

---

[13] This can only be a short outline of the very complex Residential School legacy. For further and more profound information on this subject, see e.g. Milloy and Miller.

[14] The Settlement Agreement is available online at the website of the Truth and Reconciliation Commission of Canada, http://www.trc.ca/websites/trcinstitution/index.php?p=4 (27 August 2013).

[15] As Prime Minister Stephen Harper stated in his apology, "[t]he treatment of children in Indian residential schools is a sad chapter in our history." Harper's apology followed that of Australian Prime Minister Kevin Rudd. The speech may be read here: http://www.cbc.ca/news/canada/story/2008/06/11/pm-statement.html (28 October 2013).

the work of the Truth commission. It is the concerted attack on comfortable truths and well-established master narratives that enables a change in perception, and this attack is informed by narratives of different kinds.

5 Conclusion

Joseph Boyden's novel *Three Day Road* employs familiar techniques of retelling the war – revisiting tropes, drawing on the formal and stylistic repertoire of World War I representation. However, the perspective of this particular war narrative is different, since it focuses on the experience of indigenous characters. The text thereby broadens the circle of the transnational community connected through loss and bereavement to include the aboriginal population of Canada. The 'fictive kinship' that is called upon through *Three Day Road* emerges by means of this inclusion of the indigenous, and enables this participation (cf. Winter, "Forms of Kinship and Remembrance"). The special connection that is shared by all those who have lost someone to the war is hence enlarged, widened towards a community that has been largely obliterated.

If Canadian participation in the Great War was the moment when this nation came into being, indigenous participation is difficult to ignore after having read this novel. Seen in this light, the context of World War I becomes a vehicle of how to introduce different perceptions of historical 'knowledge' into society, individuals and the national narrative. Fiction is a powerful tool to convey messages, to move people, and to evoke emotional, even sensual connections. By adhering to familiar modes of how to depict war stories, the text locates itself within all the 'possible worlds' of war narratives. This strategy is a prerequisite in order to add a second perspective, beyond that of the narrative, to the text: to shed light on the exclusion of indigenous people from the national narrative and to raise questions of identity and existence in the aftermath of colonization. Since Boyden's novel has also become a bestseller, the message is well-placed. Literature and cultural productions in general have an important role in the current reconciliation process, for they may contest, challenge and rewrite the national narrative. Thus, in Boyden's novel, one of the key stories of Canadian identity formation is revisited in order to contest and challenge traditional readings of the war's significance, for the purpose of introducing a different perspective and enabling a different reading.

Ironically enough, the alleged birth of the Canadian nation remains a paradox. Canada entered the war under imperial dependence, and left the battlefields to rise independently. That very imperial structure has imposed a system of cultural re-education on the indigenous population with the aim of destroying their culture and habits. However, the glory surrounding Canada's participation in the Great War neither rubs off on the First Nations, nor does it pose painstaking questions of the janus-faced nature of Canadian colonial history, and, hence, the origin of the liberal society as which Canada sees herself today.[16] A nation that perceives itself as being born while cutting off ties to the Crown seems unable to see the other side of the coin; that this nation was also built at the expense of its indigenous population. The most recent endeavors to achieve a reconciliation between Euro-Canadians and the First Nations resound in the narrative of *Three Day Road,* as the novel (re)claims historical agency and recognition for the indigenous people within the national narrative and enables discourses of identity negotiation. Literature thus becomes a vehicle, an amplifier, even a catalyst for struggles of constructing and maintaining identities, and, as a consequence, national structures. The context of the Great War still offers a rich reservoir to make this claim, and narratives like *Three Day Road* create a parallel timing of diverse, vibrant, more inclusive national narratives.

References

Anderson, Benedict. *Imagined Communities*. London: Verso, 2006 [1983].
Angus, Ian. "The Canadian Nation(s): Philosophy and the Critique of Empire." *Global Realignments and the Canadian Nation in the Third Millenium*. Ed. Karin Ikas. Wiesbaden: Harrassowitz, 2010. 25–34.
Assmann, Aleida. *Erinnerungsräume. Formen und Wandlungen des kulturellen Gedächtnisses*. Munich: Beck, 2003.
Bhabha, Homi, ed. *Nation and Narration*. London: Routledge, 1990.
Bölling, Gordon. "'A Part of Our History that So Few Know About'. Native Involvement in Canada's Great War – Joseph Boyden's *Three Day Road*." *Inventing Canada/Inventer le Canada*. Eds. Klaus Dieter Ertler and Martin Löschnigg. Frankfurt a. M.: Peter Lang, 2008. 253–268.
Boyden, Joseph. *Three Day Road*. London: Orion House, 2006 [2005].
Craig Brown, Robert. "Sir Robert Borden and Canada's War Aims." *War Aims and Strategic Policy in the Great War 1914–1918*. Eds. Barry Hunt and Adrian Preston. Totowa: Rowman and Littlefield, 1977. 55–64.
Das, Santanu, ed. *Race, Empire and First World War Writing*. Cambridge: Cambridge University Press, 2011.

---

16 For further reading on the difficulties that arise while Canada is trying to integrate (possible) colonial genocide into its self-image of a liberal nation, refer to McGonegal and Henderson/Wakeham.

Dempsey, James. *Aboriginal Soldiers in the First World War*. Canadian Government Archive. www.collectionscanada.gc.ca/aboriginal-heritage/020016-4002-e.html (28 October 2013).

Findley, Timothy. *The Wars*. Leipzig: Faber & Faber, 2001 [1977].

Fussell, Paul W. *The Great War and Modern Memory*. New York: Oxford University Press, 2000 [1975].

Glaser, Brigitte. "(Re)Turning to Europe for the Great War. Representations of World War I in Contemporary Anglophone Canadian Fiction." *Zeitschrift für Kanada-Studien* 30. 2 (2010): 62–75.

Grace, Sherrill, and Donna Coates, eds. *Canada and the Theatre of War*. 2 vols. Toronto: Playwrights Canada Press 2008, 2010.

Grace, Sherrill. "Sociopolitical and Cultural Developments from 1967 to the Present." *History of Literature in Canada. English-Canadian and French-Canadian*. Ed. Reingard M. Nischik. Woodbridge: Camden House, 2008. 285–290.

Granatstein, J. L., and Desmond Morton. *Canada and the Two World Wars*. Toronto: Key Porter Books, 2003.

Gruber, Eva. "Aboriginal Oral Traditions." *History of Literature in Canada. English-Canadian and French-Canadian*. Ed. Reingard M. Nischik. 27–37.

Gruber, Eva. "Literature of the First Nations, Inuit, and Métis." *History of Literature in Canada. English-Canadian and French-Canadian*. Ed. Reingard M. Nischik. 413–428.

Halbwachs, Maurice. *On Collective Memory*. Trans. Lewis. A. Coser. Chicago: University of Chicago Press, 1992.

Harper, Stephen. *National Apology*. http://www.cbc.ca/news/canada/story/2008/06/11/pm-statement.html. (28 October 2013).

Henderson, Jennifer, and Pauline Wakeham. "Colonial Reckoning, National Reconciliation? Aboriginal Peoples and the Culture of Redress in Canada." *English Studies in Canada* 35. 1 (2009): 1–26.

Hirsch, Marianne. *The Generation of Postmemory. Writing and Visual Culture after the Holocaust*. New York: Columbia University Press, 2012.

Hynes, Samuel. *A War Imagined. The First World War and English Culture*. London: The Bodley Head, 1990.

Hynes, Samuel. "Personal Narratives and Commemoration." *War and Remembrance in the Twentieth Century*. Eds. Jay M. Winter and Emmanuel Sivan. Cambridge: Cambridge University Press, 2000. 205–220.

Ikas, Karin. "Formative Years: (Dis)ability, War and the Canadian Nation." *Global Realignments and the Canadian Nation in the Third Millennium*. Ed. Karin Ikas. Wiesbaden: Harrassowitz, 2010. 35–44.

Ikas, Karin. "Global Realignments and the (Canadian) Nation in the Third Millennium: An Introduction." *Global Realignments ...* Ed. Karin Ikas. 1–24.

Kuester, Martin. "The English-Canadian Novel from Modernism to Postmodernism." *History of Literature in Canada*. Ed. Reingard M. Nischik. 310–329.

Lévy, Daniel, and Natan Sznaider. *The Holocaust and Memory in the Global Age*. Philadelphia: Temple University Press, 2006.

Löschnigg, Martin. "Memory, Myth and the Crisis of Narrative in Anglophone Canadian Novels about World War I." *Narratives of Crisis – Crisis of Narrative*. Ed. Martin Kuester, Françoise Le Jeune, Anca-Raluca Radu, and Charlotte Sturgess. Augsburg: Wißner, 2012. 108–125.

McGonegal, Julie. "The Great Canadian (and Australian) Secret: The Limits of Non-Indigenous Knowledge and Representation." *English Studies in Canada* 35. 1 (March 2009): 67–83.

Miller, J. R. *Shingwauk's Vision: A History of Native Residential Schools*. Toronto: University of Toronto Press, 2009.

Milloy, John S. *A National Crime: The Canadian Government and the Residential School System, 1879–1986*. Winnipeg: University of Manitoba Press, 1999.

Morris, David B. "Narrative, Ethics and Pain: Thinking *with* Stories." *Narrative* 9. 1 (2001): 55–72.

Nora, Pierre, and Lawrence D. Kritzmann, eds. *Realms of Memory. The Construction of the French Past*. New York: Columbia University Press, 1996.

Novak, Dagmar. *Dubious Glory. The Two World Wars and the Canadian Novel*. Berlin: Peter Lang, 2005.

Renan, Ernest. "What Is a Nation?" *Nation and Narration*. Ed. Homi K. Bhabha. London: Routledge, 1990. 8–22.

Ricoeur, Paul. *Memory, History Forgetting*. Chicago: University of Chicago Press, 2004.

Rigney, Ann. "Portable Monuments. Literature, Culture and the Case of Jeanie Deans." *Poetics Today* 25. 2 (2004): 361–396.

Rosenthal, Caroline. "English-Canadian Literary Theory and Literary Criticism." *History of Literature in Canada*. Ed. Reingard M. Nischik. 291–309.

Rothberg, Michael. *Multidirectional Memory. Remembering the Holocaust in the Age of Decolonization*. Stanford: Stanford University Press, 2009.

Sen, Amartya. *Identity and Violence. The Illusion of Destiny*. New York: Norton, 2007.

Sengupta, Indra, and Hagen Schulze, eds. *Memory, History and Colonialism: Engaging with Pierre Nora in Colonial and Postcolonial Contexts*. London: German Historical Institute, 2009.

Thompson, Eric. "Canadian Fiction of the Great War." *Canadian Literature* 91 (1981): 81–96.

Ulm, Marco. "'The Rumours Continue Until They Become the Truth': Stereoptypes in Joseph Boyden's *Three Day Road*". *Narratives of Crisis – Crisis of Narrative*. Ed. Martin Kuester et al. 91–107.

Williams, David. "The Underlying Crisis of Media Change: From *Generals Die in Bed* to *Three Day Road*." *Narratives of Crisis – Crisis of Narrative*. Ed. Martin Kuester et al. 76–90.

Winegard, Timothy C. *Indigenous Peoples of the British Dominions and the First World War*. New York: Cambridge University Press, 2012.

Winter, Jay M. "Forms of Kinship and Remembrance in the Aftermath of the Great War." *War and Remembrance in the Twentieth Century*. Eds. Jay M. Winter and Emmanuel Sivan. Cambridge: Cambridge University Press, 2000. 40–60.

Winter, Jay M. *Sites of Memory, Sites of Mourning – The Great War in European Cultural History*. Cambridge: Cambridge University Press, 1998 [1995].

Christina Spittel
Nostalgia for the Nation? The First World War in Australian Novels of the 1970s and 1980s

> I have read World War I like most people; I found it reasonably tiresome reading because I didn't know what it meant. They kept speaking about words such as "glory"; "climbing those unscalable heights," – well, if the damn things were unscalable, how did they get up there? And then when I went to Gallipoli [...] I could go up and down it before lunch. So what was there in it?
>
> Patsy Adam-Smith, "Gallipoli"

1 Re-reading the First World War

For Australians, the First World War had immediately been turned into a foundational narrative of national history, even as it was still being fought. But by the 1970s, this story of white men's courage, mateship, ingenuity, and humour on distant battlefields – Australians had fought on Gallipoli, in the Middle East and on the Western Front – seemed an anachronism (cf. Beaumont 552 f.). Popular historian Patsy Adam-Smith was not alone in finding Australia's First World War "tiresome reading". Then, just at the moment when connections with living memory began to wear thin, Australian writers, raised on family stories and commemorative ritual surrounding the 60,000 war dead, reworked this lumpy heritage for a contemporary audience.

Indeed, some felt that the truth about that war could only now be revealed. In an article entitled "Who Owns The Great War," novelist and poet Roger McDonald responded by drawing on *The Great War and Modern Memory* (1975): "'The greatest irony,' writes Paul Fussell [...], 'is that it is only now when those that remember the events are almost dead, that the literary means for adequate remembering and interpreting are finally accessible'" (McDonald, "Who Owns the Great War" 3). Fussell's now classic account resonated with Australians writing in the aftermath of Vietnam: David Williamson, script-writer for Peter Weir's *Gallipoli* (1981), called it his favourite book (qtd. in Kiernan 289); for literary scholar Robin Gerster it was "an inspiration (and an awesome standard) for anyone interested in the literature of war" (x). Yet looking for versions of "modern memory" in their own libraries, these writers were frustrated: "In our country," wrote Peter Weir, "we had no Wilfred Owen, no Robert Graves, no Sassoon, no great war poets who could tell us about the lost generation" (qtd. in Rayner 101). Instead, Robin Gerster detected an "assured and aggressive [...], absurdly old-fashioned" streak in Australian war writing (5).[1]

This chapter deliberately reads 'literary' novels alongside novelisations, filmic narratives and popular histories to argue that Australians writing in the 1970s and 1980s took a range of forms, and recovered a range of truths. The work of a previous generation, reprinted or even issued for the first time, further added to this conversation around what the First World War might mean to a community for whom it was fast receding into the distant past, beyond autobiographical memory.

2 New Frameworks of Memory

In 1977 newspapers in all Australian capital cities ventured to count the survivors of the Gallipoli campaign. 1,766 men answered their call. *The Sydney Morning Herald* listed 393 men from New South Wales in its Anzac Day issue. Most of them were 82 or 83 years old, the youngest 78 and the oldest 99 (cf. Parfitt, "The Gallipoli Muster"). As these ageing veterans looked back on their lives, a number of memoirs entered Australian bookshops (cf. Ziino 129). At the same time, private records passed from deceased estates into public possession, doubling the number of war letters and diaries available by 1980 (cf. Stanley 99). From the 1970s, professional historians and curators took over the custodianship of the Australian War Memorial, previously in the hands of veterans; and a new Australian War Memorial Act (1980) tasked the reinvigorated institution with encouraging research and publications about the Australian experience of war.

A concern that fuelled this research and rendered the old Anzacs visible again was the urgent need for national narratives in the onset of global decolonisation. Australia's volunteer army had sailed off for King and Country, as the Australian *Imperial* Force; a fifth of its men had been born in Britain (cf. Seal 173). Now the United Kingdom's decision to join the European Economic Community and to withdraw its troops from East of Suez ushered in a period of soul-searching "for a more self-sufficient, self-sustaining idea of the people, in place of the 'old' nationalism with its entanglements in wider networks of British belonging" (Ward 232). Milestones of the 'new nationalism' of the 1960s and 1970s include the *Australian*, a newspaper founded in 1964; the *Australian Dictionary of Bio-*

---

[1] See Caesar and my own work for accounts that seek to nuance these claims.

graphy, whose first volume appeared in 1966; Sydney's Opera House, unveiled in 1973, as well as Australia's first ministry of culture, founded in 1971. Funding for the arts increased significantly, in the hope that revitalised film and publishing industries might project an image of Australia to its citizenry and the world. Grants for Australian writers were not an invention of the 1970s, but the much more generous budget of the newly founded Literature Board helped Australian publishing to a boom.[2] Seven of the applications approved for funding revisited Australia's First World War.

Marianne Hirsch has pointed out how "one trauma can recall, or reactivate, the effects of another" (104), and for some of these writers, Australia's experience of the Vietnam War did that. The heated debates over conscription seemed to echo those of 1916–1917, creating the impression that, as historian Bill Gammage recalled, "the same script was being acted out" again ("The Broken Years" 15). Some of the most prolific workers of Great War memory were members of the peace movement: Roger McDonald and David Malouf, for example, had contributed poems to an anti-war anthology, *We Took Their Orders and Are Dead* (1971). Geoff Burrowes, the producer of the TV mini-series *Anzacs* (1985), had taken part in the protest marches, as had his historical adviser, Patsy Adam-Smith, for whom the frustration with the American ally marked a moment of national self-awareness: "What Vietnam did do was to make us face the fact that our age of innocence and dependence on others is gone" ("Age of Innocence").

From the vantage point of the 1970s and 1980s, the landscape of the Great War could become the *ur*-scene of a long century of industrialised violence. Roger McDonald, for example, saw the "universal anxiety about nuclear destruction, surely the climax of modernist frustration, [...] prefigured in the WWI experience. Those who came home carried with them a vision of Armageddon" ("Who Owns the Great War" 5). For poet Geoff Page, Ronald Reagan's brinkmanship was part of a long continuum that re-connected Cold War Australia with 1914–1918, "the culmination of all that had been developing steadily since the mass destruction of World War One" ("Should Non-Combatants Write About War" 105). Such hindsight made the monuments of Australia's First World War appear like "the symbolic tombs of an ideal", as Patsy Adam-Smith put it (*The Anzacs* 358), and rendered accounts that cast the conflict itself as futile and ironic – hardly the war to end all wars – particularly pertinent.

---

2 Founded in 1908, the Commonwealth Literary Fund had a budget of $ 250,000 in 1972; in the following year, the Literature Board set out with a fund of over one million dollars, which had reached 2.8 million dollars by 1986. (Gelder and Salzman 2)

3 New Points of Entry: The Popular Histories of Bill Gammage and Patsy Adam-Smith

In the 1950s and 1960s, the history of war had been the "preserve of old and serving soldiers, collectors of militaria and enthusiasts" (Stanley 91 f.); in the 1970s two works of popular history made Australia's First World War accessible to a much wider readership, whom the war had previously left untouched, even alienated. Christina Twomey has argued that, "changing ideas about trauma and victimhood which emerged from the 1980s, played an important and insufficiently recognised role in the reinvigoration of Anzac for contemporary times" (85). Even before then, Bill Gammage's and Patsy Adam-Smith's fresh narrative choices made Anzac legible as a story of national suffering *and* courage, commanding sympathy, understanding and pride, not critique or rebellion.

Gammage was 32 when *The Broken Years* (1974) came out. The Anzac Days of his childhood had been a "mechanistic affair," rendering visible the gulf between those who had been "there" and marched, and those who had not, and looked on.[3] *The Broken Years* sought to heal these divisions with a narrative that combines the words of the young historian with those of the men themselves, transcribed from previously untapped sources: letters and diaries, as well as interviews with survivors. Thus, reading about Gallipoli becomes an intimate act of witnessing:

> At some point during those hectic hours, or perhaps during the following day or so, Private McAnulty snatched a few moments to confide, *I've pulled through all right so far, just got a few minutes to spare now. I'm all out, can hardly stand up. [...] We were right out in the open. [...] I yelled out to the other 4 chaps, 'This is suicide boys. I'm going to make a jump for it'. I thought they said alright we'll follow. I sprang to my feet in one jump*
>
> At that moment he was killed, as he was writing. (*The Broken Years* 70–71)

Here Gammage 'unlocks' and preserves what Jan Assmann has called the communicative memory of lived experience: his protagonists are the young men of 1914–1918, not the octogenarians of the Anzac Day marches. They are hopeful and idealistic; some spell as they speak – "I thorrt I would join the army"; all retain their civilian identities – a footnote identifies Private McAnulty as a clerk from Melbourne, killed in action 7–12 August 1915, aged 26 (10, 69).

Frieze-like, these epitaphs form a miniature roll of honour that points to the book's cultural function, for Gammage refreshes *and* reframes Australia's story

---

[3] Conversation with the author, 6 August 2008.

of the war. His soldiers constitute a lost generation, fighting a bitter, hopeless, depressing and ultimately tragic war, "in no way of their own making" (3), facing the "ceaseless, merciless, murderous guns," much like the doomed youth of Wilfred Owen's poetry (170). Distances to Europe, once the location of the Mother Country, are remeasured: Gammage's men "travel to the uttermost ends of the earth" (3). And yet, Gammage's futility narrative is shot through with traces of high diction. The men are glorious, ardent, dashing, even chivalrous (277, 58, 139); above all, they are *Australians* carrying "the harsh antipodean frontier in their souls" (96) and waiting "excitedly before the gates of history" (51). Theirs is a tale of sadness *and* pride which can only now be fully resolved, for in Gammage's elegiac, leftist reading it divided a young optimistic (and apparently classless) nation, previously held together by the utopia of creating a "social paradise in Australia" into those back home (who were in turn split over conscription), and those who had gone and now "lived in a world apart" (278, 263).

Four years later, popular writer Patsy Adam-Smith revived Gammage's success formula, but significantly extended his scope, including prisoners of war as well as nurses. Most importantly, perhaps, *The Anzacs* (1978) included herself. Readers first see her growing up in interwar Australia, navigating the shadows of the war – her mother's loss, her father's memories, family friends' broken bodies – all part of her quest "for reality" (358). Her conclusions are similar: "The men had gone to war for the sake of Honour and Glory, God, King and Country, and it was to be fifty years before these abstractions would be openly questioned and, where necessary, put down" (347). All in upper case, "Honour and Glory, God, King and Country," literally stick out of Adam-Smith's prose – strange ruins from another era, empty "abstractions" beyond the writer's imagination, and beyond that of her readers, too. One rejoiced: "Patsy Adam-Smith pares away all the Anzac myths, all that Union Jack and King and Country drivel inflicted on generations of school kids" (Carlyon).

Between them, Patsy Adam-Smith and Bill Gammage 'repatriated' an entire lost generation: those who had never returned from the battlefields, and who were brought to life again through their letters and diaries, and those who had survived, but whom commemorative rhetoric and ritual had removed from everyday life in 1970s Australia. Among Adam Smith's and Gammage's readers were film-makers, TV producers and novelists who would mine their narratives and scrutinise their conclusions for their own versions of that conflict.

4 Heritage Fictions: *Gallipoli, Anzacs* and *The Lighthorsemen*

For Adam-Smith, Anzac had cinematic appeal: "If America had it, Hollywood would make more films about it than they have about the trek West" ("Gallipoli" 37). Indeed by 1979, Gammage was historical adviser on Peter Weir's *Gallipoli* (1981); and Adam-Smith, having already sold the film and television rights for her book, was working towards the TV mini-series *Anzacs* (1985).[4] The impact of these two narratives is only lessening now, in the twenty-first century; a third, Simon Wincer's *The Lighthorsemen* (1987), faded more quickly. Scholars have criticised them as conservative, finding *Anzacs* "utterly conventional," offering "no redefining" (Reynaud 213), even promoting "the glorification of war" (Wieland 12). Sylvia Lawson saw "almost no ideological space" between *Gallipoli*'s mythopoetic shots of Australian soldiers at the pyramids (where they were based for training) and similar scenes in Australia's first Gallipoli feature, Alfred Rolfe's *The Hero of the Dardanelles* (1916) (qtd. in Reynaud 196).[5]

Yet Australians had hardly frozen in silent agreement over the Great War's place in cultural memory since Rolfe's recruiting movie had its athletic protagonist beat up a pacifist and drown a Turkish sniper before returning to his well-deserved sweetheart. 1980s Australia needed (and got) something different – on its cinema and TV screens, *and* in its bookshops, where a range of novels entered into a debate around the war's meaning. The teenage hero of *The Lighthorsemen* risks his life for the horses, but cannot shoot a Turk; *Gallipoli*'s men only engage in man-to-man combat during a farcical exercise in Egypt; and *Anzacs*' closing words are spoken by the young pacifist reverend. An implied viewer close to those who protested against Vietnam and nuclear armament, he invests Anzac with a peace-loving compassion as he dedicates the new war memorial. Placed in the open country, the small obelisk occupies the land the dead might have worked, had they survived. On the Western Front, one of the characters explains: "Do you know that Australia is two thirds desert? [...] such an unforgiving country like ours, we're gonna need the very best, resilient people. [...] The ones being shot out here."

---

4 Patsy Adam-Smith to Michael Davie, 7 August 1979. Papers of Patsy Adam-Smith, LaTrobe Library, Melbourne, PA89/64 box 11.
5 See, however, Graeme Turner's argument that "*Anzacs* [...] rewrites history as mythic, even epic narrative" (236). Turner's notion that this reminds audiences of Australians fighting on the Western Front, may be ignoring Adam-Smith's and Gammage's accounts of the Western Front here, as well as several novels, discussed below.

Of the tie-in novels flanking each release, Jack Bennett's *Gallipoli* (1981) stands out. Godfrey MacLeod's *Anzacs* (1985) and Elyne Mitchell's *The Lighthorsemen* (1987) were short-lived paperbacks; but Bennett's *Gallipoli* (1981) saw several reprints, most recently in 2005, to mark the ninetieth anniversary of the Gallipoli campaign, branded as "The classic story that captures the Anzac spirit." Its career began in hardcover, in supermarkets as an advertisement for the film *and* a literary work in its own right. Written in eight weeks, from David Williamson's (20,000 word) script (cf. Humphries 42), the novel offers an interesting commentary on Weir's film, which Bennett had not seen. By beginning with the protagonist's birth in the bush, it bolsters the narrative's distinctly Australian frame. Most importantly, it adds a woman to the all-male cast that goes to war, "to give [...] another perspective", as Bennett explained (qtd. in Humphries 42).

Forty-year old Alice Cooley is modelled on Alice Kitchen, a nurse in Adam-Smith's *The Anzacs*. The first to leave for Europe, Cooley is always ahead of the men. Her diary entries help uphold the film's tragic framework: they put readers – including those lacking historical knowledge – in the 'know', thus highlighting the young men's innocence. But Alice is also Weir's first critic:

> the artists who paint those glorious pictures which show the last stand of some regiment or other at some exotic place [...] have never been present at an amputation; *they* have never seen major stomach wounds; *they* have never had to hold on his bed a twenty-year-old boy who has had his skull laid open [...]. (184, emphases retained)

Weir's mythopoetic cinematography avoids such scenes, neatly freezing the young protagonist into a Christ-like figure once he is hit.

These filmic narratives coloured in the accounts which Adam-Smith and Gammage had produced in the 1970s, putting in place a repertoire of tropes for visualising Australia's Great War: a strong sense of place – both for the foreign battlefields, still out of bounds for most Australians, and for the Australian hinterland, which now afforded a post-imperial frame for the futility narrative. On 1980s celluloid the war becomes a conflict between young men thoroughly at home in Australia, and their elders – parents who still locate 'Home' at the uttermost end of the world, as well as British 'vintage generals,' embodiments of an Empire as obsolete as their ideas of warfare. Such strategies had their critics: "Another dose of Aussie war heroes," moaned one journalist, about *The Lighthorsemen*:

> If you reckon stupid Pommie generals almost lost the war and victory was only guaranteed by the bravery of the Aussie boys [...] [a]nd if you can handle wooden actors, the same old faces speaking the same old banalities, worry no more and make a date with this patriotic little picture. (Colvin)

Yet a reader's letter to novelist Gwen Kelly shows just how persuasive the New Wave's heritage framework of memory was, with its attractive young casts, beautiful locales and elaborate costumes. Kelly's reader enquired whether anything had been done about film rights for *Always Afternoon* (1981), her "charming" novel about the Australian home front: "It seems to me a perfect story for an Australian film – in fact I keep seeing it as though I were watching a movie with Sigrid Thornton as a heroine."[6]

5 Alternative Readings: Thomas Keneally, Roger McDonald, David Malouf, Gwen Kelly and Geoff Page

Always Afternoon entered Australian bookshops together with Jack Bennett's novelisation of *Gallipoli* in April 1981 – a reminder that Australia's Great War always exists in several, competing versions. The dust jackets of the two hardback editions speak to each other in interesting ways: Bennett's depicts a stylised beach and sea in wavy brushstrokes ranging from ochre to navy; Kelly's a photograph of a beach in soft pastels. Where Bennett's has splatters of blood, Kelly's features a girl in a white dress – a new metaphor for Australian innocence: "[I]t is left to the man, journalistic Jack Bennett," one reviewer commented sarcastically, "to leave out the hearts and flowers and give us the blood and guts" (Mills 22). But Gwen Kelly offers something more complex than that. She is one of a diverse group of writers engaged in a very conscious effort to re-map literary terrain. They reveal the contrasting poles of innocence and experience, British and Australian, war and peace that organise the worlds of *Gallipoli*, *Anzacs* and *The Lighthorsemen* as fluid and unstable; and offer the literary novel as a place where history's inner, emotional dimensions can be explored, and the constructed, contested nature of memory can become apparent.

The first of these re-mappings came in 1975, when Thomas Keneally's *Gossip in the Forest* tried "something you can't do on stage, or film, or television," as Keneally put it, to "express human experience [...] in ways that break the old moulds of literally observed time, place, character" (qtd. in Cole-Adams 15; "Keneally" 45). Keneally eschews "the old moulds" of Anzac altogether, offering

---

[6] Anne Pembroke to Gwen Kelly, 28 January 1984, in possession of Gwen Kelly. This was *before The Lighthorsemen*, but after *The Man from Snowy River* (1982), in which Thornton plays the female lead.

instead an episode in trans-national memory: the eponymous forest is the Forest of Compiègne, where Marshal Foch presides over the negotiations for the armistice, hoping to impose his conditions on Germans and British alike: "We shall do it by the extent of our perceptions. By the dominance of our ideas concerning the nature of the event" (*Gossip from the Forest* 92). Foch's remark is also an aside to Keneally's Australian readers, whose "ideas concerning the nature of the event" the novel challenges by withholding familiar tales and reading patterns.

A collage of dialogue, narrative commentary, documents and anecdotes, Keneally's novel implicates its readers in the writing of history, as much participants in the negotiations as the characters themselves, who are seen reading dossiers, telling anecdotes, weighing evidence. Here the memory of the war is one of the spoils of victory. The German delegates have trouble procuring papers; already, they observe the destruction of records in war-ravaged Germany. Marshal Foch, on the other hand, carefully composes what is to be handed to posterity. It is here that the novelist intervenes, revealing the manipulated nature of the historical record, and supplementing it with his own. At a time when oral history is becoming increasingly recognised as an important form of historical research, Keneally offers himself as an oral historian of a special sort, a privileged record-keeper who garners the "gossip" surrounding the event as it unfolds. His readers get so close that they can see the sleeping Marshal's "hairy earholes" (19): "we feel that there is time to hunt about the dark cabin for signs of his fallibility and age. What was he reading at bed-time? And where are his teeth stored, and his old handkerchiefs?" (119) Readers also observe the "informal discussions" (151) in which characters seek to shape the outcome of the event, or at least their appearance in the history books: "Vanselow made a gesture with his hand that said, it doesn't matter, I beg you [...] not to report my behaviour to historians" (146).

While Keneally's forest may appear "blessedly beyond Australia" (Pierce, "The Sites of War," 452), Keneally shows that Australians, too, inhabit the world whose design was laid down in France. Sydney features in a haphazard list of places where Foch is remembered in "parks, avenues, and bandstands" (27). Even more importantly, the novel's epigraph shows how the past intersects with the present, the private with the public, the European forest with an Australian beach: "In the season in which this book was written, the French government persisted in exploding nuclear devices above the ocean where my children swim."

Roger McDonald's *1915* (1979) was advertised as a quintessential Australian tale: "*1915* means Gallipoli, and the birth of the Anzac myth, the year when so many Australians and New Zealanders sailed off in high hopes of adventure, but instead, found themselves face to face with disaster."⁷ But McDonald plays with expectations of war – his readers' and his characters'. In the middle of the novel, one of his protagonists reads the "tiny notebook" of a dead soldier:

> October 20: Left Sydney on "Euripides" (A14)
> October 26: Arrived Albany
> October 31: Left Albany
> November 9: "Emden" sunk
> November 17: At Colombo
> November 25: Aden
> December 2: Port Said
> December 3: Alexandria
> December 4: Mena Camp
> April 4: Left Mena
> April 12: Arrived Lemnos
> April 25: The day
> Not even a thumbprint marked the white silence of the remaining pages. (209)

This gestures to Bill Gammage and Patsy Adam-Smith, who helped McDonald in his research,⁸ but also to the novelist's very own, very different memory work. The notebook's teleological narrative neatly conflates history ("'Emden' sunk") and memory ("Left Sydney"). Unlike Gammage's and Adam-Smith's chronological accounts, McDonald's novel, conceived as "an introspective tale with the period as a background,"⁹ moves in loops to follow the minds of its characters: "Walter's senses crackled through the past or raced forward in electric dashes. He tried to add himself up, to make something of his past self to thrust into the future whole and unbreakable" (132). These 'additions' factor in the characters' pre-war struggles, to which half the novel is dedicated, and the women on the Australian home front, less easily left behind than the notebook suggests.

For McDonald's protagonists – Walter and Billy, two young men from the country and their lovers, Frances and Diana, two young women from Sydney – Australia is not so much a wide, open space of unlimited opportunities as the backdrop to various entrapments: social, geographical, physical. "McDonald shows," writes Peter Pierce, "how far a nation that had allegedly come of age in that battle [on Gallipoli] had already established its rituals, its pieties and its class differences" (507). Frances looks longingly at the European ocean liners, hailing from where "things *happened*" (100, emphasis retained). The "immobile prison"

---

[7] Extract from Press release for Roger McDonald, *1915*, 26 January 1979. Papers of Roger McDonald, National Library of Australia, MS 5612/5/14/54.
[8] An entire chapter in Patsy Adam-Smith's *Anzacs* is entitled "All Those Empty Pages" (62–81).
[9] McDonald to Gammage, 30 October 1975. Papers of Roger McDonald, NLA MS 5612/5/12/38.

(74) of poverty renders Frances' upper-class home and Walter's university out of bounds for Billy. The war seems to offer respite from Australian entrapments, bringing Billy the recognition otherwise denied him, and promising Walter the "soft heaven of a new epoch" (135–136). But this soon proves "a dead end" (385) for both. Gallipoli represents not a romantic backdrop to acts of chivalry, but "a beauty disdainful of effort" (299).

This Gallipoli is McDonald's version of "the troglodyte world" (Fussell 36): "an underworld" (278) of "constricting burrows" (243). Even when the men temporarily leave their trenches, they remain trapped in "a cave with a painted roof where clouds hang motionless over modelled gullies and a plaster beach" (299). Bill's hopes of pastoral bliss are buried here, when he receives news of his pregnant lover's death; Walter is captured, lost in the gun pits of a previous conflict, the Balkan War of 1912–1913. Readers are similarly denied hope or orientation: the important place name 'Gallipoli' is used only three times (294, 423, 425) – as if to avoid the frameworks of cultural memory that might open up the story to larger meanings. And McDonald mocks expectations of Australian heroism when he has Billy return, not as a battle-proven Anzac but with cropped hair that makes him look like a German.

David Malouf's *Fly Away Peter* (1982) similarly subverts notions of national birth on foreign battlefields. At the heart of this novella, Malouf's protagonist, Jim Saddler, and his fellow soldiers breakfast behind the lines of the Western Front. They are spreading bread with "golden-green melon and lemon jam" – Australia's national colours – when an explosion catapults them into the air and covers Jim with the blood and entrails of a friend, revealing "the promise of thick, golden-green sweetness" (82) to be profoundly ironic. On McDonald's Gallipoli, death had "become a matter of geography" (*1915*, 362), rather than national history; on Malouf's mythopoetic Western Front, it is similarly sudden and unexpected, delivered by an enemy who remains unseen. It also renders visible old entrapments, forcing Malouf's insular, narrow-minded protagonist to reconsider the world and his place in it, to conclude that "he had been living [...] in a state of dangerous innocence. The world when you looked from both sides was quite other than a placid, slow-moving dream, without change of climate or colour and with time and place for all. He had been blind" (103).

Jim Saddler is the exact opposite to the adventurous youths of the three filmic narratives: "New views of things didn't interest him" (50). Like Roger McDonald's Walter and Billy, he enlists for entirely personal reasons:

> If he didn't go, he had decided, he would never understand, when it was over, why his life and everything he had known were so changed, and nobody would be able to tell him. He would spend his whole life wondering what had happened to him and looking into the eyes of others to find out. (55)[10]

This recalls Malouf's own, post-memory predicament: Malouf grew up listening to stories of the First World War, and wondering about his cousin's well-being in the Second; joined the University Air Squadron at the age of seventeen, thinking of having to fight in Korea; wrote poetry in protest against the war in Vietnam; and admits to feeling guilty to "have been so sheltered from history" (qtd. in Hergenhan 340). For Malouf the First World War was

> a landscape that I have always known I must one day enter and try to understand. [...] It is, one suspects, for writers of my generation an area that can't be avoided, the source of so much that we are and that we believe, [...] so much local and family history, that if we are to enter deeply into our own lives we must go there. And this for a particular reason that the present story also articulates: that the first war never ended. We are still living it. It was the beginning of what happened to us and is still happening.[11]

Thus, Malouf's Western Front is "a new landscape [...], newly developed for the promotion of war" (67), an infrastructure of mechanised, industrialised killing, the precursor of the railway network that sped six million Jews to their deaths – hardly a place for "great deeds" (*Anzacs*, novel, 194).

Gwen Kelly's *Always Afternoon* (1981) and Geoff Page's *Benton's Conviction* (1985) share the preoccupation with their characters' personal conflicts that sets the Great War fictions of Keneally, McDonald and Malouf apart from the action-packed, plot-driven filmic narratives. Kelly's and Page's protagonists are civilians, whom the War touches no less deeply, melting the distance between the foreign battlefields and the small Australian communities to which Kelly and Page confine their gaze.

Always Afternoon opens in spring 1915, but this is the Australian spring – half a year into what Freda, the protagonist, calls "the Anzac episode" (73). In the coastal settlement of Arakoon Freda feels "shut in [...] mentally and physically" (115), much as Frances had done in McDonald's *1915*. But while Frances is

---

10 Peter Pierce argues that "Walter becomes a patriot" (507), and Robin Gerster senses in *1915* a self-conscious nostalgia for a time when it was still possible for patriotism to propel men into an enterprise "larger than oneself" (254). Such readings may overestimate the very personal nature of Walter's commitment: "He'd wanted change – here it came!" (*1915*, 122).
11 Papers of David Malouf, University of Queensland, Fryer Library, UQFL164, Folder 2, 163/B/VII-1-N/VII-3, 133–134. See also Malouf, "Anzac and Why I Write," and McDonald, "Anzac and Why I Write."

last seen gazing at a darkened harbour with her arms wrapped around her legs, Freda's story closes with her running down a bush path, resolved to leave Arakoon's "country horizons" (115), which her encounter with a German prisoner of war and her experience of the bitter conscription campaigns have challenged: "She looked at life with newly opened eyes [...]. There was a wider, more interesting world on her very doorstep" (115).

Ken Inglis has suggested that "for Australians [...] the squalid peculiarity of their own nation's origins made the performance of the AIF especially precious" (*Sacred Places* 436). For Kelly, Australia's Great War continues rather than outshines that other, darker chapter: the Germans are interned in the old convict prison. Where *Anzacs* had closed by re-uniting its fictional community – civilians and soldiers, old and young, men and women – around the new war memorial, *Always Afternoon* exposes remembrance as fraught, embattled territory: upon their return, Arakoon's soldiers destroy the memorial that the German prisoners have erected to their dead.

In *Benton's Conviction*, Geoff Page reveals memory as a multimedia-collage, and the war as a textual beast whose meaning is subject to debate and conflict. As the vicar of the small town of Geradgery, his protagonist David Benton is charged with maintaining the religious framework of memory in which the war has been enshrined as the "Great Christian struggle" (102). The citizens of Geradgery, therefore, "did not separate him from it, no less a part of the process than the nameless German sniper who'd begun it" (26). Patriotism itself has been turned into a religion. According to Michael McKernan, whose work on Australian churches in the Great War inspired Page's novel, "churchmen had synthesised war and Christianity so that support for the war effort became an act of high Christian virtue [...]" (McKernan 110). In Page's fictional world, the recruiting posters represent "almost a liturgy" (25), and David "preached the Union Jack" (28). He soon finds, however, that this neat framework of memory can no longer hold his own experiences of delivering the telegraphs that convey the news of a soldier's death to his next-of-kin. They sit uneasily alongside the newspaper headlines, official communiqués, songs and speeches which puncture Page's text, increasing the gap between his "publicly articulate" persona and his "privately silent self" (20).

There is a veritable war of words: recruitment posters, echoing the recruiting officer's "parade-ground staccato" (4), bellow at passers-by; newspapers are penetrated with "the brilliant 'cold steel' of the journalists" (9); and Benton feels "outmanoeuvred from the start" as he senses his Bishop's "arguments lined up against him, neat, comprehensive, impenetrable" (7). Different texts and voices jar, as they challenge and contradict each other. In *Gallipoli*, *Anzacs* and *The Lighthorsemen*, written documents integrate seamlessly into the narrative; in Page's novel, the different facets of Australia's Great War are not so easily reconciled.

6 (Re)surfaced from the Archives: Leonard Mann, Martin Boyd, Jack Lindsay, Lesbia Harford

Four novels by Australian writers who had lived through the First World War further added to the diversity of interpretations available to Australian readers. Leonard Mann's *Flesh in Armour* (1932) was reprinted in 1973 and 1985; Martin Boyd's *When Blackbirds Sing* (1962) saw new editions in 1971 and 1988. Mann and Boyd had both fought on the Western Front, and the changing fates of their novels are indicative of the changes in Australian attitudes to their War. In the 1960s, both had met with rejection. Angus & Robertson found Mann's novel "not popular enough in one way, not up-to-date enough in another way," and refused to reprint it;[12] Boyd's was eventually published, but met with "dead silence," as he recalled later (*Day of My Delight*, 277). Boyd charts his protagonist's multiple disillusionments: on the Western Front, in England, where his aristocratic family lives, and in Australia, where he is married. Mann's is a more nationalistic tale, but also one of lasting destruction: none of his three protagonists survives; one is so traumatised that he takes his own life.

Archival collections yielded further work: Jack Lindsay's *The Blood Vote* (1985) had been written in 1937; and was brought back from England, where Lindsay was living, by University of Queensland Press editor Craig Munro. Lesbia Harford's *The Invaluable Mystery* (1987), written between 1921 and 1924, resurfaced in the National Archives of Australia. Both novels are stories of initiation, set on the Australian home front. Harford's female protagonist, Sally Putnam, has a German father and moves in Sydney's socialist circles; Lindsay confronts Grant, his main character, with the debates about the conscription referendum in Brisbane. Grant comes to look at the class struggle as a war within the war, and is deeply disillusioned; Harford's protagonist finds herself emancipated at the end – freed, almost accidentally, from the men who dominate her life when her father and brother are interned, and her Russian lover disappears.

7 "sixty years to get it right"?

"It has taken us sixty years to get it right," Les Carlyon marvelled at Patsy Adam-Smith's *The Anzacs*, a confident, intimate account which removed the patina of

---

[12] Memo, Douglas Stewart to Beatrice Davis, 5 December 1967. Papers of Angus & Robertson, Mitchell Library Sydney, MLMSS 3269/453, item 359. For a detailed analysis of this novel's career, see Spittel, "A portable monument."

imperial loyalty to fetch the Anzacs into 1970s Australia. Working at a critical juncture, Adam-Smith and Bill Gammage reclaimed a lost generation of innocent young men, sacrificed in a tragedy beyond their grasp. This impression was heightened when young Australian actors impersonated them in *Gallipoli*, *Anzacs* and *The Lighthorsemen* as characters from an Eden-like, far-away Australia who lose their innocence in scenes of harrowing violence. These fairly schematic worlds with their mono-dimensional characters did not translate easily into the novels that accompanied the films. Indeed, *Anzacs* and *The Lighthorsemen* never returned to Australian bookshops; while Bennett's *Gallipoli* survived longer, on the coat-tails of Weir's hugely successful film, on whose shortcomings it comments.

In the bookshops of 1970s and 1980s Australia, a plurality of voices located Australia's experience of the First World War in the lives of Australian men and women, soldiers and civilians, as well as German settlers and European politicians. Some, like Kelly's *Always Afternoon* and Harford's *The Invaluable Mystery* were female coming-of-age stories which took some of their cues from the legend; others, such as Keneally's *Gossip from the Forest* and Page's *Benton's Conviction*, revealed the novel as a flexible medium of (counter)memory, through which the struggles over the war's meaning could become visible. Together, these texts created a debate about what that war might mean, to post-imperial, post-Vietnam Australia. Thus, one reviewer contrasted Malouf's *Fly Away Peter* with Weir's *Gallipoli*. He commended Malouf for depicting "the multi-faceted, dehumanising horror of the battlefield" and concluded, with a stab at Weir: "we need no more Gallipolising" – no more accounts of a war "screwed up by the Poms" (Davidson). Yet each of these texts saw in the First World War a foundational moment, a historical caesura, for Australians in the twentieth century.

Australia's literary reckonings with Anzac continue.[13] In the aftermath of a bitter and protracted engagement in Afghanistan, now Australia's longest war, the futility narratives of the 1970s and 1980s may well regain salience. In 2013 former Prime Minister Paul Keating delivered a sombre address at the national Remembrance Day service, evoking the First World War as "the horror of all ages," "a cauldron of destruction the likes of which the world had never seen," and today's Australians "as too wise to the world to be cannon fodder of the kind their young forebears became: young innocents who had little or no choice" (Keating 2013).

---

[13] See Clare Rhoden's chapter in this volume, and my own discussion of grief in recent Australian Great War fiction ("The Deepest Sorrow").

Acknowledgments

I thank Peter Londey for his comments and Christina Twomey for sharing her forthcoming article in *History Australia*.

References

Adam-Smith, Patsy. *The Anzacs*. Camberwell, Vic.: Penguin, 1978.
Adam-Smith, Patsy. "Gallipoli." *A Common Wealth of Words*. Eds. Maureen Freer and Ken Goodwin. Spring Hill: Boolarong Publication, 1982. 36–46.
Adam-Smith, Patsy. "Age of Innocence." [Preview of Patsy Adam-Smith's *The Anzacs* by unknown author.] *Adelaide Advertiser* (11 November 1978).
Beaumont, Joan. *Broken Nation: Australians in the Great War*. Sydney: Allen & Unwin, 2013.
Bennett, Jack. *Gallipoli*. Sydney: Angus and Robertson, 1981.
Boyd, Martin. *When Blackbirds Sing*. London: Abelard & Schumann, 1962.
Boyd, Martin. *Day of My Delight: An Anglo-Australian Memoir*. Melbourne: Lansdowne, 1965.
Caesar, Adrian. "National Myths of Manhood: Anzacs and Others." *The Oxford Literary History of Australia*. Eds. Bruce Bennett and Jennifer Strauss. Melbourne: Oxford University Press, 1998. 147–165.
Carlyon, Les. "Real People in a Real War." *The Melbourne Age* (11 November 1978): 26.
Coates, Donna. "Lesbia Harford's Homefront Warrior and Women's World War I Writing." *Australian Literary Studies* 17. 1 (1995): 19–28.
Cole-Adams, Peter. "Novelist in Search of the Irreplaceable." *The Melbourne Age* (17 November 1973): 15.
Colvin, Ian. "Another dose of Aussie war heroes." *Sunday Tasmanian* (20 September 1987): 5.
Davidson, Jim. "We don't need any more Gallipolis." *The Sydney Morning Herald* (25 September 1982): 34.
Fussell, Paul. *The Great War and Modern Memory*. Oxford: Oxford University Press, 2003 [1975].
Gammage, Bill. *The Broken Years: Australian Soldiers in the Great War 1914–18*. Canberra: Australian National University Press, 1974.
Gammage, Bill. "*The Broken Years: Australian Soldiers in the Great War 1914–18.*" *Writing Histories: Imgination and Narration*. Eds. Ann Curthoys and Ann McGrath. School of Historical Studies, Monash University: Monash Publications in History, 2000. 14–17.
Gelder, Ken, and Paul Salzmann. *The New Diversity: Australian Fiction 1970–1988*. Melbourne: McPhee Gribble, 1988.
Gerster, Robin. *Big-Noting: The Heroic Theme in Australian War Writing*. Melbourne: Melbourne University Press, 1987.
Harford, Lesbia. *The Invaluable Mystery*. Fitzroy: McPhee Gribble, 1987. [Written between 1921–1924].
Hergenhan, Laurie. "Discoveries and Transformations: David Malouf's Work." *Australian Literary Studies* 11. 3 (1984): 328–341.
Hirsch, Marianne. "The Generation of Postmemory." *Poetics Today* 20. 1 (2008): 103–128.
Humphries, Adam. "*Gallipoli* – the book." *Financial Review* (7 August 1981): 42.

Inglis, K. S. *Sacred Places: War Memorials in the Australian Landscape*. Melbourne: Melbourne University Press, 2008 [1998].

Keating, Paul. "Remembrance Day commemorative address." *The Australian* (12 November 2013). http://www.theaustralian.com.au/national-affairs/policy/they-serve-australia-still/story-e6frg8yo-1226757270589. (12 November 2013).

Kelly, Gwen. *Always Afternoon*. Sydney: Collins, 1981.

Keneally, Thomas. *Gossip from the Forest*. London: Collins, 1975.

Keneally, Thomas. "Thomas Keneally." *Speaking of Writing: Seventeen Leading Writers of Australian and New Zealand Fiction Answer Questions on Their Craft*. Ed. R. D. Walshe. Terrey Hills: Reed Educational, 1975. 43–47.

Kiernan, Brian. *David Williamson: A Writer's Career*. Port Melbourne: Heinemann, 1990.

Lindsay, Jack. *The Blood Vote*. St Lucia: University of Queensland Press, 1985 [1937].

Malouf, David. *Fly Away Peter*. London: Chatto and Windus, 1981.

Malouf, David. "Anzac and Why I Write." *War: Australia's Creative Response*. Eds. Anna Rutherford and David Wieland. St Leonards: Allen & Unwin, 1997. 331–332.

Mann, Leonard. *Flesh in Armour*. Melbourne: Phaedrus, 1932.

McDonald, Roger. *1915*. St. Lucia: University of Queensland Press, 1979.

McDonald, Roger. "Who Owns the Great War." *The Age Monthly Review* 4. 5 (1983): 3–5.

McDonald, Roger. "Anzac and Why I Write." *War: Australia's Creative Response*. Eds. Anna Rutherford and David Wieland. St Leonards: Allen & Unwin, 1997. 334–335.

McKernan, Michael. *Australian Churches at War: Attitudes and Activities of the Major Churches, 1914–1918*. Sydney: Catholic Theological Faculty, 1980.

McLeod, Godfrey. *Anzacs*. North Ryde: Methuen, 1985.

Mills, John. "War at home and abroad." *Adelaide Advertiser* (20 June 1981, 2nd edition): 22.

Mitchell, Elyne. *The Lighthorsemen: From the original screenplay by Ian Jones*. Ringwood, Vic.: Penguin, 1987.

Page, Geoff. *Benton's Conviction*. Sydney: Angus and Robertson, 1985.

Page, Geoff. "Should Non-Combatants Write About War?" *Association for the Study of Australian Literature: Sixteenth Annual Conference 3–8 July 1994, Proceedings*. Eds. Susan Lever and Catherine Pratt. Canberra: ASAL, with the assistance of the Department of English University College Australian Defence Force Academy, 1995. 105–107.

Parfitt, Carolyn. "The Gallipoli Muster." *Sydney Morning Herald* (25 April 1977): 7 f.

Pierce, Peter. "Minding Everybody's Business: The Languages of Recent Australian Fiction." *Meanjin* 38. 4 (1979): 501–515.

Pierce, Peter. "The Sites of War in the Fiction of Thomas Keneally." *Australian Literary Studies* 12. 4 (1986): 442–452.

Rayner, Jonathan. *The Films of Peter Weir*. London: Continuum, 1998.

Reynaud, Daniel. *Celluloid Anzacs: The Great War Through Australian Cinema*. Melbourne: Scholarly Publishing, 2007.

Seal, Graham. *Inventing Anzac: The Digger and National Mythology*. St Lucia: Queensland University Press, 2004.

Spittel, Christina. "Remembering the War: Australian Novelists in the Interwar Years." *Australian Literary Studies* 23. 2 (2007): 121–139.

Spittel, Christina. "'The Deepest Sorrow in Their Hearts': Grief and Mourning in Australian Novels about the Great War." *When the Soldiers Return: November 2007 Conference Proceedings*. Ed. Martin Crotty. School of History, Philosophy, Religion and Classics, University of Queensland, Brisbane, 2009. 26–33

Spittel, Christina. "A portable monument? Leonard Mann's *Flesh in Armour* and Australia's Memory of the Great War." *Book History* 14 (2011): 181–214.

Stanley, Peter. "War Without End." *Australian History Now*. Eds. Anna Clark and Paul Ashton. Sydney: UNSW Press, 2013. 90–106.

Thomson, Alistair. *Anzac Memories: Living with the Legend*. Melbourne: Monash University Publishing, 2013 [1994].

Turner, Graeme. "*Anzacs:* Putting the Story Back Into History." *War: Australia's Creative Response*. Eds. Anna Rutherford and David Wieland. St Leonards: Allen & Unwin, 1997. 229–238.

Twomey, Christina. "Trauma and the Reinvigoration of Anzac: An Argument." *History Australia* 10. 3 (2013): 85–108.

Ward, Stuart. "The 'New Nationalism' in Australia, Canada and New Zealand: Civic Culture in the Wake of the British World." *Britishness Abroad: Transnational Movements and Imperial Cultures*. Eds. Kate Darian-Smith, Stuart Macintyre and Patricia Grimshaw. Melbourne: Melbourne University Press, 2007. 231–263.

Wieland, James. "The Romancing of Anzac." *Overland* 105 (1986): 11–12.

Ziino, Bart. "'A Lasting Gift to His Descendants': Family Memory and the Great War in Australia." *History and Memory* 22. 2 (2010): 125–146.

Manuscripts

Papers of Angus & Robinson, Mitchell Library, Sydney.
Papers of Patsy Adam-Smith, La Trobe Library, Melbourne.
Papers of Bill Gammage, National Library of Australia, Canberra.
Papers of David Malouf, Fryer Library, University of Queensland, Brisbane.
Papers of Roger McDonald, National Library of Australia, Canberra.

Clare Rhoden
Even More Australian: Australian Great War Novels in the Twenty-First Century

> The Unknown Soldier [...] is a reminder of what we have lost in war and what we have gained.
>
> Prime Minister Paul John Keating

Nearly a century of writing about the Great War has defined a unique and enduring Australian perspective. In many canonical texts of other nations, Great War soldiers are sacrificed needlessly because the war achieves nothing but ruination. Mainstream Australian works, by contrast, tend to position the Great War as a foundational event in the nation's history as well as a tragic catastrophe. As we enter the twenty-first century, another generation of writers incorporates robust Australian features into narratives that both reprise and challenge the notion of the Great War as the nation's foundation. In a number of ways, these works restate both the desolation and the affirmation encapsulated in Prime Minister Keating's Eulogy for the Unknown Soldier on Remembrance Day 1993.

This chapter examines three recent novels to explore the ways in which they renew and reject the traditional Australian narrative of the Great War.[1] Peter Yeldham's *Barbed Wire and Roses* (2008) reprises the challenge to imperial authority; Brenda Walker's *Wing of Night* (2005) privileges a female, home front perspective; and Chris Womersley's *Bereft* (2010) takes us deep into the scarred heart of the returned soldier. The use of both innovation and tradition in these novels is best seen in the context of the historical and cultural importance of the Great War to Australia, so a brief overview is provided below. An analytical framework for considering Australian narratives then precedes a more detailed discussion of the novels.

---

[1] Some content of this chapter was previously published in a different format in Clare Rhoden, "Innovation Meets Tradition in Brenda Walker's *The Wing of Night*." *Westerly* 56.1 (2011): 118–134. See Appendix for a short list of twenty-first century Australian texts dealing with the Great War.

1 Australia and the Great War: A Cultural Overview

In 1993, at the Australian War Memorial in Canberra, Prime Minister Keating delivered a eulogy at the burial of the Unknown Soldier (historian Don Watson was Keating's speech writer at the time). Keating's assertion that this tomb signifies "what we have gained" as well as "what we have lost" reflects the mainstream Australian view that the Great War brought benefits as well as losses to the nation. That the Unknown Soldier represents the archetypal Anzac,[2] rather than the specific individual, is clear throughout the Eulogy. Twenty years later, the Eulogy is recognised as "one of Australia's stirring and almost spiritual speeches [...] even admired by those who do not quite subscribe to the version of Australian history embedded in it" (Blainey 47).

While strenuously contested, the Great War features in "the version of Australian history" embedded in the Eulogy as the most important foundation act of the nation's modern society. Despite the fact that this can be challenged on several levels, the Great War is largely accepted as the single most important event identifying Australia as an entity separate from the overarching British Empire. Down the generations, historians, scholars, patriots, critics, veterans, and the bereaved have all proposed alternative conceptions of the Great War and its importance to Australian society,[3] but the Anzac legend remains remarkably indestructible.

In the most general terms, Australian prose accounts favour a heroic tradition that European and American authors abandoned for a modern, disillusioned style. The Australian attitude contends that the Great War was, for most of its contemporaries, justifiable and worthwhile, and part of a continuous and honourable historical tradition of fighting for precious values. Australian authors, often raising the status of the Anzac above that of his international fellow-soldiers,

---

[2] The 'Anzac' is the generic name for the Australian soldier. Though the acronym represents the combination of Australian and New Zealand troops (Australian and New Zealand Army Corps), 'Anzac' in Australia most often refers solely to Australians. 'Anzac' is also used as an adjective to denote culturally desirable virtues and characteristics, as in 'the Anzac spirit.' The word at first only applied to Gallipoli veterans but has since been extended to all service personnel.

[3] For example, fourteen years prior to Gallipoli, the Federation of January 1901 created Australia as a single political state. Australia had arguably already witnessed war on its own shores, through decades of European invasion and the repression and dispossession of indigenous peoples. Post-WW2 migration patterns have radically altered the cultural heritage of Australians, rendering an old imperial master less relevant. Additionally, the Great War is typically read as more like a funeral than a baptism by the post-nuclear-disarmament generation, and the dominance of Gallipoli has been moderated by better understanding of the Australian losses and achievements on the Western Front (Palestine is still relatively little known). All of these notions suggest, to some, more palatable and salient starting points for the nation than Gallipoli.

consistently propose that the Great War was worthwhile on a number of levels, as if to underscore that the actions of the Anzac were justified.

While European and American writers increasingly regarded the Great War as the destroyer of civilisation, many contemporary Australian narratives report that Australians built their civil life from the ruins. A protagonist in Leonard Mann's 1932 novel *Flesh in Armour* ponders the post-war homeland:

> Perhaps they would be going home soon to mingle again with their own people in their own land. Some effect that return must have. They were a people. The war had shown that. The AIF – was it not the first sign that they were [a people], the first manifestation that a spirit had begun to work in the material mass? How long would it be before there was some other sign, [...]. It seemed, now he was leaving the war and the old familiar landscape of death, that his life and the life of this generation was finished. They were the dung for the new flowering and fruit of the future. (347)

In this passage, Mann, a veteran of the conflict, recognises both the foundational legacy of the war and the tragic sacrifice of the AIF:[4] affirmation and desolation in equal measure. Importantly, he also proposes that it is "only by science, letters, art" that a society created from such a beginning "can become great": thus the literature of the conflict becomes itself a "[manifestation] of a small creative ferment," and the war a fundamental element of the nation's developing greatness (347).

Nevertheless, most literary commentary on Great War narratives since the 1930s is based on the cultural view in which the war is meaningless and individuals are victims. From this perspective, no benefit is achieved, even by the victors. The appropriateness and value of ambiguity in attitudes to war has been too little recognised (see Wohl 219; Rhoden, "What's missing ...?"), with the result that the complexity present in most narratives of all nations has been ignored. This complexity is especially under-recognised in Australian Great War literature, with many historians and literary critics dismissing the Anzac story as a simple political device employed to convey conservative values. Some further criticize the Anzac legend as an over-simplified, over-militarised, inappropriately heroic version of Australian history (cf. for instance Lake et al., *What's Wrong with Anzac?*), overlooking the range of complex responses. However, others have demonstrated the diverse assortment of patriotic, nationalistic, propagandist, idealistic, pacifist and elegiac Australian texts spawned by the war (cf. for instance Triolo), effectively refuting the notion that only heroic narratives exist.

---

4 The Australian Imperial Force – the AIF – was the general term for the Australian troops during the Great War. Even this name distinguishes Australian soldiers as a distinct part of an imperial army, a distinction which became of increasing importance to the troops and the nation.

On the contrary: a combination of desolation and affirmation within the one text is peculiarly Australian, and is identifiable in the most recent offerings as well as contemporary texts.

A number of defining features of the Australian literary response to the Great War have been identified. Robin Gerster's exceptional critique demonstrated the decided preference for heroic portrayals (cf. 14); John Laird noted a number of Australian differences from the canon such as less emphasis on the soldiers' sacrifice (cf. 6); Richard Nile distinguished the tropes of dislocation and absence (cf. 50–55); and Bart Ziino showed how the Australians saw their war through 'the lens of tourism' (cf. 39). These features combine to differentiate a distinct Australian style for writing about the Great War. Some peculiarly Australian features are discernible in the texts under discussion in this chapter. Overviewed and extended by Rhoden (cf. "What's Missing..."; "Ruins or Foundations"), Australian Great War style dictates that:

- Heroic tropes are privileged over victimization, enabling Australian narratives to propose that the individual's actions are meaningful.
- Much of the narrative occurs outside the trench, allowing less time for passivity and fear, and emphasising the fact that the war is far from home.
- Australian protagonists actively prosecute war, being more likely to kill than their canonical counterparts, thus contrasting the Antipodean man of action with the victim infantryman of canonical novels.
- Australian stories eschew homoerotic and homosexual themes, because homo-social mateship dominates; any eroticism is decidedly heterosexual.
- Australians explore their dislocation, with tropes of adventure and tourism marking their war as both memorable and divorced from their usual lives.
- Women are either notably scarce, or distinctly feminine, supportive and tender; this contrasts with the sometimes malevolent women in canonical novels.
- The older generation is less likely to be blamed for the war's prosecution, because Australians divert the canonical disgust for authority to a simplified allocation of blame to 'the British'.
- The Australian home front is stable and supportive, delivering no or few surprises to the fighting man.
- The Australian attitude towards the war is that it is a task to be done, involving all the danger and discomfort of difficult tasks, rather than a sacred crusade for ideals.

Today, Australian writers continue to explore a number of aesthetic and ethical themes through Great War narratives, such as conscription and politics; women and war; manly love, homosexuality and mateship; killing and dying; racism and parochialism; nobility and obscenity; futility and purpose; imperialism and nationalism; and the place of the war in the twenty-first century. While more Australians now accept the Great War as reasonless slaughter, popular reverence for the Anzac has increased. At first this appears counter-intuitive, but convincing Australians that the war was unmitigated senselessness and horror has only contributed to the Anzac hero's popular stature instead of reducing it to the victim-infantryman status of disenchanted protagonists. In contrast to the victim-protagonist of the canonical novels, the Anzac is generally an active agent, a competent killer and defender, ennobled not only by suffering but by the scale of the task and his selflessness and stoicism in pursuing it. Thus the apparently irreconcilable notions of 'war as travesty' and 'humanity as noble' are conflated in the heroic Anzac.

Australian texts have many (largely overlooked) similarities with the canon, but the present discussion revolves around some under-examined differences. Australian Great War style is not distinguished solely by its self-congratulatory loyalty to traditional heroic narration. Australian authors proffer an interpretation of war's participants as noble and worthy, and of their actions as worthwhile rather than futile. Undertaking a more meaningful task, Australian protagonists have more agency than their canonical counterparts. They inhabit a simpler world that is both more comprehensible and more malleable. Much Australian Great War fiction presents the "great adventure" narrative, privileging ancient literary tropes of journey, action and danger (Zweig 4–5) above the inner experiences of individual characters. Zweig contends that "the warrior's duel with death provides culture with its essential tools, its founding myths, its knowledge of the world" (223). This construction could well describe the popularly understood foundational relationship of Australian Great War writing to Australian culture.

Australian wartime confrontation with mortality in fact celebrates life, even contingent life, and living, as opposed to simply affirming the futility of war and mourning war's victims. This optimism can be read as an intrinsic and defining aspect of Australian national character traceable to the pioneering bushman ethos, as well as a rejection of the dehumanisation so ably described in Great War narratives of disillusion. It is an insubordinate style that both celebrates life and rejects the trappings of war (behaving, perhaps, as irreverently as Australian soldiers did when out of the line). The Australian style of writing war is different, idiosyncratic: in the narratives – if not in the history – the war experience is not just horrific, but *also* worthwhile, adventurous, and constructive. The continuance of these Australian themes is discernible even in the twenty-first century. A brief discussion of a few recent Great War novels published in Australia (from among the proliferation on offer as the centenary approaches) will serve to demonstrate the persistence of the Anzac themes.

2 A Challenge to Imperialism: *Barbed Wire and Roses*

Australian Peter Yeldham's *Barbed Wire and Roses* (2008) defies factual history to hold the death penalty over the head of its Australian protagonist. Reflecting latter-day attitudes to capital punishment as well as definite nods to Australian Great War style, *Barbed Wire and Roses* reinvigorates a classic Australian theme of anti-imperialism. The fact that Australian military courts never enacted the death penalty for military crimes during the Great War speaks to the supposed cultural divergence of the Australians from the rest of the British and Dominion forces. In the classic war novels, execution acts not only to reinforce the horror and inhumanity of the war, but also to increase sympathy for the soldier-victim by intensifying the story's pathos and drama. In *Barbed Wire and Roses*, the Australian immunity is posed, somewhat anachronistically, as a more ethical model of military discipline, matching the sensibilities of latter-day society.

In some recent British narratives of the Great War, executions encapsulate the horror of all the manifold forms of death which occur in war (see, for example, Michael Morpurgo's *Private Peaceful*, 2003). In such novels, it is death rather than killing which is the business of war, and passive victimhood is more salient than active killing of the enemy. Joanna Bourke notes that "readers of military history books might be excused for thinking that combatants found in war zones were really there to be killed, rather than to kill" (2); this could also be said of many latter-day novels.

Multiple reasons have been proposed for the historical refusal of executions by the Australian government. The death penalty was included in the Australian Defence Act, for actions such as desertion to the enemy, treachery, or mutiny (cf. Pugsley 131–132). However, local political as well as ethical reasons prevented the Australian Governor General from ever approving any of the 120-plus death sentences delivered by Australian courts martial (see Corns and Hughes-Wilson for a larger discussion of the death penalty for British and dominion troops). Owing to a long colonial tradition of sparing volunteer soldiers the threat of execution (cf. Stanley 173), the general mood of Australian society disapproved of any man being executed for failing in a duty for which he had bravely volunteered. On the other hand, Australian voters would be unlikely to agree to conscription if unwilling conscripts were to become subject to the death penalty for failing in a duty which they had never wanted to perform in the first place. As the war continued and not one but two pro-conscription referenda were narrowly defeated, there was little chance of the Australian Government implementing any of the death sentences which the army's legal system delivered. It is not impossible, too, that as the war went on and disabled veterans began to arrive home, the true conditions faced by the ordinary fighting man were related to the general population. A citizenry which still kept the example of Breaker Morant in mind,[5] however muddled their view of his case, was unlikely to licence further executions by the British Army. The losses were great enough without adding a further lethal condition, and the AIF's sense that it was being exploited by the Empire had been communicated home. Australian soldiers had enough to face without the death penalty, no matter that the civil codes of the day included it.

Despite this historical refusal of the Australian government to approve any of the capital sentences decreed by Australian courts martial, the death penalty is enlisted into *Barbed Wire and Roses* when Yeldham commandeers an ill-intentioned officer from outside the AIF. In particular, the upper class British officer, superior in power to his Australian counterparts and representative of everything rotten at the heart of the old exploitative Empire, serves Yeldham's purpose well. Protagonist Stephen Conway is "well and truly fitted up" and eventually sentenced to death by "a pompous and vindictive British officer [...] an overdressed, gutless wonder" (297). Even readers unfamiliar with the Australian vernacular can recognize the manly sneer at the officer's attention to his immaculate uniform, and the inference that his limited courage resides in the uniform rather than his intestinal fortitude: a potent combination of Australian prejudices. This depiction also echoes the traditional Australian resentment and defiance of British authority: veteran-author George Mitchell, in *Backs to the Wall* (1937), says of "the long endurance of the AIF" in the front line during 1918, that "the Diggers had a theory that Haig had made a bet [...] that he could break the Australians' hearts" (263).

Yeldham's British officer, so effeminately concerned with his appearance that he "looked out of place with his polished Sam Browne [belt] and spotless uniform" (56), deliberately listens to an irreverent conversation between Australians in the trenches, and reports Stephen for insubordination and offensive behaviour. This initial encounter sets up a strong antipathy between the two men, and every succeeding meeting increases their antagonism. The intensification of the conflict between them is heightened when the intransigent officer presides over Stephen's trial for desertion.

Stephen experiences extensive ordeals throughout his war. In addition to the archetypical difficulties of trench life and battle, he suffers the unexpected death

---

[5] Harry Morant was executed in 1902 for murdering prisoners in Pretoria, South Africa, during the Boer War. His sentence has continued to be controversial in Australia, and to some his execution represents the cruel expedience of the British. A sympathetic Bruce Beresford film released in 1980 popularised this viewpoint. For details of the case see the *Australian Dictionary of Biography* at http://adb.anu.edu.au/biography/morant-harry-harbord-breaker-7649.

of the woman he loves while their relationship is still unconsummated. His affections drift gradually but definitely from those at home. Stephen's war is remote from Australia and his dislocation from home is complete, admitting no possibility of the classic adventurer's return. Every one of his friends is killed in the conflict, rendering him emotionally, isolated and increasingly vulnerable. After being shell-shocked and evacuated to a psychiatric hospital in England, Stephen is, curiously and quite a-historically, deployed into a mixed battalion comprised of reinforcements, conscripts and previously wounded from all over the Empire. This pragmatic deployment renders him unprotected by the Australian immunity from the death penalty when events conspire to place him at the mercy of the vengeful Britisher; the fabricated situation is a narrative device which increases the drama and pathos of the story. It also functions to underscore the differences between the cruel imperial master and the honourable-but-exploited dominion.

Chairing the court martial, Stephen's old enemy delivers the death sentence. Their individual enmity overshadows Stephen's life in a much more threatening manner than do the Central Powers. He is saved by the intervention of a humane Australian officer who, strenuously arguing Stephen's AIF status, reinstates his antipodean immunity at the last moment. Thus the Australian-ness of the condemned man and of the intervening officer, rather than the large historical chance that the death sentence would not be carried out,[6] effect Stephen's deliverance.

To save his wife and parents from the awkward truth that he had been court-martialled and sentenced to death, the army notifies Stephen's family that he was killed in action. Unfortunately, a later army error lets them know that he is alive and in disgrace. In a departure from Australian tradition, Stephen's wife begs him not to come home in order to spare the family's good name. Conway is thus completely detached from his natural sources of support and comfort. Like Winterbourne in Richard Aldington's *Death of a Hero* (1929), he is isolated and pitiable. Unlike the classic victim Winterbourne, however, who in effect offers himself to a machine gunner (cf. Aldington 372), Conway perseveres with his life

---

[6] Only 7.7% of (total 46) officers and 3.6% of (total 38,584) men tried for desertion were executed (cf. Corns and Hughes-Wilson 325). Most allied governments (including Britain, France, Canada and New Zealand) have pardoned their executed soldiers in recent years, following pressure from organizations such as 'Shot at Dawn' in Britain. However, investigations into the circumstances of each of the 306 British executions for military crimes reveal that very few men (about 24) were shot for cowardice or neglect of duty (cf. Corns and Hughes-Wilson 104), and that notwithstanding tragic exceptions, most executed men were repeat offenders whose crimes would also have attracted capital punishment in the contemporary civilian courts (cf. 103). Corns and Hughes-Wilson estimate that only one man in six may have had the severity of his punishment, but not the guilty verdict for his crime, overturned under a modern reconsideration of the evidence (cf. 458).

in a stoic Colonial fashion, with the sole support of a sympathetic nurse (a female character who embodies the Australian norm of support and tenderness). Despite his losses, Stephen's stoicism affirms the value of his life, and of life in general.

In *Barbed Wire and Roses*, the threat of execution emphasises Stephen's heroic endurance and completes the severing of his ties to his former life. That is, the execution trope, which historically hung over all but Australian soldiers, is here used to intensify both this Australian protagonist's value as a heroic individual and his situation as pitiable. The reader is left to reflect upon the apparent moral high ground of the Australian authorities, but this reflection speaks more to today's values than to contemporary attitudes. If "Australians have become proud that their government refused to allow what are now seen as barbarities of the British and other governments" (Stanley 173), then it is a selective pride that rejoices in the discovery of a value which can be universally applauded now, and elides other less attractive (by today's standards) attitudes, such as racism and misogyny, both of which were arguably enshrined in Australia's legal, societal and literary values of the time. Most importantly, *Barbed Wire and Roses* presents Australian readers with a palatable narrative which centres blame for the Great War's destructiveness directly on the British rather than on the aggressive acts of the enemy forces. In the twenty-first century, we are shown how – and why – imperialism is something we can well do without, and why Australian values are worth honouring; perhaps – in the current era of Afghanistan and Iraq – we are also reminded that going to war in the service of our international allies is costly and abhorrent.

3 The Women at Home: *The Wing of Night*

Brenda Walker's *The Wing of Night* (2005) breaks in fundamental ways from the general characteristics of Australian Great War style. Importantly, Walker focuses on the home front. In addition, this home front is dangerous and unpredictable, a very different presentation from the traditional Australian story. Women live alone on bush properties and are anxious about the constant threat of assault and rape: both during and after the war, rootless men prowl the bush in a frightening premonition of Great Depression days. Women "are afraid of wandering swagmen, afraid of rape and robbery" (41) during the war, and afterwards, there are "plenty of crazed men travelling the road just below [Elizabeth's] farmhouse" (169). Apparently all the local men have enlisted, and shiftless characters from other places have arrived to prey on their families.

In another departure from explicit Australian norms, class divides *The Wing of Night's* characters: "rich people were allowed to be mad in ways not open to the poor" (Walker 6); "the rich did not lose fingers in farm machinery" (11); "the rich used surnames" (124). Indeed, for Elizabeth to meet chicken-farming Bonnie "would be a breach of local custom. Men mixed freely in the bush, but well-off women were less likely to meet poorer women as equals" (63). Walker here draws a clear distinction between women's experiences and the archetypal (male) Anzac theme of egalitarianism.

The war is not the major actor here: all the women in *The Wing of Night* are damaged previously: Elizabeth by her mother's death in her childhood, and by two shattering miscarriages (cf. 46, 61); Bonnie by her orphaned upbringing, abusive marriage, and the suicide of her husband (cf. 64–68); Annie by the tragic death of her daughter (cf. 103). The war then takes their men from them. Elizabeth's husband dies at Gallipoli (cf. 76), and Annie's husband in France (cf. 104), while Bonnie's sweetheart Joe is so emotionally damaged that he rationalises he cannot return to her until he stands on an equal financial footing (cf. 136), something that was never considered pre-war. Joe's mother is also a damaged female character, having "been mad, before and after the death of his father" (34). She dies early in her second marriage and Joe, a doctor's son, suffers a drop in social class which reduces him to labourer status, emphasising the class distinctions in Walker's novel.

Unlike the traditional Australian hero described by Gerster (and also unlike for example Patrick White's archetypal Stan Parker, a decorated, competent and silent veteran in *The Tree of Man*, 1955), Joe does not 'big-note' himself or his war experience. Joe hangs himself in a police cell while hallucinating about his accidental murder of a Turkish prisoner. Unusual for an Australian novel, there are few opportunities for redemption for any of these characters, and the war is more a complicit actor in their tragedy than a large-scale historical event that temporarily interrupts their lives. After the war, the hostile landscape is even more desolate. Joe and his generation have been sacrificed and the home front is lonely. Nevertheless, the child represents continuation and also the shared life which Elizabeth and Bonnie have gained: Joe, returned from war, gives Elizabeth the child she craves, while Bonnie achieves a continuity of her relationship with Joe (through his son) which appeared impossible previously. In the desolate landscape, new life begins.

In addition to these tropes of both desolation and affirmation, *The Wing of Night* has similarities to other traditional Australian features previously described. In typical Australian Great War style, there is an implicit rejection of the homoerotic in Walker's work, as Joe and Louis explicitly only sleep close to each other when "the cold drove them" (185). Joe's suicide is prompted by his guilt over killing the helpless prisoner, rather than the death of his friends, the relentless shelling, or his near-death experiences with explosives. Joe's suicide is associated with his active killing, not his passive victimhood, though it is clear war is guilty of damaging him.

Like the Australian officer who saves Stephen Conway in *Barbed Wire and Roses*, Walker's representation of Joe's commander shows him to be "a steady old fellow who knew his men and his horses" (11). This local officer argues constantly with the colonel, "brought in from the east and put above [him] and the first thing he did was complain about Brazier's troops. The officers had their own little war, even before they left Australia" (11). This "little war" (historically noted between Brazier and Antill) is a similar clash of cultures to that occurring in other Great War narratives: here, between the divergent Australias of the west and east; in canonical works, between the classes, the genders, and the generations; in many Australian accounts including *Barbed Wire and Roses*, between the Empire and Dominions.

On Gallipoli, Walker shows Brazier wishing to protect his men, and engaging in comparatively informal, egalitarian exchanges: Brazier becomes angry when he calls Joe by the wrong name, thus failing the clichéd Australian expectation of officers and men being on first-name terms:

> "You're Harry when I'm around," he said.
>
> The soldier shrugged when he should have saluted.
>
> Brazier was suddenly ashamed. "Have a drink," he said, handing over his own flask. (21)

The sharing of the flask reinstates the Australian norm of the relationship, which we see demonstrated when the men reciprocate Brazier's egalitarian attitude:

> One of the men who were yarning climbed to his feet and reached into the small supply of firewood. He followed Brazier and offered him some branches. Wood was scarce.
>
> "Sir," said the soldier.
>
> Brazier turned, his face white with cold. He took the branches and tucked them under his arm as if they were a baton and he on a parade ground. He could barely smile. He patted the back of the soldier's hand. (28–29)

Here we see the typical, egalitarian Australian interlocutory style and the implicit relationship of mutual care between the ranks.

Although *The Wing of Night* is influenced by the ethos and understandings of the twenty-first century, particularly in its presentation of the woman's perspective, it maintains resonant echoes of the traditional Australian style. Walker's novel shows a recognisably comforting provincial continuity, at the same time testing conventional Australian tropes to expose the dismaying barrenness of emotional life and the lack of reciprocal integrity in the bush. Walker uses the Great War to explore the fractures in Australian society and the hollowness of martial aspiration, while at the same time affirming egalitarian ideals in both intimate relationships and wider society. In transcending some of the more bombastic Anzac features while reinterpreting other more positive ones, *The Wing of Night* invests in an Australian style which combines desolation and affirmation, assimilating some contested notions into a composed whole.

4 The Return of the Anzac: *Bereft*

In Chris Womersley's *Bereft* (2010), the reader is drawn into a gothic mystery, resolved through a magical realism which allows scenes from the war to invade the New South Wales countryside. Returning to Flint, the bush town of his birth, Womersley's protagonist Quinn Walker embodies the desolation and affirmation so consistently present in Australian Great War narratives. Quinn is returning, neither as the conquering hero nor the pitiful victim, but because "there is something [he] need[s] to set right" (17). As a man who has lost much, he still invests in the task he has set himself, a task for which, perhaps, only the war could have prepared him.

In typical Australian Great War style, the major difficulty of this protagonist's life does not begin with or stem from his war experiences. Although Quinn has suffered a disfiguring injury and is faced with a rather unwelcoming homeland in the grip of pandemic influenza, this novel does not posit the war as the root cause of the collapse of Quinn's world. It is instead the rape and murder of his younger sister Sarah, an event which occurred in 1909: now in 1919, "the world looked the same, but it had been thrown off course forever by Sarah's murder" (21). Traumatized by finding Sarah's body and cleverly designated the murderer by the true wrongdoer (his Uncle Robert), the young Quinn flees Flint in an excess of terror – and of guilt, for failing to protect his sister. Surviving through hard work and putting distance between himself and his home, Quinn grows into a silent and lonely young man, "remote and wary" (10), who enlists when he "foolishly [thinks] the war an elegant affair with clear results" (45). Already damaged and isolated by the murder, Quinn joins up because "[war] was exciting, and he [...] felt part of something – a sense that had been missing from his life for so many years" (45). Though later he grows to realise that war is "nothing but ruin and din" (45), Quinn at first believes that something can be achieved. This demonstrates clearly the Australian attitude that, in the midst of terrible events, it is possible for life to continue with hope of better outcomes in the future. Indeed, his persistence with life following Sarah's murder speaks convincingly of his underlying belief in future reparation.

Throughout the war, and despite his estrangement and grief, and the terrible, undeserved reputation he has of being a rapist and murderer, Quinn rejects the victim-status so common in canonical Great War narratives. Retaining agency and purpose, he matches traditional Anzac expectations by earning so high an honour as the Military Cross. Like many a heroic Anzac protagonist before him, Quinn cannot clearly recall the events for which he was decorated: "In the war they gave me a medal for bravery. I can hardly remember what I did to earn it" (122). Nevertheless, his citation makes it clear that he selflessly rescued others in danger (10). He displays archetypical Australian disrespect for formal recognition, and stereotypical heroic self-deprecation: "[O]f all the things in his life of which he had reason to be ashamed, he was perhaps most ashamed of this medal [...] What a bloody joke. He cared not a jot for his own safety: that was not the same as bravery" (10). In a nod to the famous war poet Siegfried Sassoon, he throws his medal into the sea on the voyage home. The return voyage is, for Quinn, rather a-historically over-populated with suicides who, apparently in numbers, "[clamber] onto the railing and [launch] themselves into the air" (11), with amputees, and with the "tubercular, mutilated and blind" (12). He decides that "the return from war [is] surely worse than the leaving" as it does not assuage "all that ailed him: his homesickness, his guilt, his sorrow" (13). Clearly, the war figures as a sideshow in – to Quinn's mind – the larger, unresolved tragedy of Sarah. This fits both the desolation and the affirmation tropes of Australian Great War literature, because the war is terrible, but it is also an event to simply endure until the real focus of living can be resumed, a focus which will enable a future.

Having explored the horror of war and the influenza-depopulated world of home in an almost Gothic atmosphere of isolation and desolation, Womersley's narrative draws in aspects of the uncanny, the magical, and the fractured, as Quinn negotiates his quest. The appearance and centrality of the orphaned Sadie – a potent semi-reincarnation of Sarah – draws our attention to the vulnerability and promise inherent in life: "Quinn had the sense that, without his having noticed it, a grain of happiness had lodged by his heart" (203). Quinn, wary by nature but tempered to endurance by war, fulfils his soldierly role as protector and saviour of Sadie, while she enables his revenge on his treacherous uncle. Together they resolve the question of the murderer's guilt, uncover the underworld of the town's morals, and relieve Quinn's dying mother of her sorrow for his loss. Together, they survive in this bitter post-war-in-contagion world, achieving mythical status as they visit lethal vengeance on the murderer, and then disappear into an unknown future. What happens to them is uncertain, but what is clear is that their situation encompasses both sorrow for past losses and the challenging promise of the future: "How amazing, [Quinn] thought, to be in the world. To be in *this* world. Where nothing was out of the question, where anything was possible. He felt a curious and liberating exhilaration" (200). *This* world can only be Australia, post-war.

How well this fable fits the Australian style is arguable, given that, like *The Wing of Night*, *Bereft* deals with a time and/or location not common in contemporary novels: the post-war home front. However, Quinn displays many of the traditional Anzac features: he is a survivor with agency, not a passive victim. He has little compunction about killing in a good cause, an ability perhaps awakened in him by the war itself.[7] Quinn protects and defends Sadie, simply because she needs protection and defence rather than for any specific claim she has on him, beyond her representative role as a reincarnated Sarah. Quinn has flashbacks about the war, but none as terrifying as the murder. He returns an able if scarred veteran, admirably suited to the life situation which confronts him, and determined to proceed with life post-war.

5 Conclusion: Even More Australian?

For almost a hundred years, Australian literature has dealt with the Great War in a wide range of genres, media and perspectives, from autobiographical accounts to speculative fiction. All Australian texts navigate the contested territory where the war figures, at one extreme, as a foundational event, and at the other, as a devastating national tragedy from which the country has yet to recover. This chapter, in reviewing a sample of twenty-first century Australian narratives about the Great War, traces its indelible mark on the national culture. As both a tragic event and an opportunity for growth, the Great War figures as a contested but salient fixed-point in the national story. While all the novels discussed show features more resonant with their time of writing, they demonstrate remarkably persistent echoes of the Anzac's literary and cultural legacy. Sometimes in defiance of the historical record, these novels assert a robust Australian vision of independence,

---

[7] The capability to kill in a sufficient cause is a feature sometimes overlooked by those who read Great War novels as pacifist tracts. A number of protagonists who reject killing in the war are shown to be capable of murderous actions in private causes, for example Harry in Australian John Charalambous' *Silent Parts* (2006), and Robert Ross in Canadian Timothy Findley's *The Wars* (1977).

self-reliance and centrality. While they incorporate the current concerns of their own times to deliver a contemporary authenticity, the stories also review the past with a vision shaped by ongoing Australian preoccupations.

References

Aldington, Richard. *Death of a Hero*. London: The Hogarth Press, 1984 [1929].
Blainey, G. "Book of Relics: a Kind of Secular Family Bible." Review of Nola Anderson's *Australian War Memorial: Treasures from a Century of Collecting*. *Australian Book Review* 350 (2013): 47–48.
Bourke, Joanna. *An Intimate History of Killing: Face-To-Face Killing in Twentieth-Century Warfare*. London: Granta, 1999.
Charalambous, John. *Silent Parts*. St Lucia: University of Queensland Press, 2006.
Corns, Cathryn M., and John Hughes-Wilson. *Blindfold and Alone: British Military Executions in The Great War*. London: Cassell & Co, 2001.
Findley, Timothy. *The Wars*. London: Macmillan, 1978 [1977].
Gerster, Robin. *Big-Noting: the Heroic Theme in Australian War Writing*. Carlton: Melbourne University Press, 1992 [1987].
Laird, John Tudor, ed. *Other Banners: An Anthology of Australian Literature of the First World War*. Netley, SA: The Australian War Memorial and the Australian Government Publishing Service, 1971.
Lake, Marilyn, Henry Reynolds, Mark McKenna, and Joy Damousi. *What's Wrong with Anzac: The Militarization of Australia's History*. Sydney: NewSouthBooks, UNSW, 2010.
Mann, Leonard. *Flesh in Armour* (1932). Columbia: University of South Carolina Press, 2008 [1932].
Mitchell, George Deane. *Backs to the Wall: a Larrikin on the Western Front*. St Leonards: Allen & Unwin, 2007 [1937].
Morpurgo, Michael. *Private Peaceful*. London: Collins, 2003.
Nile, Richard. "War and Literature: Imagining 1914–1918." *Writers and Intellectuals: Essays on Twentieth Century Australia from Ten Urban Hunters and Gatherers*. Eds. Richard Nile and Barry York. London: Edward Blackwood, 1992. 46–66.
Pugsley, Christopher. *On the Fringe of Hell: New Zealanders and Military Discipline in the First World War*. Auckland: Hodder & Stoughton, 1991.
Remembrance Day Speech transcript (The Eulogy). Delivered by the Prime Minister, The Hon. P. J. Keating, MP, at the funeral service of the Unknown Australian Soldier, 11 November 1993. http://www.awm.gov.au/commemoration/keating.asp. (10 July 2013).
Rhoden, Clare. "What's missing in this picture? The 'middle parts of fortune' in Australian Great War literature." *Philament* (2010): 21–33.
Rhoden, Clare. "Ruins or Foundations: Great War Literature in the Australian Curriculum." *Journal of the Association for the Study of Australian Literature*, 12. 1 (2012): Field, Curriculum, Emotion. http://www.nla.gov.au/openpublish/index.php/jasal. (10 July 2013).
Sassoon, Siegfried. *Memoirs of an Infantry Officer*. London: Faber & Faber, 1930.
Stanley, Peter. *Bad Characters: Sex, Crime, Murder and Mutiny in the Great War*. Sydney: Murdoch Books, 2010.

Triolo, Rosalie. *Our Schools and the War*. North Melbourne: Australian Scholarly Press, 2012.
Walker, Brenda. *The Wing of Night*. Camberwell: Viking, 2005.
White, Patrick. *The Tree of Man*. Ringwood: Penguin, 1984.
Wohl, Robert. *The Generation of 1914*. Cambridge/MA: Harvard University Press, 1979.
Womersley, Chris. *Bereft*. Carlton: Scribe, 2010.
Ziino, Bart. "A Kind of Round Trip: Australian Soldiers and the Tourist Analogy, 1914–1918." *War & Society* 25. 2 (2006): 39–52.
Zweig, Paul. *The Adventurer: the Fate of Adventure in the Western World*. Princeton: Princeton University Press, 1974.
Yeldham, Peter. *Barbed Wire and Roses*. Camberwell: Penguin, 2008.

Appendix 1: A brief list of narratives dealing with the Great War published in Australia since 2000

Callinan, Ian. *After The Monsoon*. Rockhampton, Qld: Central Queensland University Press, 2004.
Charalambous, John. *Silent Parts*. St Lucia, Qld: University of Queensland Press, 2006.
Conte, Steven. *The Zookeeper's War*. Sydney: Fourth Estate, 2007.
Daisley, Stephen. *Traitor*. Melbourne: Text Publishing, 2010.
French, Jackie. *A Rose for the Anzac Boys*. Sydney: Angus & Robertson, 2008.
Hague, Graeme. *And in the Morning*. East Roseville, NSW: Simon & Schuster, 2002.
Hartnett, Sonya. *The Silver Donkey*. Camberwell, Vic: Viking, 2004.
Hoy, Catriona, and Benjamin Johnson. *My Granddad Marches on Anzac Day*. South Melbourne, Vic: Lothian, 2006.
Jorgensen, Norman, and Brian Harrison-Lever. *In Flanders Fields*. Fremantle, WA: Sandcastle Books, 2002.
McConnell, Peter. *A History of the Great War: a Novel*. Yarraville. Vic: Transit Lounge, 2008.
Metzenthen, David. *Boys of Blood and Bone*. Camberwell, Vic: Penguin, 2003.
Metzenthen, David. *Black Water*. Camberwell, Vic: Penguin, 2007.
Small, Ian. *The Kurrajongs: a Work of Fact and Fiction*. Adelaide: Ian Small, 2003.
Stanley, Elizabeth. *Night Without Darkness*. Melbourne: Viking, 2001.
Ural, Serpil. *Candles at Dawn*. Trans. B. Toker. Balmain, NSW: Limelight, 2004.
Walker, Brenda. *The Wing of Night*. Camberwell, Vic: Viking, 2005.
Walker, Shriley. *The Ghost at the Wedding*. Camberwell, Vic: Penguin, 2010.
Womersley, Chris. *Bereft*. Carlton, Vic: Scribe, 2010.
Wong, Alison. *As the Earth Turns Silver*. Sydney: Pan Macmillan, 2009.
Yeldham, Peter. *Barbed Wire and Roses*. Camberwell, Vic: Penguin, 2008.

Daniel Reynaud
National Versions of the Great War: Modern Australian Anzac Cinema

1 The Anzac Legend as National Narrative

While many nations generated myths of loss and tragedy from the Great War, Australia has forged a positive myth of identity, built on the national narrative of the Anzac legend which encapsulates what it means to be truly Australian (cf. Seal 6-9). The Anzac story has become seminal to the Australian identity since the landing of the Australian and New Zealand Army Corps (ANZAC) at Gallipoli on 25 April 1915. The Anzac soldier, or 'digger,' has drawn together the salient features of earlier national mythic archetypes such as the convict, squatter, selector, bushranger, gold digger and sportsman, as neatly encapsulated in Russel Ward's influential classic *The Australian Legend*. Seal argues that from a "private, spontaneous and authentic" digger tradition, the Anzac myth has been "invented [...] [as] a deliberate ideological construct which, in collusion with the digger tradition, operates hegemonically within Australian society" (3-4).

The Anzac legend therefore did not spring fully formed from the beaches of Gallipoli. It has its own history, and its progression is vital in understanding the nature of the potency of the legend in Australian post-memory, for its origins were in many ways far removed from its modern form. It evolved from a pre-Great War desire for a unifying national story more potent than the petty politics of the federation of the Australian colonies in 1901, one which would confirm the contemporary theories of the superior British race in the Antipodes through the crucible of war. The publication in May 1915 of English journalist Ellis Ashmead-Bartlett's colourful report of the landings of the Australian Imperial Force (AIF) at Anzac Cove offered such a narrative, prompting an enthusiastic response from the Australian public and authorities, and it soon found its way into the school curriculum, was credited with boosting recruitment, and inspired the nation's first Gallipoli movie. *The Hero of the Dardanelles* (dir. Alfred Rolfe) was released in July 1915 to capitalise on the popularity of the story and to boost recruitment in line with government pressure on the film industry. The Anzac hero promoted in this film was an upper-class city boy in the best British mould, about as far removed as possible from the modern iteration of the ideal Anzac (cf. Reynaud, *Celluloid Anzacs*, 21-22). What they had in common was that they defined the ideal Australian male for their generation.

Federal and state governments seized upon the embryonic legend, shaping and promoting it to their purposes to enhance the war effort (cf. Beaumont 150–151). The Anzac image they fostered was fiercely loyal to the Imperial ideal, with few Australian qualities at all. Wartime cinema was tightly controlled to ensure support for the British Empire's efforts. No fewer than nineteen war dramas were released during the war, the majority of the commercially successful ones in the first eighteen months of the war, before war weariness shifted the market towards bush comedies and, for a brief time, war documentary (cf. Reynaud, "The Effectiveness of Australian Film Propaganda"). While Australia had had a booming pre-war movie industry, with an emphasis on local legends such as bushrangers, wartime war movies lacked distinctively Australian characters, and many of them featured no Australian subjects at all, such was the deference to an Imperial British outlook. By the end of the war, the local cinema had been largely displaced by American films (cf. Reynaud, *Celluloid Anzacs* 53–54, 80–82).

After the Great War, conflict over the legacy of Anzac emerged. In fact, in contrast to the smooth rhetoric of unity in the modern post-memory of Anzac, the war was a deeply divisive event, provoking conflict within and between social classes, political parties, religious faiths, generations, racial origins, national and imperial ideologies, and categories of war service or non-service, and these wounds remained sensitive for decades, lasting more or less as long as there was living memory to sustain it, or at least until the handful of survivors were too old to fight the ideological battles. Conservative governments exerted strenuous efforts to eliminate unacceptable versions, particularly those advocated by returned soldiers of radical republican, pacifist or larrikin persuasion. Government censorship helped sanitise undesirable representations, including the negative books and films emanating from a disenchanted Europe (for instance Erich Maria Remarque's *All Quiet on the Western Front* was banned), and official support for the conservative Returned Soldiers and Sailors Imperial League of Australia (RSSILA, now known as the RSL) in conflicts with anti-war groups ensured its triumph as the sole surviving organisation officially representing veterans (cf. Donaldson & Lake 72–88). The tradition of Anzac Day marches grew during the interwar period, and became entrenched by the 1930s. However, it was still a divisive issue, and many veterans refused to take part in Anzac Day marches.

Australian cinema of this era, struggling to compete with Hollywood, sought out local topics, including a handful of war stories, which strove for the middle ground in representing Anzac, both to avoid censorship and to maximise potential audiences. In the process, they made archetypical Australian characters central to their narratives. Three actors in particular, Arthur Tauchert, Pat Hanna, and Chips Rafferty, came to embody the Australian bushman Anzac, fixing the screen image of the Anzac permanently to that of a resourceful, comic, irreverent, unsophisticated but fundamentally decent and loyal mate. The British characters who featured in films such as *Diggers* (dir. F. W. Thring, 1931), and *Forty Thousand Horsemen* (dir. Charles Chauvel, 1940) were different from the rank-and-file Australians, but shared honourable qualities with the Australian officers, and the films themselves were able to promote Australianness without disrupting the Imperial connection. They began the process of smoothing over and reconciling differences in how the Anzac legend was viewed, the first step to a myth which could be truly unifying across the nation (cf. Reynaud, "The Influence of Dramas" 15).

The Second World War saw a temporary rise in the profile of the Anzac legend to boost the new war effort, followed by a post-war eclipse driven by the marginal impact of Australian troops in the war (especially its later phases), the popularity of British and American war stories, particularly in the cinema, and the Imperial outlook and policies of Prime Minister Robert Menzies. After the hardships of two world wars and a great depression in the preceding three decades, the peaceful prosperity of the extended economic boom and growing anti-war sentiment made the populace less interested in wartime myths (Thomson 188–190). This period saw the virtual disappearance of Australian cinema and, naturally with it, Australian war cinema.

A revival of Australian nationalism only began to be felt as the restless baby boomer generation emerged into young adulthood in the 1960s, eager to throw off the social restraints of the conformist Menzies era. The 1970s saw the consolidation of an overt nationalism that, in its attempts to shake off paternalistic Britain, often targeted it as its antithesis. Two cultural features benefitted and then in turn contributed to this: first, a revived and updated Anzac legend profiting from its relative invisibility over previous decades, and from the rapid removal through death of Great War veterans' living memories, and second, a reinvigorated national film industry. Fostered by historians, government, the RSL and the Australian War Memorial, a new Anzac legend was aggressively championed which successfully fused potentially disparate qualities. Fashionable anti-war attitudes and anti-British sentiment integrated seamlessly with the heroic larrikin, the laconic and egalitarian bushman, and the unsoldierly digger who was a fighter of natural and incomparable skill, embodying all that was good and great about Australia (cf. Thomson 190–193; McKenna 113). While the late 1960s and 1970s sowed the seeds of these changes, they came to rampant bloom in the cinema of the 1980s, with Anzac movies and television productions forming a significant element of the jingoistic period cinema which dominated the decade. Preceding the Anzac productions was a string of hit films and television programmes that glorified the 'Ocker' Australian, presenting him (the typical Australian was always male) as egalitarian, uncouth, naive yet savvy, woman-shy, and addicted to beer. Films such as *The Adventures of Barry McKenzie* (dir. Bruce Beresford, 1972) popularised the archetypical Australian larrikin, who would make repeated appearances in later Australian war films as the archetypical digger.

2 The Classic Anzac Films and Miniseries of the 1980s

Anzac film and television of the 1980s played an important role in the development of the Anzac legend, interacting with political and social factors to promote a version of the legend best suited to the nationalistic aspirations of the times, and for the first time presenting one around which there was widespread consensus. There were nine movies and television productions in the decade 1981–1990 which centred on the First World War, with three other mini-series devoting some attention to it. Two representations in particular dominated the period and have remained as the normative, even definitive representations since then.

Preceding the two was a film about the Boer War proto-Anzac legend, Bruce Beresford's *Breaker Morant* (1980), a well-crafted film based on real characters that successfully articulated the key themes of the new Anzac legend: the Australian larrikin bushman-soldier as the epitome of Australianness, and the injustice of the class-bound British high command. The film perpetuated some of the popular misconceptions about Morant that have proved difficult to change, and set the tone for the first movie-length representation of Gallipoli since 1916.

Peter Weir's defining film, *Gallipoli* (1981), was a magnificent and moving piece of cinema. *Gallipoli* presented to Australian audiences a readily acceptable version of the Anzac story and remains to this day its best-known representation. Its story contrasts two young Western Australian runners, Frank, a town man with values a little corrupted by his background, and Archy, a pure and innocent country lad, who become friends at a race, enlist, meet again in Egypt, and end up as Lighthorsemen on Gallipoli. At the battle of the Nek, Frank unsuccessfully tries to stop a futile attack, and Archy becomes the sacrificial lamb, shot down running toward the Turkish lines. Weir's film captures with clarity the key Australian themes of egalitarian mateship, practical bush values, larrikinism and the virtue of unvarnished and unpolished characters over those of metropolitan Britain, with its superficial class distinctions and snobbery, and failure to deal with reality. The film makes strong visual links between Anzac and Australia: both the Egyptian desert and Gallipoli peninsular landscapes feature heavily, and the similarities to the Australian outback, also featured, help make it feel natural that Australians identify with Anzac Cove. Of course, the naturalisation of the 'Turkish' landscapes of the film is largely because they are actually Australian, with a variety of South Australian locations standing in for the Gallipoli Peninsula.

The influence of the movie is difficult to overestimate. One critic considered it potentially the definitive film not just of Anzac, but of Australia in the period (cf. Stratton 22). It was popular with audiences and most critics alike, although some noted that it merely restated the Anzac legend without asking any hard questions about it (cf. Lawson 11). It is probably the most widely discussed Australian film of all time, and is the subject of a formidable body of work, both scholarly and popular. Anecdotally, it appears to have influenced the understanding of many Australians about the Gallipoli campaign, evidenced by Prime Minister Bob Hawke's visit to the Nek in 1990 (cf. Burness 156–157). In all likelihood, probably more people have seen this film than have read any of the major books on Gallipoli. In any case, the emotional impact and memorability of moving image over text means that it has probably been a more significant shaper of contemporary Australian attitudes to Gallipoli than any written text.

However, there was nothing leading up to its release which made its success appear inevitable, as post-Vietnam anti-war sentiment was strong and knowledge of, and perhaps therefore interest in, the Anzac legend was weak amongst the post-memory younger generation (who had been subjected to World War Two stories, but relatively few from the previous war), but a convergence of influences made it a timely film. It touched a generation seeking for an alternative to the staid and insipid imperial culture of their parent's generation, and offered a robust, oppositional view of their identity, not as a derivative outpost of the empire, but as a proud and fiercely independent nation with its own identity clearly in contrast against that of Mother England. It featured the collaboration of an Anzac historian (Bill Gammage), a young director with a vision for telling significant Australian stories (Peter Weir), and a screenwriter with a reputation as an incisive observer of Australian society (David Williamson). The film was inspired by Weir's own visit to Gallipoli, was partly financed by Rupert Murdock, whose own father had played a critical role in the anti-British sentiment growing out of the campaign, and its famous final image was drawn from a line of Bean's official war history (cf. Reynaud, *Celluloid Anzacs*, 186–195). And it did not act alone, forming part of the increasingly pervasive presentation of the Anzac legend through popular media outlets, school curriculum, Anzac Day events, war memorials and RSL clubs, political rhetoric and popular discussion, each largely reinforcing each other. And as awareness developed that the last of the surviving Great War veterans were passing away, a nationalistic post-memory nostalgia grew around their legacy.

The other influential representation of Australia in the Great War was *Anzacs* (dir. John Dixon, George Miller, Pino Amenta), screened on Channel Nine in 1985. The five-part mini-series followed a platoon in the 8th Battalion of the AIF, largely drawn from rural Victoria. Choosing to represent a rural battalion continued the trend of portraying the Anzacs as bushmen, begun by C. E. W. Bean, who in his monumental official war history emphasised the bush influence in forming the distinctive characteristics of the Anzacs – this despite the fact that about 80% of the Anzacs were town or city men. The characters of the mini-series reflect some diversity of representation, with a couple of Danes, some Englishmen, a German-Australian, and some cowardly and dislikeable Australians (for example "Dingo" Gordon). However, in the best Bean tradition, these exceptions are kept as exceptions, and the true Australian spirit of the Anzac legend is the overwhelming theme (cf. Thomson 197). For example, issues of class distinction are present, but they are smoothed over, typified when the squatter's son Martin Barrington forms a relationship with working-class girl nurse Kate Baker. In a similar vein, while "Dingo" Gordon is an unpleasant character, he is presented as atypical of the true Anzacs, the exception that proves the rule. Perhaps the most memorable figure in the series is that of Pat Cleary, played by Paul Hogan. The character embodies all of the clichés of the archetypical Australian: an anti-establishment Irishman, drinker, resourceful scrounger, gambler, sideline entrepreneur, loyal mate and 'fair dinkum' bloke. Hogan played the character as an extension of his already popular Hoges television persona, soon to be subsumed in the character of Crocodile Dundee, and the spiritual heir to the mantle of Chips Rafferty.

Despite the character simplifications and stereotypes, *Anzacs* was a huge ratings success, and garnered some critical approbation as well. It has also aged well, proving to be a popular DVD purchase into the twenty-first century, with recent customer reviews on an outlet website consistently rating it five stars, with comments such as "a simply wonderful series-scripting, acting, production values are just marvellous" (ABC Shop). While this is true of much of the miniseries, it fails to recognise its tendency to soap-opera and its adherence to the popular peddling of mythic versions of the Anzac legend. The serious issues are dealt with superficially and the heritage of the war, as portrayed in the final postwar reunion, is saturated with warm nostalgia, reducing the actual war's legacy of tensions, strife and division to virtual non-existence and leaving a feel-good mood perfectly pitched to the modern unifying national myth of Anzac.

Several other productions of the period align with the portrayal of the classic Anzac legend, but failed to create the same impact, partly due to lapses in quality and partly due to increasing audience fatigue with flag-waving period pieces. One of these was *The Lighthorsemen* (dir. Simon Wincer, 1987), an earnest attempt to produce a film that was both entertaining and historically accurate, yet which ended up somewhere in between. It has many fine moments, but did not ignite audiences. Another was "Private John Simpson," an episode from *Willesee's Australians* (1988), made for the bicentenary celebrations. It abandons history almost entirely to create an exaggerated retelling of the legend of John Simpson Kirkpatrick, but its excesses also failed to persuade (cf. Reynaud, *Celluloid Anzacs*, 231–233).

3 Negotiated Representations

Such was the output of Anzac productions that one critic complained that "most desperate of all, we seem to be averaging one Gallipoli saga every year" (Glover 18), while several historians bemoaned the uniformity of those representations, concerned that they were useless for interrogating the myth of Anzac (cf. Beaumont xix; Clancy 4–5; Thomson 196–197). While their fears held some truth in terms of how the productions were received, they are not fair in terms of how certain productions provided a level of balance in representing the legend, and how some even interrogated it. In particular, two mini-series showed a much more even-handed approach to the story of Anzac.

The first of these was *1915* (dir. Chris Thomson and Di Drew, 1982), a seven-part series screened on ABC TV, with a screenplay by Peter Yeldham that refused simplistic approaches to Anzac. While many of the clichés of the Anzac legend were present (humour, egalitarianism, making hand grenades from jam tins, and medics with donkeys), they were subtly undermined or counterbalanced by other features. The hero Walter Gilchrist ended up in a Turkish prisoner-of-war camp, while Billy, the other lead character, went mad from a head injury. Mateship was represented, but major conflicts were shown between the Anzacs themselves, and anti-British rhetoric was largely absent. The tone of the series was gritty and realistic, with little romanticism or glorification of Anzac. In particular, it showed how the stress of war made victims of everyone, leaving no real heroes at the end. Overall, it was a well-made mini-series which was popular with audiences and critics, most of whom however failed to read the nuances and saw it as a continuance of *Gallipoli*'s themes (cf. Reynaud, *Celluloid Anzacs* 203).

The second production that exhibited subtlety in its representation of Anzac was *A Fortunate Life* (dir. Marcus Cole and Henri Safran, 1986). The four-part mini-series screened on commercial television, and did justice to the text it adapted, Albert Facey's artless autobiography of his harsh childhood and youth, with the fourth episode depicting his time on Gallipoli. In focusing on one man's story, showing both the positives and the negatives, it demonstrated an even-handed, unsentimental approach that makes it one of the best representations of Anzac in Australian cinema. There is the expected heroism and mateship, as well as the belittling of the British. But there is also boorish racist and sexist Australian behaviour which is not excused or even glamorised as mere light-hearted larrikinism, and there are depictions of inter-Australian conflicts and incompetent Australian leadership. Facey's actions on Gallipoli would befit a hero, but are refused that status by the narrator's dry, undercutting statements. And surprisingly, Facey is both a teetotaller and a non-smoker, qualities most usually associated with dour wowsers, not Anzac heroes, in Australian cinema.

These productions had the capacity to qualify the more simplistic and extreme features of the popular version of Anzac, but their nuances were lost in the increasingly hegemonic Anzac legend. Audiences and critics alike saw what they wanted to see. With their subtleties ignored, they merely became two additional texts in propagating a legend free of ambiguity and tension.

4 Counter Narratives

There were three productions late in the decade which went further than merely qualifying the legend; they represented the Great War in ways that suggested shame or farce. Two mini-series were screened on the non-commercial broadcasters in 1988, *Always Afternoon* on SBS (dir. David Stevens), and *The Alien Years* on the ABC (dir. Donald Crombie). Both focused on the xenophobic treatment of Germans in Australia during World War One, and neither shied from the uncomfortable truth that Australia had mistreated its Germanic residents, many of them Australian born and bred. *Always Afternoon* explored the relationship between a German musician and an Australian girl, noting the tensions in divided loyalties when loved ones belonged to each of the Australian and German camps in wartime. Partly funded by German finance, it was hardly surprising that it took a balanced approach to the issue, but this does not detract from the merits of its portrayal of wartime Australia. *The Alien Years*, again with a script by Peter Yeldham, was broader in historical scope and more melodramatic in treatment, though lacking the restraint of *Always Afternoon*. However, it also openly showed the ugly politics behind the demonising and incarceration of German Australians – the need to whip up paranoia in order to encourage recruiting. The attitudes it portrayed are frighteningly like those fostered by wartime Prime Minister Billy Hughes' extremist rhetoric, and reminded modern audiences of the blatant racism of White Australia that underpinned the nation's participation in the First World War, an attitude elided from modern memory of Anzac. While *Always*

Afternoon garnered excellent reviews, and *The Alien Years* moderately good ones, neither attracted huge Australian audiences. These two productions attacked some of the comfortable myths on which the Australian identity reposed, which may have affected their capacity to appeal to broader audiences, but they also screened to an audience weary of rose-tinted Australian period drama, which had reached a saturation point by the bicentennial year, and they screened on non-commercial channels with smaller niche audiences.

The other mini-series to attempt to deflate the Anzac legend was *The Private War of Lucinda Smith* (dir. Ray Alchin, 1990). The third of Yeldham's forays into Anzac television with a twist, it was the most startlingly different from anything ever attempted before. Gone was the heroic treatment, the reverence for the Anzac legend, the central role for the bronzed Anzac from the bush, and even any attempt at a credible historicity. Instead in came a bawdy story of an Australian chorus girl leading a German and an Englishman in a merry dance to compete for her very evident favours, in German New Guinea at the outbreak of the war. It was the visualisation of every Great War recruiter's nightmares: female sexual charms keeping men from their military obligations. Ironically, the film *Satan in Sydney* (dir. Beaumont Smith 1918) had been made during the Great War warning specifically against this very scenario (cf. Reynaud, *Celluloid Anzacs 76*)! *The Private War of Lucinda Smith* poked fun at everything. It offered a feminist heroine, but its nudity was in stark contrast to the usual prudishness evident in Anzac literature and film. The Anzac platoon in the story better resembled the buffoonery of *Dad's Army*, as overweight officers ordered incompetent soldiers around, and national stereotypes, both German and Australian, were exploited for humour. The flagrant lack of interest in historicity was emphasised by anachronistic attitudes and dialogue, and the casting of Polynesian Samoan extras (where it was filmed) as the natives of Melanesian New Guinea. The light-hearted mini-series was designed to be a ratings blockbuster, and while performing well enough, it was not the hoped-for hit. Perhaps it touched too many sensitivities: it was too much of a period piece for those weary of them, and not reverential enough for those who still hankered after that. The bawdiness could not compensate for the slap in the face of Australian manhood.

Just as the subtle screen versions of Anzac were subsumed into the larger, simpler picture, so also did these three potentially disruptive productions sink in the popular imagination, leaving not a ripple on the surface. Having told stories that offered alternative interpretations of the Great War for modern Australia, the series have not been revived and form no ongoing part of the public dialogue about Anzac. The modern Australian popular memory of the First World War is proving to be remarkably resistant to any change that might lessen its role as idealised definer of the best of what is truly Australian.

5 Post 1990 Screen Anzac Silence and Renewal

While the 1980s produced Anzac pieces of varying quality and success, there is no denying that the legend had been given a thorough public airing and had at times achieved stunning popular and critical acclaim and impact. In particular, *Gallipoli* and *Anzacs* continued to fare well in repeated screenings and then in video and DVD sales. What is curious then, is the total absence of new Anzac-related cinema or television for two decades afterwards. In part, it can be explained by an audience reaction against period cinema, having overindulged on the surfeit of the 1980s.

However, the absence of new Great War productions for twenty years does not point to any decline in the vigour and centrality of the Anzac legend in Australia. On the contrary, the legend continues to go from strength to strength, with rising numbers at Anzac Day dawn services, and on pilgrimages to the Gallipoli battlefields and cemeteries, while the topic constitutes a veritable publishing industry of its own in vibrant health, not to mention its popularity in various media. The absence of new screen Anzac representations will have to turn to another explanation. It can perhaps best be understood by the fact that *Gallipoli* and *Anzacs* remain for many Australians as definitive statements about the war, despite being more than three decades old. There have been no new productions because there remains nothing new to say about Anzac. This is a testament to the robustness of the version of the Anzac legend and the associated Anzac myth that emerged in the 1980s: for the first time in its history, it has achieved a stable form, with the only significant change coming in its increasingly pervasive penetration into all aspects of Australian society and public life.

Another silence in the Anzac legend on screen is the relative absence of representations of other wars, in particular World War Two, or of more recent wars such as Korea or Vietnam. The Second World War lacked the sheer volume of raw material that its predecessor offered. The Second AIF had just two notable battles that have passed into popular consciousness, the siege of Tobruk and the Kokoda Track, both in the first half of the war. The rest of the war was played out in trivial campaigns, sidelined by the spotlight-seeking American General Macarthur in the Pacific and by the big stories coming out of the European war. It took some effort to turn the defeat of Singapore into the heroic story of the prisoners of war, showing how much the Anzac legend had to evolve in order to accommodate its new generation of heroes. A handful of Australian productions gave the Second World War the same Anzac legend treatment as the First, but with the exception of the Kokoda track and perhaps Tobruk, none of these stories has entered into the popular Anzac imagination. This is evident in the movies made: only *Attack Force Z* (dir. Tim Burstall, 1982) and *Kokoda* (dir. Alister Grierson, 2006) are primarily Anzac stories. The others, *Blood Oath* (dir. Stephen Wallace, 1990), *Paradise Road* (dir. Bruce Beresford, 1997), and *Australia* (dir. Baz Luhrmann, 2008), feature the war either incidentally or are not specifically Australian stories. The Second World War plays relatively little part in Australia's war memory. Vietnam managed just one appearance on the big screen in *The Odd Angry Shot* (dir. Tom Jeffrey, 1979) and one extended and insightful exploration on television in *Vietnam* (1987), the Boer War has one as already noted, and the Korean War is entirely absent. These silences merely reinforce the centrality of the Great War in Australian memory and national consciousness.

But even the Great War Anzac had to wait over twenty years for a comeback on cinema screens with *Beneath Hill 60* (dir. Jeremy Sims, 2010), a feature film about an Australian tunnelling unit on the Western Front. Based on a war memoir, it offered some novelty in focusing on a unit other than the infantry or light horse, and was the first big-screen production about the Western Front since *Diggers in Blighty* in 1933 (dir. Pat Hanna). The film featured an unfortunate re-run of some Anzac clichés, including the condescending English officer, and the tough sergeant with a heart of gold, but it also moderated its rhetoric, so that the net effect is less strident than many of the productions of the 1980s. Its faithfulness to its source made it better history than cinema, but it was still on the whole a well-crafted film. It had modest success with critics and at the box office, and on the whole, sits comfortably enough inside mainstream views on Anzac without being totally conforming.

Great War Anzacs made their first fresh television appearance since 1990 in the tele-feature *An Accidental Soldier* (dir. Rachel Ward) on ABC television in September 2013. The story breaks bold new ground for an Anzac theme, as its central character, Harry Lambert is a baker pressured into volunteering, whose expectations of a quiet job behind the lines in a service unit are ruptured by an emergency call to arms after the German Spring Offensive of 1918. He deserts the front out of an unwillingness to kill, rather than from fear, and takes refuge with a French woman, Colombe Jacotot, who is mourning the death of her own son at Verdun after she talked him into returning to the front when he deserted. Her German Alsatian husband has disappeared, leaving her in trouble with the gendarmes who suspect her of spying for the enemy. The unlikely couple, neither speaking the other's language, find empathy with each other, their defiance of submission to the war effort bringing them together. Eventually Harry and Colombe are arrested by their respective authorities, and both are sentenced to imprisonment for their crimes. Economically told, with a handful of flashbacks to fill in Harry's military service in France, it is exquisitely filmed with "luminous simplicity" (Blundell 26), with the intimate lighting and camera work reinforcing strong performances from the cast. While producer Sue Taylor described it as more of a love story than a war story, lead actor Dan Spielman made a revealing statement about its military perspectives:

> The Australian military myth is a very powerful one; the notion of mateship, of camaraderie, of glory in battle has formed a big part of our psyche. And I think it is a very exclusive myth in a lot of ways and there's not a lot of room allowed by the general Australian public to see all of the contradictions and mysteries within it. (Yeap)

Its overt engagement with the Anzac narrative is principally at each end of the film. It begins with an unfavourable portrayal of the social pressure placed on Australian men to volunteer, and closes with text describing the treatment of deserters in some armies of the British Empire. In between are moments showing the impact of war on soldiers and the attitudes of the Australian authorities to their deserters. One appreciative reviewer argues that "We have to understand [our wars] as a reality and not merely as national myth or a stereotyped piece of news reporting" (Blundell 26). Time will tell if Australian audiences are ready for this kind of interrogation and complication of the Anzac myth, where a pacifist and deserter can be a central hero in an Anzac narrative.

There is more Great War cinema to come, as Channel Nine has promised a new miniseries titled *Gallipoli*, which will form part of the 2015 centenary celebrations of the Anzac landings. Already in preproduction, it is touted as "the definitive dramatization of the battle that shaped the Anzac legend" (Channel Nine Gallipoli). Given the hype that already surrounds the centenary of the Anzac landings, it will be interesting to see what approach the mini-series takes and how it is received.

6 Conclusion

The Great War has always been given a prominent and positive construct in the Australian public memory. Since the first news of the landings at Gallipoli a combination of governments, veterans' organisations, war memorials, the media, historians and the public have worked in synergy to create a national narrative fulfilling the task of both legend and myth embodying what it really means to be Australian. However, it took about six decades to eliminate dissident voices and achieve a consensus, emerging only in the post-memory generation, where there was the creative space to shape the legend according to present need rather than the dictates of living remembered experience. There is much about the form of the post-memory Great War that is particular to Australia, although shared to some extent with New Zealand and even Turkey. Australia's memory of the Great War is one of pride, of national achievement and uniqueness; it has become central to the definition of what it means to be Australian, and is frequently invoked by politicians and the media. In a famously secular nation, many commentators have noted how the Anzac legend has become the new secular state religion, with its national cathedral (the Australian War Memorial), its provincial temples (RSL clubs and local war memorials), its holy day, 25 April, and its own rituals and celebrations that unite the nation. It has embraced those people and ideologies it formerly excluded, as Anzac Day marches feature non-military organisations, and non-white children are strongly represented in school bands playing at the marches in honour of a war that was fought for the freedom to keep Australia white, British and openly militaristic, yet whose memory is now celebrated in terms that are multicultural, anti-Imperial and generally anti-war.

Despite its troubled and contested development, Anzac has developed into "the most powerful myth of nationhood" (McKenna 111), backed by a strong popular consensus. Nowadays, a number of Australian historians are the main ones contesting the hegemony of the Anzac legend, but by and large, the discussions are literally and metaphorically academic, as their voices are having little impact in the popular dissemination of Anzac. Perhaps the elaborate memorial centenary celebrations planned for 2015 will lead to a backlash against the hype of Anzac, but on the other hand they may merely entrench it deeper into the national psyche.

A powerful contributing factor to the new Anzac legend has been the Australian cinema. Working hand in hand with other forces such as state, education curriculum, veterans' groups, the press, and a number of historians, the cinema has created a limited variety of representations of Anzac, which had been further edited down in the public memory by an audience craving something black and white. Led by a few iconic productions, Australian film and television have offered an accessible, simplified, and easily digestible version of Anzac that has resonated with the modern Australian national imagination. Given the huge reach and impact of film and television, their version has played a key role in both shaping and reflecting what post-memory Australians wish to believe and remember about the Great War, a war shorn of its racism, Imperialism and legacy of strife and division in Australia, and refashioned as one of unity, Australianness and inclusivity.

References

Beaumont, Joan, ed. *Australia's War 1914–18.* Sydney: Allen & Unwin, 1995.
Blundell, Graeme. "Virgin Soldier." *Weekend Australian* (14–15 September 2013): 26–27.
Burness, Peter. *The Nek.* Sydney: Kangaroo Press, 1996.
ChannelNine Gallipoli. http://channelnine.ninemsn.com.au/article.aspx?id=8575307. (12 August 2013).
Clancy, Jack. "The Triumph of Mateship: The Failure of Australian War Films Since 1970." *Overland* 105 (1986): 4–10.
Donaldson, Carina, and Marilyn Lake. "Whatever happened to the anti-war movement?" *What's Wrong with Anzac? The Militarisation of Australian History.* Eds. Marilyn Lake and Henry Reynolds. Sydney: UNSW Press, 2010. 71–93.
Glover, Richard. "A Soap with more Grit than Bubbles." *Sydney Morning Herald* (21 May 1986): 18.
Lawson, Sylvia. "*Gallipoli*: You are being told what you are to remember." *Filmnews* 11 (1981): 11–12.
McKenna, Mark. "Anzac Day: How did it become Australia's national day?" *What's Wrong with Anzac?* Eds. Lake and Reynolds. 110–134.
Reynaud, Daniel. "The Effectiveness of Australian Film Propaganda for the War Effort 1914–1918." *Screening the Past* 20 (2006). http://tlweb.latrobe.edu.au/humanities/screeningthepast/20/australian-film-propaganda.html. (8 August 2013).
Reynaud, Daniel. "The Influence of Dramas on the Anzac Legend between the Wars." *Illusions* 32 (2001): 9–15.
Reynaud, Daniel. *Celluloid Anzacs: The Great War Through Australian Cinema.* Melbourne: Australian Scholarly Publishing, 2007.
Seal, Graham. *Inventing Anzac: The Digger and National Mythology.* Brisbane: University of Queensland Press, 2004.
Stratton, David. *The Avocado Plantation: Boom and Bust in the Australian Film Industry.* Sydney: Pan Macmillan, 1990.
Thomson, Alistair. *Anzac Memories: Living with the Legend.* Melbourne: Oxford University Press, 1994.
Ward, Russel. *The Australian Legend.* Melbourne: Oxford University Press, 1958.
ABC Shop. http://shop.abc.net.au/products/anzacs-1. (9 August 2013).
Yeap, Sue. "WWI Love Story filmed in WA." *The West Australian* (9 September 2013). http://au.news.yahoo.com/thewest/entertainment/a/-/entertainment/18842252/wwi-love-story-filmed-in-wa/. (13 September 2013).

Filmography

1915. Dir. Chris Thomson and Di Drew, Australian Broadcasting Corporation, 1982.
An Accidental Soldier. Dir. Rachel Ward. Goalpost Pictures, 2013.
The Adventures of Barry McKenzie. Dir. Bruce Beresford. Longford Productions, 1972.
The Alien Years. Dir. Donald Crombie. Australian Broadcasting Corporation, 1988.
Always Afternoon. Dir. David Stevens. Afternoon Pictures, 1988.
Anzacs. Dir. John Dixon, George Miller, and Pino Amenta. Burrowes-Dixon Company, 1985.

Beneath Hill 60. Dir. Jeremy Sims. Lucky Country Productions, 2010.
Breaker Morant. Dir. Bruce Beresford. 7 Network, 1980.
Diggers. Dir. F. W. Thring. Efftee Film Productions, 1931.
A Fortunate Life. Dir. Marcus Cole and Henri Safran. Nine Network Australia, 1986.
Forty Thousand Horsemen. Dir. Charles Chauvel. Universal Pictures, 1940.
Gallipoli. Dir. Peter Weir. Australian Film Commission, 1981.
The Lighthorsemen. Dir. Simon Wincer. Australian Film Commission, 1987.
The Private War of Lucinda Smith. Dir. Ray Alchin, Resolution Films, 1990.
The Hero of the Dardanelles. Dir. Alfred Rolfe. Australasian Films, 1915.

Richard Slotkin
The "Lost Battalion" of the Argonne and the Origin of the Platoon Movie: Race, Ethnicity, and the Transformation of American Nationality

We are watching a movie about American soldiers at war. A small unit is about to engage the enemy. They form ranks and the sergeant calls the roll, reeling off a list of names (the camera shows their faces one by one), which is obviously intended to represent the mixture of ethnic, regional and racial groups that comprise America's heterogeneous population. The movie might be *Bataan* (1943), *A Walk in the Sun* (1946), *Fixed Bayonets* (1951), *Pork Chop Hill* (1960), *The Dirty Dozen* (1965), *Platoon* (1986), or *Saving Private Ryan* (1998).

The formulas of the Platoon Movie are more than a cinematic cliché. They express a myth of American nationality that remains vital in our political and cultural life: the idealized self-image of a multi-ethnic and multi-racial democracy, hospitable to difference but united by a common sense of national belonging. We find the same kind of blended groups aboard the space ships in films like *Star Trek*, *Aliens*, and *Starship Troopers*; in the squad rooms of television's *Hill Street Blues*, *NYPD Blue*, *Homicide*, *CSI*, *Law and Order* and dozens of other cop shows; in the hospitals of *ER* and *Grey's Anatomy*. The platoon trope has become a part of our language. In *Achieving Our Country*, the philosopher Richard Rorty refers to "platoon movies" as modeling a new kind of nationality which reconciles nationalism with cultural diversity (100). He never explains the reference. He confidently expects that every reader will know what he means. Platoon Movies celebrate the success with which post-1945 American society has naturalized immigrants of every race and nationality, a success which European states have struggled to match. As the historian Gary Gerstle observes, "no narrative of nation building [has been] more important" than the Platoon Movie in shaping the development of American society and politics in the post-war period (42).

The Platoon Movie was developed as a genre in Hollywood during the Second World War. However, the movies built upon – and also effaced – the earlier pre-cinematic history of American engagement in the First World War, and our first attempt at mythologizing a multi-ethnic American nationalism. Two stories, propagated through the journalism of 1917–1918, gave that myth its original shape. The most celebrated was that of the "Lost Battalion," an outfit raised in New York City's immigrant melting-pot, which fought a kind of 'Last Stand' in the Argonne Forest. The second was that of the Harlem Hell Fighters, an African-American regiment which became a powerful symbol in wartime debates over racism and civil rights. Their histories offer a window into the processes of social and cultural change that produced both the Platoon Movie and the ideal of blended nationality that it fostered.[1]

On 2 April 1917, President Wilson asked Congress to declare war on the German Empire, "to make the world safe for democracy." But as of January 1917, the total strength of all U.S. uniformed services was fewer than 250,000. The British Army had lost that many men in only three weeks fighting on the Somme in 1916. To make a significant impact, the U.S. would have to form an army of at least one million and get it to France within the year, with 2 or 3 million more to follow. The necessity of raising an army of millions exposed the embarrassing fact that the democracy for which the world was to be made safe had not resolved the most fundamental questions of its own organization: who counts as an American, and what social and political rights belong to the citizen? Between 15% and 20% of the population were Blacks, Native- or Mexican-American. But for forty years White Americans in the South had been systematically depriving non-Whites of the civil rights they had won during Reconstruction, creating the system of racial segregation, subjugation and lynch-law known as Jim Crow.

In 1917 one third of the American population were either foreign born or had one foreign-born parent. Since 1881, millions of new immigrants had been arriving every year from Eastern and Southern Europe, people whose language, religion and ways of life seemed repellently alien to White Americans of predominantly British and German origins. In the vocabulary of American culture, such differences were interpreted by reference to color-based racialism: the new immigrants (Jews, Italians, Poles, Slavs) were seen as being in some way more like Negroes, Indians or Asians than like 'real' White people. In the mid-1890s, a powerful anti-immigrant movement began, led by the Immigration Restriction League, whose members included men of power and social standing, among them Senate Republican leader Henry Cabot Lodge, and President Lawrence Lowell of Harvard. Lowell declared that "Indians, Negroes, Chinese, Jews and *Americans* cannot all be free in the same society" (qtd. in Chase 110). A nation can only thrive, and enjoy freedom with safety, if its people descend from "a single race, with substantially the same social and political instincts, the same standards of conduct and morals, the same industrial capability" (Tichenor 71). In 1907, President Theodore Roosevelt commissioned a report on *Races and Immigrants in American Life* by labor historian John R. Commons, which defined each immigrant nationality as a distinct race, and declared that no race was qualified

---

[1] The histories of the two regiments are detailed in Richard Slotkin's *Lost Battalions: The Great War and the Crisis of American Nationality* (2005).

for citizenship unless it met the White Anglo-Saxon standard for "intelligence, manliness, and cooperation" (6–7). The Report declared that the U.S. must choose between cutting off the immigration of undesirable races, or restricting the civil rights of immigrants already here in the same way that Black civil rights had been taken away in the South.

When the U.S. was drawn into the European War in 1917, the unresolved status of racial and ethnic minorities became a crisis. It was simply impossible to raise an army of millions without the *active* cooperation of minority communities. If 'hyphenated Americans' – African-Americans and 'new immigrants' – could not be trusted with civil rights, how could they be relied upon to fight for the nation in time of war? And if these groups were excluded from full citizenship, why should they be *willing* to serve? Almost overnight, the nation's leadership rediscovered the principle that "all men are created equal." Instead of insisting that race defined nationality, official publications, training manuals and public propaganda began to describe the U.S. as a "vast, polyglot community," in which "common ideals have transformed men and women of all these races, and kindreds, and tongues, into ONE nation." The War Department gave the ideal substance, establishing a Foreign Soldier Service and a Committee on Training Camps to work with the leaders of minority communities to develop citizenship programs for Black and immigrant soldiers: "Soldier after soldier [is to be] turned out fit and eager to fight for liberty under the Stars and Stripes, *mindful of the traditions of his race and the land of his nativity* and conscious of the principles for which he is fighting" [my italics]. The official ideologists of America's Great War were offering the minorities a new social bargain: full recognition as Americans in exchange for loyal service in wartime.[2]

The bargain the soldiers accepted was not a simple quid pro quo, the granting of specific political or economic rights in exchange for service. What was promised was something vaguer and more fundamental: a recognition that these social groups, which had been considered alien, inferior, and unfit to be associated with 'real Americans,' were to be accorded a full measure of dignity and respect – without requiring that they deny or compromise their ethnic difference from standard Americans. But the only way they could prove their qualification to be Americans – to prove their loyalty, and meet the Anglo-Saxon standard of "intelligence, manliness, cooperation" – was to serve effectively in battle.

---

2 See Nancy Gentile Ford, *War and Ethnicity: Foreign Soldiers and the United Sattes* (1994), 3–10, 26, 38–39, 51–55, 61–67, 71–73, 113–114, 235–238, 245 and ch. 6; Ronald Schaffer, *America in the Great War: The Rise of the War Welfare State* (1991), 177–178; U.S. Committee on Public Information, *Home Reading Course for Citizen-Soldiers* (1917), 3, 6, 10, 12–14, 17–18, 22–24, 55, 57; U.S. Committee on Public Information, *Meaning of America* (1918), *passim*.

Two regiments came to symbolize the role of racial and ethnic minorities in the war, and the complex way the social bargain worked. The 369th Infantry was an African-American regiment, recruited in the Greater New York area, nicknamed the "Harlem Hell Fighters." They compiled a superb combat record fighting as part of the French army. Their last and greatest achievement was to spearhead five days of continuous combat assault, culminating in the capture of the town of Sechault, for which the entire regiment was awarded the French Army's medal of valor, the Croix de Guerre. The price of that citation was a 66% casualty list. The 308th Infantry was raised among recent immigrants in Manhattan, Brooklyn and the Bronx, and its personnel were a sample of the City's 'melting pot.' Jews from Eastern Europe were the largest single ethnic group, but there were ample numbers of Italians, Poles, Irishmen, Germans and even some Chinese. It won national fame, and near legendary status, as the "Lost Battalion": six of its companies were trapped after breaking through the German lines in the Argonne Forest, and held their ground for six days under heavy attack, suffering nearly 75% casualties.

The Hell Fighters were from the first an important symbol in American racial politics. Strenuous efforts by Black politicians and White racial liberals had led to their formation in 1916 as a Colored regiment of the New York National Guard. Their mission was to demonstrate that African-Americans possessed the same soldierly virtues as Whites. Such demonstrations were critical to the civil rights movement. The basis of civil equality is the presumption that the individual is entitled, self-evidently and *by nature*, to dignity and respect. It is that presumption which compels his fellow citizens, his government, and the laws of the nation to take seriously his suits, petitions, appeals for justice. But slavery had created, and Jim Crow had perpetuated, the identification of citizen-dignity with racial 'Whiteness.' Blackness implied the opposite: a presumptive entitlement to "personal disrespect and mockery, [...] ridicule and systematic humiliation" (DuBois 102).

Newspapers and magazines mocked the training of Black troops as minstrel-show slapstick, in articles with titles like "Mobilizing Rastus." Tin Pan Alley songs popularized such attitudes. One was titled, "When the Boys from Dixie Eat Melon on the Rhine," and another called "Mammy's Chocolate Soldier." The mission of the Harlem Hell Fighters was to replace this ridiculous image with something heroic. As a Black lieutenant wrote:

> [N]ow is our opportunity to prove what we can do. If we can't fight and die in this war just as bravely as white men, then we don't deserve equality with white men [...] But if we can do things at the front; if we can make ourselves felt; if we can make America really proud of the [regiment] [...] then it will be the biggest possible step toward our equalization as citizens. The whole [regiment] has the same spirit. (*Crisis* 164, 179, 187)

But the regiment itself was a microcosm of a segregated nation. The enlisted men were lower-middle and working-class. Among the half-dozen Black officers were a prominent lawyer, Napoleon Marshall, and the jazz pioneer and entertainment entrepreneur James Reese Europe. But most of the officers were White, and belonged to the social and political elite. Colonel William Hayward was a wealthy socialite, and among his officers was Hamilton Fish, scion of one of the nation's oldest political families. The White officers saw themselves as missionaries from an intellectually advanced people to an underdeveloped race. One officer admonished himself to remember that, "if mental strength was to govern brute strength, there must be no apparent doubt of its superiority upon the part of the advocate of mentality" (Little 4–6, 16, 31, cf. Slotkin, *Lost Battalions*, ch. 3).

The same structure pertained in the melting-pot regiments. The officers were overwhelmingly drawn from the City's social and business elite, who had received officer training in summer camps organized by Theodore Roosevelt and General Leonard Wood. The officers were repelled at first by the working-class Jews, Poles, and Italians assigned to their units. They seemed "the worst possible material from which to make soldier-stuff [...] thick-set, stupid looking, extremely foreign" (Miles 7). The Army *Manual of Instruction for Medical Advisory Boards* informed them that "The foreign born, and especially Jews, are more apt to malinger than the native born" (qtd. in Bendersky 5, 38).[3]

Officers and men had to work hard to realize each other's humanity – and to a remarkable extent they succeeded. Hayward and Fish earned the affection of their soldiers, and identified themselves completely with the regiment. The officer who had thought his Jewish and Italian troops the worst possible material ended by finding them "lovable men [...] ready, willing, and ambitious to become good soldiers" (Rainsford 10–11, Tiebout 17).

The Hell Fighters were first to see action. In the spring of 1918 the American high command was unwilling to brigade the lone Black regiment with White organizations, so the 369th was sent to serve with the French IV Army during the Germans' spring 1918 offensive. They performed well as a unit, but it was a small outpost affair that made them, for a while, the most famous American unit in France. On 13 May 1918, a German raiding party attacked one of their outposts, hoping to capture and interrogate its defenders. Privates Henry Johnson and Neadom Roberts fought off the raiders in a hand-to-hand battle that saved the outpost and left a dozen enemy dead. The French Army awarded both the Croix de Guerre – the first medals awarded to U.S. soldiers in France. Press coverage of the

---

3 See L. Wardlaw Miles, *History of the 308th Infantry, 1917–1919* (1927), 7; Adler, *History of the 306th Infantry* (1935), ch. 1.; Joseph W. Bendersky, *The "Jewish Threat": Anti-Semitic Policies of the U.S. Army* (2000), 5, 38.

American army was heavily censored, but, because the 369th was serving with the French, its deeds could be openly described. Within a day or two Colonel Hayward and his officers had been interviewed by every important American journalist on the Western Front. On 21 May the story, now called the "Battle of Henry Johnson," hit the New York papers. With the exception of William Randolph Hearst's New York *American* – always hostile to Black interests – every paper presented the story as vindication of the Negro race's soldierly aptitudes. Theodore Roosevelt declared that the two Negroes had "shown themselves to be of the heroic type." Irvin Cobb, a Southern writer known for creating ridiculous Negro stereotypes, wrote about Johnson in one of the most widely quoted stories of the war, which culminated in these words: "I am of the opinion [...] that as a result of what our black soldiers are [doing] [...] that hereafter n-i-g-g-e-r will be merely another way of spelling the word American" (287–289).[4]

The regiment would go on to even more distinguished service, spending 191 days in combat – one of the longest stints by an American regiment – and qualifying for the role of assault leader in the final offensive. In September 1918 the regiment led the attack of the French IV Army, stormed the fortified heights of Bellevue Ridge, captured and held the strategic road junction of Sechault against German counterattack, losing two-thirds of its men in the process. The entire regiment was awarded the Croix de Guerre – but this ultimate achievement and tragedy was overshadowed in the press by the story of the 308th Infantry's Lost Battalion (see Slotkin, *Lost Battalions*, ch. 10). That battle was fought in the Argonne Forest, a jungle-like wilderness criss-crossed with German entrenchments and ambush positions. After a week of blind slugging, six companies of the 308th led by Majors Whittlesey and McMurtry found a gap in the German lines, and seized a strategic position behind the German front. Before their division could send them supplies or reinforcements, the Germans sealed the break and cut them off. For a week they held their perimeter against increasingly powerful German attacks, while the Army tried to rescue them and exploit their advance.

The Wall Street officers and their tenement soldiers had to maintain their unity and will to resist, and more, their will to fight, to counter-attack in an environment of inescapable disgusting filth, deepening and unsatisfiable hunger and thirst, with communication cut off and the chances of rescue unlikely. They

---

4 See Slotkin, *Lost Battalions*, esp. 141–151, which details press coverage. See also Little, ch. 30; Arthur E. Barbeau and Florette Henri, *The Unknown Soldiers: Black American Troops in World War I* (1974), 8, 77, 117, 232; Irvin Cobb, *The Glory of the Coming: What Mines Eyes Have Seen of Americans in Action in the Year of Grace and Allied Endeavor* (1918), 287–289; Cobb, "Young Black Joe," *Saturday Evening Post* (24 August 1918), 294–307.

were continually sniped and pinned down by machine-gun crossfire, subjected to murderous assaults: "[Such] a mess you never did see. Some of our men were dead, other[s] dying and moaning for help. Some were already buried and some just in pieces," "The stink was almost unbearable. Many wounded men would almost rot before they died" (qtd. in Slotkin, *Lost Battalions*, 348). When they called for artillery support, they were hit by a friendly fire bombardment that tore up their position and killed or wounded eighty of the 550 men then holding out in the Pocket. They were starving, but when their division tried to air-drop food the parachutes drifted, and they could hear the Germans cheering as they enjoyed packets of American tinned meat, chocolate and cheese.

It was vital that someone get through the German lines to guide a relieving force to their position. Half a dozen men tried, and all were killed. Finally, Abe Krotoshinsky, always described as a little, stoop-shouldered, long-nosed Polish Jew, volunteered to make the attempt. Late that afternoon the Germans made their heaviest attack, behind a mortar barrage, volleys of grenades, and flamethrowers. The Americans had only one machine-gun left at each end of the perimeter, and a few automatic rifles. But the assault was driven to ground by their gunfire, and while the enemy were in the open the tenement rats heaved themselves out of their funk holes, staged a counterattack that killed the German commander and drove his troops back in disorder. A few hours later Krotoshinsky reappeared, leading the relief force.

What the "Battle of Henry Johnson" had done for Black Americans, the Lost Battalion did for immigrants in general, and East European Jews in particular (cf. Slotkin, *Lost Battalions*, ch. 11). The New York *Globe* identified their whole division (the 77th) as "an east-side division, and to be even more explicit a Yiddish division." Abe Krotoshinsky's heroism made him for a moment the personification of the transforming power of Americanization:

> By a clever alchemy America transmutes *blighted* raw material into men [...] In less than a generation the Russian Jew has got out of his soul the consequences of centuries of tyranny and oppression. He went into the melting pot with many fears clouding his spirit; he emerges a full grown man, who looks with level and unlowered eyes at the arrogant Prussian. Who, ever again, would dare hold up to scorn the fighting capacity of the downtown New York Jew? [...] The Yiddishers fight like wildcats![5]

The Lost Battalion would be the best-remembered episode of the war, the name itself becoming part of the language, like the Alamo and Custer's Last Stand. A film would be made (*The Lost Battalion*, 1919) intercutting studio scenes with

---

[5] See American Jewish Committee, *War Record*, 39–40; [Anonymous], "The Yiddish Division," *American Hebrew* (18 October 1918), 610; [Anonymous], "The Yiddish Battalion," 630.

footage of some of the original participants, including Major Charles White Whittlesey. But even as the soldiers fulfilled their part of the bargain in France, Americans at home were changing its terms.

Mobilization had brought to the surface of American cultural life the implicit contradiction between democratic ideals and the reality of racial inequality, and compelled policy-makers to choose between them. They had publicly affirmed the promise that American citizenship after the war would indeed provide liberty and justice for all who had served. Black and ethnic minority soldiers paid the blood price demanded by that social bargain. But the fears and hatreds stirred by war propaganda roused the latent racialism of American culture.

To rouse and intensify public commitment to the war, government agencies and civilian organizations whipped up anti-German propaganda, first against the German Empire and its troops, but then against Americans of German origin, and anyone opposed to or critical of the war effort. In early twentieth-century America the most intense enmity always had a basis in racism. To identify Germans as a racial enemy, it was necessary to show their likeness to non-Whites. Theodore Roosevelt showed how easily this racial transformation could be effected. He had once shaken hands with the German Emperor, but, he explained, that was before the war, "when [the Kaiser] was a white man." When government propagandists wanted to explain just how horrible was the character of the German enemy, they resorted to the iconography of Jim Crow and its fantasies of racial rape. The most popular war poster of the period shows the German enemy as a giant gorilla, an image stereotypically associated with Blacks, in a spiked helmet, with glaring fangs, and a ravaged half-naked white woman draped over one arm (cf. Slotkin, *The Lost Battalions* 219).

Racial symbolism could also attach to certain groups of American Whites. German-Americans were the obvious first targets. Starting in the late summer of 1918, however, the 'new immigrants' (especially Jews and Italians) were also marked as *racial* enemies of White America. The precipitant was the Russian Revolution, and the months of struggle leading to the Bolshevik takeover. A Congressional committee investigating subversive movements in the U.S. gave credence to claims that "Yiddish Jews" from the Lower East Side of New York had financed and actually led the Bolshevik Revolution. One witness, who had been in Petrograd during the revolution, testified: "I have a firm conviction that this thing is Yiddish, and that one of its bases is to be found in the East Side of New York." He also declared that "some of my best friends are Jews," the first time that classic bit of hypocrisy appeared in print (Slotkin, *Lost Battalions* 382–390).[6] The

---

[6] See also U.S. Congress, 66th Congress, 1st Session, Senate, Document No. 62. *Brewing and Liquor Interests and German and Bolshevik Propaganda*, 3: 112–116, 127–129, 135–136, 140, 142–143,

anti-Bolshevik propaganda played upon a new set of fears that began to emerge as the war drew towards a close. There was widespread concern about a postwar economic collapse, fear of mass unemployment as four million soldiers were demobilized, and resentment by White and native-born workers – north as well as south – of the gains in wealth, employment, and respectability made by Blacks and immigrants during the war.

The result was a wave of social violence that began in 1919 and lasted into the 1920s. Hundreds were killed in bloody race-riots in Washington DC, Chicago, Omaha, Tulsa, and a wave of lynchings and mob violence against Blacks surged throughout the South and Midwest. At the same time, there was widespread violence (both official and vigilante) against socialists of all kinds and against labor unions in the steel, coal, textile, lumber, maritime, and civil service industries. The government used war-time powers to put all Black and labor organizations under surveillance; used agents provocateurs and illegal arrests and mass deportations to break up these organizations. East European Jews and Italian immigrants were identified as the groups most likely to provide Bolshevik agitators; and African-Americans, as the nation's most oppressed class, were thought to be the group most likely to be persuaded by the appeal of revolution.

In this atmosphere, the promise that had been made to the soldiers, of civil equality in exchange for loyal service, was broken. Two legislative issues set the tone for future policy – the immigration reform bill; and the Dyer anti-lynching bill. Lynching was the most disreputable and therefore most vulnerable aspect of Jim Crow, and the Dyer Bill would have made it a Federal crime. The Republican Party nominally supported the bill; but while it was being debated, President Warren Harding accepted an honorary membership in the Ku Klux Klan. Southern Congressmen easily blocked the bill, justifying lynching as a spontaneous expression of White racial manhood, a God-given "instinct of racial preservation" and "the call of the blood."[7]

For immigrants, the counterpart of Congress' rejection of the Dyer bill was the Johnson Reed Act, which excluded new immigrants on an explicitly racial basis. Social scientists testifying in support of the bill asserted Jewish racial difference by invoking the 'one-drop' rule hitherto used only for Blacks:

> [It] has taken us fifty years to learn that speaking English and wearing good clothes and going to school does not transform a Negro into a white man [...] Americans will have a similar experience with the Polish Jew, whose dwarf stature, peculiar mentality, and ruth-

---

444; Chase, *Legacy*, 359, and Bendersky 41–43, 63, 137, 141, 406–408.

7 See Slotkin, *Lost Battalions*, ch. 13, 451–453; the debate is in U.S. Congress, *Congressional Record*, 67th Congress, 2nd Session (1922), 786–807, esp. 797–799; and also U.S. Congress, *Congressional Record*, 66th Congress, 1st Session, 8029–8030.

less concentration on self-interest are being engrafted upon the stock of the nation. [...] the cross between a white man and a Negro is a Negro; [...] the cross between any of the three European races and a Jew is a Jew. (qtd. in Chase 171–172)[8]

Passage of the act not only cut off immigration, it also signaled official approval of discrimination aimed at keeping Jews and Italians out of the American mainstream, by restricting their access to housing, university admissions, and professional employment. As a 1922 article in the *Atlantic Monthly* put it, "It is not only the individual [immigrant] whom we [must] exclude, but [...] his descendants, whose blood may [...] mingle with and deteriorate the best we have" (qtd. in Slotkin, *Lost Battalions* 460). That was the same principle that had justified racial segregation in the South.

Jewish, Italian and African-American veterans' organizations, and civic organizations representing these communities, cited the war record of their respective groups in appealing against the wave of post-war discrimination. However, the public was disillusioned with the war itself, eager to forget what it considered a costly and thankless intervention, unwilling to support President Wilson's plans for post-war reconstruction – and resistant to the claims of veterans for jobs or financial benefits.

For the minority communities of Blacks and new immigrants, the inter-war period was marked by the persistence and intensification of discrimination (both institutional and informal). However, there was also a countervailing tendency for these communities to become increasingly politicized and militant in seeking equal rights. Veterans and their organizations were prominent in these movements, and reflected the belief that the soldiers had earned on the battlefield the rights they were being denied. The cut-off of new immigration meant that the growing population of these groups would also be increasingly well-assimilated. Their numbers and possession of the right to vote gave the immigrants and their children, and Blacks in the northern states, political power. And both groups acquired a growing cultural power, especially in the music business – and Hollywood.

The era of the Great Depression and the New Deal (1929–1938) accelerated these positive tendencies. Jews, Italians and other ethnic Whites became essential components of the political coalition that sustained President Roosevelt's policies of reform, relief, and regulation. Although Blacks in the South remained disenfranchised, those in the North also increased their political influence. Most

---

[8] See also Slotkin, *Lost Battalions* 455–456; Rep. Raker, *Hearings ... on Immigration*, 68th Congress, 1st session, 540–542; 570–573, 608–616; Chase,166, 170–173, 252–285, 293–294; Slotkin, *Gunfighter Nation: The Myth of the Frontier in Twentieth Century America* (1992), 198–202.

importantly, the social-justice ideology of the New Dealers began to shift the cultural discourse back toward that vision of multi-ethnic and multi-racial equality that had been invoked in 1917 and betrayed in 1920.

After 1937, the growing menace of Nazi Germany, Fascist Italy, and Imperial Japan crystallized this liberal tendency into a distinct cultural and political program. In different ways, each of these enemy powers asserted the claims of a "Master Race" to rule lesser breeds – which in their view would include Americans. Nazism in particular exemplified the evil potential of racialist beliefs and practices. The moral embarrassment of Jim Crow was heightened by the perceived likeness between Southern discriminatory laws and the legal proscription and persecution of Jews in Nazi Germany. The outbreak of the Second World War accelerated these tendencies. Although public opinion was sharply divided on U.S. participation, anti-Nazi feeling was also strong. The Roosevelt administration offered the Allies material support short of engagement, and worked in various ways to prepare for U.S. engagement. Hollywood joined in that preparation, as studios responded to explicit suggestions from the administration, and responded to the shifts in the public mood. As the chief purveyor of public myth, its most important contribution was the cinematic reassessment of warfare.

After the celebratory *Lost Battalion* of 1919, American films had taken a uniformly dark view of U.S. engagement in the Great War. Silent films like *Wings* (1927) and *What Price Glory?* (1927), and sound pictures like *All Quiet on the Western Front* (1930), *A Farewell to Arms* (1932) and *Lost Patrol* (1934) represented the war as an exercise in futility, a waste of lives and hopes. After 1938 that view was strongly revised. *Fighting 69th* (1940) and *Sergeant York* (1941) portrayed the war as an idealistic crusade, and death in battle as a necessary sacrifice for a good cause. Both films also represented ethnic mixture as typical of American military units, and used Jews as the embodiment of that mixture – as they had been in the time of the original Lost Battalion.[9]

The public, and Hollywood story and research departments, had been reminded of that story by Thomas Johnson and Fletcher Pratt, whose history of *The Lost Battalion* was published in 1938. Based on interviews with the surviving veterans, *The Lost Battalion* was a fable of successful Americanization, in which the stress of combat brings the varied constituents of the American population into perfect solidarity (cf. Slotkin, *Lost Battalions* 527–530). It also provided a recipe for the kind of war film Hollywood would make after the U.S. entered the war in 1941: focused on the actions of a small unit, developing larger meanings by implication.

---

[9] For an overview see Clayton R. Koppes and Gregory D. Black, *Hollywood Goes to War: How Politics, Profits and Propaganda Shaped World War II Movies* (1987), esp. chs. 2, 9, 10.

Bataan, made and released in 1943, would set the pattern for those films, by drawing on the essentials of the Lost Battalion story, and adapting them to a new war and a new social and political context.[10] The film refers to fighting in the Philippines during the early months of the war, when U.S. forces fought a doomed defensive battle in hopes of delaying the Japanese advance. Faced with a new and difficult subject, the researchers and writers who prepared the script sought precedents and models on which they could build. They drew on and referred to legendary precedents like Custer's Last Stand and the Alamo, and on the more recent legend of the Lost Battalion, recovered by the work of Johnson and Pratt. The script was officially considered to be a remake of *Lost Patrol*, a 1934 film which implicitly invoked the Lost Battalion motif (cf. Basinger 45, 340).

There are many analogies between the Lost Battalion and the last stand depicted in *Bataan*. Everyone who wrote about the Argonne described the forest as a figurative 'jungle' – in the movie the jungle is literal. The Germans who fought in the Argonne were described as a treacherous enemy, who honeycombed the jungle with snipers and pillboxes, who would feign surrender (or death) and then kill U.S. troops. The Japanese in *Bataan* repeat both of these patterns. The uniforms, helmets, and weaponry were essentially the same as those used in 1918, as are the tactics used in the film – an alternation of trench-line defense anchored on heavy machine guns, with fixed-bayonet counterattacks "over the top" (cf. Slotkin, *Lost Battalions* 552–557). The most significant borrowing from the Lost Battalion, however, is the use of an ethnically and racially mixed unit to symbolize American nationality. The same ethnic types could be used in *Bataan*, since there had been little change in either the constituents of the melting-pot or in ethnic and racial stereotypes. The unit is not a battalion but an infantry squad, in which the range of ethnic, racial and social types are represented by single figures. There are six White Anglo-Saxon Protestants and six racial/ethnic characters. Captain Lassiter and Lieutenant Bentley are WASP West Pointers. The tough top-sergeant is Bill Dane, whose name suggests Nordic derivation. Corporal Todd is an urban gangster figure; Purckett a small-town all-American boy. The medic Hardy is a Conscientious Objector who will die fighting. The ethnic characters are a Jew (Feingold), an Irishman (Malloy), a Pole (Matowski), a Hispanic (Ramirez), and two representatives of the American empire – the Filipinos Salazar (a Moro) and Katigbak. Originally, the unit was to have contained a Native American, whose grandfather had fought against Custer at Little Big Horn. The character was replaced by Salazar, whose Moro people supposedly have the same 'savage' qualities as Native Americans. The only significant ethnicity of the origi-

---

10 On the formula see Basinger, *World War II Combat Film*, ch. 1; Slotkin, "Unit Pride: Ethnic Platoons and the Myths of American Nationality," *American Literary History* 13. 3 (2001): 469–498.

nal Lost Battalion that is entirely omitted from the *Bataan* group is the Italian-American – replaced by the Latino Ramirez.

The most significant addition to the roster is a Black man, Wesley Epps. He belongs not to the Lost Battalion tradition, but to the Harlem Hell Fighters. His presence in *Bataan* is remarkable, even revolutionary in its implications. The American army in World War II was racially segregated, like the Jim Crow South. There was no racial integration below the regimental or company level, African-Americans and Japanese Americans served in racially segregated units, for the most part under White officers. *Bataan*'s unit is racially integrated only because the Army has been defeated, its segregated regular organizations broken up. But Epps' presence in the unit is accepted without any comment whatsoever, and he is treated as an equal member of the squad, respected for his skills. He has a close and easy friendship with Pvt. Matowsky. At one point the men are sharing cigarettes and water, and Epps passes his canteen to Cpl. Todd – imagine the scene playing in a Southern theater with separate White and Colored drinking fountains.

The inclusion of a Black soldier was deliberate and consciously political. Moreover, *Bataan*'s lead was followed in later films like *Sahara* (1943) and *Guadalcanal Diary* (1943). Hollywood seems to have implicitly accepted the "Double V" program linking victory over Nazism to the destruction of race-prejudice. That commitment is reflected in the fact that some film-makers persisted in trying to place African-Americans in their war stories, even when the premise for including them was rather thin (cf. Koppes and Black, "Blacks" 400–401, 405). The multi-ethnic multi-racial 'platoon,' as modeled in *Bataan*, represents a military unit that could not have existed in the American army as then constituted, and symbolizes an American community which did not yet exist. Clearly there is an intention in the film to create, not a mirror of Americans, but an ideal projection, a myth of what America *ought* to be. The fact that the ethnic platoon has since become a cultural cliché, and the 'Good War' a national myth, testifies to the success of the myth-makers, and to the authenticity of the social values and human aspirations to which they appealed.

The paradox of *Bataan* is that the emotion which enables the platoon to transcend racial prejudice is itself a virulent expression of racial hatred. The final heat which blends the ingredients of the melting pot is rage against an enemy who is fully dehumanized as a race of "dirty no-tail monkeys" – a linguistic replication of the infamous 1918 poster of the German 'Hun' as a gorilla-rapist. The defect in the Platoon Movie myth is that the degree of toleration with which *internal* racial and ethnic differences are treated in the platoon movie is proportional to and dependent on the extreme dehumanization of the *external* enemy.

Nevertheless, the good intentions of films like *Bataan* made a great deal of difference in the way Americans think about themselves. The Hollywood platoon was a utopian projection of the kind of nation that Hollywood, acting as custodian of public myth, thought we should and could become, through the testing and transformation of the war. This myth had a significant impact on the national culture that emerged from the war, especially the movements against ethnic discrimination and anti-Semitism, and the civil rights movement for racial equality. But the mythic Platoon of World War II has effaced our memory of the units who, in the First World War, fought for a nation in which "common ideals have transformed men and women of all these races, and kindreds, and tongues, into ONE nation." Since 1919 only one film has been made about the Lost Battalion – the made-for-TV movie released in 2002. No film has ever been made about the Harlem Hell Fighters.

References

Adler, Julius O. *History of the 306th Infantry*, 1935. www.longwood.k12.ny.us/history/index.htm.

American Jewish Committee. *The War Record of American Jews: First Report of the Office of War Records, American Jewish Committee, January 1, 1919*. New York: American Jewish Committee, 1919.

[Anonymous]. "The Yiddish Battalion." *American Hebrew* (25 October 1918): 630.

[Anonymous]. "The Yiddish Division." *American Hebrew* (18 October 1918): 610.

Barbeau, Arthur E., and Florette Henri. *The Unknown Soldiers: Black American Troops in World War I*. Philadelphia: Temple University Press, 1974.

Basinger, Jeanine. *The World War II Combat Film: Anatomy of a Genre*. Middletown: Wesleyan University Press, 2003.

Bendersky, Joseph W. *The "Jewish Threat": Anti-Semitic Policies of the U.S. Army*. New York: Basic Books, 2000.

Chase, Allan. *The Legacy of Malthus: The Social Costs of the New Scientific Racism*. New York: Knopf, 1977.

Cobb, Irvin. *The Glory of the Coming: What Mine Eyes Have Seen of Americans in Action in the Year of Grace and Allied Endeavor*. New York: George H. Doran Co., 1918.

Cobb, Irvin. "Young Black Joe." *Saturday Evening Post* (24 August 1918): 294–307.

Commons, John R. *Races and Immigrants in America*. Second edition. New York: MacMillan Co., 1920.

Crisis 16. 4 (August 1918): 164, 179, 187.

DuBois, W. E. B. *The Oxford W. E. B. DuBois Reader*. Ed. Eric J. Sundquist. New York: Oxford University Press, 1996.

Ford, Nancy Gentile. *War and Ethnicity: Foreign-Born Soldiers and the United States*. Ph. D. Dissertation, Temple University, 1994.

Gerstle, Gary. *American Crucible: Race and Nation in the Twentieth Century*. Princeton, NJ: Princeton University Press, 2001.

Johnson, Thomas M. and Fletcher Pratt. *The Lost Battalion*. Introduction by Edward Coffman. Lincoln: University of Nebraska Press, 2000.

Koppes, Clayton R., and Gregory D. Black. "Blacks, Loyalty, and Motion-Picture Propaganda in World War II." *JAH* 73. 2 (1986): 383–406.

Koppes, Clayton R., and Gregory D. Black. *Hollywood Goes to War: How Politics, Profits, and Propaganda Shaped World War II Movies*. Berkeley: University of California Press, 1990.

Little, Arthur W. *From Harlem to the Rhine: The Story of New York's Colored Volunteers*. New York: Covici Friede Publishers, 1936.

Miles, L. Wardlaw. *History of the 308th Infantry, 1917–1919*. New York: G. P. Putnam's Sons, 1927.

Patton, Gerald W. *War and Race: The Black Officer in the American Military, 1915–1941*. Westport, CT: Greenwood Press, 1981.

Rainsford, W. Kerr. *From Upton to the Meuse with the Three Hundred and Seventh Infantry: A Brief History of Its Life and of the Part It Played in the Great War*. New York: D. Appleton & Co., 1920.

Rorty, Richard. *Achieving Our Country: Leftist Thought in Twentieth Century America*. Cambridge: Harvard University Press, 1998.

Schaffer, Ronald. *America in the Great War: The Rise of the War Welfare State*. New York: Oxford University Press, 1991.

Slotkin, Richard. *Gunfighter Nation: The Myth of the Frontier in Twentieth Century America*. N.Y.: Atheneum, 1992.

Slotkin, Richard. "Unit Pride: Ethnic Platoons and the Myths of American Nationality." *American Literary History* 13.3 (2001): 469–498.

Slotkin, Richard. *Lost Battalions: The Great War and the Crisis of American Nationality*. New York: Henry Holt, 2005.

Tichenor, Daniel J. *Dividing Lines: The Politics of Immigration Control in America*. Princeton, NJ: Princeton University Press, 2002.

Tiebout, Frank B. *A History of the 305th Infantry*. New York: The 305th Infantry Auxiliary, 1919.

United States. Committee on Public Information. Division of the Four-Minute Men. *The Meaning of America*. Bulletin No. 33. Washington: Committee on Public Information, June 29, 1918.

United States. Committee on Public Information. Division of the Four-Minute Men. *Home Reading Course for Citizen-Soldiers*. War Information Series No. 9. Washington: Committee on Public Information, October 1917.

U.S. Congress. 66th Congress, 1st Session, Senate, Document No. 62, Vol. 1. *Brewing and Liquor Interests and German and Bolshevik Propaganda. Reports and Hearings of the Subcommittee on the Judiciary, United States Senate*. 3 Volumes. Washington: Government Printing Office, 1919.

U.S. Congress. *Congressional Record: Proceedings and Debates of the 1st Session of the 66th Congress ... Volume 58*. Washington: Government Printing Office, 1920.

U.S. Congress. *Congressional Record: Proceedings and Debates of the 1st Session of the 67th Congress ...* Washington: Government Printing Office, 1921.

U.S. Congress. *Congressional Record: Proceedings and Debates of the 2nd Session of the 67th Congress ... Volume 62, Part 1*. Washington: Government Printing Office, 1921.

U.S. Congress. 68th Congress 1st Session. *Restriction of Immigration, Hearings before the Committee on Immigration and Naturalization of the House of Representatives*. Washington: Government Printing Office, 1924.

Maurizio Cinquegrani
Place, Time and Memory in Italian Cinema of the Great War

> If people bring so much courage to this world the world has to kill them to break them, so of course it kills them. The world breaks every one and afterward many are strong at the broken places. But those that will not break it kills. It kills the very good and the very gentle and the very brave impartially. If you are none of these you can be sure it will kill you too but there will be no special hurry.
>
> Ernest Hemingway, *A Farewell to Arms*

King Vidor's adaptation of Ernest Hemingway's *A Farewell to Arms* (1957) was largely filmed on location in the Italian Alps, the frontline of Italy's war against Austria. Despite location shooting, this version of Hemingway's novel maintains an overtly melodramatic focus on the love story between expatriate American Frederic Henry and Catherine Barkley, a British Voluntary Aid Detachment cadre; the war itself, the historical and political issues at stake, are largely absent. Thirteen years later the same mountains were denied to Italian filmmaker Francesco Rosi on the ground of his anti-militarist politics, and his *Uomini Contro* (*Many Wars Ago*, 1970) had to be filmed at the Centralni Filmski Studio Kosutnjak, in Belgrade, Serbia. *Uomini Contro* reads the events of the Great War in line with Marxist political cinema of the 1960s and belongs to a small group of films about the Great War made in Italy after the cultural and political events of 1968. These films, whose political stance had been anticipated by Mario Monicelli's *La Grande Guerra* (*The Great War*) in 1959, should be understood as counter-points to previous fictional accounts of the events of 1915–1918 and, in particular, focus on class and regional division in opposition to the myths of unity emerging from films made from the beginning of the First World War to the second post-war period and well into the 1950s. They also present a broader analysis of the idea of war, any war, understood as a recurring event evolving against social justice and the common good. Through a comparison with earlier films and war memoirs, this chapter addresses these issues of memory and historicity in relation to *Uomini Contro*, *La Grande Guerra*, *I Recuperanti* (*The Scavengers*, dir. Ermanno Olmi, 1970) and *La Sciantosa* (dir. Alfredo Gianetti, 1971).[1]

---

[1] The term 'sciantosa' refers to a female stock character that developed in Italian variety shows at the turn of the twentieth century.

Uomini Contro is loosely based on Emilio Lusso's *Un anno sull'altipiano*. Lusso, whose work also inspired *La Grande Guerra*, was an infantry captain during the Great War and his book a narrative account of his experience in the trenches. In *Un anno sull'altipiano* General Leone explains that "the enemy might have rifles, machine guns, artillery: with our Farina cuirasses we can break through their lines" (Lusso 92). The Farina cuirasses were composed of a helmet and frontal armoured plate for trench warfare, and were in fact completely ineffective when opposed to modern machine guns. This episode is included in *Uomini Contro*, in the sequence where Francesco Rosi presents a grotesque image of Italian soldiers wearing these cuirasses, advancing towards the enemy lines only to be killed or severely injured by Austrian artillery. A long shot taken from the point of view of the sniper shows a small contingent of armoured Italian soldiers systematically killed, with the cuirasses clearly limiting their field of vision. Ironically, General Leone had told the soldiers that the Romans triumphed in battle thanks to their cuirasses and, indeed, the most remarkable feature of this sequence lies in its anachronistic quality. These cuirasses seem to belong to another time, to a Roman centurion or a mediaeval knight rather than to modern warfare. Throughout the nineteenth century new technologies penetrated everyday life and affected industry, transport, sciences and popular entertainment. Progress and bourgeois well-being, as Henri Lefebvre suggests, was short-lived, as the escalation of technological progress was soon applied to armaments, the threat of war and eventually to war itself (cf. 178–179). Technological progress affected the Great War on a very large scale, and the image of the Farina cuirasses seems to belong to a distant past, a long-gone era of forgotten warfare. In *La Guerra e il Sogno di Momi (The War and the Dream of Momi*, dir. Giovanni Pastrone, 1917), an old man reads to his grandchild, Momi, a letter written by the boy's father at the front and including adventurous tales of war and courage. Momi later falls asleep and dreams of tin soldiers and trenches in a series of sequences that presented one of the earliest sophisticated uses of stop-motion animation in Italian cinema. These tin figurines remind one of Italian soldiers wearing the Farina cuirasses; in 1917, only the fantasy of a child and the misjudgement of the high-ranking military officials could have contemplated a war of armoured knights facing the new pneumatic trench mortars.

Technological progress applied to warfare was to come into its own, with its full potential, only in the Second World War, with the systematic destruction of cities through aerial bombing, industrialised mass-murder, and the atom bomb. Nevertheless, machine warfare had already been glorified in the *Futurist Manifesto* of Filippo T. Marinetti (1909) and the Great War saw the use of caterpillar-tracked armoured vehicles and poison gas onto the battlefield, the first timid attempt to use air warfare and the submarine as means to either kill civilians or starve them by stopping seaborne supplies (cf. Hobsbawm 27–30). These developments should be sufficient to deprive the image of this war of any sense of romanticism and heroism, and yet the image of the battlefield that emerges from films is one of romanticised action or nihilist destruction, depending on the time of their production. As we shall see, the attempt to strip mass death of its most disturbing features was indeed central to the representational strategies of war films produced in Italy during the Great War and in the following four decades.

Jay Winter has studied the mythical and romantic war imagery produced in France after the outbreak of the war, and his argument can also be applied to the Italian context. In his investigation of the relationship between film and *Images d'Épinal*, a series of traditionalist and naïve prints on popular subjects, Winter argues that both media aimed at representing the war as a mythical or romantic adventure that did not correspond to the reality of the battlefields. As they carried the tradition of *Images d'Épinal*, films provided a popular iconography of the nation at war and explicitly aimed at an escape from a reality too hard to bear. In the darkness of the cinema, concludes Winter, the supernatural aura of the war emerged sanitised, magical and mundane (cf. *Sites of Memory* 119–144). Italian cinema of the war initially reiterated this attempt at romantic escapism. Not until the second half of the twentieth century did Italian cinema acquire a more profound socio-historical stance towards the Great War, a perspective influenced by Emilio Lusso's narratives and by the work of hermetic poet Giuseppe Ungaretti, whose collection of poems *L'allegria* (*The Joy*, 1931) captures his experiences at the front and answers to what he described as a universal need of poetry: "Si sta come / d'autunno / sugli alberi / le foglie" ["Here we stay / like leaves / on trees / in autumn"] ("Soldati," *Vita d'un Uomo* 86. Trans. M. C.) This poem, "Soldiers," refers to the uncertainty of soldiers' lives in the trenches; an existence as precarious as that of leaves on trees during the autumn. It is not romanticised or sanitised; it implies death, like later films about the Italian front.

Both war newsreels and fiction film produced in the period 1915–1918 operated on a series of selections, omissions and emphases in the treatment of their subject matter. The newsreel *Tra le Nevi e i Ghiacci del Tonale* (*Amid Snow and Ice on Mount Tonale*), produced by the Cinematographic Section of the Italian Army, was filmed just before the Italian final offensive of June–July 1918 on a series of key locations including River Piave, River Camonica, Mount Presena, Mount Tonale, and Ponte di Legno. Suffused by subjectivity like any other historical source, *Tra le Nevi e i Ghiacci del Tonale* introduces the viewer to that wintry landscape, characterised by snow, mud and wind, which will later become a recurring feature in films such as *Uomini Contro* and *La Grande Guerra*. This film shows convoys of motorised and horse-drawn vehicles carrying food, fodder and equipment to Mount Tonale and the River Piave valley. They follow a mountain road through small villages, including what was left of Ponte di Legno – a town that had almost been razed to the ground by Austrian cannons in 1917. Alpine soldiers can be seen carrying dismantled Maxim machine guns up to their positions, where they reassemble the weapons and fire them. Stovepipe mortars bombard the Austrian positions while Alpine soldiers capture the enemy's artillery. The film ends with images of Austrian prisoners escorted to the valley, where they are fed and eventually marched to the collecting station. *Tra le Nevi e i Ghiacci del Tonale* also shows the use of mule-drawn flatcars, dog sledges and skis for transport. While a valuable historical record, this film presents a sanitised image of a front haunted by the deaths of the Alpine soldiers, the Austrians, the civilians of Ponte di Legno, and yet cleared of its darkest features, the seriously injured, the disfigured, the fear that inhibits solidarity, ultimately and unavoidably, the noises:

> Un urlo non umano ma di belva ferita rompe, staziante l'aria a cento metri da noi. Pochi istanti dopo vedo un soldato che a salti segue il sentiero mentre tiene con una mano a la gamba penzoloni. Nessun soldato gli offre aiuto, soltanto quando egli è vicinissimo alle rocce delle mani lo soccorrono (Fabi 274).

> [A hundred yards from us a cry, not human, but the cry of wounded beast breaks, heart-rending, the air. A few moments later I see a soldier coming down the path with one hand holding the leg hanging loosely to his body. No soldier offers his help, and only when he is very close to the rocks a pair of hands come to his aid.] (Trans. M. C.)

This extract from the diary of an Alpine soldier deployed in Carnia explains how the Austrian mortars injured a soldier while his comrades were occupied playing a board-game. The gruesome image is made more upsetting by the admission of a fine line between fear and bravery, with other soldiers unwilling to take the risk and help the victim; hardly material for propaganda films.

As Pierre Sorlin suggests, unlike war memoirs, an ordinary newsreel "hides neither the destruction nor the suffering of the soldiers but never reveals a corpse, a mutilated body or a wounded man" (11). Similarly, fiction films made during the war hardly evoked the sense of annihilation that characterised the battlefields. Italian film production during the war was dominated by melodramatic and sensationalist narratives starring famous actresses such as Lydia Borelli and Francesca Bertini – whose photograph on a film poster is constantly admired by Sicilian soldier Rosario Nicotra (Tiberio Murgia) in *La Grande Guerra*. Films like *Il Canto della Fede* ("Hymn to faith," dir. Filippo Butera, 1917) focused on the home front and promoted an idea of unity among classes and a fictitious sense of solidarity that reflected the perspective of contemporary newsreels; the frontline was safely distant. *Il Canto della Fede* aimed at selling a myth of national unity implying that all classes were united in war and ignored the fact that conscription affected social classes differently. Industrial workers, for example, were exempt from conscription and more than half of the five million men called into the army were peasants, often illiterate and with little understanding of the causes of the war (cf. Nicolle).

This imbalance was only addressed in film well after the end of the Second World War. In *La Sciantosa*, the slogan *Abbasso la Guerra* ("down with war") is misspelled on a wall graffiti as "Abbaso la guerra"; the film thus reveals an association between illiteracy, class and hostile feelings towards the war as reiterated by several comments made by working-class characters throughout the film. In *1900* (dir. Bernardo Bertolucci, 1976), Olmo (Gérard Depardieu) – an illegitimate peasant – enlists with the Italian army and goes to the front while Alfredo (Robert De Niro) – the scion of a wealthy family of landowners – avoids the battlefields and learns from his father how to run his family's large plantation, with significant repercussions on their lives. On the contrary, social cohesion was advocated by films such as *Maciste Alpino* (*The Warrior*, dir. Luigi Romano Borgnetto and Luigi Maggi, 1916) in their attempt to exploit the widespread patriotism that accompanied Italy's intervention with an escapist narrative of heroic actions anticipating fascist rhetoric. This particular perspective has been discussed by Gian Piero Brunetta in terms of an 'inverted telescope' relying on the categories of distance and absence rather than those of nearness and presence. Brunetta investigates the ways in which newsreels produced by the Ministries of Army, War or Navy provided an answer to the propagandistic aims of the Italian Government and aimed at boosting the morale of the public. Consequently, the action on the front-line trenches was not deemed a suitable subject for the newsreels, and films often represented the supply, artillery and support lines (cf. 273–282). They focused on auxiliary military actions such as those depicted in *Tra le Nevi e i Ghiacci del Tonale* or, alternatively and with emphasis, on the celebrations following Italian victories. For example, the defeat of Caporetto, where over 10,000 Italian soldiers died, was filmed for the newsreels with a focus on the damaged buildings and the orderly retreat of the Italian army, with no evidence of the mass death caused by German poison gas, flamethrowers and hand grenades.

A romanticised ideal of the Great War seen through the lenses of this 'inverted telescope' continued to define Italian cinema in the interwar period. During the fascist era a relatively small number of fiction films depicted the events of the 1915–1918 war. Anticipating a new war, the most significant titles were released in the mid-thirties and until the fall of Benito Mussolini's regime in 1943: *Cavalleria* ("Chivalry," dir. Goffredo Alessandrini, 1936), a patriotic portrait of an air force pilot; *Tredici Uomini ed un Cannone* ("Thirteen Men and a Gun," dir. Giovacchino Forzano, 1936), a whodunit narrative focusing on thirteen soldiers guarding a long-barrelled cannon; *Passaporto Rosso* ("Red Passport," dir. Guido Brignone,

1936), a story of Italian immigrants in South America returning to Italy to fight for king and country; *Le Scarpe al Sole* ("Shoes in the Sun," dir. Marco Elter, 1935), an heroic depiction of life in the trenches that was awarded a prize by the Ministry of Propaganda at the Venice Film Festival; *Piccolo Alpino* ("Little Alpine Soldier," dir. Oreste Biancoli, 1940), a film about a small child who is taken prisoner by the Austrians during the occupation of the north-eastern territories of Italy and who escapes, proving himself as courageous as an Alpine soldier. During the Second World War, Marcello Albani directed *Redenzione* ("Redemption," 1943), a film in which the Great War is used as a narrative device to deliver a message about the Second World War: an Italian communist who deserted the front in 1915 finally embraces the patriotic cause, fights and dies for Mussolini. After the Second World War, imagined views and narratives of the previous world conflict fell into oblivion and, until the release in 1959 of the pivotal film *La Grande Guerra*, only a few, largely unsuccessful, titles about the First World War were produced: *Senza Bandiera* ("Without Flag," dir. Lionello De Felice, 1951), a spy-story before the background of the Great War; *La Leggenda del Piave* ("The Legend of River Piave," dir. Riccardo Freda, 1952), a film about the conflict between a patriotic woman and her husband engaged in criminal activities during the war; *Fratelli d'Italia* ("Brothers of Italy," dir. Fausto Saraceni, 1952), the biopic of Austrian-born Italian irredentist and sailor Nazario Sauro; *Bella Non Piangere* ("Bella, Don't Cry," dir. Davide Carbonari, 1954), about a disabled man working as a postman at the front; *I Cinque dell'Adamello* ("The Adamello Five," dir. Pino Mercanti, 1954), the story of an heroic mission to recover the bodies of five Alpine soldiers killed by a landslide in 1918. Less directly propagandistic than their fascist predecessors, these films continue to present a romanticised image of the Great War, a patriotic memory of a war fought and won to juxtapose to the outcome and the remembrance of the Second World War.

Monicelli's *La Grande Guerra* – filmed on location in Venzone, Sella Sant'Agnese, Palmanova and Nespoledo di Lestizza, Friuli, and inspired by Lusso's narrative of the Italian front – anticipated a series of key films made after 1968 which deconstructed the sanitised heroic image of the war that had emerged from earlier films. *La Grande Guerra* portrays the fear experienced by young soldiers at the front. Franco Calderoni argues that the Great War was interpreted by the Italian people in a jingoistic and largely inaccurate manner due to the country's tendency to forget, to conform, to over-celebrate its triumphs and hide its failures. Between 1918 and 1959, the arts only sporadically addressed the events of the war and, Calderoni continues, Italian attitudes towards the conflict had irremediably been damaged by the unreliable treatment of the war in the newspapers of that time. Italian journalists failed to portray the war in an objective manner and emphasised each victory, while ignoring the major failures of the army (cf. 17–19). A rejection of this patriotic image of war also emerges from *La Grande Guerra*, in the scene where Giovanni reads an extract from *Domenica del Corriere*, a morale-bolstering illustrated magazine characterised by richly jingoistic undertones. The cover illustration by Achille Beltrami shows soldiers celebrating Christmas in the trenches, and the text claims that boredom characterises life at the front before the next offensive. A Venetian soldier argues that they should report on the miserable quality of their food and the limited supplies. This cinematic approach to the war was unheard of and met with strong opposition in the Italian press – still engaged in its unreliable treatment of the conflict. On 10 January 1959, the newspaper *La Stampa* reported the news of a film in pre-production to be presented by Dino De Laurentis, directed by Mario Monicelli and starring two of the most popular comic actors of the time, Alberto Sordi and Vittorio Gassman. Paolo Monelli, who signed the article 'Simplicissimus,' expresses his concerns for the comic elements of a film dealing with events such as the Defeat of Caporetto and, more specifically, for the presence of two comic actors destined to portray two Italian soldiers as mediocre and slightly cowardly individuals constantly tempted to desert; over the following four days, other Italian newspapers – including *Il Giorno, Il Mattino, Il Giornale d'Italia* – reported on the film, and despite Monicelli's reassurances they feared that the film would express contempt for the army and those who died in the trenches (cf. Calderoni 72–79).

Films made after *La Grande Guerra* continued to contribute to an in-depth understanding and to challenge the idea of a collective memory of the war while addressing the profound changes in Italian society that caused such memory to fade and re-emerge as the reflection of an altered historical and political context. In the first sequence of *La Sciantosa*, Anna Magnani looks repeatedly at an old leather-bound album of photographs containing images of the actress at a younger age. One of these photographs was taken in 1936 and portrays Magnani on the set of *Cavalleria*. Both *La Sciantosa* and *Cavalleria* are set during the Great War, and the intertextuality of this scene provides Magnani's character with a fictitious past emerging from a previous narrative of the war. Alfredo Gianetti, as Emiliano Morreale suggests, thus presented a "sublimation of Magnani's long-gone beginnings in the variety show" (113). In *La Sciantosa*, Magnani interprets Flora, an aging diva of the *café-chantant*, whose career has dramatically declined. She receives an invitation to visit the supply and support lines behind the front and to sing for the army. Flora decides to sing a jingoistic military march and appears on stage wearing an Italian flag and a crown resembling that of the House of Savoy. The singer realises that she has been invited to sing, not for the front-line soldiers, but for the wounded, and she is profoundly moved by the sight of these young men, who have been disfigured on the battlefields. She interrupts the band, removes her crown and the flag – thus revealing a black dress evoking mournful feelings – and sings *'O surdato 'nnammurato*, a Neapolitan song written by Enrico Cannio in 1915 about the sadness of a young soldier who is fighting at the front and pining for his beloved. Her performance is later interrupted by Austrian artillery. The contrast between the patriotic image of Flora wrapped in the flag at the notes during the military march, and the tearful image of the singer performing a moving interpretation of a popular song is striking, and reveals the conflicting vision of a war of heroes and patriotism versus a humanist understanding of the shattering violence and pointlessness of war. With films such as *La Grande Guerra* and *La Sciantosa*, the war is no longer seen through the lenses of an 'inverted telescope' nor presented in terms of heroism and the celebration of battlefield action. Rather, its image acquires a critical interpretation that challenges earlier representations of the conflict and their patriotic hero-worship narratives.

The war was fought in the northern regions of Italy and, disregarding the participation of soldiers from all over the country, the memories of civilians in the Veneto or Friuli regions ought to defer from those of non-combatants in Lazio or Sicily. In 1915, the Italian nation was just over fifty years old and profound differences existed between regions; the language itself was a barrier to the ideal of unity put forward by the propaganda. The regional dimension of the war was often emphasised in film through the use of dialect. In *La Sciantosa*, for example, the words "Ciao Tosa" – 'tosa' meaning 'girl' in the Venetian dialect – are written on one of the carriages taking the soldiers to the front, while the main male character, Tonino (Massimo Ranieri), has a pronounced Neapolitan accent. In *La Grande Guerra*, the contrast between Oreste's Milanese and Giovanni's Roman accent is also striking. Other characters in *La Grande Guerra* are originally from Tuscany, Apulia, and Sicily. Unable to recognise regional accents, Oreste claims that south of Parma Italians are all *romani*. The regional issue reminds one that historical memory changes according to its context. As Jorge Luis Borges puts it, "already a fictitious past occupies in our memories the place of another, a past of which we know nothing with certainty – not even that it is false" (*Tlön, Uqbar, Orbis Tertius*; qtd. in Lowenthal 1985).

The memory of the Great War, and the way in which it is reflected in film, is indeed a changeable construct, depending on its time and place. Non-inscriptional and textual memories of the event should be understood in terms of an open-ended, and largely problematic, process. Thus, for example, *Uomini Contro* is largely concerned with the idea of memory. Historically, films reflect memories of war in a diverse manner, never directly or in an unmediated manner, and always depending on the time of their making. Memory works differently for those who lived through the war and those who 'remember' it through mediated narratives of arguable authenticity. Jay Winter has challenged the ways in which 'collective memory' is used without interrogation, and has argued in favour of a greater rigour in the use of the concept. Winter defines film as one of a series of collective languages of mourning, searching for some redemptive meaning (cf. *Remembering War*, 183–200). Film has the power to affect the ways in which viewers think and 'remember' the past: "while film mediates the construction of individual and group memories, and in particular memories of war, it does so in ways which are never mechanical and which, in their variety and subtle power, reach different collectives in different ways" (*Remembering War*, 185). Winter focuses on the ways in which shared mediators, including films, do not correspond to shared common memories; different cohorts cannot simply be added to a vague concept of collective memory, and thus both film and memory are difficult to relate to a political contestation about ideas of nation and communities.

Italian films of the Great War released in the 1970s reflect this ambiguity. Rosi's *Uomini Contro*, for example, was made at a time of great political turmoil in Italy and, rather than presenting an answer to the nation's need to cling nostalgically to its history, it reconstructs the past in relation to the present – a present which is itself explained by the past. Rosi interpreted Lusso's work – originally deprived of a coherent political affiliation – through a Marxist perspective in line with his commitment to the so-called *cinema d'impegno*. *Uomini Contro* distances itself from previous glorifications of war and yet represents a radical attempt to find meaning in the shattering experience of the trenches, in the meaningless mass slaughter. *Uomini Contro* addresses soldiers' desertion and cases of self-harm. The latter was a common recurrence in the trenches, with over 10,000 soldiers found guilty of self-harm in 1916 alone (cf. Cosulich 37). Ultimately the film is about war and dialectic materialism. For both Rosi and Lusso the fact that the war was fought by working-class men on both fronts was a major preoccupation:

> Per la prima volta si rendevano conto che la guerra la facevano solo i contadini, i pastori, gli operai, gli artigiani. E gli altri dov'erano? Altra scoperta: anche dall'altra parte, la guerra la facevano i contadini e gli operai. (Lusso, 1951)

> [For the first time we realised that the war was only fought by countrymen, shepherds, workers and artisans. Where was everyone else? Another discovery: the Austrian army was also made of countrymen and workers.] (Trans. M. C.)

However, whereas the book broadly reflected Lusso's sense of betrayal – in 1914 he had been in favour of intervention – the film portrays its main character, Lieutenant Ottolenghi (Gian Maria Volonté), as a committed socialist embracing the fight of his soldiers against the military establishment. His actions reflect a position which was not shared by Lusso himself and which can be associated with other political memoirs of the Great War.

On 28 August 1917 Giuseppe Garrone, commander of the sixth unit of the Battaglione Alpini Tolmezzo, wrote a letter to his father from the front in Carnia:

> Grazie! Anche i codici sono arrivati! Che effetto mi ha fatto rivedere questi libricini che da più di due anni avevo persino dimenticato che esistessero. E non ero il solo ad averli dimenticati in questi tempi. Com'è strano il mondo. Anche la somma giustizia sociale che scaturirà dalla Guerra, sarà l'effetto, sia pure parziale, di tante piccole e flagranti ingiustizie. (Garrone 394)

> [Thank You! The codes have arrived! I had forgotten all about these books and was so happy to see them again! These days I am not the only one who has forgotten the codes. The world is a strange place. Even the ultimate social justice resulting from this war is going to be the consequence of a number of injustices, great or small.] (Trans. M. C.)

Giuseppe Garrone was killed by enemy fire on 16 December 1917. In his letter he anticipates a social justice based on a broad notion of patriotism and fairness rather than a revolutionary aspiration in the fashion of Volonté's character in *Uomini Contro*. Garrone's nephews, Alessandro and Carlo, were among the leaders of the Resistance during the Second World War and communist militants; their generation had experienced fascism, and this was reflected in their ways of seeing the war as a political fight against the regime.

Instead of ultimate social justice, it was fascism that was to result from the war, and films made after 1968 reveal this failure. *La Sciantosa*, for example, departs from any belief in a social justice brought about by the war, portraying instead a series of working-class individuals with little interest in the politics of war and a sceptical attitude towards any potential benefit resulting from it. Ottolenghi's unfulfilled hope, at odds with earlier films of the war, is shared by Oreste in *La Grande Guerra*. Gassman's character claims that the only just war is the war against inequality, and that the country needs reforms and not fallen soldiers. He reads Mikhail Bakunin, revealing an often confused support for revolutionary processes, and claims that nobody has the right to order a man to meet his death in the trenches. Francesco Rosi's narrative of the Great War is informed by later events – fascism, the Second World War, political conservatism in post-war Italy – and departs from a purely historical understanding of the conflict to use the trenches of the Italian front as a social and political reflection on the country. Whereas *La Sciantosa* exemplifies the lack of beliefs in a more just society expressed by the working classes during the conflict, *Uomini Contro* offers an alternative, the hope in a more just society emerging not from the conflict itself but from a socialist revolution.

After the war, fascism rapidly suffocated genuinely revolutionary forces, and fifty years later, when Rosi directed *Uomini Contro*, the opposition between radical left- and right-wing groups was central to the wave of terrorism and political turmoil known as the Years of Lead. Rosi himself admitted that one of the main aims of *Uomini Contro* and its representation of history as the product of class struggles was to understand the wars that followed and thus the present (cf. Cosulich 60). In his film, the image of a soldier dying on the barbed wire, shot and unable to move, echoes images of the barbed wire of the concentration and extermination camps of the Second World War. As he departs from Lusso's original intent, Rosi presents a reflection on war and men's behaviour when facing death in the trenches, and by doing so he introduces the audience to events that can be interpreted as the starting point of the political division which characterised twentieth-century Italy. As Maurice Halbwachs argued, an understanding of the processes of reshaping operations applied to the past implies an understanding of the ways in which the present social milieu influences the reproduction of the past (cf. 49). Rosi re-imagines the Great War under the influence of the sociopolitical landscape of the Years of Lead. In the trenches of the Great War, in Rosi's view, one can see the emergence of the revolutionary forces and the reactionary powers whose opposition delineated future historical events during fascism and republican Italy.

A reading of the First World War that focuses on its continuing impact on Italian politics throughout the century is also provided by Ermanno Olmi in *I Recuperanti*. In August 2012, over two hundred twenty-pound grenades from the Great War emerged from the Vedretta di Nardis glacier near Trento.[2] Although such a large find is a rare event, small or large relics of the war can easily be found in the old battlefields of the north-eastern Italian front. Well into the second half of the twentieth century, scavengers made a living out of recuperating noble metals from the former trenches. This activity is portrayed by Olmi in his film. Gianni (Andreino Carli), a demobilized Alpine soldier, returns to the Altopiano di Asiago from the Second World War and, unable to find decent employment, teams up with an old scavenger. The pair recovers metal remains of war weapons, including old unexploded bombs, grenades, bullets, and pieces of guns and cannons, and other relics left behind from the First World War in the rocks and meadows of the Altopiano, through hidden bunkers and depots. Made at the time of increasing political tension and violence in Italy, *I Recuperanti* addresses issues of memory and historicity in relation to the two wars and the second immediate post-war period. This film illustrates well-known social issues previously addressed by neo-realist filmmakers in the immediate post-war years, such as unemployment

---

2 See "Il ghiacciaio si scioglie e spunta arsenale risalente alla Grande Guerra," *Il Gazzettino* (31 August 2012) http://www.gazzettino.it/nordest/trento/il_ghiacciaio_si_scioglie_e_spunta_arsenale_risalente_alla_grande_guerra_foto/notizie/20/216804.shtml. (11 April 2013).

and more broadly that "crisis of self-esteem and self-identity" which defined neorealist characters such as Antonio Ricci in Vittorio De Sica's *Ladri di biciclette* (*Bicycle Thieves*, 1948) and which, as Mark Shiel suggests, "indicated the crisis of an entire people at a unique moment in their history" (98). In *I Recuperanti*, Andreino Carli's character is unable to find a secure job, contemplates emigration to Australia, and experiences the failure of the woodcutters' cooperative. His crisis is the crisis of an entire community incapacitated by post-war austerity.

However, Ermanno Olmi is not only concerned with the specific context of the late 1940s, his film aiming at a more profound historical consideration of the impact of war between nations on a community inhabiting a landscape which has often been a theatre of conflict. The Altopiano di Asiago, where both *Uomini Contro* and *I Recuperanti* are set – although only the latter was filmed on location – had already been one of the battlefields of the Italian wars of independence against the Austrian empire in the mid nineteenth century. Between 10 and 25 June 1917, the Italian and Austro-Hungarian armies fought for possession of Mount Ortigara in the Asiago Plateau: over 31,000 soldiers were killed or seriously wounded. In 1945 Pedescala, near Asiago, saw one of the most infamous massacres of civilians at the hands of the Wehrmacht, Waffen-SS and Italian fascists. In *Amore di Confine* ("Love of Frontiers," 1986), a collection of short autobiographical stories about the Second World War, Mario Rigoni Stern – one of the scriptwriters for *I Recuperanti* – reminds the reader that Asiago had already been burnt to the ground by Sigismund, the Archduke of Austria, in 1446 and again by the Austrian artillery in 1916: "Era un paese di montagna, dico era perché nel 1916 la guerra lo ha prima incendiato e poi distrutto e raso al suolo; e anche se tra il 1919 e il 1922 è stato ricostruito, ora non è più quello" ["Asiago was a mountain village; I say it was because in 1916 the war destroyed it and burnt it to the ground; it was rebuilt between 1919 and 1922, but it is no longer the same place"] (Stern 6. Trans. M. C.).

In *I Recuperanti*, Du, the old scavenger (Antonio Lunardi), echoes Stern's words and represents a generation that experienced two world wars and that saw war as an inevitable and recurring event: "la guerra e una brutta bestia, gira e gira il mondo e non si ferma mai. [...] Tiri su case che poi la guerra le buttera giu e io verro qui a trovare bombe" ["War is a nasty beast – he explains – it goes around and around the world and never stops [...]. You build houses and war tears them down and here I come, looking for relics"] (Trans. M. C.). Similarly, in *La Grande Guerra* Oreste argues that centuries of wars have not brought any greater good to peoples and nations. Du's words imply the concept of historic recurrence, whereas repetitive patterns in the history of a country, place or community exhibit the striking similarities of specific events as they converge and resonate in what is understood as a collective memory or a collective dissipation of memory (cf. Trompf). Soon after their first encounter, Du invites Gianni "to look at things the way I do." Here, Du is inviting Gianni to look at the landscape of the Asiago Plateau with particular attention to the copper, brass, iron and lead remnants left behind from the Great War; he is also inviting Gianni to see and understand the impact of the cyclical repetition of history on the place and its community, the processes according to which the wounds of war struggle to heal. Central to the narrative are the metal remains of the war, relics bearing witness to history while providing an unmediated impression of the past made available to the senses by their physicality. Du uses these relics to make the past seem credible and to illustrate the coexistence of the narrative's present, 1945, with the past, 1914–1918. Olmi, on the other hand, uses the scavenger's activity to display the coexistence of the film's present, 1970, and the violent history of the plateau in the two world wars. *I Recuperanti* – like *Uomini Contro*, *La Grande Guerra* and *La Sciantosa* – is thus concerned with historical processes and events, and their long-lasting effects on the landscape and people of Italy.

References

Calderoni, Franco. *La Grande Guerra: dal Soggetto al Film*. Bologna: Cappelli, 1959.
Cosulich, Callisto. *Uomini Contro: dal Soggetto al Film*. Bologna: Cappelli, 1970.
Brunetta, Gian Piero. "L'immagine della prima Guerra mondiale attraverso il cinema." *Operai e Contadini nella Grande Guerra*. Ed. Mario Isnenghi. Bologna: Cappelli, 1982. 273–282.
Fabi, Lucio. *Gente di Trincea: la Grande Guerra sul Carso e sull'Isonzo*. Milan: Mursia, 2009.
Garrone, Giuseppe and Eugenio. *Lettere e Diari di Guerra 1914–1918*. Milan: Garzanti, 1974. 394.
Halbwachs, Maurice. *On Collective Memory*. Trans. Lewis A. Coser. Chicago: University of Chicago Press, 1992 [1952].
Hobsbawm, Eric. *Age of Extremes: the Short Twentieth Century 1914–1991*. London: Abacus, 1995.
Lefebvre, Henri. *Introduction to Modernity*. Trans. John Moore. London and New York: Verso, 1995 [1962].
Lowenthal, David. *The Past is a Foreign Country*. Cambridge and New York: Cambridge University Press, 1985.
Lusso, Emilio. *Un anno sull'altopiano*. Torino: Einaudi, 2005 [first edition Paris: Edizioni italiane di cultura, 1938].
Lusso, Emilio. "La Brigata Sassari e il Partito Sardo D'Azione." *Il Ponte* (1951): 9–10.
Morreale, Emiliano. *L'invenzione della nostalgia. Il vintage nel cinema italiano e dintorni*. Rome: Donzelli, 2009.
Nicolle, David. *The Italian Army of World War One*. Botley, Oxford: Osprey Publishing, 2012.
Shiel, Mark. *Italian Neorealism: Rebuilding the Cinematic City*. London: Wallflower Press, 2006.

Sorlin, Pierre. "Cinema and the Memory of the Great War." *The First World War and Popular Cinema: 1914 to the Present*. Ed. Michael Paris. Edinburgh: Edinburgh University Press, 1999. 5–26.

Stern, Mario Rigoni. *Amore di Confine*. Turin: Einaudi, 1986.

Trompf, Garry W. *The Idea of Historical Recurrence in Western Thought: from Antiquity to the Reformation*. Berkeley: University of California Press, 1992.

Ungaretti, Giuseppe. *Vita d'un Uomo – Tutte le Poesie*. Segrate, Milan: Arnoldo Mondadori Editore, 1969.

Winter, Jay. *Sites of Memory, Sites of Mourning: the Great War in European Cultural History*. Cambridge: Cambridge University Press, 1998 [1991].

Winter, Jay. *Remembering War: The Great War between Memory and History in the 20th Century*. New Haven, CT: Yale University Press, 2006.

Filmography

1900. Dir. Bernardo Bertolucci. Produzioni Europee Associati (PEA), 1976.
Bella Non Piangere. Dir. Davide Carbonari. Excelsa Film, 1954.
Il Canto della Fede. Dir. Filippo Butera. Cleo Film, 1917.
I Cinque dell'Adamello. Dir. Pino Mercanti. Cinemontaggio, 1954.
Cavalleria. Dir. Goffredo Alessandrini. I.C.I., 1936.
A Farewell to Arms. Dir. King Vidor. The Selznick Studio, 1957.
Fratelli d'Italia. Dir. Fausto Saraceni. Dino de Laurentiis Cinematografica, 1952.
La Grande Guerra. Dir. Mario Monicelli. Dino de Laurentiis Cinematografica, 1959.
La Guerra e il Sogno di Momi. Dir. Giovanni Pastrone. Italia Film, 1917.
La Leggenda del Piave. Dir. Riccardo Freda. Produzione Film Colamonici Tupini, 1952.
Maciste Alpino. Dir. Luigi Romano Borgnetto and Luigi Maggi. Italia Film, 1916
Passaporto Rosso. Dir. Guido Brignone. Societa Anonima Stefano Pittaluga, 1936.
Piccolo Alpino. Dir. Oreste Biancoli. Manderfilm 1940.
I Recuperanti. Dir. Ermanno Olmi. RAI Radiotelevisione Italiana, 1970.
Redenzione. Dir. Marcello Albani. Andros Film, 1943.
Le Scarpe al Sole. Dir. Marco Elter. Artisti Associati, 1935.
La Sciantosa. Dir. Alfredo Gianetti. RAI, 1971.
Senza Bandiera. Dir. Lionello De Felice. Elfo Film, 1951.
Tra le Nevi e i Ghiacci del Tonale. Prod. Cinematographic Section of the Italian Army, 1918.
Tredici Uomini ed un Cannone. Dir. Giovacchino Forzano. Pisorno Cinematografica, 1936.
Uomini Contro. Dir. Francesco Rosi. Prima Cinematografica, 1970.

Marzena Sokołowska-Paryż
The Great War and the Easter Rising in Tom Phelan's *The Canal Bridge*: A Literary Response to the Politics of Commemoration in Ireland

This may have been a sheer coincidence, but there seems to be something very symbolic about the fact that Tom Phelan's novel about the Great War was published in the same year in which the Prime Minister of the Republic of Ireland, Bertie Ahern, publicly declared that the ninetieth anniversary of the Easter Rising of 1916 would be commemorated by an official military parade, as was the custom prior to the outbreak of the Troubles in Northern Ireland.[1] *The Canal Bridge* (2005) opens with a memorial list citing the names of men from Mountmellick, County Laois, Ireland, who "were in uniform during the Great War" (n.p.). In the following acknowledgments, the author recalls his battlefield tour to "the Somme, Ypres, Passchendaele and many other sites where the bodies of the young soldiers of World War I are still being found," and he pays a special tribute to "a delegation from the North" whom he met at the site of the Menin Gate Memorial in 1999: "You had come to Belgium to lay wreaths on soldiers' graves and at the monuments erected in their memory. Young men you were, former members of the security forces in Ulster. [...] As we shook hands you told us that in the laying of wreaths you were honouring the dead, not because of where they had come from, but because of who they were" (vii–viii). These introductory pages perform a commemorative function and provide a significant interpretative framework for Phelan's fictive story about the citizens of Ballyrannel, whose lives are shattered equally by the consequences of the carnage on the battlefields of Flanders and France and by the violence unleashed by a national uprising on the home front. The novel consists of a series of personal reminiscences, the more poignant as most of these monologues are the voices of the dead.

In Tom Phelan's novel, the dominant leitmotif of a childhood song about the eponymous bridge connecting the opposite sides of the canal may be read as a powerful call for the depoliticization of conflicting national memories. The pivotal point in Irish history was undoubtedly the year 1916, which saw the British suppression of the Easter Rising in Dublin and the initially successful assault of the 36th Ulster Division on Thiepval Ridge on the first day of the Somme offensive:

---

[1] The controversies sparked by this decision are outlined in Beiner 366–367.

"Ireland is deeply troubled by evocative memories of its past, not least of 1916, which inhabits a mythic time and space reverberating with resonances that range far beyond the events of that year" (Beiner 366). In the aftermath of the Great War, the political appropriation of the Easter Rising by the nationalists and the republicans, and the Somme battle by the unionists, led to the formation of divergent national myths of the Great War, where myth should be understood as "not a falsification of reality, but an imaginative version of it, a story of war that has evolved, and has come to be accepted as true" (Hynes ix). The national apotheosis of the insurgents redefined Irish involvement in the war as "a great mistake, a profound betrayal, one that could only be compensated for by Irish neutrality in the Second World War" (Boyce 202), whereas "the losses of the Ulster Division on the Somme came specifically to be associated with the freedom of Ulster Unionists to run their own policy [...] in what emerged as Northern Ireland. For them the 'blood sacrifice' of the Somme was equal and opposite to that of Easter 1916" (Jeffery 133).

Keith Jeffery argues that the contemporary "longer historical perspective" provides the opportunity of a profound reassessment of the conflicting political myths: "if we view the development of 'advanced nationalism,' the outbreak of the Easter Rising in 1916, and so on not as some completely separate narrative distinct from the world war, but as an integral part of essentially the same story, then the Great War becomes the single most central experience of twentieth-century Ireland, not just, or least, for what happened at the time, but in its longer term legacy and the meaning which we can draw from it today" (2). By including a memorial list in his book, Phelan makes his position clear: the Irishmen who fought in the Great War deserve recognition and remembrance as soldiers. He demands an empathic acknowledgment of these men, regardless of the motivations that led them to enlist and the cause their uniform aligned them with. He is in perfect agreement with Jeffery in that "fatally obsessed with difference, in Ireland we too often fail to perceive the similarities in our predicament, upon which we must build if any lasting 'peace' is to be established on our island" (3). Irishmen, whether Protestant unionists or Catholic republicans and nationalists, went through the same hell of trench warfare, and neither suffering nor death distinguished between the Irish and the English. Paraphrasing the words of Richard Grayson, the doubts as to the righteousness of the cause of the war do not need to exclude the possibility of paying tribute to the men who fought in it (181).

Phelan's mention of the Menin Gate Memorial thus resonates with specific implications, for it is a British national/imperial monument. It is useful at this point to adopt Arthur Danto's distinction between monument and memorial: "We erect monuments so that we shall always remember and build memorials so that we shall never forget. [...] Monuments make heroes and triumphs, victories and conquests, perpetually present and part of life. The memorial is a special precinct, extruded from life, a segregated enclave where we honor the dead. With monuments, we honor ourselves" (152). The Menin Gate was intended as a monument raised in tribute to the victorious British Empire, as overtly stated in the Report of the British National Battlefields Memorial Committee, dated 24 February 1921: "consideration of sentiment and history were strongly in favour of at least one general memorial at some outstanding locality which would serve to commemorate in an adequate manner the actions of the troops of the whole Empire" (qtd. in Quinlan 373–379). The Menin Gate was also endowed with a very poignant memorial purpose, with the Hall of Memory at its center, listing the names of almost fifty-five thousand officers and soldiers who had lost their lives in the infamous Ypres salient and thus conforming to the need of "naming [which] recalled each individual victim and returned to him an individual existence against the oblivion to which he had been consigned on the battlefield" (Goebel 29).

These meanings of the Menin Gate Memorial add an important interpretative dimension to the predicament of the most prominent characters in Phelan's novel, Matthias (Matt) Wrenn and Cornelius (Con) Hatchel, Irishmen who willingly join the ranks of the British army in 1913, impressed by the stories of faraway exotic lands told by the Anglo-Irish landowner for whom they worked. The beginning of the novel creates a contrast between the pre-war fascination with the British Empire, shared by many Irishmen, and the war-forged disillusionment of men who felt they had been unfairly and brutally deprived of their youth and future by a cruel twist of history: "a dark cloud of disappointment descended on the ship and it did not stir for two days as we all tried to get used to two new terrible ideas: we were not going to India and we were going to war. It was like we'd had a double-barrelled, rotten trick played on us" (74). The first year in the British Army is recalled by Matt as the most fascinating time of his life, holding a promise of "places where the sun was shining all the time, [...] – India and Kenya and Australia and Rhodesia and Jamaica and Malaya and Burma and Ceylon and Borneo, too and New Zealand" (44). He is awed by the vastness of the British Empire, with countries "so big that Ireland would fit into them a couple of hundred times" (44). These passages are a powerful reminder that many young men, including Irishmen, were enticed by an idea of the British Empire, the glamour of its immensity and omnipotence. However, the reason why Irishmen from small towns and villages joined the British Army was also more mundane, namely the desire to escape poverty: "I'd march from here to Timbuktu on a feed of onions and liver and spuds" (46).

The initial "unease for joining the English army" (43) quickly dissipates among the Irishmen, and Con notes with satisfaction their physical and mental transformation: "We were country bumpkins changing into golden-skinned warriors, peasants turning into knights who could look any man anywhere in the eye; paupers we had been, but now we were men with a jingle in our pockets" (55–56). They take pride in their British uniforms and exalt in the assumed supremacy of their newly acquired imperial masculinity: "Bulging with energy in every muscle, we were brimming with life, young as the sun, invincible, indestructible, immortal" (54). The physically-fit and perfectly-trained male body was looked upon as a guarantee of military prowess and spiritual fortitude.² Phelan shows how this ideal of hegemonic imperial masculinity is brutally shattered by the realities of fighting in conditions which Eric Leed has so aptly defined as the "industrialized war": "the dominance of long-range artillery, the machine-gun, and barbed wire [which] had immobilized combat, and immobility necessitated a passive stance of the soldier before the forces of mechanized slaughter" (164).

The moment of initiation into war comes not with the first battle but with the first sighting of the wounded and the dead. The horrifying wounds suffered by soldiers as well as the corpses in varying stages of decomposition were unnerving because they demonstrated, in the most revolting way, the vulnerability of the human body. As Joanna Bourke states, the shock of the First World War derived from the unparalleled scale of the physical mutilation that men suffered and witnessed: "The severity of [the] mutilations was unprecedented: nothing in British history [...] was adequate preparation for the physical devastation of the First World War. All parts of the body were at risk: head, shoulder, arms, chest, intestines, buttocks, penis, leg, foot" (33). Phelan's Irish soldiers are stretcher-bearers, witnessing on a daily basis the degradation of men to sheer corporeality: "there was something obscene about it, the way any part of the body isolated looks strange. I hated seeing heads in the muck, or legs, or arms" (90). Following the advice of an English doctor never to bring back wounded when "what's left of them wouldn't want to be kept alive if he was you," Matt kills the fatally wounded

---

[2] The ideological concept of imperial masculinity is strongly rooted in the "muscular Christianity" movement in the late nineteenth century, associated predominantly with the English public school. It promoted the ideal of an "elite masculinity," based on the virtues of "aggressive spirituality and physical prowess" (Bourke 13), which served to legitimate the hegemonic nature of English manhood, i.e. "their capacity to govern others" (qtd. in Shephard 19). This ideal is, however, equally pertinent to the issue of Irish manhood, depicted in the following passage of James Joyce's *A Portrait of the Artist as a Young Man* as derivative from the British model: "he had heard about him the constant voices of his father and of his masters, urging him to be a gentleman above all things and urging him to be a good catholic above all things. [...] *When the gymnasium had been opened he had heard another voice urging him to be strong and manly and healthy* [italics mine] and when the movement towards national revival had begun to be felt in the college yet another voice had bidden him be true to his country and help to raise up her language and tradition" (88).

and horribly disfigured soldiers in an act of compassion: "No matter who it was – English, Irish, French, German, Indian, Senegalese – [...] I sang quietly when I was using Knifey" (91).

There is an interesting parallel to be found between Joanna Bourke's emphatic assertion that "the most important point to be made about the male body during the Great War was that it was intended to be mutilated" (33) and the description of soldiers going over the top in Phelan's novel: "they ran against moulded chunks of metal shrieking toward them to whip out their guts, rip off their legs and arms, smash their hard skulls into smithereens, explode their brains into grey puffs, rip out their balls and send them flying in [...] tiny fragments" (98). When one looks at a military conflict solely from the perspective of the threat combat poses to the male body, then the personal reasons and national causes for which men came to serve in the war cease to have any meaning; what is more, the way the soldier is perceived changes diametrically. Bourke focuses on photographs in which "the cowering, agonized expressions on the faces of the soldiers struggling back from the front lines suggest recognition of their inability to struggle against the forces determined to wreak havoc on their bodies" (33), whereas Eric Leed redefines the combatant of the Great War: "Trench warfare [...] eroded officially sponsored conceptions of the soldierly self as an agent of aggression. It produced [...] a defensive personality, moulded by identifications with the victims of a war dominated by 'impersonal' aggressors of chemicals and steel" (106). In *The Canal Bridge*, Con sees animals and men as different sorts of "poor dumb beasts": "at least when the level of violence and cruelty against them had risen to unbearable, the [animals] had fought to escape. The soldiers didn't fight to escape, to live. They lived to fight, lived to jump out of a hole into a barrage of bullets as destructive as the whirring steel teeth of a pulper against the solid flesh of a turnip" (97).

Con recalls with anger the first day of the Somme offensive when "fifty thousand casualties were counted" (146). A year later soldiers march on to capture Passchendaele, where "seventy thousand men became so minced up with the mud that no trace was ever found of them. [...] Seventy thousand – the population of one hundred and forty Ballyrannels" (98). It is not the German soldiers who are the enemy: "the soldiers across the way looked just like us, same height, same coloured skin, same coloured hair, same age, every bit as dirty" (144). Trench warfare rendered all men indistinguishable in their predicament, and the following point made by Leed perfectly summarizes Phelan's portrayal of the soldiers of the Great War: "[it was] a war in which all combatants were victims of material [and] in which an industrial technology was the 'true' aggressor" (107). This confrontation of men and technology does not mean that the idea of the enemy ceases to have any relevance, for where there is a crime (war) there must be a perpetrator. Con's rage is directed against the men-in-command, who, according to him, devised the entire madness of the war, pitilessly sacrificing men and ruthlessly prolonging the carnage. He confronts Field Marshal Douglas Haig, with dire consequences for himself, in an implausible and yet highly evocative scene. There is a marked contrast between Con's appearance as "a human rat" and that of Haig and his staff officers: "so clean and creased and polished and spitted and relaxed and well fed" (193), clearly indicating that the latter is completely out of touch with the conditions men have to endure at the front. Con claims himself to be a messenger from the soldiers: "I came from the trenches and no-man's-land, and there's bits of dead soldiers in my boots and on my uniform and in my pockets, and that's why I stink like an open grave" (194). He invites the dumbfounded Haig to descend from his immaculate headquarters into the hell he created for his troops, "to enjoy the muck, and the rats, and the shite, and the piss, and the rotten corpses, and rotten horses" (195).

It is the prerogative of fiction writers to imagine whatever situations they please, however incredible. Yet this confrontation does not appear in the text solely because the author had such a whim. Con's last words to Haig have an ostentatiously prophetic quality: "Surely they'll make a statue of you on a horse after the War to pretend to themselves how great the War was [...]. Remember me, Mr. Haig, when they pull the cover off the statue [...] listen to the hissing and the booing of the young lads you sent to the butcher, not for a pound of beef, but to get butchered themselves" (198). Phelan creates here an overt contrast between the post-war practice of commemorating the BEF's commander-in-chief in the form of equestrian statues (the Earl Haig monument in Edinburgh, the Douglas Haig Monument at Montreuil-sur-mer, and the Field Marshal Earl Haig monument at Whitehall, London) and one of the most ingrained assumptions at the core of the British myth of the Great War: "[Haig] seems to epitomize everything that was wrong with the generalship of the First World War. This popular view sees him as stubborn, stupid, callous, uncaring; a man who spent his war safe in a comfortable and well-appointed château miles behind the lines while troops suffered and died in rat-infested trenches" (Sheffield 134). It is also evident why the battles of the Somme and Passchendaele are given so much prominence in his novel: "If most of the British public know only of the Somme when thinking about the Great War, then that portion that knows a little more will have heard of Passchendaele, where Butcher Haig, having learned nothing from the slaughter of the Somme in 1916, spent 1917 in again throwing the flower of British manhood against impregnable German wire and machine guns, through waist-deep mud, to no avail" (Corrigan 333).

Con is accused of deserting his post and sentenced to death. His act of defiance is an ostentatious gesture of empathic solidarity with all the men in the trenches, his personal sacrifice made in the name of all the dead and dead-to-be, all the mutilated and mutilated-to-be. Phelan makes a powerful point that there was nothing political about the hardships the soldiers were forced to endure, the agony of the wounded, and the horrific ways in which men died. This argument is augmented by the fact that Phelan's Irishmen serve as stretcher-bearers in the war, i.e. they do not fight but bring help to the suffering. *The Canal Bridge* perfectly supports Richard Grayson's thesis that the conviction of the vast majority of Irishmen that "[the First World War] was a pointless and futile war" is "little different to the popular version of history that prevails in Great Britain" (171). Phelan deliberately foregrounds the fact that the grief felt for the loss of a son is the same for an Irish Catholic (Con Hatchel's mother) and an Anglo-Irish Protestant (Mrs. Hodgkins, who lost her son Lionel in the battle of Passchendaele).

The Canal Bridge serves the evident purpose of recovering the memory of Irishmen serving in the Great War from "national amnesia" (Boyce 191). Speaking about his preparation to write a novel about the Great War, Phelan mentions an incident that took place on his return to Dublin via Manchester from a battlefield tour. He and his wife were wearing poppies they had got in Manchester for Remembrance Day: "shortly after we stepped off the plane, a woman stopped us and said, 'We don't wear those here'. [...] we were in Ireland – a country that had sent a quarter of a million young men to Europe between 1914 and 1918, that had lost 35,000 on the battlefield, that had persuaded its youth they would be fighting for Ireland. [...] Thus were the men who fought for Ireland in Europe consigned to Ireland's ash pit" ("Notebook"). Phelan was aware, however, that, in order to restore the Irish soldiers of the Great War to their rightful place in national memory, it was necessary to rewrite W. B. Yeats's version of the Easter Rising as the spiritual triumph of men whose willing sacrifice gave birth to a new Ireland.[3]

Historical facts about the Easter Rising are relentless. The leaders surrendered after only a week of fighting without gaining widespread national support: "[I]t was a very small-scale affair and was not immediately either very popular or very successful. It was perceived as a mainly German-inspired rising, not least because of the pro-German sentiments expressed by the Volunteers" (Jeffery 49). Irishmen serving at the front, regardless of their political convictions, were generally not very enthusiastic about the outbreak of the uprising, the more so with

---

[3] Fran Brearton points to W. B. Yeats's contribution to the formation of Irish cultural memory: "Yeats is culpable, not for ignoring the war since he did not do so, but for helping [...] to consolidate the view that the tragedy of the Great War was primarily an English not an Irish tragedy, and, as such, that it was remote from cultural life" (44). Nuala C. Johnson writes of the importance of proclamations of support for the insurgents by members of the literary establishment: "The public intervention of well-known people such as George Bernard Shaw, who claimed the rebels should be treated as prisoners of war rather than traitors, elevated the rebellion to the international stage and effected public opinion towards the rebels and their fate" (143).

instances of Germans exploiting the event with an obvious intent of creating a friction between Irish and English soldiers (Jeffery 54–55). Phelan includes these reactions in his novel, with Matt voicing the soldiers' discontent with the atmosphere of distrust generated by the news of the events in Dublin: "[W]e were all young lads in this dung heap together [...]. But after Pearse played out his fantasies [...], we Irish were suspect and the Germans made things worse by putting up signs in their trenches inviting the Irish to come over to their side, promising to treat us better than the English had treated the Easter rebels" (102).

What was a downright political and military defeat quickly gained a new meaning after the leaders of the uprising were executed by order of the British military authorities. Phelan highlights in his novel the historical paradox behind the mythologization of the insurgents, namely that they owed their ultimate reputation of national martyrs to the decisions made by those against whom they rebelled: "[I]f the English had only given them all a good kick in the arse and sent them home to their mothers the whole thing would have been over and done in a matter of days. [...] the lads in Dublin were eejits when they were alive but heroes when they became corpses. The magic was done by the English with their firing squad" (107). For Matt, the execution of the Rising's leaders had little significance in comparison with "the twenty-seven thousand [soldiers] down in four hours" in the most excruciating circumstances on the Somme. He is bitterly aware, however, that these deaths would capture the public imagination and usurp the memory which the men "lying in the muck" more righteously deserved: "all that Ireland could think of was twelve bastards who stabbed in the back every Irishman fighting against the Germans. Couldn't they have waited? Did they need to be heroes so badly?" (93)

The executions provided the opportunity to 'translate' a complete failure into "a blood sacrifice, [...] which in acknowledging and accepting the futility of the gesture overcame futility in the very act of making the gesture" (Brearton 19). Phelan's criticism of the Easter Rising derives from his more general disapproval of what Guy Beiner calls the "republican model of martyrdom," which effectively redefined the failed anti-English insurrections from the eighteenth century onwards:

> Shortly after the suppression of the 1798 Rebellion, the dissemination of memories of grievances in the popular press began elevating the vanquished United Irish leaders into heroic martyrs. [...] A republican model of martyrdom was more clearly formulated after remaining United Irishmen defiantly rose up again in rebellion in 1803. [...] In the nineteenth century, this pattern repeated itself in the construction of nationalist republican memory of the seemingly negligible rebellions of Young Ireland in 1848 and of the Fenians in 1867. Through the publication of countless hagiographic histories and street ballads, these humiliating defeats were remembered as exemplary events. (Beiner 374–375)

The most fervent advocate of this "model of martyrdom" was Patrick Pearse, a member of the Irish Republican Brotherhood, and one of the seven signatories of the proclamation of the Irish Republic (alongside Thomas J. Clarke, Seán Mac Diarmada, Thomas MacDonagh, Éamonn Ceannt, James Connolly, and Joseph Plunkett). After the suppression of the Rising, he was subsequently court-martialled and sentenced to death by the British military authorities.

According to Seán Farrell Moran, "Patrick Pearse's unique contribution to Irish political history was his expression of the 'mythic' ideas which served as the moral basis of physical-force nationalism" (630). These ideas, Moran writes, "border[ed] on the psychopathic" because "Pearse failed to see that what he was really doing was attempting to reinvent the myth mimetically. Since myth is by definition impossible to invent, the reasons behind living a myth out in life seem to be irrational if not pathological" (639):

> Pearse desired an apocalypse which could release him and his generation from a present which was shameful. [...] Ireland was not free because it had allowed itself to be emasculated, and this emasculation had led to an acceptance of the impotence and dishonor of peace. [...] In Irish culture the idea of personal redemptive transformation [existed] in the transformation symbolism of the Eucharist, and in the *Táin*, where Cúchulainn was transformed into an unstoppable warrior by his warp spasm. [...] It was the transforming power of myth that attracted Pearse; he wanted to accept its offer of a wholeness which destroyed all self-doubts and inadequacies. Ultimately that wholeness came from a death which coupled the dead with the nationalist martyrs of the past and those who suffer for it in future. (Moran 637, 641)

Phelan is full of scorn about Pearse's myth-based ideology: "[he] inebriated himself on Irish lore, gore, legend and history. For him, Ireland was a woman, and Pearse would redeem her from England and give her a rightful place among the nations of the Earth" ("Notebook").

There is an interesting similarity between Moran's view that "Pearse's unique contribution to Irish political history derived from his personal experience of despair, irresolution, the need to escape his personal situation, failure, and ambivalence" (625) and the derogatory opinion voiced by one of the soldiers in Phelan's novel that "we cursed the stupidity of Pearse who'd been so taken up by being a martyr for Ireland that he couldn't hold on a job for long. He had lived with his mother and sister to save himself from dying from hunger while he scrawled poetry in his garret. A few hours in a trench in France on a wet day would have knocked the illusions out of the lad" (102). It is, however, the monologue of Father Kinsella that contains the most scathing condemnation of Pearse as a politically irresponsible and egotistic fanatic: "so badly he wanted to be a mythical or mystical hero he just couldn't wait to get himself killed. [...] There was no need for anyone to be a martyr for Ireland, unless they wanted to occupy a niche in the national pantheon of mindless zealots, have had songs written about them to be sung in drunken and tuneless voices forever. [...] Dead idiots. Mindless zealots. Blind idealists" (85–86).

In Phelan's *The Canal Bridge*, the most repulsive character is Johnjoe Lacy, who accuses Matt and Con of betraying Ireland by their decision of joining the British Army. It is telling that Lacy, though he plays a prominent role in the plot of the novel, is always spoken about and quoted by others. There is no space in Phelan's novel for a monologue (even if entirely fictive) of a fervent devotee of the "republican model of martyrdom," instead, the author focuses on the tragic consequences of a fanatical belief in violence as the only righteous path towards national independence. Phelan aims to show in his novel how "opportunistic supporters of the executed rebels then took up the fight against England on Irish soil" ("Notebook"). There is gossip about Lacy among the inhabitants of Ballyrannel that he was involved in acts of sabotage during the Easter Rising, "derailing the train on the main line near Mabra to slow down the English soldiers going to Dublin when the shooting started at the Post Office" (105). He bullies the simple-minded road brusher Ralphie Blake into joining the "anti-English activity [that] was heating up round the country" (106).

The Ballyrannel to which Matthias comes back after the Great War is infested with nationalistic rancour. It is only a question of time when this aggressive political mood evolves into outright acts of violence, aimed to 'free' Ireland from its alleged enemies (Anglo-Irish Protestants) and traitors (Irishmen who served in the British Army). Phelan creates a parallel between simple villagers like Ralphie, who follow the IRA against their common sense, and the men in the trenches, who went over the top on orders of their leaders: "dumb lads at the mercy of the men who led them from behind" (92). It is also telling that the author presents two excruciating examples of death by fire in the last part of the novel, intentionally creating a connection between the victims of war and the victims of politically motivated violence. Sarah Hodgkins, daughter of Anglo-Irish landowners and a former VAD, recalls the death of her friends, all young nurses, burnt alive after their tent at the casualty clearing station caught fire from a falling flare: "It was the screams – that was the worst part; the high-pitched screams" (227). Kitty Hatchel, Con's sister and Matt's beloved, is traumatized by the memory of the sight of two old men dying in the fire that engulfed their home, set by the IRA, and only because the owners were Protestants: "I shivered at the remembrance of the two old brothers, struggling to escape the flames but dying inside – the pain, the screams" (212). When Enderly, the Anglo-Irish 'Big House,' is targeted by an IRA group, Matt, Kitty and Sarah make a stand, fighting the men off, but at a high price. In a symbolic scene, Matt, who miraculously survived the Great War, is fatally wounded by Lacy, a zealous IRA member.

The very last monologue in the novel, spoken by Kitty, is dated 1970. She is the only survivor from among the group of close friends, Catholic and Protestant, who had once lived together in harmony until the war came, and with it the Easter Rising. This last monologue accounts for the novel's composition based on a series of personal memories: "When I die, gone forever will be the pain created by the loss of Lionel and Con, and Matt, and now Sarah. [...] There will be only knowledge. History books cannot pass on the pain endured, the anguish, the terror of the times. [...] Even a headstone in a cemetery, leaned on and wept for years, becomes just one more piece of cold granite when the final rememberer dies" (278). The path to understanding the Irish past, beyond the contending political interpretations of the Great War and Easter Rising, leads through the thoughts and emotions of the people of that particular time, even if these people are only figments of the author's imagination. It is the thoughts and emotions that the reader is to identify with, which also explains the preference for voices as the structural foundation of the narrative. In *The Canal Bridge* Phelan sets out, therefore, to validate fiction as a means of forging historical empathy which, in the case of Ireland, can potentially contribute to the ethically desirable depoliticization of national memories, for "empathy discloses an ontological kernel of otherness in the other that is worthy of respect – and, in that sense, has a core integrity that points towards morality" (Agosta 72). Though the bibliography cited at the end of the novel is indeed impressive, Phelan's aim is less to produce an accurate reconstruction of Irish history than to foreground views that may effectively change the perception of this history in the present, to re-tell and re-remember both "an untold and eventually forgotten story [of the Great War]" (Grayson 172–173) as well as the officially commemorated and constantly articulated story of the Easter Rising in a way that would bring an end to "the total polarization of [Irish national and British national/imperial] identities" (Hennessey 239).

The role of literature in determining which historical events are collectively acknowledged as defining national identity cannot be overestimated. As Fran Brearton writes, "the Rising's legacy has, as it appears, almost completely sidelined the legacy left by the Great War in the Republic of Ireland. Ireland does not have an anthologized or canonized tradition of Great War literature, but it does have an anthologized canon of Easter Rising literature" (15). The more important, therefore, is the growing literary interest in the Irish soldiers of the Great War. One may say that the incentive came from Jennifer Johnston's highly acclaimed novel *How Many Miles to Babylon?* (1974), adapted for television by the Northern Irish poet Derek Mahon (1982, BBC). The play *Observe the Sons of Ulster Marching Towards the Somme* (1985) by the Irish Catholic Frank McGuinness captured the public imagination in both Éire and Northern Ireland, and "it has come to be regarded as a genuinely sympathetic, if critical, exploration of the minds and hearts of the [Ulster loyalists] who fought on 1 July 1916" (Kiberd 279). James Carroll's *Supply of Heroes* (1986) was inspired by the discovery of a family grave in Tipperary: "To my surprise, [my mother's uncle's] tombstone was that of a British soldier, and it told me that he had been killed in France in the Great War. So, I begin by acknowledging the memory of my great-uncle, whose fate as an Irishman fighting for England, instead of against her, has tugged at my imagination all these years" (vii). Sebastian Barry said in an interview that his novel *Long Long Way* (2005) was intended as an imaginary resurrection of the un-remembered Irish soldiers: "In this moment not only are the 36,000 who died in the war gone, but also every last man of the 160,000 or so that survived. That made it feel somehow urgent to describe their suffering and their resilience, and all the rest [...] To understand them, to identify with them, and silently and with enormous friendship to salute them." All such works are an important step towards changing what Nuala C. Johnson has defined in her title as the "geography of remembrance" in Ireland. In the same interview, Sebastian Barry notes with satisfaction how, after the publication of his novel, "the numbers of people at readings and in letters [...] suddenly realize that they have this strong connection, and remember they had great-uncles or whatever at the war, and are suddenly appalled by what they went through, and, in many cases, suddenly proud, suddenly amazed, suddenly thankful, which is wonderful." It is appropriate, however, to end this chapter with Tom Phelan's words: "It is time for the Irish to demand that the guards at the gates of the pantheon of Irish heroes stand aside and admit their grandfathers and great-grandfathers who fought in the Great War. It is time for them to wear the poppy on Remembrance Day" ("Notebook").

References

Agosta, Lou. *Empathy in the Context of Philosophy*. New York: Palgrave Macmillan, 2010.
Barry, Sebastian. Interview by Mark Harkin. 2005. http://www.threemonkeysonline.com/als/_a_long_long_way_sebastian_barry_interview.html. (15 June 2010).
Beiner, Guy. "Between Trauma and Triumphalism: The Easter Rising, the Somme, and the Crux of Deep Memory in Modern Ireland." *Journal of British Studies* 46. 2 (2007): 366–389.
Bourke, Joanna. *Dismembering the Male: Men's Bodies, Britain and the Great War*. London: Reaktion Books, 1999.
Boyce, D. G. "'That party politics should divide our tents': nationalism, unionism and the First World War." *Ireland and the Great War: 'A War to Unite Us All?'* Eds. Adrian Gregory and Senia Pašeta. Manchester and New York: Manchester University Press, 2002. 190–216.
Brearton, Fran. *The Great War in Irish Poetry: From W. B. Yeats to Michael Longley*. Oxford and New York: Oxford University Press, 2003.
Carroll, James. *Supply of Heroes*. New York: Signet Books, 1987.
Corrigan, Gordon. *Mud, Blood and Poppycock: Britain and the First World War*. London: Cassell, 2004.
Danto, Arthur C. "The Vietnam Veterans Memorial." *The Nation* (31 August 1985): 152.
Goebel, Stefan. *The Great War and Medieval Memory: War, Remembrance and Medievalism in Britain and Germany, 1914–1940*. Cambridge: Cambridge University Press, 2007.
Grayson, Richard S. *Belfast Boys: How Unionists and Nationalists Fought and Died Together in the First World War*. London and New York: Continuum, 2010.
Hennessey, Thomas. *Dividing Ireland: World War I and Partition*. London and New York: Routledge, 2010.
Hynes, Samuel. *A War Imagined: The First World War and English Culture*. London: The Bodley Head, 1990.
Jeffery, Keith. *Ireland and the Great War*. Cambridge: Cambridge University Press, 2011.
Johnson, Nuala C. *Ireland, The Great War and the Geography of Remembrance*. Cambridge and New York: Cambridge University Press, 2007.
Joyce, James. *A Portrait of the Artist as a Young Man*. London: Penguin Books, 1992.
Kiberd, Declan. "Frank McGuinness and the Sons of Ulster." *The Yearbook of English Studies* 35: *Irish Writing since 1950* (2005): 279–297.
Leed, Eric J. *No Man's Land: Combat and Identity in World War I*. London, New York and Melbourne: Cambridge University Press, 1979.
Moran, Seán Farrell. "Patrick Pearse and the European Revolt Against Reason." *Journal of the History of Ideas* 50. 4 (1989): 625–643.
Phelan, Tom. *The Canal Bridge*. Dublin: The Lilliput Press, 2005.
Phelan, Tom. "Notebook." *Newsday* (12 November 2005). http://www.newsday.com/opinion/notebook-1.596246 (5 April 2013).
Quinlan, Mark. *British War Memorials*. Hertford: Authors On Line, 2005.
Sheffield, Gary. *Forgotten Victory. The First World War: Myths and Realities*. London: Review, 2002.
Shephard, Ben. *A War of Nerves: Soldiers and Psychiatrists, 1914–1994*. London: Pimlico, 2002.
Yeats, W. B. "Easter 1916." *Yeats's Poems*. Ed. A. Norman Jeffares. London and Basingstoke: Macmillan, 1989. 287–289.

Angela Brintlinger
The Great War through 'Great October': 1914/1917 in Russian Memory

Nastoiashchii – ne kalendar'nyi – Dvadtsatyi Vek.
[Not the calendar – but the real Twentieth Century]

Anna Akhmatova, Poem without a Hero

Esli tvoia khata s kraiu...
[If your hut is on the edge of the settlement...]

Valentin Pikul'

Those Russians who experienced the First World War wrote about it, most famously perhaps Mikhail Sholokhov in his *Quiet Flows the Don* and Boris Pasternak in *Doctor Zhivago*. But later generations rarely focused on the events of 1914–1918, their attention distracted by developments far more momentous for the Russian people. The two Russian Revolutions of 1917 (including the socialist revolution, which came to be called 'Great October'), the ensuing and devastating Civil War, the construction and consolidation of the new Soviet state, Stalin's 'Great Terror,' and of course the Second World War, which the Soviets called the 'Great Fatherland War,' all overshadowed the events of the Great War.[1] As topics for fiction and film, Russians chose those other wars, particularly the Second World War, which dominated Russian fiction and film throughout the second half of the twentieth century and continues to be a live topic today.[2]

Only in the 1970s did the theme of World War One emerge. Two prominent writers turned to the Great War for fictional material, but for very different reasons. Both lived in the Soviet Union at the time, and both were marginalized, also for very different reasons. After almost a decade of prison camp and exile, Alexander Solzhenitsyn (1918–2008) had returned to central Russia and the pages of Soviet literary magazines with his groundbreaking novella, published in *Novyi Mir* in 1962, about the Soviet GULag system. With the express permission of General Secretary Nikita Krushchev, *One Day in the Life of Ivan Denisovich* brought the

---
[1] Karen Petrone has explored the interwar representations of World War I in her recent book *The Great War in Russian Memory* (2011), very useful as background to the post-memory era.
[2] On films during and about the war see Youngblood.

world – and language – of *zeks*, or prisoners, into the Soviet mainstream. But the author himself, writing from the margins of society as a former exile and an outspoken critic of Soviet history, became *persona non grata* in Soviet publishing. By 1970 he spent his days hiding out in the homes of friends, working on his epic historical work, *August 1914*.[3] Soviet novelist Valentin Pikul' (1928–1990), living in Riga, Latvia, on the edges of the Soviet empire, also turned to the events of World War One in his own epic story of love and danger, *Moonzund*, a popular novel set near the Moonzund Archipelago in the waters off Estonia.

Both authors, again each in their own way, were writing from a position of patriotism. Solzhenitsyn tackled Tolstoy in writing what critics inevitably saw as a twentieth-century *War and Peace*, and in what we might call the 'peace' sections he immersed himself in the spaces of southern Russia and its sprawling agricultural life. In his turn Pikul' interwove a love story featuring a lady spy with the narrative of a World War One naval battle, hitting all the right patriotic, nationalistic, and Bolshevik notes, and tying events on shipboard to the October Revolution. One of dozens of Pikul's historical stories and novels, *Moonzund* captivated mainstream Soviet audiences of his day.[4] The novel was published in 1973 and was made into a film by Alexander Muratov in 1987, starring the young dreamboat actor Oleg Menshikov.[5]

Having been awarded the Nobel Prize in 1970, Solzhenitsyn felt the eyes of the world on him despite his complications with his own government. In 1971 he released the first 'knot' or 'nodal point' of his elaborate cycle of historical novels (collectively known as *The Red Wheel*). This first book of the cycle, *August 1914*, drew on a research paper Solzhenitsyn had written decades earlier as an undergraduate[6] and incorporated into its war scenes knowledge of the geographical area gained when Solzhenitsyn himself fought in the Second World War. Published in 1971 in Russian by the Parisian émigré publishing house YMCA-Press,

---

[3] I will quote from the English version of the novel: Alexander Solzhenitsyn. *August 1914*. Trans. Michael Glenny (1972).

[4] According to Richard Stites, Pikul' was "the most widely read author in the Soviet Union from the seventies" through the early 1990s (151). I will quote from Valentin Pikul', *Moonzund (Roman-khronika). Miniatiury* (2008).

[5] Menshikov's roles since then have included the NKVD officer in Nikita Mikhalkov's 1994 award-winning *Burnt by the Sun*, the hero of Régis Wargnier's *East-West* (1999), a film about Russian émigrés returning to the Soviet Union after WWII, and the title character in the recent TV serial film of *Doctor Zhivago* (2006).

[6] Solzhenitsyn wrote an undergraduate thesis in 1937–1938 on Samsonov's defeat at Tannenberg; see Dunlop, Haugh and Nicholson 365.

the novel was quickly translated into a number of languages[7] and had a warm reception in the United States and England, but could not be published in Russia until 1993.

Solzhenitsyn felt strongly that the Russian voice on the Great War needed to be heard and saw his novel standing in for the missing chorus. Aware of the vastness of the task, he wrote:

> I couldn't portray the whole of the First World War [in the first node], even though its history has never been told in our country. I decided to choose a single event – a battle – and through it show the whole war. I had made this choice as early as 1937, when I was only nineteen (qtd. in Scammell 730).

The novel was about more than the war, though. As biographer Michael Scammell put it, "[O]ne of his aims in publishing his big series of novels was to reverse the consequences of the October Revolution, [but] the other was to restore unity to his divided and suffering people" (736). Solzhenitsyn reached out to émigré readers and to the West in a quixotic quest to undo "Great October" by writing about the Great War.

Significantly, though set in pre-Soviet times and buttressed by historical research, both of these works of fiction draw on personal experience. Pikul' and Solzhenitsyn paint portraits and highlight the "masses" and the "elites," the behavior of proto-Bolshevik and Bolshevik sailors and soldiers, while also exploring Russian officers' attitudes toward German invaders of imperial lands and waters. Patriotic notes of nationalist pride sound in descriptions of competent military behavior; at the same time the authors express disappointment and disdain in chronicling the behavior of selfish, corrupt, or cowardly men, regardless of their rank or political affiliation.

As Karen Petrone has recently argued, traditionally scholars of the Great War have believed that Russia and the Soviet Union "failed to reflect" on the meaning of the First World War. In fact, she argues, Soviet discourse about World War One "was formed, suppressed, revised, rehabilitated, and sometimes suppressed again" (289, 291). Soviet history in all its complexity – the ever-moving Communist party line, changing censorship priorities, and local events, policies, and personalities – cannot be reduced to a simplistic notion about Soviet Russia ignoring the 'imperialist' war.

---

[7] For the saga of how Solzhenitsyn managed to publish the novel abroad while still living in the Soviet Union, and how the issue of rights and translations was handled – and bungled – see Scammell 729–736.

In a closer look at these two opposite writers – the Soviet Pikul' and the anti-Soviet Solzhenitsyn – the present chapter demonstrates that no matter the political or personal agenda, or indeed the level of artistic talent, Russian writers could only look at the Great War by tying it to their own home front events, Revolution and Civil War. This era struck some writers as an essential experience in the formation of Soviet and twentieth-century Russian identity, an experience that could tell historians and readers much about what the Soviet Union came to mean as a political and social entity.

It is not surprising that while participating in the European memory project about the Great War, Russians filtered history through their own lens, the lens of the so-called 'Great October.' But the members of the post-memory generation, whose fathers served in the First World War, experienced and even participated in the Second World War. The personal histories of Solzhenitsyn and Pikul' and their generation do much to explain why these authors returned to the pre-revolutionary era and the Great War in their fiction.

1 A Panorama of War and Peace

In an interview about Solzhenitsyn's novel, Roman Jakobson talks about the "ethos of life-long temporal distance" which informed *August 1914*.[8] And indeed, Solzhenitsyn deliberately participated here in a tradition of Russian historical fiction. For contemporary readers of the novel, the historical flavor of Solzhenitsyn's work on the Great War confirmed his talents as an author. His earlier work had primarily been based on personal experience: his prison term resulted in two major works about the Gulag (*One Day in the Life of Ivan Denisovich*, *The First Circle*), and his bout with cancer in the epic *Cancer Ward*.

In contrast, *August 1914* brought Solzhenitsyn into the pantheon of Russian writers of historical fiction whose novels have gained from temporal distance. Alexander Pushkin's *The Captain's Daughter* (1836) and Leo Tolstoy's *War and Peace* (1869) had also been written from a post-memory perspective, fifty years after the cataclysmic military events they describe.[9] Thus Solzhenitsyn, and to an extent his pro-Soviet popular counterpart Valentin Pikul', in enacting a post-memory approach to war at the borders of Russia wrote themselves into Russian literary history. Modern Russian writers have been obsessed with history, and

---

8 For the full interview, see Philip Rahv, "The Editor Interviews Roman Jakobson."
9 The Pugachev Rebellion (1772–1774) and Napoleonic wars, respectively. See Struve 394.

these two brought that obsession into the 1970s with their fictional judgments on the First World War.

For Solzhenitsyn, historical fiction – and even non-fiction – always had an eyewitness quality about it: in his two-volume *Gulag Archipelago*, which he termed in the subtitle a "literary investigation," his narrative voice became more convincing because he himself had served a sentence in the Soviet prison camps. *First Circle* was set in a special prison for radio technology research similar to the one where Solzhenitsyn had been incarcerated, and even though *One Day in the Life of Ivan Denisovich* has a central character who is a simple peasant, the details of the labor camp gained authenticity from Solzhenitsyn's own personal experience.

By turning his attention to the First World War, which had ended exactly one month before his birth, Solzhenitsyn would seem to have been moving into unknown territory. In fact, even *August 1914* has personal resonance for the author, since his father had fought for the Tsar in the Great War, coincidentally taking part in battles in the very areas of East Prussia where the son would find himself twenty-some years later fighting the Nazis. Thus while we can certainly characterize Solzhenitsyn's work as 'post-memory,' there is a degree of family history essential to the novel – from the character of Isaakii, based on his father and known by his own nickname of Sanya, to the memories of peacetime Rostov, which during Solzhenitsyn's childhood between the wars bore a clear resemblance to the pre-war city, to other 'fictional' characters drawn from portraits of his friends and family members (Scammell 731).

Scholars have called *Red Wheel* a "detailed study of the causes and consequences of the Russian Revolution."[10] Solzhenitsyn sometimes abbreviated the cycle in his notes as *R-17*, clearly noting that although the events described in the first 'knot' predate revolutionary conflicts in Russia by almost three years, *August 1914* was really about the 1917 Russian revolutions. Andrew Wachtel, an expert on Russian historical fiction, maintains that Solzhenitsyn used narrative voice to shape his project, deliberately choosing a specific kind of narrative stance:

> the archaic position of a chronicler, [thus] rejecting the formal constraints and esthetic expectations connected with artistic literature as well as historiography [...] in order to enable him to describe the origins of the Soviet Union and at the same time explain in his own way that illness from which his country has suffered for 70 years. ("Nazad k letopisiam," 646. Trans. A. B.)

---

10 The final work, consisting of four novels, was published in ten volumes, 6,000 pages in all in the Russian edition. See Ericson, Jr. and Klimoff 151.

According to Wachtel, the first 'knot,' *August 1914*, retains a similarity to historical fiction, with several chapters at a time addressing one plot line or set of characters, but by the later novels in *Red Wheel*, Solzhenitsyn moves toward a chronicle-like methodology, reviving the "never-quite-forgotten indigenous historical genre" (*An Obsession with History* 218).[11] It was historical methodologies and the 'illness' of Bolshevism, rather than the conflict between emperors, that drove Solzhenitsyn's prose.

Contemporary critics praised Solzhenitsyn's ability to tell his story from a variety of points of view – "from the viewpoint of the rank-and-file and from that of the higher-ups, the commanders in the field as well as the staff officers in the rear. The result is a highly comprehensive view of war [...]" (Rahv, "In Dubious Battle" 357). But some of Solzhenitsyn's characters, when contemplating the cause of the war, see the whole enterprise as pointless and needlessly destructive:

> Now that the lush and prosperous years had started to come to Russia, the last thing she needed was a war; they should have just said a Requiem Mass for that Archduke Franz Ferdinand, after which the three emperors of Germany, Austria, and Russia should have drunk a glass of vodka at the wake and forgotten the whole affair (*August 1914*, 64).

Such thoughts, put into the head of a successful Ukrainian farmer, demonstrate that the tsarist regime had little connection, in Solzhenitsyn's view, with the people themselves; the royal family's ties to other European heads of state made a mockery of the war and its claims of nationalism and patriotism.

Real patriotism, and the missing love of Russia that might have saved the country both from its imperial entanglements and the disease of Bolshevism, blossomed in Solzhenitsyn's other characters. Isaakii was a "typical son of the steppe" with his "tousled, wavy, corn-colored hair" (8) and a Tolstoyan by conviction. Another central hero, Colonel Vorotyntsev, firmly believed that "Russia was inexhaustibly strong, even if she was governed by a pack of fools" (111). These two, and several others, represent the good and true Russian – thoughtful, hardworking, filled with a "pity" for Russia (11) that made them fight in Samsonov's army, though they could see that the efforts were misdirected and pointless.

Published abroad, *August 1914* nonetheless had an impact at home as well. The official Soviet newspaper *Literary Gazette* published a scathing review, and readers in the Soviet Union strove to obtain a *tamizdat* or *samizdat* copy of the novel to read it for themselves. And read it they did, as the little book *August 1914 is Being Read in its Homeland*, published in Russian by YMCA-Press in Paris

---

11 Wachtel focuses his discussion on *March 1917*, by which time the *style indirect libre* has taken precedence over any other narrative mode (208).

in 1973, attested. In articles, anonymous reactions, and documents, the volume presented a fascinating spectrum of contemporary reader response from behind the iron curtain. Most importantly, *August 1914* was read as part of a tradition, in the context of previous Russian historical novels: Leo Tolstoy's *War and Peace* and Boris Pasternak's *Doctor Zhivago*, among others. As one contemporary wrote:

> Solzhenitsyn has written a book that is huge in its scope and scale and extremely important for our time, even though it is a historical narrative [...] He entered into an argument with Leo Tolstoy [...] Solzhenitsyn showed how the people were victorious and the commanders were losing [...] Everything is already present in this first book of the epopeia: the deepening chasm between the people and those in power. ("Avgust chetyrnadtsatogo chitaiut na rodine" 106. Trans. A. B.)

With its many characters and many points of view, *August 1914* frustrated some of its readers, as they strove to make sense of Solzhenitsyn's depiction of what Anna Akhmatova called "not the calendar, / but the real Twentieth Century" (176; trans. Carl Proffer) which began in 1914 with the first salvos of the war. Some of his characters are misguided, others are short-sighted; some are too self-focused, while others seem helpless to struggle against events as they unfold. One critic identifies a particular "historical measure" for weighing good and evil during the years of war and revolution: was an individual concerned with the right thing? That "vital subject of concern," he wrote, was the "fate of the fatherland, the history of Russia" (Tropinin 93).

August 1914 careened toward its ending, detailing errors – both individual and military – in this first set of battles in the war with Germany. Solzhenitsyn's narrator identified an apocalyptic sense in the first decades of the twentieth century; with the defeat of the Russo-Japanese war hanging over the army,

> [i]t only needed two or three such defeats in succession for the backbone of the country to be put out of joint forever and for a thousand-year-old nation to be utterly destroyed [...]. The present war might either herald a great rebirth of Russia or the end of her altogether. (112)

But it was not only the spirit of the army that would determine the outcome; as one officer muses: "In Russia there's always said to be an 'extreme shortage of funds' for the army. Yet, although there's never any money for the army, there's plenty to spare for the court. They want victories and glory without paying for them" (154). The Russian attitude of *tiap-liap*, of doing things carelessly, is in the end blamed for the catastrophe. The Great War had one great effect in Russia – the end of the autocracy and the beginning of an entirely new political system, one that would eventually expel the "son of the steppes," Solzhenitsyn.

2 Intrigue on the High Seas

If Solzhenitsyn had become a pariah by the early 1970s, his countryman Valentin Pikul' was thriving. Pikul' published in official venues and sold millions of books (by some counts the numbers exceeded 20 million volumes in his lifetime).[12] Pikul's career opened and closed with works about the Second World War: his first novel, *An Ocean Patrol*, set in the Barents Sea, was published in 1954, and his final novel, *Barbarossa*, was published posthumously in 1991. In a way, Pikul' was an anti-Solzhenitsyn: known primarily in the Soviet Union, loyal to the Soviet authorities, and the recipient of Soviet, not international, awards, Pikul' also wrote from the margins, as an amateur historian who lived much of his adult life in Riga. Certainly 'mainstream,' Pikul' did not embrace the official literary doctrine of his era, instead avoiding Socialist realist production as a theme altogether. Pikul' believed that he could perform a service for his country in the ranks of Russian historical novelists. Even though he was not wanted in the military, Pikul' found a way to serve his fatherland too in a different way.

Called by critics the "perennial king of the historical fiction market" (von Geldern 855–856),[13] Pikul' let no war escape him: it is indicative of his broad interest that the five films made from his stories range across modern European history: the Seven Years' War, Russo-Turkish War, Russo-Japanese War, and the two world wars. As one historian notes, Pikul' "has no equal in number of books written or number of copies printed" (Dotsenko 118). Pikul' favored naval fiction, and his works include such titles as "Torpedo Boats Head Out to Sea," "The Retired Naval Warrant Officer," and "From Odessa through the Suez Canal." Even off the battlefield, military lives preoccupied him, such as in "Forgotten Lieutenant Il'in" and "Eighteen Bayonet Wounds."

This preference for naval themes emerged from Pikul's personal history. Not only did his father serve in the Baltic Navy on a torpedo boat and then become a military shipbuilder, both father and son served in the navy during the Second World War. Pikul' was only eleven when his father was transferred to the naval base at Molotovsk (later Severodvinsk). In 1941, the young boy and his mother returned to Leningrad for the summer and were caught in the Nazi blockade of that city. They escaped via the "road of life" across Lake Ladoga, but were not fated to reunite as a family. The senior Pikul' was transferred from the Belomor

---

[12] In 2008 his wife made the fairly preposterous claim that the total had reached 500 million. Quoted in "In Murmansk a new monument to Valentin Pikul was dedicated," http://tvkultura.ru/article/show/article_id/35125, from an interview on 21 July 2008.

[13] Von Geldern goes on to note that Pikul's "lush epics of tsarist politics have long been the target of intellectual scorn" (856).

Flotilla to the Stalingrad front, where he perished in 1942. Valentin ran away to the Solovki Islands to the naval school for boatswains and cabin boys founded by Peter the Great and finished out the war as a signaller on the torpedo boat *Grozny*.[14]

These were dramatic events in a young boy's life: separation from his father, a hard, cold, hungry winter among fellow citizens trapped in the city known both as the European Russian capital and the cradle of Revolution, followed by a daring escape and the chance to plunge directly into adulthood as he himself joined the struggle against enemy invaders. The loss of his father capped this tragic childhood – but Pikul' would not in the end follow his father's military legacy.

In fact, Pikul's nascent naval career came to an abrupt halt soon after the war's conclusion when he was expelled from the Leningrad Higher Naval Academy in 1946 for lack of knowledge. Undaunted, Pikul' continued to consider himself a 'navy man' and to popularize naval history with a broad readership.[15] His personal connection to the Baltic Fleet and his experience in naval battles with the Northern Fleet as a young man during the Second World War informed his writing and gave him credibility with a mass audience, despite the naval illiteracy of which professional historians continue to accuse him.

Like others of Pikul's works, *Moonzund* gives the impression of being grounded in archival research – details of division numbers, troop and ship movements, names of both German and Russian officers suggest a deep knowledge of the decisive land-sea battle.[16] Described as a "*roman-khronika*" in its subtitle, *Moonzund* explores the many attitudes toward war and death that we find amid the Russian navy in the beginning of the war. The question is not one of success or even survival: "for some time," as the protagonist Sergei Arten'ev states, "I have been much more concerned with how to die well" (73). Throughout the novel

---

14 *Grozny*, an adjective related to *groza*, or storm, means 'Awesome' or 'Dread,' but it is probably not a coincidence that one of the key characters in *Moonzund* is the Bolshevik Trofim Semenchuk, who serves on the torpedo boat *Grom*, or Thunder.

15 Dotsenko critiques Pikul's abilities as a historian, a novelist, and even a linguist, claiming that Pikul' lacked fluency in naval terminology and filled his novels with precise descriptions of naval moves that were essentially meaningless (124). Another critic (N. N. Molchanov) disagrees, asserting that "Books by Pikul the naval chronicler are distinguished by their knowledge of the sea, people, psychology, the history of the navy, of military technology" (509).

16 A recent publication refutes that impression: the book *Moonzund 1917: Poslednee srazhenie russkogo flota* (*Moonzund 1917: Last Battle of the Russian Navy*), published in 2009, reprints the translated diary of German officer A. G. von Chishvitz as well as a 1928 study by military historian A. M. Kosinsky, and demonstrates that these were the primary and secondary sources on which Pikul drew to construct his tale.

characters consider how to fight the enemy from without (the Germans), but also from within (274) – including hardline monarchists, opportunists out to save their own skins, and capitalists looking to extract profit from the war – and many come to terms with their own inevitable extinction.

Winning the war, though, does not enter into the equation. "*We don't mourn defeats or exult at victories. The source of our mood is: vodka, no or yes?*" (23). With this stylized couplet, one of the engineers on Pikul's ship, the navy reserve man Leonid Deichman, conveys his disdain for the daily news of the war from the front. "Ripped by the war from the plentiful sleepiness of his rural Ukrainian village, where he had left behind his beloved garden of radishes, dill and cucumbers," Deichman serves as raisonneur to the novel's protagonist, Sergei Arten'ev, and together both sound the theme of the book in its early pages: Russia, and the sailors and soldiers particularly, had tired of war. The military was vulnerable, susceptible to the "bacillus of Bolshevism" (10).

The German-sounding name of this wholly positive character from the depths of the Russian countryside underscores another aspect of the book: writing from the margins, Pikul' explores the multinational character of the Russian empire by setting his novel in and around Riga and Libava[17] and by drawing German-influenced characters, ranging from the lowly engineer Deichman to commander Karl Joachimovich von Den (ultimately forced to commit suicide). "There are too many barons in the navy," one character notes. With discussions of goings on at the Russian imperial court and the unholy influence of Grigory Rasputin on the tsarina and her family, a Shakespearean motif of rot and corruption also permeates the novel from the early chapters of the book: "Something is rotten in the state of Denmark" (65), thinks Arten'ev.

Of course, the First World War presented a complicated set of problems and loyalties across Europe, but for the Russian empire, with its Germanophile autocrat and German empress, its German-influenced territories in the west and its plethora of foreign aristocrats in the officers' corps, boundaries of allegiance were more blurred yet. Not for nothing did Tsar Nicholas strive for peace accords with the major European powers in 1914. Even the "state of Denmark" comment is no mere quotation from *Hamlet*, given Nicholas II's close blood ties to the Danish royal family. It is these issues and more that create conflict among characters in Pikul's *Moonzund*.

Despite its marginal geographic setting, *Moonzund* is about central Russian concerns. As part VI of the novel opens, Pikul' announces: "Reader! [...] If your

---

[17] Now Liepāja, Latvia, this port was a part of the Russian empire from the time of the third partition of Poland (1795) until 1918 and reentered the Russian sphere of influence when Stalin signed the Molotov-Ribbentrop pact in 1939. From May 1915 it was occupied by Germany.

hut is on the edge of the settlement [...] don't bother with this book" (373). For Pikul', the "Russian idea" (as defended by the intelligence agent Klara), the value of honor and glory, and the passion of love and the sea are all wrapped up in the historical novel. By the last scenes Arten'ev, who has held himself apart from the sailors and retains characteristics of the old upper classes [*byvshie liudi*] in his personal habits,[18] announces to the commissar: "Consider me sympathetic" to the Bolshevik cause (435). He may have no real place in the Communist future, but the course of this naval battle and the debates raging around it have changed his allegiances. The rot among the officer corps and especially the royal family and Russian government convinced him that the end of the Russian monarchy was nigh.[19]

By evoking the peasant saying, and peasant ethos, of the "hut on the edge of the settlement," Pikul' reifies the rise of the lower classes. Throughout the novel he has portrayed positive and negative phenomena associated with the masses, but his purest characters all come to see that the war with the Kaiser spells the end of the tsarist regime. The success, or failure, of naval battles is ultimately irrelevant, merely more tragic and bloody events on the way to a newly Red Russia.

3 Memory and Post-Memory

In the wake of the Great War itself, Maxim Gorky characterized it as an "absurd war," "stunning proof of our moral weakness, of the decline of culture." A supporter of the Revolution, Gorky characterized the era as "days of victorious cruelty and brutality" (375). But it was *tiap-liap*, *razgildiaistvo*, and basic irresponsibility that many blamed for the downfall of the Russian empire.

A contemporary American critic of Solzhenitsyn's novel believed that "Solzhenitsyn place[d] Leninist 'revolutionary defeatism' [the worse, the better], Tsarist corruption, and the well-intentioned ineffectuality of the Samsonovs under the same rubric of gross irresponsibility," an irresponsibility from numerous angles that brought about the "national disaster" of the Russians' participa-

---

[18] Among other things, Arten'ev collects miniatures – portraits from a by-gone era – and frequents antique stores and booksellers, all habits that do not mesh with emerging Bolshevik culture. At one point he contemplates what his career might have been under different historical circumstances and imagines himself as an antique dealer.

[19] As the 1987 film hero puts it in a critical scene with common sailors: "I am not against your revolution, I am against the sloppiness you are covering up in its name." That same *tiap-liap*, here called *razgildiaistvo*, is the downfall of the Russian navy as well as Samsonov's army in *August 1914*.

tion in World War One and the ensuing revolution (Ehre 369–371). Both novelists work from the "ethos of life-long temporal distance" – a historian's attempt to sum up the forces that created the society in which he lived and suffered.

In that sense, post-memory has added power in the context of Russian culture. On one hand, in Soviet Russia the events of the First World War appeared to have been forgotten – rarely commemorated, lost in the chaos of ensuing domestic violence. But on the other hand, by the 1970s a return to those dramatic battles served as analytical material for considering how the Revolution happened at all. Whether disastrous like the Prussian campaign of General Samsonov that opened the first world war for the Russian army, demonstrating the superiority of the German forces, or with mixed results, like the Moonzund naval battle that protected St. Petersburg from the German fleet while losing "Germanic" ground, events of the Great War were like runes to be read in order to understand how Bolshevik Russia came to be.

Demonstrating that in the years 1915 and 1916 conspiracies bubbled from the left and from the right, Pikul' showed that in the midst of a war with Germany and Austria, the class conflict within Russian society was ripening, awaiting its moment, and those revolutions came in February and October of 1917. One of the more successful of Pikul's historical stories and novels, *Moonzund* made for an exciting naval-themed film: brimming over with naval vocabulary, details of ships and transports, and the cityscapes of coastal towns and ports, *Moonzund* answered the desires of seafarers and landlubbers alike, with the politics of the Great War a mere backdrop to the internal politics of a "diseased Russia."[20] The fate of the fatherland lay in the balance between 1914 and 1917, and the 'short twentieth century,' the Soviet century, began with the opening salvos of the imperialist war.

In 1985, at the height of *glasnost*, critic Lev Anninsky heralded a new era in World War Two films, declaring that the Great Patriotic War had passed into memory; those born during and after the war now only knew that war from stories, as "legend," and it was up to this post-memory generation to "sing their own songs about the war" (Anninskii 58). This reassessing of legends, exploring myths with new research, new film scripts, new novels, and frequently new agendas, has characterized the late Soviet and post-Soviet periods of Russian literary and film culture.

The First World War, however, remained a 'forgotten war': forgotten in its time due to powerful historical and ideological events at home, and forgotten in the long run. Only a few recalled it: those, like Solzhenitsyn, who wanted to

---

[20] "When a person is mortally ill, doctors even study his feces in order to save the person […] in this case we are speaking of Russian society as a whole that is diseased" (*Moonzund* 215).

explain the revolutionary tumult that visited Russia in the wake of the Great War and to undo more than a half-century of Soviet history, or those, like Pikul', who sought in the 1970s to distract their contemporaries from the stagnation that eventually superseded the tumult and to revive the waning fervor of Bolshevism. In great part this sense, that World War One was 'forgotten,' has been forged in contrast to Russia's European neighbors and their cults of the Great War. Petrone has argued that in the interwar period World War One was rather "decentered" than forgotten entirely.[21] Some traces of that first war with Germany remained, and in the post-memory world they could be accessed – on land and on sea – to make an argument about the meaning of Russia and its national destiny – an argument that has become important again today in the post-Soviet era that Solzhenitsyn and Pikul' anticipated.

References

Akhmatova, Anna. *Selected Poems*. Trans. Walter Arndt, Robin Kemball, and Carl Proffer. Woodstock and New York: Ardis, 2003.

Anninskii, Lev. "Tikhie vzryvy: polemicheskie zametki." *Iskusstvo Kino* 5 (1985): 56–69.

Dotsenko, V. D. "Fenomen Valentina Pikulia." *Mify i legendy russkoi morskoi istorii*. St. Petersburg, 1997. 118–125.

Dunlop John B., Richard S. Haugh and Michael Nicholson, eds. *Solzhenitsyn in Exile: Critical Essays and Documentary Materials*. Stanford: Hoover Institution Press, 1985.

Dunlop, John B., Richard Haugh, and Alexis Klimoff, eds. *Aleksandr Solzhenitsyn: Critical Essays and Documentary Materials*. Belmont, MA: Nordland Publishing Company, 1973.

Ehre, Milton. "On *August 1914*." *Aleksandr Solzhenitsyn: Critical Essays and Documentary Materials*. Eds. Dunlop, Haugh and Klimoff. 365–371.

Ericson Jr., Edward E. and Alexis Klimoff. *The Soul and Barbed Wire: An Introduction to Solzhenitsyn*. Wilmington, DE: ISI Books, 2008.

Gor'kii, A. M. "Letter to Romain Rolland" (January 1917). *Sobranie sochinenii v tridtsati tomakh* 29 (Moscow, 1955): 374–375.

Petrone, Karen. *The Great War in Russian Memory*. Bloomington: Indiana University Press, 2011.

Pikul', Valentin. *Moonzund (Roman-khronika). Miniatiury*. Moscow: Veche, AST, 2008.

Rahv, Philip. "In Dubious Battle." *Aleksandr Solzhenitsyn: Critical Essays and Documentary Materials*. Eds. Dunlop, Haugh and Klimoff. 356–364.

Rahv, Philip. "The Editor Interviews Roman Jakobson." *Modern Occasions* (1972): 19–20.

Scammell Michael. *Solzhenitsyn: A Biography*. New York, London: Norton and Company, 1984.

Solzhenitsyn, Alexander. *August 1914*. Trans. Michael Glenny. New York: Farrar, Straus and Giroux, 1972.

---

21 Petrone gives a detailed description of the Moscow "All-Russian War Cemetery" to explain the process of memory and forgetting in the period between the two world wars. See her introduction to *The Great War in Russian Memory*, 1–5.

Stites, Richard. *Russian Popular Culture. Entertainment and Society since 1900*. Cambridge: Cambridge University Press, 1992.
Struve, Nikita. "The Debate over August 1914." *Aleksandr Solzhenitsyn: Critical Essays and Documentary Materials*. Eds. Dunlop, Haugh and Klimoff. 393–407.
Tropinin, I. "*Avgust chetyrnadtsatogo* i russkoe istoricheskoe samosoznanie." *Avgust chetyrnadtsatogo chitaiut na rodine*. Paris: YMCA-Press, 1973. 83–99.
von Geldern, James. Review of Rosalind Marsh, *History and Literature in Contemporary Russia* (NYUP 1995). *American Historical Review* (1997): 855–856.
Wachtel, Andrew Baruch. *An Obsession with History: Russian Writers Confront the Past*. Stanford, CA: Stanford University Press, 1984.
Wachtel, Andrew Baruch. "Nazad k letopisiam: Solzhenitsynskoe *Krasnoe Koleso*." *Solzhenitsyn: Myslitel', istorik, khudozhnik. Zapadnaia kritika, 1974–2008: sbornik statei*. Ed. Edward E. Ericson, Jr. Moscow: Russkii put',' 2010: 627–647.
Youngblood, Denise. *Russian War Films: On the Cinema Front, 1914–2005*. Lawrence, Kansas: University of Kansas Press, 2010.

Part 4: **Interrogations: Cross-Cultural and Trans-Historical (Re)Interpretations of the Great War**

Geert Buelens
"They wouldn't end it with any of us alive, now would they?": The First World War in Cold War Era Films

"Yes, the French are in it, and all them little countries. Austria, Hungary, Belgium, Spain."

Charlie Allnut in *The African Queen*, 1951

In 2007 *Military History Magazine* published a "Special Collector's Edition" on what the editors considered the "100 Greatest War Movies" (*100 Greatest War Movies*). Featuring a self-assured looking Tom Hanks in *Saving Private Ryan* on its cover, which also promised inside information on "*Das Boot, Glory, Patton, M*A*S*H*, Napoleon, Zulu, Gettysburg, Open City, The Longest Day*" etc., this special issue seemed to conform to what one would expect from an American military history buff publication: excitement, terror, gore, glory, heroism and, incidentally, a satiric or even war-critical moment. Yet, the two top movies on the list turned out to be *All Quiet on the Western Front* (1930) and *Paths of Glory* (1957), famous First World War films that have proven instrumental in establishing that conflict as the exact opposite of excitement, glory and heroism. These films' impressive battlefront scenes undoubtedly contributed to their status as classics of the genre, but they seem to have influenced our very idea of what war is on a more fundamental level. Today, unqualified jingoism is hardly ever, if at all, a part of respected war films. Even those films that celebrate a specific war accomplishment, like *Gallipoli* about the 'birth' of the Anzac Spirit or, indeed, *Saving Private Ryan*, which has been interpreted convincingly as an example of American post-Cold War triumphalism (cf. Auster), never fail to emphasize the physical and moral price that was paid. In that respect 'the war to end all wars' seems to have set the standard for the way warfare is portrayed.

Nevertheless, it seems safe to say that to most Western audiences war film in the 1950s, 1960s and 1970s referred to pictures about the *Second* World War. Filmmakers in the United States as well as Eastern, Central and Western Europe grew ever more obsessed with that conflict during these decades, foregrounding the martyrdom of resistance fighters in occupied countries, the heroism of Allied forces that brought about the final victory over the Axis powers, and the horror of the Holocaust as the ultimate proof that this was a 'just war.' While the Second World War reminded audiences of the *just* price one ought to be willing to pay when it came to *just* causes, the First World War seems to have accommodated everyone's pacifist conscience and maybe even utopian dreams during the Cold War era. Despite the huge commercial and critical success of *M*A*S*H** (1970) the Korean war never became a staple in the film industry and Vietnam only did so after that war had finished (*Coming Home, The Boys in Company C* and *The Deer Hunter* all date from 1978, *Apocalypse Now* was released in August of 1979).[1]

In countries like France, Italy, Britain and Belgium the First World War remained the *Great War*, but – increasingly – it also became *that other war*, a conflict more distant and therefore less likely to evoke memories as intense and livid as World War Two. This does not imply, as David Lescot and Laurent Véray seem to suggest, that the memory of the First World War is not charged with conflicts and dissent.[2] Despite the ubiquity of mud, trenches, shell holes and mass slaughter in First World War films from every era and place, it does matter when and where these films were shot. Local political and cultural sensitivities, as well as geopolitical convolutions and constraints, have played a significant role in the production, distribution, and reception of WWI films. An almost systematic disregard for artistic practices beyond the United Kingdom, the United States, France, Germany and Italy in First World War cultural studies, however, has tended to obscure this.[3] To study classic WWI films like *Paths of Glory* (1957), *King and Country* (1964) and *Uomini contro* (1970) alongside examples from Bulgaria (*The Peach Thief*, 1964), Romania (*Forest of the Hanged*, 1965), and Poland (*Austeria*, 1982; *Pismak*, 1985; *H. M. Deserters*, 1986), not only brings the often neglected Eastern and Balkan fronts into the picture, it also opens up perspectives on themes that are rarely discussed in this context, most importantly ethnic versus imperial nationalism and the plight of the Jews – which tied in with two very prominent themes during the Cold War, postcolonialism and the Holocaust.

---

[1] John Wayne's *The Green Berets* from 1968 is the rare mainstream exception. For a list of both fiction and documentary films about Vietnam, see Dittmar and Michaud (Appendix B).

[2] Cf. "De nos jours, on continue de tourner des films sur la Grande Guerre. Sans doute parce que c'est un conflit à propos duquel les Européens peuvent se retrouver, où les mémoires sont comparables – ce qui n'est pas du tout le cas de 1939–1945" (Lescot and Véray 36).

[3] Four cases in point when it comes to the cinema: Kelly (whose book opens with an analysis of a 1914 Danish film – *Ned med Vaabnene/Lay Down Your Arms* – but in the other chapters only discusses American, French, German and British films), Marcus (an otherwise excellent article which adds the Australian *Gallipoli* to the major powers corpus), Véray (which in its *Filmographie* mentions 30 Great War fiction films made after the Second World War, 21 French ones, 3 British, 2 Italian, 1 Australian, 1 Canadian and 1 Belgian/French one) and Sorlin ("Film and the War"; his selected filmography of 30 titles includes 10 French ones, 7 German, 5 British, 5 American, 1 British-American coproduction, 1 Italian and 1 Australian one). Noted exceptions are the edited volumes by Dibbets & Hogenkamp (which only discusses pre-1945 films) and Paris (which also includes chapters about Russia, Poland, Australia and Canada).

1 Waves of First World War Films

First World War films tend to come in waves.[4] After the dozens of films released immediately following the war, the next series of major films was produced in the thirties, signaling that Western societies were finally ready to face and debate the war (Sorlin, "Cinema and the Memory" 18). Another series of European films arrived around the fiftieth anniversary of the war: full-length WWI-movies were released both by Western European countries involved in the conflict on the Allied side: *King and Country* (1966), *Thomas l'imposteur* (1965), *L'Horizon* (1967), *The Blue Max* (1966), *Le Roi de Coeur* (1966) and by Eastern European states that had supported the Central Powers (*The Peach Thief*) or the Allies (*Forest of the Hanged*), whereas Sweden saw the production of two films dealing briefly with the effects of the war on this neutral country – Mai Zetterling's *Älskande par* (*Loving Couples*, 1964) and Jan Troell's *Här har du ditt liv* (*This Is Your Life*, 1966). One of the most successful films of the postwar era, *Doctor Zhivago* (1965), does not deal primarily with the Great War, but it does feature very interesting scenes about it.

The biggest wave of First World War films arrived only a few years later, from 1969 to 1972, during the height of the anti-Vietnam movement and the rise of the New Left, though only a few of these films (*Johnny Got his Gun*, 1971, and *Uomini contro*, to some extent also *Oh! What a Lovely War*, 1969, and *Louisa, een woord van liefde*, 1972) can be seen directly in that light.[5] It is hard to evaluate Sorlin's suggestion that the arrival of these films in a group around 1970 signals that there finally was a window, an opportunity "to look back at the conflict which had opened the century" ("Cinema and the Memory" 23) in between the fifteen years of immediate WWII-obsession and the later series of Vietnam films beginning in the late 1970s. For one, Vietnam films really were an American business only, and apart from Dalton Trumbo's pet project *Johnny Got His Gun* American studios and directors did not make films about the American involvement in the First World War in the late 1960s and early 1970s.[6] It was mainly French, Belgian, British and Italian directors who chose the Great War as the setting or topic for ruminations about state sanctioned violence and loss.

---

[4] Chapman distinguishes between two waves, one around 1930, the second in the late 1950s and '60s (121–137).
[5] Véray also associates Jacques Rouffio's *L'Horizon* (1967) with Vietnam (163). For a discussion see Jacquet (53–54) and Véray (162–167), who also stresses its feminism.
[6] Roger Corman's 1971 *Von Richthofen and Brown* (also known as *The Red Baron*) deals with German and British aces (the title character Brown was a Canadian who had joined the RAF). Also in 1971, Franklin J. Schaffner's Romanov-saga *Nicholas and Alexandra* was released, a film featuring interesting WWI scenes, especially about the Russian government's mobilization decision in 1914, but again, without any reference to the American war effort.

2 Neither Heroes Nor Foes

The forms of adventure and heroism that have always been central to World War II films rarely feature in their World War I counterparts. Only films about air warfare tend to depict combat in chivalric terms – like *The Blue Max*, *Zeppelin* (1971) and *Von Richthofen and Brown* – and, intriguingly, they are also the only ones having German main characters, often portrayed with sympathy and respect.[7] But even in these cases the conflict itself is framed as a cruel and absurd endeavor organized by sadistic military leaders, as in this telling remark by Canadian ace pilot Brown in *Von Richthofen and Brown*, when a journalist with the *Toronto Star* suggests the war might soon be over: "How can it be over? There's still some of us alive. They wouldn't end it with any of us alive, now would they?" The happy ending of *Zeppelin* consists of the bicultural English/German hero arriving in neutral Holland, enabling him to wait for the end of the war in peace. It is hard to imagine similar quotes or plot twists in adventure films about the American Civil War or the Second World War. The Great War, it seems, has become the war where the real enemies are the war itself and the leaders waging it. The official enemy of the jingoist war-time propaganda (e.g. 'The Hun') is conspicuously absent. This might also help explain why post-WWII Hollywood never showed a real interest in the Great War: it did not fit its Manichean tradition.

The First World War as a conflict where the soldiers of belligerent armies were not enemies but fellow-victims of the carnage is a premise of most Western European and American WWI films since *All Quiet on the Western Front*: whether they are German or French or British troops, the soldiers are all scared, overwhelmed and essentially innocent. There are exceptions to this theme, of course, particularly in World War II-era films like *The Life and Death of Colonel Blimp* (1943),

---

[7] In these three cases the Germans are shown as courageous and technologically advanced aviators, yet there is a catch to every one of these films. *The Blue Max* excels in sheer endless air scenes full of dogfight bravado, but the main character – a German working class boy all too eager to win the highest medal and the esteem of his aristocratic colleagues – is without scruples and so, it turns out, is the German High Command which makes him into a war hero to enthuse the war-weary masses, although the commanding General knows the pilot disobeyed orders and deserves to be court-martialled. In *Von Richthofen and Brown*, the gallant Red Baron is presented as a chivalrous hunter ("My ancestors were Teutonic knights; I've merely exchanged my horse for an airplane"), but near the end of the film the rise of fascism is announced (including the stab-in-the-back myth, anti-Semitic remarks and ace fighter pilot Hermann Goering joining this right wing faction). The zeppelin of the eponymous film is built by a brilliant German scientist and his wife, but he feels abused by his employer when mustard gas is being used. (Film quotations in this article are transcribed by the author, often based on the English subtitles on the DVD-editions and/or the Quotes-section on the Internet Movie Database.)

where the German brutality theme of 1914–1918 propaganda is taken up again, often rephrased to apply to (or tune in with) contemporary Nazi acts of violence. After 1945, this 'All Soldiers of the Great War Were Victims' theme returned with a remarkable twist. From *Paths of Glory* onwards the enemy was no longer to be found on the other side of No Man's Land, but high and dry at the often opulent tables of the own High Command. There are no *Platoon*-like condemnations of atrocities by common soldiers or junior officers (neither Entente nor Central) in these First World War films.[8] Only high commanders seem to have committed war-crimes against their own men. The most extreme indictment in this respect is surely Francesco Rosi's *Uomini contro*, where the Italian Army's main occupation seems to be butchering its own soldiers. The Austrian enemy is out there as well, of course, killing Italians with artillery and snipers but it seems hardly as brutal as the utterly vindictive, die-hard General Leone, who orders supposedly morale-boosting decimations and executions of his own troops for all sorts of offenses, from what could be labeled innocent mistakes or misjudgments of a given military situation up to acts of cowardice, insubordination, mutiny and desertion. This point is emphasized most emphatically in a scene where scores of Italian soldiers are mowed down in an open field and the Austrians themselves ask them to return to their trenches ("We can't keep killing like that. Go back!").[9]

3 Desertion as Pars Pro Toto

The theme that dominates post-1945 films depicting the First World War is desertion. In reality, despite the horrendous circumstances in which soldiers had to live, desertion was a rare phenomenon during the First World War and the number of executed soldiers was relatively low,[10] which suggests that painting a representative picture of life in the trenches was not the film directors' main concern in this respect. From *Paths of Glory* to *Blanche Maupas* (2009), the plight of those soldiers too shell-shocked, numbed or appalled to fight on, only to be brutalized and eventually shot by their own military seems to have become directors' preferred pars pro toto to demonstrate this conflict's quintessential cruelty and injustice.

---

[8] Tavernier's *Capitaine Conan* (1996) is a rare, post-Cold War counterexample in that it also deals with court-martials for looting and violence against civilians.

[9] With 750 executions and another 250 Italian dead as a result of retaliatory decimation, the Italian army was by far the cruelest against its own soldiers (cf. Kramer 127). About the film see also Véray 172–176.

[10] In the main modern armies about 0.1 to 0.3 % of the soldiers were convicted for desertion. See Jahr 436. For the British Army see Kelly (176) and Simkin.

Films featuring scenes about desertion or executions include *A Farewell to Arms* (1957 version), *La Grande Guerra* (1959), *Der brave Soldat Schwejk* (1960), *King and Country*, *Forest of the Hanged*, *Le Roi de Coeur*, *L'Horizon*, *Uomini contro*, the "Joining Up" episode of Ken Loach's *Days of Hope* (1975), *Pismak*, *H. M. Deserters*, *Capitaine Conan*, *Le Pantalon* (1997), *Un long dimanche de fiançailles* and *Les Fragments d'Antonin* (2006). In this long series of films, one not at all central to the canon of WWI films stands out because it is the only film in which the deserters seem to win out in the end: *Doctor Zhivago*. This is how this scene is narrated, mainly in voice-over, by Dr. Zhivago's half-brother, a Soviet General:

> Gen. Yevgraf Zhivago: By the second winter [of World War I, G. B.], the boots had worn out ... but the line still held. Even Comrade Lenin underestimated both the anguish of that 900-mile long front ... as well as our own cursed capacity for suffering. Half the men went into action without any arms ... irregular rations ... led by officers they didn't trust.
>
> Officer: [to soldiers] Come on, you bastards!
>
> Gen. Yevgraf Zhivago: And those they did trust ...
>
> Pasha: [leaps out of the trench and begins leading his men in a charge] Come on, Comrades! Forward, comrades! Earth-shakers!
>
> [an artillery shell explodes in front of him; he falls to the ground, and the soldiers retreat to their trench]
>
> Gen. Yevgraf Zhivago: Finally, when they could stand it no longer, they began doing what every army dreams of doing ...
>
> [the soldiers begin to leave their trenches]
>
> Gen. Yevgraf Zhivago: They began to go home.

Communist General Zhivago brings this story as the prelude to the Revolution, but compared to the other First World War films of the time this second most popular film of the 1960s unintentionally conveys a rather peculiar implicit message:[11] if only more men had had the guts to leave the trenches, the war could have ended sooner and millions of lives would have been saved.[12] But only very few soldiers

---

11 Only *The Sound of Music* reached a bigger audience.
12 The 1957 version of *A Farewell to Arms* also includes a passage that can – unintentionally, one would presume – be read as pro Bolshevik. When Lt. Frederick Henry, the American hero of the story, explains his desertion to his English lover Catherine, he uses exactly the same phrase ("I've made a separate peace") that was used earlier on in the film, when an Italian officer discussed the Brest-Litovsk Treaty. Catherine's reply ("It's not your army, or your country") was

left their trenches and those who did were treated as criminals and sometimes executed. From the 1950s onwards this raised the question as to who the real enemy of these soldiers had been.

4 The Real Enemy

Within the context of the Cold War this 'Enemy Within' theme gained extra significance. With the McCarthy witch-hunts still in everybody's memory and the Fifth Column rhetoric very much a staple of Western propaganda this was no light allegation: the enemy was not to be looked for within the ranks of artists and intellectuals, but in the upper classes of politics and the military. The fact that Joseph Losey, director of *King and Country*, one of the most vehement indictments of these deserters' executions, was a victim of blacklisting himself only reinforced this point.[13] Stanley Kubrick's sardonic *Dr. Strangelove* (1964) brought the same point home in an eerily contemporary setting, right after the Cuba Missiles Crisis. In a telling Great War reference, the responsibility of both generals and politicians for the war madness is made abundantly clear:

> General Jack D. Ripper: Mandrake, do you recall what Clemenceau once said about war?
>
> Group Capt. Lionel Mandrake: No, I don't think I do, sir, no.
>
> General Jack D. Ripper: He said war was too important to be left to the generals. When he said that, 50 years ago, he might have been right. But today, war is too important to be left to politicians. They have neither the time, the training, nor the inclination for strategic thought. I can no longer sit back and allow Communist infiltration, Communist indoctrination, Communist subversion and the international Communist conspiracy to sap and impurify all of our precious bodily fluids.

Considering the Freedom *vs.* Oppression narrative the Western powers used during the Cold War, the simple fact that such openly critical films could be made and screened might have had some propagandistic value in itself. But the thing was: even Western nations did not always allow these films to be shown.

---

supposed to refute the suggestion of desertion, despite the fact that the Americans had joined the war, making them official allies of the Italian army Henry had just left.

13 In Belgium, of the many outlets reviewing this film only the communist newspaper *Le Drapeau Rouge* mentioned Losey's blacklisting ("A propos du dernier film"). Trumbo, director of *Johnny Got His Gun*, was also blacklisted. As one of the Hollywood Ten, he refused to testify before Congress and spent 11 months in jail (see also Jacquet 59–60).

The most notorious case is *Paths of Glory*, which only saw a general release in France in 1975, after initial screenings in neighboring Belgium in 1958 had been disrupted by French officers, threats had been expressed towards theater owners and the French Embassy had asked not to show the film again.[14]

Other Western films faced problems as well. In Italy, for instance, the production of Mario Monicelli's 1959 *La Grande Guerra*, the first ironic treatment of the conflict, was initially boycotted by the Italian army and right-wing politicians, journalists and veterans called for its suppression.[15] A few years earlier, the script of *A Farewell to Arms* had to be rewritten on the urging of the Italian Defence Minister, which not only led to the resignation of director John Huston (Gundle 106), but perhaps also helps to explain this remarkable caption during the opening credits:

> We tell a story out of one of the wildest theaters of World War I – the snowcapped alpine peaks and muddy plains of Northern Italy. Here between 1915 and 1918 the Italians stood against the German and Austrian invaders. No people ever fought more valiantly, no nation ever rose more gallantly out of defeat to victory.[16]

---

[14] My account is based on newspaper clippings in the Brussels Cinematek (an overview of the affair in *Gazet van Antwerpen* ["Brusselse studenten betoogden"]); on Lanneau (for the French-speaking reception in Belgium), on "Accueil critique" (for the reception in France), and, in particular, on Véray (149–159), who stresses how the highly politicized debate surrounding the film in 1975 did not really differ from the original reception in the late 1950s and how the representation of the Great War was not really the bone of contention but rather what was perceived as the film's stance against the French military (compromised during the infamous Battle of Algiers in 1957). Based on recently released diplomatic documents Véray also reconstructs earlier French attempts to prevent the film's distribution, how as a form of retaliation Kirk Douglas's French wife was no longer invited to the Cannes Film Festival and, above all, how the French basically blackmailed United Artists not to present the film to the official Censorship Board in France (if they were to present the film there, the French authorities would ban for three months any film by the producing studio and distributor of *Paths of Glory*). The French Foreign Office also asked its Embassies to do all they could to prevent the local distribution, a campaign which lasted until late in 1959 and which was successful in both Israel and Switzerland and, for a very short while, also in West-Berlin. In this context it might be worth noting that in Claude Chabrol's *Les Cousins* (1959), in a scene set in April of 1958, a copy of *Les Sentiers de la Gloire*, the French translation of the novel Kubrick based his film upon, is clearly shown in the window of a Paris bookshop. For those on the left promoting the film, this clearly must have been a small act of rebellion at a time when – as is mentioned by Véray (156) – on 22 March 1958 the leftist *Libération* had predicted that this important film would not be shown in France because the parallels with the current military missteps were all too clear.

[15] See Gundle (106). *La Grande Guerra*'s final Italian censorship label was Not under 18, whereas the Dutch board judged it Not under 14 ("La Grande guerra").

[16] Interestingly, the 1932 version of *A Farewell to Arms* directed by Frank Bozarge featured a similar opening caption, added at the urging of Italian fascist officials (Gundle 103), linking the

The Charles Vidor film did not mention that the Italians were the initial invaders at the Isonzo, but for the first time the less than heroic parts of that Italian 'defeat' (the disorder, desertion and executions during the retreat following the Battle of Caporetto) were shown in a film. Other controversial war films (*La Grande Guerra* and *Uomini contro*) about the Italian campaigns would follow suit, each of them encountering censorship problems (cf. Gundle 105–106).

5 The 'Communist' Take

Ironically, it seems as if Eastern European (Communist bloc) films about desertion and the execution of one's own soldiers had fewer problems with the local censors. Of course, the political system had dramatically changed since 1918 in these countries. Any criticism of political and military leaders in these films could easily be labeled as directed against war time imperialist and bourgeois enemies of the people. The most striking element of these Eastern European films, however, is the way they point to ethnic nationalism as the crucial factor in these cases of desertion.

Essential to a good understanding of the war in Central Europe is the fact that nations/people who found themselves on both sides of enemy lines were forced to fight their own. Such was the plight of the Jews all over Europe, but also of the Polish, Czech, Romanian, Ukrainian, Croatian and other soldiers conscripted into either the Russian or the Prussian and Austro-Hungarian armies. The official Communist doctrine had it that "a nation is a historically constituted, stable community of people, formed on the basis of a common language, territory, economic life, and psychological makeup manifested in a common culture" (Stalin qtd. in Fowkes 5). Although a case could be made that the Communist States in Eastern and Central Europe functioned not so much as satellites but as *colonies* of the Soviet Union (Judt, ch. VI, esp. 167–171), the official view was that they were separate entities with their own national culture, all of them with ethnic minorities and differences within these states which were, by and large, recognized and respected (Fowkes ch. 4). Apart from these different national identities – particularly exemplified during Olympic Games or other sport tournaments – these countries were supposed to share an internationalist and communist identity.

Italian "glory" at the Piave with that of the Marne – a remarkable equation considering the fact that the Battle of the Marne stopped the German invasion, whereas the Piave victory in 1918 marked the final stage in a battle that was started by the Italians.

During the Habsburg rule, internationalism had a completely different ring to it. Austria-Hungary was a multi-ethnic state which recognized the many languages and identities – even in the army – as long as the nation itself came first. To those ethnic communities striving for independence, Austria-Hungary was an imperialist and chauvinist state or maybe even occupier.[17] The World War One implications of Austro-Hungarian policies for the ethnic minorities are dramatically evoked in the 1964 Romanian film *Pădurea spânzuraților* (*Forest of the Hanged*), for which Liviu Ciulei received the Best Director Award in Cannes a year later. Drafted in the Austro-Hungarian Army, ethnic Romanian First Lieutenant Bologa is forced to fight Romanians and interrogate and punish Romanian peasants who allegedly disobeyed an order not to plough near the frontlines. Appalled, he tries to desert and, in the final moments of the film, is hanged in a scene echoing the opening minutes, where under Bologa's supervision a Czech deserter was executed after being court-martialled. *Forest of the Hanged* offers many scenes where ethnic Czech, Romanian, Polish, Ruthenian, Hungarian and Austrian soldiers and civilians deal with one another in respectful, caring and even loving ways. But the military system, represented by the Austrian General von Karg, shows no mercy. When Bologa asks to be transferred to another front, where he would not have to fight his fellow Romanians, von Karg responds that this question shows a lack of love for his fatherland.

This tension between the official (legal) and ethnic (sentimental) forms of belonging is also present in a Polish comedy from 1986. The following scene from Janusz Majewski's *C. K. Dezerterzy* (*H. M. Deserters*) suggests that while the many ethnic groups in Austria-Hungary did not find it hard to live and work together, they lacked a common, national identity. The new Austrian Oberleutnant von Nogai is confronted by the insubordination of his garrison:

Lt von Nogai: Have you arranged the company according to my orders?

Sgt: Yes, sir!

Lt: We'll see. Austrians, step forward!

[nobody moves]

Lt: It seems our company has no Austrians.

---

17 Again, to some extent the same could be said about the Soviet Union, but in the post-Stalin era it proved very well possible to produce films in Eastern and Central Europe that could be interpreted as explicit denunciations of Austria-Hungary and allegorical/implicit comments on Soviet policies.

Sgt: I would like to report that we're all Austrians.

Lt: All of us? Then why did no one step forward?

Sgt: You wanted me to arrange them by nationality, so we have Czechs, Slovaks, Slovenes, Bosnians, Herzegovians, and Poles.

Lt: In other words, a bunch of wretches not fit for regular life. Where are the Germans?

Sgt: You interrupted me, so I didn't have time to say that the Germans are on the left.

Lt: So there are some. Bravo. Order them to sing the National Anthem.

[complete silence]

Lt: Didn't you understand? The National Anthem.

Sgt: Attention! The National Anthem!

Lt: Sing!

[one soldier starts singing "Gott erhalte, Gott beschütze" in a very high voice]

Lt: An eunuch? We have an eunuch in this brothel?

Sgt: Company, sing!

[only one soldier starts singing "... Unsern Kaiser, unser La-a-and", he winks at the Sgt]

Sgt: I would like to report, that this is because they do not know German. They know the Anthem, but can't sing it.

Lt: They know it, but can't sing it? I'll teach it to you so well you'll be singing it in your sleep! You'll be singing it with tears in your eyes, you politically suspected pigs!

This lot of 'Austrian' soldiers deserts and only escapes execution because the Kaiser seems to have stepped down. Prisoners and soldiers alike start celebrating until a German regiment arrives, eager to shoot these Habsburg renegades (and by doing so making it absolutely clear who is really in charge of the Central Powers operations). With the German rifles directed against their former allies, a courier arrives. Without a word, the Germans leave. The war is over. A big celebration starts, with the soldiers enthusiastically waving their Polish and Hungarian flags. The implication is clear: they did not just lose the war, by losing they gained national independence.

But not all inhabitants of Austria-Hungary were winners. Jerzy Kawalerowicz's 1982 *Austeria* is a loving, nostalgic but also painful paean for the Polish

Jews, presenting their world "moments before its tragic holocaust."[18] As such it also provides a forceful corrective to Poland's troubled dealings with its Jewish population. By setting his film on the first day of the war and showing all sorts of violence towards Jews (and others, it should be added), the director clearly links the many pogroms of the First World War to the Holocaust during the Second World War. Nationalism seems not an issue at all, here. As Ewa Mazierska noted, none of the characters care about Poland or Austria-Hungary: "They identify not with a state, a country or a nation, but their own town or [...] their house and place of work" (211). In that respect *Austeria* "celebrates the multiculturalism of pre-war Galicia" (212), like many of the other Cold War era WWI-films produced behind the Iron Curtain.

More than a decade before Jean-Jacques Annaud would tackle the war effort of African soldiers in *La Victoire en chantant* (cf. Filmography), Vulo Radev's *The Peach Thief* showed how white and black French prisoners lived and made music together on the Balkan Front. More controversial today is the film's representation of the Bulgarian and Serbian armies.[19] During the war they were enemies (Bulgaria having entered the war by declaring war on Serbia in 1915); during the Cold War they were socialist neighbors. Set in the old Bulgarian capital of Veliko Turnovo at the end of the war, the film tends towards the latter position. While the Serbs, as part of the Entente and winners of the war, can be seen as co-responsible for the trauma of the Treaty of Neuilly, which had cost Bulgaria dearly in territory, money and prestige, *The Peach Thief* does not frame them as adversaries. Title character Ivo, a highly endearing, civilized, French-speaking Serbian prisoner of war is the doomed love-interest of Liza, the wife of a war-weary yet proud Bulgarian officer. Ivo believes in the Revolution, as do rioting Bulgarian soldiers who are fed up with the war and who dream of world peace and a true brotherhood of man. In one of their tender love scenes Liza caresses the very different buttons on Ivo's uniform:

> Liza: English, Serbian, Romanian ... And this eagle?
>
> Ivo: Austrian.
>
> Liza: Why an Austrian too?
>
> Ivo: Buttons don't fight each other.

---

[18] Director's notes in *26th London Film Festival Programme Notes* (Cinematek, Brussels).
[19] Some extremely nationalist Bulgarian (anti-Serbian) reactions on *YouTube* have been removed.

In the final scene Ivo is shot, implying that this utopia of a peaceful harmony was not exactly realized. But the longing for such a world is very much central to Eastern and Central European films about the First World War. While these countries' sacrifices in the Second World War had been even greater, it was the Great War they most of all tended to frame as the cause of their pacifism.

6 Western Europe: Integration and Reconciliation

On an institutional level, political and cultural life in Western Europe in the 1960s and 1970s was marked mainly by European integration based on French-German reconciliation, a Never Again attitude towards war and, consequently, a unison denunciation of fascism and everything it stood for. The result was a form of historical political correctness in which the animosity of the former enemies tended to be downplayed and dissenting voices were silenced. In France in particular this led to forced amnesia which was only very rarely alluded to. François Truffaut does so in *Domicile conjugale* (1970) when a neighbor of the newly-weds claims that he will not leave his apartment until Marshall Pétain is reburied in the grave prepared for him at Verdun.[20] But the general attitude towards the Germans is one of prudent respect. From the Italian-Yugoslav exploitation spy-thriller *Fräulein Doktor* (1969) up to the Anglo-American air ace films discussed earlier, German characters are never the ruthless Nazi butchers of many World War Two films. In that respect, the fascist era is seen as a cruel but essentially a-historical parenthesis in European relationships, while the First World War becomes not so much a conflict of Allied versus Central Powers but of outdated oligarchs out of touch with the brotherly feelings ordinary Europeans have for one another.

Truffaut's *Jules et Jim* (1962) forcefully extends a theme of Jean Renoir's *La grande illusion* (1937), the friendship and respect between a French and a German World War One soldier. In Truffaut's film the war seems no more than a violent interlude in the protagonists' passionate friendship. This strong sentiment is echoed in the sacred chapel of Truffaut's *La chambre verte* (1978), where Great War veteran Julien also honors a German soldier – a photograph of Oskar Werner/ Jules in uniform – whose plane he shot down: "when you look at this photo, it's difficult to think of this man as an enemy." A quite extraordinary example of French-German reconciliation happens at the end of the fourth episode of

---

[20] The Vichy leader died in prison on the Île d'Yeu and was buried close by. The neighbor's point is that Pétain's merits as a First World War hero should not be eclipsed by his World War Two actions.

Maurice Pialat's *La maison des bois* (1971). After a German warplane has been shot down by a French pilot, the small town where the series is set flocks towards the site of the crash to look at the wreck. French officers follow suit and solemnly salute the German pilot, dead in the cockpit. In the final, wordless three minute scene we see an extremely long shot with the camera slowly zooming in on the plane, used as bier for the covered corpse, and a French soldier guarding it. For the first time since the opening scene of the episode music is used: a slow, mournful chamber orchestra version of Haydn's melody known as "Deutschland über Alles". This is neither about patriotism nor revanchism, but all about heartfelt respect and an overwhelming feeling of loss.

Mourning is central to most French treatments of the First World War, most explicitly so in *La maison des bois* (where the vibrant mother and foster mother Jeanne dies of grief after her son is killed in action), *La chambre verte* (the story of a man who lives to honor the dead) and Bertrand Tavernier's 1989 *La vie et rien d'autre* (about the identification of unknown soldiers after the Armistice). A peculiar film in this respect is the Belgian-French production *Rendez-vous à Bray* (André Delvaux, 1971) about a Luxembourg musician who is supposed to meet his mobilized French friend but the soldier never shows up. Even those who remain neutral during the war are tainted with a feeling of loss and emptiness. The war itself is neither seen nor heard in the film, but we do see the trembling of a chandelier – as a marker of the distant cannons. The main character plays the piano in a movie theater where (unlike in Troell's *Här har du ditt liv*) not war images are screened, but *Fantômas*, the phantom of the war.[21] These pictures hardly contain any battlefield scenes and focus mainly on the grief and the aftermath of the war.

7 Imperialism

British depictions of the war from the 1960s up to the 1980s are much more political. In keeping with the dramatic social transformations and tensions of British society in these decades they tend to reframe it basically as a class war (cf. Kelly 178–180; Sorlin, "Cinema and the Memory" 24; Marcus 296; Chapman 132–134; Véray 170). In only one case is this analysis extended to the most notorious and violent bone of contention of British postwar politics, the Irish question.[22] In 1975 – two years after both the UK and Ireland had joined the European Economic

---

[21] See also Martin.
[22] *Oh! What a Lovely War* explicitly sympathizes with both Scottish and Irish nationalist tendencies.

Community and while the Troubles and sectarian killings were escalating – Ken Loach in *Days of Hope* has seventeen-year old Ben, brother-in-law of conscientious objector Philip, have the following argument with his sister/Philip's wife after he has been accepted into the army in 1916 and it turns out he will not be fighting the Germans:

Ben: We're off to Ireland, like.

Sarah: You're going to Ireland?

Ben: Oh, don't start your politics, our kid.

Sarah: I'm saying nowt.

Ben: You don't need to say owt. Your face says it for you. I got to do what I'm told, don't I?

Sarah: I expect that's what the German army said as they marched into Belgium.

Ben: [in disbelief] You're not comparing us with them, are you?

Sarah: Why not? The Irish have as much right to fight for their freedom as the Belgians have.

Ben: Get off.

In Ireland Ben's regiment is ordered to raid houses of suspected IRA-members, just like his own house was raided by British police at the beginning of the film, looking for his brother-in-law. Again, the real adversary turns out to be one's own defense force. It's telling that in this *Days of Hope* episode the only enemy we see is a ten-year old Irish boy who leads a British soldier into a mine (neither Irish nor German military are shown) and that this soldier was born in London from Irish parents. In Loach's view the First World War as well as the conflict in Ireland placed David against David, while (upper-class, capitalist) Goliath remained unchallenged. His take proved extremely controversial.[23]

A year before Jean-Jacques Annaud's *La Victoire en chantant* (*Black and White in Color*) would scoop up the Academy Award for Best-Foreign Language Film with a comedy about the First World War in Africa, many people in Britain still proved unable to see the war in Ireland as essentially a colonial conflict too. Postcolonial issues have been central to Western societies since the 1950s, but apart from Annaud's farcical treatment of the Western powers' behavior in the African

---

[23] McKnight lists contemporary press and viewers reactions with telling headlines like "Where was the Army's heroism?" and "'Days of Hope' serial goes Communist" (203–205).

theater of war and the few films about the Australian and Canadian involvement, the plight of subalterns during the Great War still has to be represented on the big screen by Western film makers.[24]

8 Distance and Memory

From the 1950s onwards the First World War is explicitly linked to issues of memory and distance in time. *La chambre verte* and *La vie et rien d'autre* are essentially about remembrance, but earlier on as well the war was treated as something of a past era. Films as different as *La Madelon* (1955), Axel von Ambesser's *Der brave Soldat Schwejk*, *Jules et Jim*, *King and Country*, *Här har du ditt liv*, *Johnny Got His Gun* and, more recently, *Les Fragments d'Antonin* and *The Wipers Times* (2013) use shaky black-and-white archival footage or pictures to evoke the war. The overall effect is one of alienation: what a strange, far-away and primitive world this was, where Tsars and Kaisers ruled and people moved so jerkily. In *La Madelon* the archival silent images are integrated quite nicely into the black and white feature film. The cutting of *Jules et Jim*, on the other hand, deliberately adds to the jerkiness and "unrealism" (see Insdorf 87). In *Les Fragments d'Antonin* the trembling of the shell-shocked soldiers is underscored by the jerky images.[25] Films with contemporary political aims (like *Johnny Got His Gun* in the time of Vietnam) were not necessarily helped by these antiquated images. Overall they reinforced the idea that in truly modern times a conflict such as the Great War was no longer possible, which raises the question why a world such as ours, so convinced of its own modernity and structural difference vis-à-vis the era of the First World War, seems increasingly obsessed with this ancient conflict? Are we exorcising ghosts when we are watching this old footage? Does our current World War One cult function as a way to soothe our bad conscience or darkest fears about armed conflicts in our day and age?

The steady stream of First World War films made during the Cold War poses these questions in an even more uncanny way: the trenches might have been something from the past, as thermonuclear warfare threatened to kill all people, soldiers and citizens alike. In that respect the Great War maybe functioned as

---

24 Both John Huston's *The African Queen* and Peter R. Hunt's *Shout at the Devil* (1976) are set in Africa during the war, but they are adventure films without a specific (post)colonial focus. Cf. Anne Samson's chapter in the present volume.
25 On the 'period charm' the 1914-era accumulated in the 1960s–80s and our tendency to imagine that seemingly far-away world as an "Edwardian costume drama," see Clark xxv.

some form of displacement: the sepia-tinted images of a film like *King and Country* evoke the past as a cruel and violent but above all far-away place.

In essence that past and place could not be communicated. Or so Edgar Reitz seems to suggest in the opening scene of his epic, sixteen-hour *Heimat – Eine deutsche Chronik* (1984). In May 1919, Paul Simon returns from the war. Home in the small rural village of Schabbach after a six-day walk from France he joins his father in the forge, embraces his mother and, urinating on the dunghill, re-connects with his native soil. But when the family and neighbors flock in to welcome him and discuss their own war-time experiences, Paul remains silent. His best friend Helmut, who died in Russia, appears to him in a vision and talks about the white shroud the fallen soldiers received in heaven, like angels. Paul stares in wonder. Throughout this eighteen-minute scene he only mutters the words "Wait a moment, mother." About the war he does or cannot talk.

References

100 Greatest War Movies: The Best Films Ranked, Reviewed, Deconstructed ...: Plus 191 Pop-ups, 420 Secrets from Behind the Scenes. Leesburg, VA: Weider History Group, 2007.

"Accueil critique des films de Stanley Kubrick." *La Cinémathèque française*, n. d. http://www.cinematheque.fr/fr/dans-salles/hommages-retrospectives/revues-presse/kubrick.html. (24 September 2013).

"A propos du dernier film de Joseph Losey. King and Country (Pour l'exemple)." *Le Drapeau Rouge* (15 May 1965).

Auster, Albert. "Saving Private Ryan and American Triumphalism." *Journal of Popular Film and Television* 30. 2 (2002): 98–104.

"Brusselse studenten betoogden tegen schorsing van Amerikaanse oorlogsfilm. Rolprent komt volgende week waarschijnlijk opnieuw op het programma." *Gazet van Antwerpen* (1 March 1958).

Chapman, James. *War and Film*. London: Reaktion, 2008.

Clark, Christopher M. *The Sleepwalkers: How Europe Went to War in 1914*. London: Penguin Books, 2013.

Dibbets, Karel, and Bert Hogenkamp, eds. *Film and the First World War*. Amsterdam: Amsterdam University Press, 1995.

Dittmar, Linda, and Gene Michaud, eds. *From Hanoi to Hollywood: The Vietnam War in American Film*. New Brunswick: Rutgers University Press, 1990.

Fowkes, Ben. *Ethnicity and Ethnic Conflict in the Post-Communist World*. New York: Palgrave, 2002.

Gundle, Stephen. "Hollywood, Italy and the First World War: Italian Reactions to Film Versions of Ernest Hemingway's *A Farewell to Arms*." *Culture, Censorship and the State in Twentieth-Century Italy*. Eds. Guido Bonsaver and Robert S. C. Gordon. London: Legenda, 2005. 98–108.

Insdorf, Annette. *François Truffaut*. Cambridge: Cambridge University Press, 1994.

Jacquet, Michel. *La Grande Guerre sur grand écran: une approche cinématographique de la guerre de 1914–1918*. Parcay-sur-Vienne (Indre-et-Loire): Anovi, 2006.
Jahr, Christoph. "Desertion." *Enzyklopädie Erster Weltkrieg*. Eds. Gerhard Hirschfeld, Gerd Krumeich, and Irina Renz. Paderborn: Schöningh, 2003. 435–437.
Judt, Tony. *Postwar: A History of Europe since 1945*. New York: Penguin Press, 2005.
Kelly, Andrew. *Cinema and the Great War*. London; New York: Routledge, 1997.
Kramer, Alan. *Dynamic of Destruction: Culture and Mass Killing in the First World War*. Oxford: Oxford University Press, 2007.
"La Grande guerra (1959 I)." *Cinema Context. Mediastudies UvA*, n.d. Web. 24 September 2013.
Lanneau, Catherine. "Quand la France surveillait les écrans belges: la reception en Belgique des Sentiers de la gloire de Stanley Kubrick." Histoire@Politique. *Politique, culture, société* 8 (2009). http://www.histoire-politique.fr/index.php?numero=08&rub=autres-articles&item=48. (24 September 2013).
Marcus, Laura. "The Great War in Twentieth-Century Cinema." *The Cambridge Companion to the Literature of the First World War*. Ed. Vincent B. Sherry. Cambridge; New York: Cambridge University Press, 2005. 280–301.
Martin, Marie. "Les nuits de 1914–1918. Fantômes, théatralité et onirisme dans Thomas l'imposteur (Cocteau, Franju) et Rendez-vous à Bray (Gracq, Delvaux)." *Les Mises en scène de la guerre au xxe siècle: théâtre et cinéma*. Eds. David Lescot and Laurent Véray. Paris: Nouveau monde éditions, 2011. 99–116.
Mazierska, Ewa. "Between Parochialism and Universalism: World War One in Polish Cinematography." *The First World War and Popular Cinema: 1914 to the Present*. Ed. Michael Paris. New Brunswick, N. J.: Rutgers University Press, 2000. 192–216.
McKnight, George. *Agent of Challenge and Defiance: The Films of Ken Loach*. Westport, CT: Greenwood Press, 1997.
Simkin, John. "Executions in the First World War." *Spartacus Educational*. Spartacus Educational Publishers Ltd, Sep. 1997. http://www.spartacus.schoolnet.co.uk/FWWexecutions.htm. (24 September 2013).
Sorlin, Pierre. "Cinema and the Memory of the Great War." *The First World War and Popular Cinema*. Ed. Michael Paris. 5–26.
Sorlin, Pierre. "Film and the War." *A Companion to World War I*. Ed. John Horne. Oxford: Wiley-Blackwell, 2010. 353–367.
Véray, Laurent. *La Grande Guerre au cinéma: de la gloire à la mémoire*. Paris: Éditions Ramsay, 2008.

Filmography

The African Queen. Dir. John Huston. Romulus Films, 1951.
Älskande par [Loving Couples]. Dir. Mai Zetterling. Sandrews, 1964.
Austeria. Dir. Jerzy Kawalerowicz. Zespól Filmowy "Kadr," 1982.
Blanche Maupas. Dir. Patrick Jamain. BE-FILMS, 2009.
The Blue Max. Dir. John Guillermin. Twentieth Century Fox Film Corporation, 1966.
Der brave Soldat Schwejk. Dir. Axel von Ambesser. Central Cinema Company Film, 1960.
C.K. Dezerterzy [H. M. Deserters]. Dir. Janusz Majewski. Mafilm, 1986.
Capitaine Conan. Dir. Bertrand Tavernier. Canal+, 1996.

La chambre verte. Dir. François Truffaut. Les Films du Carrosse, 1978.
Les cousins. Dir. Claude Chabrol. Ajym Films, 1959.
Doctor Zhivago. Dir. David Lean. Metro-Goldwyn-Mayer, 1965.
Domicile conjugal. Dir. François Truffaut. Les Films du Carrosse, 1970.
Dr Strangelove or: How I Learned to Stop Worrying and Love the Bomb. Dir. Stanley Kubrick. Columbia Pictures Corporation, 1964.
A Farewell to Arms. Dir. Frank Borzage. Paramount, 1932.
A Farewell to Arms. Dir. Charles Vidor. The Selznick Studio, 1957.
Les Fragments d'Antonin. Dir. Gabriel Le Bomin. Dragoonie Films, 2006.
Fräulein Doktor. Dir. Alberto Lattuada. Avala Film, 1969.
La Grande Guerra. Dir. Mario Monicelli. Dino de Laurentiis Cinematografica, 1959.
Här har du ditt liv [*This Is Your Life*]. Dir. Jan Troell. Svensk Filmindustri, 1966.
Heimat – Eine deutsche Chronik. Dir. Edgar Reitz. Edgar Reitz Film, 1984.
"Joining Up." *Days of Hope*. Dir. Ken Loach. British Broadcasting Corporation, 1975.
Johnny Got His Gun. Dir. Dalton Trumbo. World Entertainment, 1971.
Jules et Jim. Dir. François Truffaut. Les Films du Carrosse, 1962.
King & Country. Dir. Joseph Losey. BHE Films, 1964.
Крадецът на праскови [*The Peach Thief*]. Dir. Vulo Radev. Boyana Film, 1964.
The Life and Death of Colonel Blimp. Dirs. Michael Powell and Emeric Pressburger. Rank Organisation, 1943.
Un long dimanche de fiançailles. Dir. Jean-Pierre Jeunet. 2003 Productions, 2004.
Louisa, een woord van liefde. Dir. Paul Collet and Pierre Drouot. Showking Films, 1972.
La Madelon. Dir. Jean Boyer. Filmsonor, 1955.
La maison des bois. Dir. Maurice Pialat. Office de Radiodiffusion Télévision Française, 1971.
Nicholas and Alexandra. Dir. Franklin J. Schaffner. Columbia Pictures Corporation, 1971.
Pădurea spânzuraţilor [*Forest of the Hanged*]. Dir. Liviu Ciulei. Filmstudio Bucuresti, 1965.
Le Pantalon. Dir. Yves Boisset. France 2 (FR2), 1997.
Oh! What a Lovely War. Dir. Richard Attenborough. Accord Productions, 1969.
Paths of Glory. Dir. Stanley Kubrick. Bryna Productions, 1957.
Pismak [*L'écrivain*]. Dir. Wojciech Has. Zespol Filmowy "Rondo," 1985.
Rendez-vous à Bray. Dir. André Delvaux. Ciné Mag Bodard, 1971.
Le Roi de Coeur [*King of Hearts*]. Dir. Philippe de Broca. Fildebroc, 1966.
Shout at the Devil. Dir. Peter R. Hunt. Tonav Productions, 1976.
Thomas l'imposteur. Dir. Georges Franju. Filmel, 1965.
Uomini contro [*Many Wars Ago*]. Dir. Francesco Rosi. Prima Cinematografica, 1970.
La Victoire en chantant. Dir. Jean-Jacques Annaud. Artco-Film, 1976.
La vie et rien d'autre. Dir. Bertrand Tavernier. Hachette Première, 1989.
Von Richthofen and Brown. Dir. Roger Corman. Corman Company, 1971.
The Wipers Times. Dir. Andy De Emmony. Trademark Productions, 2013.
Zeppelin. Dir. Etienne Perier. Getty & Fromkess Corporation, 1971.

Richard Smith
Post-Colonial Melancholia and the Representation of West Indian Volunteers in the British Great War Televisual Memory

In November 1915, the first contingent of volunteers set sail from Jamaica on board the *Verdala*, heading for Seaford Camp on the south coast of England. The spectacle was captured on film by the Fox Film Company, who had established a studio in Kingston to shoot movie scenes for the orientalist spectacular, *A Daughter of the Gods* (cf. Soloman 24). The newsreel of the departing troops was shown to Jamaican audiences the following February. An editorial in the *Daily Gleaner* alluded to the power of moving images to reinforce a sense of national purpose and belonging, even among those who had witnessed or taken part in the depicted event. This media effect had a particular potential when representing masculine sacrifice in battle:

> We knew that the crowd was great ... but it has been left to the cinema camera to show us how dense it was: we saw our boys as they filed through the thronged streets ... but they seem to leap more conspicuous to the eye as we watch them on the film. While, as in the light of the descending sun the *Verdala* moves slowly out of Kingston harbour with her freight of loyal and courageous souls, there is a touch of pathos about that scene which it must do each and every one of us enduring good to have felt ... We want all Jamaicans to see it ... to remember always what voluntary effort is accomplishing here for the Empire and for the honour of the country (24 February 1916, 8).

British media and historical studies have acknowledged how Great War television documentary serves as a vehicle for national mourning and commemoration (cf. Hanna, *The Great War on the Small Screen*). Renewed interest in the Great War during the early 1960s restated the conflict as a tragedy during which a promising Lost Generation, having basked innocently in the warm summer of 1914, were either slaughtered in the trenches or returned home disfigured or emotionally scarred (cf. Bond; Harvey; Todman). The early 1960s also gave rise to a parallel strand in British national identity formation which carried similar emotional resonances around mourning and nostalgia, the decline of Empire and the emergence of a multicultural society shaped by the mass migration of former imperial subjects, which began after the Second World War (cf. Gilroy).

As the fiftieth anniversary of the outbreak of hostilities approached, the ground-breaking, twenty-six part television series, *The Great War* (BBC 1964) stirred the popular memory of the conflict. Other key influences included Alan Clark's book *The Donkeys* (1961), which challenged the competency of the army leadership, the stage and film versions of *Oh! What a Lovely War* (1963 and 1969 respectively) and the incorporation of Wilfred Owen's poetry into the secondary school syllabus (cf. Badsey; Hanna, "A Small Screen Alternative"). Re-imaginings of the war emphasised the human cost of the conflict, evident in many literary and artistic accounts, and sought to address human experiences rather than questions of military strategy, leadership and state policy. Interest in the wartime role of women and changes in gender relations attributed to the exigencies of war also emerged from this critical shift (cf. Woollacott; Higonnet). Such a climate provided additional impetus to recover the involvement of imperial subjects whose experiences called out for attention, particularly within the context of a burgeoning multicultural society.

It was not until 1999 that broadcasters began to acknowledge the confluence of war memory and the rise of multicultural Britain by commissioning documentaries which acknowledged the contribution of imperial subjects to the war effort between 1914 and 1918. As the BBC begins to roll out 2500 hours of programming to commemorate the centenary of the Great War between 2014 and 2018, it is appropriate to examine how imperial troops are represented in popular television (BBC 2013). Since the end of the Great War, significant transitions have taken place which have impacted on the identity formation of imperial volunteers and their descendants, as well as on the experiences of national belonging in Britain, the former seat of empire. The processes of nationhood, initiated in the wake of the First World War and gathering pace after the Second, involved the passage from imperial subject to independent citizen and, if the promise of opportunity in the Mother Country beckoned, the journey to British nationality.

This chapter discusses television documentary which evokes the experience of British West Indians in the Great War. Since the arrival of the Windrush generation in the 1940s and 1950s, West Indian migration has occupied a significant place in the shifting landscape of post-imperial Britain. It casts a specific light through which to explore shifts in British national memory and the identities of the migrants and their descendants. The chapter will also touch on wartime media representations of the West Indian volunteers to trace continuities and disruptions in the processes of memory. For many West Indian veterans, migration experiences in the United States and Latin America and exposure to Pan-Africanism were additional elements in the process of identity formation, underlining the complex relationship between military service, national memory and mourning. In contrast to contemporary mainstream British grieving processes which denote war as tragedy, the commemoration of the West Indian war contribution tends to inculcate mourning as masculine (dis)honour, forgetting and shifting geographies of home.

Untold: Mutiny was broadcast in October 1999, as part of Channel 4's Black History Month season. The documentary was the first moving image study to explore the Great War contribution of British West Indians. It presented a history of the British West Indies Regiment (BWIR) structured around interviews with three veterans who, by the late 1990s, were counted among the handful of West Indian volunteers from the Great War still alive. Filmmakers Tony T. and Rebecca Goldstone were pioneers, not only in terms of reaching a national television audience, but also in generating wider media attention in the broadsheet press. Aside from the brief academic studies by W. F. Elkins and C. L. Joseph, the West Indian war experience had not been addressed since post-war official and commemorative accounts. These included Cipriani (1940), De Lisser (1917), Cundall (1925) and C. L. R. James' political study of the war and the West Indies published in 1932.

Mutiny highlights the deep-seated attachment to the Empire in the minds of many British West Indians at the outset of the war. This was a loyalty born of faith in what were perceived as British values of justice and the belief that the British monarchy had personally intervened to abolish slavery. A petition or memorial to London was regarded by the black peasantry and working class as a means of sidestepping the authority of the local plantocracy. *Mutiny* describes how Marcus Garvey's Universal Negro Improvement Association, founded in Jamaica as hostilities commenced, immediately sent a declaration of loyalty to the Secretary of State for the Colonies.

Described as "black patriots" by the narrator, the three veterans interviewed for *Mutiny* recount the remembered emotions associated with their enlistment in the British West Indies Regiment (BWIR) formed in November 1915. Some black West Indians were so enthusiastic to serve that they stowed away on ships bound for Britain. A desire to leave parochial small island communities provided motivation for some; others were desperate to escape poverty wages of "9 pence per day." "I was so joyful to go and fight for England", declared Eugent Clarke of Jamaica, aged 106. "All of us felt glad that we were going – we were glad to go, man", enthused Gershom Browne of Guyana (101). "The English are great. The greatest in the world" asserted Clifford Powell (110), who was interviewed in the British West Indian Welfare Centre in Guantanamo, Cuba with the Jamaican national flag and Union Jack visible in the background. At the time of filming, Powell was thought to be the oldest surviving West Indian veteran of the war. Powell's testimony of admiration and loyalty is particularly striking, for he was one of the four thousand West Indian veterans who migrated to Cuba after the war when promises of land and employment did not materialise. Many West Indian migrants were forcibly repatriated by the Cuban authorities during the economic depression of the 1930s. However, sufficient numbers remained, or returned to serve at the U.S. base during the Second World War, to warrant the establishment of the Centre in 1946.

The outpourings of loyalty and enthusiasm to enlist exhibited by many West Indians were not greeted with equal enthusiasm by the British War Office. West Indian recruitment schemes were initially discouraged on several grounds, including the suggestion by Lord Kitchener, Secretary of State for War, that black soldiers would be too visible on the battlefield. Spurious claims such as these, diverted attention from the underlying concern that black men might outperform white men on the battlefield, potentially raising the confidence of black imperial subjects and leading to greater pressure for self-determination. As Clifford Powell remarked, "When black people have rifles in their hands, don't joke with them. They mean to fight." White masculine authority had already been brought into question during the South African War (1899–1902), when Britain struggled to find physically fit recruits, an anxiety which festered in the minds of the imperial establishment.

Despite the reliance on black and Indian soldiers in many imperial campaigns of the nineteenth century, black volunteers were derided to deflect attention from the anxiety around white masculine performance. *Mutiny* recounted how C. L. R. James was ridiculed when he tried to enlist in the Trinidad Merchants' Contingent, formed to recruit white middle-class volunteers directly to British regiments. Similar schemes emerged for whites in other West Indian territories. In *Beyond a Boundary* (1963), James recalled his rejection from the Contingent, despite excellent educational and sporting credentials, on account of his dark skin. This proved to be a defining moment which helps to explain the central place James attributed to the war in his pioneering 1932 study of West Indian nationalism.

As *Mutiny* explores, the intervention of George V in April 1915 forced the recruitment of West Indians to be taken more seriously. The king and his advisors were keen to present the image of a united Empire, but also recognised that the continued refusal of recruits might undermine British rule. By May, preparations were well under way to send representative contingents from the British West Indies, including the mainland territories of British Guiana (Guyana) and British Honduras (Belize). In October 1915, the formation of the British West Indies Regiment as an infantry unit was formally announced, and over 15,000 men were eventually recruited, each of them volunteers.

Mutiny recounts how the volunteers sang "we want to catch the Kaiser if we get a chance" but notes that the response to the war by those who stayed behind was often less enthusiastic. Some were reluctant to fight a "white people's war" and regarded the volunteers as "German bait." The loyalty of even the most pro-British black recruit would soon be tested by the institutional racism of the British Army, as well as the harsh realities of war. Some of the subsequent poor treatment meted out to the British West Indies Regiment may also have been the result of incompetence rather than racism. This was clearly illustrated during a later, ill-fated voyage of the *Verdala*, which in March 1916 left Jamaica carrying the third war contingent of around eleven hundred officers and men.

The vessel was diverted via Nova Scotia to avoid German submarines. However, the men were not issued with winter uniforms, and the *Verdala* had not been fitted out to serve as a troop carrier. Many on board succumbed to frostbite and over one hundred suffered amputation of exposed toes, feet or lower legs. The documentary frames the *Verdala* incident as a Jamaican Gallipoli, marking the arrival of Jamaica on the world stage in the same way as the Dardanelles fiasco is often presented as the birth of the Australian nation.[1] The military authorities in London provided the bungling foil to the heroism of the Jamaican volunteers, whose qualities of endurance and stoicism were reported in the Jamaican press at the time. The Jamaican *Daily Gleaner*'s report of the third contingent's departure opened with an excerpt from Bret Harte's poem "Reveille," evoking the image of an emergent nation cast into the heat of battle. Harte's words, written for the Union cause in the American Civil War (cf. Scharnhorst 229) were particularly apposite for black volunteers who, on occasion, had been urged to fight and so prevent the reintroduction of slavery by the Germans. The lines presciently raised the possibility of an opportunity lost to prove national manhood in battle:

> Hark! I hear the tramp of thousands,
> And of armed men the hum;
> Lo! a nation's hosts have gathered
> Round the quick-alarming drum –
> Saying, "Come, Freemen, come!
> Ere your heritage be wasted" (*Daily Gleaner*, 7 March 1916, 6)

As reports of the *Verdala* disaster reached Jamaica, the press was swift to deny any local culpability and to reassure future recruits that sacrifices away from the line of fire were just as heroic. The victims of the episode were incorporated not only into the glorious annals of the imperial military effort but also into the national memory of an implied future independent Jamaica:

> Blunders occur; they occurred at Loos, they occurred at Neuve Chapelle ... And men suffer, as it is inevitable they must: they suffer and endure like the heroes that they are. The men who left us the other day could not guess that ever before they saw the Germans or Turks they would have to suffer wounds. Yet, as the Governor very truly puts it, these men "have suffered in the cause of their country quite as much as those who are damaged in action" (5 April 1916, 8).

---

[1] See the chapters by Christina Spittel, Clare Rhoden and Daniel Reynaud in the present volume.

In November 2008, a BBC local television news feature suggested West Indian soldiers who died before reaching the battlefield should be claimed within contemporary British, rather than Caribbean, national memory. Cousins Timothea Fevrier and Nicolas Jean Baptiste were shown visiting the grave of their forebears, Nelson and Dennis Fevrier, two St. Lucians who volunteered for the BWIR. The two brothers were interred in the war cemetery at Seaford in January 1916, having succumbed to disease shortly after their arrival from the West Indies. The discovery of the graves provides resolution for the Fevrier family, who had been unaware of the exact location of the graves for over ninety years. Baptiste relates how "the connection has been made [...] and the story has been told." The Fevriers' personal history also serves as a symbol of the national family's process of unforgetting and reimagining. In the words of presenter Kurt Barling, "Our diverse present is rooted in the contributions of our cosmopolitan forebears; Dennis and Nelson [are] symbols of the sacrifice so many made" (BBC 2008).

While the *Verdala* incident may have dissuaded West Indians from volunteering, *Mutiny* recounts a more deep-seated hostility towards black imperial recruitment from the military establishment. Such opposition threatened to undermine the efforts of the colonial establishment to portray the war as a universal struggle against Germanic authoritarianism. Under military law all black men, whether British subjects or otherwise, were regarded as aliens and could not rise above non-commissioned rank. More significantly, with the exception of the first two battalions of the BWIR who were deployed against the Turkish army during 1917 and 1918, the remaining ten battalions were not regarded to be of the calibre required for armed combat. They were assigned instead to labour battalion duties, such as unloading supplies, road building and transporting ammunition. Despite the vital importance of such tasks, the West Indians regarded their status as deeply inferior, particularly as they were denied the opportunity to fire a shot in anger, although routinely serving within range of enemy shellfire and experiencing casualties as a result.

The decision to use the BWIR as labour battalions, rather than combat troops, and the rising tide of discriminatory treatment characterised the history of the BWIR as a "heart-breaking tale of humiliation and disillusion" in the words of Lieutenant-Colonel Charles Wood-Hill, commander of the first battalion. *Mutiny* does not address the more ambiguous, reactionary side to Wood-Hill, who thought nothing of striking the men under his command (cf. Cipriani). It was an obsession with military honour and discipline, rather than a desire to oppose racial discrimination, which spurred Wood-Hill to champion the BWIR. This was highlighted in a letter written by Wood-Hill to the West India Committee after the war, in which he expressed the hope that military discipline would make West Indians immune to political radicalisation (cf. *Daily Gleaner*, 27 June 1921, 4/6).

However, while West Indian soldiers were prepared to accept authority and endure hardship in exchange for post-war recognition, they would not suffer undue indignity and discrimination without resistance. As *Mutiny* recounts, on 6 December 1918, shortly after the Armistice, Lieutenant-Colonel Willis, commander of the ninth battalion BWIR, based in the port of Taranto, Italy and notorious for his harsh approach to discipline, was surrounded by angry soldiers when he ordered them to clean latrines used by Italian labourers. The men dispersed quietly, but the following day, the ninth and tenth battalions refused to work. The men were disarmed, but not before unrest had spread to other battalions. War Office secret telegrams reveal that a battalion of white troops with a machine-gun company were requested to forestall any further unrest among the West Indies battalions.

Subsequently, sixty West Indian sergeants met to form the Caribbean League, a pivotal episode in the emergence of Anglophone Caribbean nationalism. *Mutiny* reports that at a subsequent meeting of the League, one soldier asserted "that the black man should have freedom and govern himself [...] and that force must be used, and if necessary bloodshed to attain that object", a statement which perhaps explains the reticence of an empire arming those it had repressed for so long. But it is also important to recall the relatively modest aims of the League – "the Promotion of all matters conducive to the General Welfare of the islands constituting the British West Indies and the British Territories adjacent thereto" ("Notes of meeting held at Cimino Camp" 1918). This was a distinctly social democratic agenda, but one which British imperialism and the West Indian plantocracy would find impossible to meet in the post-war economic crisis.

The attitude of the British military hardened in the wake of the mutiny at Taranto, culminating in the 'Reign of Terror' established by the South African base commandant, Brigadier-General Carey Barnard. Eugent Clarke recalled how the men were barred from recreational facilities, "You couldn't even go to the gate, let alone into town [...] he was a rough man." Gershom Browne reported how the West Indians were rejected by their erstwhile white comrades, "they didn't seem to want any attachment with us [...] we had always seemed to get on good together in Egypt." An anonymous black sergeant complained to the Colonial Office that the men were treated "neither as Christians nor as British citizens, but as West Indian niggers."

Discriminatory experiences such as these were compounded by the rejection of most West Indian battalions for front-line combat. This sense of exclusion was underpinned by masculine discourses that privileged arms-bearing above all other forms of military duty. Equally vital services provided by non-combatant labour at the front, in the lines of communication and supply chain were implicitly diminished. Within this schema, betrayal is a denial of manhood. Although the burden of loyalty shifts from the colonial subject to the imperial establishment, the patriarchal ideal that the ultimate test of manhood lies on the battlefield remains unchallenged. For the white soldier in the popular consciousness, death in battle is represented as tragedy and a cause for anger and mourning. For the black soldier, exclusion from combat becomes the focal point for the emotions of loss. For Peter Lennon, reviewing *Mutiny* in the *Guardian*, "Britain betrayed its black soldiers." The BWIR was the "Dishonoured legion" who volunteered in the hope of fighting "for king and country", but "were victimised by racist officers and kept from the front so the Germans wouldn't think the Empire needed the help of 'savages'" (7 October 1999). The documentary, *Not Forgotten: Soldiers of Empire* (2009) declared that the "eager, unproved black volunteers of the West Indies" did not get "what they hoped for. The chance to prove themselves equal on the field of battle."

Recovery from this hurt through the processes of remembering and unforgetting becomes an urgent task; one that is ever-present in black history. The titles of documentaries dealing with the black experience during the Great War respond to this concern, including the docu-drama *Walter Tull: Forgotten Hero*[2] and *Not Forgotten: Soldiers of Empire*. Who rediscovers and tells these histories, however, is a complex political issue. In *Walter Tull: Forgotten Hero*, black British actor Nicholas Bailey, best known for his role as Dr Trueman in the long-running soap opera, *Eastenders*, undertakes a personal journey of discovery to uncover the life of the first black officer to serve in the British Army during the war.

Soldiers of Empire presents a very different approach. Ian Hislop, the white presenter and producer of the documentary, appears as the chief agent in the rediscovery of this aspect of black history as he peruses documents in the archives and consults newspapers of the period. Hislop interviews Nola and Jahrome Stair, two grandchildren of Stanley Stair, the last known West Indian veteran of the war who died aged 107, eighteen months before *Soldiers of Empire* was transmitted. Through this popular family history format, the effect is to resurrect the metaphor of the imperial family in which race determines one's role and in which the language of duty and service is deployed to downplay discrimination and thus minimise discomfort in the audience.

This framing is highlighted earlier in the documentary when the continuing family connections of the descendants of an Indian soldier, Manta Singh, and those of the white officer whose life he saved are explored. As members of the martial races, Indians were regarded more favourably within the imperial family and were deployed to France in the early months of the Great War. At the battle

---

[2] On Tull, see Michael Paris' chapter in the present volume.

of Neuve-Chapelle, Manta Singh rescued a wounded officer, Captain Henderson, under heavy fire. Singh was himself wounded and died of his injuries at the Brighton Royal Pavilion, converted into a military hospital for Indian troops. Today, the two soldiers' grandsons, Jaimal Singh Johal and Ian Henderson, sustain a familial friendship also continued by their respective fathers, who served in the Indian Army during the Second World War. Hislop observes that Indian "independence does not seem to have ruptured this link" of "loyalty and mutual respect", suggesting that not only the values of the military comradeship, but the values of empire which these are believed to embody, still pertain in contemporary multicultural Britain.

The men interviewed for *Mutiny* are presented as irrevocably changed by a war which for them has never ended, leaving a lasting impression. Eugent Clarke highlights a separation from civilian life that is never resolved: "Miss the war – you feel like you're out of place." These sentiments are reiterated by Gershom Browne, who with the words, "I'm glad I'm a soldier. Thank God for the life as a soldier," suggests the possibility of a permanent West Indian soldier for whom the war has become *the* defining experience (cf Smith forthcoming; see also Fussell and Bourke). Most moving of all is the palpable sense of relief Browne expressed in recalling how he had remonstrated to stop his comrades bayonetting surrendering Turkish soldiers in cold blood. Browne's modestly understated act of humanity highlights how the West Indian soldier rose above the barbarism of modernity, despite experiencing discriminatory treatment.

In the wake of the Taranto mutiny, the military and colonial authorities were anxious that the BWIR should be demobilised as rapidly as possible, and most of the regiment "never saw Blighty" nor attended victory parades. On their return home, the authorities dispersed the veterans to their parishes so quickly that, as Eugent Clarke remembers, "they never gave us a welcome." But the war irrevocably changed the attitude of the veterans to imperial authority, even if affection for things British still clearly lingered in the minds of Browne, Clarke and Powell when *Mutiny* was recorded. Barbara Wickham, the surviving younger sister of veteran Clennell Wickham, relates how on his return to Barbados he was asked to vacate a church pew reserved for whites. Wickham stormed from the church, never to return. He later became editor of the radical weekly *Barbados Herald*. In the words of Gilbert Grindle, Assistant Under-Secretary at the Colonial Office in London, "the black man has come to think and feel of himself as good as the white."

It could be argued that in an era of global migration, a military history informed by past imperial relationships may be less relevant than the increasing numbers of contemporary British citizens drawn from origins beyond the former empire. Indeed, many will have ancestors who fought for the Central Powers or who lived in non-combatant nations during the Great War. Television documentary about the Great War tends to present a familiar vision of the British past. Even documentary which tackles new perspectives on the war recycles footage that has often been seen many times over by television audiences (see Haggith and Smith). Programmes with a critical view of the military establishment, or which challenge earlier perceptions of the war, may still be well-received by an audience mourning changes to British society resulting from global migration patterns. Sections of this audience may have started to accommodate the changes wrought by migration from former colonies, and many will have been born into the realities of multicultural Britain, while some perhaps still struggle to come to terms with the end of Empire. Equally, despite the changes wrought to contemporary Britain by global migration patterns, descendants of the migrants who arrived from the former empire from the 1940s onwards still strive to stake their rightful place in British society. Recovery of the forgotten memory of military service by their ancestors is a powerful image to enlist in that struggle.

References

Badsey, Stephen. "The Great War since The Great War." *Historical Journal of Film, Radio and Television* 22. 1 (2002): 37–45.
BBC. "BBC reveals 2,500-hour World War I season." 16 October 2013. http://www.bbc.co.uk/news/entertainment-arts-24552194. (25 October 2013).
BBC. BBC London News. First broadcast BBC1, 6 November 2008, 18:30.
Bond, Brian. "A Victory worse than a Defeat? British Interpretations of the First World War." Annual Liddell Hart Centre for Military Archives Lecture, 1997.
Bourke, Joanna. *An Intimate History of Killing: Face-to-Face Killing in Twentieth-Century Warfare*. London: Granta, 1999.
Cipriani, Andrew A. *Twenty-five Years After: The British West Indies Regiment in the Great War 1914–1918*. Port of Spain: Trinidad Publishing Co., 1940.
Daily Gleaner, 24 February 1916, 8; 7 March 1916, 6; 27 June 1921, 4, 6.
De Lisser, Herbert George. *Jamaica and the Great War*. Kingston, Jamaica: Gleaner Co., 1917.
Elkins, W. F. "A Source of Black Nationalism in the Caribbean: the Revolt of the BWIR at Taranto, Italy." *Science and Society* 33. 2 (1970): 99–103.
Fussell, Paul. *The Great War and Modern Memory*. New York: Oxford University Press, 1975.
Gilroy, Paul. *After Empire: Melancholia or Convivial Culture?* London: Routledge, 2004.
Giovannetti, Jorge. "The Elusive Organisation of 'Identity': Race, Religion, and Empire among Caribbean Migrants in Cuba." *Small Axe: A Caribbean Journal of Criticism* 19 (2006): 1–27.
Haggith, Toby, and Richard Smith. "'Sons of our Empire': Shifting Ideas of 'Race' and the Cinematic Representation of Imperial Troops in the First World War." *Empire and Film*. Eds. Lee Grieveson and Colin MacCabe. London: Palgrave, 2011. 35–54.
Hanna, Emma. "A Small Screen Alternative to Stone and Bronze: The Great War Series and British Television." *European Journal of Cultural Studies* 10. 1 (2007): 89–112.

Hanna, Emma. *The Great War on the Small Screen: Representing the First World War in Contemporary Britain*. Edinburgh: Edinburgh University Press, 2009.
Harvey, A. D. *A Muse of Fire: Literature, Art and War*. London: Hambledon Press, 1998.
Higonnet, Margaret. *Behind the Lines: Gender and the Two World Wars*. New Haven: Yale University Press, 1989.
James, C. L. R. *Beyond a Boundary*. London: Stanley Paul, 1963.
James, C. L. R. *The Life of Captain Cipriani: An Account of British Government in the West Indies*. Nelson, Lancs: Coulton, 1932.
Joseph, C. L. "The British West Indies Regiment 1914–1918." *Journal of Caribbean History* 2 (1971): 94–124.
Lennon, Peter. "Dishonoured Legion." *Guardian* (7 October 1999). http://www.theguardian.com/theguardian/1999/oct/07/features11.g23. (25 October 2013).
"Notes of meeting held at Cimino Camp, Italy." National Archives, Kew, UK, CO318/250/2590.
Smith, Richard. "The First World War and the Permanent West Indian Soldier." *Empires in the First World War*. Eds. Rick Fogarty and Andrew Jarboe. London: I. B. Tauris [forthcoming].
Smith, Richard. *Jamaican Volunteers in the First World War: Race, Masculinity and the Development of National Consciousness*. Manchester: Manchester University Press, 2004.
Scharnhorst, Gary. *Bret Harte: Opening the American Literary West*. Norman, OK: University of Oklahoma Press, 2000.
Soloman, Aubrey. *The Fox Film Corporation, 1915–1935: A History and Filmography*. Jefferson, NC: McFarland and Co, 2011.
Todman, Dan. *The Great War, Myth and Memory*. London: Hambledon, 2005.
Wood Hill, Lt. Col. Charles. *A Few Notes on the History of the British West Indies Regiment*. n.p., n.d.
Woollacott, Angela. *On Her Their Lives Depend: Munitions Workers in the Great War*. Berkeley: University of California Press, 1994.

Filmography

Not Forgotten: Soldiers of Empire. Dir. Sarah Feltes. British Broadcasting Corporation, 2009.
Untold: Mutiny. Dir. Helena Appio. Channel 4, 1999.
Walter Tull: Forgotten Hero. Dir. John MacLaverty. British Broadcasting Corporation Scotland, 2008.

Anne Samson
Fictional Accounts of the East Africa Campaign

The war in East Africa began on 8 August 1914, when the German wireless station at Dar-es-Salaam was bombed by a British ship. It ended on 25 November 1918, when the German troops under General Paul von Lettow-Vorbeck surrendered in Northern Rhodesia. Within the first month of war, German troops in East Africa had attacked forces in Belgian Congo, British East Africa (Kenya), Portuguese East Africa (Mozambique), Nyasaland (Malawi) and Northern Rhodesia (Zambia). In addition to local forces from the territories already mentioned, South Africa, Southern Rhodesia (Zimbabwe), India, Britain, Belgium, Portugal and West Africa also participated in the war. Unlike the war in Western Europe, the war in East Africa was a mobile one, with few set battles throughout the four years of campaigning. In addition, there were encounters on each of the major lakes – Tanganyika, Nyasa, Victoria – as well as in the Rufiji Delta. Air power too was used, both combatively and for observation purposes. Finally, apart from having to deal with the human enemy, all forces had to contend with the weather, which alternated between the dry and rainy seasons when roads became impassable, with wild animals which roamed the land freely, and with insects such as bees, jigger fleas, mosquito and tsetse fly, which caused discomfort and spread diseases such as malaria and sleeping sickness.[1] This chapter will explore the most important themes that have inspired fictional accounts of the campaign and evaluate the extent to which these reconstructed memories compare with the known reality of the campaign.

1 Settlers and the Outbreak of the Great War

The first theme, that of settlers, features in the earliest fictional account identified to date. *Follow After* by Gertrude Page (1915) graphically captures the challenges and anxieties the early colonists faced at the outbreak of war and the impact it had on the local white communities in Southern and Northern Rhodesia, where one of the first battles of the campaign took place (*The Spectator*, 1915). Her second

---

[1] The best overview of the military aspect of the campaign is Paice, *Tip and Run: The Untold Tragedy of the Great War*. For a political overview of the campaign, see Samson, *Britain, South Africa and the East Africa Campaign*.

war-time book, *Far from the Limelight* (1918),[2] continues the theme through five short stories which focus on the settlers themselves and the challenges they faced in determining whether or not to join the war effort. For Page, the war becomes a backdrop for settler issues to be discussed – one of which was whether the Rhodesias should join in the Union of South Africa. In 1915, this was a pressing issue as the Charter the British South Africa Company held over the territories was due for renewal that year. The decision was finally made in 1925 that the Rhodesias would become independent territories outside of Charter control and not part of the Union to prevent being swamped by the dominant Boer culture. The challenges of returning 'home' from Africa are further explored in Page's writing, and what is clear, is that although there are challenges and hurdles to overcome, the colonies were not completely cut off from the 'motherland' in the same way that the German colonies were: Page and her husband were two settlers in Southern Rhodesia, who made their way back to Britain to help the war effort there.

For those in the colonies and dominions, determining where one's allegiance lay proved a challenge which was not easily overcome. This was particularly noticeable in South Africa in mid-1915, when recruitment for Europe and East Africa was taking place at the same time as an election was approaching. If too many government or pro-Empire supporters left the country, there was a strong possibility that the anti-Empire element would win, thereby jeopardising British control in southern Africa.

Settlers appear in both English and German fictional accounts of the campaign. This is not surprising as the settlers were concerned about the impact war would have on their livelihoods and their relationships with the indigenous populations. Although many hoped that if there was a war in Europe it would not extend to Africa, preparations were taking place for the eventuality of conflict. In *An Ice-Cream War* (1983), William Boyd intersperses the story of Cobb, who is sent to India and then East Africa, with the experiences of an American settler in British East Africa whose farm is on the border of German East Africa. Temple Smith is neighbours with a retired German army officer who has an English background, reminiscent of Tom von Prince, who farmed in the Usambara mountains on the border. Although the latter dies at the battle for Tanga, in Boyd's account the German survives the campaign, providing an opportunity to explore the relations between neighbours and cultures as their paths cross during the course of the war. In Wilbur Smith's *Assegai* (2009), underlying the apparent calm and friendliness between the two colonies lurked a darker side – preparation for war. For the Germans, it was developing air power and finding ways to support the Boers in

---

[2] Although this was Page's second war-time publication, at least four others were published during the war. Many were reprinted through to the 1930s.

South Africa; for the British, it was about finding out what the Germans were up to. An intricate spy network is set up, reminiscent of Consul Norman King's work in Dar-es-Salaam in the months before the outbreak of war and later, during the war, that of Richard Meinertzhagen; a character who features in William Powell's *Chui and Sadaka* (2011). Part of this spy network was making use of the Masai, a people which had been split across borders when the 'scramble for Africa' had taken place, but who disregarded borders and were allowed to. Their loyalty was to those they trusted and is explored by both authors in different ways – Smith through allegiance and Powell through rejection.

The outbreak of war and the emotions it aroused are the focus of a number of novels. Those mentioned above explore reactions of the settlers in Africa on the outbreak of war, whilst a few such as *Jim Redlake* (1930) and *Cupid in Africa* (1920) look at the reactions of those in Britain as war is declared and the discovery that they are to proceed to Africa rather than Europe for their military service. *Jim Redlake* also looks at the differences in outlook by Boer and British in South Africa and is an insightful description of the interplay between settler and visitor.

2 Minorities

There are very few fictional accounts which explore the relations between the soldiers and indigenous populations. Three early novels stand out: Francis Brett Young's *Jim Redlake*, P. C. Wren's *Cupid in Africa* and Percy Westerman's *Wilhelmshurst of the West Frontier Force* (1918). Post 2000, in line with a growing recognition of the price paid by the indigenous populations in the development of the war, there have been a number of novels embracing the diversity of culture involved. These include Powell's *Chui and Sadaka* (2011), Alex Capus' *A Matter of Time* (2009) and Smith's *Assegai* (2009). This is a rather high percentage (twenty-five per cent) when compared with the eleven per cent of non-fictional titles which were identified dealing with peoples who were not white (cf. Samson, "A Century of Remembering..."). As with the non-fiction accounts there is very little which focuses only on black, Indian and Coloured involvement, despite these troops playing a fundamental role in the success of the campaigns – both German and British and the large number of porters involved. Although these diverse forces outnumbered the whites, they are regarded as a minority due to their absence of voice.

The war in East Africa appears unique in that men from twenty different countries, or groupings, participated (cf. Samson, *World War I in Africa*). Soldiers of all colours from India, South Africa, Kenya, Nigeria, Ghana, the West Indies,

Zimbabwe, Zambia, Malawi, Uganda and Britain served alongside each other and in the same regiments as need demanded. The novels written by the men who fought in the campaign are far more reconciliatory and positive about the relationships whereas the later authors tend to emphasise the racial stereotypes. These insights, often missing from official or more formal accounts, are significant for social historians and others trying to understand why certain actions succeeded and others did not.

A racial group which features proportionately more in the novels than in non-fiction accounts is the Indian. Indian contribution to the campaign (from India, British East and South Africa) was significant in terms of manpower and material support, yet there were questions over their effectiveness as soldiers. This is perhaps why they do not appear as much in the histories and accounts – at a time when Britain was extolling the successes of its soldiers, it would be awkward to include a narrative which was too complex and seemingly peripheral to the Western Front. The novel, however, allows comment to be made more easily as noted by Francis Brett Young in a letter to his wife about *Jim Redlake* (cf. Leclaire).

Another group of people who were more involved in the campaign than is evident in the non-fiction accounts is that of women. The novel, through the introduction of romance permits this often ignored group of participants to feature. *Assegai* (2009) has the female spy, *Chui and Sadaka* (2011) the female spy and prisoner, *An Ice-Cream War* (1983) and *Cupid in Africa* (1920) the nurse, *Ghosts of Africa* (1980) the spy and camp follower whilst in *The African Queen* (1935), *A Matter of Time* (2009) and Page's books (1915, 1918) women are stoical, pushing men to do their duty amongst other supporting roles. Two German novels have women as their lead characters: *Die weiße Jägerin* by Rolf Ackermann (2007), which tells the story of Margaret von Trappe, who travelled with her husband during the war, and *Afrika, mon amour* by Chris Schnalke (2007), serialised for television by Carlo Rola in Germany. In the latter, the scorned woman betrays her country. Women in the East Africa campaign were involved in a myriad of ways – looking after farms to release the men to fight, as camp followers working with munitions and supplies and nursing. Although these roles were similar in title to what women in Europe were doing, the conditions in Africa differed. Karen Blixen transported material to her husband and others on the front-line, and the German women generally followed their men as refugees rather than become prisoners although, when Tabora fell to the Belgians in 1916, a number of German women including Ada Schnee, the German Governor's wife, became prisoners – the start of a tactic to put additional pressure on allied resources.

3 Battles and military encounters

As intimated in the introduction, action in the East African theatre took place during August 1914 on most borders, irrespective of whether or not the invaded country was neutral.[3] By the end of 1914, the Germans occupied the only British territory they would during the war – a town in British East Africa – only to give it up in 1916, when a major offensive was launched by the British using South African troops. This is the starting point of Hamilton Wende's *The King's Shilling* (2005). Other early skirmishes and battles are mentioned in Page's *Follow After* (1915), Smith's *Shout at the Devil* (1968), Balder Olden's *On Virgin Soil* (1930), and in Mader (1927, 1938) and Viera's (1943) short stories.

Most captivating are the events which involved water. Percy Westerman's role in the Royal Navy and being based at Portsmouth enabled him to write *Rounding up a Raider* (1916). Westerman draws on various events in the war involving the Germans disguising ships as raiders, and the sinking of the German cruiser *Königsberg* in the Rufiji Delta. The *Königsberg*, which took eight months to put out of action, is the focus of a number of novels, reflecting the impact this cruiser had on the British psyche, although interestingly, the season's tea harvest being destroyed does not feature in any of the fictional accounts. Novels which cover the *Königsberg* include Wilbur Smith's *Shout at the Devil* (1968), which was also made into a major film (1976) starring Lee Marvin, Roger Moore and Barbara Parkins, and William Stevenson's *Ghosts of Africa* (1980).

By far the most captivating encounter of the war in East Africa was the Lake Tanganyika Expedition, when the British sent two boats overland from Cape Town to Albertville to assume command of the lake. The first of four novels on the Lake Tanganyika Expedition was *The African Queen* (1935) by C. S. Forester, following serialisation in the *News Chronicle* (1934). The later award-winning film was directed by John Huston and starred Katherine Hepburn and Humphrey Bogart. The film has limited references to the war, whereas the book has a few more mentions, such as the involvement of the Belgians. At the end of the book, the reader is introduced to the star-attraction of the expedition, the flamboyant Commander Geoffrey Spicer-Simson, while in the film, the German boat featured is the original *Graf von Goetzen*, which today services Lake Tanganyika as *MV Liemba* and is the focus of the National Geographic documentary, *The Jungle Navy* (1999).

Alan Scholefield's *The Alpha Raid* (1980) is loosely based on the expedition, covering the basics: the trip across land from Cape Town to Albertville (Kalemie) in Congo and an eccentric commander who dislikes and distrusts the Belgians,

---

[3] Belgium became involved in the war when Germany invaded the country in August 1914, and Portugal declared war on Germany in March 1916.

leading to a fraught relationship between the allies. Using the events of the war, the South African born author explores the relationships between individuals in terms of class, race, education and aspiration. Another feature of the tale is the frustration by all sides of having to fight the war in Africa – a struggle which is seen as futile and, as the character Justine noted, unfair to the blacks whose country is being ravaged for no benefit to them.

Alex Capus's *A Matter of Time* (2009) is the English translation of the German novel *Eine Frage der Zeit* (2007). Although termed a novel, it is the closest historical account in English of the German side of the struggle for supremacy on Lake Tanganyika. The story charts the journey of the *Graf von Goetzen* from Papenburg to Kigoma and its painstaking reconstruction, which is interrupted by the outbreak of war. The factual account of the ship's progress provides a backdrop and context for Capus to explore the military and civilian relations amongst the Germans as well as German relations with the local inhabitants. The German account is interspersed with the British organisation of the Lake Tanganyika Expedition. The straightforward telling of the story enables Capus to portray Spicer-Simson more sympathetically than so far evidenced in any English novel or historical account of the expedition. The tale ends with the sinking of the *Goetzen* after only two voyages across the lake in order to prevent it falling into Belgian or British hands.

The fourth book is Christopher Dow's *Lord of the Loincloth* (2012). An Amazon review (Shabbyhouse) criticises the author for not having undertaken any new research and for rehashing what is already known. The author had a tough act to follow as Giles Foden's *Mimi and Toutou Go Forth* (2006) and Peter Shankland's *The Phantom Flotilla* (1968) are both well-regarded factual accounts of the expedition.

Water again features in David Bee's *Our Fatal Shadow* (1964), who found inspiration in the naval events on Lake Nyasa. Bee, who worked for the British colonial service in Tanganyika between 1958 and 1961 was inspired by stories he heard told round the lake, from his father who had served as the medical officer on HMS *Hyacinth* after the sinking of the *Königsberg* and his two uncles who served in Jan Smuts's 1st Mounted Brigade in East Africa. Rather than write a history of the events, Bee decided to reach a wider audience by turning the accounts into fiction, although he sets out in the introduction what he changed. He covers the main events of the campaign, including the capture of the German vessel on Lake Nyasa which gave the British control of the waters and enabled them to move troops more easily along the length of Nyasaland.

The final water story is based on the diaries of Nis Kock (1938), a sailor who joined the German forces in East Africa until his forced surrender in 1917. The Danish novel by Christen P. Christensen, *Sønderyder forsvarer Østafrika 1914–18*

(1937) was translated into English as *Blockade and Jungle* in 1941 and tells the story of Kock's experiences as a South Jutlander or Danish sailor on the German-commandeered ship *Kronborg*, also known as the *Rubens*. It shows how Germany used the guise of neutrality to send reinforcements to a force which was ostensibly completely cut off from what was happening in Europe, and whose actions would have little or no impact on the outcome of the conflict. The success of this blockade runner, as well as the *Marie*, gave a great boost to German morale as the forces realised they had not been forgotten by the homeland. As with Olden's *On Virgin Soil* (1930), these two novels provide some insight into the logistics and organisation which allowed the German *schutztruppe* to achieve what it did.

Remaining on the theme of ships, the next most fascinating topic is that of L-59, the airship or zeppelin which was sent to Africa by Germany but which never made it. It is the feature of Viera's main story (1943) and of *Assegai* (2009). The zeppelin and other flying accounts feature in *Ghosts of Africa* (1980), *Shout at the Devil* (1968) and *Cupid in Africa* (1920).

The theme of ships in East African fiction – both water and air-borne – provides exotic interludes in what was a side-show of the war in Europe. The daring and expectation the various actions resulted in were at the time significant, which is what has made them attractive for the novelist. Each of these tales impacted on the direction of the campaign in some way – more so than many of the skirmishes and battles on land. Although the zeppelin never made it to the Makonde plateau, it buoyed the Germans to know they had not been forgotten, and although the British destroyed the *Königsberg*, the Germans salvaged the guns which were used during the remainder of the campaign.

Of the land encounters, the battle for Tanga has featured most frequently. The battle which took place in early November 1914 was regarded as a fiasco by both sides although the Germans had the more successful encounter. The battle was significant on numerous fronts, it resulted in a change in British command structures, it placed the German military commander firmly in the lead over the Governor, who was technically responsible for the military actions of the German colony, and led to the idea that the Germans had successfully trained bees to attack their opposing forces (cf. Samson, *World War I in Africa*; Paice). The main English fictional accounts are found in Young's *Jim Redlake* (1930), Stevenson's *Ghosts of Africa* (1980) and Boyd's *An Ice-Cream War* (1983), whilst the German accounts are related as short stories by Mader (1927, 1938) and Viera (1943).

In contrast to the military encounters, P. C. Wren's *Cupid in Africa* (1920) tells a similar story to that of *Jim Redlake*, with long periods of no fighting and endless waiting or marching through the bush and rain, and an almost pre-occupation with insects. These two stories in particular were written by men who had served in Africa, and their accounts are supported by many of the diaries which have been left behind.

Although a relatively minor theme, prisoners of war appear in a number of the fictional accounts of the campaign. In *An Ice-Cream War* (1983), Boyd brings all the characters in his book together through the romance which develops between a German nurse and a British prisoner of war who is severely injured at Tanga. *The White Rhino Hotel* by Bartle Bull (1992) starts with a prisoner of war discussing the end of war with his German captor, whilst Bee's *Our Fatal Shadows* (1964) also features prisoners. The camaraderie between the prisoners and their captors referred to in various novels is not unfounded as explained by Arnold Wienholt (1922), an Australian hunter who was an intelligence scout in the campaign. His encounter with Lettow-Vorbeck features in the film *The Young Indiana Jones: The Phantom Train of Doom* (1993). In contrast, the fear of being taken prisoner appears in Wilbur Smith's *Shout at the Devil* (1968) and *Assegai* (2009), and in William Powell's *Chui and Sadaka* (2011), whilst Forester in *The African Queen* (1935) has his lead characters fall into the hands of the Germans. For the majority of these last-mentioned novels, the fear of being captured invariably corresponds with the stereotypical view of the savage black man.

4 Final Comments on Authors: Nation, Race, Gender

The above discussion has covered the main themes of the fictional accounts so far identified of the East African campaign, though there are many more, analysed extensively, among others by Dirk Göttsche and Doret Jordaan. For the historian, being able to identify the trends and frequency with which events or characters feature in the texts provides an insight into what popular memory there is of the campaign. An analysis of when the texts were produced as well as the focus of each, allows the historian to draw inferences of potential influences.

An assessment of the fictional accounts identified to date accords with the divisions identified by Jay Winter and Antoine Prost in their study of literature around the Western Front. A few novels and short story compilations appeared during the war years, followed by a slight surge in the 1920s and later war years, but with none in the 1950s – the time Winter and Prost have identified as the transition between the veteran generation writing from a personal perspective and that of secondary accounts. This is not surprising given the Eurocentric background of the authors and their associated literary traditions. The recent surge in fictional accounts, eight identified since 2005, aligns with the advent of genealogical studies and easier access to information on obscure theatres of war through the internet (cf. Samson, "A Century of Remembering").

Of the identified English fiction writers of the campaign, four were born in Africa, five, including three Americans and one Canadian, spent time working in Africa and three were involved in the campaign. Some of the English-speaking authors have given clues as to their reasons for writing about the campaign: Young used the novel to express views he felt had been censored when he wrote *Marching in Tanga* (1917), his non-fiction account of the campaign. Bee was inspired by various stories he had heard. Forester, who was too young to serve during World War I, was old enough to pick up on newsworthy stories, and when pressed by his publisher to write a book in the 1930s, he took inspiration from a tube poster advertising the 'Dark Continent' (C. S. Forester Society, 2012). Stevenson heard about the campaign from his son, who was working in the Selous Game Reserve, which was named after Frederick Selous, the famous hunter who was killed there in 1916. Westerman is the exception – not having spent time in Africa; his wartime service and stories he gleaned from returning sailors provided the starting points for his novels.

Winter and Prost note that from the 1980s "authors marry family history and national history in powerful ways. Some writers heard of the war when they were young from their grandparents, and see it as a foundational myth, a story of great power and appeal" (188–189). This may well be the case for fiction about the war in Europe. However, in the case of the East African side-show, the inspiration for writing appears to be based on the stories others have told combined with an experience of the territory concerned. In the language of Winter and Prost, the "foundational myth [with its] great power and appeal" has been transferred to a wider audience. Another contrast between the fiction produced around the Western Front and that of the East Africa campaign concerns film. Where Winter and Prost have noted that "filmic representations of the war have helped turn it into an icon of futility" (190), the films produced on the campaigns in East Africa tend to emphasise the success of the white man over nature in achieving his aim.

The German accounts were written by five authors, two of whom, Olden and Viera, fought in East Africa. Ackermann lives in Namibia, having worked in Tanzania, Schnalke spent some time in India, while Mader had African links of some sort, although exactly what and when is not clear. The fifth author, Capus, is Swiss, with no clearly discernible link to the theatre, although Dirk Göttsche notes that Capus has a long-standing interest in Africa; his first novel, *Munziger Pasha* (1997) was set in Egypt (cf. *Rediscovering Africa*). There has been an increase in German literature on the colonies from about mid-1990, as the centenary of Germany's colonial wars in South West Africa approached, "effectively reinscribing colonialism in German cultural memory" (Hofmann 171). Göttsche attributes the increased interest to the multiculturalism of German speaking countries and the fascination of the wider world engendered by growing up in certain regions (cf. Interview). This contrasts with the post-1980 English authors who came to the campaign through working in Tanzania or Kenya.

There was one book in Danish by Christen P. Christensen, who says in the English translation: "These reminiscences then tell the story of an ordinary man [...] but it seems to me to give fine expression to a whole people's courage, devotion to duty and ready sacrifice in the service of a foreign power" (9). Bjarne Bendtsen, who has studied the Danish books published on the East African campaign, explains that "Christensen's version of Kock's memoirs seems to have struck a chord of interest in the Danish public in the late 1930s, when otherwise Nazi Germany loomed as a large threat over Denmark as imperial Germany had done a good twenty years earlier" (Bendtsen). In doing so, Christensen "underlines the racial kinship between Danes and Germans" (Bendtsen).

Christensen's novel uses literature for propaganda purposes. Of the novels written during Hitler's time in power, 1933–1945,[4] only four new books were published on the campaign – two in German (1938 and 1943), one in Danish (1937) and one in English (1935). Of these, the German and Danish texts are perhaps the most politically inspired. This tentative conclusion is drawn from the attempt by Christensen to reinforce the "kinship between Danes and Germans" (Bendtsen) and that both Viera (1943) and Mader's short stories (1938) focus on the first major German victory in the colonies at a time Germany was looking for *lebensraum* and to reclaim its lost African colonies. This is an area which would benefit from greater research.

One can continue to draw inferences as to why these authors felt drawn to write about this side-show and what this might tell us, but what is perhaps more significant is an assessment of who has not written anything about it. All the authors mentioned in this paper are white – there is no black, Indian or Coloured (South African mixed race) contribution to the fictional genre or interpretation of the campaign. Apart from those who fought in the campaign, the views of local inhabitants are fairly stereotypical or glossed over, a view supported by Göttsche (cf. Interview), although Powell's novel *Chui and Sadaka* about two mixed-race girls is an exception to the rule. Why it is that only authors of white extraction have written about the campaign when it had a huge impact on the lives of all resident in what is today Tanzania is an area for further research and beyond the scope of this chapter. The claim that it was a 'white man's war' fought by white

---

4 Used here only as a well-known, clearly discernible period.

men for white ideals is too superficial and stereotypical to explain this gap in the literature of the campaign.

Other significant omissions include the names of well-known authors Elspeth Huxley and Karen Blixen, or Isak Dinesen as she was sometimes known. The former was a young girl in British East Africa during the war whilst the latter helped transport food and supplies to the British troops. The war features in their non-fiction works, but so far no reference has been found in their fictional accounts. Similarly, the novels by authors who experienced the war focus very little on the actual violence of war – it is there and suspense is built but most of it is hinted at. This contrasts with novels written from the 1980s onwards, where the violence becomes more graphic – for example, *Ghosts of Africa* (1980), *The King's Shilling* (2005) and *Assegai* (2009).

5 Conclusion

In some respects this study has raised more questions than answers. The study has identified where memory of the campaign exists – predominantly amongst people with some experience of Africa and countries which had some involvement in the campaign. This may seem obvious, but it does not account for the fact that only white authors have written on the campaign. Given that at least 150,000 white men fought in East Africa and almost a million black porters were involved in the campaign, why are there so few books on the theatre and why do they focus mostly on the same events? Why does there appear to be a greater interest in the East African campaign by American authors compared to British authors, when the territory fought over was adjacent to a British colony and became a British mandate in the 1920s? While a link with Africa may account for the English interest in the campaign, the same clear-cut links cannot be made for the texts in German and Danish. Is there a difference in memory between authors from countries which were victorious in the war and those which were not?

The challenge for historians is that the fictional accounts are not always historically accurate and need to be mediated. Determining the validity of accounts can provide a dilemma for the historian. The writings on the Lake Tanganyika Expedition provide a useful example. Most of the accounts written on the expedition are unreferenced, although Giles Foden provides a brief bibliography of the sources he has used in *Mimi and Toutou Go Forth: The Bizarre Battle of Lake Tanganyika*. Dirk Göttsche, in *Rediscovering Africa: The Rediscovery of Colonialism in Contemporary German Literature* refers to the accounts by Foden and Peter Shankland as novels (cf. 121). The latter wrote his book *The Phantom Flotilla: The*

Story of the Naval Africa Expedition 1915–16, using interviews with the doctor of the expedition. Yet, for scholars of the campaign, they are regarded as the main secondary texts; the referenced text being Edward Paice's *Tip and Run: The Untold Tragedy of the Great War*. Similarly, one of the best overviews of the entire campaign is an unreferenced text, Charles Miller's *Battle for the Bundu*; again the referenced text being that by Paice. Literary critics may well have terms and definitions to describe these nuanced differences; for the historian, the unreferenced text is, invariably, the beginning of a journey of discovery. As this chapter has indicated, a study of fiction can be useful to explore trends and themes which in turn can provide insights into where there is a memory of a previous time.

References

Bendtsen, Bjarne. "Danes at War in East Africa: The Case of the Blockade Runner SS." Kronborg. Forthcoming conference paper. Great War in (East) Africa Association, 2012.

C. S. Forester Society. "African Queen." *Reflections* (November 2012) http://csforester.files.wordpress.com/2011/03/reflections-233.pdf. (25 September 2013).

Foden, Giles. *Mimi and Toutou Go Forth: The Bizarre Battle of Lake Tanganyika*. London: Penguin, 1995.

Göttsche, Dirk. *Rediscovering Africa: The Rediscovery of Colonialism in Contemporary German Literature*. Rochester: Camden House, 2013.

Göttsche, Dirk. Interview about *Rediscovering Africa: The Rediscovery of Colonialism in Contemporary German Literature*. http://www.boydellandbrewer.com/content/docs/Remembering.20Africa.20FINAL.20with.20links.pdf. (25 September 2013).

Hofman, Michael. *Deutsch-afrikanische Diskurse in Geschichte und Gegenwart: literatur- und kulturwissenschaftliche Perspektiven*. Amsterdam: Rodopi, 2012.

Jordaan, Doret. "The usage of African languages in three selected contemporary German novels set in Africa." *Inkanyiso* (Issue 1, 2010). http://www.inkanyiso.uzulu.ac.za/journals/inkanyisovol2issue12010.pdf. (25 September 2013).

Kock, Nis. *Sønderjyder vender hjem fra Østafrika. Fra Krig og Fangenskab til Frihed og Fred*. Copenhagen: C. A. Reitzels, 1938.

Leclaire, Jacques. *Tanga Letters To Jessie. Written by Francis Brett Young to His Wife from German East Africa 1916–1917*. Francis Brett Young Society, 2006.

Miller, Charles. *Battle for the Bundu*. London: Macmillan, 1974.

Paice, Edward. *Tip and Run: The Untold Tragedy of the Great War*. London: Weidenfeld & Nicolson, 2007.

Samson, Anne. *Britain, South Africa and the East Africa Campaign, 1914–1918: The Union Comes of Age*. London: IB Tauris, 2006.

Samson, Anne. "A Century of Remembering the Great War in East Africa." Paper presented at Imperial War Museum, London. July 2012. http://www.academia.edu/1754139/A_century_of_remembering_the_Great_War_in_East_Africa. (25 September 2013).

Samson, Anne. *World War I in Africa: The Forgotten Conflict Among the European Powers*. London: IB Tauris, 2013.

Shabbyhouse, "Absolute Rubbish." Amazon, 29 November 2011. http://www.amazon.co.uk/Lord-Loincloth-Christopher-Dow/dp/0979696801. (25 September 2013).
Shankland, Peter. *The Phantom Flotilla: The Story of the Naval Africa Expedition 1915–16*. London: Collins, 1968.
The Spectator, 10 July 1915: Review. http://archive.spectator.co.uk/article/10th-july-1915/23/readable-novelfollow-after-by-gertrude-page-hurst. (25 September 2013).
Von Herff, Michael. *"They walk through the fire like the blondest Germans": African Soldiers Serving the Kaiser in German East Africa (1888–1914)*. Unpubl. Master of Arts Thesis. Montreal: McGill University, 1991. http://digitool.Library.McGill.CA:80/R/-?func=dbin-jump full&object_id=60565&silo_library=GEN01. (25 September 2013).
Wienholt, Arnold. *The Story of a Lion Hunt; with some of the Hunter's Military Adventures during the War*. London: Andrew Melrose, 1922.
Winter, Jay, and Antoine Prost. *The Great War in History: Debates and Controversies, 1914 to the Present*. Cambridge: Cambridge University Press, 2005.

Novels about East Africa

Ackermann, Rolf. *Die weiße Jägerin*. Munich: Droemer Knaur, 2005.
Bee, David. *Our Fatal Shadows: A Story of German East Africa and Tanganyika* [also known as *The Curse of Magira*]. London: Geoffrey Bles, 1964.
Boyd, William. *An Ice-Cream War*. London: Penguin, 1983.
Bull, Bartle. *The White Rhino Hotel*. New York: Viking, 1992.
Capus, Alex. *A Matter of Time*. Trans. John Brownjohn. London: Haus, 2009.
Christensen, Christen P., ed. *Blockade and Jungle: From the Letters and Diaries etc. of Nis Kock*. Trans. Eleanor Arkwright. London: Robert Hale, 1940.
Dow, Christopher. *Lord of the Loincloth: The Adventures of the Royal Naval African Expedition*. Houston: Phosphene, 2007.
Forester, C. S. *The African Queen*. Harmondsworth: Penguin, 1935.
Mader, Friedrich Wilhelm. *Am Kilimandjaro: Abenteuer und Kämpfe in Deutsch-Ostafrika (Die Helden von Ostafrika, erster Teil)*. Stuttgart: Union Deutsche Verlagsgesellschaft, 1927.
Mader, Friedrich Wilhelm. *Die Schlacht bei Tanga: Erzählung aus dem Weltkrieg*. Gütersloh: C. Bertelsmann, 1938.
Olden, Balder. *On Virgin Soil*. Trans. Lorna Dietz. London: McCauley, 1930.
Page, Gertrude. *Follow After*. London: Hurst & Blacket, 1915.
Page, Gertrude. *Far from the Limelight*. London: Cassell, 1918.
Powell, William. *Chui and Sadaka*. Kuala Lumpur: EAF Press, 2011.
Schnalke, Christian. *Afrika, mon amour*. Berlin: Ullstein Verlag, 2007.
Scholefield, Alan. *Lion in the Evening*. London: Heinemann, 1974.
Scholefield, Alan. *The Alpha Raid*. London: Heinemann, 1976.
Smith, Wilbur. *Assegai*. London: Macmillan, 2009.
Smith, Wilbur. *Shout at the Devil* London: Heinemann, 1968.
Stevenson, William. *The Ghosts of Africa*. New York: Harcourt, Brace & Jovanovich, 1980.
Viera, Josef S. *Deutsch-Ostafrika unverloren! Erzählung aus den deutschen Kolonialkämpfen im Weltkrieg mit Kartenskizze und Bildern nach Federzeichnungen von Willy Planck*. Stuttgart: Loewe, 1943.

Wende, Hamilton. *The King's Shilling: A Novel*. Johannesburg: Jacana, 2005.
Westerman, Percy. *Rounding up the Raider: A Naval Story of the Great War*. London: Partridge, 1916. http://www.gutenberg.org/ebooks/36499. (25 September 2013).
Westerman, Percy. *Wilmshurst of the Frontier Force*. London: Partridge, 1918. http://www.pgs.org.uk/wp-content/uploads/2013/02/website-Percy-Westerman-by-J-Sadden.pdf. (25 September 2013).
Wren, P. C. *Cupid in Africa: Or the Making of Bertram in Love and War – A Character Study*. London: Heath Cranton 1920. http://www.gutenberg.org/files/37544/37544-h/37544-h.htm. (25 September 2013).
Young, Francis Brett. *Jim Redlake*. London: Heinemann, 1930.

Alicia Fahey
Voices From the Edge: De-Centering Master Narratives in Jane Urquhart's *The Stone Carvers*

> The margin or the border is the postmodern space *par excellence*, the place where new possibilities exist.
>
> Linda Hutcheon, The Canadian Postmodern

The first chapter of Jane Urquhart's novel *The Stone Carvers* (2001) begins with a group of women engaged in an act of storytelling about the origins of their village. The women believe "the story connected them, through ancestry, through work and worship, and through vocation to the village's inception" (6). Indeed, both the listening to and telling of stories is of primary importance in the novel; *The Stone Carvers* is about the production and dissemination of stories across the boundaries of time and space. In particular, Urquhart draws upon the historical narrative of the Battle of Vimy Ridge that took place during the First World War in April 1917. Due to an abundance of official histories and state initiatives that argue Canada's victory at Vimy was a formative event for the Canadian nation, Vimy has achieved the status of a master narrative in the collective memory of Canadian citizens.

Master narratives are stories of transcendent or universal truths that promote a comprehensive and totalizing view of past events and usually represent state interests. In his popular history *Vimy* (1986), Pierre Berton explains how the master narrative of the Battle of Vimy Ridge achieved such prolific heights:

> It has become commonplace to say that Canada came of age at Vimy Ridge. For seventy years it has been said so often – in Parliament, at hundreds of Vimy dinners and in thousands of Remembrance Day addresses, in newspaper editorials, school texts, magazine articles, and more than a score of source books about Vimy and Canada's role in the Great War – that it is almost an article of faith. Thus it is difficult to untangle the reality from the rhetoric. (294–295)

As a result of the various state initiatives instituted to inundate the public with the narrative of Vimy as Canada's originary moment, the rhetoric of myth was eventually accepted as a historical given by Canadian citizens. The Vimy master narrative was further reinforced by the construction of sculptor Walter Allward's massive monument at the site of the battle during the inter-war period, which demonstrates Daniel Sherman's observation that monuments, as the main feature of commemorative practice, are used to "[channel] mourning in a direction that conforms to the dominant perceptions of national interest" (7).

Allward's monument and its commemorative function play an important role in Urquhart's representation of Vimy. *The Stone Carvers* is a historical fiction about a woman named Klara Becker, who travels to Vimy, France, to help construct the monument in order to commemorate the loss of her lover in the First World War. However, instead of reinforcing the homogenous and totalizing discourse that the master narrative purports, Urquhart's novel de-centers the official version of Vimy by opening the story to voices that are marginalized or even absent from the official record. This re-positioning does not replace official history with a new master narrative; instead, *The Stone Carvers* uses various narrative strategies to undermine the hegemony of the master narrative and to connect Vimy to other stories that take place in Canada and abroad. What is at stake in *The Stone Carvers* then, is memory itself, as the novel portrays memory as a process and reveals how the meanings of past events continue to change as time progresses. Marianne Hirsch uses the term "postmemory" to describe a "structure of inter- and trans-generational transmission of traumatic knowledge and experience of the past from the direct experience of a first generation to later generations through a connection felt so deeply that it is experienced as memory" (106). Urquhart herself has chronicled her deeply felt connection to Vimy through her mother's personal accounts and collection of material memories of Vimy Ridge, such as postcards, souvenirs, books, needlework, and soldier folk art, so that when Urquhart visited the monument in 1974, she "wasn't prepared for [her] own reaction" of being moved to tears (Urquhart, "Our Lost and Found Memories" A6). In both contesting and expanding the national narrative of Vimy Ridge, *The Stone Carvers* reconsiders the place and meaning of the First World War in Canada's contemporary post-memory culture.

1 Historical Context: Laying the Foundation of the Master Narrative

Historical fictions that revisit and reconsider the past have proliferated in Canadian literature since the late twentieth century, and master narratives are often the focus of these re-writings.[1] In his introduction to *The Postmodern Condition:*

---

[1] Studies that investigate contemporary Canadian historical fictions include: Andrea Cabajsky and Brett Grubisic's *National Plots: Historical Fictions and Changing Ideas of Canada* (2010);

A Report on Knowledge (1984), Jean-François Lyotard describes "incredulity" towards master narratives as a defining factor of the postmodern condition (xxiv). After arguing that master narratives have been delegitimized as a result of postmodernism's suspicious tendencies, Lyotard poses the question, "Where, after the metanarratives, can legitimacy reside?" (xxiv–xxv). And yet, in his foreword to Lyotard's seminal text, Fredric Jameson points out that replacing the old regime with a new legitimizing narrative runs the risk of "reproduc[ing] the very polemic in which Lyotard's own book wishes to intervene" (ix). With Jameson's warning in mind, rather than evaluating the validity of competing versions of Canadian identity and the First World War, this chapter considers *how* Urquhart's treatment of Vimy participates in destabilizing the hegemony of the master narrative.

The Stone Carvers engages in the process of subverting official history by presenting multiple versions of the master narrative, including counter-histories that remember Vimy by contesting, denying, and reconfiguring the official version. Katharine Hodgkin and Susannah Radstone argue that memory is the site of a struggle over meaning and that there are political implications in the "divergences, inconsistencies, different versions at different times" because variations are indicative of "the culture in which these memories have been built and emerge, and about the workings of memory itself" (5). The destabilizing function of *The Stone Carvers* thus demonstrates that – unlike master narratives – memory is not static. The tenuous condition of memory is made explicit near the end of the novel by the narrator's claim that "[n]o one knows anymore what the allegorical figures [of the Vimy monument] represent. No one cares" (378). The novel's depiction of Vimy as a failed "site of memory," which Pierre Nora describes as, "any signifying entity, of a material or ideal kind, which has through human will or the work of time become a symbolic element of the memorial patrimony of a given community" (qtd. in Sherman 3), provokes questions about Canadian culture. By examining the effects of the First World War on Canadian citizens engaged in combat and on the home front through stories that bring about discord with the national version, *The Stone Carvers* queries how we commemorate (publicly and privately) the casualties of war, as well as investigating the possibilities and limitations of art and narrative as modes of representation. Additionally, the novel describes memory as a process that needs to be continuously reconstituted so that it remains relevant in contemporary contexts. The alternative – an indiffer-

---

Gabriele Helms's *Challenging Canada: Dialogism and Narrative Techniques in Canadian Novels* (2003); Manina Jones's *That Art of Difference: Documentary Collage and English-Canadian Writing* (1993); Martin Kuester's *Framing Truths: Parodic Structures in Contemporary English-Canadian Historical Novels*; Herb Wyile's *Speculative Fictions* (2002) and *Speaking in the Past Tense* (2007).

ence or resistance to memory and a failure to perpetuate its transmission (in other words, if "no one cares") – is that the past will eventually be forgotten.

How, then, to commemorate the First World War? T. G. Ashplant, Graham Dawson, and Michael Roper identify two dominant paradigms in which war memory is primarily represented: the state-centered ("political") paradigm that concentrates on collective national identity and the ("psychological") paradigm of mourning through which individuals attempt to come to terms with the incomprehensibility of war (7). Both paradigms are produced and disseminated through what the authors call "narratives of articulation":

> [these] refer to shared formulations within which social actors couch their memories. They extend, in social range, political power and symbolic potency, from hegemonic official narratives cementing international alliances or binding together a nation-state, through oppositional or other sectional accounts of subordinated experiences striving for public recognition, to locally common or shared, and even individual (sometimes fragmentary), memories. (16)

With this in mind, the master narrative that is reconsidered in *The Stone Carvers* is that Canadians "came of age" as a nation in April 1917 during the Battle of Vimy Ridge. This state-centered narrative of articulation is a hegemonic official narrative that functions to bind together the nation-state of Canada by endorsing a narrative of independence that characterizes Canadian soldiers, and, by extension, the imagined community of Canada, with the shared qualities of bravery, courage, and ingenuity. The "shared formulations," which Ashplant, Dawson and Roper describe as framing "templates" (34) and which resemble Hayden White's discussion of narrative tropes that constitute all forms of narrative discourse and reveal the ubiquity of narrative as a mode of representation, are used to sediment the narrative of independence in the collective memory of Canadian citizens. "The narrative," White argues, "is not the icon; what it does is describe the events in the historical record in such a way as to inform the reader what to take as an icon of the events so as to render them 'familiar' to him" (52). White continues: "This historical narrative thus mediates between the events reported in it and the generic plot-structures conventionally used in our culture to endow unfamiliar events and situations with meanings" (52). The mythic rendering of Canadian participation in the First World War and Vimy Ridge corresponds with White's observation that history is a combination of reported events and generic plot structures. Similarly, Jonathan Vance argues that the "Great War" (an appellation that is itself loaded with mythic implications) achieved the status of myth in Canadian society in order to "fill the needs" of grieving citizens – in other words, to justify, in various ways (e.g. consolation, entertainment, explanation), the vast scale of loss and destruction caused by the war (cf. 8–9). The generic plot structure of myth proved to be an adequate signification of these needs.

In *The Stone Carvers*, the primary mode of perpetuating the transmission of a state-centered narrative is the construction of the Vimy monument at the site of the battle in France. The sculptor who designed the monument, Walter Allward, uses allegorical figures and religious iconography to represent the over 60,000 Canadians who died in the First World War and, specifically, the more than 11,000 whose bodies were never recovered. Allward's figures draw on recognizable templates that function to solidify the memory of Vimy in the minds of the Canadian public.² The monument also utilizes the template of familial succession, represented by the statue of Mother Canada (a personification of the Canadian nation) weeping for her lost sons. Graham Carr discusses the use of generational motifs as part of an "ecology of war remembrance" and argues that the idea of generation is used as a narrative device that naturalizes the transmission of historical understanding and "subtly manoeuvers the focus from 'objective' history to 'subjective' memory'" (61). It is therefore through the familiarity of these recognizable templates or narrative tropes of religion and family that the memory of the First World War, and especially the Canadian victory at Vimy Ridge, is transmitted from national memory to individual memory. This brings to mind Arthur Danto's distinction that "we erect monuments so that we shall always remember and we build memorials so that we shall never forget [...]. Monuments commemorate the memorable and embody the myths of beginnings. Memorials ritualize remembrance and mark the reality of ends" (153). The power of the Vimy monument as a site of memory during the time period in which it was created lies in Allward's use of the psychological paradigm of mourning to assert the national narrative, thus blurring the boundaries between private and public commemoration and rendering the memory of Vimy in a recognizable form so it could be readily consumed and internalized by the Canadian public. Whether or not these narrative frames of religion, allegory, familial succession, and myth remain relevant in a contemporary Canadian context is one of the questions presented by Urquhart's novel.

Immediately following the war, the Canadian narrative of the Battle of Vimy Ridge as a national bildungsroman was adopted with such rigor that conflicting narratives could not impede the epic proportions of the myth of national origin. Today, contradictory narratives are more widely circulated, although they remain the minority. On the ninetieth anniversary of the battle of Vimy Ridge, Michael Valpy, writer for the Toronto *Globe and Mail* newspaper, argued that "Canadians, and only Canadians, call it the Battle of Vimy Ridge [...]. In everyone else's histori-

---

2 For further discussion of the use of religious iconography in Canadian war art see Laura Brandon's important study *Art or Memorial? The Forgotten History of Canada's War Art* (2006).

cal lexicon, it was a limited tactical victory in the First World War's horrendous Battle of Arras, which the British and their allies lost" (F4). And yet, while alternative narratives to the state-centered paradigm did and continue to exist, they draw upon and, ironically, reinforce the very narrative they wish to contest. Urquhart portrays a dissenting version of the war through Klara's brother, Tilman, who loses his leg while engaged in combat at Vimy Ridge. When Tilman's friend Giorgio inquires about the battle, Tilman replies:

> I don't think a single one of us who was there knew whether or not there was a victory. We barely understood where we were when it was all over. And let's not overlook the fact that thirty-five hundred guys died, and three times as many were injured. I didn't even hear about the grandness of the victory until the war was finished, and then I thought the fellow telling me had things all wrong. (306)

By focusing on his individual experience of the battle instead of a retrospective symbolic meaning imposed on it, Tilman presents a counter-narrative to the battle of Vimy Ridge that undermines the notion of victory and focuses, instead, on the death and destruction that more closely resembles Valpy's description of the event.

Similarly, Urquhart's description of the system of tunnels running below Allward's monument operates as what James Young refers to as a counter-monument: monuments that express a deep distrust of monuments and function to challenge and de-naturalize viewer's assumptions about memory and the past (27–28). Unlike Allward's use of abstract concepts (e.g. "love" and "sacrifice") and aesthetic unity to appeal to a general audience – his obsessive quest for "flawless" stone takes years because it must contain "no previous history of organic life" (269) – the tunnels are a heterogeneous subterranean archive of inscriptions, paraphernalia, and art created by the soldiers who fought in the battle of Vimy Ridge. As Giorgio tells Klara, "there is *some* authenticity left, down here, or at least the remnants of it" (359). The narrative of the tunnels is polysemous and fragmentary, drawing on the subordinated and locally shared experiences of the soldiers whose individual memories form a collective memory that contests, but simultaneously reinforces, the abstraction of the monument above them; this double signification of meaning establishes a supplementary relationship between Allward's monument and the tunnels that run below it.[3]

The difficulty of separating the dominant narrative from subordinate narratives is further complicated by the fact that all of the versions generally refer to the same historical record of events. In contrast, it is the *interpretation* of the

---

[3] Jacques Derrida (1974) explains that the supplement has double signification because it is both an accretion of meaning and a substitution, or intervention of meaning (cf. 144–145).

events (the templates or generic plot structures used to represent and transmit the memory of Vimy) that generate conflicting versions. There are two facts that form the foundation of the many narratives of articulation of Vimy Ridge. First, that Canadians managed to capture the ridge after French and British troops failed to do so. Second, that the battle of Vimy Ridge was the first time the four divisions of the Canadian Corps fought together as a cohesive unit (in previous battles the Canadians were amalgamated with the British troops). As Vance points out, "[i]t was the image of provincial unity that gave the Battle of Vimy Ridge such import. […] For many people, that battle came to symbolize the potential of Canada if such cooperation could be realized on an ongoing basis" (233). And yet, in *The Stone Carvers*, the potential for unity lies not in trying to resolve the tensions between the dominant, monologic narrative and the heterogeneous experiences of marginal characters but in accepting the simultaneous existence of these competing versions.

2 Construction: Conflicting Artistic Visions

Linda Hutcheon first used the term historiographic metafiction to refer to postmodern fictions (and other art forms) that "are both intensely self-reflexive and yet paradoxically also lay claim to historical events and personages" (*A Poetics of Postmodernism* 5). In addition, Hutcheon's book *The Canadian Postmodern* (1988) identifies what she claims to be distinctly Canadian postmodern ideologies that influence contemporary Canadian fiction. The concept of the margin is central to her discussion of postmodernism and is referred to in the epigraph that begins this essay: "The margin or the border is the postmodern space *par excellence*, the place where new possibilities exist" (*The Canadian Postmodern* 4). This quotation illustrates Hutcheon's observation that, influenced by postcolonial, poststructural, and feminist theories, contemporary Canadian authors turned to the marginalized and/or silenced aspects of history in order to assert alternative narratives of articulation. According to Hutcheon, "Since the periphery or the margin might also describe Canada's perceived position in international terms, perhaps the postmodern ex-centric is very much a part of the identity of the nation" (*The Canadian Postmodern* 3). Canada's perception of itself as marginal derives from a resistance to being subsumed by the culture of the United States as well as negotiating the nation's colonial legacy.

Although *The Stone Carvers* is not as explicit an example of historiographic metafiction as other Canadian novels (in particular, Timothy Findley's *The Wars* of 1977 set the precedent for historiographic metafictions about Canada and the

First World War), the novel does exhibit some historiographic and metafictional qualities. Urquhart's use of marginal characters (a female spinster, a homosexual soldier/physically disabled veteran, Canadians of non-British heritage) to challenge the master narrative of Vimy is reinforced by the form of the novel, which resists linearity and singularity by weaving together multiple narratives in a non-chronological sequence. Also, the novel's aiming to open the existing narrative rather than to propose a new totalizing narrative is characteristically postmodern. In an interview with Herb Wyile, Urquhart explains how historical figures "act as a hook to draw [her] into the texture of time, and then gradually the person in question will withdraw to the outskirts of the story" (81–82). In the case of *The Stone Carvers*, Allward represents the official narrative, and his role in the novel is minimalized in order to make space for alternative voices. This de-centering of official history and assertion of marginalized or ex-centric figures is the primary way in which Urquhart contests and expands the national narrative.

If Urquhart relocates Allward's character in order to focus on the personal experience of a woman mourning the loss of her lover in the war, this is both a postmodern and political manoeuvre. Of course, the fact that Klara travels to Vimy disguised as a man in order to participate in the construction of the monument complicates any easy division into personal and private commemoration, and into male and female gender roles. The complexity of Klara's character is located, in part, in her frequent transgression of the social boundaries imposed on her gender. From her geographically marginalized residence on a hill outside of town, she secures her economic independence by performing traditionally male-dominated trades such as farming, carving, and tailoring (10). Having never married, but lacking the conservative deference necessary for a life of religious duty, Klara occupies a liminal space in the community of Shoneval.

Thus, it is Klara's resistance to social and cultural conventions that makes her a likely character to contest official history. According to Dawn Thompson, "memory becomes political when it is employed to rewrite notions of subjectivity and reality, especially the realities lived and narrated by minority subjects who are trying to change that reality and/or their position within it" (4). *The Stone Carvers* attempts to rewrite the meaning of the national narrative of the Battle of Vimy Ridge by supplementing the historical record with the experiences of a woman and the home front. Klara most explicitly challenges the national narrative in a culminating act of defiance near the end of the novel when she alters Allward's sculpture in order to make "[h]er own mark" (334). She does so by turning the allegorical figure of the torchbearer into a portrait of her dead lover, Eamon. Allward's initial reaction to Klara's revision reveals the totalizing impulse behind his artistic vision:

> He had wanted this stone youth to remain allegorical, universal, wanted him to represent everyone's lost friend, everyone's lost child. He had wanted the stone figure to be the 66,000 dead young men who had marched through his dreams when he had conceived of the memorial. Even in its unfinished state this face had developed a personal expression, a point of view. This had never been his intention. (337)

Klara's narrative of articulation is reminiscent of Jay Winter's assertion that war memorials are "sites of symbolic exchange" whose meanings are "highly personal." He continues to explain that monuments use, "collective expression, in stones and ceremony, to help individual people [...] to accept the brutal facts of death in war" (94). Furthermore, Klara's personal expression of mourning interferes with Allward's national narrative that draws on the template of generational succession, whereby the torchbearer will symbolically bequeath the memory of Vimy to future generations. The two modes of discourse are deployed for different ideological purposes, and the power struggle between Allward and Klara is thus a matter of representation and of voice: Who gets to tell the national story? Whose interests does the national story serve?

Although Allward's character is more complex than an embodiment of official history (he does recognize Klara's talent and allows her to complete her alternative narrative), he later accuses Klara of "suffering from an excess of originality" (346), as though she were impaired by her individuality. In contrast, the new possibilities of meaning that are represented by Klara's alternative narrative of articulation suggest that memory is a malleable process subject to change and variation. And yet, it is the instability of memory that requires continual reassessment in order to secure its relevance and transmission to later generations. Robert Zacharias's compelling analysis of Vimy emphasizes the positive potential of revisionist narratives. He argues:

> When Joseph Boyden's *Three Day Road* places Cree sharpshooters as fighters at Vimy Ridge, or Jane Urquhart's *The Stone Carvers* inserts a same-sex love story into the construction of the Vimy Ridge Monument, we ought to recognize that, in returning to Vimy, these authors are returning to the mythological birthplace of Canada to insert difference – Aboriginal, queer – into the very heart of the national narrative. (128)

The impetus of revisionist history is therefore political; it questions how we make meaning of past events and whose memory is being represented in the various versions available in the present. Moreover, the discourses and conventions deployed to convey different versions of memory are themselves invested in power struggles.

3 "Always Remember the Bones": Form and Structure

In addition to de-centering the master narrative of Vimy through counter-histories and marginal characters, Urquhart inserts difference through the form of the novel itself and its narrative structure; language and narrative are thus implicit in the struggle of voice in the novel. In Margaret Atwood's novel *The Robber Bride* (1993), Tony, a professor of history at the University of Toronto who specializes in the study of war, delivers a lecture to her students that identifies pertinent historiographical issues:

> Where to start is the problem, because nothing begins when it begins and nothing's over when it's over [...]. History is a construct [...]. Any point of entry is possible and all choices are arbitrary. Still, there are definitive moments, moments we use as references, because they break our sense of continuity, they change the direction of time. We can look at these events and we can say that after them things were never the same again. They provide beginnings for us, and endings too. (4)

Tony's assertion that history is a construct is reminiscent of White's discussion of the literary nature of historical narrative. White reminds us that "no given set of events attested by the historical record constitutes a story manifestly finished and complete" (43). In other words, not only is the structure of story inevitably imposed on the chronicling of historical events, but objectivity is made impossible by this narrative necessity.

With this in mind, formal aspects of *The Stone Carvers* demonstrate the arbitrary nature of historical points of entry by locating the narrative of Vimy within other historical moments. This repositioning, narrated by the third person omniscient voice of history, supplements the master narrative of Vimy with alternative stories of origin. The narrative of the obsessive sculptor Walter Allward and the construction of his monument at Vimy is de-centered to incorporate three other stories: the story of an early settlement village in southern Ontario during the mid-late nineteenth century; the story of the descendants of those settlers also living in the village – now named Shoneval – during the twentieth century; and that of the eccentric, castle-building patron of the arts, King Ludwig II. of Bavaria. The trans-generational stories are woven together by Klara Becker, thereby establishing a woman as the nexus of the otherwise male-dominated narratives. The four plot lines are not told in isolation; rather, they interact with one another, effectively democratizing the narrative and diminishing any sense of hierarchy that may be conveyed by a more traditional linear narrative form. The oscillation between past and present, Europe and Canada therefore equalizes the historical significance that each story performs in the novel's construction of Canada's identity. Additionally, Andreas Huyssen argues that a resistance to chronological narrative is a common characteristic of post-memory culture; it is a "welcome critique of compromised teleological notions of history rather than being simply anti-historical, relativistic, or subjective" (6). To this end, interruption of the traditional form and trajectory of linear narrative in *The Stone Carvers* is a self-reflexive representation of history-as-construct.

Equally important, the novel's four interacting stories are evocative of White's reduction of narrative to generic plot structures. Urquhart plays with this reductive formula in order to make connections that redistribute the relations of power amongst the stories. In their most minimal form, each story in *The Stone Carvers* is a quest narrative about a man whose obsession ultimately leads to his downfall: Father Gstir is obsessed with obtaining a bell for his church and then, once obtained, he is unable to bear the "profound responsibility of it" (146); the extravagant palaces that King Ludwig designs become the site of his containment and his death, under mysterious circumstances, in the nearby Starnberger See; Eamon's Icarus-like obsession with airplanes leads to his enrollment in the war and his untimely death; Allward's obsession with stone and perfection prolongs the completion of the monument and earns him a negative reputation that prevents any future commissions. The combination of international, national, local, and personal narratives supports White's observation "that historical narratives are not only models of past events and processes, but also metaphorical statements which suggest a relation of similitude between such events and processes and the story types that we conventionally use to endow the events of our lives with culturally sanctioned meanings" (51). Thus, when the "heavy red cloth" used by Klara's grandmother for the Corpus Christi procession (24) later appears when Klara orders "heavy red cloth" for Eamon's coat (113), or the ropes that hang from the scaffolding at the Vimy monument during its construction rub together and remind Allward of "the sound of two pines scraping against each other in a wind-filled Canadian forest" (2), Urquhart is alluding to this relation of similitude between the events and processes of Canadian history over time and space and the role of artistic representation (whether it be modest constructions or extravagant structures) in commemorating these events. Further, the fact that the same modes of representation are available to both personal and state-centered narratives undermines the hegemonic privilege of the Vimy master narrative.

In addition, the narrative of Shoneval provides an alternative story-of-origin for Canada that predates the master narrative promoted by official historians that Canada's originating moment transpired at Vimy Ridge. Gordon Bölling observes that, interestingly, Father Gstir arrives in Canada in 1867, which is the same year as the beginnings of Confederation (cf. 301). Gstir's arrival therefore parallels another unifying master narrative of national origin. However, rather than substituting Confederation for Vimy, the story of the predominately German settlement in Ontario is infused with national difference. Most importantly, the genealogical history of the citizens of Shoneval contradicts the claim made by the master narrative that Canadians joined the First World War as a patriotic gesture to their mother country. In contrast, Urquhart reveals that European immigration to Canada was largely motivated by a desire to avoid the wars in Europe. As a result, "nobody [in Shoneval] wanted to enlist because they had spent the Sunday afternoons of their childhoods listening to grandparents count their blessings – the most important of which was freedom from armed conflict" (136). Only two men (boys, really) from Shoneval enlist in the war, and the circumstances under which they sign up – poverty and homelessness in the case of Tilman, youthful hubris in that of Eamon – contradict the national narrative of loyalty to Britain. In fact, none of the main characters in the novel have familial ties to Britain; Britain is barely mentioned, aside from a critique of the mother-country's insatiable hunger for Canadian lumber, which, as Neta Gordon provocatively argues, operates as a metaphor for the British recruitment of Canadian soldiers and the ensuing annihilation of a generation of Canadian men (cf. 66). Furthermore, the German ancestry of Tilman and other settlers of Shoneval complicates the 'us' *versus* 'them' and 'victim' *versus* 'perpetrator' binaries at the very heart of master narratives of war. Since the characters in the novel are outside of the margins of British culture, the master narrative promoted by official historians such as Jack Granatstein and Desmond Morton that Canadians went to war because of Britain (cf. 177) loses its consolidating force.

Not only is the depiction of Vimy as an originary event challenged by *The Stone Carvers* through the incorporation of other stories of origin, but the two beginnings to the novel also reveal the ambivalence of historical points of entry. The opening scene that precedes the first chapter functions as an untitled prologue and is spoken by a third person narrator in the objective and distanced voice of official history. It begins: "In June of 1934, two men stand talking in the shadow of the great unfinished monument" (1). Although it begins the novel, the sentence resists the concept of a beginning since it makes the story begin *in medias res*, during the construction of the monument in the inter-war period. Further, while the reader can infer that the two men are Allward and his assistant, their identities are not disclosed in the opening scene. The narrative voice thus reveals the limitations to official representations of history, which, by attempting to maintain the illusion of objectivity, can render individual identities into abstraction.

Conversely, a narrative shift occurs in the chapter following the untitled prologue. Whereas the introductory scene resembles a panoramic point of view because it is distanced and generalized (it offers no insight into the characters' thoughts or emotions), the narrative voice deployed in the first chapter develops a sense of intimacy and proximity when it is focalized through Father Gstir and Klara Becker. Additionally, the use of free indirect discourse allows for a proliferation of points of view – yet another way in which Urquhart democratizes the narrative.[4] The first chapter begins with an archetypal narrative opening in the voice of oral history: "There was a story, a true, if slightly embellished story, about how the Ontario village was given its name ..." (5). The juxtaposition of the narrative voices of official history and oral history implies a connection between the discourse of myth and the mythologizing objectives of official history and calls attention to the narrative necessity of historical representation.

The remainder of the novel is narrated in the informal voice of the first chapter until the final paragraph, when the distanced voice of official history returns. In the final paragraph, the narrator directly implicates the reader in the story by a brief shift to second person reference: "If *you* stand in certain parts of the valley *you* can see them [Allward's monument, Father Gstir's church, King Ludwig's castles] shine" (390, emphasis added). In addition to the strategic collapsing of spatial and temporal boundaries in this closing remark – again drawing on the similitude of historical experience and its representation – the use of the second person extends the responsibility of memory to the present-day reader. The implications of the sentence, namely that different positions allow for different vantage points, encourage readers to be self-reflexive about the values implied through their own positions and points of view when they engage in the act of bearing witness.

4 Conclusion: Restoration

If, as I have been arguing, the function of revisionist narratives is to reconsider the place and meaning of history in contemporary post-memory culture, then Jane Urquhart's novel *The Stone Carvers* is one of the many recent novels in Canada to mark the emergence of a critical turn in contemporary thinking about the First World War. The act of storytelling that begins this essay – Klara telling the nuns the story of Shoneval's origin – demonstrates the performative aspect of

---

[4] According to Gérard Genette, focalized narrative is "told by a narrator who is not one of the characters but who adopts the point of view of one" (168). He defines free indirect discourse as when "the narrator takes on the speech of the character or, if one prefers, the character speaks through the voice of the narrator, and the two instances are then *merged*; in immediate speech, the narrator is obliterated and the character *substitutes* for him" (174, emphasis in original).

storytelling. The women believe that the story-of-origin connects them to the village's inception, and they "[cling] to the story, as if by telling the tale they became witnesses, perhaps even participants in the awkward fabrication of matter" (6). Through this act of reconstruction, both teller and audience participate in their local history by bearing witness to the past and, in doing so, continue the perpetuation of its shared memory. In contrast, the inability of both the viewers in the novel and of Canadian citizens in the present to remember the meaning of the allegorical figures that collectively form the Vimy monument suggests a failure of the monument to reflect the changing recognizable frameworks of an increasingly secular post-war society.

Vimy does, however, continue to maintain its hold on the Canadian consciousness. In 2007, a rededication ceremony (preceded by years of restoration) took place on the 90th anniversary of the monument's unveiling. The restoration and subsequent rededication raises questions as to whether these undertakings were an attempt on behalf of the Canadian government to reassert the legitimacy of the master narrative of Vimy Ridge, or whether it demonstrates the succession of the memory of Vimy being 're-membered' for a contemporary post-memory audience. Urquhart's novel – which was published prior to the anniversary – also acknowledges the uncertainty of Vimy's place in a post-memory culture but does not provide any easy solutions or answers. Instead, *The Stone Carvers* brings together the paradigms of personal and public memory in order to expose their similarities and, as a result, undermine the hegemony of the master narrative of Vimy Ridge. The success of the local transmission of Shoneval's history through the act of storytelling suggests that personal and/or local narratives of articulation are necessary supplements to national narratives.

If the narratives of articulation of past wars continue to operate as frames through which we comprehend later conflicts, then there is a reciprocal relationship between the past and the present that needs to be cultivated for future generations. The rededication of the Vimy monument and the proliferation of recent Canadian literature that examines the First World War suggest that Canadians *are* interested in preserving their past at both the state and local levels, but there is no consensus as to whose voices and interpretations warrant representation. All things considered then, *The Stone Carvers* suggests that plurality is perhaps the most viable framework for representing Vimy at this present juncture.

References

Ashplant, T. G., Graham Dawson and Michael Roper, eds. *The Politics of War Memory and Commemoration*. London and New York: Routledge, 2000.
Atwood, Margaret. *The Robber Bride*. Toronto: McClelland & Stewart, 1993.
Berton, Pierre. *Vimy*. Toronto: Anchor Canada, 1986.
Bölling, Gordon. "Acts of (Re-)Construction: Traces of Germany in Jane Urquhart's Novel *The Stone Carvers*." *Refractions of Germany in Canadian Literature and Culture*. Eds. Heinz Antor et al. Berlin and New York: Walter de Gruyter, 2003. 295–317.
Carr, Graham. "War, History, and the Education of (Canadian) Memory." *Contested Pasts: The Politics of Memory*. Eds. Katharina Hodgkin and Susannah Radstone. London and New York: Routledge, 2003. 57–78.
Danto, Arthur. *Wake of Art: Criticism, Philosophy, and the Ends of Taste*. New York: Routledge, 1998.
Derrida, Jacques. *Of Grammatology*. Trans. Gayatri Spivak. Baltimore and London: Johns Hopkins University Press, 1974.
Genette, Gérard. *Narrative Discourse*. Trans. Jane E. Lewin. Ithaca, New York: Cornell University Press, 1980.
Gordon, Neta. "The Artist and the Witness: Jane Urquhart's *The Underpainter* and *The Stone Carvers*." *Studies in Canadian Literature* 28. 8 (2003): 59–73.
Granatstein, J. L., and Desmond Morton. *Canada and the Two World Wars*. Toronto: Key Porter, 2003.
Hirsch, Marianne. "The Generation of Postmemory." *Poetics Today* 29. 1 (2008): 103–128.
Hutcheon, Linda. *The Canadian Postmodern: A Study of Contemporary English-Canadian Fiction*. Toronto, New York and Oxford: Oxford University Press, 1988.
Hutcheon, Linda. *A Poetics of Postmodernism: History, Theory, Fiction*. New York and London: Routledge, 1988.
Huyssen, Andreas. *Twilight Memories: Marking Time in a Culture of Amnesia*. New York: Routledge, 1995.
Jameson, Fredric. "Foreword." Jean-François Lyotard. *The Postmodern Condition*. vii–xxi.
Lyotard, Jean-François. *The Postmodern Condition: A Report on Knowledge*. Trans. Geoff Bennington and Brian Massumi. Minneapolis: University of Minnesota Press, 1984.
Sherman, Daniel. *The Construction of Memory in Interwar France*. Chicago: University of Chicago Press, 1999.
Thompson, Dawn. *Writing a Politics of Perception: Memory, Holography, and Women Writers in Canada*. Toronto: University of Toronto Press, 2000.
Urquhart, Jane. *The Stone Carvers*. Toronto: McClelland & Stewart, 2001.
Urquhart, Jane. "Our Lost and Found Memories of Vimy Ridge." *Globe and Mail* [Toronto], 8 April 2012: A6.
Valpy, Michael. "Vimy Ridge: The Making of a Myth." *Globe and Mail* [Toronto], 7 April 2007: F4.
Vance, Jonathan. *Death So Noble: Memory, Meaning, and the First World War*. Vancouver: UBC Press, 1997.
White, Hayden. "The Historical Text as Literary Artifact." *The Writing of History: Literary Form and Historical Understanding*. Eds. Robert H. Canary and Henry Kozicki. Madison, Wisconsin: University of Wisconsin Press, 1978. 41–62.

Winter, Jay. *Sites of Memory, Sites of Mourning: The Great War in European Cultural History*. Cambridge and New York: Cambridge University Press, 1998.

Wyile, Herb. *Speaking in the Past Tense: Canadian Novelists on Writing Historical Fiction*. Waterloo, Ontario: Wilfrid Laurier University Press, 2007.

Young, James. *The Texture of Memory: Holocaust Memorials and Meaning*. New Haven: Yale University Press, 1993.

Zacharias, Robert. "'Some Great Crisis': Vimy as Original Violence." *Shifting the Ground of Canadian Literary Studies*. Eds. Smaro Kamboureli and Robert Zacharias. Waterloo, Ontario: Wilfrid Laurier University Press, 2012. 109–128.

Brigitte Johanna Glaser
Women and World War I: 'Postcolonial' Imaginative Rewritings of the Great War

During the last few decades, a time when globalisation and transnational exchange have flourished but have also evoked a rethinking of the idea of the nation, a surge in the imaginative preoccupation with the past has been noticeable in postcolonial writing. The fact that this interest in history and in narrating historical events has produced a striking number of texts dealing with the First World War may in part be owing to the approaching centenary of the war's outbreak. It may also be seen, however, as a late postcolonial response to an especially devastating experience which has haunted the involved countries for a long time and which has been dwelt on extensively in Canada and New Zealand or which, in the case of Australia, had led to decades of silencing.[1] In fact, these countries' concerns may be read as attempts to imaginatively reconstruct history from an ex-centric position, and therefore as a belated repositioning of the authors with regard to their countries' past. Stuart Hall has commented on the importance of highlighting the particular cultural inflections of (fictional) representations of history: "We all write and speak from a particular place and time, from a history and a culture which is specific. What we say is always in context, *positional*" (qtd. in Walder 13). It does, therefore, not come as a surprise that postcolonial authors pay attention to aspects that are specific to their countries,[2] signalling thereby their concern with what had previously been silenced,[3] and that they seem to be aware of the fact that for some of their countries the experience of the Great War retrospectively emerged as a transitional moment which intensified the growing distance from the motherland.[4]

World War I fiction had for a long time been dominated by descriptions of soldiers' involvement in war action, hence men's experiences of the conflict, while the place of women in that war was of limited interest. Especially women in the colonies were, owing to their geographical location and their gender, in a posi-

---

[1] The Australian scholar Richard Nile has been researching this topic and is currently preparing a monograph on "Recovering Australia's Lost Literatures of the First World War."
[2] Among the aspects they now address from a postcolonial perspective are their respective indigenous populations, the colonial social conditioning of their ancestors, or the gendered power relations that were in place in their countries.
[3] A recent novel addressing the involvement of First Nations members in the First World War is Joseph Boyden's *Three Day Road* (2005).
[4] Interestingly, Australia, Canada and New Zealand all gained complete sovereignty only in 1931 through the Statute of Westminster.

tion seemingly twice removed from the centre of the action, but they were nevertheless affected by or even drawn into the war that was fought across the ocean. Almost one hundred years later, novelists from Anglophone countries, most of them former settler colonies, are imaginatively reconstructing the situations women were in during and shortly after the war years. Among the fictions exploring women's experiences as nurses or as individuals coping with life on the home front are two Canadian novels, Frances Itani's *Deafening* (2003) and Jane Urquhart's *The Stone Carvers* (2001), two Australian novels, Chris Womersley's *Bereft* (2010) and Thomas Keneally's *The Daughters of Mars* (2012), as well as *Mansfield: A Novel* (2004) by the New Zealand author C. K. Stead. Doris Lessing's *Alfred and Emily* (2008), a hybrid text by a British writer born in Persia and growing up in Rhodesia, combines fictional, factual and autobiographical elements and shares the preoccupation with the colonial past. What these texts share is their authors' concern with the marginal colonial position of their countries during the time of the Great War and their interest in the similarly restricted agency of female participants in war activities. Furthermore, they explore the hitherto silenced and marginalised involvement of women in the war against the background of a 'nostalgic' reassessment of the colonial history of their countries, the objectives being to recover and redeem their respective country's contributions to the war, to offer a new perspective on the past, and to reposition themselves with regard to the centre-margin dichotomy.

1 Postcolonial Nostalgia and Women's Experiences

The notion of "postcolonial nostalgia" has been theorised by Dennis Walder in connection with fictional reconstructions of the past as a means of reassuring oneself of one's position in the present. Referring to E. J. Hobsbawm's study on *The Age of Empire*, which draws attention to the "twilight zone between history and memory; between the past as a generalized record [...] and the past as remembered part of, or background to, one's own life" (qtd. in Walder 2), Walder sees literary texts as tools that allow writers to reassess history: "situating ourselves in time and space involves us in constructing a thread of meaning that enables us to know, or think we know, who and what we are in the present" (6). This reassessment of history through historical fiction not only constitutes a way of dealing with the problem of colonial silencing or misrepresentation, since it creates perspectives and voices that run counter to the official histories produced by those in power, but it also allows for a confident self-positioning within a community of equally affected countries.

Furthermore, Walder associates nostalgia with creativity. Doing so, he draws on Svetlana Boym who, in her study *The Future of Nostalgia*, distinguishes between two extremes of nostalgia. While "restorative" nostalgia "does not think of itself as nostalgia, but rather as truth and tradition" (Boym xviii) and tries to restore the past, considering it "the lost home, or homeland" (Walder 11), "reflective" nostalgia, so Boym, "dwells on the ambivalences of human longing and belonging and does not shy away from the contradictions of modernity" (xviii). Here the individuals engaged in it "realise the partial, fragmentary nature of history or histories, and linger on ruins and loss" (Walder 11). Influenced by Boym's notion of "reflective" nostalgia, Walder claims that occasionally postcolonial nostalgias also reveal:

> a positive side, which admits the past into the present in a fragmentary, nuanced, and elusive way, allowing a potential for self-reflexivity or irony appropriate for former colonial and diasporic subjects trying to understand the networks of power relations within which they are caught in the modern world. (16)

Regarding nostalgia not so much in terms of sentimental feelings for things gone or as a "source of individual self-indulgence" (3), Walder rather emphasises "its potential as a source of understanding and creativity" by pointing out that "nostalgia often involves a projected future," since it is concerned with "processes of communal and individual experience that constitute the present and, by implication the future" and thereby "reveals a process that reconnects the individual to his or her past, and to a community" (18). Nostalgia, so he claims, draws attention to the gap between past and present and provokes an imaginative engagement with the past: "Exploring nostalgia can and should open up a negotiation between the present and the past, leading to a fuller understanding of the past and how it has shaped the present, for good and bad, and how it has shaped the self in connection with others, a task that may bring pain as well as pleasure" (9). Placing themselves in a long line of writers who have taken up the Great War in their fiction, the authors of the selected novels indicate that the painful past has not yet been dealt with adequately and that there are still aspects and details that need to be addressed, such as the role of women in this conflict. At the same time, they draw attention to national specifics of war experiences and thus move their countries to the centre.

As the studies of Sarah Glassford and Amy Shaw, Susan R. Grayzel, Anne Powell, Angela K. Smith, Gill Thomas, and Janet S. K. Watson comprehensively show, women were involved and affected by the First World War in a variety of ways: the war was most closely experienced by nurses; it was fought and endured on the home front by women involved in politics, by mothers, sisters and wives worrying about the young men who had left for the battlefields across the sea, and by loved ones who had to deal with the injured and traumatised who returned; it was written about by women who imaginatively tried to come to terms with its fallout; and it was remembered by way of a memorial culture that has been maintained until today. As the selected texts to be explored show, Australian, British, Canadian, and New Zealand authors have chosen to depict women in a variety of situations, always emphasising the importance of their contributions and the significance of their suffering and thus constructing the notion of a female heroism.

2 Being Close to the Action: Nurses in the First World War

Only a very few authors have chosen to associate their female protagonists with the immediate war action, since women and war have traditionally been situated on opposite sides and their places were seen on the home front rather than the trenches. The closest women were able to get to the actual war was through their work as nurses. As Grayzel points out in her study, approximately 650 New Zealand and some 2500 Australian nurses served in the First World War (40). Although initially not admitted into military service and therefore forced to work for other organisations or to organise themselves, they were eventually welcomed, supposedly because of "their allegedly natural capacities for caring and nurturing" (Grayzel 37). The motivations for women to contribute to the war varied, the most frequent being a sense of duty and the wish to serve one's country, the desire to remain connected to loved ones serving overseas, and the wish to have an adventure. When it became obvious that there was a great need for nurses, active recruitment especially among the educated, middle and upper classes set in, which meant that some of the hired women were expected to perform previously unthinkable tasks. However, even trained nurses were confronted with injuries and illnesses they had never seen before and, when placed on hospital ships or in casualty clearing stations, were subjected to unimaginable working conditions, since they were often ill equipped and understaffed.

With his novel *The Daughters of Mars*, Thomas Keneally presents a narrative in which the experiences of World War I nurses are followed closely and thus lays the ground for a reassessment of women's contributions in terms of a heroism that is now exerted by the other sex.[5] Keneally describes the experiences and fates of two sisters, Sally and Naomi Durance, who leave their rural home in the Macleay Valley of New South Wales behind in order to work first on the Red Cross hospital ship *Archimedes* stationed in the Dardanelles before they are sent on to France to serve in different places along the Western Front. Keneally's novel is dedicated to "the two nurses, Judith and Jane," by which he refers to his wife and his sister-in-law, and it is based on extensive historical research, one of his main sources notably being "the diaries kept by the Australian nurse Sister Elsie Tranter" (Caterson).

What is remarkable about *The Daughters of Mars* is the ex-centric perspective the author brings to bear in his text when he places the emphasis on characters who have been twice removed from the action by way of gender and geography, and when he is concerned less with the war action than the immediate aftermath, that is, "the bloody result and the people who are responsible for cleaning it up" (Limprecht). In Keneally's novel the war is described from the periphery in more than one way: it is witnessed on the hospital ship or the casualty clearing station several kilometres away from Gallipoli or the places of action along the Somme respectively; it is focalised through a point of view dominated by rural Australian inexperience; and it is passed in review by an author positioned almost a century after the events occurred. This typically postcolonial perspective, which takes into account previously marginalised positions, has also been emphasised in various reviews of the book. While Caterson draws attention to the particularity of the Australian experience when he comments on the two sisters' "moving from the margins of history to the very centre, self-consciously trying to leave behind what they consider their 'bush clumsiness,'" Walton highlights the author's interest in representing the war from a new and hitherto untried angle: "Of course, Keneally has long been interested in how Australians, tucked away blamelessly at the bottom of the world, have often found themselves at the dark centre of European history. And of course too, seeing it through the entirely unprepared eyes of these young women is one of the ways in which he restores the war's essential 'strangeness.'"

Keneally's novel merges public and private history, taking two women of obscure origins to exotic, fascinating and dangerous places of the Old World and thus offering them a testing ground for their courage and moral constitution. Prompted to volunteer for active service in the army for a variety of reasons, among them a sense of guilt and the need for expiation after the death of their

---

5 Because of its similarity in plot development and the details presented, the novel *Lives We Leave Behind* (2012) by New Zealand writer Maxine Alterio will not be considered.

mother[6] as well as the wish to escape boredom and experience adventures, the two trained nurses first embark on a journey to Egypt, the Dardanelles and the island of Lemnos before they take up positions in Northern France. They quickly learn to work in extreme circumstances: they are forced to treat venereal diseases among soldiers; they deal with shrapnel wounds they could never have imagined and for the treatment of which they lack proper tools and medication; they are subjected to discrimination and exploitation; and they finally witness the effects of mustard gas and air raids. Keneally highlights friendship and solidarity among the nurses and depicts the young women in terms of the personal relationships they establish and cultivate. Visiting museums, churches and cafés in Rouen, Boulogne, Paris and London, they furthermore "experience the allure of the Old World" (Riemer), by which their lives "are made more exciting and interesting, though at the same time more complicated and fraught" (Caterson). Above all, they encounter the randomness of death and learn about the arbitrariness of life, not only through the sheer number of critically wounded young men who pass through their hands but also through their own exposure to the Spanish influenza towards the end of the war.

Apart from presenting specific historical details relating to Australian soldiers such as the referendum-based refusal to introduce conscription or the option of conscientious objection, *The Daughters of Mars* above all offers readers a glimpse of the opportunities the First World War held out for women as well as the historical disadvantages it prolonged. As the novel succinctly shows through the large cast of female characters, nurses allowed to go on active service were carefully selected and, if they were sent home (as is the case with Naomi Durance and Matron Mitchie), were sometimes given a second chance in one of the voluntary hospitals. Set up through private funding, these hospitals showed greater flexibility concerning their staff, hiring also nurses who did not have a formal training and occasionally even employing female doctors (Keneally presents such a rare example in the case of Airdrie, a young Scottish doctor who is employed by Lady Tarlton in her Australian Voluntary Hospital at Chateau Baincthun). Keneally furthermore renders correctly the particular restrictions nurses faced during the First World War. As pointed out by Grayzel, relationships among soldiers and their nurses were seen as a problem, to the extent that nurses were made honorary 'officers' in order to prevent their fraternisation with other ranks (41; see also Holmes). Keneally's example for such a relationship is the connection of Nurse Nettice and Lieutenant Byers, which leads to her removal to a 'rest compound' in order to put a distance between them. Later she is sent back to Australia together

---

6 They are haunted by the idea that the death of their mortally ill mother has been caused by the pain-killing medication they gave her.

with Byers. In addition, nurses were considered "to be 'innocent' and in need of protection" (Grayzel 41), and yet there were also fears and suspicions concerning their sexuality (cf. Grayzel, 62–78). This ambivalent attitude towards women is depicted by Keneally in the case of Nurse Freud, who is raped by a young Australian soldier on the island of Lemnos. Although she reports the violation and identifies the perpetrator, he is not put on trial. Instead, it is the nurse who experiences severe recriminations.

Undoubtedly, the Australians played a central role in the final victory at the Western Front. Keneally acknowledges these contributions, not only through his references to military successes achieved by the battalions under the command of General Monash[7] but also through his many examples of individual heroism. It is, however, striking that throughout the novel he particularly emphasises women's heroism, most explicitly in the nurses' behaviour during the sinking of the torpedoed *Archimedes*. In this traumatic event they are shown to display great courage and tenacity, unlike the similarly afflicted men:

> Sally leaned her forehead against the raft's black rubber flank while Naomi began to lift Nettice, who was vulnerable for lack of a preserver. Nettice was light to lift and of surprising agility. The sergeant did not help but not out of ill-will. After so much presence and command he had gone suddenly silent. The high intoxication of his reaching the raft waned in him. He lost his powers of command as awful surprise and cold entered him. (Keneally 145)

Several of the nurses are depicted as standing out for their display of courage and calmness in the face of death, to such an extent that Naomi Durance wonders about the believability of their experiences: "They'll never be able to print the story of *Archimedes* because we weren't hysterical enough" (165). Naomi's words clearly imply that gender-specific conduct loses its importance in extreme situations created by the war. Instead, these situations give rise to unexpected behaviour and dispositions such as female heroism and the loss of courage in men. By highlighting this crossing of supposed boundaries, Keneally at the same time undermines conventional constructions of Australian national identity that have favoured masculinity and excluded women (cf. Langer 144–149).

With his ambivalent ending, which leaves open the question of which of the two sisters survived the war, Keneally emphasises once more that, despite their

---

7 Sir John Monash is well remembered as a scholar, engineer and soldier. He joined the army at age 19 and quickly rose through the ranks, making use of his knowledge in engineering, transport, supply and intelligence. In 1914 he took part in the fighting at Gallipoli and was the only Australian brigade commander to survive unharmed. By 1918 he led the entire Australian Corps and was subsequently honoured for his many contributions to Australia's military achievements.

heroic conduct, the nurses were as much afflicted by the arbitrariness of historical events as the soldiers were. By placing them and their work at the centre of his narrative (in part through focalisation), he adds a new perspective from which contemporary readers may view the First World War and thus contributes to the continuing revaluation of Australia's involvement in the events overseas.

3 Women on the Home Front

Quite contrary to being placed close to the action, most women in the colonies remained at home during the First World War, waiting for news from or about their loved ones, and coping with their lives which were dominated by fears, the experience of personal loss and, in some cases, the need to care for the injured and the traumatised. While in the early stages of the war their opinions and sentiments tended to be influenced by a government-driven propaganda meant to evoke enthusiasm for the war efforts (Grayzel 9–22), disillusionment and despair subsequently shaped their views. In Frances Itani's *Deafening* and Chris Womersley's *Bereft* the lives of women on the Canadian and Australian home fronts respectively are imaginatively rendered in differing ways. The concerns that both texts share, however, are questions regarding women's treatment by men and the extent of women's suffering.

Itani's *Deafening* accompanies a young couple, Grania O'Neill and Jim Lloyd, during the war years. While Jim joins the Canadian Army Medical Corps' field ambulance and serves at an Advanced Dressing Station in France. Grania remains at home. Although she is a trained nurse, she is not wanted overseas; hearing-impaired and hence in need of help, she moves back into her parents' home while her husband is away in Europe. Itani alternates perspectives and thus juxtaposes both the diametrically opposed lives the two characters lead in Canada and France and the assumptions they have about each other's experiences. She thus highlights the huge gap that is between them as well as the limited knowledge women are left with, not only because of censored postcards and letters, but also because of men's reservations about describing what they have been exposed to. Women like Grania are shown to live in relatively protected surroundings. Their quiet and remarkably peaceful existence is shattered only when there are casualty reports or when the wounded and the traumatised are brought home. At that point, however, the aftermath of the war hits these women with full force, since they are confronted with men who need full-time care, given the seriousness of their injuries, who are unable to communicate about their experiences, and who occasionally turn violent out of a need to vent their anger. Thus for women at home, so Itani seems to suggest, the struggles and heroic efforts only begin when the fighting has ceased and when they have to assume the role of caregivers.

By contrast, the Australian author Chris Womersley presents a dark vision of women on the home front. His novel *Bereft* deals with the impact the war has on women who have been left behind without protection. At the centre is the 26-year-old Quinn Walker, who in 1919 returns from Europe to his native rural New South Wales, suffering from shell shock and a severely damaged face. Ten years earlier he had left his home after the violent death of his 12-year-old sister, Sarah Walker, since he had mistakenly been regarded as her rapist and murderer. Quinn, a witness to the crime, knows the perpetrators but, despite the dangers involved for him, returns home because he wishes to be close to his family. He arrives just in time to witness the slow death of his mother from the Spanish influenza.

The gothic narrative features a second central person, the 12-year-old Sadie Fox, a neglected orphan who is struggling to survive in an environment that is marked by both the harshness of the bush and the vicissitudes of living in a strongly patriarchal society. Sadie's toughness and ability to prevail over adverse circumstances mirror, as Quinn quickly realises, the defiance, intelligence and occasional bossiness of his sister Sarah, and thus trigger in him an interest in and brotherly feelings for her.

Sadie Fox is depicted as a victim of the events at the time: she is left behind when her brother Thomas joins the Australian war efforts across the ocean, never to return home, and when her mother succumbs to the flu. The novel addresses the problems of unprotected women during and after the Great War. It indicates that women were exposed to dangers because men had left their families, because men were incited to act violently (even within their families), and because men were injured and weakened as a result of the war. Being 'bereft' of a secure and supportive family environment, Sadie is shown to have descended to an animal level and to act upon her instincts in order to survive. Deprived of the possibility of personal development through a loving upbringing and an education, she has no alternative but to live in a man's world (the extreme sides of which are alluded to by Womersley in the suspicious dealings and mutual dependence of the rapist Robert Dalton and his companion Gracie, the tracker).

His concern for Sadie offers Quinn the chance to redeem himself, especially when in a strange repetition of the events that had occurred a decade earlier a 12-year-old girl is once again subjected to male violence (by the same man, his uncle Dalton). Quinn, who, from the perspective of his 'mates' Dalton and Gracie, appears effeminate, is not taken seriously and is confronted in an aggressive way. He fails to save the girl from rape but subsequently becomes the "angel of death" (Womersley 221) she had longed for and wields out his revenge, while Sadie heroically tries to put her violation behind her. The future, the novel suggests, is that of two mentally scarred individuals who will have to move forward carrying the burdens of their traumatic pasts.

Both Itani and Womersley end their narratives on a sombre note, indicating thereby that the consequences of the war will have to be dealt with for a long time to come. None of them idealises the situations women at home were left in but both rather focus on different kinds of hardship these women were faced with, thus drawing attention to the ways in which women courageously dealt with the aftermath of the First World War even in faraway places.

4 The Impact of War on the Imagination

While the number of women who were close to combat was indeed very small, most of them were aware of living in a changed world because of the war. As the autobiographical accounts of women writers during and after the war years as well as the fictional renditions of the Great War by female novelists, especially in British modernist writing, indicate,[8] the conflict's aftermath had impressed itself on people's minds and needed to be dealt with. The psychological impact of the First World War on artists and subsequently on the directions their artistic creations would take, is addressed also in contemporary fiction, where it is either linked with the postcolonial self-positioning of the respective artists (C. K. Stead and Jane Urquhart) or where it is evoked in order to explain an artist's semi-autobiographical approach to fiction (Doris Lessing).

In an imaginative recreation of five crucial European years (1915–1919) in the life of the New Zealand expatriate writer Katherine Mansfield, C. K. Stead pursues the question of how artists were affected by the First World War. While undoubtedly placing his emphasis on the female writer, Stead presents, through changing focalisation (as is also indicated in the chapter titles), a variety of perspectives on both the war and the changing relationships among the historical figures he has recourse to. Among the various forms of response to the war are on the one hand those of active participation or reluctant participation, and on the other hand those of critical distance and reservation. While the novel abounds with references to Siegfried Sassoon as one of the best known poets who joined the action and wrote about it, the figures representing involvement Stead has chosen

---

[8] See for example the memoir *Testament of Youth* (1933) by Vera Brittain, the pseudo-autobiography *Not So Quiet ... Stepdaughters of War* (1930) by Evadne Price, the autobiographical novel *We That Were Young* (1932) by Irene Rathbone, as well as numerous novels and short stories by May Sinclair, Rose Macaulay, Rebecca West, Enid Bagnold, Katherine Mansfield and Virginia Woolf (cf. Smith 105–180; Watson 240–261).

are Leslie Beauchamp, Mansfield's promising young brother, who dies shortly after arriving at the front, and Fred Goodyear, a young writer deeply in love with Mansfield, who succumbs to death some time after having been seriously injured. John Middleton Murry, Mansfield's long-time partner and subsequent husband, is in turn depicted as only reluctantly joining the war efforts: considered unfit for action, he enters the War Office in 1916, probably under the (partially self-imposed) pressure exerted on him. In contrast to these pro-war attitudes, Stead also depicts the critical stances widespread in various artists' enclaves, among them the Lawrences and larger Bloomsbury (the representative positions of the latter being offered through the views of T. S. Eliot and Bertrand Russell). Caught among these diverse leanings is Katherine Mansfield.

The evaluation Stead gives of the impact the war has on Mansfield clearly indicates a redirection of her art. The young woman who is twice removed from the action through both her colonial background and her gender is portrayed as repeatedly seeking contact with those who are engaged in the war, evidently because she wishes to comprehend what she perceives of as a mystery:

> What was wrong with her? There was no answer; or there were many answers. There was the war for example. Did that explain it? She looked up at the swaying compartment and of course there were uniforms, two of them, two moustaches, two caps, two long coats – officers carrying with them the mysterious knowledge of what it was like, *really* like, "at the Front". [...] For a moment she amused herself, first with the idea of asking them ("Excuse me, gentlemen, but do tell me, *What is it like at the Front*?") and then with the fantasy that "*at the Front*" was a fiction, nothing more than a secret society, a club where soldiers went and met with the enemy, and joked about civilians, and together made up stories, all linked together into one big story called "the Great War," which they brought home and pretended to be reluctant to tell, so friends and families and neighbours and reporters had to squeeze hard to get a few drops from the lemon of their secret and unspeakable experience. (16–17)

Feeling deprived of this rare and very specific knowledge of the war, Mansfield is shown to long for closeness to those who are engaged in the war or about to enter it. Thus she tries to capture its essence through personal interaction. Francis Carco, Leslie Beauchamp and Fred Goodyear are the three young men who, from her perspective, enable her to feel the closeness of the war and experience its aftermath. The loss of all three of them in the course of only two years and the difficulty to accept their deaths lead her to the realisation that she will never understand what it is all about: "'The War' was an abstraction, a puzzle, a nightmare. She knew she couldn't write about it – not directly" (213). Her personal losses trigger, however, a rethinking of the substance of her art. Especially the death of her brother directs her attention away from recording ephemeral impressions of travel experiences (as reworked in her short story collection *In a German Pension*) towards writing about what she is familiar with. Out of a need to preserve his memory, she begins to conjure up moments of the past and images of a distant land:

> She looks up at the photograph of Leslie above her desk, stares into his eyes until it seems there is a momentary flicker, a living response. She knows what he wants of her – that she should write recollections of their own country. In the past she has avoided New Zealand; rejected it. Since Leslie's death the memories, the sense of places and people, have filled her consciousness. There is a "sacred debt" to be paid because of Leslie; and the idea of it no longer goes against the grain of her ambitions. (103)

Only because of this devastating loss of her brother, so Stead suggests, does Mansfield acknowledge her expatriate position and begin to cultivate her ex-centric perspective, the outcome being her turning to new themes and a new form.

While Stead describes how much the extreme pain caused by personal loss triggers a moment of awareness in the New Zealand writer and a subsequent redirection of her creativity, other authors address the long-term effects the war had on women, often in the form of depicting the traumatisation the afflicted suffer from or suggesting ways of coping with loss. While Jane Urquhart recreates in *The Stone Carvers* the lasting grief which the death of her first love Eamon O'Sullivan has caused the German-descended protagonist Klara Becker, Doris Lessing dwells on the impact of the war on several generations in her novella-plus-memoir *Alfred and Emily*. In both cases, art is shown to provide relief from pain.

Urquhart's Klara is one of those young women who were left behind when their young fiancés or husbands set out for the war, often in search of adventure and completely unaware of the misery that awaited them. Against the wishes of Klara and his own Irish-Canadian community, Eamon joins the army out of his great love for flying aeroplanes and leaves for Europe, never to be heard of again. Inspired by a Canadian artist's vision of creating a monument[9] to honour the country's men lost in the First World War, the family-trained sculptress Klara travels to France fifteen years later to become part of this project. Disguised as a man, she is hired as one of Allward's carvers and thus enabled to commemorate Eamon through her art. Her objective being "to recall the face of one who has died" (332), she leaves on *The Spirit of Sacrifice*, a sculpture of two young men, the image of her beloved's face, thereby laying Eamon to rest and overcoming her grief.

By emphasising the diverse ethnic backgrounds of those involved in the war on behalf of Canada as well as those contributing to the memorial after the war, Urquhart positions Canada as a heterogeneous country in which pre-war,

---

[9] Walter Allward is the Canadian monumental sculptor who created the famous Canadian National Vimy Memorial France. See Alicia Fahey's chapter in the present volume.

Old World distinctions between friends and foes are no longer upheld. Instead, the author stresses individual experience, having her own approach articulated through the fictional Allward when she has him reflect on Klara's clandestine action: "This woman had brought a personal retrospection to his monument, and had by doing so allowed life to enter it" (340). For Klara – and also for Urquhart – it is less the country's losses and the bravery of its men that matter than the impact the war has on individuals, families and communities. By highlighting the post-war period the author furthermore shifts heroic action away from the soldiers to those who mourn and remember them. Her brief projection of a shared future for those who meet while working on the monument provides a glimpse of the cross-cultural life possible in a country like Canada, even at a time when another war is looming.

While Urquhart renders the ways in which her fictional(ized) characters respond to the aftermath of the war, Lessing reworks her own experiences. In "an idiosyncratic combination of personal history, public history and fiction" (Cheuse), Lessing investigates the trauma that had afflicted her own family and was responsible for the "dark cloud hovering over her childhood" (James). With *Alfred and Emily* she presents a hybrid text, consisting of three parts: a 'what-if?' narrative which projects the kind of life her parents (Alfred Tayler and Emily McVeagh) might have led had they not been involved in the war; a brief and inserted "Explanation" in which she states her objective and provides her readers with family photographs; and an autobiographical account of her growing up with parents who were deeply traumatised by what they had experienced in the trenches and the hospital wards respectively. Lessing juxtaposes a life without war with her family's real life, indicating the difference not only through alternative personal decisions and developments but also through a change in style. The first, quietly engaging part of her narrative presents her parents in a prosperous and war-free England and permits Alfred Tayler to pursue his dream of becoming a gentleman farmer and to marry the kind and loving Betsy, while it depicts the nurse Emily McVeagh as briefly married to a doctor before she leads the more satisfying life of a rich widow and philanthropist. Tayler and McVeagh meet when they are young and remain friends, but they never marry and never leave for Rhodesia. The second half of Lessing's narrative, rendered in a fragmentary and disjointed style and largely told from the perspective of the child the author once was, gives an account of her parents' painful and wasted existence, of lives which remained in the grip of the war even though this war had ended many years before. It describes the unhappy marriage of two individuals who continued to be haunted by their war experiences, not only because their bodily injuries daily reminded them of the past (as was the case with her father, who had lost his leg due to shrapnel wounds) but also because horrifying memories of what they had seen or heard pursued them throughout their lives.

Lessing stresses the fact that it was not only combatants who were suffering from long-term effects but that also women, working as nurses (as did her mother) or even growing up after the war (as she herself was), could become victims of the war. Hence she describes her childhood in Rhodesia in the 1920s and 1930s as being marked by this past:

> Even as a child I knew his obsessive talking about the Trenches was a way of ridding himself of the horrors. So I had the full force of the Trenches, tanks, star-shells, shrapnel, howitzers – the lot – through my childhood, and felt as if the black cloud he talked about was there, pressing down on me. I remember crouching in the bush, my hands tight over my ears: 'I won't, I will not. Stop. I won't listen.' My mother's voice? I could have listened, but it was all too much. The fate of parents who most terribly need their offspring to listen. […] Later, much later, did I see that my mother's wartime ordeals were ravaging her from within just as my father's Trenches were eating away at him. […]. (170)

> It took me years – and years – and years – to see it: my mother had no visible scars, no wounds, but she was as much a victim of the war as my poor father. (172)

Lessing's repeated return in her writings to her war-infested childhood, for example in her essay "My Father" (1963), in her autobiography *Under My Skin* (1994) and – at almost 90 years of age – in *Alfred and Emily*, as well as her continuing preoccupation with her mother, whom she had resented for much of her life, indicate that she felt the need to work through the traumatising effect the First World War seems to have had on more than one generation. Imaginatively reshaping her family experiences evidently constituted "a way for Lessing to give artistic shape to her own indignation" (James) about having to deal with the war's aftermath.

5 Conclusion

Almost a century after the event, the First World War still exerts its influence on the imagination of writers. Even though Lessing does not fit the label of 'postcolonial' author, she grew up in one of Britain's colonies and clearly saw herself as a woman affected by the war. Her repeated return to her family's history has to be seen as a painful confrontation of the past in order to position herself in the present as an author approaching her subjects in a semi-autobiographical manner. The other writers discussed above draw on the Great War in order to reassess their countries' positions. Keneally presents a well-researched fictionalised account of Australian nurses' involvement in the war activities, Itani and Womersley are concerned with some of the consequences women left behind in their home countries had to deal with, and Stead and Urquhart imaginatively explore the impact the war had on the creativity of colonial female artists. All of these authors are tentative with regard to the eventual outcome of the particular war experiences they describe, offering open or alternative endings or indicating that the confrontation of this traumatising phase of their country's history is as yet unfinished. In a move that is informed by postcolonial nostalgia they review historical events from a slightly different angle. By presenting heroic conduct as detached from the immediate war action and as emanating from women rather than men, they widen the spectrum of achievements accomplished by members of their respective countries. They thus move to the centre what had so far been marginalised in historical accounts of the First World War and by doing so write themselves into the canon of Great War literature.

References

Boym, Svetlana. *The Future of Nostalgia*. New York: Basic Books, 2001.
Caterson, Simon. "History's Master." *The Sydney Morning Herald* (23 June 2012). http://www.smh.com.au/action/printArticle?id=3396877. (29 August 2013).
Cheuse, Alan. "Doris Lessing Mines Gold in *Alfred and Emily*." *npr books* (12 August 2008) www.npr.org/templates/story/story.php?storyId=93528963. (29 August 2013).
Glassford, Sarah, and Amy Shaw, eds. *A Sisterhood of Suffering and Service: Women and Girls of Canada and Newfoundland during the First World War*. Vancouver: UBC Press, 2012.
Grayzel, Susan R. *Women and the First World War*. London: Longman, 2002.
Holmes, Katie. "Day Mothers and Night Sisters: World War I Nurses and Sexuality." *Gender and War: Australians at War in the Twentieth Century*. Eds. Joy Damousi and Marilyn Lake. Cambridge: Cambridge University Press, 1995.
Itani, Frances. *Deafening*. Toronto: HarperCollins, 2003.
James, Caryn. "They May Not Mean to, but They Do." *New York Times Sunday Book Review* (10 August 2008). www.nytimes.com/2008/08/10/books/review/James-t.html?pagewanted=all. (29 August 2013).
Keneally, Thomas. *The Daughters Of War*. London: Sceptre, 2012.
Langer, Beryl Donaldson. "Cultural Space and Women's Place." *Australian/Canadian Literatures in English: Comparative Perspectives*. Eds. Russell McDougall and GillianWhitlock. Melbourne: Methuen, 1987. 144–150.
Lessing, Doris. *Alfred and Emily*. London: Fourth Estate, 2008.
Limprecht, Eleanor. "The Daughters of Mars." *The Sydney Morning Herald* (1 July 2012) http://www.smh.com.au/action/printArticle?id=3417871. (29 August 2013).
Powell, Anne. *Women in the War Zone: Hospital Service in the First World War*. Stroud: Sutton, 2008.

Riemer, Andrew. "Where angels fear to tread." *Brisbane Times* (2 June 2012). http://www.brisbanetimes.com.au/action/printArticle?id=33381165. (29 August 2013).
Smith, Angela K. *The Second Battlefield: Women, Modernism and the First World War*. Manchester: Manchester University Press, 2000.
Stead, C. K. *Mansfield: A Novel*. London: Harvill Press, 2004.
Thomas, Gill. *Life on all Fronts: Women in the First World War*. Cambridge: Cambridge University Press, 1992.
Urquhart, Jane. *The Stone Carvers*. Toronto: McClelland & Stewart, 2002 [2001].
Walder, Dennis. "Introduction: The Persistence of Nostalgia." *Postcolonial Nostalgia: Writing, Representation, and Memory*. New York and London: Routledge, 2011. 1–19.
Walton, James. "The Daughters of Mars by Thomas Keneally: Review." *The Telegraph* (1 November 2012). http://www.telegraph.co.uk/books/bookreviews/9633521/The-Daughters-of-Mars-by-Thomas-Keneally-review.html. (29 August 2013).
Watson, Janet S. K. *Fighting Different Wars: Experience, Memory, and the First World War*. Cambridge: Cambridge University Press, 2004.
Womersley, Chris. *Bereft*. Melbourne: Scribe, 2010.

Contributors

JEAN ANDERSON is Associate Professor and Programme Director for French at Victoria University of Wellington, and editor of the *New Zealand Journal of French Studies*. Her recent publications include "Seeing Double: Representing Otherness in the Franco-Pacific Thriller," in *The Foreign in International Crime Fiction: Transcultural Representations* (Continuum, 2012), which she co-edited with Carolina Miranda and Barbara Pezzotti. They are currently working on a book on serial crime fiction.

MARLENE A. BRIGGS is Assistant Professor of English at the University of British Columbia. Her research focuses on questions of memory, mourning, and trauma in her teaching of twentieth-century literature. Her research examines the legacies of the First World War in three generations of British writers ranging from Wilfred Owen to Carol Ann Duffy. She has published on D. H. Lawrence, Doris Lessing, Virginia Woolf, and others.

ANGELA BRINTLINGER is Professor of Slavic Studies at Ohio State University. She holds a PhD in Slavic Languages and Literatures from the University of Wisconsin and MA degrees in Russian from Wisconsin and Middlebury College. She is the author of two monographs: *Chapaev and his Comrades: War and the Russian Literary Hero across the Twentieth Century* (2012) and *Writing a Usable Past: Russian Literary Culture, 1917–1937* (2000), as well as a number of edited collections, including *Chekhov for the 21st Century* (2012), *Madness and the Mad in Russian Culture* (2007), and the translation into English of Vladislav Khodasevich's biography of the Russian poet Gavriil Derzhavin (2007). In Spring 2013 she was honored to hold the Fulbright Distinguished Chair in Slavic Studies at Warsaw University.

GEERT BUELENS is Professor of Modern Dutch Literature at Utrecht University, guest professor of Dutch Literature at Stellenbosch University (RSA) and Kluge Fellow at the Library of Congress (2008). His research deals primarily with the intersections between literature and society. He has published widely on the Flemish avant-garde writer Paul van Ostaijen and on twentieth-century avant-garde poetry, nationalist literature and poetry of the First World War. He is the author of *Van Ostaijen tot heden. Zijn invloed op de Vlaamse poëzie* (Vantilt/KANTL, 2001, 2001^2, 2008^3, winner of the Flemish Culture Prize for Essay and Criticism, 2003), a collection of essays on poetry and society, *Oneigenlijk gebruik* (Vantilt, 2008) and a monograph on European First World War poetry (*Europa Europa*, Ambo, 2008 – ABN-AMRO Award for Best Non-Fiction Book of 2008), translated into German as *Europas Dichter und der Erste Weltkrieg* (Suhrkamp 2014); an English translation will be published in 2015 by Verso. He edited the anthologies *De beste gedichten van 2001* and the largest collection of First World War poetry, over 200 poems from thirty languages (*Het lijf in slijk geplant*, Ambo, 2008). He is co-editor of the *Journal of Dutch Literature* and a regular contributor to Belgian and Dutch newspapers. His current research is on the cultural history of the 1960s, the writing of national and international literary histories, neutrality and the First World War and the interplay between poetry and song writing since the Romantic Era.

MAURIZIO CINQUEGRANI joined Film Studies at the University of Kent in September 2012, having previously taught at London Metropolitan University, Birkbeck College, and King's College London. In 2011 he participated in the Camden Town Group in Context research project at Tate Britain with a contribution looking at the relationship between early film practices and the work of Walter Sickert, Malcolm Drummond and other artists. In 2012 he also worked as filmic cartographer at the University of Liverpool in an AHRC-funded research project entitled Cinematic Geographies of Battersea: Urban Interface & Site-Specific Spatial Knowledge. He received his PhD in Film Studies from King's College London in 2010, with a thesis on early British cinema and urban space. He has an MA in Contemporary Cinema Cultures from King's College London and a BA in Film Studies from the University of Bologna. His first monograph, *Of Empire and the City: Remapping Early British Cinema*, was published in 2014 by Peter Lang.

ALICIA FAHEY is a Doctoral Student in the Department of English at the University of British Columbia and a specialist in Canadian literature and visual studies. Her research examines exhibition catalogues of Canadian war art from the First and Second World Wars and the ways in which these catalogues, when read in conjunction with other literary and visual representations of the Wars, re-enforce or re-imagine Canadian master narratives and official histories. Recent publications include the exhibition and catalogue "The Iron Pulpit: Missionary Printing Presses of British Columbia" with the University of British Columbia's Rare Books and Special Collections, as well as research and editorial contributions to the production of an edition of P. K. Page's poetry, *Kaleidoscopes*, and an edition of Page's *Mexican Journal*. Alicia is currently working on a critical edition of Sheila Watson's *The Double Hook*.

PHIL FITZSIMMONS is an Associate Professor of Education at Avondale College of Higher Education. Prior to taking up this appointment he was Director of Research at the San Roque Research Institute, Santa Barbara, California. His research interests are in the fields of literacy and literature, and in particular visual literacy in new modalities of adolescent reading. Recent publications related to this particular research agenda include: "Connectivity and Text: Finding Self Through the Use of Graphic Novels," in press, in *Connectivity Across Borders, Boundaries and Bodies: International and Interdisciplinary Perspectives* (Oxford: Interdisciplinary Press); "When There's Love Inside There's a Reason Why. Emotion as the core of authentic learning in one middle school classroom," *in Literacy Learning in the Middle Years* 19. 2 (2011); "Popular Culture as Possibilities, Paradigms and Prerogatives for Literacy Learning: Giving voice to middle school students," in *Talking Points* 21. 2 (2010); and "A Rebirth of Myth and Monster: An old sign in a new framework" in *Myth and Symbol* 4. 2 (2007).

BRIGITTE JOHANNA GLASER (Prof. Dr.) teaches English Literature and Cultural Studies at the University of Göttingen (Germany). She has published two monographs on eighteenth-century fiction and seventeenth-century autobiographical writing respectively. During the last few years her research focus and publications have been on colonial and postcolonial literature as well as transnational writing. A co-edited volume of essays on *The Canadian Mosaic in the Age of Transnationalism* appeared in 2010.

SHERILL GRACE is a University Killam Professor at the University of British Columbia. Her research interests include Canadian Literature and Culture, Theatre, Autobiography and Biography, Modernism, Literature and the Arts (Interdisciplinary Studies), Theory, Editing, Women's Literature. She has published over 200 articles, chapters, and review articles, as well as 24 books, including *Sursum Corda!*, the two-volume edition of Malcolm Lowry's letters, the monographs *Inventing Tom Thomson* (2004) and *Canada and the Idea of North* (2001; 2007), and the co-edited book, *Theatre and AutoBiography* (2006). Her most recent books are the biography *Making Theatre: A Life of Sharon Pollock* (2008), *On the Art of Being Canadian* (2009), and the co-edited volume *Bearing Witness: Perspectives on War and Peace from the Arts and Humanities* (2012). Her major study of post-1977 Canadian literature and culture, *Landscapes of Memory: Canadian Literary and Artistic Representations of the Two World Wars, 1977 to 2007*, appeared in the spring of 2014. Professor Grace has received many prizes and awards for her research, including the Queen Elizabeth II Diamond Jubilee Medal for Service and Scholarship in 2013.

TY HAWKINS is Assistant Professor of English at Walsh University of Ohio, USA. He is the author *of Reading Vietnam amid the War on Terror* (Palgrave 2012), as well as several articles on the literature and rhetoric of American warfare. His scholarship has appeared in *College Literature, Papers on Language and Literature,* and *War, Literature & the Arts,* among other venues.

MARTIN LÖSCHNIGG is Associate Professor of English at the University of Graz, Austria, where he is also chair of the English Department's section on post-colonial literatures, and deputy director of the Centre for Canadian Studies. His main fields of research are narrative theory, autobiography, the English novel, the literature of war, and Canadian literature, and he has published widely on these subjects. Book publications include *Intimate Enemies: English and German Literary Reactions to the Great War 1914–1918* (co-ed., with Franz Karl Stanzel; Heidelberg 1993, 2nd edn. 1994); *Der Erste Weltkrieg in deutscher und englischer Dichtung [The First World War in German and English Poetry]* (Heidelberg 1994); *Die englische fiktionale Autobiographie [English Fictional Autobiography]* (Trier 2006); *Kurze Geschichte der kanadischen Literatur [A Short History of Canadian Literature]* (co-author, with Maria Löschnigg; Stuttgart and Leipzig 2001); *Migration and Fiction: Narratives of Migration in Contemporary Canadian Literature* (co-ed., with Maria Löschnigg; Heidelberg 2009), and *Europe – Canada: Transcultural Perspectives* (co-ed., with Klaus-Dieter Ertler and Yvonne Völkl; Frankfurt a. M. 2013).

DAVID MALCOLM is Professor of English Literature and Chair of the Department of English-Language, Literatures and Cultures in the Institute of English and American Studies at the University of Gdańsk in Poland. He is co-author (with Cheryl Alexander Malcolm) of *Jean Rhys: A Study of the Short Fiction* (Twayne, 1996), and author of *Understanding Ian McEwan* (2002), *Understanding Graham Swift* (2003) and *Understanding John McGahern* (2007, all University of South Carolina Press). He is co-editor of *The British and Irish Short Story, 1945–2000*, volume 319 of the *Dictionary of Literary Biography* (Thomson-Gale, 2006). The *Blackwell Companion to the British and Irish Short Story*, which he edited with Cheryl Alexander Malcolm, was published in autumn 2008. His study *The British and Irish Short Story Handbook* was published by Wiley-Blackwell in February 2012. He has published essays on nineteenth-century and twentieth-century British, Irish, and US literatures in scholarly journals and collections in the UK, the USA, Germany, Austria, France, Spain, the Czech Republic, and Poland. He writes reviews for the *Times Literary Supplement*.

MARGOT NORRIS is a retired Professor of English and Comparative Literature at the University of California, Irvine, where in addition to teaching the works of James Joyce and other modernist writers she also offered courses on modern war literature. She is the author of the 2000 study *Writing War in the Twentieth Century*, with chapters on World War I fiction and trench poetry, the Manhattan Project, the films of *Schindler's List* and *Apocalypse Now*, and journalistic accounts of the Gulf War.

MICHAEL PARIS FRHistS, is Professor Emeritus of Modern History at the University of Central Lancashire. Publications include *The First World War and Popular Cinema* (Edinburgh, 1999), *Warrior Nation: Images of War in British Popular Culture, 1850–2000* (Reaktion, 2000), and *Over the Top: The Great War and Juvenile Literature in Britain* (Praeger, 2005). He is also editor of *Repicturing the Second World War: Representations in Film and Television* (2007).

MAREK PARYŻ is a Professor of English and the Chair of the section of American Literature at the Institute of English Studies, University of Warsaw. He has published three books, most recently *The Postcolonial and Imperial Experience in American Transcendentalism* (Palgrave Macmillan 2012). He has edited or co-edited four volumes of academic essays, including *Projecting Words, Writing Images: Intersections of the Visual and the Textual in American Cultural Practices* (with John R. Leo, Cambridge Scholars 2011). He is the editor of the *Polish Journal for American Studies* and senior editor of the literature and culture section of the *European Journal of American Studies*. In 2007 he was a Senior Fulbright Scholar at the University of Illinois at Chicago.

CAROLINE PERRET is currently Research Associate for the Group for War and Culture Studies at the University of Westminster, and researches the impact of war on cultural production. She is particularly interested in art, illustrated books, literature, films and poetry in the historical, political, social, and cultural context of WWI and WWII in both Britain and France.

DANIEL REYNAUD is Dean of the Faculty of Arts & Theology at Avondale College of Higher Education. He has published widely on the topic of Australia's war cinema, including *Celluloid Anzacs: The Great War through Australian Cinema*, and has worked with the Australian National Film and Sound Archive to recover and partially reconstruct four significant silent war films from 1915–1928.

CLARE RHODEN teaches in the English Program of the School of Culture & Communication at the University of Melbourne, Autralian. Her research concentrates on Australian literature of the Great War and Australian writers. Her book about the Australian style of writing the Great War, based on her PhD *The Futility of Purpose*, is currently in press.

ANNE SAMSON is an independent historian and co-ordinator of the Great War in Africa Association, and an Associate Researcher at Stellenbosch University, South Africa. She is the author of *Britain, South Africa and the East African Campaign, 1914–1918: The Union Comes of Age* (2005). Her second book on the East Africa campaign was published by IB Tauris in 2013, entitled *World War I in Africa: The Forgotten Conflict Among the European Powers*. She has contributed various articles on aspects related to the campaign.

THOMAS F. SCHNEIDER (PD Dr.) is Director of the Erich Maria Remarque Peace Center, which is run by the town and university of Osnabrück. He also teaches literature at Osnabrück University and at the Universität der Bundeswehr in Munich. His special interests are the German literature of World Wars I and II, comparative twentieth-century war and anti-war literature (Germany, Britain, United States, France), German Exile Literature and questions of the representation of modern war in the media. He is co-editor of the journal *Krieg und Literatur/War and Literature* and a member of the editorial board of *Journal of War & Culture Studies*. Among his recent publications are: "How to Treat the Germans. Emil Ludwigs politisch-publizistisches Engagement im US-amerikanischen Exil," in Jürgen Egyptien (ed.). *Erinnerung in Text und Bild. Zur Darstellbarkeit von Krieg und Holocaust im literarischen und filmischen Schaffen in Deutschland und Polen*. Berlin 2012; "Narrating the War in Pictures. German Photo Books on World War I and the Construction of Pictorial War Narrations," in *Journal of War & Cultural Studies* 4 (2011). He is also the co-editor of *Wahrheitsmaschinen. Der Einfluss technischer Innovationen auf die Darstellung und das Bild des Krieges in den Medien und Künsten* (2010); *Bilderschlachten. 2000 Jahre Nachrichten aus dem Krieg. Technik – Medien – Kunst* (2009); *Die Autoren und Bücher der deutschsprachigen Literatur zum Ersten Weltkrieg 1914–1939. Ein bio-bibliographisches Handbuch* (2008); *Information Warfare* (2007), and *Huns vs. Corned Beef: Representations of the Other in American and German Literature and Film on World War I* (2007).

PAUL SKREBELS is a Senior Lecturer in the Writing and Creative Communication program at the University of South Australia. He is a member of the University's Narratives of War Research Group, and has produced articles and books on literature, film and military history topics. He and colleague Claire Woods have edited a Great War Australian soldier's memoir, *There and Back with a Dinkum*, published 2013. Since December 2011 he has been editor of *Sabretache*, the journal of the Military Historical Society of Australia.

RICHARD SLOTKIN is the Olin Professor of American Studies (Emeritus) at Wesleyan University, and the author of *Lost Battalions: The Great War and the Crisis of American Nationality* (2005), a study of Black and immigrant soldiers in World War I. He is best known for a trilogy of scholarly books on the myth of the frontier in American cultural history. *Regeneration Through Violence* (1973) was a Finalist for the 1974 National Book Award, and received the 1973 Albert J. Beveridge Award of the American Historical Association. *The Fatal Environment* (1985) is a standard reference in American Studies. *Gunfighter Nation* (1992) was a Finalist for the 1993 National Book Award. *No Quarter: The Battle of the Petersburg Crater, 1864* (2009), is a study of the political and military forces that shaped the Civil War's largest racial massacre. His latest book is *Long Road to Antietam: How the Civil War Became a Revolution* (2012), which deals with the political and strategic crisis that led to the Emancipation Proclamation. He has also written three historical novels: *Abe: A Novel of the Young Lincoln* (2000) received the Michael Shaara Award for Civil War Fiction (2001) and the Salon.com Book Award (2000); *The Return of Henry Starr* (1988); and *The Crater: A Novel of the Civil War* (1980).

RICHARD SMITH (Dr) is a Lecturer in the Department of Media and Communications, Goldsmiths University of London. He has written widely on the experience of West Indian troops in both World Wars and the race and gender implications of military service in the British Empire, including *Jamaican Volunteers in the First World War: Race, Masculinity and the Development of National Consciousness* (2004, 2009). Richard's current research focuses on representations of black and Asian troops in popular history documentary and the role these images serve within the national memory of multicultural society. He also continues to research the black presence in Britain 1900-1945; the role of the mass media in the British Empire, and comparative history approaches to colonial soldiery in modern empires. Richard's expertise is regularly sought by broadcasters, museums and archives and he is involved in a number of academic and local history initiatives marking the centenary of the First World War.

MARZENA SOKOŁOWSKA-PARYŻ is Associate Professor at the Institute of English Studies, University of Warsaw, where she teaches courses on contemporary British and Commonwealth literature, with specific emphasis on war fiction and film in relation to history, memory, and national identity. She is the author of *Reimagining the War Memorial, Reinterpreting the Great War: The Formats of British Commemorative Fiction* (2012) and *The Myth of War in British and Polish Poetry, 1939-1945* (2002). She has contributed to a wide variety of journals and edited volumes, writing on "Poet Laureates 'Remember' the Last Veteran," "Images of the Past: History and Memory as Photography in Graham Swift's *Out of this World*," "The Great War Revisited: The Laughter of the Fool and the Shame of the Coward in Paul Bailey's *Old Soldiers*," "Reimagining the Great War in Grand-

Historical Narratives," "The Great War in British Detective Fiction," "The Naked Male Body in the War Film," "The Narration and Visualization of Rape and the Inadvertent Subversion of the Anti-War Message in Brian De Palma's *Redacted* and *Casualties of War*," "The Second World War in Recent Polish Counterfactual and Alternative (Hi)stories." She has also published papers on post-1945 British poetry, as well as contemporary Australian film and fiction.

CHRISTINA SPITTEL is a Lecturer in English at the University of New South Wales, Canberra. She has published on Australian war writing, the teaching of Shakespeare in the Third Reich and the publication of Australian communist writing in socialist East Germany. She is currently completing a book on the First World War in Australian novels (based on her PhD from the University of Freiburg) and an article on the career of Erich Maria Remarque's novel *All Quiet on the Western Front* in Australia.

HANNA TEICHLER has studied English, French and Portuguese philology at Johann-Wolfgang-Goethe University in Frankfurt am Main (focus on anglophone and francophone postcolonial studies, New Literatures in English) and graduated in May 2011 with an MA degree. After having worked as a research assistant for an interdisciplinary project at the University of Siegen (History Department), she was accepted as a PhD candidate in Frankfurt in December 2011 (New Literatures in English). Her dissertation project examines possibilities of reconciliation in a postcolonial context and focuses in particular on performative aspects of memory, identity and history in an increasingly complex media landscape. She has participated in the Mnemonics Conference for young researchers in September 2012, hosted by Aarhus University, Denmark, and presented at the Gendered Memories of War and Political Violence Conference (Central European University, Budapest) in December 2012.

ROSS J. WILSON is Senior Lecturer in Modern History and Public Heritage at the University of Chichester. He has written on the experience, representation and memory of the First World War in Britain and the United States. His first book assessed the relationship between the British soldiers on the Western Front and the materials and spaces they encountered on the battlefields and behind the lines (*Landscapes of the Western Front*, 2012). His second book has examined the ways in which the First World War is remembered within contemporary British society with particular regard to how the war functions as a focus of identity for individuals and communities (*Cultural Heritage of the Great War in Britain*, 2013). His current research focuses on the 'war cultures' of British and American troops during the war and comparative studies of memory across the former combatant nations.

Index of Names

Ackermann, Rolf 400, 405
Adam-Smith, Patsy 255, 257–261, 264, 268, 269
Akhmatova, Anna 349, 355
Albani, Marcello (dir.) 326
Alchin, Ray (dir.) 297
Aldington, Richard 280
Alessandrini, Goffredo (dir.) 325
Ambesser, Axel von (dir.) 380
Amenta, Pino (dir.) 294
Andrews Del 110
Andrews, Lyn 51
Annaud, Jean-Jacques (dir.) 376, 379
Ashby, Hal (dir.) 118
Ashmead-Bartlett, Ellis 289
Attenborough, Richard (dir.) 83
Atwood, Margaret 219, 235, 420

Bagnold, Enid 436
Barbusse, Henri 205, 208, 212
Barker, Pat 1, 29, 30, 53, 85, 161
Barnett, Corelli 136
Barry, Michael (dir.) 135
Barry, Sebastian 346
Bassett, Michael (dir.) 48
Bee, David 402, 405
Bennett, Jack 261, 262
Beresford, Bruce (dir.) 279, 292, 299
Bergman, Ingmar (dir.) 91
Biancoli, Oreste (dir.) 326
Blixen, Karen (Isak Dinesen) 400, 407
Blunden, Edmund 44, 97
Borden, Mary 139, 141
Borges, Jorge Luis 328
Bourcy, Thierry 203, 208, 211, 213
Boyd, Martin 268
Boyd, William 398, 404
Boyd, William (dir.) 47, 139
Boyden, Joseph 50, 239, 241, 245, 248
Brecht, Bertolt 25, 83, 167
Brignone, Guido (dir.) 325
Brittain, Vera 136, 436
Bull, Bartle 404
Burrows, Robyn 52

Burstall, Tim (dir.) 298
Burton, Geoff (dir.) 49
Butera, Filippo (dir.) 324
Butler, William 173

Capus, Alex 399, 402, 405
Caputo, Philip 104
Carbonari, Davide (dir.) *326*
Carroll, James 346
Chabrol, Claude (dir.) 372
Charalambous, John 286
Chauvel, Charles (dir.) 291
Chesney, George Tomkyns 173
Chislett, Anne 154, 162, 166
Cimino, Michael (dir.) 118, 391
Ciulei, Liviu (dir.) 374
Claudel, Philippe 208
Clem, Robert (dir.) 5, 121–132
Cloete, Stuart 139
Cobb, Irvin 310, 398
Cobb, Humphrey 82
Cole, Marcus (dir.) 295
Conroy, Robert 178
Coppola, Francis Ford (dir.) 118
Corman, Roger (dir.) 367
Cothias, Patrick 193
Cowan, Paul (dir.) 156
Crane, Stephen 21, 95
Crombie, Donald (dir.) 296
Cummings, E. E. 121

Daeninckx, Didier 203, 208, 209, 210, 213
Dante, Joe (dir.) 112
De Felice, Lionello (dir.) 326
De Sica, Vittorio (dir.) 332
Deighton, Len 173
Delvaux, André (dir.) 378
Dick, Philip K. 173
Dixon, John (dir.) 294
Dorgelès, Roland 205, 208, 212
Dos Passos, John 121
Drew, Di (dir.) 295
Dugain, Marc 210

Index of Names

Dupeyron, François (dir.) 210
Dwan, Allan (dir.) 112

Eisenstein, Sergei (dir.) 89
Eliot, T. S. 4, 8, 123, 437
Elter, Marco (dir.) 326
Elton, Ben 51

Facey, Albert 295, 296
Faulkner, William 121, 122
Faulks, Sebastian 139
Fick, Nathaniel 99
Fimeri, Wain (dir.) 53
Findley, Timothy 1, 9, 153–156, 167, 219–224, 227–228, 230, 231–235, 244, 286, 417
Fisher, John Hayes (dir.) 49
Fitzgerald, Francis Scott 121
Foden, Giles 402, 407
Ford, Ford Madox 161
Forester, C. S. 401, 404, 405
Forzano, Giovacchino (dir.) 325
Freda, Riccardo (dir.) 326
French, David 154, 159

Gallagher, Matt 98
Gammage, Bill 257–261, 264, 269, 293
Garnhum, Dennis 168
Gianetti, Alfredo (dir.) 321, 327
Gidron, Martin J. 175, 179
Gorky, Maxim 359
Grautoff, Ferdinand 173
Graves, Robert 7, 44, 256
Gray, John 154, 156, 157
Grierson, Alister (dir.) 298
Griffith, D. W. (dir.) 89
Gross, Paul (dir.) 44, 48

Hanna, Pat (dir.) 290, 299
Harford, Lesbia 268–269
Harris, John 139
Haynes, Brad (dir.) 48
Hayward, William, Colonel 309, 310
Heller, Joseph 123
Hemingway, Ernest 95, 98, 100, 121, 182, 321
Hindmarch, Carl (dir.) 139, 140, 142, 143
Hodgins, Jack 51, 153, 164
Hodson, James Lansdale 139

Hooper, Louise (dir.) 4, 29, 36
Hughes, Ted 4, 59–62, 69–77
Huston, John (dir.) 372, 401
Huxley, Elspeth 407

Itani, Frances 52, 161, 428, 434–436, 441

Jackson, Pat (dir.) 138
James, Henry 7
Japrisot, Sébastien 208
Jarman, Derek (dir.) 139
Jarrold, Julian (dir.) 29, 48
Jeffes, Jane (dir.) 49
Jeffrey, Tom (dir.) 299
Johnston, Jennifer 345
Joyce, James 338

Kawalerowicz, Jerzy (dir.) 375
Kelly, Gwen 262, 262, 266, 267, 269
Keneally, Thomas 262–263, 266, 269, 428, 430
Kerr, Don 153, 154, 165, 166
Kipling, Rudyard 33, 143–146
Kirk, Brian (dir.) 48, 143
Kowalski, David J. 175
Kubrick, Stanley (dir.) 82, 112, 116, 371, 372
Kwei-Armah, Kwame 147, 149
Lattuada, Alberto (dir.) 82
Laurence, Margaret 164
Le Rouge, Gustave 203, 206, 213
Leiber, Fritz 174
Leroux, Gaston 203, 204–207
Lessing, Doris 436, 438, 439, 440
Le Queux, William 173
Lindsay, Jack 268
Loach, Ken (dir.) 379
Losey, Joseph (dir.) 371
Lucas, George (dir.) 88
Luhrmann, Baz (dir.) 299
Lusso, Emilio 322, 323, 326, 329, 331
Lydon, Dan 149

Macaulay, Rose 436
MacKinnon, Gillies (dir.) 4, 29, 30, 36, 85
MacLeod, Ian R. 178, 179, 261
Mader, Friedrich Wilhelm 401, 403, 405, 406

Maggi, Luigi (dir.) 325
Mahon, Derek 345
Majewski, Janusz (dir.) 374
Major, Kevin 153–154, 159, 160, 166
Malick, Terrence (dir.) 112
Malins, Geoffrey 141
Malouf, David 2, 3, 257, 262, 265, 266, 269
Mann, Delbert (dir.) 4, 17, 18, 20, 41, 27, 84, 113–118
Mann, Leonard 268, 275,
Mansfield, Katherine 11, 436, 437, 438
March, William 5, 121–131
Marinetti, Filippo Tommaso 322
Martin, Philip (dir.) 139
Massicotte, Stephen 154, 161, 167
Masters, Edgar Lee 122
McCarthy, Cormac 104, 187, 371
McCrae, John 161
McDonald, Roger 255, 257, 262–266
McDowell, J. B. 141
McGuinness, Frank 345
McKenna, Brian (dir.) 48
Meckert, Jean (Amila) 208
Mercanti, Pino (dir.) 326
Milestone, Lewis (dir.) 17–27, 82, 109–118
Miller, George (dir.) 294
Mitchell, Elyne 261
Mitchell, George 279
Monicelli, Mario (dir.) 321, 326, 327, 372
Moorcock, Michael 173, 176, 179
Moore, Ward 174
Morpurgo, Michael 50, 278
Morselli, Guido 173
Munro, H. H. 173
Murry, John Middleton 437

O'Brien, Jim (dir.) 123
O'Brien, Tim 96
Olden, Balder 401, 403, 405
Owen, Wilfred 4, 29–41, 85, 113, 146, 164, 182, 256, 259, 386
Ozanne, Dominic (dir.) 48

Pabst, G.W. 135
Page, Geoff 257, 262, 266, 267
Page, Gertrude 397, 398
Pasternak, Boris 349, 355

Pastrone, Giovanni (dir.) 322
Patrice, Ordas 193
Paul, Heinz (dir.) 137
Pécherot, Patrick 203, 208, 212, 213
Peterson, Eric 154, 156
Phelan, Tom 10, 335–346
Phillips, Robin (dir.) 154, 220
Pialat, Maurice (dir.) 378
Pikul', Valentin 10, 349, 350, 350, 351, 352, 356–359, 360, 361
Poirier, Léon (dir.) 137
Pound, Ezra 123
Powell, William 399, 404, 406
Powers, Kevin 95–104
Pratt, Fletcher 315, 316
Prévost, Guillaume 203, 208, 210, 213
Price, Evadne 436
Pushkin, Alexander 352
Pynchon, Thomas 123

Radev, Vulo (dir.) 376
Rathbone, Irene 436
Reitz, Edgar (dir.) 381
Remarque, Erich Maria 4, 7, 17–27, 82, 84, 85, 91, 95, 109–118, 290
Renoir, Jean (dir.) 377
Resnick, Mike 177, 178
Robinson, Derek 139
Rolfe, Alfred (dir.) 260, 289
Rosi, Francesco (dir.) 321, 322, 329–331
Russell, Bertrand 437

Safran, Henri (dir.) 295
Saraceni, Fausto (dir.) 326
Sassoon, Siegfried 7, 29, 30, 37–39, 44, 85, 136, 256, 285, 436
Schnalke, Christian 400, 405
Shankland, Peter 407
Shears, Owen 173
Sherriff, R. C. 135
Sholokhov, Mikhail 349
Siebert, Detlef (dir.) 143
Sillitoe, Alan 4, 59–70, 72, 76, 77
Sims, Jeremy (dir.) 299
Sinclair, May 436
Smith, Beaumont (dir.) 297
Smith, Wilbur 398, 401, 404

Solzhenitsyn, Alexander 10, 349–356, 359–361
Sordi, Alberto (dir.) 327
Spielberg, Steven (dir.) 112
Spillebeen, Geert 143
Stead, C. K. 428, 436–438, 441
Stevens, David (dir.) 296
Stevenson, William 405

Tardi, Jacques 190, 196, 197
Tavernier, Bertrand (dir.) 369, 378
Tennyson, Alfred 161
Terraine, John 136
Thiessen, Vern 153, 154, 157, 158, 159 157–159, 163, 167
Thomson, Chris (dir.) 295
Thomson, R. H. 154
Thorpe, Adam 52
Thring, F. W. (dir.) 291
Tolstoy, Leo 350, 352, 354, 355
Troell, Jan (dir.) 367, 378
Truffaut, François (dir.) 377
Trumbo, Dalton (dir.) 367, 371
Turtledove, Harry 177, 178

Ungaretti, Giuseppe 323
Urquhart, Jane 11, 52, 153, 157, 411–424, 428, 436, 438–439, 441

Vanderhaeghe, Guy 154, 161, 164, 165, 167
Vasili, Phil 149

Verhoeven, Paul (dir.) 112
Vidor, Charles (dir.) 373
Viera, Josef S. 401, 403, 405, 406
Vonnegut, Kurt 104
Vuillaume, Maxime 207

Walker, Brenda 273, 281–284
Walker, Roger Wade 149
Wallace, Stephen (dir.) 299
Ward, Rachel (dir.) 299
Watt, Harry (dir.) 138
Weir, Peter (dir.) 44, 112, 255, 260, 261, 269, 292, 293
Wende, Hamilton 401
West, Rebecca 436
Westerman, Percy 399, 401, 405
White, Patrick 282,
Williamson, David 255, 261, 293
Wincer, Simon (dir.) 260, 294
Womersley, Chris 273, 284–286, 428, 434–436, 441
Woolf, Virginia 123, 436
Woolfe, H. Bruce (dir.) 137
Wren, P. C. 399, 403

Yeats, W. B. 341
Yeldham, Peter 51, 273, 278–281, 295–297
Young, Francis Brett 399, 400

Zetterling, Mai (dir.) 367

Index of Titles

1901 (Conroy) 177, 179
1906. Der Zusammenbruch der Alten Welt (Grautoff) 173
1915 (McDonald) 263–266
1915 (dirs. Thomson and Drew) 295

An Accidental Soldier (dir. Ward) 299
Aces High (dir. Gold) 84, 91
The African Queen (Forester) 400, 401, 404
The African Queen (dir. Huston) 365, 380
Afrika, mon amour (Schnalke) 400
Alan Sillitoe's Nottinghamshire (Sillitoe) 60
Alexander Nevsky (dir. Eisenstein) 89
The Alien Years (dir. Crombie) 296, 297
Alfred and Emily (Lessing) 11, 428, 438, 439, 440
All Quiet on the Western Front (dir. Mann) 4, 5, 17, 17–27, 84, 85, 89–92, 113–118
All Quiet on the Western Front (dir. Milestone) 5, 17–27, 82, 109–113, 315, 365, 368
All Quiet on the Western Front (Remarque) 17, 18, 19, 22, 24, 25, 26, 27, 95, 290
All the King's Men (dir. Jarrold) 29, 48, 136
The Alpha Raid (Scholefield) 401
Always Afternoon (Kelly) 262, 266–267, 269
Always Afternoon (dir. Stevens) 296–297
L'Ambulance 13 (Cothias and Ordas) 190, 193–196, 198
Les Âmes grises (Claudel) 208
Angels of Mercy (Andrews) 51
Un anno sull'altipiano (Lusso) 322
Another World (Barker) 53
"Anthem for Doomed Youth" (Owen) 30, 33
The Anzacs (Adam-Smith) 257, 259, 261, 268
Anzacs (dirs. Dixon, Miller and Amenta) 257, 260, 262, 294, 298
Anzacs (MacLeod) 261, 262, 266, 267, 269
Apocalypse Now (dir. Coppola) 118, 366
Armageddon (dir. Woolfe) 137
As I Lay Dying (Faulkner) 122
Assegai (Smith) 398, 399, 400, 403, 404, 407
Attack Force Z (dir. Burstall) 298

August 1914 (Solzhenitsyn) 10, 350, 352, 354, 355, 359
Austeria (dir. Kawalerowicz) 366, 375, 376
Australia (dir. Luhrmann) 299
Australians at War (dir. Burton) 49
Aventures effroyables du capitaine Hyx (Leroux) 206

Backs to the Wall (Mitchell) 279
The Bad Seed (March) 124
Barbed Wire and Roses (Yeldham) 51, 273, 278–281, 283
Bataan (dir. Garnett) 128, 305, 316, 317, 318
La Bataille invisible (Leroux) 206–207
"The Battle of Dorking" (Chesney) 173
The Battle of Jutland (dir. Woolfe) 137
The Battle of the Somme (dirs. Malins and McDowell) 141
Battle of the Somme: The True Story (ten Cate) 143
Battles of Coronel and Falkland Islands (dir. Woolfe) 137
Bella Non Piangere (dir. Carbonari) 326
Beneath Hill 60 (dir. Sims) 299
Benton's Conviction (Page) 266, 267, 269
Bereft (Womersley) 273, 284–286, 428, 434, 435
Billy Bishop Goes to War (Gray and Peterson) 153, 154, 156–157, 163, 227, 228
A Bird in the House (Laurence) 164
Birdsong (Faulks) 139
Birdsong (dir. Martin) 139
Blackadder Goes Forth (dir. Boden) 1, 44
Blanche Maupas (dir. Jamain) 369
Blood Oath (dir. Wallace) 299
The Blood Vote (Lindsay) 268
The Blue Max (dir. Guillermin) 367, 368
Le Boucher des Hurlus (Meckert) 208
Der brave Soldat Schwejk (dir. von Ambesser) 370, 380
Breaker Morant (dir. Beresford) 279, 292
Bring the Jubilee (Moore) 174, 179
Broken Ground (Hodgins) 51, 153, 164

Broken Sun (dir. Haynes) 48
The Broken Years (Gammage) 257, 258
The Butterfly Plague (Findley) 221, 224

C'était la guerre des tranchées (Tardi) 190, 196–197, 198
"The Calls" (Owen) 30
Can You See Me, Yet? (Findley) 221
Canada: A People's History (dir. Turbide) 54
The Canal Bridge (Phelan) 10, 335–345
Cancer Ward (Solzhenitsyn) 352
Il Canto della Fede (dir. Butera) 324
Capitaine Conan (dir. Tavernier) 368, 370
The Captain's Daughter (Pushkin) 352
Catch That Zeppelin! (Leiber) 174
Catch-22 (Heller) 123
Cavalleria (dir. Alessandrini) 325, 327
La Chambre des officiers (Dugain) 210
La Chambre des officiers (dir. Dupeyron) 210
La chambre verte (dir. Truffaut) 377, 378, 380
"The Charge of the Light Brigade" (Tennyson) 161
Le Château noir (Leroux) 204
Chui and Sadaka (Powell) 399, 400, 404, 406
I Cinque dell'Adamello (dir. Mercanti) 326
C. K. Dezerterzy (dir. Majewski) 366, 370, 374
Coming Home (dir. Ashby) 118, 366
Company K (dir. Clem) 5, 121, 124–132
Company K (March) 5, 121–123, 125, 129, 131
The Company of the Dead (Kowalski) 175, 179
Contro-passato prossimo (Morselli) 173
La Cote 512 (Bourcy) 203, 211
Les cousins (dir. Chabrol) 372
Covenant with Death (Harris) 139
Les Croix de bois (Dorgelès) 205
Cupid in Africa (Wren) 399, 400, 403

Dancock's Dance (Vanderhaeghe) 153, 154, 161, 162, 163, 164, 165–166, 167
The Daughters of Mars (Keneally) 436
Day of My Delight (Boyd) 268
Days of Hope (dir. Loach) 370, 379
Deafening (Itani) 52, 161, 428, 434
Deathwatch (dir. Bassett) 48
The Deer Hunter (dir. Cimino) 118
Le Der des ders (Daeninckx) 203, 208, 210

Diggers in Blighty (dir. Hanna) 299
Diggers (dir. Thring) 291
Doctor Zhivago (dir. Lean) 367, 370
Doctor Zhivago (Pasternak) 349, 355
Domicile conjugal (dir. Truffaut) 377
Douaumont (dir. Paul) 137
Dr Strangelove or: How I Learned to Stop Worrying and Love the Bomb (dir. Kubrick) 371
"Dulce Et Decorum Est" (Owen) 30, 31, 32, 85

Elmet (Hughes) 60, 69–76
Les Étranges Noces de Rouletabille (Leroux) 204

Famous Last Words (Findley) 221, 224n9
Far from the Limelight (Page) 398
A Farewell to Arms (dir. Borzage) 315, 372
A Farewell to Arms (Hemingway) 98, 102, 321
A Farewell to Arms (dir. Vidor) 321, 370, 372
Le Feu (Barbusse) 205
The Fighting Days (Lill) 154, 155, 160, 161
The First Casualty (Elton) 51
The First Circle (Solzhenitsyn) 352, 353
Flesh in Armour (Mann) 268, 275
Fly Away Peter (Malouf) 265, 269
Follow After (Page) 397, 401
The Forbidden Zone (Borden) 139
Forest of the Hanged (dir. Ciulei) 366, 367, 370, 374
The Forgotten Five (anonymous) 190–193, 194, 195, 198
A Fortunate Life (dirs. Cole and Safran) 295
Forty Thousand Horsemen (dir. Chauvel) 291
Les Fragments d'Antonin (dir. Le Bomin) 370, 380
Fratelli d'Italia (dir. Saraceni) 326
Fräulein Doktor (dir. Lattuada) 82, 86, 87, 88, 89, 90, 92, 93, 377
Full Metal Jacket (dir. Kubrick) 112

Gallipoli (Bennett) 260, 261, 262, 267, 269
Gallipoli (dir. Weir) 1, 44, 49, 112, 255, 260, 269, 292–293, 295, 298, 300, 365, 366
The Ghosts of Africa (Stevenson) 400, 401, 403, 407
Gossip from the Forest (Keneally) 263, 269

La Grande Guerra (dir. Monicelli) 321, 322, 323, 324, 326–327, 328, 330, 332, 333, 370, 372, 373
La grande illusion (dir. Renoir) 377
Gravity's Rainbow (Pynchon) 123
The Great War (Kerr) 153, 154, 165, 166
The Great War (dir. McKenna) 48
The Great War (dirs. Terraine and Barnett) 136, 385
The Great War: American Front (Turtledove) 177, 179
"Greater Love" (Owen) 30
La Guerra e il Sogno di Momi (dir. Pastrone) 322

Haber (dir. Ragussis) 86, 87
Här har du ditt liv (dir.Troell) 367, 378
Headhunter (Findley) 224
Heimat – Eine deutsche Chronik (dir. Reitz) 381
The Hero of the Dardanelles (dir. Rolfe) 260, 289
L'Horizon (dir. Rouffio) 367, 370
How Many Miles to Babylon? (Johnston) 345
How Young They Died (Cloete) 139

An Ice-Cream War (Boyd) 398, 400, 403, 404
"In Flanders Fields" (McCrae) 161
"Insensibility" (Owen) 30
The Invaluable Mystery (Harford) 268, 269
The Invasion of 1910 (le Queux) 173
The Invasion of England Told Twenty Years After by an Old Soldier (Butler) 173

Jim Redlake (Young) 399, 400, 403
Johnny Got His Gun (dir. Trumbo) 367, 371, 380
Journey's End (Sherriff) 135
Jules et Jim (dir. Truffaut) 377, 380

Kaboom (Gallagher) 98
The Kid Who Could Not Miss (dir. Cowan) 156
King and Country (dir. Losey) 366, 367, 370, 371, 380, 381
The King's Shilling (Wende) 401, 407
Kipling's Keuze (Spillebeen) 143
Kokoda (dir. Grierson) 298

The Last Day of World War One (dir. Fisher) 49
"The Last Laugh" (Owen) 30
La Leggenda del Piave (dir. Freda) 326
The Life and Death of Colonel Blimp (dirs. Powell and Pressburger) 368
The Lighthorsemen (Mitchell) 261, 262, 267, 269
The Lighthorsemen (dir. Wincer) 260, 261, 294
Un long dimanche de fiançailles (Japrisot) 208
Un long dimanche de fiançailles (dir. Jeunet) 370
Long Long Way (Barry) 346
Lord of the Loincloth (Dow) 402
The Lost Boys (Thomson) 153, 154, 162, 163, 165, 167
Louisa, een woord van liefde (dirs. Collet and Drouot) 367
Loving Couples (Zetterling, dir.) 367

Maciste Alpino (dirs. Borgnetto and Maggi) 325
Mad Jack (dir. Gold) 136
La Madelon (dir. Boyer) 380
La maison des bois (dir. Pialat) 378
The Man in the High Castle (Dick) 173
Mansfield: A Novel (Stead) 11, 428
"Maps and the Great War" (Sillitoe) 63
Marching in Tanga (Young) 405
Mary's Wedding (Massicotte) 153, 154, 158, 161, 162, 165, 166, 167
A Matter of Time (Capus) 399, 400, 402
Mimi and Toutou Go Forth (Foden) 402, 407
The Monocled Mutineer (dir. O'Brien) 136
Mons (dir. Woolfe) 137
Moonzund (Pikul') 10, 350, 357–359, 360
Mother Courage and her Children (Brecht) 25
My Boy Jack (dir. Kirk) 48, 135, 139, 143–147
Mystère de la chambre jaune (Leroux) 204

Nicholas and Alexandra (dir. Schaffner) 367
Nineteen Twenty-One (Thorpe) 52
No Man's Land (Major) 153, 154, 159–160, 163, 166

A Nomad of the Streams of Time (Moorcock) 176
Not Forgotten (dir. Jeffes) 49
Not Forgotten: Soldiers of the Empire (dir. Feltes) 392
Not So Quiet ... Stepdaughters of War (Price) 436

Observe the Sons of Ulster Marching Towards the Somme (McGuinness) 345
The Odd Angry Shot (dir. Jeffrey) 299
Oh! What a Lovely War (dir. Attenborough) 1, 83, 87, 92, 93, 156, 367, 378, 386
On Virgin Soil (Olden) 401, 403
One Bullet Away: The Making of a Marine Officer (Fick) 99
One Day in the Life of Ivan Denisovich (Solzhenitsyn) 349, 352, 353
Our Fatal Shadows (Bee) 404
"Over There" (Resnick) 177

Le Pantalon (dir. Boisset) 370
"The Parable of the Old Man and the Young" (Owen) 30, 146
Parade's End (Madox Ford) 161
Paradise Road (dir. Beresford) 299
Paris menacé, Paris sauvé (Vuillaume) 207
Passaporto Rosso (dir. Brignone) 325
Passchendaele (dir. Gross) 44, 48
Paths of Glory (dir. Kubrick) 82, 112, 116, 365, 366, 369, 372
The Peach Thief (dir. Radev) 366, 367, 376
The Phantom Flotilla (Shankland) 402, 407
The Piano Man's Daughter (Findley) 221
Piccolo Alpino (dir. Biancoli) 326
Platoon (dir. Stone) 128, 305, 369
A Portrait of the Artist as a Young Man (Joyce) 338
Private Peaceful (Morpurgo) 50, 278
The Private War of Lucinda Smith (dir. Alchin) 297

Quiet Flows the Don (Sholokhov) 349
Quiet in the Land (Chislett) 154, 162, 163, 166

Raw Material (Sillitoe) 59, 60, 63–69, 76, 77
I Recuperanti (dir. Gianetti) 321, 331–333
The Red Badge of Courage (Crane) 21, 95
Redenzione (dir. Albani) 326
Regeneration (Barker) 1, 85, 161
Regeneration (dir. MacKinnon) 4, 29, 30, 32, 36–37, 40, 85, 92
Remains of Elmet (Hughes) 60, 70, 72, 73
Rendez-vous à Bray (dir. Delvaux) 378
Resistance (Shears) 173
Return to the Wood (Hodson) 139
Revealing Gallipoli (dir. Fimeri) 53
The Road (McCarthy) 104
Le Roi de Coeur (dir. de Broca) 367, 370
Rouletabille chez Krupp (Leroux) 204, 207
Rouletabille chez le Tsar (Leroux) 204
A Rumor of War (Caputo) 104

The Sands of Iwo Jima (dir. Dwan) 112
Satan in Sydney (dir. Smith) 297
Saving Private Ryan (dir. Spielberg) 112, 128, 305, 365
Le Scarpe al Sole (dir. Elter) 326
"The Sentry" (Owen) 30
The Seventh Seal (dir. Bergman) 91
The Severed Wing (Gidron) 175, 179
Senza Bandiera (dir. De Felice) 326
Shout at the Devil (dir. Hunt) 380
Shout at the Devil (Smith) 401, 403, 404
"The Show" (Owen) 30, 32
Silent Parts (Charalambous) 286
Slaughterhouse-Five (Vonnegut) 104
Small Soldiers (dir. Dante) 112
Soldier's Heart (French) 153, 154, 159, 162, 164, 165, 167
The Somme (dir. Hindmarch) 135, 139–143, 147
The Somme – From Defeat to Victory (dir. Siebert) 143
Spoon River Anthology (Masters) 122
"Spring Offensive" (Owen) 164
SS-GB (Deighton) 173
Star Ship Troopers (dir. Verhoeven) 112
Star Wars (dir. Lucas) 81, 88
The Stone Carvers (Urquhart) 11, 52, 153, 157, 411–424, 428, 438

"Stones" (Findley) 221
"Strange Meeting" (Owen) 30, 39
The Summer Isles (MacLeod) 178, 179, 180
Supply of Heroes (Carroll) 346

Tannenberg (dir. Paul) 137
Target for Tonight (dir. Watt) 138
Tea Tree Passage (Burrows) 52
Testament of Youth (dir. Armstrong) 136
Testament of Youth (Brittain) 436
The Thin Red Line (dir. Malick) 112
The Things They Carried (O'Brien) 123
Thomas l'imposteur (dir. Franju) 367
Three Day Road (Boyden) 9, 50, 153, 239–240, 244–248, 250, 251, 419, 427
Timothy Findley's The Wars (Garnhum) 154, 155, 166, 167
Les Traîtres (Bourcy) 212
Tranchecaille (Pécherot) 203, 212, 213
Tredici Uomini ed un Cannone (dir. Forzano) 325
The Trench (dir. Ozanne) 48
The Trench (dir. Boyd) 47, 139
Tull (Vasili) 149

Under My Skin (Lessing) 440
Uomini Contro (dir. Rosi) 321, 322, 323, 328, 329, 330, 331, 332, 333, 366, 367, 369, 370, 373

La Valse des gueules cassées (Prévost), 203, 210
Verdun, visions d'histoire (dir. Poirier) 137
La Victoire en chantant (dir. Annaud) 376, 379
La vie et rien d'autre (dir. Tavernier) 1, 378, 380
Vimy (Thiessen) 153, 154, 157, 158, 163, 165, 167, 411
Vita d'un Uomo (Ungaretti) 323
Von Richthofen and Brown (dir. Corman) 367, 368

Walter Tull: Footballer, Soldier, Hero (Lydon and Walker) 149
Walter Tull: Forgotten Hero (dir. MacLaverty) 149, 392
Walter's War (dir. Riley) 135, 139, 147–150
"War" (Findley) 221
War and Peace (Tolstoy) 350, 352, 355
War Requiem (dir. Jarman) 139
War Story (Robinson) 139
The Wars (Findley) 1, 9, 153, 219–221, 223–235, 244, 286, 417
The Wars (dir. Phillips) 154
We That Were Young (Rathbone) 436
Die weiße Jägerin (Ackermann) 400
Western Approaches (dir. Jackson) 138
Westfront 1918 (dir. Pabst) 135
When Blackbirds Sing (Boyd) 268
When William Came: A Story of London under the Hohenzollerns (Munro) 173
The White Rhino Hotel (Bull) 404
Wilfred Owen: A Remembrance Tale (dir. Hooper) 29–39
Wing of Night, The (Walker) 273, 281–284, 286
Winged Warfare (Bishop) 156
Wings (Thomas) 136, 315
Winter Pollen (Hughes) 71, 72
The Wipers Times (dir. De Emmony) 380

The Yellow Birds (Powers) 5, 95–105
You Went Away (Findley) 221
Ypres (dir. Woolfe) 137

Zeebrugge (dir. Woolfe) 137
Zeppelin (dir. Perier) 368

www.ingramcontent.com/pod-product-compliance
Lightning Source LLC
Chambersburg PA
CBHW050847160426
43194CB00011B/2063